Eighth Edition

Social Inequality

FORMS, CAUSES, AND CONSEQUENCES

Charles E. Hurst

The College of Wooster

PEARSON

Boston Columbus Indianapolis New York San Francisco Upper Saddle River
Amsterdam Cape Town Dubai London Madrid Milan Munich Paris Montreal Toronto
Delhi Mexico City Sao Paulo Sydney Hong Kong Seoul Singapore Taipei Tokyo

Editorial Director: Craig Campanella
Editor in Chief: Dickson Musslewhite
Publisher: Karen Hanson
Editorial Assistant: Joseph Jantas
Director of Marketing: Brandy Dawson
Executive Marketing Manager: Kelly May
Marketing Assistant: Janeli Bitor
Director of Production: Lisa Iarkowski
Senior Managing Editor: Maureen Richardson
Production Project Manager: Maggie Brobeck

Art Director, Cover: Jayne Conte
Cover Image: © elavuk81/Fotolia LLC
Media Director: Brian Hyland
Lead Media Project Manager: Thomas Scalzo
Supplements Editor: Mayda Bosco
Full-Service Project Management and Composition: TexTech, Inc.
Printer/Binder: Courier Westford
Cover Printer: Courier Westford
Text Font: Times

Credits and acknowledgments borrowed from other sources and reproduced, with permission, in this textbook appear on the appropriate page within text.

Library of Congress Cataloging-in-Publication Data

Hurst, Charles E.
  Social inequality : forms, causes, and consequences / Charles E. Hurst.—8th ed.
      p. cm.
  Includes bibliographical references and index.
  ISBN-13: 978-0-205-06477-9
  ISBN-10: 0-205-06477-9
  1. Equality—United States. 2. United States—Social conditions. I. Title.
HN90.S6H87 2013
305.0973—dc23

                                                    2011040216

10 9 8 7 6 5 4 3 2 1 V013

ISBN 10: 0-205-06477-9
ISBN 13: 978-0-205-06477-9

To Mary Ellen

with love always for who you are.

CONTENTS

PART 2   General Explanations of Inequality

PART 3   Consequences of Social Inequality

PREFACE

In 2011 economic inequality in the United States was greater than at any time since the Roaring Twenties. As a result, the last few years have been difficult for many middle- and working-class families whose financial well-being was strained because of lost jobs, declines in pensions and stock values, mortgage difficulties, and increases in health insurance premiums. During the 2007 to 2009 recession, those at the top gained in wealth; at the same time almost two-thirds of American families suffered economic losses. While the richest 20 percent owns almost 85 percent of all wealth, well over 40 million people are poor in the United States. Individuals in the middle and working classes wonder about their own economic future and that of their children. Widening gaps in wealth and income, continued racial and sexual discrimination, threats to the democratic process, persistent child poverty, hunger, and homelessness continue to tear at our social fabric.

Like past editions, this eighth edition of *Social Inequality: Forms, Causes, and Consequences* is intended as a user-friendly introduction to the study of social inequality. The assumptions on which it is based are the same as in previous editions: (1) inequality is multidimensional; (2) explanations of the various forms of inequality are necessary for any resolution of inequality's undesirable consequences; (3) demonstrating inequality's vast extent and forms provides motivation for understanding how it is to be explained; (4) couching a discussion of inequality in its broader historical, cultural, and international context provides a deeper understanding of the nature and role of inequality in society; and (5) an evenhanded approach covering the full range of perspectives and information on inequality is most appropriate, especially for students being exposed to this material for the first time. My goal is to convey, as simply but as compellingly as I can, a sense of the pervasiveness and extensiveness of social inequality in the United States within a comparative context, to show how inequality can be explained, how it affects all of us, and what is being done about it.

This edition benefits from a variety of changes that, I believe, have significantly strengthened the text.

1. At the suggestion of a reviewer, I have placed the chapter on poverty and welfare near the beginning of the book after the one on income and wealth since both deal with economic inequality. Within that chapter, the discussion on the poor and welfare has been reorganized.
2. I have added more extensive discussions on White privilege, the racialization of welfare, gender identity, bullying, and the significance of education.
3. Also added have been new sections on the impact of inequality on trust and stability in society, and theories of global inequality.
4. In several chapters, there has been a more concerted effort to illuminate the specific mechanisms by which inequality is produced and maintained. This includes presenting more details on how status inequality is created, how inequality encourages crime, and how education is involved in the process linking social background with social mobility and attainment.
5. The chapters in Parts One, Three, and Four have been revised, often extensively, with up-to-date information and research so that readers can be made aware of the latest findings on inequality and its consequences.

6. To illustrate major points, new examples have been drawn from recent news on education, race, sexuality, wealth, and law. These include discussions on Arizona law and immigration, U.S. Supreme Court decisions on campaign financing, Title IX cases involving sex discrimination, military policy on sexuality, and school choice.

7. Many new critical questions, photos, and Nutshell features have also been added.

8. Finally, with an eye toward increasing student involvement and class discussion, new to this edition are nine "mini-cases" that have been scattered throughout the text, and film suggestions that have been added at the end of most chapters.

The eighth edition is divided into four major parts. *Part One* examines the extent of economic, status, and political inequality in a general sense, as well as the impact of gender, sexual orientation, and race/ethnicity on economic status and political inequality. Specific theories on gender and racial/ethnic inequality are also presented in detail. *Part Two* covers in-depth discussions of general explanations of inequality. The classical arguments included are those of Marx, Weber, Durkheim, and Spencer, while the contemporary theories discussed include functionalist, social constructionist, reproduction, and labor market theories, along with explanations of inequality between nations. Rather than placing them at the beginning as other texts usually do, I have placed the theory chapters after discussions of the extent of inequality because I believe students will be more inclined to study theories once they realize how extensive inequality is in society. Though scholars often think deductively, students are more likely to start with their own lives, and see what is going on around them before becoming inquisitive about the causes of what is happening in society. The chapters in *Part Three* demonstrate how inequality affects our personal life chances in the forms of physical health and mental well-being as well as how it impacts society's crime rates, environmental inequities, social trust, and social movements. There is no question that inequality's effects are pervasive. Finally, *Part Four* addresses processes of change and stability in the structure of social inequality through discussions of social mobility and attainment, and the justice and legitimacy of inequality. The book concludes with a Glossary of many of the basic terms used in the text.

SUPPLEMENTARY MATERIALS AVAILABLE FOR THE INSTRUCTOR

The following supplements are available to qualified instructors who have adopted this textbook.

INSTRUCTOR'S MANUAL AND TEST BANK (ISBN 020506602X) This resource provides an Overview for each chapter followed by Multiple Choice, True/False, and Essay Questions. The Instructor's Manual and Test Bank is available to adopters at www.pearsonhighered.com.

MYTEST (ISBN 0205066054) This computerized software allows instructors to create their own personalized exams, to edit any or all of the existing test questions, and to add new questions. Other special features of this program include random generation of test questions, creation of alternate versions of the same test, scrambling question sequence, and test preview before printing. Please visit www.pearsonmytest.com.

POWERPOINT PRESENTATION (ISBN 0205066062) The slides follow the chapter outline and feature images from the textbook integrated with the text. The PowerPoint slides are available to adopters at www.pearsonhighered.com.

MYSEARCHLAB This resource contains writing, grammar, and research tools and access to a variety of academic journals, census data, Associated Press news feeds, and discipline-specific readings to help you hone your writing and research skills. In addition, a complete eText is included. MySearchLab can be purchased with the text (ISBN 0205852009) or separately (ISBN 0205699421).

ACKNOWLEDGMENTS

Although any shortcomings in the book are my own responsibility, any improvements in this edition are due in large part to others. These include my friends and colleagues Christa Craven, Raymond Gunn, David McConnell, and Dale Seeds at the College of Wooster, and the reviewers of the eighth edition, Melodie Toby, Kean University; Scott Dolan, the University at Albany; and Tanetta Andersson, Case Western Reserve University, who provided many thoughtful suggestions for improvement of the text. I am grateful for all their detailed comments.

I also want to thank Karen Hanson and Maggie Brobeck at Pearson Higher Education for making the process of writing smoother by being on hand to answer my numerous questions. The continual guidance by and careful copyediting by John Shannon and Leslie Connor were invaluable in raising the quality of the writing. I deeply appreciate their efforts.

Finally, and as always, I am deeply indebted to my wife, Mary Ellen, for her continued love, moral support, and sense of perspective. She really keeps me grounded, and is one of the unsung, real heroes in my life. In an unequal world, she is without equal.

CHAPTER 1

An Introduction to the Study of Social Inequality

Was there, or will there ever be a nation whose individuals were all equal, in natural and acquired qualities, in virtues, talents and riches? The answer in all mankind must be in the negative.

JOHN ADAMS (1735–1826)

First Daniel was demoted and saw his hours cut. Then, like thousands of others, Daniel lost his job. Still, he scrambled to find a new job because he was almost out of money (Chura, April 28, 2009, p. B5). Daniel joins millions of others who are worried about keeping afloat economically. For most people in the United States, the last few years have been a time of economic pain. The number of individuals living in poverty is at an all-time high. This includes the "new poor," a group of people who have never experienced poverty, but who have lost their jobs and fallen on hard times. In 2009, one in five Americans suffered declines in their incomes of at least 25 percent. More people are without insurance to pay medical bills. And as the ranks of the poor and unemployed have swelled, the gap between the richest and poorest has continued to widen, and a 2010 poll indicates that most Americans believe that gap will continue to grow (Pew Research Center, June 22, 2010). All of these events have helped to foment greater feelings of economic insecurity among individuals and strengthened tendencies toward social fragmentation in society.

This is a book about social inequality in all its forms, and how it continuously affects not only social conditions in U.S. society but also our personal lives on the most intimate levels. While social inequality has been a topic of concern at least since the days of Aristotle, the international economic crisis of the last few years has crystallized and intensified its significance and the problems associated with it.

Of course, these problems weigh unevenly across the U.S. population. Individuals are affected more or less by them because of their economic position, ethnicity, race, and gender.

People also reside in places that vary in terms of culture, economic resources, and potentials. Together, a person's individual attributes and how these are interpreted, along with family background, and the political, social, and economic contexts in which people reside, affect their specific attitudes, orientation to life, and their chances for decent and satisfactory lives. Consider your own situation. Imagine that you had come from a family of noticeably different wealth or from a different region or nationality, or that you were of a different race or sex. How would your experiences, perceptions, and opportunities be different?

Inequality is present and affects us at all stages of our lives. Think of your own experiences. Even when young, we hear of people as being from the "wrong side of the tracks," as not being "our kind," as being "above" or "below" us. We hear epithets aimed at persons because of their race, ethnicity, sex, or sexual orientation. As youths, we notice that because of the way they dress, where they live, and who their parents are, some children are treated differently and have more or fewer opportunities than others. We are also smart enough to see that there are class differences associated with different neighborhood schools, and even churches. These economic differences show no sign of disappearing.

Economically, the gap between the top and the bottom has increased and class mobility has stagnated in the last few decades. Analyses by newspapers as divergent as the *Wall Street Journal* and the *New York Times* have publicized the growing inequality. "As the gap between rich and poor has widened since 1970, the odds that a child born in poverty will climb to wealth—or a rich child will fall into the middle class—remain stuck," writes David Wessel in the *Journal* (May 13, 2005, p. A1). In the last 30 years, class "has come to play a greater, not lesser, role in important ways," agree Scott and Leonhardt in the *Times* (May 15, 2005, p. A1).

Statistics confirm the extensive inequality. For example, in 2009, almost 44 million people, or 14.3 percent of the U.S. population, were classified as poor by the Census Bureau. Over 14 million of these were children under 18 years of age. For a single person under 65 years old, this meant having an income below $11,161, and for a family of two adults and two children, having an income of no more than $21,756 (U.S. Census Bureau, September 2010a). In 2009, the median household income in the United States was $49,777—even less than what it was 10 years earlier. Households whose incomes were in the top 20 percent had incomes that were almost 15 times those of households in the poorest 20 percent. And the 2009 compensation of chief executive officers (CEOs) in the top 500 U.S. corporations was 263 times that of the average worker (Anderson et al. 2010). The gap in income has been fueled recently by a combination of a growth in corporate profit in 2009–2010 and major layoffs in the top 500 U.S. corporations. "Companies are doing much better than workers; that's a defining characteristic of today's economy" (Samuelson, August 2, 2010, p. 26). This earnings gap is one indicator of the increasing polarization of incomes in the United States. Since the late 1990s, the incomes of the bottom 20 percent of families have declined by about 3 percent while those of the top 20 percent have increased over 9 percent (Bernstein, McNichol, and Nicholas, April 2008). As we will see in the next chapter, wealth is even more highly polarized than income in the United States, with a small percentage controlling most of the resources. Indeed, economic inequality thrives in the United States.

Recent events have intensified the trend toward greater inequality. To further strengthen their economic positions, for example, an increasing number of companies have been able to successfully pass off their pension obligations to the federal government; consequently, workers will likely receive only a small proportion of their originally promised pensions. "It's a hammer blow to thousands of retirees who will have to somehow make do with lower pension checks," complained Joseph Tiberi, a representative of the International Association of Machinists and Aerospace Workers, after United Airlines withdrew its pensions plans. "The promises United made to them are worthless" (Maynard 2005, p. C2). Similarly, James Roberts, who worked for

Bethlehem Steel for 33 years but had to retire early because of serious health problems, lost a large percentage of his pension benefits and free health care when the company passed on its obligations to the federal government. The pension was money he counted on to "use for food or . . . for entertainment or . . . to help my kids who are in school. . . . The promises were not kept. That makes me angry, because we gave up things in order to get those promises" (Dale 2005, p. D2). Among those especially hard-hit have been blue-collar workers whose manufacturing plants have moved or shut down. Jeffrey Evans's plight is a common one. His truck-parts plant in southern Ohio closed, leaving him unemployed in a part of the state where nearly one-third of the population is living below the poverty line. At 49, he found himself moving back in with his mother: "I lost everything I worked for all my life" (Eckholm 2008a, p. A12).

The injurious impact of inequality is not confined to the working class and poor, however. In recent years, as companies downsize to meet competition and maintain profits, the effects of social and economic forces pushing people into different economic circumstances have been increasingly felt by those in the white-collar ranks. In Toledo, 56-year-old Rob Noonan was laid off from his construction management job, and not only lost his $140,000 salary but much of his retirement savings as well. But he still goes into work because work is so central to his identity. He knows that many of his unemployed friends are "mad at life." He also knows that he could blame his predicament on forces beyond his control or he can put responsibility on himself and try to solve his problem (Slevin, May 10, 2009, p. A4). Unfortunately, Rob's story is not unique. In 2009 alone, almost 2.8 million workers applied for unemployment insurance because of mass lay-offs in the private sector. This was the highest level ever. About 27 percent of these insurance claims were by workers in manufacturing (U.S. Department of Labor, January 27, 2010).

The streamlining and downsizing of businesses have left millions of experienced, specialized workers with temporary part-time jobs or without jobs. Frequently, their immediate response is like that of Edoardo Leoncavallo, an unemployed, middle-aged architect who knows the family problems that result from downward mobility: "I think my wife initially felt resentment. I think she felt, Why can't you bring home the bacon?" (Labich 1993, p. 42). At the same time, advances in computer and information technologies have created opportunities for others to become phenomenally rich. In the early 1990s, few people had heard of Michael Dell. Yet in 2010, this 46-year-old from Austin, Texas, who is the driving force behind Dell computers, was among the richest Americans, with wealth in excess of $14 billion (*Forbes 400,* 2010).

Certainly, individuals disagree on what causes people to wind up in the economic positions they are in. Erma Goulart, a 67-year-old retiree and widow with only a high school diploma, believes that she "worked hard for what I have" but feels that "[t]he rich get more benefits and tax breaks and the poor people don't." In contrast, Steve Schoneck, a 39-year-old college graduate and accounting official for a utility company, thinks that "[y]ou always have the opportunity to try and move forward financially. . . . Over all, I've achieved the American dream. I'm happy" (Scott and Leonhardt 2005, p. A16). These assessments suggest the different emphasis that people place on the relative roles of individual and extra-individual factors in explaining their class positions, and the fact that those who are less successful are less likely to be fully content with their positions.

SOME CONTROVERSIAL ISSUES OF SUBSTANCE

Inequality and its effects are all around us. Consider the impact of inequality one is likely to see during a lifetime involving differences in possessions, places, wealth, experiences, bodies, races, genders, and power. The extensiveness of such inequality is almost overwhelming. And yet, there is a great deal of controversy about social inequalities. Are social inequalities inevitable, especially in a capitalist society that stresses competition and individual success? Why do some people have more than others? Is this natural or unnatural? Do "you always have the opportunity to try" as Steve Schoneck suggests, and does "hard work" always pay off despite the odds against average people that Erma Goulart believes exist? Is inequality a *social* problem or an *individual* one? Is it desirable or not? Is inequality a source of divisiveness or a basis for integration in U.S. society? Are social *classes* really present in the United States, and, if so, are they the most important dimension of inequality in our society? Can equality in political power even exist if economic resources are distributed unequally? Or does the golden rule operate— those with the gold rule? Does the globalization in the world economy strengthen or weaken inequality? These are among the most intriguing and consequential questions that have been raised in the study of social inequality. We now examine some of these in more detail.

Is Inequality Inevitable?

Perhaps the most basic issue relates to the inevitability of inequality. It is important to clarify that reference is being made here to *institutionalized* rather than *individual* inequality (i.e., structured inequality between categories of individuals that are systematically created, reproduced, legitimated by sets of ideas, and relatively stable). We would not be studying this phenomenon if it was not a prominent feature of contemporary society with significant consequences. To ask whether it is inevitable is to address the origins of inequality (i.e., whether it is caused by natural or artificial factors). If social inequality is directly linked to conditions inherent in the nature of groups of individuals or society, then little might be expected to eliminate it. On the other hand, if such inequality arises because of the conscious, intentional, and freely willed actions of individuals or the structures they create in society, then perhaps it can be altered.

One side argues that inequality is always going to be present because of personal differences among individuals either in the form of basic

differences in their own makeups or differences in the amount of effort they expend. A large majority of Americans would appear to agree. Recent polling suggests that most people rank "hard work" more often than any other factor as being critical for economic success (Hanson and Zogby 2010). In explaining his own success, Steve Schoneck believes he took advantage of the opportunities available to everyone and, as a result, was able to achieve the American dream. In his view, he had what it took to get ahead. If there is an open society and if people vary in their talents and motivations, then this would suggest that inequality is inevitable, a simple fact of society. "Some inequalities come about as a result of unavoidable biological inequalities of physical skill, mental capacity, and traits of personality" argued Cauthen (1987, p. 8) in his treatise on equality. Some early philosophers also argued that there are "natural" differences between individuals; in fact, some people still maintain that differences of this type separate the sexes, resulting in the inevitability of inequality. Aristotle took the position that "the male is by nature superior, the female, inferior; and the one rules, and the other is ruled" (in Kriesberg 1979, p. 12). More recently, Goldberg (1973) argued that male dominance and higher achievement are probably inevitable because of the biological differences that he says exist between males and females. These and other explanations of inequality will be discussed in detail later.

Other theorists have argued that inequality is inevitable because as long as certain kinds of tasks are more necessary for the survival of the society than others, and as long as those who are able to perform those tasks are rare, social inequality of rewards among individuals is needed to motivate the best people to perform the most difficult tasks. Under these conditions, the argument goes, inequality cannot be eradicated without endangering the society.

On the other side of the fence are those who argue that economic inequality is not inevitable and is largely the by-product of a system's structure and not the result of major differences in individual or group talents, characteristics, and motivations. Rousseau, for example, linked the origins of inequality to the creation of private property (Dahrendorf 1970, p. 10). It is the characteristics of the political economy and the firms and labor markets within it that are primary determinants of differences in income and wealth. Where a person works and in what industry have major effects on income. Certainly, the job changes resulting from downsizing would suggest this. Essentially, then, this argument states that it is not human nature and individual differences but rather structural conditions that determine where an individual winds up on the ladder of economic inequality. Discrimination is another of those conditions.

Clearly, Erma Goulart suspects that her situation may be at least partially determined by forces (e.g., tax policies) beyond her control. If the conditions that generate social inequality are artificial creations of human actions, then they can be changed, and economic inequality is not inevitable, nor is it necessarily beneficial for the society and all its members. We will examine this controversy more thoroughly in later chapters.

Is Inequality Desirable or Undesirable?

Some scholars think of inequality as a source of integration in society. The functionalist view, for example, which we will explore later, argues that inequality in rewards is a way of making sure that critical occupations are filled with the most qualified persons. That is, since rewards provide motivation to do certain tasks, the structure of inequality is really an incentive system that helps the whole society survive. Other analysts contend that economic and other kinds of inequality create divisiveness between the haves and the have-nots, men and women, minorities and majorities. This is in large part because these groups are not equally likely to believe that the system of inequality is fair. Nor do they agree that inequality works to the benefit of the entire society rather than only a few select groups. Because of this, inequality is more likely to instigate conflict than it is to strengthen cohesion between groups and in society in general.

A variety of studies have asked Americans how they feel about equality and inequality, and it is clear that they have mixed emotions. Americans are decidedly ambivalent about what should be done about social inequality. National studies of U.S. adults suggest that while Americans do not want equality for everyone and that some differences are needed to motivate people to work hard, they think the present degree of income and wealth inequality is too great and unfair and should be reduced (Page and Jacobs 2009; Norton and Ariely 2011). While they tend believe in freedom and individual responsibility, they also feel that governmental help should be given when opportunities for some are blocked and when others need help because of disabilities.

In some ways, Americans are attracted to equality; in other ways, they view inequality as justified. Part of the problem here is that people think about different things when they think about inequality, and people feel differently about the various kinds of equality/inequality; thus, the meaning of equality/inequality is not self-evident. For example, Bryan Turner (1986) identified four basic kinds of equality: (1) equality of human beings—that is, the notion that basically we are all the same and equally worthy as persons; (2) equality of opportunity—the idea that access to valued ends is open to all; (3) equality of condition—that is, that all start from the same position; and (4) equality of results or outcome, or equality of income. The latter is the most radical of the four and the one most likely to incite controversy.

Americans feel quite differently about equality of opportunity than they do about equality of income, and groups feel differently about the fairness of the system. A study of over 2,700 leaders in various areas, for example, showed that they feel any fair distribution of goods should be based on equality of *opportunity* rather than equality of *result*. We will examine the tangle of American beliefs about inequality and its fairness more fully in Chapter 15.

Are There Classes in the United States?

The economic differences that exist among families and among individuals can be easily recognized, but does that mean that social *classes* exist in the United States? There is much to discourage the belief in classes, including the traditional American value system, which stresses individualism, liberty, and the notion that all can get ahead if they work hard. It is inconsistent with these values to believe in or to have class inequalities in which a person's fate is largely determined by the group to which he or she belongs. The value of equality—that we are all one people, that, underneath, U.S. citizens are all "common folk" without formal titles (e.g., duke, lord)—also helps to reinforce the basic notion that all Americans are equal and not members of different classes. To believe otherwise would be un-American.

In addition to some central U.S. values, other conditions moderate the belief in the existence of classes. First of all, a lack of agreement in conceptualization of "class" makes it difficult for there to be agreement on the existence of classes. Second, in contrast to race and sex, there are far fewer reliable and clear-cut physical clues to class position. Walking down the street, it is much easier to tell accurately whether someone is Black or White and male or female than it is to tell what class he or she occupies. Class is often invisible, and therefore we seem to be less often confronted by it. People do not always wear their class positions on their sleeves, so to speak. Think about it: Can you reliably and accurately tell the class positions of your classmates simply by their appearance?

Third, this very invisibility makes it much easier to create and manipulate ideas about the existence of classes in society. It is much easier to say that classes simply do not exist. Finally, the increasing concern for privacy and personal security in U.S. society, which isolates people from each other, enhances the belief in the absence of classes. It is hard to recognize classes and the predicaments of others if we live in shells. Any individual differences in wealth would be viewed as a continuum along which all individuals and families could be located. Here, the image of a system of inequality is one of a tall but narrow ladder. Discrete, wide, separate class layers would not be a part of this perspective.

In fact, some social theorists have argued that the term *social class* has no relevance for the United States, at least in its Marxian definition. In this view, social classes, as unified class-conscious groups with their own lifestyles and political beliefs, do not apply to the United States, whereas they may still fully apply to European countries that have a tradition of class conflict, like Italy or France. There may be differences in lifestyle and status between different occupational groups, but these differences are not thought to be class based. Much of the traditional research in the field of inequality, in fact, has focused on social lifestyle differences between groups rather than on economic-class differences. The focus of research is, of course, conditioned by the historical context in which it occurs, the cultural milieu, and the events of the times. As we shall see, this is clearly the case in research by Americans on social inequality in the United States.

One position, then, is that social classes as full-fledged antagonists do not characterize present-day U.S. society. A second view is that fairly distinct classes exist at the extremes of the inequality hierarchy but not in the middle, which is considered largely a mass of relatively indistinguishable categories of people. A third position is that distinct classes have always existed and continue to exist in the United States, and that class conflict, especially in the institutionalized form of union–management friction, continues to this day. Distinct disparities in the incomes of those in different occupational categories would appear to reinforce the notion that classes exist in the United States, and the increasing polarization of incomes and wealth might further crystallize the image of a class structure in the minds of individuals.

But even if classes do exist, does this mean that they are the most important dimension of social inequality in the United States? Certainly, there are other bases and forms of inequality that are important, such as those between the sexes and between races. Moreover, inequality not only can take an economic form, but also can appear in a social or political form. We will be examining all these forms in the next several chapters, beginning with those forms of inequality that appear more as *outcomes* (i.e., economic, status, political) and then moving on to those forms that can be viewed more as *bases* for those outcomes (i.e., gender, sexual orientation, race/ethnicity). As we will see, Max Weber conceived of each of the three outcomes above as aspects of the distribution of power in society. Power can take each of these forms, and how much power one has in these areas appears to be at least partially *based* on one's gender, sexual orientation, and race/ethnicity. Oftentimes, the latter three bases intersect in their impact or have compounding effects. The combination of being not only a woman but also Black rather than White, for example, can have distinct effects on how far one can get economically, socially, and/or politically. In several of the following chapters, we will have occasion to look at the impact of this "intersectionality" on inequality outcomes.

Can Capitalism and Democracy Coexist?

Do economic and political inequality necessarily go together? The *economic* system of **capitalism** has been linked to the *political* system of democracy in both a positive and a negative manner (Almond 1991). It has been viewed as a determinant as well as an enemy of democracy. Can capitalism and democracy effectively coexist? Pure capitalism demands that markets be open and free and that individuals be able to freely pursue their economic goals, competing with others within the broad framework of the legal system. Capitalism's ideal conditions assume *equality of opportunity,* regardless of sex, race, or any other category. Presumably, individual talents and motivations are the prime determinants of how far a person goes in the system. This is how many would explain the high executive salaries noted previously. "The company pays what it has to pay to recruit and retain a person. . . . A person is worth what the market is willing to pay for him," said Charles Peck, an analyst for the Conference Board (Gladstone 1988, p. 4). A system like this presumably would result in the best people being in the highest positions, with the consequence being an efficiently run economy. But if this type

of competitive capitalism operates in the United States, then economic inequality is unavoidable, since the talents and motivations of individuals and supply and demand for them vary. There is a potential for economic concentration under these circumstances, with a few having much while many have little.

Alongside the U.S. capitalistic economic system exists a political democracy in which everyone is supposed to have a vote in the running of the government. "One person, one vote" is the rule. *Equality of result* is expected in the political arena in the sense that power should be equally distributed. The question is, Can equality of political power and inequality in economic standing coexist? Or does economic power lead to inordinate, unequal political power, thereby making a mockery of political equality? Can open economic capitalism and political democracy exist harmoniously alongside each other? John Adams, one of the Founding Fathers of the United States, expressed concern that "the balance of power in a society accompanies the balance of property and land. . . . If the multitude is possessed of the balance of real estate, the multitude will have the balance of power and, in that case, the multitude will take care of the liberty, virtue and interest of the multitude in all acts of government" (Adams 1969, pp. 376–377). Bryan Turner wrote, "Modern capitalism is fractured by the contradictory processes of inequality in the marketplace and political inequality at the level of state politics. There is an inevitable contradiction between economic class and the politics of citizenship" (1986, p. 24). How do individuals who lack economic resources react politically to this situation? Does the contradiction generate resistance? Is it possible to have a society that is both capitalistic and democratic? During the recent economic crisis, which exposed extensive fraud and inequality, government intrusion into market mechanisms suggested that capitalism and democracy are inherently antagonistic to each other. Conversely, the Supreme Court's recent decision to allow unfettered corporate funding to political campaigns would appear to open the door to greater political power for those who have the money.

Conservatives and liberals generally take different positions on each of the issues we have been discussing. Conservatives tend to praise the virtues of open capitalism and emphasize its benefits for the individual, rather than to see the internal contradictions between capitalism and democracy. Liberals, on the other hand, view unbridled capitalism as destructive of human beings and stress the linkage between economic and political power, seeing money as a contaminant of the political process. Conservatives also tend to view social inequality as inevitable, if not necessary and desirable, and perceive the United States as being largely classless, seeing the similarities among Americans as being more fundamental than the differences. In sharp contrast, liberals conclude that inequality is neither inevitable nor desirable, that the United States is a class society, and that basic social, economic, and political conditions create deep divisions within the population.

Does Globalization Reduce or Increase Inequality?

As a whole, U.S. society is increasingly susceptible to conditions and developments beyond its borders. Many of these are economic, but others are political, social, cultural, and sometimes even religious in nature. The weakening of national boundaries that attends globalization has allowed nations to trade, borrow, and transport goods and services more easily. At the same time, it has also meant a greater flow and interchange of currencies, peoples, and influence. As a worldwide force, has globalization had a positive or negative effect on inequality? As we will see later, some argue that free trade and exchange of ideas and technologies encourage the leveling out of differences and inequalities among nations, while others contend that open markets favor the powerful and are used by economic powers to strengthen and deepen their hold on global economic operations. The former argue that open exchange fosters the dissemination of technology and medicine to nations in need of help, leading to benefits such as the development of larger middle classes in places like India and China. The latter allege more negative

outcomes: Freedom and open borders advantage wealthy countries and disadvantage poorer ones. Transnational corporations and other international organizations can bypass restraints and regulations by individual countries, thereby weakening the power of national governments over them. The opening up of broader markets and labor supplies also gives corporations more leverage over local governments and workers.

Whatever its effects, the impact of globalization is not simply economic. Open exchanges among nations have political, social, and cultural consequences as well that affect the shape and character of national systems of inequality. Globalization's rapid expansion has made international relationships much more complicated and difficult to understand because of the vast differences in histories, traditions, and cultures that exist among partners in the world marketplace. The combination of open borders and a lack of full understanding of other countries and peoples can breed feelings of insecurity and encourage protectionist tendencies by national governments. Those in power can then feed worries about dangers like terrorism to push policies that help to maintain their power (Beland 2008). These policies often take the form of more restrictive immigration and trade policies. The inflow of immigrant workers with cultures and behaviors quite different from those of native or dominant populations increases the significance of status differences and inequality, and can inflame hostilities within the working class. Because it makes borders more permeable, globalization also breaks down a country's insulation from a multitude of problems originating in other nations. The increasingly dense network of relationships around the globe means that changes and conditions in one place can reverberate throughout the whole international system. Consequently, the full impact of globalization on the economic, status, and power balance *among* countries and economic, social, and political inequality *within* them has yet to be completely mapped out. But there appears to be little question that globalization's impact across the world, at least for the near future, will continue unabated.

ISSUES OF METHODOLOGY

In addition to the preceding substantive controversies, there are also important methodological issues that must be considered in the study of inequality, most of which you will encounter as you read through the following chapters. How these questions are handled by scholars heavily affects the conclusions they draw about the nature and extent of social inequality. These issues frequently involve questions about definitions and measurement of concepts, levels of analysis, and the relative impacts of race, class, sex, and gender on individual lives.

Definitional Problems

One of the most fundamental questions involves the measurement of social class and poverty. As noted later, *social class* has been defined in different ways, using different indices. Some consider social classes simply as different categories of people in which individuals in the same category happen to have similar levels of education, income, and occupational **prestige**, whereas others view different classes and organized groups in conflict with each other. Still others focus on lifestyle as the critical factor that distinguishes social classes. These different definitions result in different measures of social-class position. Hollingshead's Two-Factor Index of Social Position, for example, involves objectively rating a person from 1 to 7 on occupational and educational scales (Hollingshead and Redlich 1958). Wright's measure of social class, in sharp contrast, uses exploitation as its defining characteristic, and consequently separates different types of exploitation that individuals use or are exposed to while they work (cf., e.g., Wright and Cho 1992).

As in the case of social class, *poverty* has also been defined and measured in different ways. Some argue that being poor means more than not having money—it also means a lack of status and power. Even when money is used as the measure of poverty, there is disagreement about whether it should be gross or net income, whether it should include income from government programs, whether it should be current or long-term income,

and so on. Currently, the federal government sets income thresholds to determine one's poverty, and uses gross income from all sources as the measure of a person's income. Other methodological issues arise when examining additional dimensions of social inequality. How to measure discrimination when discussing racial or gender inequality, how to measure the openness of a society using its mobility rates, how to measure political power, and how to gauge the comparability of situations when discussing how the degree of social inequality in the United States stacks up against that found in other countries—all are methodological issues of significance and difficulty.

Why are these differences in measurement and definition so professionally and practically important? Professionally, varying definitions and measures make comparability of results difficult and raise problems of communication among scholars supposedly studying the same phenomenon. Practically, these different perspectives are significant and involve heated discussion among politicians because how such things as openness, discrimination, poverty, and class are measured affects what kinds of policies they think should be pursued. For example, the measure of poverty affects how much poverty exists, how big a problem it is, and how much, if anything, needs to be done about it. Simply recognizing poverty as a social problem, in fact, is the result of some individuals or groups "making claims" about poverty's problematic nature and then using a particular style to convince others that it is a problem (Ibarra and Kitsuse 2003). Others may not see poverty as a social problem or may not be convinced by the styles used to demonstrate that poverty really is a social problem. The definition and measurement of poverty, therefore, is a political hot potato because so much rides on which approach is accepted at the time.

In addition to class and poverty, "race" is also a contested concept because while we have traditionally thought of it as designating innate and fixed biological differences between individuals, it has increasingly been shown to be a concept that has been *socially constructed* over time. Rather than an inherent quality of individuals, it is seen as a manufactured product, resulting from social conflict and power arrangements in society. Racial classifications and positions within them change as political, social, and other shifts occur in society. I will discuss the theory of racial formation more fully in Chapter 8.

With respect to the discussion of women, the trend in terminology has been to use the term *gender* rather than *sex* when discussing differences and inequalities between men and women. However, they mean different things. When we speak of a person's *sex,* we ordinarily are referring to the biological status of being *female* or *male. Gender,* however, denotes the definitions, assignments, and behaviors that different groups and cultures assign to the sexes, and these can vary across societies. These are definitions and assignments "built into" the roles and positions in the economy and other institutions, creating a gendered social structure (Lorber 2001). In other words, *gender* is a "cultural construct" (Caplan 1987; see also Ortner and Whitehead 1981).

As we will see, some have argued that *sex* is also a product of culture, which would give the usually biological term a decidedly cultural, that is social scientific, interpretation. From the 1960s onward, many social scientists have embraced the above distinctions between sex and gender, and have even emphasized the term *gender* over *sex,* sometimes avoiding the latter term altogether. Perhaps this is in part because the latter smacks of biology, an alleged basis of behavior that has been submerged in social science. "Dropping sex and adopting gender buried biology," contends Dorothy Smith. "Although legitimate as a political move, it has left us with no way of recognizing just how biology enters into relations among women, men, and children. I think of my bodily experience, particularly as a mother, and I am powerfully aware of how biological fundamentals entered into that experience" (Smith 2009, p. 76). There are biological components to who we are as beings (e.g., menstruation, hormones), even how we react to them is largely a cultural phenomenon. While analytically separate, sex and gender almost always intersect.

Thus, the terms *sex* and *gender* will both be used in the text. When the focus is on inequalities between males and females as sexes (e.g., income and poverty differences), the term *sex* will be used. When the focus is on social definitions or roles, often socially ranked and culturally assigned to males or females, **gender** will be used. For example, occupations are often "gendered" (i.e., associated with or considered most appropriate for either men or women). One would think that it is indisputable that there are only two sexes. But even that is open to question, as the discussions in Chapter 7 will show. This suggests that definitions are always socially constructed.

Finally, the concept of *power* is also a fuzzy one. Power can exist in many forms and can be viewed on several levels. In the discussion of political inequality in Chapter 5, I will focus initially on power in decision-making processes in the *political institution.* It is not unusual for us to think of power solely as a property of the political or governmental realm. But power inequality can also exist in the employment relationships between men and women, bosses and workers, Blacks and Whites. Since work dominates the everyday lives of most adults, I will also examine power relationships in the work environment.

In addition to the definitional issues swirling around all these concepts, there is also a dilemma involving their interrelationship. Can one effectively separate the independent effects of race, class, sex, and gender on the individual? Although each is a distinct variable, all are inextricably intermixed in the lives of actual individuals. Persons simultaneously occupy positions on each of these, and, in real life, they are deeply interconnected. We must recognize both their separateness and their interconnectedness when considering their roles in people's lives.

Levels of Analysis

The study of social inequality is concerned with both individuals and groups, personal positions as well as structural arrangements. Thus, analysis proceeds on several levels. For example, we are interested in how an individual's class-related characteristics affect the probability of that person being arrested, but we are also interested in how the structure of inequality itself affects the crime rate for the society as a whole. We are interested in the process by which individuals attain higher or lower status positions, but we are also interested in how class structures shift in society and how changes in occupational structures affect rates of social mobility. We will look not only at how an individual's race or sex affects his or her income but also at how institutionalized discrimination affects the overall structure of inequality between the races and sexes. Many of the chapters to follow take into account these important methodological issues.

ORGANIZATION OF THE BOOK

The text is divided into four major parts. Part One addresses the extent of inequality in its various forms. Chapters 2, 3, 4, and 5 focus on specific forms of inequality that concern resource *outcomes* (i.e., income/wealth, poverty, social status, and power) which are distributed unequally among individuals and groups in the United States. Inequalities related to sex, sexual orientation, and race, while viewed as specific forms of inequality in their own right, are also significant *bases* for inequalities in resource outcomes. They are addressed in Chapters 6, 7, and 8. Sex, sexual orientation, and race affect the distribution of wealth, status, and power in our society. Unlike other inequality texts, I have included a chapter on sexual orientation because, as many recent examples of bullying, harassment, and discrimination in the United States indicate, it is a significant basis for social and economic inequality. Finally, to place the U.S. structure and dynamics of inequality within a broader framework, I will briefly discuss the global context of U.S. inequality at the end of each of these chapters. The reader will then be able to see how the United States stands in relation to other nations.

Several of the chapters in Part One include *specific* causes of given forms of inequality. Part Two presents the major *general* explanations for social inequality, with Chapter 9 including discussions of Marx's, Weber's, Durkheim's, and Spencer's classical perspectives on inequality.

Chapter 10 analyzes more contemporary explanations, ranging from functionalist theories, to social reproduction and constructionist theories, to labor-market theories of inequality.

Having discussed the extent and explanations of inequality in Parts One and Two, Part Three demonstrates the pervasive *consequences* of inequality for individuals and society. Physical and mental health, hunger, and homelessness are all subject to the influences of individual positions in the hierarchy of social inequality. These personal effects are the focus of Chapter 11. The long arm of inequality reaches far into personal and private worlds, but its effects also extend into the wider society as well. In Chapter 12, the effects of inequality on crime, environmental equity, social trust, and solidarity are explored. Specifically, the effects of socioeconomic position, race, and sex and gender on criminal justice are examined, ranging from the chances of being arrested to the likelihood of being given a long sentence. Street crimes, white-collar crimes, and hate crimes are each discussed. Inequality also has played a role in generating high crime rates, and raising questions about environmental justice. As we will see when examining the negative effects of inequality in a global context, the United States does not always fare well when compared to other rich industrial nations.

On a broader level, the labor, civil rights, and women's movements can be viewed as reactions to inequalities based on class, race, and gender, respectively, inequalities that are perceived as unjust. Chapter 13 surveys the history of these movements and their relationship to inequality.

Part Four of the book examines what has been happening to the system of inequality and how people feel about it. Chapter 14 asks whether there is a great deal of mobility in U.S. society. Do rags-to-riches stories provide a typical picture of the careers of most Americans? How does the United States compare with other countries in its rate of mobility? Is it more open than others? Have African Americans and women become more upwardly mobile in recent years? What determines how far up people go in the occupational hierarchy? Finally, Chapter 15 discusses the thorny issue of the equity of inequality. What do Americans think about their system's inequality? Is it fair or not? What do they think determines or *should* determine how far one gets in the system? These comprise some of the central questions addressed in Part Four.

Each chapter ends with a short set of questions, and in some cases, films, addressing some critical issues raised by the chapter. They are aimed at forcing you to come to grips with central problems in inequality, often by looking at inequality in your own life. *Web Connections* sections suggest various websites where you can get more information and which you can use as bases for course exercises. These should broaden and deepen your understanding of inequality. Many chapters also contain a brief *Nutshell* covering a topical issue from the popular press or a *mini-case* addressing a specific issue to be analyzed. Each issue is introduced to serve as a point of departure for classroom discussion. Finally, a *Glossary* of basic terms used in the text follows the last chapter.

The lines separating the social sciences are often vague, the result being that discussions in the book often will draw on the work of economists, anthropologists, as well as sociologists, and others. In addition, there is material from other countries. These inclusions, hopefully, result in a more thorough and well-rounded perspective on the structure and process of social inequality in the United States.

Critical Thinking

1. Try to think of a personal relationship you have with someone who is unequal to you in some way, and yet the inequality appears to have few negative effects on you or your relationship. What characteristics lessen the impact of the inequality in this relationship? Discuss some lessons from this relationship that might be used to diminish the negative effects of inequality in society as a whole.
2. Is social inequality a problem that demands the full attention of society or is it merely a personal problem of those living below the middle class? Explain your answer.
3. Is it possible for *equality* in political power to exist alongside economic *inequality*?
4. Gazing into your crystal ball, do you think the long-run impact of increasing relationships among peoples around the world will lead to a leveling of inequalities among them or will it solidify or increase existing inequalities?

Web Connections

Several of the following chapters use information obtained from national polls, many of which are published on the Internet. The National Council on Public Polls suggests that among the questions you should consider before accepting poll results are the following: (1) Who sponsored and who conducted the poll? (2) Is the sample large enough and representative of the whole population? (3) Were any important groups excluded from the poll? (4) Was the technique used in the interview likely to affect the answers received? (5) Was the wording of the questions neutral or biased in some way? (6) Are the survey results still valid or are they out-of-date? (*Source:* Carr 2005.)

CHAPTER 2

Class, Income, and Wealth

Two nations; between whom there is no intercourse and no sympathy;
who are as ignorant of each other's habits, thoughts, and feelings,
as if they were dwellers in different zones, or inhabitants of
different planets. . . . You speak of . . . the rich and the poor.

BENJAMIN DISRAELI (1804–1881)

In the next several chapters, we will be considering several forms of inequality: economic, status, gender, racial, and political. In this chapter, we examine economic inequality in the form of social class and income/wealth differences. Chapter 3 considers the extent of poverty and attempts to address it. We begin with economic inequality because other aspects of inequality are often strongly related to economic or class inequality in a society. As we will see in later chapters, economic position has a significant impact on the prestige, power, and life chances that individuals possess. Consequently, a discussion of social class and economic inequality is critical for a full understanding of other forms of inequality.

THE EVERYDAY REALITY OF CLASS

In general, Americans do not like to talk about **class**. "Class is not discussed or debated in public because class identity has been stripped from popular culture. The institutions that shape mass culture and define the parameters of public debate have avoided class issues. . . . [F]ormulating issues in terms of class is unacceptable, perhaps even un-American" (Mantsios 2004, p. 193). But their reluctance to discuss class does not mean that Americans do not have a mental picture of the class structure or their position in it. The meaning of class for the public is rooted in their everyday experiences and relationships. Awareness of class differences begins early; even pre-school children categorize individuals as rich or poor. Early in elementary school, they already have a distinct image of how occupations vary in prestige (Ramsey 1991).

Class structure is also a subjective reality for adults. When asked about it, people in the United States are much more likely to agree on and have clear images of the top and bottom of the class structure than they are of the middle classes, which are seen as more amorphous and heterogeneous. The perceived distinctiveness of the top, for example, is based not only on their wealth, but also on the social and cultural boundaries that are seen as separating them from those below. Because of their extraordinary wealth, those at the top of the economic hierarchy often take on notoriety or celebrity status (e.g., Bill Gates, the Kennedy family). Those who have "old wealth" are often very guarded about who is let into their group and who is not, which again identifies them as unique and different from those below them (cf., e.g., Kendall 2002; Frank 2005). The popular image of the bottom is similarly clear, with that perception being dominated by stereotypes of individuals who are chronically on welfare, homeless, and often of minority status. The economic middle, in contrast, is seen as mainly made up of white-collar professionals, semiprofessionals, and highly paid blue-collar "aristocrats," that is, a loose collection of widely varying individuals not nearly as homogeneous in the public's eye as those at the top and bottom. Below them, the working class is often described as being composed of those in less-skilled, routine white-collar and blue-collar positions.

Most Americans feel at least fairly strongly that they belong to a particular class (Jackman and Jackman 1983). When asked to place themselves in the class structure, usually 80–90 percent of adults say that they are either "middle" or "working" class. In 2003, a survey by the Gallup Organization indicated that 63 percent of the adults interviewed considered themselves as "middle" or "upper-middle" class, while 28 percent classified themselves as "working" class. Only 1 percent thought they were "upper class" and 7 percent labeled themselves "lower" class (Robison 2003). A 2005 *New York Times* poll found similar results—57 percent and 35 percent of respondents, respectively, considered themselves as belonging either to the middle class or to the working class (Scott and Leonhardt, May 15, 2005).

But on other aspects of class structure, individuals vary in their perceptions. When asked in past surveys to describe the nature of the class structure in the United States, individuals' images have differed depending on their own class positions. Historically, middle-class respondents have described the class structure more as a relatively smooth continuum with few major breaks between classes, while those in the working and lower classes have been more likely to see classes as discrete, distinct groups, and to perceive a smaller number of classes. A recent poll found that 61 percent of Blacks compared to only 38 percent of Whites believe that the United States is divided into the "haves" and "have-nots." However, these percentages have grown over the last two decades corresponding to growth in the polarization of incomes and wealth (Ludwig 2003). Generally, those in the lower classes are more likely than those in higher classes to believe there is a greater distance between the top and the bottom (cf., e.g., Ossowski 1963; Vanneman and Pampel 1977).

Criteria used to place individuals in a given class also vary. Occupational positions that are seen as requiring mental ability or as having authority over others are generally classified as at least middle class rather than working class (Jackman and Jackman 1983). Class position itself affects what individuals think distinguishes persons in different class positions. For example, those in the working and lower classes are more likely to see the upper class as being distinguished by *money,* while those in the higher classes see their main distinction as deriving from their *lifestyle.* Indeed, individuals in the higher professions are significantly more likely than persons in other occupational statuses to engage in "highbrow" cultural activities (Katz-Gerro 2002). With respect to other criteria, married men and women vary in how much they consider their separate incomes and educations when describing their class position. Married men and women, for example, agree that both the husband's and wife's incomes affect their class position equally, but they differ on whether their own as well as their spouse's educations help define their class position (Yamaguchi and Wang 2002). What all these research results suggest is that while Americans tend to agree on some broad ideas about U.S. class structure, there are also many ways in which their views vary, resulting in the absence of a single crystallized image of the U.S. class structure as a whole.

TWO VIEWS OF U.S. CLASS STRUCTURE

Mirroring popular disagreements are debates among scholars about the nature of the class structure in the United States. Some portrayals of class structure use sets of very diverse criteria, following closely a socioeconomic definition of class, whereas others try to be more faithful to Marxian criteria. Neither of these approaches is inherently better than the other, and each focuses on criteria that have been found to have separate effects on individuals' life conditions. Each approach attempts to identify meaningful breaks in the class system, and, as such, each is useful in characterizing different aspects of economic inequality. Consequently, rather than presenting only one model of the U.S. class structure, in the following sections we will examine both socioeconomic and Marxian images of the U.S. class system.

Class Structure as a Continuum

Traditionally, U.S. researchers have defined social class statistically in terms of occupational status, education, and/or income. Individuals or families that fall in the same category on these dimensions are then said to be in the same social class. Generally, persons receive a score based on their placement on these variables; in essence, social class is determined by a statistical score. Since these scores are continuous, with small differences in scores between individuals in adjacent positions, the class hierarchy is frequently viewed as a continuum where the boundaries between classes are not always clear and distinct. Classes

may merge imperceptibly into one another and, as a result, boundary determination becomes an important problem.

Another characteristic of this approach is that the dimensions used to measure social class are not all purely economic in nature. Occupational status is essentially a measure of the *prestige* of an occupation—that is, it reflects the subjective judgment of individuals about an occupation. Education is also a noneconomic phenomenon. The result is that this measure of social class is multidimensional in that it mixes economic with social dimensions of inequality. Consequently, this measure is often referred to as **socioeconomic status**.

Finally, this measure does not assume any kind of necessary relationship between the classes. There is no assumption, for example, that the upper and working classes are in conflict with each other. Classes are merely the result of scores on a series of socioeconomic dimensions. In sum, the traditional, more conservative measure in the United States assumes that the structure of social class, or socioeconomic status, is (1) a continuum of inequality between classes, (2) partly the result of subjective judgments as well as objective conditions, (3) multidimensional, and (4) nonconflictual in nature.

As an example of this approach to class, Gilbert defined social class as "a large group of families . . . approximately equal in rank to each other and clearly differentiated from other families. . . . The various stratification variables tend to converge and jell; they form a pattern, and this pattern creates social classes" (2003, pp. 14–15).

Using the socioeconomic criteria of income, education, and occupation, Gilbert (2003) proposed that the United States contains six major classes. A condensed version of his model is presented here. The percentage of households in each class is enclosed in parentheses.

1. *Capitalist Class (1%):* Graduates of high-ranking universities who are in top-level executive positions or are heirs who have an income average of $2 million mainly from assets.

2. *Upper Middle Class (14%):* Individuals with at least a college degree who are in higher professional or managerial positions or owners of medium-sized businesses who have incomes of about $120,000.
3. *Middle Class (30%):* Individuals who have high school degrees and maybe some college who are in lower managerial or white-collar, or high-skilled, high-pay, blue-collar occupations who make about $55,000 a year.
4. *Working Class (30%):* Persons with high school degrees who are in lower-level white-collar (e.g., clerical, sales workers) or blue-collar positions (e.g., operatives) whose incomes are about $35,000 per year.
5. *Working Poor (13%):* Those with some high school who are service workers, or are in the lowest paid blue-collar and clerical positions who have average incomes of $22,000.
6. *Underclass (12%):* Individuals with at best some high school education who work part-time, are unemployed, or are on welfare, and who have incomes under $12,000.

In surveying different models of U.S. class structure that use several kinds of socioeconomic criteria, there are some remarkable *similarities* as well as differences among them. These models usually see the structure as being composed of five to seven classes, rather than as a dichotomy or trichotomy. Also, the proportion of the population said to be in each class in each model is very similar. Generally, the working and middle classes, in which the majority of the population is placed, are considered to be about equal in size, and the upper class is generally said to be around 1 percent. Then, depending on whether employed as well as unemployed are included in the lower class, its percentage can range from 10 to 25 percent.

Some of the most significant *differences* in traditional models center on the criteria used to place individuals in various classes. One notable difference lies in the distinctions made about the lower class. Some researchers simply include all those who are poor, while others draw a line between those who are poor but work and those

who are chronically unemployed and poor for long periods of time. The term **underclass** is frequently used to refer to the latter group. There is some debate about the actual size of the underclass. A conference of experts on the issue agreed on the definition of the underclass as "poor people who live in a neighborhood or census tract with higher rates of unemployment, crime, and welfare dependency" (McFate 1987, p. 11). By this definition, the underclass would include 5–10 percent of the population.

Another difference among the models of class structure concerns the way they treat white-collar and blue-collar occupations. Traditionally, blue-collar work has been considered manual in nature, while white-collar work has been defined as nonmanual. Manual work was generally viewed as requiring primarily physical and routine rather than mental and intricate skills/tasks. Recently, however, the lines distinguishing the nature of blue-collar and white-collar jobs have become blurred. The routine nature of much low-level white-collar work has encouraged some analysts to place individuals who do this kind of work into the working class, and to place those who do complex, high-skilled, well-paying blue-collar work into the middle class. As technological change occurs, and some physical labor by humans is replaced by machines, the character of the working class changes correspondingly.

The question of the relative importance of the manual/nonmanual and level-of-complexity criteria is the subject of some debate and has become focused in the debate about the **proletarianization** of some white-collar work and the **embourgeoisement** of some blue-collar work. Briefly, the proletarianization argument states that a significant and increasing number of white-collar jobs are routine and boring, demand little skill, and involve little worker control. Qualitatively, this makes them no different from many blue-collar jobs. Some have described those who occupy those positions as a "new working class," especially as the economy advances and becomes more automated. Generally, Marxists tend to view the U.S. class structure in a manner consistent with the proletarianization thesis.

In contrast, the embourgeoisement thesis, embraced more often by those with a more conservative bent, proposes that complex, high-paying blue-collar jobs take on many of the sociocultural characteristics of the white-collar middle class. As society moves into a postindustrial phase and its labor force becomes more saturated with white-collar service positions, the size of the blue-collar workforce shrinks. Most people become middle class in their standards of living and lifestyles.

Although several past studies have found that clerical positions have become deskilled (e.g., Crompton and Jones 1984), others have found a distinct trend toward *deproletarianization*. There has been an increase in the proportion of the labor force who are managers, experts, or supervisors, providing more support for the postindustrial theories than the Marxist thesis of proletarianization. Wright and Martin (1987) proposed that these results may simply mean that capitalism has internationalized itself and has shifted more proletarianized occupations into Third World countries. Examination of occupational shifts during the 1990s suggests that changes have occurred throughout the economy, resulting in multiple trends. The expansion of high-tech jobs near the top of the occupational hierarchy accompanied an increase in low-paying service jobs at the lower rungs of the occupational ladder. In between these extremes, the middle suffered the decline of unionized, high-paying manufacturing jobs (Wright and Dwyer 2003). The Department of Labor anticipates that between 2006 and 2016 occupational growth will be highest in the broad professional and service fields (Dohm and Shniper 2007). If these shifts continue, they may signal a faster movement toward a more polarized occupational structure.

Class Structure as Antagonistic Categories

In contrast to the continuum approach, Marxian sociologists generally object to the mixing of economic, status, and other socioeconomic variables because they believe it dilutes what Marx considered to be the core economic meaning of social class. Marx believed class was basically an economic phenomenon and was defined by an individual's position in the social relations of production, by control over the physical means (property) and social means (labor power) of production. In other words, class is not defined by income or occupation but rather by ownership/control in the system of production. In this view, introducing other socioeconomic variables, such as prestige or occupational status, only distorts the meaning of social class. Thus, in the Marxian definition, class is much less multidimensional in nature. Moreover, the crucial differences between the social classes are qualitative in nature—that is, the class system is not a continuous hierarchy in which the lines between classes blur and classes merge into each other. Rather, the boundaries between the classes are discrete and clear. Finally, classes in this view are defined by the exploitation that exists between them and by the interconnection between the functions of each class. This means that a given class is defined by its relationship to another class. Workers are members of the working class, for example, *because* of the nature of their relationship to capital and capitalists. Different classes perform distinct but interrelated functions in capitalist society.

While some Marxists define class strictly in terms of structural position, others incorporate a social-psychological dimension into their conception, arguing that **class consciousness** or a shared sense of belongingness and organized opposition must also be present for *social* classes to be present—that is, individuals must identify with each other and understand their real relationship to other classes and act on that knowledge. Ollman (1987) stated flatly that the concept of class has both subjective and objective dimensions, the subjective element being a sense of unity that develops as a class emerges. People "tend to acquire over time other common characteristics as regards . . . lifestyle, political consciousness and organization that become, in turn, further evidence for membership in their particular class and subsidiary criteria for determining when to use the class label. Here, class is a quality that is attached to people" (Ollman 1987, p. 64). In this approach, people become a real *social* class when they acquire a common culture and political awareness. In addition to occupying the same location or position in relation to the means of production, then, people in the same social class "share the distinctive traditions common to their social position" (Szymanski 1978, p. 26). This common identity, especially when it involves awareness of common exploitation and engagement in class struggle, Marx suggested, is what welds an aggregate of people into a social class, or a "class-for-itself" (Bottomore 1966).

The existence of a class-for-itself means that it exists as a self-conscious group ready to advance its own interests. The strength of this kind of class consciousness among the working class in the United States has been moderate at best, and it pales in comparison to some European countries like Sweden, France, and Italy. There have been specific instances when workers have banded together and fought corporations despite dangers to each worker's welfare (McCall 2008). But while evidence suggests that there is some consistency between class position and attitudes toward corporations and management, American workers as a whole have not acted on their beliefs in the political arena. The lower level of unionization and the absence of a working-class political party in the United States have slowed the development of class solidarity (Brooks 1994; Wright 1997).

As we have seen, there is lack of agreement on the exact definition and measurement of social class even among Marxists. Marx never gave an explicit, clear-cut definition of class. He suggested various definitions and different numbers and types of social classes at different points in his writing. Nevertheless, his approach and that of contemporary Marxian analysts are clearly different from those discussed earlier who define class in broader socioeconomic terms. In sum, Marxists generally view classes as (1) discrete rather than continuous, (2) real rather than statistical creations, (3) economic in nature, and (4) conflict-ridden. In contrast, traditional conservative approaches define classes as existing along a continuous hierarchy, largely statistically created, and being multidimensional and relatively harmonious in their relationships.

Perhaps the most sophisticated recent attempt to analyze the class structure of the United States in Marxian terms comes from Erik Wright. Wright's characterization of U.S. class structure uses exploitation as the defining element (Wright and Cho 1992; Western and Wright 1994). Classes and class locations are distinguished by an individual's ability to exploit or be exploited on the basis of (1) property, (2) organizational authority, or (3) expertise or skill.

Combining these three criteria, Wright identified several class "locations" within this structure of class relationships. The most elemental distinction involves those who have property from those who do not (owners vs. nonowners). Among *owners,* Wright has separated capitalists who employ others (employers) from those who do not (petty bourgeoisie). Application of the other two criteria of class location, authority and expertise, results in distinctions among *employees,* which create a number of class locations. Considering the criterion of bureaucratic authority, there are those who have it and those who do not (managers and nonmanagers). Individuals are considered managers if they are involved in policy decisions and are in a position to impose sanctions on others. Employees also differ in level of skill or expertise, which is the third criterion of class position. There are (1) managers and professionals who are experts, (2) workers and managers who are not experts, and (3) semiprofessionals (such as those in technical jobs) who are in between. In this scheme, the owners might be considered the capitalist class and the workers compose the working class. The remaining groups among employees (managers, professionals, semiprofessionals) might be viewed as the middle class because they have characteristics of both those above and below them. In a real sense, as Wright has put it, these employees occupy "contradictory" locations because not only are they exploited as employees but they also exploit other employees because of their authority and/or expertise assets. Frequently, this group of employees is referred to as a "new"

OWNERS (approximately 15 percent)
(are self-employed in the system of production)

includes

(1) employers, (2) petty bourgeoisie

EMPLOYEES IN CONTRADICTORY (MIDDLE) LOCATIONS
(approximately 45 percent)
(have expertise and/or authority but are not owners)

includes

(3) manager/experts, (4) other managers, (5) professionals, (6) semiprofessionals

WORKERS (approximately 40 percent)

includes

(7) those who are in nonowner/nonexpert/nonmanagerial positions

FIGURE 2.1   Wright's Class Structure

middle class because of its relatively recent growth within capitalism. Figure 2.1 graphically depicts Wright's class structure.

The figure gives a rather static, broad view of the class structure and how persons might be located within it. But Wright has pointed out that class position also depends on the relationship a person has with others in his or her family— relationships that may link the individual to different classes. In other words, a person's own position is "mediated" by the position of others. For example, two individuals may both be professionals, but one lives in a family made up primarily of workers while the other lives in a family in which all the adults are professionals. These varying sets of relationships connect each of these professionals to the class structure in different ways. The subjective meaning of social class and how they place themselves in the class structure may be different for college professors whose parents are working class, for example, than it is for professors who come from a fully professional family. One can easily see how the life experiences and lifestyles of these individuals would likely differ.

In addition, two individuals may be in the same class at a given time, but one is located on a clear and recognized career path that will take that person to a higher position (e.g., being on the "fast track" to an executive position at a corporation) while the other person is in a dead-end job. This "temporal" aspect of class position means that to define class location fully, one must take into account the span of the broader career trajectory in which the current position is embedded. The addition of the concepts of mediated and temporal class position makes Wright's characterization of class structure more complex as well as realistic.

Common to this Marxian conceptualization of social class is the idea that classes are tied together by relationships of exploitation. In addition to Wright, Sorensen (2000) suggested a measure of class that uses exploitation as its central characteristic. He defined *exploitation* in terms of the ownership or control of assets that produce returns or "rents" for the individual. "Rents are returns on assets that are in fixed supply because single owners of the asset to the market control the supply of those assets. . . . I propose to define *exploitation class* as structural locations that provide rights to rent-producing assets" (p. 1525). Consequently, the class structure consists of classes who do or do not own such assets and that are fixed in an antagonistic relationship to each other. While Wright agreed with Sorensen on the importance of using exploitation to define class relationships and structure, recall that he believes the bases of exploitation and the nature of the relationships between exploiter and exploited are more complex than what is suggested by the concept of rent-producing assets.

Several critics have raised questions about Wright's measure of class position. Meiksins (1988) argued that it is not necessarily true that those with skills or credentials exploit those below them. This is an empirical issue and cannot simply be settled by conceptual fiat. Resnick and Wolff (2003) have further suggested that the recent emphasis on basing a Marxian class model on the concept of exploitation has led to neglect in the use of another central concept in Marx's theory as a basis for class modeling, namely, "surplus value." Resnick and Wolff argue that classes of employees can be distinguished according to whether they (1) produce surplus, (2) appropriate (i.e., take) it, or (3) are given part of the distribution of the surplus that is produced. This would suggest that there are three main classes in a capitalist society like the United States. In a word, they view workers as *producing* the surplus, capitalists as *appropriating* it, and managers/supervisors as receiving *distributed* surplus because they provide the conditions under which workers produce surplus. Following Marx, Resnick and Wolff define workers as "productive" because they actually create the surplus, while capitalists, managers, and the like are classified as "unproductive." Resnick and Wolff do not contend that their class model is better than Wright's, but only that there are potentially several models, each of which taps a different part of social and economic reality and, therefore, helps us to understand some parts of class reality while ignoring others.

SOME GENERALIZATIONS   As you have seen, all analysts of U.S. class structure wrestle with recurrent issues of where to place given sets of individuals within the class structure. Most prominent among these issues are (1) whether to place lower white-collar positions (i.e., routine clerical, service, sales occupations) within the middle or working class; (2) whether to place high-level managers within the middle or upper class, or in a separate category such as the corporate class; (3) how and where to incorporate the rising number of "knowledge" workers or professionals within the class structure; and (4) whether to include the poor and/or unemployed among the

working class or to consider them a separate lower class or underclass. As the nation's economy experiences downsizing and similar corporate moves, another increasingly relevant issue will be to figure out how temporary, floating, and new entrepreneurs fit into the U.S. class structure.

In reviewing both the multidimensional socioeconomic and Marxian models, a few generalizations may be made about U.S. class structure. *First,* there appears to be general agreement across all these models that the upper or capitalist class makes up only a very small percentage of the population, about 1 to 2 percent. *Second,* most of these schemes suggest that the working class comprises at least close to half of the population. *Third,* estimates of the lower class or underclass range from approximately 5 to 12 percent. *Finally,* most of these models place lower-level routine white-collar occupations in the working class rather than in the middle class. These scholarly assessments are broadly consistent with the popular perceptions of Americans discussed earlier.

If you were to consider each of these conceptualizations of social class, how would your perception of U.S. class structure change as you went from one to another? Certainly, the definition a person has of something affects what he or she sees. This is no less true of class perceptions.

TECHNOLOGY AND THE SHAPING OF THE U.S. CLASS STRUCTURE

The class structure of any society is shaped by the political, cultural, economic, and technological context in which it is embedded. *Politically,* changes in rules and resources governing labor–management conflict, including unionization of workers, affect class conditions and relationships. Government trade and immigration policies, poverty programs, tax laws, and restrictions on business help determine the size and composition of classes, the extent of income and wealth differences, and the channels for moving up and down the class ladder. *Culturally,* broad-based values about democracy, equality, and justice can serve to temper the extent of social inequality, whereas the presence of prejudice, stereotypes, and derogatory ideologies about different groups can perpetuate such inequality. Finally, *economic* and *technological* developments have become increasingly significant for the changing composition of classes and for shifts in the distribution of individuals among classes. These developments need to be emphasized.

In recent years, technological developments have sped the integration of national economies into a global network. What happens to steelworkers in Ohio, textile employees in North Carolina, and electronic-component workers across the country is directly tied to the international context within which the U.S. economy operates. The ties created between nations make each more vulnerable to economic and political shifts in other countries. Like a giant web, pressure on any part causes reverberations throughout the system. The growth of China and India as economic powers, political instability in the Middle East, economic changes in Russia, the economic union of European countries, and attempts by Latin American nations to better integrate their economies, all have economic repercussions for the United States.

The demand for goods produced by U.S. employees fluctuates with economic and political changes in other countries. For example, the disappearance of almost 170,000 U.S. manufacturing jobs in recent years is linked to economic problems experienced in Asian markets and the subsequent decline in prices for goods and reduction of U.S. exports to those countries. In the 1990s, as economic crises occurred in Asian markets, their currencies were devalued, prices of their goods dropped, and importation of these goods into the United States became more attractive (Slater and Strawser 1998; Goodman and Considine 1999). In the early 2000s, declines in the value of the U.S. dollar made American products more attractive and stimulated their export and encouraged tourism. In 2009–2010, the United States complained that the Chinese government had manipulated the value of its currency so as to make their exports more attractive, resulting in lower demand for U.S.-made goods.

Downsizing, lean production, and the exportation of jobs to cheaper foreign labor markets have been primary ways used by U.S. manufacturers to reduce costs and respond to foreign competition. *Successful* penetration of U.S. firms into foreign countries may mean higher profits for some, but it also spells lower incomes for many workers, white-collar and blue-collar alike. Higher unemployment means lower incomes for those affected, in part because it means lower pressures for increased wages. Not surprisingly, job loss and fear of job loss dampen appeals for wage increases, as does the weakness of U.S. labor's power (Volgy, Schwarz, and Imwalle 1996; Aaronson and Sullivan 1998). *Unsuccessful* foreign penetration by U.S. corporations, on the other hand, means fewer exports for U.S. firms, lower profits, and very likely, lower stock prices. The latter means declines in the wealth of those who own these stocks. Thus, individuals throughout the entire class system are affected by international economic events, but not in the same ways.

Just as international events and conditions affect economic fortunes in the United States, so too do U.S. activities affect economic conditions in other countries. The deep economic crisis of 2008–2009 originated in the United States but had worldwide implications. American mortgage problems and falling house prices, for example, devalued stocks in markets in Europe and elsewhere. This, in turn, reduced the wealth of many average citizens. The very interconnectedness of nations means that problems in one of them, especially a dominant one like the United States, have severe repercussions for others.

Progress in the technology of communication networks and information systems, which has brought together larger networks of individuals and organizations around the globe, has intensified the interconnectedness of the world economy. Technology also has repercussions for the occupational structure. Increased computer usage in all kinds of organizations has provided the impetus for increases in jobs for systems analysts, software programmers, and computer technicians. Between 2006 and 2016, for example, employment in information technologies is expected to grow by 212,000 jobs, and the software, telecommunications, and Internet industries

Abandoned factories like those in the upper Midwest and Atlantic states are an indicator of the decline of U.S. manufacturing jobs in recent decades. Many of those jobs have moved abroad where cheaper labor and better corporate tax advantages are available. The jobs lost are often those that had been unionized and paid well, and provide one reason for the earnings gap in the United States. (© Peter D./Shutterstock)

are projected to expand by almost 40 percent (U.S. Department of Labor 2008). Whether recent economic crises will alter this development remains to be seen.

In addition to their effects on occupational distribution, advances in computer technology and the rapid growth of the Internet have also created greater possibilities for flexible work patterns and new forms of economic organizations. Because technology allows for the dispersion of workers across space, even across countries, work groups are being formed in cyberspace, resulting in the creation of "virtual organizations" (Crandell and Wallace 1998). The Internet has opened up scores of opportunities for individuals who are adept at using it. New companies made possible by powerful computer technologies have arisen overnight and their stocks have rocketed so suddenly that

their youthful creators have become millionaires in a very short time. Amazon.com, eBay, Google, Facebook, and similar companies have made their management very wealthy on paper. More individuals have become billionaires since 1985 in the United States than in its entire previous history, and technical knowledge and opportunity have provided the bases for their wealth (Thurow 1999).

While technological change itself does not appear to explain the rise in wage inequality in recent decades (Mishel, Bernstein, and Shierholz 2009), variations across socioeconomic groups in technology usage do have an impact. Higher-status individuals are more likely than those in lower-statuses to have access to information technologies (IT), own better IT equipment, and know how to use the Internet in ways that strengthen their economic standing (DiMaggio and Bonikowski 2008; Zillien and Hargittai 2009; Stern 2010). This **digital divide** forms another basis for economic inequality.

Employment and unemployment patterns are also being dramatically affected by computer technology and the Internet. The freedom from restrictions of space and time that the Internet provides means that the line between home and work can easily become blurred. Employees can stay at home and still be employed in computer tasks. Even though the success rates of such businesses are low and self-employment accounted for less than 1 percent of all job growth in the United States in the 1990s, enterprising employees can start their own businesses and become entrepreneurs. Workers who are interested in moving but wish to remain employees are not limited in their job searches by local newspaper advertisements. Rather, they can search the Web for employment in a wide variety of geographic areas. Conversely, because of new communication technologies, employers can hire qualified individuals who live in very diverse locations. Knowledge and skills in new computer technologies have become a critical avenue for success. These possibilities hold the potential to complicate the processes of status attainment and diversify the compositions of given classes.

Moreover, new technology has made corporations and their workers less loyal to each other.

It has created employment for some, unemployment for others; higher profits for some, and lower incomes for others. All this means that some will benefit from the ongoing technological revolution while others will remain onlookers, lacking access to and/or participation in it.

INCOME INEQUALITY

Because social class has been first and foremost thought of as an economic phenomenon, it should not be surprising that "income" has frequently been used as a measure of class position. As such, its distribution can provide clues about the character of U.S. class structure and trends within it. *Money income,* as defined by the Census Bureau, includes money from virtually all sources, including wages or salaries, Social Security, welfare, pensions, and others. There are some advantages to using *total money income* when assessing the extent of economic inequality. In the first place, it is certainly more immediately quantifiable than many other measures, such as real estate. Second, income is highly valued in U.S. society and serves as a base on which people are evaluated by others. Third, income inequalities saturate and are reflected in a number of other economically related areas. Unemployment, inflation, farm and food prices, rent control, women's liberation, racism, and welfare are all areas that involve income-differential issues. In your own case, think about

the number of ways that income is implicated in different areas of your life. Income, then, at least at first glance, would appear to be a more than adequate measure of economic inequality.

However, when interpreting the following statistics, several limitations should be kept in mind. First, income is only a partial measure of a family's or individual's economic well-being. It does not include the value of stocks, real estate, or other noncash economic assets, and, second, if it is *current* income, it does not take into account the income trajectory an individual may be on if, for example, he or she is just beginning in a lucrative career. Third, some of the estimates of income are based on pooled findings from several government studies that are not always identical in methodology or measures of income. Finally, and most significantly, the U.S. Census Bureau contends that income is underreported, with some sources of income being more likely to be reported than others. Tax filers tend to underreport their incomes on their income tax forms, and not all persons are required to file income tax returns. Independent estimates suggest that incomes from government benefit programs and property income are among those most likely to be underestimated (U.S. Census Bureau, August 2008).

Table 2.1 presents information on how U.S. households are distributed among different income categories. The top and bottom lines indicate that although the percentage of families with

TABLE 2.1 Percentage Distribution of Households by Income Level: 1980–2009

Income*	1980	1990	2000	2009
Under $15,000	15.5	14.0	12.1	13.0
$15,000–24,999	12.7	11.8	11.1	11.9
$25,000–34,999	12.1	11.2	10.5	11.1
$35,000–49,999	16.4	15.7	14.5	14.1
$50,000–74,999	21.4	20.0	18.4	18.1
$75,000–99,999	11.5	12.2	12.7	11.5
$100,000 and over	10.4	15.0	20.6	20.1
Median income	$43,892	$47,637	$52,301	$49,777

*Measured in 2009 adjusted dollars.

Source: U.S. Census Bureau, *Income, Poverty, and Health Insurance Coverage in the United States: 2009.* Current Population Reports, Series P-60, No. 238, September 2010, Table A-1, p. 33.

incomes below $15,000 has declined over time (from 15.5% in 1980 to 13.0% in 2009), the percentage of those with incomes of at least $100,000 went up much more during that same time (from 10.4% to 20.1%). The percentages of those in the $25,000–$74,999 categories have generally declined. While shifts in the top and bottom categories in this table may suggest that economic conditions have improved since 1980, we need to reserve judgment until we explore the matter further.

One way in which income inequality shows up clearly is when comparisons are made between racial and **ethnic groups**. About 24 percent of Black and more than 16 percent of Hispanic households had incomes below $15,000 in 2009, compared to under 11 percent of non-Hispanic White households. On the other end of the income scale, 23 percent of non-Hispanic White households had incomes of at least $100,000 in 2009, compared to about 10 percent of Black and Hispanic households (U.S. Census Bureau, September 2010a). Not surprisingly then, as they have in the past, the median incomes of households varied as well in 2009, ranging from

$32,584 for Black to $38,039 for Hispanic to $54,461 for White households.

Incomes also vary between family types. As might be expected, households with married-couple families are generally better off than those headed by only males or females, regardless of race. But as Figure 2.2 demonstrates, Blacks and Hispanics are worse off than non-Hispanic Whites in each type of family. Female-headed families have the lowest incomes within each racial and ethnic group. Overall, such families have less than half of the income of married-couple families.

IS THE MIDDLE CLASS SHRINKING?

Regardless of how it is measured, most of the analyses on the middle class indicate a shrinking in the size and prosperity of the middle-income groups. The decline in the percentage of families in the $25,000–$74,999 categories is only one indication. Horrigan and Haugen (1988) further examined this issue, using family income and two ways of comparing changes in family income distributions over time. They found that the middle

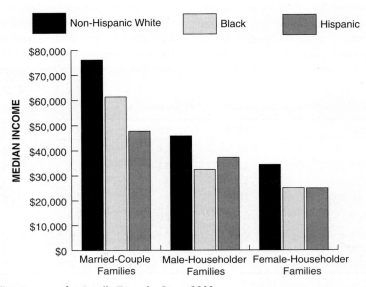

FIGURE 2.2   Median Incomes for Family Types by Race: 2009

Source: U.S. Census Bureau, Table FINC-01 at http://www.census.gov/hhes/www/cpstables/032010/faminc/new01_000.htm.

shrank between 1969 and 1986. The constriction of the middle class continued into the 1990s, in part due to declines in upward mobility from the bottom (Gottschalk in Bernstein 1996, p. 90).

The apparent decline of the middle class has significant ramifications for a democracy. Scholars as far back as Aristotle have stressed the importance of a large and prosperous middle class for the stability, cohesiveness, and productivity of a society (Pressman 2007). Yet throughout the United States, the number of middle-class neighborhoods has declined, while poor and rich neighborhoods have grown (Galster, Cutsinger, and Booza 2006). A recent analysis puts the matter bluntly: *"Middle-class prosperity in the late twentieth and early twenty-first centuries is an illusion"* (Leicht and Fitzgerald 2007, p. 4; italics in original).

Since the late 1970s, income inequality has continued to grow, with the top 10 percent getting more than 90 percent of all the gains in income in the last 30 years, thereby further distancing themselves from the rest of the population. The shares of total income of the bottom 90 percent experienced declines during this period (Mishel, Bernstein, and Shierholz 2009; McCall and

Percheski 2010). The extent of income concentration is higher in 2009 than it has been since the late 1920s, and the real incomes of middle-class families were lower in 2008 than they were in the mid-1940s. In 2009, the mean household income of the top 20 percent was more than 14 times that of the poorest 20 percent. In contrast, 30 years ago it was 11 times as great (U.S. Census Bureau, September 2010a). Part of the explanation lies in the fact that an increasing proportion of the national income has gone to profits and capital, and less to wages and salaries (Mishel, Bernstein, and Allegretto 2007). Changes in tax policies which favored high-income groups and high unemployment rates have also contributed to the increase in income inequality (Mishel, Bernstein, and Shierholz 2009).

Figure 2.3 confirms the decline in income shares going to those below the top 20 percent. As the figure indicates, the percentage of all income going to the bottom and middle quintiles of the population has declined since 1980, while that going to the top 20 percent increased from 44.1 percent in 1980 to 50.3 percent in 2009. The top 5 percent alone received almost 22 percent of all income in 2009.

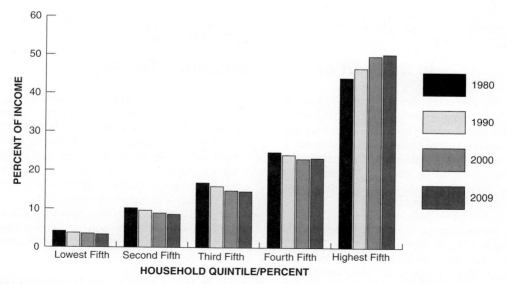

FIGURE 2.3 Percentage Share of Aggregate Income Received by Each Fifth of Households: 1980–2009

Source: U.S. Census Bureau, *Income, Poverty, and Health Insurance Coverage in the United States: 2009.* Current Population Reports, Series P-60, No. 238, September 2010, Table A-3, pp. 45–47.

Trends in the Gini ratio—which measures the extent of discrepancy between the *actual* distribution of income and a *hypothetical* situation in which each quintile of the population receives the same percentage of income—also indicate increasing concentration of income in the United States. The ratio has a possible value range of 0 to 1; 0 indicates complete equality and 1 indicates complete inequality. In 1980, the ratio stood at 0.403; by 2009, it had risen to 0.468.

The middle and lower classes are well aware of the recent declines in their economic fortunes. In 2008, most of the 58 percent who said their incomes were lagging behind the cost of living were in the middle- and lower-income groups. Well over half of them said they had trouble paying basic household bills (Pew Research Center, February 14, 2008). This may be attributed to the fact that, in contrast to those with higher incomes, a significant majority of these individuals feel they are underpaid in their jobs (Jacobe 2008a). On average, about three-fourths of a family's income comes from employment earnings, and an even greater proportion accounts for the incomes of middle-class families (Mishel, Bernstein, and Shierholz 2009). It should not be surprising then, that the acceleration in income inequality since 1980 is due heavily to the increase in earnings inequality, especially between those in the top 10 percent and the rest of the working population. As noted earlier, the compensation of CEOs at top corporations was 263 times that of average workers, and the CEOs of those companies that laid off the most workers earned even more (Anderson et al. 2010). When workers are let go to increase company efficiency, the company's stock often rises, and stock options are a major part of CEO compensation. Those earnings differences also reflect a polarizing increase in both high- and low-paying jobs alongside a decrease in middle-wage positions (Autor, Katz, and Kearney 2008; Mouw and Kalleberg 2010).

Recent high unemployment rates, shifts in the occupational structure, declines in the power of unions, a lagging minimum wage, and globalization account for most of these changes (Mishel, Bernstein, and Allegretto 2007). Economic instability, resulting in the need for workers to change or find new jobs, also contributes to a stagnation or decline in their wages (Fuller 2008; Mouw and Kalleberg 2010).

MINI-CASE 2.1

To Support or Not to Support a Factory

Traditionally, unions in different countries, including the United States, have fought for higher wages, better benefits, and safer working conditions for their members. Private companies have tended to be hostile to union organization and higher minimum wages because they drive up costs. And a high unemployment rate has intensified the pressures felt by workers who need and want to work but cannot earn a decent wage.

A recent event in Newcastle, South Africa illustrates some of the pressures that workers and government representatives face (Dugger, September 27, 2010). South Africa has one of the highest unemployment rates in the world. So unskilled, poorly educated people are willing to take jobs that they would not accept if the labor market was tighter. Chinese clothing factories that moved into South Africa have argued that they need to pay wages which are significantly below the minimum wage established by South Africa's national union/employer council. Some of these companies have been shut down because their wages fall short of the minimum standard. But many of these poorly paid workers who lost their jobs are actually angry at the shutdowns. So, as the manager of the national council said: "We're at a crossroads" (Dugger, p. A8). Should we punish factories that violate minimum-wage regulations or should we ignore the violations and let the factories remain open and provide jobs at sub-minimum wages? Should workers continue to support a factory that doesn't provide a living wage but does provide jobs? What should be done?

Source: Based on Celia W. Dugger. September 27, 2010. "Efforts Meant to Help Workers Squeeze South Africa's Poorest?" *New York Times*, pp. A1 and A8. ▪

The decline of the middle class appears to be linked to a heavy dependence by average individuals on wages and the market to sustain their incomes. International evidence indicates that when compared to countries in which governments create specific policies to maintain equality, countries with governments that provide limited federal support for individuals have experienced a larger shrinkage of the middle class (Pressman 2007).

One immediate contributor to the growing inequality in wages and salaries has been the gap between CEO and average-worker pay. In 2007, the gap between CEO compensation and the average worker's was 10 times what it was three decades ago (Anderson et al. 2008). Wages and salaries make up a much larger portion of the average worker's compensation than is the case for CEOs, whose compensation packages contain a large amount of nonsalary benefits. Since 1979, the average wages of middle- and lower-level workers have declined. In 2007, for example, the median wage for men was more than 4 percent below what it was in 1979 (Mishel, Bernstein, and Shierholz 2009), and it has stagnated since then even as the number of full-time male workers has declined (U.S. Census Bureau, September 2010a). In 2010, the average weekly earnings for production and nonsupervisory employees was estimated to be $636 (U.S. Department of Labor, January 2011.)

Looking at this chapter's figures and tables, it is clear that there has been a rise in income inequality in recent decades, and a variety of long-term factors seem to be involved. Among them are the following:

- Declines in earnings growth, a rise in the proportion of workers with low earnings, and resultant rises in earnings differences between low-skilled and higher-skilled workers
- Shifts in the economy from production of goods to services, which contain wider variations in salaries and wages
- Market manipulations and changes in economic transactions and contracts
- Recessionary and expansionary forces in the economy

- Shifts in the demands for high- and less-skilled workers, in part creating more temporary positions with few benefits
- Changes in employment rates with a tighter labor market in the late 1990s
- Changes in the age structure of the population and labor force (e.g., influx of the baby-boom generation into the labor market) and in the composition of households (e.g., rise in single-parent families)
- An influx of poorly educated immigrants into the workforce and the rising use of less-expensive foreign labor
- Declining unionization and power of unions
- Industrial streamlining, reengineering, and downsizing
- Governmental policies such as minimum wage changes, tax reform, and cuts in programs for the needy
- Effects related to globalization

WEALTH INEQUALITY IN THE UNITED STATES

As significant as the increase in income inequality has been, wealth inequality in the United States is even more noteworthy. This is not only because inequality in wealth is much greater than income inequality, but also because wealth is a more complete measure of a family's economic power, since it consists of the value of all the family's assets minus its debts. Wealth includes the value of homes, automobiles, businesses, savings, and investments.

But although the amount of personal wealth gives a fuller picture of an individual's or family's economic position, even it does not fully reflect the access of the wealthy to a greater number of economic tools that serve to enhance their economic opportunities and market situation. For example, ownership of a great deal of stock in a corporation that is interlocked or directly connected with other corporations may give an individual indirect influence over the economic behavior of the latter organizations. Like poverty, wealth has economic implications beyond the actual size of the holdings. Economic opportunities are at least in part a function of the economic tools a person has at his or her disposal.

Consensus about the methodology used to uncover the distribution of wealth does not exist to the degree that one would desire. Some of the difficulties associated with present methods are clear. Information about wealth is difficult to obtain. Virtually all data about it come from various field surveys and administrative records. Often, individuals are hesitant to be interviewed, and this is especially true of the wealthy who, for several reasons, may be sensitive about their wealth. "As a rule," stated Allen (1987), who has conducted an extensive analysis of the country's richest families, "the members of wealthy capitalist families refuse to divulge even the most rudimentary details of their wealth. . . . In order to maintain their anonymity, the members of corporate rich families typically refuse to disclose even basic biographical information about themselves" (pp. 26–27). What is requested of individuals in surveys and what is given are frequently not the same (J. D. Smith 1987).

Social scientists, in general, have produced hundreds of studies of the poor and poverty, even the middle class, but good broad-based information about the wealthy and wealth concentration has always been and remains difficult to find. Another problem with wealth data is that personal items such as jewelry, antiques, and art are often undervalued. Finally, researchers use different units of analysis in discussing the distribution of wealth. Sometimes the unit used is the individual, while in others the family or consumer unit is the basis of analysis. I will discuss the sources of data on wealth distribution in greater detail later. But first, let us examine wealth differences in their historical context.

Wealth Concentration before the Civil War

If ever there was a time when equality was present, it surely must have been when the United States was first being established. When this nation was forming politically, many citizens had left their European homelands because of oppression of one kind or another to escape to the "land of the free," where the streets were thought to be paved with gold. The Founding Fathers, using "the voice of justice," forged a document that not only enumerated the offenses committed against the then new American people but also demanded freedom and equality for all. While some, such as Alexander Hamilton and Thomas Jefferson, argued about whether the government should or should not take a strictly egalitarian form, many believed the period was an "era of the common man" (Pessen 1973). The Founders recognized the belief that "all men are created equal" and later devised a constitution that had among its objectives to "establish justice." In his famous visit to the United States, Alexis de Tocqueville (1969) was surprised by the "equality of conditions" that seemed to prevail in the youthful country. And although he believed wealth was certainly present, no one group held a monopoly on it. Indeed, Tocqueville believed that wealth moved about quite a bit in the country.

Recent studies have simply not borne out these beliefs. Social historians, poring over probate records, tax forms, and old census documents, have found a decidedly different America than one might have expected. Studies of wealth distribution in the early United States consistently point to the fact that wealth inequality was a clear and constant condition during this period. This was especially true for the period between the Revolution and the Civil War, a time in which inequality was on the rise.

Before the Revolution, however, the increases in inequality do not appear to have been as great or as consistent, but differences in wealth were quite noticeable. Studies in Philadelphia and Chester County, Pennsylvania; Boston and Salem, Massachusetts; and Hartford and rural Connecticut point not only to evident variations in wealth among people, but also in some cases to increasing differences as time passed (Pessen 1973). Uniform evidence about a trend toward increasing inequality before 1776 does not exist; but after 1776, the trend toward increasing inequality is present everywhere.

In his studies of cities in New England, the Middle Atlantic, the South, and the Midwest, Sturm (1977) found some sobering results for believers in the "romantic hypothesis." Using probate data, he found distinct and increasing inequality in estate wealth for the period from 1800 to 1850. During this time, per capita holdings of the very wealthy went up about 60 percent (Sturm 1977). An examination by Pessen for this period in Brooklyn and Boston likewise confirms the general trend toward inequality. In Brooklyn in 1810, 1 percent of the population held 22 percent of the private wealth, and in 1840, 1 percent owned 42 percent (Pessen 1973, p. 36). Figures for Boston and New York echo these findings.

Concentration of wealth in the nineteenth century appears to have peaked during the period from 1850 to 1870. Soltow (1975) found that while wealth inequality remained fairly constant during this period, it was also very high. Using census data on real and personal estate holdings among free adult males, he found that in 1860, the top 1 percent owned almost 30 percent and the top 10 percent owned about 73 percent of estate wealth, again demonstrating a strong degree of wealth concentration. During the period from 1850 to 1870, "there very definitely was an elite upper group in America in terms of control of economic resources" (Soltow 1975, p. 180). A small percentage had great wealth, but large numbers had little, if any. In 1850, over half of free adult males owned no land even though it was quite cheap. Nor did the situation change much in the years following 1850 (p. 175).

Given the period, as one might expect, a person was more likely to be an owner of real estate if that person was native born, older, and a farmer (Soltow 1975). In 1860, there were an estimated 41 millionaires, 545 in 1870, and 5,904 in 1922. But if one uses constant 1922 dollars, the real estimate for 1870 would be between 1,800 and 2,600.

The main conclusion from all these data is that at least from the mid-eighteenth to the mid-nineteenth centuries, wealth concentration was high and tended to increase during that period. Little is known about the extent of wealth concentration during 1870 to 1922 "except that it was lower after the Civil War than before and lower in 1922 than it was to become by 1929" (Lindert and Williamson 1976, p. 31).

Wealth Concentration in the Contemporary United States

Estimates are that the richest 1 percent held about 30 percent of all wealth during the 1920s, although their wealth decreased to under 30 percent in the 1930–1950 period. By the late 1950s, however, their assets increased to almost 35 percent of all wealth (Keister and Moller 2000). During the first half of the 1970s, the proportion of wealth going to the top 1 percent declined, but then began to rise significantly during the late 1970s and continued through the 1990s although at a slower rate (Nasar 1992; Wolff, May 1992). Between 1990 and 2004, the concentration of wealth remained fairly constant but grew slightly after 2004. In 2007, the richest 1 percent controlled over one-third and the top 20 percent owned 85 percent of all privately held wealth in the United States. Projections to 2009 suggested even greater wealth concentration (Wolff 2010).

In 2007, the median wealth or **net worth** of households, that is, the value of all their assets minus their debts, was over $120,000. The richest 20 percent had an average of $2.3 million in wealth, while the bottom 40 percent averaged only $2,200. Between 1983 and 2007, the number of households with wealth of at least $10 million increased sixfold, but the percentage of households with zero or negative wealth, also rose going from 16 to 19 percent. As Figure 2.4 shows, *the wealthiest 20 percent owned 85 percent of all wealth in 2007, while the bottom 40 percent held under 1 percent. The top 1 percent alone owned over 34 percent of all privately held wealth in the United States, more than twice as much as the bottom 80 percent of the population.* While the proportion of private wealth owned by the top 20 percent has grown since 1983, those in the middle quintile saw their share of net worth decline from 5.2 percent to 4.0 percent in 2007 (Wolff 2010). During the 2007–2009 recession, more than 60 percent of families experienced a

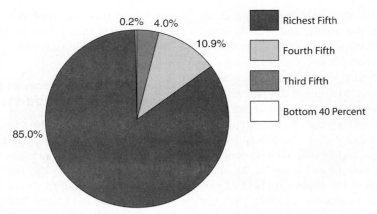

FIGURE 2.4   Distribution of Net Worth by Quintile and Bottom 40 Percent: 2007

Source: Based on Edward N. Wolff, "Recent Trends in Household Wealth in the United States: Rising Debt and the Middle-Class Squeeze: An Update to 2007." March 2010. Working Paper No. 589, p. 44, Table 2. The Levy Economics Institute.

decline in wealth, with a median decrease of 18 percent. About 50 percent of those in the bottom wealth quartile suffered losses, compared to about three-quarters of those in the top quartile. Overall, however, wealth increased 27 percent for the top quartile during this period while it decreased by over 50 percent for those in the bottom quartile (Bricker et al. 2011).

Financial or *non-home* wealth, that is, wealth involving only stocks, mutual funds, and other investments, was even more concentrated than overall net worth in 2007. The top 20 percent possessed 93 percent of all stocks, mutual funds, and other investments. In contrast, the bottom 90 percent owned only about 7 percent of all financial wealth (Wolff 2010). In sum, all the evidence indicates a highly unequal distribution of wealth in the United States.

The reasons for the increasing concentration of wealth in recent years are related to the differences in the types of wealth held by various income groups. That is, their assets are distributed differently. Those on the top are more likely to have much of their wealth in stocks, bonds, and related kinds of investments. In 2007, the vast majority of the wealth of the richest 1 percent was in stock, mutual funds, financial securities, or business investments; only 10 percent of their

wealth was in their principal home (see Figure 2.5). Stocks did very well in the late 1980s and the 1990s, and those who had invested profited handsomely. In contrast, those with much less wealth are likely to have their wealth in savings accounts and home ownership (see Figure 2.5). In 2007, 65 percent of the wealth of the middle 60 percent of households was in their homes. Under 4 percent was in stock, mutual funds, or financial securities (Wolff 2010). Consequently, the recent decline in home values along with stagnant incomes has led to greater debt among those in the middle class.

Most of the households in the middle and at the bottom rely almost completely on wages and salaries to pay their bills. Many are heavily in debt. In 2004, over one-quarter of the poorest 20 percent had debts that exceeded 40 percent of their total incomes (Mishel, Bernstein, and Allegretto 2007). Given these debts, most people in the middle and lower quintiles have little money to invest in the stock market; nor can they save for the long term. Only about one-third of the poorest 25 percent and those without a high school diploma save at all, compared to about three-quarters of the richest 10 percent and those with college degrees (Bucks, Kennickell, and Moore 2006). Needless to say, mounting debt and

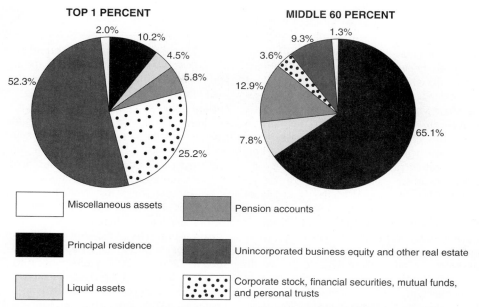

TOP 1 PERCENT

MIDDLE 60 PERCENT

FIGURE 2.5   Distribution of Asset Types in Top 1 Percent and Middle 60 Percent of Wealth: 2007

Source: Based on Edward N. Wolff, "Recent Trends in Household Wealth in the United States: Rising Debt and the Middle-Class Squeeze: An Update to 2007." March 2010. Working Paper No. 589, p. 48, Table 6. The Levy Economics Institute.

the inability to save make wealth accumulation extremely difficult, and directly affect the transmission of wealth to the next generation.

The constraints placed on poorer families mean that they are less able to provide inheritances to their children, leaving the latter with little or no wealth on which to build. This is another reason why wealth inequality is so important—its accumulation has direct implications for economic inequality among the children of today's families. As a basis for future economic status, wealth (or its absence) helps to stabilize, reproduce, and even exacerbate economic inequality in future generations (Oliver and Shapiro 1995). Inheritances contribute to the maintenance of wealth inequality over generations because these "head-start assets . . . often include paying for college, substantial down-payment assistance in buying a first home, and other continuing parental financial assistance . . . [This inherited wealth allows its recipients to live] economically and

socially beyond where their own achievements, jobs, and earnings would place them" (Shapiro 2004, pp. 2–3). Education, occupational attainment, and home ownership can contribute to wealth accumulation, but this especially has been the case for Whites rather than Blacks, who have suffered historically from discrimination in these areas. Moreover, Blacks do not benefit from education and occupation economically as much as Whites. The presence of single-parent families also makes it difficult for Black families to accumulate wealth (Campbell and Kaufman 2006).

The large amounts of wealth owned by a very small percentage of the population raises questions about where the wealth comes from and who the wealthy are and are not. Historically, family and inheritance have been major sources of wealth among the corporate rich in the United States. Only a minority obtained their initial wealth through entrepreneurship or personal saving. Gift and estate laws have done little to stem

NUTSHELL 2.1   Sources of Wealth Measurement

The observations drawn about the extent of wealth inequality rely heavily on the work of economist Edward Wolff, who uses data from the Survey of Consumer Finances (SCF) conducted by the Federal Reserve Board since 1983. This data source yields a more accurate picture of wealth distribution because it uses a broader and more inclusive definition of net worth and a sample that includes a better representation of the wealthiest households. The SCF is the source used most often in investigations on wealth distribution (Keister and Moller 2000). Other surveys, such as the U.S. Bureau of the Census's Survey on Income and Program Participation (SIPP) and the Panel Survey of Income Dynamics (PSID), underrepresent the richest families and, therefore, significantly understate the wealth of the richest segments of society and the extent of wealth inequality in the United States. Consequently, Wolff contends that these two surveys "are probably useful for studying the wealth accumulation behavior of the middle class, but are not reliable for analyzing the behavior of the very rich" (Wolff 1998, p. 134). Moreover, since the sample used in the SCF is different from those of the two other surveys, so is the composition of the wealth found in its top 20 percent and bottom 80 percent.

Two of the important terms used by Wolff in his analyses are *net worth* and *financial wealth*. **Net worth** refers to "the current value of all marketable or" cash-convertible "assets less the current value of debts" (Wolff 1998, p. 133). It includes the value of housing, real estate, cash, savings, certificates of deposit, money market accounts, bonds, stocks, and equity in businesses and trust funds owned by the household. It also includes the cash value of retirement, life insurance, and pension plans. Wolff believes that this measure is important because it "reflects wealth as a store of value and therefore a source of potential consumption" (p. 133). Spilerman also views wealth for its potential "as a capitalized income stream" (2000, p. 500). Wolff goes on to say that "I believe that this is the concept that best reflects the level of well-being associated with a family's holdings" (Wolff, April 2000, p. 3). In contrast to net worth, **financial wealth** is a narrower concept and is defined as one's net worth less the net equity in one's house. Financial wealth includes only those forms of wealth that are easily convertible to cash. Therefore, home equity is excluded because "it is somewhat difficult to liquidate one's housing wealth in the short term" (Wolff 1998, p. 133).

---

the flow of inherited wealth to subsequent generations. Wealth is kept in the family, and this is one reason why the extended family is such an important institution among the rich. The social, cultural, and economic capital passed on to children helps them maintain and even increase their wealth.

In addition to the historical importance of inheritance, however, technology innovation is becoming a much more prevalent source of wealth. Three-quarters of the individuals on Forbes 2010 list of the 400 richest Americans obtained their wealth in the service, food and beverage, manufacturing, media, technology, or investment industries. Many started their own businesses or are self-employed. Few achieved their vast wealth because of inheritance. To be included on the 2010 Forbes-richest list, one's

wealth has to have been at least $1 billion. Together, the net worth of these 400 individuals totaled $1.27 trillion. But these 400 do not represent most Americans. For most, inheritance still plays an important role in laying a foundation for wealth accumulation.

What characteristics are related to the amount of wealth one has? Certainly race and ethnicity are factors that are involved. As Table 2.2 demonstrates, Blacks and Hispanics generally have significantly less wealth than Whites. In 2007, the median net worth among non-Hispanic Whites was about 16 times that of non-Hispanic Blacks, and the median non-home wealth was about 88 times greater among non-Hispanic Whites. Both Blacks and Hispanics are more than twice as likely as Whites to have zero or negative wealth (Wolff 2007).

TABLE 2.2 Mean (Median) Household Net Worth and Non-Home Wealth by Race and Hispanic Origin: 2007 (in thousands)

	Mean Net Worth	(Median)	Mean Non-Home Wealth	(Median)
Non-Hispanic Whites	652	(144)	495	(44)
Non-Hispanic Blacks	123	(9)	71	(0.5)
Hispanics	170	(9)	96	(0.4)

Source: Edward N. Wolff, "Recent Trends in Household Wealth in the United States: Rising Debt and the Middle-Class Squeeze: An Update to 2007." Working Paper No. 589. March 2010, Table 10.

Wealth also varies by family type, with married-couple households without children possessing about three to four times the wealth of single-headed households with children. The wealth of married-couple families with children is more than twice that of single-parent families with children. Among age groups, those in the 65–74 age bracket had the most net worth, and those under 35 the least. Finally, in 2007 the wealth of those with college degrees far exceeded that of less educated individuals (Bucks et al. 2009).

CONFRONTING ECONOMIC INEQUALITY

Although little attention has been given by policymakers to programs that directly address the reduction of social inequality, the federal income tax system and government transfers purportedly address the issue of distribution of economic resources among individuals in the United States.

The Effects of Taxes and Transfer Programs

The tax system is supposed to be "progressive"—that is, to lessen income differences between income strata by taxing higher-income groups at higher rates. To what extent does it accomplish this goal? Looking at Table 2.3, we find that inequality is greatest under "market income," which essentially is pretax income gained only from the market, and does not include income from government insurance and welfare programs.

In this case, the poorest 20 percent receive only 1.5 percent of all income, while the top 20 percent receive almost 54 percent of all income. The **Index of Income Concentration** shows that the degree of income inequality declines when the benefits from government programs are added to the income definition, as in "post–social insurance income." Inequality declines even further when taxes are taken into account, as in "disposable income." These changes indicate the redistributional effects of both taxes and governmental assistance programs. Of the government programs, Social Security has the greatest impact on reducing poverty (Zandvakili and Mills 2001).

When compared to other industrial countries, however, the effects of taxes and transfers in the United States on inequality and poverty are small. International studies reveal that U.S. programs were less effective than all others in reducing inequality and poverty rates (Defina and Thanawala 2004; Kenworthy 2009). The direct effect of taxes on reducing economic inequality in the United States is minor, but they do have an indirect effect because they are used to fund government transfer programs, which have a greater impact on inequality. However, the regressive effect of sales and payroll taxes weakens any positive consequences that come from income taxes (Kenworthy 2009).

Part of the reason for the lower effect of taxes on reducing inequality has been the recent decline in the progressive nature of the federal tax system, as indicated by declines in the number of tax brackets and cuts in tax rates for wealthy individuals. Most of the benefits from tax cuts in

TABLE 2.3 Median Income and Income Inequality under Four Definitions of Income: 2005

| Income Measure | Median Income | Index of Income Concentration | Percent of Income Received By | |
			Lowest Quintile	Highest Quintile
Market income	$43,701	0.493	1.50	53.83
Post–social insurance income	$47,975	0.447	3.24	51.03
Disposable income	40,843	0.418	4.42	47.28
Money income	$46,326	0.450	3.42	50.34

Note: "Market income" is all cash income before taxes, including capital gains and rental income, minus government cash transfers and work expenses. "Post–social insurance income" is market income plus the addition of non-means-tested government cash transfers such as Social Security. "Disposable income" includes money from all sources except lump-sum payments from insurance companies, workers' compensation, or pension plans, and includes the value of non-cash government transfers such as food stamps and subsidized housing, minus federal, state, and property taxes. "Money income" is money from all sources except capital gains, before taxes and expenses.

Source: U.S. Bureau of the Census, *The Effect of Taxes and Transfers on Income and Poverty in the United States: 2005,* Current Population Reports, Series P-60, No. 232, March 2007, Tables 1 and 3, pp. 3 and 6.

2001 and 2003 went to the wealthiest 2 percent (Zuckerman 2006). In addition, the past two decades have seen the adoption of 14,000 tax loopholes that allow many to reduce their tax payments (Sawhill, May 27, 2008). Tax breaks are most beneficial for those with higher incomes. Consequently, data from the Internal Revenue Service indicate that the effective average tax rate for the 400 individuals with the highest incomes was only 17 percent in 2007 (Ohlemacher, April 18, 2011). This might help account for the finding that almost half of all Americans think that wealth should be distributed by taxing the wealthy more heavily (Newport 2008b).

Nevertheless, the wealthy provide most of the individual tax payments received by the Internal Revenue Service. In 2007, the top 10 percent were responsible for over one-half of federal tax revenue, with the top 5 percent contributing more than 44 percent (Ohlemacher, April 18, 2011). In 2009, almost half of all Americans paid no income tax; most of these were from low-income groups who receive federal tax credits, which cancel out their tax liability (Williams 2010). All this may suggest to some that the government is taking away from the rich more than

from the poor, and indeed, the official tax rates are higher for those in higher income brackets. Three points should be kept in mind, however. *First,* tax rates have declined most precipitously for the highest-income groups in the past two decades (Orr 2010). *Secondly,* since most of the wealth of the wealthiest is in the form of stocks, a much higher percentage of the incomes of the wealthy derives from capital gains, which are taxed at a lower rate than earnings from employment. The latter is the principal source of income for those in the middle and working classes. Consequently, the *percentage* of their incomes that is paid in taxes by the wealthiest is generally lower than the percentage that is paid by those whose incomes are derived largely from job earnings. This suggests the *third* point, namely, that the higher *amount* paid by the wealthy is testament to the large size of their incomes. Conversely, the much smaller amounts of taxes contributed by those on the bottom give evidence to the meagerness of their incomes.

When considering the mild effect of *individual* federal income tax on income inequality, it should be noted that *corporate* taxes are not included, nor is the value of nonincome wealth.

Tax breaks often go to corporations as an incentive to keep jobs and companies in a community, so some corporations pay a lower percentage in federal taxes than many workers. (Photo by Brendan R. Hurst.)

The proportion of total federal government revenue that comes from corporate taxes steadily declined throughout the twentieth century. In 2003, only 9.9 percent of Internal Revenue collections came from corporate taxes compared to 50.5 percent from individual income taxes (U.S. Census Bureau 2005). According to the Government Accountability Office, between 1998 and 2005, about two-thirds of U.S. corporations paid no federal income taxes at all, and a similar percentage of foreign corporations operating in the United States avoided taxes as well ("Most Firms," August 12, 2008). Increasingly, U.S. corporations have sought to incorporate parts of their businesses outside the United States in order to avoid payment of corporate taxes. As of 2002, such "inversions" as they are called, were legal under U.S.

law. Locating elsewhere allows companies to benefit from advantageous tax and banking laws in the chosen countries (Barry 2002). The Internal Revenue Service recently estimated that about $70 billion in taxes were lost in 2001 because of offshore accounts. At the same time, the agency has made it more difficult for lower-income individuals to qualify for earned-income tax credits, credits they receive because of their low incomes (Walsh, April 25, 2003). A recent federal bankruptcy law has also made it more difficult for average citizens to evade payment of their debts, debts that are in large part due to costs derived from medical bills, divorce, and loss of jobs. These are not costs that are the result of a lavish lifestyle.

Just as corporations benefit from current law, so too do the wealthy who benefit from recent changes in estate tax laws. The latter changes allow individuals to pass on more of their wealth (eventually up to $1 million) without being taxed on it. This encourages the **sedimentation** of wealth. Consequently, the inequality of economic resources is not reduced by either corporate or estate taxes, both of which allow the well-to-do to keep more of their wealth. Maintenance of wealth is also optimized by the fact that those with incomes above $100,000 are three times *less* likely than the working poor to be audited by the IRS (Johnston 2002). As a whole, the current tax system has not done much to make the income distribution more equal.

Other Suggestions Reducing Inequality

Taxes and transfers are only two of the programs that relate to the issue of economic inequality. Not surprisingly, many of the suggestions for alleviating poverty and reducing inequality focus on attempts to maximize incomes for those at the bottom. These include proposals to (1) raise the minimum wage, which has not kept up with inflation; (2) extend the Earned Income Tax Credit (EITC) to different types of households; (3) subsidize health insurance for low-wage employees; (4) make the tax system more progressive; and even to (5) encourage greater unionization (Wolff, May 2002; Danziger and Danziger 2006). Several modern administrations also considered proposals for a guaranteed annual income for all citizens that would replace many traditional welfare programs. One of the principal reasons these proposals failed during the Kennedy, Nixon, and Carter presidencies is that the guaranteed income, by applying to all citizens, lumped everyone together, thus violating a deep cultural belief in the distinction between deserving and undeserving individuals. This belief is part of what shapes the way policymakers frame their views on welfare (Steensland 2006).

Compared to citizens in other Western industrial countries, Americans in general also have a greater "taste for inequality" and a stronger belief that the market rather than the government should determine income (Crutchfield and Pettinicchio 2009; Birchfield 2008), both of which would also discourage acceptance of a guaranteed income for all. In addition, some argue that a guaranteed income would encourage an individual's dependence on the government and lead to a massive exodus from the workforce, thereby endangering the whole economy. Others say that a government program that offers access to health care, education, child care, and housing would be a more efficient and effective way than universal cash grants to reduce inequality (Bergmann 2006). On the positive side, others contend that a universal basic income would provide individuals with the opportunity to explore additional productive activities without having to worry unduly about wages. It may also help to equalize power between classes because it would make available to workers a source of income other than wages (Wright 2006). Passage of new income distribution proposals, of course, depends in part on the sympathies of government officials. Historically, the policies of conservative democratic governments tend to increase economic inequality, while those of liberal governments appear to reduce it (Bartels, February 2004; Brady and Leicht 2008).

Perhaps the most controversial recent proposal to address broad-based inequality in the United States was put forward by Ackerman and Alstott (1999). Briefly, Ackerman and Alstott (1999) suggest that the most direct way to address economic inequality between individuals is to grant every young adult a "stake" so they can begin their adult lives on a more equal level. Specifically, they suggest a one-time stake of $80,000 for young adults to use as they wish to develop their futures. Individuals take responsibility for the success or failure of their choices, and in old age they would have an obligation to repay the stake if they are able to do so. To fund the $80,000 stakes for beginning adults, a tax of 2 percent on all wealth would need to be levied. Ackerman and Alstott believe this is fair, since "every American has an obligation to contribute to a fair starting point for all" (p. 5). They stress that all citizens are in the American enterprise together, and thus we have to work together to reach a more just society. Existing programs of the welfare state have been too divisive, and we need a plan that will invigorate common values. A "stakeholder society" will do that, say Ackerman and Alstott. They believe that beneficiaries of their proposed policy "will locate themselves in a much larger national project devoted to the proposition that all men are created equal. By invoking this American ideal in their own case, they link themselves not only to all others in the past who have taken steps to realize this fundamental principle but also to all those who will do so in the future" (p. 7). Two objections raised against this proposal are that the tax required to fund it takes away wealth from those who have legitimately earned it, and that giving individuals a large stake essentially dampens any motivation to save and accrue assets through one's own efforts (Wright 2006).

Attempts at reform have frequently gotten hung up due to the difficulty of trying to balance conservative and liberal approaches, trying to be tough but compassionate at the same time. Suggestions aim to help those who need help but also to encourage individual responsibility. American values encourage us to be generous but also to realize that there is no "free lunch." Both society and the individual have obligations. "Any successful social policy must strike a balance between collective compassion and individual responsibility," wrote Christopher Jencks (1992, p. 87). Historically, the reform pendulum has swung between these two themes.

Recent federal suggestions have mirrored some of the preceding state efforts, but have also incorporated elements of compassion. The Family and Medical Leave Act of 1993 requires those who employ at least 50 workers to provide three months of unpaid leave per year for child care or medical reasons. But only about half of the private labor force is covered, along with government workers (Landers 1993). Suggestions have also been made to increase the Earned Income Tax Credit (EITC) to low-income families. All of these efforts reflect a concern for compassion, but many aspects of current policy also reflect a laissez-faire view of income distribution. The political paralysis that often exists because of opposition from powerful economic interests and competing perspectives among officeholders suggests that what may be needed to bring about real changes in economic inequality is a broad-based, grassroots social movement (Raphael 2009).

THE GLOBAL CONTEXT AND THE IMPACT OF GLOBALIZATION

The discussions of income and wealth discrepancies just presented document the extensiveness of economic inequality in the United States. To better evaluate the significance of these economic inequalities, we need to consider them in a broader context, even though this can be difficult. Cross-national comparisons of economic-inequality systems have always been hazardous because of variations in definitions, measures of economic status, units of analysis, and data-collection times. Nevertheless, some gross comparisons can be made.

When it comes to levels of income inequality, generally countries lower in living standards by UN measures have levels that exceed those in industrial nations. Included among the most unequal are many African nations. In Zambia, for example the expenditure share of the richest 20 percent in 2000 was over 15 times that of the poorest 20 percent (United Nations 2007). In Haiti, the 2001 income of the richest 10 percent was almost 72 times as great as that of the poorest

10 percent. In 2000, in the United States, it was only 16 times as great. In many largely less technologically advanced countries, the richest 20 percent of the population possess well over half of all privately held income (United Nations 2007).

In comparison with other rich industrial countries, however, the United States possesses the highest degree of income inequality. As Table 2.4 shows, individuals in the 90th percentile of the U.S. population had 2004–2005 average incomes that were almost six times those of people in the 10th percentile. Confirming the high degree of inequality, the Gini coefficient of 0.38 for the United States was higher than that of any other rich industrial country in 2004–2005. The coefficient can vary from 0.0 (equality of income among households) to 1.0 (concentration of all income at the top). When compared to those in other industrial countries, U.S. individuals in the 90th percentile are further *above* and those in the 10th percentile are further *below* the median income in the United States than is the case in any other country (Mishel, Bernstein, and Shierholz 2009).

As in the United States, wealth is even more unequally distributed among nations than income. North America, Europe, and well-to-do Asian-Pacific countries account for almost one-third of the world's household wealth. Estimates are that the richest 2 percent of individuals hold more than half of all the wealth in the world, and the top 10 percent own 85 percent (Davies et al. 2008). The concentration of wealth in the world is comparable to a situation "for a 100-person population in which one person receives $900 and the remaining 99 people each receive $1" (Davies et al. 2008, p. 7). Thirty-nine of the world's 229 countries hold more than 80 percent of all wealth. Per capita wealth is lowest in India, Pakistan, Indonesia, and most of the central and western portions of Africa. Among the richest countries, there are significant variations in the distributions. In Australia, Germany, Ireland, and Spain, for example, the richest 10 percent own 41–45 percent of all wealth; in the United States, they possess almost 70 percent (Davies et al. 2008).

Given the widespread inequality among nations, coupled with the breakdown of national

TABLE 2.4 Income[a] Inequality among Households within Rich Industrial Countries, 2004–2005

Country	Gini Coefficient[b]	Income Ratio of 90th Percentile to 10th Percentile
Australia	0.30	3.95
Austria	0.27	3.27
Belgium	0.27	3.43
Canada	0.32	4.12
Denmark	0.23	2.72
Finland	0.27	3.21
France	0.28	3.39
Germany	0.30	3.98
Greece	0.32	4.39
Ireland	0.33	4.41
Italy	0.35	4.31
Japan	0.32	4.77
Netherlands	0.27	3.23
New Zealand	0.34	4.27
Norway	0.28	2.83
Spain	0.32	4.59
Sweden	0.23	2.79
Switzerland	0.28	3.29
United Kingdom	0.34	4.21
United States	**0.38**	**5.91**

[a] "Income" is household income from earnings, self-employment, capital, and government transfers with income taxes and Social Security taxes subtracted.

[b] The Gini coefficient measures the distribution of income across households or persons. The coefficient can range from 0.0, indicating perfect equality of income across all persons or households, to 1.0, which indicates concentration of all income with the top household or person. In other words, the higher the coefficient, the greater the inequality.

Source: Adapted from *OECD Stat Extracts* at http://stats.oecd.org/index.aspx. OECD is the Organization for Economic Cooperation and Development.

boundaries in the world economy, it is not surprising that the relationship between global economic inequality and globalization has become a hot topic of research. Does more extensive involvement of all nations in the world economy reduce the economic inequality between them? Is globalization a way out of world poverty? Has globalization reduced or exacerbated economic inequality within the United States? We need to address these questions.

Globalization itself has been defined in two basic ways, one which is narrowly economic and another which incorporates a variety of dimensions and is sometimes referred to as the "grand" theory of globalization (Goldthorpe 2002). In the latter view, globalization is seen as an economic, political, and social force that has enveloped most of the world. The broad central impact of globalization is to create greater interdependence between parts of the world and to compress the world into a smaller place (Harvey 1989; Guillen 2001). A narrower conceptualization of globalization views it as a strictly economic phenomenon, involving the increase in direct investment, flow of workers, and free trade between countries. It is this definition that we will use in our assessment of globalization's impact on inequality among nations and within the United States.

There is no theoretical agreement over whether globalization has been a primarily positive or negative force in the world at large. The positive or **"neoliberal"** view envisions globalization as raising the average economic fortunes of all nations as members of a world community through the opening up of opportunities and sharing of skills and technologies (Taylor 2002). Globalization encourages internationalism and opens up all countries to the same set of market forces. Since the global marketplace is an open competitive arena, it creates pressures on countries to use their resources efficiently and to find a niche or specialty that puts them at a comparative advantage in the market. The supposed result is a reduction in poverty, a decline in inequality between nations, and, consequently, a wholesale breakdown in the dichotomies that have characterized the world (e.g., rich–poor, core–periphery, North–South; Wade 2004). In this view, globalization should also reduce economic inequality *within* countries because it is a win–win situation for everyone involved.

The critical view, in contrast, interprets globalization as a force that strengthens the opportunity for powerful nations to take advantage of more vulnerable and less powerful ones through the dismantling of traditional protections for the less wealthy and the consequent exploitation of their labor. Transnational corporations have weakened the power of labor and unions, intensifying competition between home-based and foreign labor. The deindustrialization accompanying globalization reduces the number of high-paying manufacturing jobs and pushes more workers into lower-paying service work (Alderson and Nielsen 2002). One result is a widening of economic inequality between skilled/educated and less-skilled/uneducated workers within countries and between developed and underdeveloped nations

(Scholte 2000; Makoba 2002). Poorer countries are more likely to subscribe to this critical view, because they believe that their countries enter the world economy with many disadvantages. Free trade is supposed to operate in the global marketplace, for example, but they know that wealthy nations often subsidize their farmers, putting farmers from poorer countries at a disadvantage.

A more nuanced view of globalization states that while globalization harmed less-developed countries in the 1970s, it has more recently hurt employees in developed countries through the exportation of work to lower-wage countries. It has been argued that the effect of globalization on **world inequality** may change as different stages in the world economy and international relationships develop. As globalization becomes initially established, inequality between nations grows, but in later stages the advantages of rich nations are slowed and inequality between nations declines (Krugman and Venables 1995).

So what is the answer: Has globalization had a positive, negative, or mixed impact on economic inequality? "On this very important question, responsible opinion tends towards diametrically opposing views" (Seshanna and Decornez 2003, p. 354). Goldthorpe (2002) says flatly that globalization theorists have not made their case one way or the other.

Since the early 1800s and up to the recent past, most world inequality has been due to economic inequality *between* nations (Goesling 2001). Economic inequality between nations grew significantly during the Industrial Revolution and the twentieth century at the same time that globalization was occurring. And some argue that globalization has continued to create more inequality and has either increased or had no effect on poverty in the world (Prabhakar 2003; Seshanna and Decornez 2003; Kiely 2004; Wade 2004). They find that direct investment in the world market is concentrated in the developed countries rather than evenly spread among all countries, resulting in a concentration rather than dispersion of capital.

Others disagree, contending that in the last few decades of the twentieth century inequality among nations, though extensive, appears to have stabilized (Schultz 1998; Firebaugh 1999; Goesling 2001) or that globalization fosters a reduction in economic inequality (Minnich 2003; Dollar and Kraay 2004; Firebaugh and Goesling 2004; Weede 2008). Countries that are most globalized are more likely to thrive economically. In their study of countries across the economic spectrum, for example, Firebaugh and Goesling (2004) found that, while still large, economic inequality between nations declined in the last part of the twentieth century "primarily because of [globalization's] role in the spread of industrial technology in Asia" (p. 285). Moreover, they anticipate that it will continue to decline because of industrialization and the fact that most of the growth in the working-age population will be in these poor nations. But even though its contribution has declined, economic inequality among countries still accounts for roughly two-thirds of world inequality (Firebaugh 2000; Goesling 2001).

In sum, there are conflicting findings on whether globalization has a positive or negative effect on economic inequality among countries. It has been suggested that among the main reasons for these disagreements are differences in methodology (Mills 2009). Earlier I alluded to the difficulties of finding comparable data and definitions in assessing inequality between nations. Those who argue that globalization has reduced inequality criticize the methodology, conceptualizations, and logic of those on the other side. For example, proponents say that critics of globalization define *technology* as meaning information/communications rather than industrial technology. While the former may indeed worsen between-nation inequality, the latter does not (Firebaugh and Goesling 2004). What dimensions of globalization are included in studies also makes a difference because some dimensions may be related to economic inequality in some countries while others are not. In their study of 69 developed and less-developed nations, Reuveny and Li (2003) found that open trade reduced inequality within less-developed countries but not developed ones. Foreign direct investment by multinational corporations increases inequality in both types of countries. On the other hand, the free flow of financial capital does not seem to affect income inequality.

Despite these variations, on the whole there seems to be much more agreement that globalization raises economic inequality within countries including the United States (Alderson and Nielsen 2002; Firebaugh and Goesling 2004; Wade 2004; Moore and Ranjan 2005; Weede 2008; Massey 2009). Despite any possible slowing in international inequality, inequality *within* nations has increased and has become a greater contributor to world inequality as a whole (Goesling 2001; Guillen 2001). Declining inequality in many industrialized nations has been replaced with increasing inequality. The "great U-turn" in income inequality within advanced nations is partially explained by globalization. In the global marketplace, countries that exercise fewer controls on the movement of capital experience greater earnings inequality as a result (Mahler 2004). Examining data from 16 industrial countries, Alderson and Nielsen (2002) found that while direct investment abroad has led to more capital for employers, it has also spurred a decline in high-paying jobs, a reduction in demand for low-skilled compared to high-skilled labor, and an increase in the number of immigrants who have varying levels of skills. These developments have widened the economic gaps within advanced countries. Mishel and others add that globalization has also reduced employment in traditionally high-paying manufacturing jobs, lessened investment in the U.S. manufacturing base, and reduced the price of many goods, thereby indirectly causing a decline in the average wages of U.S. workers. They also note that competition from foreign workers can cause U.S. employees to reluctantly accept wage reductions. Finally, the "offshoring" of many high-tech white-collar service jobs and competition in trade also appear to have had a depressing effect on the salaries of U.S. white-collar professionals (Mishel, Bernstein, and Allegretto 2005). "Whatever the causes," writes Robert Wade (2004) perhaps with some exaggeration, "the fact is that the United States is now back to the same level of inequality of income as in the decades before 1929, the era of the 'robber barons' and the Great Gatsby" (p. 578).

Summary

This chapter has analyzed economic inequality as a fundamental form of social inequality. Economic inequality was defined as including social-class, income, and wealth differences in the United States. Americans have complex views of the class structure itself and on what determines their places within it. Scholars as well vary in their depictions of it, usually seeing the class structure either as a socioeconomic continuum or as a set of more discrete classes. Despite these variations in class models, there are some general agreements on the proportions found in different classes. Disagreements about U.S. class structure include the question of the placement of lower-level white-collar workers, the issue of the shrinking middle class, and the question of proletarianization or embourgeoisement of the working class.

Discussing class structure is only one way to depict economic inequality. Describing the extent of income inequality is another. Such inequality has increased in recent years, with the top 20 percent receiving a greater proportion of total income and the bottom 80 percent a smaller proportion. These differences are in part manifested in the growth in wage inequality between CEOs and other workers. In recent years, this gap has been propelled by technological and globalization processes that affect unemployment and the bargaining position of labor on the worker side, and lower costs, better tax positions, and higher profits on the CEO/corporate side.

The increases in income inequality are overshadowed by even greater wealth inequality. Recent estimates show that the richest 20 percent own about 85 percent of all wealth, while the bottom 40 percent possess well under 1 percent of all wealth. As a broad measure of an individual's or family's economic position, wealth is a better indicator than income because it incorporates a broader range of assets that can affect economic inequality across generations. In sum, whether measured by social-class indicators, income, wage, or wealth distributions, economic inequality is extensive and appears to have grown since the early 1980s in the United States.

As in the United States, there are significant differences in economic inequality among nations. Generally, economic inequality is greater in poorer countries, although there are major variations among industrial nations. When compared to its industrial counterparts, the United States ranks at the top in terms of its income and wealth inequality.

Poverty rates provide an additional measure of economic inequality and another one on which the United States ranks unfavorably among industrial nations. And, as we will see in the next chapter, poverty in the U.S. shows no sign of abating.

Critical Thinking

1. Why do you think the United States fares poorly on measures of poverty and economic inequality when compared to other industrial nations?
2. Consider the jobs you have held. What factors do you think led to your being employed and affected the earnings you received?
3. Were you surprised by the extent of income and wealth inequality in the United States? Why or why not?
4. What do you think economic and technological conditions will be like 10 years from now? How will these affect your chances of moving up or down in wealth?

Web Connections

The U.S. Census Bureau regularly collects data on income and poverty in the United States. Go to their website at www.census.gov and click on "income" and "poverty." United for a Fair Economy is an independent, nonprofit organization interested in greater equality that also gathers information on wealth, earnings, and income distribution and their relationship to race and democracy. They also write reports on this information. Visit www.FairEconomy.org. Do you think inequality undermines democracy?

Film Suggestions

People Like Us: Social Class in America (2001). A survey of the classes in the U.S. class structure and relationships between classes.

Class Dismissed (2001). Discusses stereotypical TV portrayals of working-class people.

CHAPTER 3

Poverty and Welfare

*Poverty is a great enemy to human happiness; it certainly destroys
liberty, and it makes some virtues impracticable and
others extremely difficult.*

SAMUEL JOHNSON (1709–1784)

The distribution of income and wealth discussed in the last chapter provides a portrait of economic inequality in the United States. Information about the extent and distribution of poverty within the population adds to that picture. The measurement of poverty, attitudes about welfare, and policies that are supposed to address poverty have all become contentious issues, in part, because of the popular image of the poor and because the welfare programs in which they participate are believed by many to be at odds with fundamental American values. The design of poverty policies is affected by the cognitive and emotional pictures that policymakers and the public have of the poor. Often these images are erroneous, and consequently, the bases of programs and their potential for positive impact are weakened.

This chapter begins with an analysis of public perceptions and myths regarding the poor as they relate to core cultural values. It then presents federal statistics on the measurement and extent of poverty and who the poor actually are. From there, the chapter moves to a discussion of some major antipoverty programs, welfare reform, and the effectiveness of government programs. To provide a broader perspective, the chapter concludes with a summary of how the U.S. poverty rate and programs compare to those of other countries.

HISTORICAL ROOTS OF U.S. POVERTY PERSPECTIVE

Images that we have of the poor are bound up with our explanations for their poverty. Our deeper cultural values affect the theories of poverty that we find acceptable and color our perceptions of the poor. Most of the images of the poor and the causes of poverty that have dominated U.S. history have focused in one way or another on alleged weaknesses among the poor themselves. This focus on the individual's characteristics as the basic cause of poverty emerged in fourteenth-century Europe with the rise of industrialism, the emergence of the freed wage-laborer, and the growth of international commerce. The massive economic changes occurring on the Continent and in England during this period—in addition to famines, widespread diseases, and war—generated a large number of paupers and beggars. Something had to be done to deal with these individuals. At the same time, the process of industrialization demanded the ready availability of workers.

As the dominant source of relief and welfare moved progressively out of the hands of churches and private charities and into the hands of public institutions and officials, a clear distinction between the "deserving" and "undeserving" poor developed in the late fifteenth century. Pregnant women, seriously ill individuals, and the elderly were among those who were considered worthy of help. Individuals who could but did not work were considered undeserving of assistance. The principle of "less eligibility" prevailed—that is, the idea that any relief given not be great enough to discourage work. The amount of relief was not expected to be higher than the wages of the lowest worker in the community (Dolgoff and Feldstein 1984).

The Elizabethan Poor Law of 1601 distinguished among the "able-bodied poor," the "impotent poor," and "dependent children." The former were required to work; refusal to do so meant punishment, and nonpoor citizens were forbidden to aid them. Those classified as being "impotent"—such as the disabled, deaf, blind, elderly, and mothers with small children—were given either "in-door relief" (placed in an institution or almshouse) or "outdoor relief" (allowed to stay in their own homes but given food, clothing, or other needed goods). "Dependent children" who could not be supported by their families were farmed out as apprentices, taught trades, and expected to serve in this capacity until early adulthood (Zastrow 1982). To be eligible for aid, a poor person was expected to have been a stable member of the community and without family support.

The distinction between the deserving and undeserving poor found in the Elizabethan Poor Law became deeply ingrained in the approaches taken to the poor and welfare in Britain and the United States and have remained so to this day. In early America, poverty was becoming a serious problem. Before the Civil War, upheavals in the economy, sickness, immigration, and demographic changes generated large numbers of poor individuals. Specifically, the decline in the home manufacture of goods, unemployment, the rise of low-wage labor, the seasonality of much work, and crop failures were among the economic changes responsible for poverty. Growing population pressure on the land, the changing age structure of the population, and increasing immigration also led to increased poverty levels (Katz 1986).

Reaction to the problem of poverty in the United States was heavily influenced by the English approach. Relief was considered a public responsibility, to be locally administered and controlled; it was not to be given to those who had families who could support them, and those who could work were expected to do so (Katz 1986). Even then, however, many believed that any relief would discourage the motivation to work and weaken character. Efforts were made then, as now, to seek out and eliminate the "able-bodied" from the relief rolls. The Quincy Report, a 1821 Massachusetts study of poverty and welfare, made the by-now familiar distinction between the impotent poor and the able poor. The "poorhouse," an early attempt to take care of the poor, sought to (1) eliminate the undeserving from help by requiring work and banning alcohol for residents and (2) encourage children and the deserving able poor by stressing work education and discipline in the hopes that such treatment would set them on the path out of poverty. The goal was to transform the character and behavior of its residents (Katz 1986).

The poorhouses did not work out very well. The conflict in goals that plagues many current welfare programs was already present in the early poorhouse program. A concern for order, cost, routine, and custody overshadowed the initial goal of reforming the individuals in them. Many became rundown and the care given became less than adequate. Officers of the poorhouses were often found to be guilty of graft. Inmates had greater and greater control over their behavior in the poorhouse; discipline was not enforced nor was useful work found for most inmates (Katz 1986).

EXPLANATIONS AND RACIALIZATION OF POVERTY AND WELFARE

When debating how to structure poverty programs, policymakers generally frame arguments in terms of who is deserving and who is undeserving of governmental help (Yoo 2008; Guekzkow 2010). That is, they categorize poor individuals into different groups. How subgroups among the poor are classified and viewed depends on (1) the perceived cause of their poverty, (2) the composition of the subgroup, (3) whether they are believed to be on welfare, and (4) who is doing the categorizing. Frequently, the categorization of a group by the public depends heavily on whom or what they think is responsible for the group's poverty, and people vary in the explanations they accept. Some believe that most poverty is caused by an individual's own attitudes, behavior, and/or flaws. That is, they blame the individual. Others argue that poverty is caused by conditions beyond a person's control, such as economic recession or illness. Finally, some even attribute poverty to "divine intervention" (Brimeyer 2008; Robinson 2009). Most Americans subscribe to a mix of individualistic and structural views, but a majority lean in the direction of blaming the individual (Robinson 2009). Individuals who live in an area in which the majority of people are Republicans and most of the poor are Black, are most likely believe the poor are destitute due to individual failings rather than structural problems and, thus, to view them as undeserving (Hopkins 2009). Generally, persons with less education, higher occupational status, and who are politically and religiously conservative are more likely to blame poverty on the poor themselves, while more liberal and highly educated individuals attribute poverty primarily to structural or situational causes (Robinson 2009).

Reaction to the poor also depends on the group to which they belong; some poor are thought of more positively than others. Generally, those on welfare are viewed as undeserving while those who reject welfare but are homeless or are among the working poor are defined as deserving. Those on welfare are perceived as being "poor by choice" while others are thought to be "poor by circumstance" (Robinson 2009, p. 513). Individuals on welfare are seen as undeserving because they appear to violate the widespread and deeply held belief in the work ethic and to not take advantage of chances to move out of poverty. Surveys have consistently shown that the public view *poor* individuals positively while holding a negative view of *welfare* recipients (Henry, Reyna, and Weiner 2004). Welfare itself has been widely interpreted as discouraging work and fostering dependence on government even where employment opportunities for the poor are believed to exist (Allard 2009).

Negative portrayals of welfare by the media have helped to perpetuate opposition to welfare, especially in areas where high levels of racial prejudice and large numbers of Blacks are present (Dyck and Hussey 2008; Fullerton and Dixon 2009; Hopkins 2009). During discussions and design of the 1996 welfare reform in the United States, for example, the typical welfare mother was labeled by the media as being a lazy, immature person who gave birth to multiple children and who was also an incompetent mother. This image helped to shape the requirements built into the Welfare Reform Act of 1996 (Kelly 2010). Negative mental depictions of groups during debates about who should be eligible were also operative. The presentation of immigrants as irresponsible and as coming to the United States solely to get public aid motivated politicians to make them ineligible for programs such as Supplemental Security Income (Yoo 2008).

Popular stereotypes about race are a major reason for the negative view of welfare and its beneficiaries. Poverty is believed to be a largely urban Black problem, and Blacks are thought by many to be lazy and responsible for their own lack of economic progress (Henry, Reyna, and Weiner 2004; Hanson and Zogby 2010). In other words, rather than seeing them as victims of discrimination, they are considered to be responsible for their own poverty. A primary explanation for the historically negative attitude toward welfare is that the public believes most of those on welfare are Black and, therefore, responsible for their poverty. Consequently, welfare recipients are believed to be undeserving of government aid. These racial attitudes have infiltrated popular feelings about poverty and undermine support for welfare programs (Quadagno 1994; Hopkins 2009; Robinson 2009). Programs are seen by many poor Whites as a "Black benefit" less available to poor Whites (Cleaveland 2008). In this way, welfare is racialized as being a Black program, which lowers its standing in the eyes of the public. Since those on welfare are viewed as being undeserving, this combination of seeing poverty and welfare as Black issues means that Blacks are viewed as undeserving of governmental aid. In sum, cultural values, racial stereotypes, and categorizations of the poor, all combine to reinforce American attitudes about the poor and welfare. Certain values, particularly those concerning individual responsibility and work, are especially significant in shaping our perceptions of the poor and how they should be treated.

CULTURAL VALUES AND THE POOR

Historically, perceptions of the poor have been conditioned by the cultural context. A number of U.S. values have had a significant impact on our views of the poor. Among the most central of these are (1) individualism/autonomy and (2) the belief in work, intertwined with its moral character.

Individualism/Independence

The quintessential image of the pioneer as someone who, when confronted by the rigors of frontier life, worked hard and took individual responsibility for his or her own fate, has been ingrained in the American psyche as what true Americans should be like. Despite the fact that most early Americans traveled and lived in groups, the idea of the rugged individual has held great appeal (Boorstin 1967). Basic to this ideal image of the heroic American are several components:

1. This person is physically and psychologically independent; he or she needs no help from others.
2. Individual achievement is sought despite difficult obstacles.
3. Achievement even under difficult circumstances means that anyone can succeed if he or she tries hard enough.
4. Those who do not make it either lack the ability or are lazy and therefore immoral. In any case, they do not have what it takes to succeed.
5. The possibility of material gain is needed to motivate people (Dolgoff and Feldstein 1984).

These components suggest that being poor or rich is largely the result of a struggle in which the best win and the worst fail. Individuals who are poor either do not have the personal qualities necessary to succeed or do not put forth enough effort. Moreover, being poor and on welfare indicates dependency on others, and therefore flies in the face of the ideal that Americans should be independent.

The Enlightenment of the eighteenth century and Adam Smith's economic theories provided intellectual support for belief in the autonomous individual. It was believed that intelligent individuals, equipped with modern knowledge, could do almost anything for themselves as well as society. Smith's economic theories stressed a laissez-faire approach to economic affairs. Free individuals, unencumbered by governmental and other regulations, seeking their own goals would create the most efficient and productive society. Governmental interference in the form of any aid was believed to violate the intricate processes of freely working, "natural systems." "The 'inefficient poor' like inefficient businesses, were to die off through natural selection" (Tropman 1989, p. 137).

The beliefs that individuals should be self-reliant, exercise self-restraint, and take responsibility for their own lives are still reflected today in polls that show a large majority of Americans favor policies that require work, impose time limitations on welfare benefits, and allow no increases in benefits when women on welfare have more children (Shaw and Shapiro 2002).

The Moral Character of Work

"God helps those who help themselves" goes the old saying. The belief that individuals are responsible for their own destinies can be traced back to religious doctrines consistent with a U.S. society which had a large frontier to be explored and conquered. One of these religious strands was Calvinism, which Miller has called "the most individualistic development out of the most individualistic wing of the most individualistic part of the Judeo-Christian heritage" (1977, p. 3). Calvinism is a puritanical religion that stresses the importance of the individual and his or her own work as an indication of whether he or she is among the "elected." Under this doctrine, work is considered crucial to a meaningful life. Idleness is not only a sin but a social evil as well. People who become poor do so because they lack character. Since they are not successful, it is a sign that they are not among God's elect. Calvin was against even free almsgiving to those he considered idle and lazy (Dolgoff and Feldstein 1984).

Many early American religious practitioners subscribed to these beliefs. The American Puritan minister Cotton Mather (1663–1728) confirmed the religious significance of work in his exhortations about the importance of having "a calling." Every man should have an occupation through which he contributes to society, argued Mather, otherwise he cannot expect anything from society. "How can a man Reasonably look for the *Help of other men,* if he be not in some *Calling* Helpful to *other men?*" wrote the minister. When men do not put forth their efforts, what happens? "By *Slothfulness* men bring upon themselves . . . Poverty . . . Misery . . . all sorts of Confusion . . . On the other Side . . . a *Diligent*

man is very rarely an *Indigent* man" (Rischin 1965, pp. 24–28; emphases in original). It is easy to see why those in positions of wealth and power might subscribe to these views, since they not only justify the wealth of those at the top but also locate the source of poverty in a lack of effort by the poor individual.

Although the explicitly religious character of many of these pronouncements has lessened, the hold of the essential ideas is still strong. To place the reason for economic success or failure on the individual is to exonerate society and others from being responsible for poverty, and, just as importantly, to isolate the poor from the rest of society and to foster a "them versus us" imagery among the population. The further perception, though inaccurate, of most of the poor as Black intensifies the belief that the poor are qualitatively different in character from the rest of the population. A recent poll suggested that U.S. adults are more likely to view Blacks as more lazy than either Hispanics or Asian Americans (Shaw and Shapiro 2002).

The work ethic is at the heart of the rationale for current welfare policies. The thrust is on getting able-bodied people to work outside the home so that they will not take advantage of welfare benefits. Only the deserving poor should receive help. The notion that those without jobs, especially during times of relative prosperity, are to blame for their own economic troubles goes back deep in our history. As Bremner (1956) noted in his analysis of reactions to poverty during the nineteenth century, "In normal times Americans were accustomed to think of unemployment as exclusively the problem of the inefficient and indolent. Conservatives stuck to this view even in depression years." It was also believed that the presence and fear of poverty served as incentives to work and to use one's abilities to the fullest (Bremner 1956, pp. 16–17).

The beliefs in individualism and the moral character of work influence present-day images of the poor and welfare. This is not to say that other values are not also implicated in current images. A sense of community and compassion (humanitarianism), the beliefs in achievement and success as upward mobility, and the belief that the family is supposed to play a crucial role in maintaining its members are all additional values that have helped to shape our perceptions of the poor and what is to be done about poverty. The focus here has been on individualism and the work ethic because, more often than not, these values have been most salient to and have informed the perceptions of those responsible for crafting welfare policies.

MYTHS ABOUT THE POOR

Values and beliefs often distort social reality because they suggest that most of the poor have characteristics that they, in fact, do not possess. In media portrayals of the poor, Blacks and women are generally overrepresented. The poor are presented as lazy, and poverty is too often interpreted as a solely urban phenomenon (Clawson and Trice 2000). These distortions provide one reason why individualistic explanations of poverty are so weak; too much evidence contradicts them. Blacks are often believed to make up the bulk of those who are poor and on welfare, but, in fact non-Hispanic Whites comprised 43 percent, while Blacks were 23 percent and Hispanics 28 percent of the poor population in 2009. Given their beliefs about work and their images about those on welfare, some people assume that the majority of those receiving aid are able-bodied, middle-aged men who are too lazy to work. In fact, 43 percent of the poor are either below 18 or over 65 years old. Of the remainder, roughly 14 percent of the nonaged poor have a disability of some sort and 10 percent of poor families are headed by a female parent. Thus, the majority are not able-bodied, middle-aged men. Many in the recent poverty ranks are the "new poor," that is, individuals who have been laid off or made poor because of medical expenses, and who have never been poor before.

There are other misconceptions about the poor that reinforce the belief that they are undeserving. One is that they have a significantly greater number of children than the nonpoor. This is simply not the case. There is only a slight difference in the average size of poor and nonpoor families. In 1991, the average size of U.S. families in general was 3.17, whereas that of poor families was 3.52, about a third of a person larger. In 2002, families whose heads had less than high-school educations averaged 3.36 persons compared to 3.11 for families whose heads had at least a college degree. This again indicates only a small difference in average family sizes between socioeconomic groups. There is even some evidence that higher fertility rates are occurring among couples with high incomes and elite educations (Weeden et al. 2006). A 1998 survey by the Department of Labor found that food stamp households containing minors had an average of 4.1 persons in the household with 2.4 children under 18 years of age. Non–food stamp households with minors present averaged a similar 4.0 persons in total, with 1.8 of them under 18 years of age (U.S. Department of Labor, August 2000). Thus, the differences in household composition between those on and those not on "welfare" are not nearly as great as welfare stereotypes would suggest.

Nor is there any good evidence that poor mothers have children, including illegitimate ones, to increase their benefits. Yet a majority of Americans apparently believe that the presence of welfare encourages young women to have children and discourages those who get pregnant from marrying the fathers (Davis and Smith 1989). The assumption that people have children to get more support from the government simply does not hold up when the evidence is examined (Morris and Williamson 1986). Increases in welfare benefits do not appear to have a significant impact on poor parents' decisions to have more children (Gensler 1997; Zavodny and Bitler 2010).

First, the vast majority of unmarried mothers on welfare have only one child and illegitimacy rates tend to be lower in states with higher welfare benefits (Ellwood and Bane 1984; Bell 1987). Second, welfare benefits are quite low, making it uneconomical to have more children to receive more benefits. In 2007, for example, the average per-person monthly food stamp benefit was $95.63, and in 2005 the average monthly child support payment was $425. When comparing these benefits with the estimated $140,000 it took in 2007 for a lower-income, single-parent, two-child family to raise the younger child to age 17, it becomes apparent that the economic incentive to have large numbers of children would be very low (U.S. Department of Agriculture, March 2008).

Another reason why many balk at giving the poor too many cash benefits is that they are perceived as wasting their money on frivolous purchases. However, evidence from the 2008 Consumer Expenditure Survey conducted by the U.S. Department of Labor suggests that the poor spend most of their incomes on basic needs. Table 3.1 compares the percentages and amounts of income spent on different items households in the poorest income quintile with the percentages spent by those in the richest income quintile.

Total expenditures for those in the lowest quintile are less than one-fourth of the top quintile ($22,304 vs. $97,003). In terms of how income is spent, 81 percent of the $22,304 in outlays is spent on housing, food, transportation, and utilities by the lowest-level households. An additional 7 percent is spent on health care. Significant for future quality of life, only 2 percent of the expenditures of the lowest-expenditure group is put aside for insurance and pensions. In contrast, while they spend more, in absolute terms, in each category, smaller *percentages* are spent by the richest quintile on housing,

food, and health care. But these households spend 28 times as much money as the lowest income group on insurance and pensions, providing them with a better foundation for a stable future.

Another perception of those on welfare is that they are usually guilty of fraud and cheating. But in fact, only an extremely small percentage cheat and then, in almost all cases, only a small amount of money is involved. More prevalent and more serious than cheating by recipients are the honest mistakes and errors made by public officials when determining eligibility for and level of public aid (Zastrow 1982; Bell 1987). In addition, recent exposures of pervasive fraud by building contractors and others who profit from the government's housing program, extensive overcharging by contractors charged with cleaning up polluted areas, and fraudulent charges by health care providers and fictitious clinics strongly suggest that if fraud is a problem in poverty programs, the poor are not its primary source. In fact, 2010 estimates are that Medicare fraud alone amounts to $60 billion a year (Weaver 2010).

When considering the deservedness of those who receive welfare and who they are, one should remember that many nonpoor also receive governmental welfare, although one usually does not think of middle-class or wealthy persons or corporations as receiving such aid. For this reason,

TABLE 3.1 Average Annual Expenditures and Percentages Spent in Major Categories for Lowest and Highest Income Quintiles: 2008

Major Spending Category	Lowest Income Quintile		Highest Income Quintile	
	Amount	Percentage	Amount	Percentage
Housing	$8,900	40%	$30,791	32%
Food	$3,473	16%	$10,982	11%
Transportation	$3,430	15%	$15,614	16%
Utilities	$2,238	10%	$5,177	5%
Healthcare	$1,624	7%	$4,391	5%
Entertainment	$1,082	5%	$5,673	6%
Insurance and Pensions	$532	2%	$15,126	16%
Other Expenditures	$1,025	5%	$14,426	10%
Average Annual Expenditures	$22,304	100%	$97,003	101%[a]

Source: U.S. Department of Labor, *Consumer Expenditures in 2008,* Report 1023, March 2010.

it has been called **phantom welfare** (Huff and Johnson 1993). Direct cash and credit subsidies, tax exemptions and deductions, subsidized or reduced-cost services, and various trade restrictions are among the assistance programs provided to businesses. The recent multibillion dollar "bailout" or "rescue" of financial institutions by the federal government is among the latest examples of government support for the nonpoor.

Not only businesses but also nonpoor persons receive significant amounts of aid. Among the benefits to the middle class in the "fiscal welfare system" are tax deductions for mortgages and exemptions for parents of college students (Abramovitz 2001, p. 298). Despite the many governmental benefits that flow to the nonpoor, it is generally only the poor who are perceived as receiving "welfare" and often seen as undeserving of that aid. Yet, if the degree to which it is deserved is a measure of whether governmental benefits should go to a group, then the phantom welfare that is given to nonpoor individuals and organizations needs to be given more attention than it has received.

NUTSHELL 3.1   A Dark Side of Welfare Reform

While the 1996 welfare reforms reduced the number of individuals on welfare and pushed many into the labor force, it also created a variety of problems for those who had hoped to escape poverty. In her interviews with TANF recipients in West Virginia, Melissa Latimer found that many complained about the minimal government effort to bring jobs into the region and the lack of help in job placement. Availability of and access to relevant training was also a widespread issue. When seeking help these residents also felt that they were treated poorly by human services workers:

> "These workers make you feel like a bum every time you apply for help."
> "They think you ain't much of nothing."
> "When a person signs up for help, they should not be made to feel like a failure."
> "[They should] quit putting employees in there that look down on more welfare people." (Latimer 2008, pp. 87, 95)

These findings are not unusual; the manner in which welfare recipients are treated has changed little as a result of welfare reform. The shadow of being considered "undeserving" still hangs over the poor who seek help. As Sandra Danziger recently put it: "[I]n the current cash welfare programs the poor are neither pitied nor entitled" (2010, p. 535). Some have to fight the image of being undeserving:

> "I have always worked and paid taxes."
> "I support my own children and I have health problems but I am determined."
> "I am doing my best." (Latimer 2008, pp. 88–89)

Older poor women, especially those who live in poor rural areas and seek help often face unique problems because of their age and the generation in which they were raised:

> "People like us, we were taught to do for ourselves. . . be self-reliant. But there's too many people like me (seniors) that need help . . . even if they have to swallow their pride."
> "I need to be doctored up because I'm a swellin' from my arthritis. I cain't hardly walk. But I cain't get medication for it cause I ain't got the money."
> "Since I'm over 60, there's nobody out there's gonna hire me when they find out my age." (Henderson and Tickameyer 2008, pp. 160, 161, 163)

How do we change the culture of welfare so that no poor person is automatically stigmatized when he or she seeks help?

Sources: Melissa Latimer, "A View from the Bottom: Former Welfare Recipients Evaluate the System," *Journal of Poverty* 12:77–98; Sandra K. Danziger, "The Decline of Cash Welfare and Implications for Social Policy and Poverty," pp. 523–545 in *Annual Review of Sociology*; Debra A. Henderson and Ann R. Tickameyer, "Lost in Appalachia: The Unexpected Impact of Welfare Reform on Older Women in Rural Communities," *Journal of Sociology & Social Welfare* 35:153–171.

The Poor and Incentive to Work

Perhaps the most consequential perception of the poor involves their attachment to work and the work ethic. As mentioned earlier, the value of work is deeply ingrained in U.S. culture, as is the belief that most people can succeed if they try hard enough. These beliefs force us to raise some important questions about the poor. First, are people poor primarily because they do not work? Second, do the poor believe in the work ethic or do they prefer not to work? With respect to the first question, census data indicate that a significant proportion of the poor work, many of them full-time. In 2009, 36 percent of poor individuals 16 years of age or older worked during the year, and almost one-fourth of these did so full-time, year-round. In 2009, 2.6 million poor adults worked full-time year-round, and 8 million more worked part-time, year-round. Yet they are still poor. Working 40 hours per week for 50 weeks during a year at the 2009 minimum wage of $7.25 would provide a household income of $14,500, only two-thirds of the amount needed to raise a family of four (two parents, two children) above the poverty level. Of those poor who do not work, most would not expect the 43 percent of the poor who are under 18 or over 65 to work much, if at all. In addition, there are others who are genuinely disabled and unable to work, including military veterans. In 2009, for example, the poor population included about 5 million 18–64 year-old persons who were disabled.

Low wages, in concert with a weak labor market, declining governmental supports, and increased income inequality are major factors behind the recent rise in poverty (Mishel, Bernstein, and Shierholz 2009). The level of wages is especially important because 80–90 percent of the incomes of poor families with one full-time worker come from wages. Even among single-parent families, a majority of income is derived from earnings (Urban Institute, June 2009).

The low-wage workforce is disproportionately composed of the most vulnerable groups in our society. In contrast to the rest of the labor force, women, members of minorities, youth, and workers with no more than high school educations are overrepresented among low-wage employees. Women who are single parents have been caught in a particularly difficult bind in the last 15 years because there has been increased societal pressure to both work *and* take care of their children. While both are likely to be desired by a single parent, as a young welfare mother put it, you can't have both at the same time (Hennessy 2009). Both are full-time. And yet to not do both of these is culturally unacceptable.

What these data indicate is that many poor individuals work, but despite their efforts and the difficulties they face, they remain poor. Because of the importance of earnings as a source of income for most families, it is important that programs be designed with work incentives in mind. Both the poor and the nonpoor respond to such incentives (Danziger, Haveman, and Plotnick 1986). Most Americans want to work. When asked if they would continue to work even if they did not need the money, two-thirds of American adults said that they would continue to work (General Social Survey 2006). A large number of studies have found that there is virtually no difference between the poor and nonpoor in their desire to work (e.g., Davidson and Gaitz 1974; Morris and Williamson 1986). Interviews with poor single mothers confirm these general findings. Work "gives me a feeling of accomplishment"; it shows my children "a good example." "When I don't work, I feel useless like I'm wasting my life." "I don't want to live on welfare" (Hennessy 2009, pp. 566–567). These findings should not be surprising, given that work is a hub around which many Americans' most cherished values revolve. Work is a major source of self-esteem and identity.

WHO ARE THE POOR?

This is not an easy question to answer because of continuing complaints and disagreements about how "poverty" should be officially measured. The federal poverty measure considers pretax income from all sources to determine one's income level. Consequently, it does not include the value of noncash benefits or the effect of taxes and tax credits on income. It also contains a household spending formula that is outdated. Alternative poverty measures that address these issues, such as those developed by the National Academy of Sciences, more often indicate that poverty levels are higher than suggested by the official measure. However, because longitudinal governmental data on poverty are based on it, the official poverty measure will be used in the present discussion.

In contrast to the long-term movement toward greater income and wealth inequality, trends in official poverty rates have been more erratic since 1980, going up in the early 1980s before declining and then rising again in 1989. They began to decline again in 1993 and did so for the remainder of the decade before increasing again in 2001. In 2009, the poverty rate stood at 14.3 percent (43.6 million people), up from 11.3 percent (31.6 million) in 2000 (U.S. Census Bureau, September 2010a).

Whether persons or families are defined as "poor" by the Census Bureau depends on whether their income falls below a given threshold. These thresholds vary by one's age, and family size and composition. For example, in 2009, individuals younger than 65 years were defined as poor if their total income fell below $11,161. On the other hand, a family of four with two parents and two children under 18 years of age had to have a gross income of under $21,756 to be classified as poor.

Contradicting the stereotype, most of the poor are not Black. Non-Hispanic Whites account for 43 percent of the poor, compared to Black Americans, who make up 23 percent. However, Table 3.2 shows that Hispanics and Blacks have poverty rates that are almost three times those of Whites. Hispanics have become an increasingly large part of the poverty population. In 1980, they composed only 12 percent of the poor population, in 1990, 18 percent, and in 2009, 28 percent. The increase can be linked to the increase in immigration of poor Hispanics during this period. The poverty rate for families with female householders is about five times that of married-couple families, and the poverty rate for children is noticeably higher than that for any other age group. Over one-third of those living in poverty in 2009 were children. Children in families headed by a female are four times more likely to be poor than children living in families with a married couple. Their poverty rate is 43 percent (U.S. Census Bureau, September 2010a).

While a popular stereotype is that most poor live inside principal cities, 2009 data indicate that a

TABLE 3.2 Poverty Rates by Race, Age, and Family Status: 1980–2009

	Poverty Rate (% in Poverty)			
	1980	**1990**	**2000**	**2009**
All persons	13.0	13.5	11.3	14.3
Under 18 years old	18.3	20.6	16.2	20.7
18 to 64 years old	10.1	10.7	9.6	12.9
65 and older	15.7	12.2	9.9	8.9
Whites, non-Hispanics	9.1	8.8	7.4	9.4
Blacks	32.5	31.9	22.5	25.8
Hispanics	25.7	28.1	21.5	25.3
Married-couple families	6.2	5.7	4.7	5.8
Female-headed families	32.7	33.4	25.4	29.9
Male-headed families	11.0	12.0	11.3	16.9

Source: U.S. Census Bureau, *Income, Poverty, and Health Insurance Coverage in the United States: 2009.* Current Population Reports, Series P-60, No. 238, September 2010, Table 4, p. 15, Table B-1, pp. 56–61, Table B-2, p. 62, Table B-3, p. 68.

slight majority of the poor actually live outside major cities. Geographically, poverty rates are higher in rural areas and in the core of central cities, and are higher in the South and West than in the Northeast or Midwest. Mississippi, Alabama, Arkansas, Kentucky, and West Virginia were among the states with 2009 poverty rates that were well above the national average. In contrast, the rates in Alaska, Connecticut, Maryland, and New Hampshire were significantly lower than the national average (U.S. Census Bureau, September 2010b).

Within the poor population, some people are poorer than others. Some have incomes that are very near the poverty threshold, whereas the incomes of others fall well below that poverty line. Two measures are used to indicate how far an individual's or family's income falls below their poverty threshold. One of these is a *ratio* that compares their actual income with their poverty threshold. A ratio of 1.00 indicates that their income is exactly the same as the threshold. A ratio below 1.00 is a measure of how far *below* poverty the person's or family's income falls;

conversely, a ratio above 1.00 indicates how far their income is *above* the poverty threshold. In 2007, about 44 percent of poor families, or 19 million individuals, had incomes that were *less than half* of the amount that the government uses to classify them as poor. In 2009, 7 million children lived in families with this level of income.

The second measure used to show the depth of poverty is the **income deficit**, which is the difference between a family's income and its poverty threshold. In 2009, the average poor family's income deficit was $9,042, which means that their income was actually $9,042 below their poverty threshold. Thus, they were not only poor, but *very* poor.

FLAWS IN PRE-1996 ASSISTANCE PROGRAMS

Many of the complaints that plagued assistance plans before the 1996 welfare reforms reflected the previously discussed public attitudes about the poor and welfare. In addition to concerns

It is common to associate poverty with the inner city, and indeed central cities have the highest poverty rates of any residential area. But rural poverty is also significantly higher than the national average. The poverty rate for those living outside metropolitan areas was 16.6 percent in 2009. Almost two-thirds of the poor live in the South and West. Rural states such as Alabama, Arkansas, Louisiana, and New Mexico have high poverty rates compared to others. (© Stephen Mcsweeny/Shutterstock)

about deservedness, work incentive, and family cohesion, controversies also involved questions about program equity, adequacy, and goal conflicts. Together these issues led to a major overhaul in public assistance programs, which will be summarized shortly.

The question of equity was raised in a variety of contexts. Under existing programs, not all individuals in equal need were given the same assistance because of differences in regulations and assistance levels between demographic groups and states. Individuals older than 65, for example, were more likely than others to be lifted out of poverty by governmental programs, especially Social Security. Traditionally, male heads were less likely to get assistance than female heads of families. However, females face some unique problems as a result of divorce, labor-market discrimination, and lack of adequate child care for their children. There were also geographical inequities, with some states having higher benefits or greater flexibility in their programs than others.

Lack of adequate support was a second deficiency of past programs. None of the public assistance programs had—or has—a standard benefit level that will enable a recipient to live comfortably. Since the 1970s, the value of public assistance benefits in real terms has not even kept pace with inflation. Cutbacks to programs in the 1980s exacerbated this problem. Finally, the inadequacy of existing programs is demonstrated by research showing that compared to other affluent industrialized nations, U.S. assistance programs were the least effective in lifting individuals out of poverty, largely because of the low level of benefits (Kenworthy 1999; Defina and Thanawala 2004).

Conflict in the goals of programs created additional problems. Satisfying the goal of adequacy, for example, might mean raising the cost of a program, or raising the level of benefits might endanger work incentives by making recipients feel complacent about seeking employment. This problem is complicated by the fact that the poor population is heterogeneous, and changes in one goal may be more important for one group than another. For example, how important is it that the work-incentive goal be maximized for those who

are elderly, disabled, or underage? Perhaps adequacy is more important for them.

A great deal of controversy exists over whether public assistance fosters the disintegration of marriages and encourages illegitimacy (Murray 1984). Most studies have found no relationship between benefit levels, family dissolution, and illegitimacy (e.g., Ellwood and Bane 1984; Danziger, Haveman, and Plotnick 1986; Ellwood and Summers 1986; Wilson 1987). Nor have higher state benefit levels been linked to increases in the number of female-headed households (Greenstein 1985). In fact, the number of female-headed households grew even when benefit levels declined (O'Hare 1987). Rather, changes in family composition are more closely tied to shifts in attitudes about families and divorce as well as to broader events in the economy. Family dissolution and reluctance to marry are related, for example, to the greater employment opportunities for women and the employability problems encountered by Black men (Ellwood and Summers 1986; Sawhill 1988).

Finally, many believe that public-assistance programs have built-in work disincentives (Murray 1984). Behind this belief is the conviction that "generous" benefit levels discourage recipients from seeking employment. However, this relationship is not as straightforward as it may appear. In the mid-1970s, low-income individuals were given an incentive to work in the form of the Earned Income Tax Credit (EITC). This allowed low-income workers to claim a tax credit of 10 percent of their earned income up to $5,000, giving them a maximum benefit of $500 (Levitan 1985). If low benefit levels encourage one to seek work, one would think that due to the combined effect of the EITC and the decreased value of benefits in the 1970s, unemployment would be down as individuals elected to go into the labor force. Instead, unemployment rose during the 1970s. While high benefit levels and benefit penalties if one works may have some disincentive effects, it appears that broader economic conditions are more closely related to employment rates than are welfare benefits (Danziger, Haveman, and Plotnick 1986; Sawhill 1988).

WELFARE REFORM AND CURRENT POVERTY PROGRAMS

Historically, there have been different kinds of attempts to address the problem of poverty. Some of the earliest were private and local in nature. There are still a large number of national and regional nongovernmental organizations that have as their major goal the reduction of poverty and the problems associated with it, such as homelessness and hunger. Among the most effective are Action Against Hunger USA, National Alliance to End Homelessness, Coalition for the Homeless, Action Aid International USA, Bread for the World Institute, and Second Harvest. Other programs involve different levels of governmental participation. Whether the government should fully carry the burden of solving this problem, rather than private voluntary groups, has been a source of controversy.

Consequently, there are different perspectives on how extensive the government's programs should be. The most stringent view—the **residual**, or conservative, view—holds that social welfare aid should only be given to the poor when their families and their involvement in the private economy have not been able to lift them out of poverty. In this sense, welfare is to serve a "residual" function, coming in only after other more traditional, nongovernmental sources of help have been exhausted. As this function implies, social welfare expenditures and programs are expected to be kept to a minimum and only those who demonstrate indisputably that they are in need are considered eligible for welfare help. Even then, benefits will be low and short term so as not to discourage work. Poverty is viewed as being caused primarily by individual defects and character flaws, rather than by wider social or cultural conditions. Under these circumstances, there is a social stigma for those seeking welfare. Up until the New Deal, this approach to welfare dominated the U.S. welfare system (Zastrow 1982; Bell 1987), and it still maintains a strong grip.

The second view of social welfare—the **institutional**, or liberal, perspective—has basically the opposite characteristics from the residual approach. Specifically, it assumes that social welfare programs are an integral part of the institutional structure of modern society, and that like other institutions, they play a vital role in dealing with many of the problems generated by society's social structure and events, such as business cycles and aging, which are largely inevitable. The institutional approach is consistent with the situational and structural theories of poverty. Since poverty is largely beyond the control of most poor, people should be able to expect help without a stigma being attached to such aid. Beginning with the New Deal in the 1930s, an institutional element was formally introduced on a broad scale into the general income-maintenance system of the United States. The result is that the present system is largely a mixture of both approaches.

A third view of social welfare programs interprets them differently than either conservatives or liberals. Instead of being considered either an unnecessary burden on government or as an integral and humane part of it, this *pacifying* perspective interprets social welfare programs as a means of controlling the working class and the poor. Social welfare programs expand when there is rising unrest among these groups and contract when these groups are calm (Piven and Cloward 1971). This placating function of welfare is closely related to the uneven operation of the capitalist economy. Oversupplies of labor lead to increases in government-sponsored programs. At the same time, however, the work requirements and benefit levels of welfare programs are stringent enough to ensure the availability of a cheap labor force to employers.

Despite variations in the perspectives, flaws and complaints about public assistance programs discussed earlier instigated an effort to change the structure of welfare policy, and in 1996 the Congress passed a welfare-reform package. At first glance, changes brought about by the Personal Responsibility and Work Opportunity Reconciliation Act of 1996, as its title suggests, are based on many of the same assumptions of past programs: individual characteristics are responsible for poverty, policymakers have to get tough with those on welfare to save them, people need to be pushed off welfare into work, welfare creates dependency, and single mothers form the core of those on public assistance. The 1996 Act was designed to reform the welfare system through an emphasis on making welfare recipients less dependent on public aid by pressuring them to find and accept work in the marketplace. Consistent with past policy on welfare recipients, the provisions of the law assume that those on welfare need to be pushed into work, that, if given the chance, they would prefer to remain dependent on welfare. But in contrast to past legislation, it does not guarantee public aid to a poor person. Among the Act's provisions are the following:

- Able-bodied adults are required to work after 2 years of aid or lose benefits.
- Aid is limited to 5 years over a person's lifetime.
- Block grants are given to states that can devise their own programs (Aid to Families with Dependent Children [AFDC] is eliminated).
- Future legal immigrants are ineligible for benefits in their first 5 years.
- Spending on food stamps is lowered by about $24 billion over a 6-year period, and guarantees of cash assistance for children are eliminated.
- Medicaid coverage is continued for people on welfare and for 1 year after leaving it if they are working.
- Teenage mothers are encouraged to identify the fathers of their children, stay in school, and live at home with parents.

Proponents hailed the new package as a reflection of American values of work and independence and as a way of forcing those on welfare to be "responsible." Critics claimed that it created few, if any, jobs in which welfare recipients could work and would push more than a million more children into poverty. In many ways, the new legislation appeared to have a number of the same flaws that plagued past policies.

President Clinton also signed into law an increase in the minimum wage to $5.15. Although many believe that good wages and earned income tax credits are a better way to remove people from poverty than welfare programs, this wage increase alone did not raise most poor families out of poverty. If one worked full-time, 40 hours a week, 52 weeks a year, minimum wage earnings still totaled $10,712, well below what was needed to raise an average poor family above the poverty line. Inadequacy has been a traditional weakness of American welfare programs, and, as suggested, some critics feared that more children would be thrown into poverty by the 1996 changes.

The block grants resulting from the welfare reforms of 1996 were aimed at giving states more leeway in shaping their own programs and encouraging individuals to reduce their assumed dependency on welfare by becoming employed as soon as possible. Consequently, by July 1997, every state had devised its own mixture of programs and requirements that fall within federal guidelines (National Governors' Association Center for Best Practices 1999). Some states impose lifetime limits of 60 months on assistance, while others have shorter limits. Some require individuals to be working before 2 years of aid are over, while others hold to the 2-year limit. States also vary on how they treat interstate immigrants, assistance to drug felons, available transitional child care, and the existence of caps on total assistance amounts.

A central feature of these reforms was the Temporary Assistance for Needy Families (TANF) program, which replaced AFDC. Thus, it is one of the more controversial dimensions of welfare reform. In Wisconsin, one of the first states to experiment with extensive welfare reform, the W-2 (Wisconsin Works) program replaced AFDC. Individuals participating in W-2 are "guided to the best available immediate job opportunity." In the event individuals do not find jobs, they are given subsidized or community employment, or are required to enter a work training program. The aim is to remove individuals from welfare rolls as soon as possible. After 2 years, they are on their own, and can only be in the program for a total of 5 years over their lifetimes. To provide transitional support while in employment or training, Wisconsin has provided job centers, some child support, emergency loans to keep them working, transportation assistance, and health care (Medicaid; Department of Workforce Development 1999). The programs of all the states emphasize self-sufficiency as a goal and impose time limitations beyond which individuals are no longer eligible for benefits.

One of the major changes that occurred with welfare reform was the shift from cash assistance to social service (noncash) assistance to the poor. Before 1995, more than three-quarters of welfare was in the form of cash assistance; since 1996, only one-third is in cash assistance (Allard 2009). This dispels a popular view of everyone on welfare receiving generous monthly checks. The focus on getting people to work was one source for the increased emphasis on social services.

A Profile of Some Major Programs

Current U.S. income-maintenance programs can be divided into two general parts: social insurance and public assistance. Both parts include cash and **in-kind benefits**. **Social insurance** is aimed at replacing income lost because of death, unemployment, disability, or retirement. Most of the social insurance programs were developed under the Social Security Act of 1935; they include old-age insurance, survivors' insurance, disability insurance, unemployment insurance, and, in many cases, workers' compensation. Medicare is also a social insurance program. These programs are financed by the insured through payroll taxes, by employers, and by the government. Eligibility for participation depends on the extent of a person's prior work history. As long as individuals satisfy certain basic requirements, they are automatically eligible for these programs. There is little stigma attached to participation in these programs because individuals are thought of as deserving of such benefits. These programs are most illustrative of the "institutional" perspective on welfare.

Public assistance programs, which have been more "residual" in terms of the assumptions built into them, are "means-tested" programs that aim at temporarily assisting poor individuals and families. These make up what most people think of as "welfare." The major programs included in the public assistance category are TANF, Supplemental Security Income (SSI), Supplemental Nutrition Assistance Program (SNAP), and Medicaid. SNAP was formally known as the Food Stamp Program. In addition to these programs, local general assistance and housing also are included in this category. Public assistance programs are financed by general revenues, and instead of individuals being automatic participants upon the satisfaction of basic requirements, persons wishing to receive welfare (i.e., public assistance) must prove that their income is low enough to justify their receiving aid. Thus, there tends to be more of a stigma attached to applying for and receiving welfare than is the case, for example, when one receives a Social Security check.

SOCIAL INSURANCE PROGRAMS Table 3.3 indicates the number of recipients and federal amounts for the major social insurance and public-assistance programs in 2008. Social Security was and is by far the most expensive of the income-maintenance programs. In 2008, annual payments exceeded $615 billion and the program served almost 51 million beneficiaries. Social Security provides monthly benefits to eligible retired and disabled workers, as well as to their spouses, children, and survivors. Retirement benefits make up most of these expenses. In 2008, the average monthly retirement benefit was $1,153.

Although most of the benefits from the Social Security retirement program go to nonpoor recipients, millions are protected from falling into poverty because of the program. Despite this benefit, Social Security has become a source of contention between younger and older generations. As its costs have gone up due to an aging population and a comparatively smaller base of workers to support it, younger workers resent the program's immediate cost to them and worry whether it will be able to support them when they retire.

In addition to the retirement program, survivors' and disability insurance are also a part of Social Security. Under the first type, a worker's

TABLE 3.3 Number of Recipients and Federal Expenditures for Major Social Insurance and Public-Assistance Programs: 2008		
Program	No. of Recipients/ Beneficiaries (in Millions)	Benefits/ Payments (in Billions)
Social Insurance		
Social Security (total)	50.9	$615.2
Social Security (retirement)	35.2	$409.5
Social Security (survivors)	6.5	$99.3
Social Security (disability)	9.3	$106.3
Medicare	45.2	$455.1
Public Assistance		
Supplementary Security Income	7.5	$43.0
Supplementary Nutrition Assistance	28.4[a]	$34.6
Temp. Assist. for Needy Families (2007)	3.9[a]	$10.7
Medicaid (2007)	56.8	$276.5

[a]Average number of *monthly* recipients.

Source: U.S. Census Bureau, *Statistical Abstract of the United States 2010.*

surviving dependents receive cash benefits. Disability insurance provides protection against the loss of family income resulting from a "breadwinner" being disabled. In 2008, over $106 billion was paid to disabled workers and their dependents.

In 1965, Medicare was added to the Social Security package. Its purpose is to provide hospital and medical insurance to people age 65 or older and those who are disabled but covered by Social Security. Payment under Medicare is made directly to the care provider. At the present time, Medicare does not pay for all medical services. For example, it does not cover custodial or routine dental care, nor does it pay for long-term nursing home care. The latter has been an issue of increasing concern, especially as the number of elderly increases. Medicare benefits totaled almost $455 billion in 2008 for its 45 million enrollees, more than four times the amount spent in 1990.

PUBLIC ASSISTANCE PROGRAMS The programs that we have been discussing are largely based on the assumption that their beneficiaries have contributed both to the financial support of those programs and to society in general through their years of employment. Thus, the benefits are interpreted more as a right than as a handout; that is, they are viewed as deserved. In contrast, public assistance programs are controversial in large part because many of the recipients are seen as undeserving. It is with these programs that questions about fraud, laziness, and deservedness arise most often. Groups that traditionally have been the most vulnerable to poverty conditions are most likely to receive welfare. These include women, children, minorities, and the elderly.

Under the public-assistance umbrella are TANF, SNAP, Medicaid, and SSI programs (see Table 3.3). All of these programs are *means tested*; that is, individuals are required to prove that their level of need is such that they require help. Most of them involve at least two levels of government in their administration or funding. The federal government has given states wide latitude in determining eligibility criteria. The form of benefit also varies. The benefits from the TANF and SSI programs come in the form of cash assistance, while those from SNAP and Medicaid come in the form of in-kind benefits (e.g., checks are not sent to the beneficiaries; rather it is goods or services that are provided). Let us look briefly at each of these major programs.

Largely because of its cost and the controversy surrounding it, Aid to Families with Dependent Children (AFDC) was replaced in 1996 by Temporary Assistance for Needy Families (TANF). As its name suggests, the program provides cash assistance for poor families with children. In 2007, federal and state expenditures for TANF were almost $11 billion. While TANF's overall design was created by the federal government, the program's specific eligibility rules and administration is carried out by each state. Adult recipients are required to fulfill work requirements and to pass income eligibility tests. TANF heavily emphasizes the need to work and the amount of time over which a person can receive benefits. The stated aim is to move able-bodied individuals off welfare as soon as possible. While in operation, AFDC was heavily criticized in large part because it was believed to discourage work and destroy families, and also because a large number of its recipients were thought to be undeserving.

Table 3.4 presents some of the basic characteristics of TANF participants. Contrary to the stereotype, the average TANF family tends to be fairly small, averaging fewer than two children. Most adult recipients are female, about one-third are White, another third Black, and about one-quarter are Hispanic. Over 40 percent have less than a high school education, and only 5 percent have more than a high school degree. Just over one-quarter are employed. Forty-two percent of the children in these families are under 6 years of age, and only 10 percent are older than 15.

Supplemental Security Income (SSI) is another cash-benefit welfare program aimed at people who are in financial need, and who are either 65 years of age or older, blind, or disabled. Implemented in 1974, it replaced federally reimbursed programs being run by the states to help the elderly, blind, and disabled. In 2008, over seven

TABLE 3.4 Characteristics of TANF Households and Recipients: 2008	
Average number of persons in household	2.9
Average number of children per family	1.8

Adult Recipients:	Percent
Sex	
Male	13%
Female	87%
Race/Ethnicity	
Hispanic	23%
Non-Hispanic white	35%
Black	35%
Other	6%
Education	
No formal education	5%
Less than high school	38%
High school degree	52%
More than high school	5%
Citizenship Status	
U.S. citizen	93%
Qualified alien	7%
Employment Status	
Employed	26%
Unemployed (looking for work)	47%
Not in labor force (not looking or discouraged)	27%
Receiving earned income	22%
Child Recipients	
Less than 6 years old	42%
6–11 years old	30%
12–15 years old	19%
16–19 years old	10%

Source: U.S. Department of Health and Human Services, Administration for Children & Families, *Characteristics and Financial Circumstances of TANF Recipients: Fiscal Year 2008.* Available at www.acf.hhs.gov/programs/ofa/character/FY2008/indexfy08.htm.

million persons received federally administered SSI payments totaling $43 billion. Monthly payments ranged from $393 for the elderly to $494 for disabled persons and $508 for blind individuals.

The Supplemental Nutrition Assistance Program (SNAP) is one of the major in-kind public assistance programs offered by the federal government. Although a food program operated during the period from 1939 to 1943, it was not reinstituted again until the early 1960s. Even though some experts would have preferred increases in cash benefits to a food program, the program has grown significantly since 2000. In 2008, about $35 billon in benefits were allotted and during any given month there were over 28 million recipients. Still, in 2008 only 67 percent of those eligible signed up to receive benefits. SNAP participants tend to be among our most vulnerable citizens. In 2009 more than half of the participants were children or elderly, and 58 percent of the households with children were headed by one adult, usually a female. Female-headed households accounted for just under one-third of all SNAP households. The average SNAP household contained 2.2 persons. Eighty percent of these households contained a disabled or elderly person, and were likely to receive SSI or Social Security income. Twenty-nine percent of SNAP households had income from earnings, but these households were mostly poor. The average SNAP household income was only 60 percent of the poverty level (U.S. Department of Agriculture, October 2010b). A profile of SNAP participants is provided in Table 3.5.

Medicaid is another in-kind program aimed at providing financial assistance to states to pay for the medical care of those on public assistance, children, pregnant women, and the elderly who meet basic economic requirements. It is different from Medicare in a number of ways. First, it is a selective program, whereas Medicare is a universal program. This means that applicants have to satisfy certain economic requirements before they can receive the service; that is, the program is means tested. In contrast, everyone in a particular age category is qualified to receive basic Medicare benefits, regardless of income. Second, Medicaid

TABLE 3.5 Participants in Supplemental Nutrition Assistance Program: 2009

	Percentage of Participants
Children	48%
Nonelderly adults	44%
Elderly adults	8%
Households with children	50%
Elderly person living alone	13%
Disabled nonelderly person living alone	12%
Gross household income as percentage of poverty line:	
25% or less	27%
26–50%	14%
51–75%	17%
76–100%	27%
Above poverty line	14%

Source: U.S. Department of Agriculture. Characteristics of Supplemental Nutrition Assistance Program Households: Fiscal Year 2009. Report No. SNAP-10-CHAR. October 2010b.

is a federal- and state-administered program, whereas Medicare is nationally administered. Finally, at least on paper, Medicaid covers all kinds of services, whereas Medicare is more restrictive in coverage (Dolgoff and Feldstein 1984).

To participate in the Medicaid program, states are required to cover several groups of eligible people, including some low-income elderly, women, and children, and disabled individuals. About half of all participants are children. The elderly and disabled compose less than one-fourth of beneficiaries, but they account for almost two-thirds of its costs. In 2007, federal expenditures for the roughly 57 million recipients who received Medicaid benefits totaled almost $277 billion.

There seems to be fairly widespread agreement that programs such as Medicare and Medicaid have made it possible for more people to get needed medical care. More people have used more health services than before the inception of these programs. Despite these salutary trends, however, problems still remain. Since the 1996 reform bill, the number of families getting cash benefits from public assistance programs has dropped significantly, but the number of participants in noncash programs such as Medicaid, food programs, and disability benefits has grown as problems in the economy have multiplied. Participation in the food stamp program approached record numbers in 2008 (Ohlemacher, February 26, 2007; Eckholm, March 31, 2008). Variations between states in their coverage rules and the optional facilities/services available create inequalities among individuals who are equally in need of medical care.

AN ASSESSMENT OF THE REFORM ACT OF 1996

Given the controversial nature of the Personal Responsibility and Work Opportunity Reconciliation Act of 1996, it should not be surprising that there is similar disagreement about its effects on welfare recipients. The popular press has generally emphasized success criteria that show the Act to have had positive effects, and has downplayed criteria and evidence that suggest the Act's negative impacts (Schram and Soss 2001). Indeed, whether welfare reform is viewed as having been a success depends on how "success" is measured.

By some measures—number on welfare, employment, child poverty—there has been success. First, between 1996 and the middle of 2000, the number of welfare recipients fell by 53 percent (6.5 million). The number of people on welfare is lower than it has been since 1969, and the percentage on cash assistance is the lowest it has ever been (Lichter and Jayakody 2002). Second, women who were on welfare have been pressed to end their dependency and enter the labor force in large numbers. Between 1996, the year of the reform legislation, and mid-1998, an additional 741,000 mothers who had never been married moved into the labor force (Lerman and Ratcliffe 2001). Third, the child poverty rate fell from 20.5 percent in 1996 to 16.2 percent in 2000, although it increased to 17.6 percent in 2003 (U.S. Census Bureau, August

2004). There has also been a decline since 1996 in the rate of pregnancy among unwed teenagers (Lichter and Jayakody 2002).

Even for the above positive effects, however, there is debate about the role of welfare reform in creating them. A strong economy at the time of legislation is also thought to have contributed heavily to reductions in welfare rolls and increased employment, resulting in reductions in child poverty (Corcoran et al. 2000; Kaushal and Kaestner 2001; Lens 2002). The question is whether reform will have the same effect when the economy is not so robust. Greenberg and Bernstein (2004) provide an answer to the question, noting that between 2001 and 2004, the number of people on welfare fell at the same time that the poverty rate increased. It appears that welfare reform "generally performed well during the tightest labor market in 30 years [mid-to-late 1990s] but has been far less effective amid the slack labor market that has prevailed since the 2001 recession" (p. B2). The high unemployment rate during the 2008–2009 recession and the reluctance of employers to hire in 2010–2011 because of instability in the economy also placed greater pressure on welfare programs at a time when serious concerns about government spending were beginning to grow.

Other evidence on welfare reform's effects is also less positive. The 1996 act has increased the inequalities in welfare programs between states. One consequence has been increased migration *out* of states with especially stringent welfare regulations, although the reasons for migration *into* particular states appear to be multiple and not fully understood (De Jong, Graefe, and Pierre 2005).

There have also been employment consequences. While many mothers who left welfare are employed, most are not working 40 hours per week consistently, many are in low-wage positions that do not offer many health or other benefits, and most are unlikely to move up into more stable positions with significantly higher pay. Tracking the employment transitions of young women from unemployment through work in bad jobs to work in good jobs, Pavetti and Acs (2001) estimated that by their late 20s most of the women on welfare will either still be working in bad jobs or will not be working regularly. Only a minority will be in good jobs. Consequently, many of these new workers have simply joined the ranks of the working poor, working for incomes that are often lower that those they had before leaving welfare (Abelda 2001; Bavier 2001; Cancian 2001; Lens 2002). As one scholar and former welfare participant put it: "If the goal of welfare reform was to get people off the welfare rolls, bravo. . . . If the goal was to reduce poverty and give people economic and job stability, it was not a success" (cited in Ohlemacher, February 26, 2007, pp. A1 and A3).

In her 3-year ethnographic study conducted among welfare families and at welfare offices, Sharon Hays (October 17, 2003) found that 40 percent of the women and children who had gotten off welfare had *no* source of income, and of the remaining 60 percent, about half were still poor. Similarly, Cancian and Meyer's study of former welfare participants in Wisconsin (2004) found that while more than 50 percent have gotten out of poverty, they have not achieved economic independence, and continue to rely on noncash benefits from the government. There is some evidence that the wages of former welfare recipients will grow, assuming that they can continue to gain experience and maintain full-time positions (Corcoran et al. 2000). But the latter is much less of a certainty and varies with the state of the economy and the individual's place of residence.

Most of the employment is in metropolitan rather than rural areas, even though many of the latter areas have some of the highest poverty rates in the United States. In fact, there is evidence that, because of its urban bias, welfare reform may have actually worsened economic conditions among poor rural mothers. "Rural America . . . is too often forgotten in the welfare policy debates. Most predominately rural states provide low TANF benefits in comparison to generous urban states" (Lichter and Jayakody 2002). Recent interviews with over 400 low-income rural mothers confirmed the desperate conditions that many face ("Study Examines," 2002). About 50 percent

work one to three jobs, averaging 32 hours per week and earning just under $800 per month. More hours are simply not available from their employers. As a result, child care is often unaffordable and frequently costs more than the income brought in by the job. The availability of adequate child care centers and transportation continues to be a significant issue.

The vast majority of welfare recipients who work little or do not work at all face a variety of difficulties that prevent them from entering the active labor force. These include educational and experience deficits as well as family issues like domestic violence and physical and mental problems (Butler et al. 2008; Danziger 2010). Low-income foster mothers, for example, are conflicted when faced with the policy demands to work as well as care for children who have been victims of abuse and neglect (Critelli and Schwam-Harris 2010).

A mismatch between the location of the poor and social service agencies created to help them also creates a barrier to moving out of poverty. Areas with high poverty rates have only half as many services readily available than areas with low poverty rates (Allard 2009). So the likelihood of a poor person getting the help needed is reduced.

At the present time, poor parents are caught in the gears of policies that make contradictory demands on them. For example, they are encouraged by welfare policies to work at the same time that their schools and their students are being monitored and expected to raise educational standards and performance. The more time poor parents spend working, the less time they have to help their children perform better in school. Parents need to work to support their families, but support for today is not the same as support for tomorrow. It is the degree of investment in their children's education that may very well affect the chances that the next generation will be out of poverty (Newman and Chin 2003).

These problems tend to fall disproportionately on young single mothers who have little education. Those most likely to be helped by welfare reform and to be early leavers are those who are most likely to find employment—that is, the able-bodied, better educated, skilled, and experienced. This leaves a core of less-educated, less-experienced, disabled individuals who are unlikely to be able to become self-sufficient and who find it difficult to move off welfare. It may be much more difficult to enforce TANF rules with this group (Bavier 2001; Lichter and Jayakody 2002).

The full consequences of the 1996 welfare reform legislation will probably not be known for a while. For reform to have a chance of being effective, all of the components needed to make recipients self-sufficient have to be in place. This requires solving the problems of child care, transportation, and training/education. It also demands addressing the broader issues of employment supply and sex discrimination in the workplace. At the present time, it appears that the reforms implemented in most states have not improved the lives of welfare recipients (Danziger 2010).

The persistence of poverty has suggested to some that the poor may serve basic functions for the society, and particular nonpoor groups within it. Indeed, having an "undeserving" poor population serves many functions for the rest of us, including helping us feel superior, creating social work jobs, providing an accessible low-wage labor pool, and reinforcing dominant values (Gans 1995). By indicating these and other basic functions performed by the poor in U.S. society, Gans implied that poor people are not an isolated group who are poor because of their lack of integration into the mainstream of society, but rather are an integral part of the society. Alternative poverty programs that have been suggested vary in the extent to which their recommendations focus on the poor as a unique and separate group or as an integral and integrated part of the larger society. Those that stress the former tend to believe that the root causes of poverty lie in the flawed characters and characteristics of the poor themselves, whereas those in the latter camp are more likely to argue that societal structures and processes create a poor population.

Because of widespread stereotypes of those on welfare, including those that suggest welfare recipients are personally responsible for their condition, some have argued that broader-based policies and programs must be implemented to address problems the poor face. For more than a decade, William Julius Wilson has stressed that for any program to be fully accepted by the public it must be seen as benefiting everyone, not just particular groups. "I am convinced," wrote Wilson in 1987, "that, in the last few years of the twentieth century, the problems of the truly disadvantaged in the United States will have to be attacked primarily through universal programs that enjoy the support and commitment of a broad constituency" (p. 120). Most fundamentally, Wilson believes that racial, ethnic, and other groups need to de-emphasize how they are *different* from one another, and emphasize and act on the values, goals, and destinies that they have in *common*. Organized coalitions of different groups that focus on problems that they all share are more likely to be effective. Since we are all part of one society, economic events and inequality have implications for all of our lives (Wilson 1999).

U.S. POVERTY AND WELFARE IN COMPARATIVE PERSPECTIVE

When we look across the world, we find that some populations not only have much higher rates of poverty, but also have degrees of poverty that are significantly more abject than those found in the United States. The greatest numbers living in extreme poverty are in South Asia, Africa, and East Asia, respectively. India alone is estimated to have 350 million people living in extreme poverty (Waldman 2005). In Haiti, Madagascar, Gambia, Nigeria, Rwanda, Zambia, Sierra Leone, Mali, Tanzania, and the Central African Republic, well over half the population live on $1 per day. When compared to other rich Western industrial nations, however, the United States does not fare as well. In 2000, the United States had the highest relative poverty rate. It also had the greatest percentage of children in poverty and the third highest rate of poverty among the elderly (Mishel, Bernstein, and Allegretto 2007). Taking into account taxes, government cash transfers, and family size, 17 percent of U.S. households had incomes in 2000 that were no more than 50 percent of the median income in the country. Finland, Norway, and Sweden had poverty rates that were two and a half times lower than the U.S. rate. When combining poverty levels, literacy rates, health conditions, and unemployment into an index of living standards, an analysis by the United Nations ranked the United States 17th out of 19 industrial nations (United Nations 2007). Clearly, the United States does not rate well in these comparisons of poverty levels.

Why might the United States have higher levels of poverty and inequality than most other rich democracies? Several factors are at play, including cultural values that discourage extensive government involvement in the lives of individuals,

While almost one out of five children in the United States is poor, some other countries have even higher rates of child poverty. In India, several hundred thousand beggar children roam the streets in hopes of receiving alms from sympathetic passersby. Some children are acting on their own, while others are controlled by adult criminals seeking to profit from the begging. (© TheFinalMiracle/Fotolia LLC)

a market economy that emphasizes free exchange and competition and drives the society toward greater income inequality, and welfare policies that do not have a large impact on reducing poverty.

Societies with free, largely unregulated market economies tend to have higher degrees of economic inequality than other nations where governments are more actively involved in economic matters (Birchfield 2008). In the former, given an assumption of equal opportunity for all, the operation of an open market determines the outcome and distribution of goods and resources among the people. Let the chips fall where they may, so to speak.

In the abstract, Americans tend to subscribe to conservative values of small government, a free economy, and individual responsibility. But at the same time, evidence indicates they realize that problems may arise during the actual operation of society that demand government intervention on behalf of those who are victimized or trapped. While Americans are cool toward helping those whom they believe can help themselves (i.e., are undeserving), they tend to be generous towards those they believe are poor for reasons beyond their control (i.e., are deserving). Their feelings toward groups that are usually the focus of government assistance such as the poor and elderly, are much warmer than those felt about the rich and big business, for example (Bartels 2008). Page and Jacobs's 2007 national survey revealed that most people support government assistance to the poor for their basic necessities (2009). The researchers refer to this seemingly contradictory mixture of beliefs as "conservative egalitarianism" (2009). One consequence of this ambivalent stance is that while the United States has some welfare programs, they tend not to be overly generous, and thus, do not drive down the poverty rate very much.

There appears to be little question that a generous welfare policy reduces poverty (Brady 2009). But compared to other industrial nations, the United States does not fare well. American welfare programs are less effective than those in Britain, for example, in reducing persistent poverty, speeding movement out of poverty, and alleviating the poverty problems associated with race (Worts, Sacker, and McDonough 2010). Our welfare benefits are the most meager of all Western democracies; the chances that a middle-aged adult will become poor are more than 16 times greater in the United States than in Denmark, which has the most generous welfare program (Smeeding 2005; Brady, Fullerton, and Cross 2009).

Some societies choose to devote more resources than others toward reducing poverty. As Timothy Smeeding put it: "We have more inequality and poverty than other nations because we choose to have more" (2005, p. 980). More inequality means that the richest groups in our society have moved further away from the middle class and poor. Their material interests are different and they see little need for a generous welfare program (Smeeding 2005).

Summary

This chapter has discussed many of the assumptions and perceptions of the poor that provide an important part of the underpinnings for current welfare policy. Often, these perceptions are not consistent with government data on the actual poor population.

American attitudes about the poor are frequently ambivalent. Traditional values of individualism, independence, hard work, and material success encourage a negative attitude toward those who are not economically successful. At the same time, humanitarian and community values encourage people to take care of those who are less fortunate than themselves. Believing that virtually all people can make it if they try hard enough, but at the same time knowing from historical events such as the Depression, plant closings, and market declines that not everything about their economic fates is in their hands to control, has resulted in a somewhat bifurcated approach to poverty programs for the needy. There are elements of both a residual and institutional approach in this system.

Problems of inequity, inadequacy, and goal conflict have permeated public assistance programs for the poor. In addition, questions about how they affect work incentive, family composition, and effectiveness have also generated heated debate. Alternative proposals attempt to grapple with the problems of adequacy, employment, work incentives, and so on. Many have suggested economic growth and full employment as the keys to the puzzle of poverty, as they would lead to greater self-sufficiency for everyone. Indeed, the Welfare Reform Act of 1996 focused on pushing individuals into the labor force.

Current programs fall into the broad categories of social insurance and public assistance. Social insurance programs such as Social Security retirement, disability, and Medicare insurance provide universal coverage with a minimum of stigma to a wide variety of individuals who fall into a particular demographic category. There is no means testing or demeaning administrative process suggesting that these recipients are receiving welfare. In the other category of public assistance are those who are poor but not elderly and/or disabled. Individuals with these characteristics—often women who head their own households, children, and members of minorities—must provide proof that they are indigent. They must prove that they are deserving of nutrition assistance, Medicaid, and benefits from other programs.

Follow-up investigations on the effectiveness of the 1996 reforms are decidedly mixed in their results. In many cases, policies have deepened poverty, at least in the short run. More time is needed, however, to fully assess the full impact of the states' reforms. It is clear that, when compared to other industrial countries, the United States has higher poverty rates and its programs are less effective in reducing poverty.

As difficult as poverty may be to understand, we still have not confronted the even thornier issue of economic inequality. A focus on inequality unavoidably involves all of us, since we all live out our lives within its structure. If inequality continues to grow as it has in recent years, we may be forced to address this topic. The real question is whether poverty, let alone inequality, can be eliminated within a democratic capitalist society. This brings us back to some of the core questions with which we began this book.

If poverty is generated not merely by differences among individuals, but by conditions that are part of a capitalist economy, such as unemployment and the pressure for profit and lower wages, then a permanent solution, as Morris and Williamson suggested, is very unlikely unless fundamental changes in the political economy occur. Are inequality and poverty inevitable? Given the present social structure, the answer is probably yes. Are inequality and poverty desirable? It depends. Although it is a serious problem for those who must suffer with it, poverty appears to be functional for others. It helps maintain the attractiveness of low wages and menial jobs, especially when coupled with low benefits from programs. At the same time, it provides employment for many middle-class professionals. As to the immediate future of inequality and poverty, the fact that income and wealth inequality has increased in recent years, despite the presence of income-maintenance programs, suggests that (1) we do not really consider inequality to be a major problem,

(2) we do not really know what causes it to fluctuate, and/or (3) some find inequality beneficial.

Evidence strongly suggests that what happens in the economy has a major impact on both inequality and poverty. Instability in our globalized economy has generated greater unemployment and income insecurity. At the dawn of the twenty-first century, many organizations are streamlining and downsizing in an effort to maintain profits in the face of intensified domestic and foreign competition. While executives and shareholders frequently reap the economic benefits of these leaner and more efficient organizational structures, the attendant layoffs have led many in the middle class to fall near or into poverty. These shifts have also exacerbated the poor financial conditions of those already at the bottom and are also likely to cause further tensions among racial/ethnic groups and between the sexes. In sum, the rewards and punishments of recent economic changes are clearly and unequally divided. The combination of the economic trends and their varied effects on different groups, together with our reluctance to address the problem of inequality and to recognize its social roots, are not good omens.

Critical Thinking

1. In your opinion, what would be the determining factor in setting a poverty threshold? Why?
2. What can be done to separate the ideas of race and welfare in the minds of many people? How can we stop the racialization of welfare?
3. To what extent, and under what conditions, if any, is the federal government responsible for reducing or eliminating poverty? Defend your answer.
4. Given what has been suggested in this chapter, what do you think should be the cornerstone features of any effective antipoverty plan?

Web Connections

The Finance Project is a nonprofit research and assistance firm that has an information resource center which provides information on welfare, income supplements, job training, and asset development. Visit their website at www.financeproject.org.

Film Suggestion

28 Women (2005). Depicts the experiences of single mothers trying to create stable lives.

CHAPTER 4

Status Inequality

It is impossible, in our condition of Society, not to be sometimes a Snob.

WILLIAM MAKEPEACE THACKERAY (1811–1863)

Differences in *economic* resources are not the only kind of inequality. Frequently, inequality can take a *social* form that is not necessarily rooted in one's wealth or power. Social status is about having a particular lifestyle and set of social characteristics. It is about being viewed as a certain kind of person, as a member of a specific subgroup that has attached to it a definite degree of high or low prestige. The previous two chapters discussed the various types of *economic* inequality present in U.S. society. But the ranking system is more complicated than that, and experiences in everyday life tell us that invidious distinctions are made between individuals on grounds other than economics. It is not just the *amount* of wealth, but the *kind* and *source* of wealth as well as how it is *used* that are ranked. It is not just the amount of education, but the kind and place of education. It is not just the earnings of the occupation, but the kind of occupation it is. It is not just whether one is poor, but whether one is on welfare. If economic inequality is primarily about *quantities,* status inequality is about *qualities.*

People often are evaluated and ranked on the basis of their education, religion, possession of "culture," type of occupation, and even their speech patterns and clothing styles. Think about how students are evaluated by their peers. In addition to gender and race/ethnicity, fraternity/ sorority membership, academic major, athletic status, the regions of the country they are from, and even the dormitories in which they live serve as criteria for status rankings. In each case, these function as systematic bases for high or low prestige.

Evidence presented in previous chapters supports the existence of *economic* classes, but there is no doubt that inequality includes *social* dimensions as well. More often than not, we notice these social distinctions in our contacts with others; that is, they become most salient when we interact with individuals whose characteristics and lifestyles differ from our own. Research suggests that we often rank people differently depending on those characteristics and lifestyles. Indeed, the term **social stratification** suggests that alongside economic inequality we have a system of status inequality, and often these two forms are intertwined with each other, as we shall see. Quite often, for example, an individual's economic position will affect his or her social position. But an individual's or group's social status need not be tied to either economic or political power. This requires that we examine social status as a separate form of ranking system. In this chapter, we will examine the nature of this status dimension of inequality.

THE THEORY OF SOCIAL STATUS

Social **status** refers to an individual's ranking with respect to some socially important characteristic; thus, some people are thought to be low in social status, while others are high on this scale. Max Weber, the great German sociologist, stressed the importance of distinguishing between (economic) class and (social) status inequality, even while he pointed out that they could be empirically related to each other, as when social status is dependent on *class* position. Weber viewed a person's *status situation* as "every typical component of the life fate of men that is determined by a specific, positive or negative *social estimation of honor*. This honor may be connected with any quality shared by a plurality" (Gerth and Mills 1962, p. 187). This means that status is ultimately a subjective assessment rendered by a community or another group. "Status is the sum of the evaluations that are 'located' in the minds of other people with whom one interacts" (Milner 2004, p. 29). This means that individuals are or are not given homage and respect because they possess or lack some characteristic the community considers honorable or dishonorable. That quality is social rather than economic in nature; for example, one's family name, the street where one lives, the kind and degree of education one possesses, or one's race or gender all may elicit such honor or dishonor. Weber argued that this "claim to positive or negative privilege with respect to social prestige" may be based on (1) a "mode of living," (2) "a formal process of education which may consist in empirical or rational training and the acquisition of the corresponding modes of life," and/or (3) "the prestige of birth, or of an occupation" (Weber 1964, p. 428).

Status groups that are ranked in a certain place on a community's social hierarchy are characterized by (1) a set of conventions and traditions, or lifestyle; (2) a tendency to marry within their own ranks; (3) an emphasis on interacting intimately— for example, eating only with others in the same group; (4) frequent monopolization of economic opportunities; and (5) emphasis on ownership of certain types of possessions rather than others (Weber 1964). All of these features reflect the tendency in status groups to establish and maintain the integrity of the boundaries that separate them from other groups. Wearing team jackets or particular types of clothes, associating with only particular kinds of people, and participating in an initiation process when becoming a member of a group are all signals that social status is operating.

Murray Milner Jr. (2004) explains that an individual's status within a group is dependent on conformity to the group's norms. These norms may involve expectations with respect to behavior (e.g., involvement in rituals), social relationships (e.g., friends and enemies), certain physical characteristics (beauty, race, gender), and use of appropriate symbols (e.g., dress, language). Since high status is coveted and in short supply, those at the top may change the norms or make them more complicated to maintain their position, making it more difficult for those below them to move up and displace them. One's own status is always at the expense of someone else's social position.

To be an accepted member of a status group, a person is expected to follow the normative lifestyle of the group and to have "restrictions on 'social' intercourse" (Weber 1964, p. 187). This means that the person is expected to associate intimately with only similar kinds of people. Consider what might happen when people in a distinct status group step out of line by violating the expected customs of the group. They might be confronted, ostracized, shunned, or punished in some other more physical way, and told in no uncertain terms what they need to do to get back in the good graces of their community or group. Because status groups are separated by social and cultural boundaries, the above efforts are made to maintain them. Continuous "boundary work" is needed to reinforce status distinctions between groups.

A group tries to set itself apart from other status groups, especially those that might contaminate the purity of the group. An extreme instance of this process exists when individuals of a particular status group agree to marry only among themselves (i.e., to practice endogamy) and to chastise or shun anyone who marries outside the group. Lewis Lapham recalled his own experiences in this regard (1988, p. 160): "At college I knew several boys whose mothers discouraged their sons' acquaintance with anybody who lived in towns not adequately represented in the Social Register. If a boy didn't come from Grosse Pointe or Burlingame or Fairfield County, then his place of origin was listed under the heading *terra incognita*." After all, status honor rests on "distance and exclusiveness." In her study of upper-class women's involvement in voluntary associations, for example, Diana Kendall (2002) notes how carefully new applicants are screened and the elaborate application process that is involved before a new person is accepted as a member. To maintain the integrity and value of membership, applicants need to negotiate a complex application process. The extent and intensity of the application process is a direct indicator of the strength of the social boundary of a status group. The maintenance of a status group's cultural and social integrity requires continual vigilance of its boundaries with the outside. Not just anyone can be accepted.

It should not be surprising that to be accepted as a member of a particular status group requires possessing certain credentials. Credentialism is a major tool in the practice of exclusion (Parkin 1979). Having the proper credentials might mean, for example, having a given license or educational degree, to be accepted into the "club." Because they help to control the labor supply, for example, requiring particular education credentials and/or licensing even enhances the earnings associated with an occupation (Weeden 2002).

"Exclusion" is a primary mechanism by which those in powerful status groups keep others from gaining power (Parkin 1979). Voluntary residential segregation in a secure gated community on the part of a high-status group might also be seen as an attempt at separation from people of lower status. Or men may attempt to keep their corporate positions exclusive by preventing women from moving to the top of the ladder.

The various conventions, rules, traditions, and rituals of a particular status group help to sustain it over time. Thus, it is not surprising that there are attempts to enforce them within the group. Status groups are the "bearers of all 'conventions' . . . all 'stylization' of life either originates in status groups or is at least conserved by them" (Gerth and Mills 1962, p. 191).

So far, we have seen that status groups (1) are associated with different estimations of social honor, (2) are based on a variety of socially relevant characteristics such as occupation or ethnicity, and (3) tend toward closure—that is, maintenance of boundaries with outside groups, and (4) enforce adherence to their lifestyle and social interaction expectations. In addition, status groups tend to monopolize particular types of economic opportunities and acquisitions, while they discourage the possession of other kinds. For example, a status group whose honor or prestige is based on its class position may encourage its members to acquire fancy homes in particular neighborhoods, but it may be considered bad form to spend money acquiring a new bowling ball or a gaudy automobile. Under certain conditions, social status can become the primary form of social inequality. For example, social status becomes more significant when access to other forms of power is weak (Milner 2004). When people have little else to use as leverage in social situations, they use their own status conventions and goods as a means of controlling others or enhancing their social positions. Burri (2008), for example, has shown how radiologists have used monopolization of imaging technologies to reassert their distinctiveness and strengthen their social status as a profession. Milner (2004) has demonstrated how teenagers use their consumption and buying power as mechanisms for the maintenance of status distinctions among their peers. It follows from these examples that status groups are "phenomena of the distribution of power within a community" (p. 181).

Formal gates usually mark the entrances and exits of areas populated by status groups noted for their distinctive lifestyles and cultures. Geographic spatial separation between groups, whether on a playground, in a school lunch hall, in a corporate headquarters, or in a city, creates boundaries distinguishing groups in an area. (© Andy Z./Shutterstock)

Weber argued that when social and economic conditions in a community are stable, stratification by status becomes dominant. Further, after status has been "lived in" for a while, status privileges can become legal privileges. In the United States, these conditions are frequently found in small towns where the same kin groups have lived for generations, where relationships are based on family name, and where social connections are important. Ironically, status also becomes salient when change threatens or tradition is in danger of being upset, as when politically or economically powerful newcomers come to town (Milner 2004). The "old guard" may try to maintain their high position by stressing their social status in the community, for example, the fact that they have lived there all their lives and are leaders in the culture of the community.

When legalization of status privileges occurs, a society may be on the road toward a full-fledged caste system. According to Weber, the extreme of a caste system developing out of a status system happens only when the "underlying differences . . . are held to be 'ethnic'" in nature

(Gerth and Mills 1962, p. 189). Race is a basis for deference/honor because "it is thought to represent the possession of some quality inherent in the ethnic aggregate and shared by all its members." This "essential quality" is "manifested in . . . external features such as colour, hair form, physiognomy and physique" (Shils 1970, p. 428). The existence of varying degrees of social distance among various **ethnic groups** in the United States provides ample evidence of such a ranking system. In this instance, distinctive ethnic status groups are converted into a set of hierarchically arranged groups, those on the top thought to be the most pure and those on the bottom considered to be impure, contaminating, or even untouchable. What may trigger this conversion are the differences in the degree of ownership by these groups of other highly valued characteristics (e.g., education, religion) or commodities (e.g., wealth, technology; Berger and Fisek 2006). The "pariah" groups may be tolerated only because they may perform necessary but dishonorable, dirty, and onerous work. For example, lower castes may be the only groups ritualistically permitted to collect garbage or dead carcasses from the street. While these extreme forms of separation are not as evident in the United States, tendencies for groups to avoid groups of different statuses do exist.

Groups that are dishonored or low in status may attempt to usurp prestige by creating their own ranking system. This enhances their own social status often to the denigration of other groups. One example is provided by Lamont (2000) who found that working-class men use their own criteria to distinguish themselves as an honorable and distinct status group from those above and below them. Rather than wealth or political power, which would relegate them to a lower status, these men use moral criteria (being hardworking and responsible, having integrity, etc.) to separate themselves from others. These are the kinds of criteria that define the social and cultural boundaries which distinguish their own group from others, and they are the criteria that provide them with a higher social status in their own eyes.

When ranking does occur among status groups, *deference* is expected to be shown toward those in more prestigious or honored groups. The ways by which individuals greet and compliment others, as well as similar behaviors of homage, are examples of deferential behavior (Goffman 1959, 1967). For example, students are often concerned with how they should address me: Should it be "Professor," "Doctor," "Mister," or simply "Chuck"? Some clearly feel uneasy using the latter form of address because they think it suggests a lack of respect or deference.

While those in lower statuses may show deference for those at the top, the latter can use their resources to present themselves in ways that elicit and justify such respect. They typically have the resources and motivation to appear impressive, and so manage situations to obtain the responses they desire. Through their *demeanor,* individuals of higher status can suggest that they are worthy of such deference. Demeanor is "that element of the individual's ceremonial behavior typically conveyed through deportment, dress, and bearing, which serves to express to those in his immediate presence that he is a person of certain desirable or undesirable qualities" (Goffman 1967, p. 77).

Deference behavior between individuals in differently ranked status groups can be based on a variety of criteria. A member of a group may be considered entitled to such behavior from others because of occupation, race or ethnicity, level and type of education, gender, lifestyle, political or corporate power, family name or kinship network, income, and amount and type of wealth. Service work on behalf of a community or society and formal titles also can serve as grounds for status honor in some locations. All these factors are deference relevant because they are linked with basic values and/or issues in the society. A region or area can also be the basis of deference because it is thought to be associated with a particular lifestyle or occupational role (e.g., Appalachia with coal mining, Manhattan with the stock market, etc.), with the exercise of power in a society (e.g., Washington D.C.), or with some other valued criterion (e.g., New England with quality education).

SPHERES OF STATUS IN THE UNITED STATES

As suggested earlier, the esteem in which a person is held in the United States can be related to a number of areas of life, for example occupation, education, lifestyle, and wealth. Less noticed, but also arenas of status, are physical appearance and geographic place. Finally, race and gender are also factors that elicit status rankings.

Occupation

Occupational role, of course, is frequently associated with both social class and social status, but the most commonly used measures of occupational ranking tap the prestige/esteem dimension rather than the economic one. Occupation is a basis for deference and honor not only because of its association with valued goals (income, power, etc.) but also because there are lifestyles associated with particular roles—lifestyles that receive different degrees of honor. Plumbers and professors clearly are accorded different levels of honor because of what people associate with each of these occupations. Individuals in higher-ranking occupations, for example, have been found to have broader tastes in music—that is, to enjoy and appreciate a wider range of music types (Peterson and Simkus 1992). Occupational status groups also are distinguished by the level and kinds of education and training that members undergo, as well as the types of behavior that characterize their occupations.

A good example of an occupational status group is professional musicians. Bensman (1972) argued that musicians form a "status community" in that they adhere to a particular and somewhat unique set of values that shapes their lifestyles. The institutions, behaviors, and practices that organize and constitute their lives, in turn, are based on those core values. Insiders are clearly separated from outsiders. There are regularized interactions and rituals that help keep the community cohesive. When musicians get together informally, they perform, discuss music, or attend concerts, all of which increase their allegiance to the community's values. In addition to having its own subcultural values, the music community is internally stratified according to a number of musically relevant criteria such as the instrument one plays and the skill with which it is played.

Generally, status communities based on occupation are among the most relevant for one's status. Over the years, there have been several attempts to rank occupations according to prestige or status. Early efforts to measure occupational status suffered from the fact that they generally were based on inadequate samples of respondents, were of a subjective nature, and contained prestige differences within the general occupational categories that were often almost as great as those between such categories.

Several attempts were later made to perfect an occupational status ranking, the most influential being the North-Hatt scale developed in the mid-1940s. It differed from earlier scales in that a much wider range of occupation types was considered, and it relied less on the creator's judgment of rankings. The prestige rankings obtained were based on a 1947 survey of 2,920 individuals who were asked to classify the *general standing* of each of 90 occupations. No mention was made

of prestige. The most frequently cited reasons for awarding a given occupation an excellent standing, in order of decreasing frequency, were that it paid well (18%), served humanity (16%), required a lot of previous training and investment (14%), and had a high level of prestige associated with it (14%). A replication of the study in 1963 yielded very similar rankings for the 88 distinct occupation types (Hodge, Siegel, and Rossi 1964).

However, the criterion considered most important in ranking the status of occupations appears to have changed along with the political and social climate. A 2005 Harris poll queried 1,217 U.S. adults about the degree of prestige they accorded 22 occupations. The list included a variety of blue-collar, white-collar, and service occupations in different institutional areas (Harris Poll, September 8, 2005). It was clear that association with high earnings was not enough to give an occupation a high ranking. Real estate brokers and stockbrokers were at the bottom of the list. The four occupations given a "very high prestige" ranking by at least half of the respondents were those that served humanity (fireman, scientist, doctor, nurse).

Education

Like occupation, education is also considered an important and valuable dimension of one's life in the United States. Level of education is supposed to be related to the level of knowledge and skill one has in a particular field. In addition to that, however, education also prepares one for a particular status group and ensures the continuation of status groups. The type of education as well as the place where it is received are bases for prestige. A degree from an Ivy League school such as Yale or Harvard, or a small private school such as Amherst or Smith is quite prestigious compared to a degree from a local community college. The elitism and degree of selectivity associated with a school is linked to the level of prestige accorded to it. Think about the differences in the students you might know who graduate from each type of school. Schools like to pride themselves on the kinds of students they produce. Different types of schools instill different sets of values and outlooks in their students, thereby encouraging the development of different cultural groups.

The cultural/status effects of education have been analyzed in depth. Bourdieu (1977a) suggested that higher education helps to reproduce the class structure by functioning to reinforce the value and status differences between the classes. It does this by honoring the **cultural capital** held by those in the higher classes. This capital—which consists of a group's cultural values, experience, knowledge, and skills—is passed on from one generation to the next. In organizing itself around the linguistic and cultural competence of the upper classes, higher education ensures that members of the upper classes are successful in school. This legitimates the class inequality that results because, on the surface, it appears that the inequality is largely the result of individual performance in a meritocratic, open educational system. That is, the language used, the cultural knowledge expected for success in school, and the values and behaviors honored are those of the upper class. In the words of one interpreter, "The school serves as the trading post where socially valued cultural capital is parleyed into superior academic performance. Academic performance is then turned back into economic capital by the acquisition of superior jobs" (MacLeod 1987, p. 12). The experiences in school and in the workplace of those in the working and lower classes, coupled with the general outlook and specific attitudes they have acquired because of their class milieu, lead them to believe that they cannot succeed in school, thus lowering their aspirations to do so (MacLeod 1987). The result is stratification within the educational system, which then reinforces the class stratification in the wider society.

From early childhood, middle- and upper-class parents engage in what Annette Lareau (2003) has termed "concerted cultivation," the conscious preparation of their children in the skills and values they will need to be successful and to maintain their higher position in the social hierarchy. Or as Kendall describes it in her study of how upper-class women go about perpetuating their social-class positions, "Most elite parents strongly believe that, early on in their children's lives, the parents should start putting together all the right 'building blocks' that their children will need in order to take their own places in elite circles in which the parents live, and that the parents need to continue this process of social reproduction as the children grow into adulthood" (2002, p. 81). As several of the studies indicate, schools play a central role in the social reproduction of the class structure from top to bottom.

One of the principal functions of education is to prepare students for the cultural status groups they will enter after graduation (Collins 1971). In his biting satire at the beginning of the twentieth century, Thorstein Veblen (1953) observed that elite schools of higher learning had as their primary purpose "the preparation of the youth of the priestly and the leisure classes . . . for the consumption of goods, material and immaterial, according to a conventionally accepted, reputable scope and method" (p. 239). Similarly, authors of a more recent empirical study of elite prep schools observed that "curriculum is the nursery of culture and the classical curriculum is the cradle of high culture" (Cookson and Persell 1985, p. 74). But they also observed, in sharp contrast to Veblen's emphasis on the nonfunctional learning of the "leisure" class, that the education is deadly serious.

Analysis of the history of U.S. boarding schools supports the conclusion that they were developed to help the established upper class isolate and reaffirm its cultural characteristics. Initially, the founders hoped that these schools would help separate their cultural group from the new wealth developing in industry and from the increasing numbers of lower-class immigrants. This suggests again the strong impetus toward social closure among the old rich. But the need for financial support of these schools necessitated taking in some of the sons of individuals who had become recently wealthy from industrial, manufacturing, or other enterprises in the latter part of the nineteenth century (Levine 1980). These *nouveaux riches,* consequently, infiltrated the boarding

Even the classical architecture and spacious, finely manicured grounds of prestigious prep schools conspire to create a feeling of tradition and specialness among their students. (Photo by Charles E. Hurst.)

schools even though the established patrician families winced because the former were often seen as lacking in manners and polish. One of these new-wealth parents, Phillip Armour, once described his occupation as converting "bristles, blood, and the inside and outside of pigs and bullocks into revenue" (Levine 1980, p. 83). This kind of comment is hardly the type that would have won over persons from the established old-wealth families.

While stressing the rigor and difficulty of attainment within them, studies of elite prep schools confirm the importance of cultural capital and the role of these schools in perpetuating the class system. A large part of the education for students in these status seminaries involves learning how to hide or mask their wealth, to acquire "taste," and to prepare themselves to be "soldiers for their class"—that is, to occupy and carry out the responsibilities of their class (Cookson and Persell 1985). As Shils (1970) observed, some schools are thought of as more important than others, and "those educated in them acquire more of a charismatically infused culture" (p. 426). The rules of eating, sleeping, and playing together,

along with peer expectations and formal discipline, help forge cohesiveness at the same time that the classical curriculum, the emphasis on dialogue and discussion, and extracurricular activities such as sports encourage the development of specific values. The hothouse, intense, closed setting of the prep school helps to foster a "brick wall syndrome," a belief that exclusivity should be the norm and that there is nothing wrong with the separation of this group of students from those in the outside society (Kendall 2002).

The formal and informal curricula of these schools are designed to make sure that these results occur. Even the architecture of the school and demeanor of the headmaster or headmistress conspire to create an atmosphere in which such learning and value development can take place. "The cultural capital that prep school students accumulate in boarding schools is a treasure trove of skills and status symbols that can be used in later life" (Cookson and Persell 1985, p. 30).

For their students, elite prep schools also serve as a major linchpin between parental class position and obtaining positions of power in the wider society. These students tend to get into the better colleges and universities and, ultimately, to obtain positions of influence in the leading political, cultural, legal, and corporate institutions of society. Giving admission preferences at elite universities and colleges to the sons and daughters of alumni illustrates not only the passing on of social status between generations, but also high-status schools' tendencies toward exclusivity and boundary maintenance. **Legacy** preferences help schools maintain the integrity of their lifestyle, but they also violate values associated with equality of opportunity (Kahlenberg 2010).

Studies of prep school graduates reinforce the conclusion that these students need to go on to the "right" universities, such as Harvard, Yale, or Princeton; beyond that, they have to get into the appropriate clubs and societies at these universities, and to do this a student has to come from the "right" boarding school. Getting into the right sorority or fraternity, especially one in which your parent was a member, is an important step in the process of class cultivation. Among the values and skills learned in these organizations are the importance of screening potential members, allegiance to your own kind of people, and the development of social networks that will be helpful in later years (Kendall 2002; Robbins 2004). Upon graduating from their universities, these students can take up their memberships in the most exclusive social clubs and become established in high-status Wall Street law or brokerage firms. This process, from the teen years through attainment of an occupation, helps ensure the exclusivity and survival of this high-status group.

School and Lifestyle

Status inequalities between groups can be found in a variety of school levels. Unambiguous categorization of individuals according to appearance, behaviors, values, and attitudes develops early in childhood. Social cliques and categories have been found even among elementary school children, as well as in junior and senior high schools. Attachment of a student to a social category or clique has real consequences in the school setting. Self-esteem and identity appear to be linked to the status of one's "crowd" in school (Brown and Lohr 1987; Adler and Adler 1998). If one is considered a member of a low-prestige crowd, it not only can affect one's self-esteem but also cause alterations in behavior. Sometimes this can have devastating effects, as was found recently in a survey of high school students in San Francisco. Only 37 percent of students who were eligible for the subsidized lunch program actually took advantage of it. They would rather pay for lunch themselves, even though they cannot afford it, or go without eating at all. As one student observed, lunch "is the best time to impress your peers" and being on the lunch program "lowers your status" (Pogash, March 1, 2008, p. A1). Such can be the power of status groups.

Initial analyses of school killings in the 1990s by students also suggest the significance of popularity, social isolation, and social labeling for self-esteem, identity, and conflict between groups of students. The students responsible for the deaths at Columbine High School in Colorado were linked to a category of students called the Trenchcoat Mafia. But social clusters at different schools go by many names: jocks, burnouts, preppies, trendies, leading crowd, nerds, brainiacs, goths, wannabees, earth queens, stickup boys, geeks, freaks, grits, punks. People with similar interests, backgrounds, or accomplishments join together to separate themselves from others and to solidify their identities and sense of membership at school. Belonging to a clique or category is a way of avoiding social isolation. It is also a means of ranking different kinds of individuals. From his own study of high schools, Milner (2004) suggests that the status ranking of cliques or groups in schools depends on their adherence to expectations regarding areas such as "beauty, athletic ability, clothes and style, athletic uniforms and letter jackets, speech, body language, collective memories, humor, ritual, popular music, dancing and singing, and space and territory" (p. 44). None of these is necessarily linked to income or class position, again confirming the frequent noneconomic nature of social status.

Although membership can be unstable and rankings within each of them can shift, these social clusters have many of the properties of status groups (Cairns and Cairns 1994; Eder 1995; Adler and Adler 1998). As such, they represent a type of status inequality. Among these qualities is *group ranking* in terms of popularity and prestige at school. A second feature following from this involves explicit attempts to attract certain youths while keeping others out, that is, *attempts at maintaining boundaries* between insiders and outsiders. Being mean, bullying, picking on outsiders, and "putting them down" are techniques to keep outsiders at arm's length. Careful recruitment and monitoring of behavior and attitudes are common ways of ensuring insider loyalty once in a group. "Cliques' boundary maintenance makes them exclusive. . . . The dynamics of inclusion lures members into cliques, while the dynamic of exclusion keeps them there" (Adler and Adler 1998, p. 72). People outside the cliques are thought of as different. "You don't even date outside of your clique. It's like a kind of racism," observed one female high school senior (Brett, June 8, 1999, p. A6).

A third status feature of these groups is a *lifestyle* that is perceived to be distinctive. A large part of the unique lifestyles among student groupings is suggested by the clothing and adornments they wear. Students labeled as "goths" tend to wear black clothes, whereas more mainstream "jocks" wear Polo or J. Crew. Tattoos, jewelry, and hairstyle also symbolize given social categories at school. As part of the distinctive lifestyles, involvement in school activities, musical tastes, and language also systematically vary. Fourth, *exclusive places or locations* tend to be associated with different social clusters. Physical space takes on a *social* significance. Just like gangs controlling neighborhoods, given lunch tables are "owned" by clusters, as are places where students hang out. Finally, *stigmatization and avoidance of social contamination* is also found within these school groups. Because of recurrent jockeying for status within groups, individuals pick on each other and single out some for intense ostracism. Avoidance of outsiders antagonistic to the group

is also expected. Paradoxically, meanness to others is a way of maintaining popularity in the group (Merten 1997).

Wealth and Class

Having a particular amount and type of *wealth* and/or *income* as reflected in one's class position can also be a basis for status if only because economic resources usually serve as a control on the kind of lifestyle one can afford. The right kind and level of consumption may gain one entrance into the upper class. The use of inherited wealth, family lineage, club membership, quality of education, and general lifestyle as criteria for membership into the established upper class helps maintain the exclusivity of that class. We have already seen how early boarding schools functioned in this regard. Practicing endogamy within the class helps determine who can get into "Society." Maintaining a closed circle in the face of an ostensibly open democratic society demands that mechanisms be present to keep just anyone from getting into the circle.

E. Digby Baltzell (1958), a member of the upper class himself, insisted that the United States contains a national urban upper class with its own tradition that is tightly knit and class conscious. This upper class has been buttressed historically by institutions that serve its members, such as boarding schools, select eastern universities and colleges, and the Episcopal Church (see also Domhoff 1971; Ostrander 1984). The upper class as a status group practices a particular kind of lifestyle with particular kinds of rules associated with it. Specifically, children are expected to be well-bred, with manners and a sense of their importance in society. Boarding schools are a principal source of this training, but family ties are also central. Keeping the family line intact and marrying the right kind of person are important. Marriages are not made as facilely as might be the case in other social classes. But some restricted social activities, such as debutante balls and fox hunts, which once were prominent elements in the lifestyle of the upper class, have declined in recent years. Acceptable occupations include financier, lawyer, business executive, physician, art collector, museum director, and even architect. Membership in exclusive metropolitan social clubs, often composed only of males, is also important if an individual is to be part of the upper-class status community. Living in an exclusive residence separate from middle class and other neighborhoods and maintaining a second summer home are also means by which separation from outsiders is preserved.

Upper-class families tend to be patriarchal, but even the female spouse may be a member of a private social club. Frequently, she is expected to be involved in charitable activities and other social events. There is a division of labor between the sexes in these families. Evidence suggests that members of this upper-status group are concerned with maintaining their separation from others, even in death. Their burial customs and sites tend to be different from those of lesser mortals (Kephart 1950). A historical analysis of cemeteries in the United States noted the long-term attempts by the middle and upper classes to segregate themselves physically in burial sites from those of a more lowly status, and to freely use monuments and mausoleums to proclaim their status. In recent years, mausoleums and monuments have again increased in popularity. Advertisements for these tout these structures as symbols of prestige that will remind viewers of how much success was attained during one's lifetime (Sloane 1991). As these characteristics indicate, "members of the upper class not only have *more,* they have *different*" (Domhoff 1971, p. 91).

Weber thought that status groups are ranked according to their patterns of consumption as manifested in their lifestyles (cited in Gerth and Mills 1962, p. 193). Many possessions have a level of prestige that differs drastically with their actual monetary value. For example, consider the relative prestige of a new Chevy pickup and an older BMW, both of which may cost the same amount. It is not so much the economic value per se of the consumed goods that is important, but rather the fact that these goods, especially if owned by a higher-ranking status group, serve as symbols of worth and ability. It becomes a matter of self-respect and honor to conspicuously display such goods, not merely to "keep up with the Joneses" but to surpass them if possible (Veblen 1953).

VEBLEN'S THEORY OF THE LEISURE CLASS
The linkage of class position to status is most clearly seen in the arguments of Thorstein Veblen. His discussion of status applies most directly to the periods up to the early part of the twentieth century. Veblen contended that manual labor had become defined as dishonorable and undignified, not becoming to one who wished to be considered of high social status. On the other hand, he argued that nonproductive labor, such as that of being a business executive, increased the probability of owning great amounts of property, which in turn increased one's status honor. Owning property had become, in Veblen's view, the equivalent of possessing honor. In order to show this honor and property to others, one then had to engage in ostentatious displays of wealth and status— namely, various forms of what he called "conspicuous consumption." This display served as a symbol of one's worth and ability.

Veblen argued that the modern leisure class of the industrial era engaged not only in conspicuous consumption and leisure but also in conspicuous waste. Women, for example, had become, in Veblen's view, not only the "property" of men but also an ornament with which men could display their wealth and power. Women took on a ceremonial function with the rise of the Industrial Revolution and were expected to avoid industrious, productive work. Rather, in their behavior and appearance, women were to symbolize the status of their husbands. In their attire, they were expected to be especially wasteful; that is, their dresses were to be nonfunctional waste material. "Special pains should be taken in the construction of women's dress, to impress upon the beholder the fact (often indeed a fiction) that the wearer does not and cannot habitually engage in useful work. . . . [It is] the woman's function in an especial degree to put in evidence her household's ability to pay" (Veblen 1953, p. 126).

We can summarize Veblen's ideas by indicating that he felt that people's worth and honor, in modern times, were linked to their ability to pay—that is, their wealth and possessions. The more a person can display such resources, the greater the respect attributed to him or her. This leads to an ostentatious show for others in a desire to impress and to a competition to outdo others in such display. Such display covers a wide range of possessions, even such things as better-groomed lawns, ownership of prize horses, and conspicuous dress. Everyone battles in this competition, according to Veblen, but the leisure/business class is most successful.

Since Veblen, there have been other analyses of the lifestyle of the upper class. Brooks (1979) argued that Veblen's ideas must be updated because the lower classes do not revere the upper class as in Veblen's day, nor is leisure strictly the province of the upper class today. More often, people engage in "parody display" of honored status symbols. Just as in a literary parody, people poke fun at possessions that, in the past, have commanded great respect. Brooks views this parody as the result of a mixture of admiration and ridicule by the lower classes. But still he finds that competitive display and conspicuous consumption are alive and well in U.S. society. Speech, clothing, and membership in exclusive clubs, for example, continue to be used in making invidious comparisons. Using beautiful women as ornamentation or as trophies also continues today. "'Beauty' is a currency system like the gold standard. Like any economy, it is determined by politics, and in the modern age in the West it is the last, best belief system that keeps male dominance intact" (Wolf 1991, p. 12). By encouraging women to spend a lot of time on how they look and act as they attempt to meet culturally enforced standards, the "beauty myth" weakens their ability to fully develop their mental, political, and economic potential (Wolf 1991).

Portrayals of the lifestyles and distinguishing traits of the social classes are not limited to the upper class. Widespread images of all the classes can be found in the media, and they carry consistent themes that suggest Americans' subjective views about each group. Kendall's study (2005) of newspaper and television characterizations of classes uncovered a variety of both positive and negative presentations for each class:

Upper Class: just regular people who are generous, materialistic, and worthy of emulation, but also sometimes unhappy, unfulfilled, and deviant

Middle Class: people who should be the normative standard for the country and whose problems are frequently caused by those above and below them, but who often are in debt because of inability to pay for their lifestyle

Working Class and Working Poor: hardworking, unsung heroes, but also corrupt, bigoted, without taste or "class" who are unemployed or unhappy in their jobs

Poor and Homeless: victims of circumstance who deserve help but who too often do not help themselves, have deviant lifestyles, and are dependent on welfare

To the extent that media content reflects popular beliefs, these images suggest that the public thinks about social classes in paradoxical ways but at the same time as status groups with distinctive lifestyles.

Physical Appearance and Status

Clearly, physical appearance is often a basis for social status. "In twentieth-century American society, physical beauty emerged as a resource, like wealth or talent" (Rubenstein 2001, p. 212). Apparently, the power of beauty as a resource is evident very early in life. A recent study found that parents give more attention and care to beautiful than to less attractive children (cited in Dowd 2005). While beauty is a resource, it may also be used to reinforce gender inequality. Popular folktales that have been most often reproduced (e.g., Cinderella, Snow White) are those that stress the value of female rather than male beauty. This consistent encouragement to be beautiful may discourage women from pursuing roles, activities, or positions that will make them appear less attractive.

NUTSHELL 4.1   Language as an Indicator of Status Group Membership

One of the ways that group insiders identify outsiders is through the use of terms and phrases that are unfamiliar to outsiders and that are associated with particular groups. Familiarity with a group's argot is a badge of social status, and unfamiliarity provides a group with a way of separating themselves from others, of maintaining a boundary. Consequently, a clue to an individual's status group membership can often be found in the language she or he uses. Sometimes the argots of these status groups are organized around ethnicity or race, and sometimes around specialized occupations. Below are some terms associated with the groups that are listed. See if you know the meaning of these terms.

Hip-hop discourse:

A. homie
B. get crunked
C. playahate
D. mack daddy
E. clockin

Corporate executive discourse:

A. disconnect
B. value-added
C. take-away message
D. value proposition
E. plugged in

Appalachian discourse:

A. gully washer
B. cathead
C. botherment
D. outlander
E. swoggle

Hip-hop meanings: (a) an individual from the area where one lives; (b) fired up, party surrounding; (c) jealousy over another who is successful; (d) a man with many women who manipulates them; (e) watching. *Sources:* Elaine Richardson, *Hiphop Literacies* (New York: Routledge, 2006); Geneva Smitherman, *Black Talk: Words and Phrases from the Hood to the Amen Corner* (Boston: Houghton Mifflin, 2000).

Corporate meanings: (a) failure in communication; (b) something that adds value to a service or product; (c) the main point of a statement; (d) results a customer or client can anticipate from a service or product; (e) being in the know or an insider. *Source:* Candace Goforth, "'Plug in' to the Lingo." *Akron Beacon Journal,* February 27, 2006, p. D1.

Appalachian meanings: (a) a strong rain; (b) a big biscuit; (c) an annoyance; (d) a person from outside the mountains; (e) to mix or stir. *Source:* Robert Hendrickson, *Mountain Range* (New York: Facts on File, 1997).

For men, women's entrapment in the beauty myth serves as a means of social control over women because it removes a source of potential competition (Baker-Sperry and Grauerholz 2003).

To further realize the importance of beauty, one need only look at the media to see how it is used to sell everything from automobile transmissions to cologne. Beauty implies that those who possess it have other mental and behavioral qualities that set them apart from less attractive individuals.Research has suggested that individuals who are considered physically attractive also are considered to have happier marriages, have better

mental health, and be more confident, trustworthy, and likeable than those who are considered unattractive. They also are thought to be more attentive when being interviewed, to be better performers in the classroom, to be better at important tasks in general, and to deserve more room on the street (Webster and Driskell 1983; Wilson and Eckel 2006). They also do better during their careers. Attractive employees earn more than less attractive workers and are promoted more rapidly (Hamermesh and Biddle 1994; Biddle and Hamermesh 1998; Rhode 2010). In criminal cases, defendants who are more physically attractive tend to be treated more leniently, especially in cases in which beauty is not relevant to the type of crime. When beauty is used as a weapon in a crime, however, more attractive individuals receive more severe punishments. "It is as if beauty is a gift, and its malevolent manipulation is condemned" (Rubenstein 2001, p. 215).

Research suggests that high school students who are overweight or obese are less likely than others to be chosen as friends (Crosnoe, Frank, and Mueller 2008). Obese persons are also less likely to be chosen as spouses (Rhode 2010). Younger White women, especially, are deeply conscious of and have negative feelings about their body shape and weight (Cash and Henry 1995). The widespread use by women of elective plastic surgery, liposuction, and cosmetics that promise to make them look younger suggests the importance of appearance in their lives. In 2009, over 12 million cosmetic surgeries were performed in the United States, 91 percent of them on women (American Society of Plastic Surgeons 2010). Eating disorders, such as bulimia and anorexia, are also attempts to make one look thinner and more attractive in present-day society.

Beauty, of course, is in the eyes of the beholder, but what the beholder sees and how it is interpreted are shaped by culture's values. Beauty is a social construction. The definitions of beauty and other status symbols vary among societies and over time within the same society. Whereas in East Asia the face is used as the criterion of beauty, in the United States it is the body in general that is used as a measure of beauty (Frith, Shaw, and Cheng 2005). Beauty standards can also vary among racial and ethnic groups within the same society (Kang 2006). Such standards also change over time. The beauty of the human figure portrayed in a Rubens painting is not the same ideal of beauty seen today in the clothing ads of Victoria's Secret or Ralph Lauren.

Especially in open and democratic societies, the salience and ranking of status symbols wax and wane over time. In one year, having a particular characteristic or possession may result in great status honor or prestige, but a few years later, that same possession may be of little social importance,

In the United States, physical beauty is a currency that can be cashed in for improved social status. The subjective importance placed on beauty is indicated by the more than 12 million cosmetic surgeries performed in the United States in 2009, according to the American Society of Cosmetic Surgeons. Over 90 percent of these surgeries were on women. (© Mayer George Vladimirovich/Shutterstock)

while another has ascended to a position of high prestige. In large and impersonal urban settings where individuals do not know each other personally, displays of status symbols are more common indicators informing strangers *who* their owners really are (Form and Stone 1957). It does not take long to pick up on the social meaning of what we put on our bodies. Even the smallest, seemingly insignificant adornment can suggest status. Pharoah, one of two African American elementary school children in Chicago studied intensively in *There Are No Children Here,* was eager to have a pair of glasses, even if he did not need them, because "he suggested, if he wore glasses, his teachers would choose him more often to run errands or to answer questions. They would, at the very least . . . make him look smarter" (Kotlowitz 1991, p. 62). There is no question that what we wear sends signals about our status.

It is well established that one of the most often-used status symbols in urban settings concerns fashions in clothing. Veblen (1953) observed that at the turn of the twentieth century, clothing was particularly well suited to being a status symbol since "our apparel is always in evidence and affords an indication of our pecuniary standing to all observers at the first glance" (p. 119).

Undoubtedly, how we dress affects the attitudes and behavior of others toward us (Kaiser 1985). "Clothing itself is the beginning and end of human display, touching on one side the skin of the person and reaching out on the other to announce to all what the person inside the skin is or wishes to be" (Brooks 1979, p. 201). Clothing takes on a moral character in that people assume that your dress indicates something about the kind of person you are. "A cheap coat makes a cheap man," observed Veblen long ago. The appearance of secondhand clothing stores in Washington, D.C., which cater to the not-quite affluent, for example, testifies to the importance people place on trying to make an impression. Originally expensive suits can be purchased for a low price. Noted one customer: "It pays to shop in a place like this in a town like Washington where clothes are a big part of how you are perceived" (Barringer 1990, p. 10). Such concerns start early, with parents tramping off to buy Baby Gap, Baby Dior, and Baby Ralph Lauren designer clothing. Recently, the hot debate over "saggin" baggy pants, which to some suggests a lack of respect and seriousness on the part of the wearer, has led several states to create ordinances banning the wearing of such clothing.

Some research suggests that clothing frequently brings out status-related reactions. Alison Lurie (1987) suggested a number of ways in which clothing can be used to give an impression of high status. She labeled these as "conspicuous" addition, division, multiplication, and labeling. Conspicuous addition refers to the technique of layering clothes—that is, wearing several kinds of clothing over each other, even though it is not functionally necessary. Scarves and vests, for example, when worn ornamentally, would be a demonstration of conspicuous addition and an example of what Veblen called conspicuous waste. Conspicuous division and multiplication are different forms of the technique of wearing a wide variety of different types of clothing, especially for separate occasions. The point here is that, to indicate high status, a person does not want to wear the same piece of clothing twice consecutively and does want to wear different kinds of clothes for evening, dinner, casual, and other sorts of situations.

A good example of conspicuous multiplication is found in the inner city of Harlem where status among youths is related to the number and kinds of sneakers worn ("The Well Heeled" 1988). One's status is indicated by the use of different sneakers for different occasions and activities. "A man's got to have style, or he's half a man," explained one youth named Mr. Washington. "The fact is, in the inner city you are what you wear—on your feet" (p. A1). One has to be careful not to wear the wrong brand or style of sneakers in the wrong place or on the wrong occasion. There are regions, sections of cities, even streets, that are closely identified with particular brands of shoes. "In Boston, there are Nike streets . . . and Adidas streets . . . and woe to anyone caught wearing the wrong brand on the wrong street" (p. A6). Shoes are used to identify not only one's status but also one's turf. Some youths are willing to sell drugs to keep themselves in shoes, some of which cost over $100 a pair. The youth quoted earlier, Mr. Washington, owns 150 pairs of sneakers. "Black adolescents are more likely than white adolescents to define their masculine identities through fashion" and to choose clothing that is associated with their race (Crane 2000, p. 191).

Finally, a fourth form of clothing technique mentioned by Lurie, conspicuous labeling, is a way of ensuring that the knowledgeable would be able to distinguish the high-status piece of clothing from an imitation. Otherwise, a status crisis could occur for those who wish to use clothing as a status symbol, since several brand names of clothing may look virtually identical. Labeling on the outside, rather than the inside, of a garment is an obvious way of advertising your status to those around you.

Place and Status

Think for a moment of the United States as a large geographical grid on which different groups travel and reside in particular places. If you could see this grid from above, what would it look like? Social patterns of enclaves, segregation, inclusion, and exclusion would become evident.

Historically, sociologists have not paid much attention to the role that the physical environment plays in our understanding of society's social structure. Indeed, the arrangement of space and the role of place have been neglected in the study of inequality. But in the past few years, space and place have increasingly been recognized as being related to social status (Lobao, Hooks, and Tickameyer 2007). Daphne Spain (1992) has even argued that space is used to acknowledge and reinforce inequalities between men and women. Earlier in U.S. history, the lower status of women was used to keep them out of college, and later to relegate them to separate women's colleges. At work, women's workplaces are most often open spaces characterized by a lack of doors and walls (e.g., as in a secretarial pool), in sharp contrast to the privacy found in the closed-door higher-status jobs of men. Finally, at home, different spaces and entrances have often been assigned to men and women, especially in nonindustrial societies and in nineteenth-century United States.

Where people live is also associated with their status lifestyles. Regionally, for example, high concentrations of the upper class reside in New England, Florida, and California, whereas few upper class live in heartland states such as North and South Dakota, Iowa, Kansas, Oklahoma, West Virginia, Indiana, and Arkansas (Higley 1995). The United States has neighborhood clusters, many of which are clearly and intentionally connected with specific groups occupying different status levels. The elegant mansions of the so-called blue blood estates neighborhoods in places such as Beverly Hills and Scarsdale hold those at the top of the status ladder, while the public assistance neighborhoods of West Philadelphia and Watts are disproportionately dwelling places of

African American and single-parent families. Public housing has also become increasingly occupied by female-headed families, and contains disproportionate numbers of elderly and children (Spain 1993). Throughout the status ladder are found neighborhoods known as "young suburbia," "middle America," "shotguns and pickups," and "sharecroppers." Each of these has its own core values and lifestyle. That these distinct cultural pockets exist should not be surprising: "People seek compatible neighbors who share their family status, income, employment patterns and values" (Weiss 1988). If they have appropriate resources, the neighborhoods people choose to live in are those with residents whose political and cultural values are similar to their own (Bishop 2008).

We must not forget, however, that living in a particular community or neighborhood is not always the result of free choice. Resources and status help dictate where one lives. Constraint also enters the picture when people try to keep "undesirables" out of their neighborhoods through mortgage-loan practices, building restrictions, and zoning procedures. Increasingly, one can find new housing developments for the affluent and cultured that are surrounded by walls and maintained by armed guards at secured entrances. Often, these communities are planned and monitored by electronic surveillance devices, and constitute another, perhaps more blatant, form of segregated neighborhood. Mike Davis (1992) offered Los Angeles as a good example of "where the defense of luxury lifestyles is translated into a proliferation of new repressions in space and movement, undergirded by the ubiquitous 'armed response.'" He saw this approach to living as "a master narrative in the emerging built environment of the 1990s" (p. 223). As noted earlier in this chapter, Weber made a point of identifying exclusionary tactics as devices used by higher status groups to keep their position intact. Privacy and security, and, most important, seclusion from others, mark these "walled communities" (Schneider 1992). Turf wars are perpetrated not only by those at the bottom of the status system but also by those at its pinnacle. The control of physical space is one reflection of status inequalities in our society.

INEQUALITY IN APPALACHIA

On a broader scale, not only do neighborhoods and communities conjure up different perceptions and evaluations but so do regions. There are stereotypes and lifestyles, for example, that have been attributed to Californians, New Englanders, the Old South, the New South, Midwesterners, and Appalachians. Regions can be and have been the basis for status grouping and ranking, even though the cultural, social, and sometimes even topographical homogeneity attributed to these set-apart places is usually mythical rather than factual. Nevertheless, some of these regions, perhaps most notably Appalachia, have been identified as constituting not only separate subcultures but also status groups that have been consciously ranked as being low in prestige. Its low social standing and lack of political power, combined with its reputed distinctiveness and isolation, may help account for the relative lack of socioeconomic research done on Appalachia, compared with other disadvantaged, but more publicized groups such as women and blacks (Baumann 2006). Let us explore Appalachia as an example of status based on region.

A discussion of Appalachia is informative in at least two ways. First, it allows us to examine economic inequality within a region sometimes described as a colony for more powerful economic interests. Second, it allows us to examine the cultural mystique and folklore associated with a section of the country that has often been thought to be out of touch with the mainstream of U.S. society and its culture. Associated in the public mind with mountain men, the region has been portrayed as being inaccessible and isolated. As such, it has been viewed in the popular press and mind as constituting a separate and often homogeneous culture as well as a unique lifestyle. Does Appalachia constitute a separate subculture and, if so, how is it viewed in terms of social status? What is the origin of this subculture, and how is it linked with the economic inequality that prevails in the region?

As a strip in the eastern part of the United States, Appalachia covers parts of 13 states, bordered on the north by southern New York state; on the south by parts of Mississippi, Alabama, and Georgia; on the west by the eastern sections of Kentucky and Tennessee; and on the east by the western portions of Pennsylvania, Virginia, and the Carolinas. It includes all of West Virginia. Most of the discussion of Appalachia as a subculture, however, is based on material from southern Appalachia (northern Georgia, Alabama, North and South Carolina, and parts of Tennessee and Virginia), whereas discussions of the coal industry focus on central Appalachia (Kentucky, West Virginia, southwestern Virginia, and eastern Tennessee). Northern Appalachia is composed of parts of New York, Pennsylvania, Maryland, Ohio, and West Virginia.

Poverty and Economic Development in Appalachia

Poverty and uneven economic development in Appalachia are often associated with the introduction of large-scale coal mining, timber, and other outside corporate intrusions into the region. However, historical studies of Appalachia demonstrate that the social, political, and economic conditions that had helped to perpetuate poverty in Appalachia had already been present in many places (Duncan 1999; Billings and Blee 2000). The notion that Appalachia was completely isolated from the outside world is erroneous. Even before the Civil War, for example, Appalachia was tied to the wider U.S. economy through its salt-making and iron industries. The importation of slaves into the region also fostered outside ties and allowed some to gain control of their local communities (Billings and Blee 2000). As a consequence of elites taking control of local settings, the kind of politics that was generally exercised was aimed at satisfying and maintaining their personal and narrow interests, rather than helping communities as a whole. Little investment was made in the infrastructure that would have laid a foundation for the future and spurred development and raised all citizens economically. The result was communities with strong systems of inequality on the one hand, and weak civic cultures and polities on the other. Political corruption was not uncommon and served to maintain social and economic inequality. Thus, conditions were not fertile for the elimination of poverty or inequality, but only for their perpetuation (Duncan 1999; Billings and Blee 2000).

Racial segregation and educational and employment discrimination between families further divided many communities. Rich and poor, Black and White often did not even share religious institutions. Powerful White farmers kept out new industries so that they could maintain a captive and dependent labor force who would work for low wages (Duncan 1999). Racial inequality deepened throughout the nineteenth century as White landowners strengthened their economic position while landless Blacks sank deeper into poverty (Billings and Blee 2000). Because of their poor educational facilities and lack of social and political connections, Blacks were ill-equipped to take advantage of the few new economic opportunities that did arise.

Finally, the subsistence agriculture that was practiced and the growing population provided a formula for continued poverty for many and outmigration for others. Local economies that would have allowed more independence from outside economic interests were not developed. Underemployment at low wages created a labor force that was ripe for exploitation by incoming coal, timber, and other industries (Billings and Blee 2000). In sum, the uneven development and entrenched poverty found in much of Appalachia are rooted in a history replete with economic, political, and racial inequities. That history provided a hospitable environment for further profit taking by industry.

Outside timber, mining, and manufacturing interests gained increasing access to and ownership of much of the land and other natural resources in the region. Coal became a major industry, and without understanding all the implications, many residents "sold their land and/ or mineral rights for pennies an acre to 'outsiders.' . . . Appalachians became not the entrepreneurs but the laborers" (Appalachian Regional Commission 1985, p. 8). The "patterns of corporate exploitation were established that continue to dominate the resource utilization today" (Beaver 1984, p. 82). John Tiller, a former miner from Trammel,

Virginia, described Appalachia as a colony: "It has all the earmarks—the absentee landlords; nothing built of permanence. You can look at the whole area—the poor roads, the poor schools, the lack of facilities—and realize that there's no solutions" (Carawan and Carawan 1975, p. 26). Hundreds of thousands of acres have been stripped for their lumber and coal resources by absentee owners, individuals who live outside the region but take its resources. Demand for coal in countries like China and India has had mixed effects on the living standards of families in Appalachia. Mountaintop mining, which strips hills and mountains of their trees, has accelerated in central Appalachia since the mid-1990s and has generated great controversy because of its damage to hardwood forests and tourism in the region. The damage to tourism may be especially significant for the economy of West Virginia because tourism is the state's most rapidly growing industry.

Recent census analyses indicate that, while there are variations within Appalachian subregions, economic activity in Appalachia as a whole in the 1980s and 1990s was stagnant compared with the rest of the United States, and wages continued to lag behind the national average (Foster 2003). The per capita income and wage gaps between Appalachia and the rest of the country were not much different in 2000 than they were in 1970. Appalachian per capita income is only about 82 percent that of non-Appalachian regions (Baumann 2006). Part of the reason appears to be related to differences in the distribution of employment fields; the economic returns from mining and farming are significantly lower than those from services and manufacturing (Cardiff 1999). Central Appalachia, where most of the mining occurs, also happens to be the poorest segment of Appalachia (Baumann 2006). While the percentage of full-time workers with less than a high school diploma has dropped significantly since 1970, the proportion of Appalachian workers with college educations continues to lag behind that of the rest of the nation (Baumann 2006).

The events and conditions just noted brought attention to the region, and media presentations helped form the images and conclusions outsiders

The coal produced in Appalachia more often economically benefited absentee company owners than it did local residents, exacerbating wealth differences within the region. Railroads provided transportation for coal and as well as the setting for many modest homes in places like southwestern Virginia. (© Will Griffith/Shutterstock)

developed about Appalachia. They even helped shape the perceptions of Appalachians about their own region. Since the turn of the twentieth century, when major changes in the economy and ownership had already begun, the image portrayed of Appalachian culture has been one of stagnation and backwardness attributed in large part to the supposed physical isolation of the region.

But in his study of a central Appalachian valley, Gaventa (1980, 1984) argued that the proliferation of the cultural model of Appalachia as being backward, uncivilized, and little else was a creation that helped justify the exploitation (development) of that region by outside interests. As Yale-educated, Kentucky native Jill Fraley observed: "The image of Appalachia as synonymous with poverty, deprivation, and a refusal of modern progress, was an image created and nurtured with the development of coal and timber industries in Appalachia . . . it was the creation of a capitalist, industrial majority that needed an excuse for stealing land and leveling mountains" (2007, p. 257). The presence of excess investment

capital and an ideology that encouraged development of undeveloped rural areas led to the purchase and control of Appalachian property by outside investors. Part of the justification of this easy appropriation of resources was couched in the specious argument that the inhabitants were quiescent and backward simpletons. Gaventa demonstrated, however, that this reaction was really a rational response to their condition of powerlessness. Repeated defeats, the greater resource power of outside forces, the construction of various barriers, and the perpetuation of myths and stereotypes about the Appalachian people all have conspired to create less rebellion, even though extensive grievances and discontent on a variety of issues lie just below the surface.

THE POPULAR IMAGE OF APPALACHIA
Following the Civil War, Appalachia was "discovered" by journalists and others who viewed it as an offbeat place with unfamiliar vegetation inhabited by a people with odd customs ("A Strange Land and Peculiar People" cited in Beaver 1984, p. 86). Since then, a variety of values have been

associated with Appalachians, many of them negative in nature. "The Appalachian is fatalistic," wrote Lewis (1974), "while mainstream Americans believe they can control their environment and their lives. The Appalachian is impulsive, personalistic and individualistic while mainstream Americans are rational, organized, can handle impersonal role relationships and have a social consciousness" (p. 222). Individualism, a love of and dependence on family and an attachment to home, a belief in personal liberty and independence, fatalism and resignation, a belief in the essential equality of all individuals, a disdain for and suspicion of formal education, and the centrality of personal religion, all have been characteristics frequently associated with Appalachians (cf., e.g., Erikson 1976; Batteau 1984; W. H. Turner 1986).

As was indicated earlier in this chapter, the social status given to another person or group is a subjective process, one in which the group is portrayed as having a specific lifestyle and set of beliefs that distinguish it from surrounding groups. In most groups, there is more heterogeneity than is suspected by outsiders, but it is the latter's perceptions, whether or not based on fact, that govern their reaction to the group. The fact is that despite the stereotypical view often taken of it, Appalachia is a region with varied resources, a differentiated geography, and people of varied ethnic backgrounds.

Alongside the negative image of Appalachia as a stagnant and backward region, another more patronizing image exists. This interpretation fosters the view of Appalachia as an area of great natural beauty being despoiled by greedy economic interests. Unsullied nature and the rugged individualism of mountain men are integral components of this perspective of Appalachia as an innocent victim (Batteau 1984). In this view, the mountains take on a mystical, romantic quality. This is part of the region's appeal for tourists. But this image also fosters other reactions.

A problem with such subcultural descriptions—especially of an area that has been said to be socially, culturally, and physically shut off from the rest of the country—is that they tend to become caricatures over time, ignoring internal differences within the region and changes that have occurred in its relationship with other parts of the world. These subcultural characteristics also have been interpreted as the principal causes for the unusually high rates of poverty found in Appalachia. This constitutes a form of victim blaming, however, because evidence suggests that it has not been primarily subcultural values or isolation but rather the nature of a region's ties to the outside that have exacerbated and perpetuated the high poverty rate. Numerous scholars, many from the region, have labeled Appalachia as a rich land with poor people, poor because their resources have been exploited by outsiders (cf., e.g., Gaventa 1980; Eller 1982).

Even though Appalachia is a heterogeneous area, where many lead urban and middle-class lives, few have questioned the traditional stereotypes associated with the Appalachian. Too often, images of an Appalachian character (1) are derived primarily from descriptions of adult *males,* (2) ignore the fact that many of the characteristics are shared by other Americans, and (3) minimize or deny the inconsistencies and differences found within Appalachian culture (Erikson 1976, pp. 75–78). With respect to the latter, for example, the African American ethnographer William Turner (1986) suggested that many Blacks in Appalachia do not share the values and beliefs of their White neighbors. Rather than being fatalistic, traditional, and so forth, they are attracted to materialism and individual achievement and do not identify psychologically as strongly with the land and the region as White Appalachians do.

Despite the fact that changes have occurred in the region, many traditional values have weakened, and many Appalachians are integrating culturally and socially into the wider society, stereotypes still abound. Old images die hard deaths.

The image of Appalachia as being composed of backward, fundamentalistic, individualistic mountaineers has lowered the status prestige of this region for most Americans. In the late 1960s, "in some popular and scholarly circles Appalachia was second only to Black America as a repository for social pathos" (W. H. Turner 1986, p. 279).

Appalachia occupies "the lowest rung in [our] socio-economic ladder" (Coreil and Marshall 1982). Data collected in interviews with long-term rural Kentuckians suggested that a large majority of them feel that Appalachians are given "much less respect than other Americans." Many also believed that Appalachians experience greater occupational, educational, legal, and income inequality than other Americans. They also were inclined to view the inequality involving Appalachians as being separate from racial and class inequality, suggesting that they identify themselves as a separate group when it comes to the problems of inequality (Smith and Bylund 1983).

How do the elements of this discussion of Appalachia relate to our earlier conclusion that status can be based on region? Let us review the core factors that determine status and status-group ranking. We noted that status honor/prestige is subjectively given by a community to another person or group. This perception, in turn, depends on the characteristics attributed to the person or group and on how valued these characteristics are in mainstream culture. Status honor can be based on (1) lifestyle, (2) extent of empirical-rational formal education, (3) family genealogy, and/or (4) occupation, according to Weber (1964). We also said that a distinct lifestyle and isolation from outsiders characterize status groups. Weber further argued that individuals in similar status situations tend to form cohesive communities. This cohesiveness is reaffirmed and maintained through intimate associations among themselves and by their wariness of and distance from outsiders. Status groups also are characterized by some uniqueness in their acquisitions; that is, their possessions may be exclusively associated with members of the group. Finally, higher-status groups try to avoid contaminating contact with lower-status groups, since they represent "impure" qualities and, in the extreme case, may be considered pariah groups.

The evidence we have reviewed strongly suggests that most Americans have a fairly coherent conception of Appalachians as a group and that they perceive them as having distinctive values and behaviors. Moreover, this subculture is more often than not portrayed in negative terms; that is, it is perceived as low status. The Appalachian subculture is thought to have a unique lifestyle, according to the traditional conception, that includes a denigration of formal education, a genealogy composed of so-called common folk, and traditional occupations that are usually blue collar or agricultural in nature. None of these characteristics enhances the status honor accorded Appalachians. The mountain people frequently have been portrayed as being physically, socially, and culturally isolated from the outside world, and conversely, as having close relationships among themselves, especially within families. The qualities assessed as different by the standards of the dominant culture lead to the ridicule and romanticism heaped upon mountaineers and "hillbillies" by outside urbanites. In correspondence with the romantic view of mountain culture, some of the artifacts associated with this culture, such as musical styles and instruments, have been viewed as being unique and worthy of preservation, especially by intellectual outsiders. In sum, what exists in Appalachia is an interesting confluence of economic, colonial, and status factors that must be understood within their historical context. Most importantly, our traditional image of Appalachians, while not consistent with much empirical evidence, has encouraged us to label Appalachians as a separate status group with low prestige.

THE IMPORTANCE OF SOCIAL STATUS IN THE GLOBAL ARENA

Beyond the United States, social status distinctions are also found in other societies as well. A long-term project in Britain, for example, has uncovered status and lifestyle distinctions that provide evidence for defined stratification among status groups, and these distinctions are not reducible to economic class differences (Chan and Goldthorpe 2004). In other words, Weber's argument for the analytic separation between class and status is supported. These status groups are distinguished by differences in the breadth of their consumption of cultural activities (e.g., art, music, etc.).

Members of the same status group also tend to carry out their intimate relationships with each other rather than with outsiders.

Inequality based on status group differences is widespread, and is not always reflected simply in taste differences. The violent conflicts that exist in many parts of the world also suggest the existence of status differences. In Rwanda, ethnic violence between the Hutu majority and the Tutsi minority left up to million Tutsi dead in 1994. Often these conflicts are rooted in religious differences, but they sometimes are grounded in prejudice and discrimination based on sexual orientation and ethnic membership. Violence between Christians and Muslims in parts of Africa and Central Europe, between Hindus and Muslims in South Asia, and between Jews, Muslims, and Christians in the Middle East are just a few of ongoing battles based on religion. Often, the dominant religious group oppresses the minority.

In Cameroon, rights abuses based on sexual orientation occur frequently. Individuals who are suspected of being homosexual are denied jobs and education, may be beaten by authorities, and abused in prison. Gays are stereotyped in the media, and women who do not act or dress in a "feminine" manner are persecuted (Human Rights Watch 2010).

As the above examples illustrate, status inequality is a worldwide issue. But while research has been done on the relationships between globalization, on the one hand, and economic and political inequality on the other, virtually no research has been conducted on the potential impact of globalization on status inequality or status communities. In some ways, this is rather curious because globalization generally involves the movement and intermixing of people with different cultural, religious, political, and educational backgrounds. What I will do here is briefly suggest some possible relationships between globalization and the development of new bases of status resulting in the rise and fall of status communities within and between nations. So consider the following few paragraphs as food for thought.

It seems to me that increased immigration from Latin America and Asia, public discussions about various religious groups, and concerns about the global educational and digital divide are all seedbeds for the development of new status communities and the strengthening of nascent ones. Historically, adaptation by immigrants to the United States sometimes took the form of economic, social, and cultural enclaves. Within them, immigrants could maintain their distinct cultural ways of life, creating a sometimes voluntary and sometimes involuntary boundary between themselves and the larger society. Given the continuing controversy about the economic, educational, environmental, and other effects of immigration on U.S. society, and the conviction on the part of some that we ought to severely limit immigration and be more rigorous in our monitoring of recent immigrants, it may be that the boundaries between immigrant enclaves and the rest of society will become more solidified, reinforcing any tendencies toward exclusion and exclusivity now present. The result could be more stratification by status based on immigrant position, where immigrants are labeled and stigmatized. Might this not encourage them to turn inward to develop more fully their own communities to the neglect of ties with others? The immigrant–native divide may have political and economic implications as well.

A second axis of status ranking that may become more prominent involves religion. Recent "terrorist" activities have sensitized more Americans to the religious division of Islam, Judaism, and Christianity, and have led to retributions of members of one religion against those who follow a different creed. At least in the short term, these actions and reactions solidify the boundaries that separate these religious communities both within and between countries as some individuals "look down on" members of different religions. The religious differences are often viewed with ethnic overtones, suggesting that Muslims, Christians, and other religious groups are basically viewed as being made up of different *kinds* of people, and confirming Weber's belief that status communities are perceived as groups of people who are *inherently* different. This situation can lead to the reinvigoration of religion as an important basis of status honor or dishonor.

Finally, there has also been discussion by international leaders about the "global digital divide" that separates developed from less developed nations. In 2000, members of the major economic powers in the world—the G-8 as they are called—met to assess the extent of the digital gap and propose policies that might help to close it. The gap is large: In North America, for example, there are 61 computers for every 100 individuals, whereas in South Asia there is only 0.5 computer and in sub-Saharan Africa only 1 computer for every 100 people. The Internet is rarely if ever used in these regions, whereas in North America over 50 percent of the citizens use the Internet (Chinn and Fairlie 2005). While this may change, the current situation conjures up an image of a world community in which some parts are left "out of the loop" about what is happening in the world and others are not. This again strengthens boundaries between different kinds of people, and since the rate of computer and other modern technology usage is correlated with other bases of inequality such as race, wealth, education, occupation, and gender, technological inequality further deepens and reinforces inequality along these axes. The "global e-lite" may form a new class or status group (Drori 2006). Do you think new status communities may develop as a result of globalization? Will the continuing infiltration of new values, styles, and technologies into countries create new social disparities where none have existed?

Summary

This chapter has addressed the topic of social status, a form of inequality that is analytically separate from economic inequality, even though it is frequently based on an individual's economic resources. Status also can be based on occupation, education, lifestyle, physical appearance, region, race, gender, and sexual orientation. The type of occupation one has, the kind of education one receives, the lifestyle one pursues, and the way one appears in public are each a badge of status. Each affects how others perceive us and how they treat us. Each also forms a basis for the groups with which we identify. In their extreme, status groups can be legally sanctioned where the boundaries separating insiders and outsiders are virtually impermeable. Veblen was acutely aware of the invidious comparisons that groups made with each other in the early 1900s, and these continue today. Even the labels attached to various places and regions of the country suggest that they have implications for social status. We examined Appalachia in depth because differences in economic and political power and social status all converge in this region. By analyzing the region, one can see several forms of inequality at work all at once. In Chapters 6, 7, and 8, we will turn our attention to gender, sexual orientation, and race/ethnicity as additional bases of status ranking. Clearly, the groups involved in these areas elicit images of distinct lifestyles and concerns about contamination and purity. But before exploring these groups, we turn to the political dimension of inequality.

Critical Thinking

1. Discuss the new forms or bases of status developing in the United States. What are they and how important are they? Will they replace status based on older grounds? Explain your answer.
2. How can individuals present themselves to others to indicate their membership in particular status groups?
3. On an everyday basis, how do students in junior high school and high school behave to maintain or enhance their social status among their peers? That is, how do they "do" status?
4. Does the formation of tightly knit status groups encourage fragmentation in the United States, or do they simply enrich and strengthen our diversity?

Web Connections

Appalachia has often been described in contradictory ways—as beautiful but ravaged, and as rich in resources but impoverished. The Appalachian Regional Commission's website will give you a better idea of trends in its population, employment, education, and poverty. Visit www.arc.gov/.

Film Suggestions

Killing Us Softly 4 (2010). Explores media advertising of women.

Born Rich (2003). Interviews with children born into wealthy families about what it is like to be born rich.

CHAPTER 5

Political Inequality

*Where some people are very wealthy and others have nothing, the result
will be either extreme democracy or absolute oligarchy, or despotism
will come from either of those excesses.*

ARISTOTLE (384–322 BCE)

The exercise of power and the experience of powerlessness are implicit in all the forms of inequality. The relationships between the wealthy and nonwealthy, men and women, gays and straights, and Blacks and Whites are frequently mediated by the relative economic, social, and cultural power of these groups. Power also has a narrow political meaning as well, relating to the varied involvement and impact of individuals and groups in the national government. Power differentials also shape the everyday work worlds of men and women as well. We will examine the political and work arenas of power, beginning with a discussion of images of political power structure in the United States then moving to a review of evidence that bears on those images.

PORTRAITS OF NATIONAL POWER STRUCTURE

The founding architects of the U.S. national government did not agree on how large or how strong it should be, nor did they consistently agree on whether everyone should have an equal influence on government. Washington and Adams, for example, believed in the need for a strong, centralized government, while Jefferson and Madison worried that such a government would move the country toward a European-style monarchy rather than a democracy.

Arguments on how widespread such power is have continued to this day. Basically, the debate boils down to one over the extent of inequality in political power. Most of these views can be listed under one of the following types: (1) pluralist, (2) power elite, or (3) ruling class. The principal issue on which these approaches differ is the degree to which they see power as being concentrated in the United States. After the summaries of these perspectives, a survey of the empirical evidence that bears on them will be presented.

The Pluralist View

Basically, this widely accepted position argues that there are a number of competing groups and organizations that hold much of the power in the country, but no one of these groups holds power all of the time. There is no central or **inner circle** that dominates or coordinates the connections between these groups, because each is relatively autonomous and self-interested. Each group pursues issues that are of narrow interest to its organization; in those areas it can have influence, but in others it has little or no power. Generally, social inequality is "noncumulative, i.e., most people have some power resources, and no single asset (such as money) confers excessive power" (Manley 1983, p. 369). Although there is some contact between organized groups, it tends to be inconsistent and deals with specific issues rather than broad orientations (Higley and Moore 1981). For example, conservative and liberal religious organizations may join together and have some power in their support of proposed policies revolving around rights of the unborn, but on other issues, they may differ or have no influence or interest. The shifting of power from group to group as issues fluctuate keeps power in a rough balance throughout the society. Individuals can exercise power in part by becoming members of these groups.

In sum, although the pluralist approach has spawned a number of specific theories, most share these four core ideas:

1. Power is shared rather than concentrated among a variety of groups and individuals.
2. These groups are relatively autonomous of each other and become politically active primarily when political policies are at issue that directly affect their narrow interests.
3. The average citizen can be politically influential through membership in these groups and through voices of responsible journalists and intellectuals.
4. The consequence of items 1 through 3 is that there really is no single, permanent structure of power. Power is mercurial and its distribution is somewhat balanced by the existence of varied competing groups (Riesman, Denney, and Glazer 1950; Galbraith 1952).

In these theories, one is given the impression of a society that is fundamentally based on *a broad system of values about which there is a widespread consensus,* even though the society is composed of a variety of groups with specific interests that may be different. In this society, each individual is rational and free, and interests are taken into account in one way or another by those organizations such as government or corporations that might be seen as having greater power. Power and powerlessness do not appear to be problems. The sharing of power actually helps the society to function.

A variant of the pluralist model was proposed by Keller (1969), who contended that the increasing complexity and differentiation in modern societies makes the existence of "coordinating elements" essential. To prevent this society from disintegrating because of all of its different parts, some groups must play a central role in keeping the parts together. These "strategic elites," as Keller calls them, perform this function and serve as the "guardians and creators of common purpose and . . . managers of collective aims and ambitions" (Keller 1969, p. 521). Such elites have knowledge that is both expert and critical for the functioning of the entire society. Obviously, not all organized groups in the society qualify for this elite status. Included among the strategic elites are leaders in the political, economic, military, cultural, and recreational arenas. Because strategic elites are specialized, none of them dominates according to Keller, nor do these elites constitute a ruling class.

Unfortunately, this theory is not very informative about the *degrees* of importance of each of the strategic elites; nor does it explain what happens when strategic elites, such as those in economic, political, and military domains, collide with each other. Finally, what makes these groups strategic elites is their expert knowledge in critical areas. But a theory that stresses specialized knowledge as the important basis for power neglects the fact that ideology and outlooks frequently trump knowledge as bases for power (Prewitt and Stone 1973, pp. 126–127).

For more than 50 years, **pluralism** has been roundly criticized (Mills 1956; Bachrach and Baratz 1962; Connolly 1969; Prewitt and Stone 1973). The central criticisms of pluralism frequently reflect skepticism about the reality of democracy in society today and are based on an analysis of current events on the political scene. First, the issues of concern to many people frequently are not dealt with by the government. In large part, this occurs either because these individuals are not in positions to make their interests known or because their interests are of less concern than those of people who hold positions of economic and social power and whose values are represented and reflected in the government (Connolly 1969; Prewitt and Stone 1973). Second, voluntary associations are no longer effective representatives of the average citizen as they have themselves become oligarchic in nature. In addition, individuals in positions of organizational power do not represent the average membership. Most members of voluntary associations do not have access to power (Presthus 1962; Kariel in Connolly 1969, p. 16). Finally, nondecisions and problems that never become publicly defined as issues must be examined. Pluralism examines issues but ignores "the values and biases that are built into the political system and that, for the student of power, give real meaning to those issues which do enter the political arena" (Bachrach and Baratz 1962, p. 950).

The Power-Elite View

The idea of a **power elite** differs drastically from pluralist conceptions and Keller's concept of strategic elites, but it is not the same as the ruling-class concept, which we will discuss shortly. Perhaps the most famous U.S. power-elite theory was developed by C. Wright Mills (1956). Because Mills's portrayal of the power elite has drawn an inordinate amount of attention in the years since it was written, and because it represents a prime example of a theory in opposition to the pluralist position, it is presented here in detail. Mills's essential argument is that power is centralized in a power elite.

According to Mills, certain historical changes have brought about the development of a power elite. As society has grown, institutions have become more complex, and national functions have become centralized in specific institutions—namely, economic, military, and political institutions. Mills contended that with historical changes, the tasks in top positions in each of these institutions have become so similar that it is now possible for those at the top to interchange positions. Consequently, in addition to centralization in institutions, there has been an increasing coalescence, so much so that *three* separate political, military, and corporate elites are now *one* power elite made up of individuals in the highest positions in an interconnected set of institutions. "By the power elite, we refer to those political, economic, and military circles which as an intricate set of overlapping cliques share decisions having at least national consequences" (p. 18). The nucleus of the power elite consists of those who hold high positions in more than one of the three major institutions, as well as those, such as prestigious lawyers and financiers, who serve to knit the three institutions together (pp. 288–289).

The persons within this structure have their power because of their positions. They do tend to come from the same kinds of economic, social, and educational backgrounds and do informally intermingle. Ultimately, however, it is their position that makes them powerful in national decision making.

Some may feel that Congress is part of the power elite, but Mills did not agree. Rather, he referred to Congress as a "semi-organized stalemate" made up of people who, since they have their eyes on reelection, are concerned largely with the fluctuating local issues of their constituencies back home. In other words, such groups as the farm bloc, labor unions, white-collar workers, and Congress really have little to do with decisions of national consequence. These groups, specifically Congress, make up a middle level of power in the United States. If the competition of groups in pluralism operates at all, it is at this level, as congressional members exchange favors, make compromises, and balance each other out. Mills (1956) further believed that the wealthy and political officers who are entrenched in local interests will not become nationally important. As he stated, "to remain merely local is to fail" (p. 39). Local society has, by and large, been swallowed up by the national system of power and prestige. This is in part due to increasing urbanization, increasing satellite status of smaller towns, improved transportation networks, and the World Wide Web. Again, it has been changes in the structure of the society that have resulted in the appearance of a particular kind of power structure.

On the bottom of this pyramidal power structure are the large majority of people who are quickly developing into a **mass society**. Masses are characterized by the fact that they are always on the receiving end of opinions, cannot or do not effectively respond to opinions expressed in the mass media, and really have no outlet for effective action in society. Mass media, largely controlled by those on the top of the power structure, have only served to weaken communications between the top and the bottom of the structure. The media tell people what their experiences are or should be and stereotype them. Education only serves to help people "adjust" to a society that is extremely hierarchical in terms of power. Voluntary associations, although they may be viewed theoretically as a link between the individual and the people at the top, do not perform this function because as they have grown, the individuals in them feel less powerful. Power is distant and inaccessible to average members.

It should be pointed out that Mills was not saying that there is a conspiracy on the part of a small group of individuals to control political power in the United States. Rather, it has been a sequence of historical and structural events and changes, such as the growth in major institutions, that has led to the development of such a power structure. For example, the military is not powerful because it is conspiring against civilian populations, but it is in a position of power because the United States as a nation is now within an international military neighborhood, surrounded by allies and enemies. This means that what in the past may have been simply and purely political issues have now become largely military issues. Foreign aid is no longer just an economic or political issue but a military issue as well.

The *current* power elite is a relatively recent phenomenon that, in Mills's view, came into existence only after the New Deal in the 1940s and 1950s. Before that time, the power structure passed through several other epochs in which either no single institution or one of the three major institutions was dominant. Today, the hierarchy among these institutions is much less clear, and they are much more equal and intertwined.

Mills's power-elite theory has been criticized on several grounds, including the arguments that his terminology is vague and his selection of issues to test his theory is biased. He has also been faulted for choosing data that support his theory and ignoring contrary evidence. Third, some critics have attacked his conception of power as being too narrow in that it omits the role that moral and other kinds of authority may play in offsetting the power of an elite. His argument that power is based on position rather than actual decision-making has also been contested, as has his contention that power only flows from the top down. After Mills' death, the power of civil rights and the women's movement to influence policy confirmed the ability of those on the bottom to organize and have an impact. Finally, some have argued that Mills attributed too much independent power to the military and unions and too little to the Congress (Domhoff 2006; Weston 2010).

Despite these criticisms, Mills analysis improved the quality of the debate about power differences (Prewitt and Stone 1973) and initiated a stream of research on national power structure. Moreover, recent headlines have substantiated his contention about the great power that corporate and political institutions have over average citizens (Domhoff 2006; Jenness, Smith, and Stepan-Norris 2006).

The Ruling-Class View

As we have seen, Mills's description of the power structure is one in which a group of individuals in high positions in core institutions dominate, while those at the bottom comprise an unorganized, ineffectual mass. The bottom has little power and offers little active resistance. Rather, these individuals are manipulated and educated in a manner that makes them almost willing subordinates in the society. The **ruling-class** view similarly proposes that a small group has inordinate political power in the society and that there are important interconnections between economic and political institutions. However, aside from these similarities, the ruling-class model differs from the power-elite model in three ways:

1. Rather than stressing several types of institutions as being involved in the elite, the ruling-class view emphasizes the dominance of the economic institution and position within it.
2. The ruling-class model often views the bottom of the power structure as being more active and effectual as a working class. It can organize and bring about change in the society. In the case of the power-elite model, the mass is largely passive in response to its position, whereas in the ruling-class model the working class can be class conscious and organized. Thus, the relationship between those on the top and those at the bottom is characterized more fully by conflict (Bottomore 1964).
3. The relationship between the upper class or bourgeoisie and political power is portrayed as being much tighter than is the case in Mill's power-elite theory in which the upper class and celebrities are more tangential to the political process. In Mills's view, it is strictly *institutional position,* not *personal wealth,* that leads to political power.

G. William Domhoff's argument that rich corporate owners constitute a "dominant class" that largely controls the political process is perhaps the best representation of a ruling-class theory of U.S. politics. Briefly, Domhoff (1998) contends that a cohesive power elite dominates federal governmental affairs, and it is composed of those members of the upper class whose wealth is heavily concentrated in corporate holdings and who actively become involved in corporate affairs and

political policy making. Consequently, their power is based in both class position and corporate attachment. In addition, these individuals have similar backgrounds, often know each other, and have general political and economic interests in common. Because of the cohesiveness founded on these similarities, the upper class "is a *capitalist* class as well as a *social* class" (Domhoff 1998, p. 116; emphasis added). Although there may be internal disagreements over specific policies, there is broad agreement over the general direction that policy should take. The corporate-based elite dominates the political arena through its heavy influence on public opinion, participation in lobbying through its powerful interest groups, and involvement in policy formation through foundations, board room discussions, and various research groups.

In contrast to Mills's view of the power elite, Domhoff does not suggest there is a mass society without voice and in which no group but the elite can have any power of consequence. Rather, he notes that unions and different liberal groups frequently conflict with the corporate rich, but that, generally, it is the latter group that sets the parameters within which conflict occurs. Domhoff is quick to point out that, given the size, internal disagreements, and bases of the dominant class, his is not a conspiracy theory. Rather his argument focuses on providing evidence that there is "an upper class that is tightly interconnected with the corporate community . . . [and] that the social cohesion that develops among members of the upper class is another basis for the creation of policy agreements" (1998, p. 71). In sum, while Domhoff does recognize that there are other bases of power, they pale in comparison to the inordinate power exercised by those with massive economic resources. Clearly, the pouring of huge amounts of private money into the electoral process would seem to support his emphasis on economic power.

DISTRIBUTION OF POLITICAL POWER

Each of the positions just discussed makes a different argument about political inequality on the national level in the United States. But the data that bear on them must be examined before conclusions can be drawn about the actual concentration and dispersion of political power. The degree of political power and political participation can be measured in a variety of ways, and each of these measures provides clues concerning the actual distribution of power.

Although some people feel they have little influence, perhaps they are wrong. One means by which to assess the potential political impact of a group is through its history of participation in the political process. "Participation is a potent force; leaders respond to it. But they respond more to the participants than to those who do not participate" (Verba and Nie 1972, p. 336). A group obviously has to make its desires known if it is to have the possibility of gaining political power under the present system. "Party politicians are inclined to respond positively not to group *needs* but to group *demands*, and in political life as in economic life, *needs* do not become *marketable demands* until they are backed by 'buying power' or 'exchange power' because only then is it in the 'producer's' interest to respond" (Parenti 1970, p. 528; emphasis in original). Individuals and groups can make their demands known by participating in the political process through (1) voting, (2) holding political office, and/or (3) putting pressure in the form of lobbying and monetary support.

Voting

Voting is a frequently used measure of political participation. Voting turnouts for national elections in this country are well below the 80 percent turnouts found in other industrial democratic nations. This lower voting rate is somewhat surprising, given that evidence suggests Americans tend to be more politically aware than adults in other similar countries. The party system's lack of close connection with many other social groups, along with voluntary registration, has weakened participation in the U.S. political process (Powell 1986). Thirty-six percent of voting-age citizens did not vote in the 2008 presidential election.

Across the board, as Table 5.1 indicates, members of minorities and lower socioeconomic

TABLE 5.1	Voting Rates among Citizens 18 and Older in the 2008 Presidential Election, by Selected Characteristics

	% Voting*
Sex	
Men	62
Women	66
Race and Hispanic Origin	
White, non-Hispanic	66
Black	65
Asian	48
Hispanic (any race)	50
Educational Attainment	
Less than high school graduate	39
High school graduate or GED	55
Some college or associate degree	68
Bachelor's degree	77
Advanced degree	83
Annual Family Income	
Less than $20,000	52
$20,000–$29,999	56
$30,000–$39,999	62
$40,000–$49,999	65
$50,000–$74,999	71
$75,000 and over	76
Employment Status	
Unemployed in labor force	55
Employed in labor force	66

*All percentages rounded to nearest whole.

Source: U.S. Census Bureau, *Voting and Registration in the Election of November 2008.* Current Population Reports, Series P20, No. 562, Table 2, pp. 4–5.

groups are less likely to vote than Whites or those with higher educations or incomes. The former groups are overrepresented in the nonvoting population, and as such, lose to the extent that voting is a measure of political power. The overrepresentation of lower socioeconomic individuals among nonvoters is exacerbated by the fact that organized efforts to get individuals to the polls focus on those who are most likely to vote anyway, that is, the affluent and more highly educated segments (Campbell 2007). Moreover, to the extent that individuals with higher incomes and educations vote for candidates and legislation that favor their positions, lower-ranking groups may suffer from the resulting political policies.

The power of class differences to influence voting and legislation, however, may apply primarily to White voters. Research based on exit polls of over 12,000 Black Los Angeles voters during the 1978–2000 elections suggests that race may make a difference. Among Blacks, middle-class votes appeared to align with lower-class Black sympathies (Hajnal 2007). In other words, among these voters race overrides the significance of class divisions when it comes to choosing candidates or voting for legislation. There is some concern, however, that younger Blacks view the political process differently than older Blacks, and may be less likely to vote or support the traditional agenda of the older generation (Bositis 2007).

The data for Hispanics in Table 5.1 has to be interpreted carefully as well since the data only include citizens and not all Hispanic adults. In 2000, 39 percent of Hispanics in the population were not citizens. The political impact of this ethnic group will no doubt increase as more become citizens. In fact, Hispanics have been increasingly courted by national candidates, in large part because they are expected to compose one-fourth of the U.S. population by 2050. In addition, 80 percent of the Hispanic population is concentrated in just 10 states, states that contain 80 percent of the electoral votes needed to win the presidency (Campo-Flores and Fineman 2005). Finally, religious and moral issues of the kind that have become prominent (e.g., abortion, gay marriage, etc.) are central to the lifestyles of many Hispanics. In combination, these factors make Hispanics an increasingly important political constituency.

As voting data suggest, some groups are, at best, only minimally involved in the political process. Those who are totally inactive have disproportionate numbers from low-income and low-education backgrounds, whereas "complete

activists" have an overrepresentation of high-status individuals in their ranks (Verba and Nie 1972, pp. 97–99). The complete activists are individuals who participate in a variety of ways (voting, attending meetings, making campaign contributions, contacting officials, etc.). "Wealthier and better-educated citizens are more likely than the poor and less-educated to have clearly formulated and well-informed preferences, and significantly more likely to turn out to vote, to have direct contact with public officials, and to contribute money and energy to political campaigns" (Bartels 2008, p. 252). Business and professional groups continue to be politically involved, but tend to promote the interests of the affluent and educated (Skocpol 2007). There is also evidence to suggest that this inequality in political participation is perpetuated over generations through educational differences.

Although working-class families have been among the most openly patriotic and have generally contributed their members disproportionately to serving their country militarily, they are less likely to vote or occupy political positions than are those in higher classes. (Photo by Brendan R. Hurst.)

Parents who are highly educated tend to be politically involved, provide a variety of politically relevant experiences to their children, and perhaps most significantly, maximize the chances of their children becoming highly educated themselves. "In turn, well-educated offspring are likely to . . . have challenging and financially rewarding jobs, to develop civic skills and to receive requests for participation in non-political institutions, to be politically informed and interested, and so on. . . . Most of the proximate causes of political participation have their roots, at least in part, in social class background" (Verba, Burns, and Schlozman 2003, p. 58). These differences in preparation and participation means that "ordinary Americans speak in a whisper while the most advantaged roar" (quoted in Dionne 2004, p. B2).

Historically, the less advantaged have also been less organized and less powerful when attempting to influence the political system. While some organizations and movements advocating their interests have sprung up in recent years, other groups such as unions have declined in membership. Union members have higher rates of voting than nonmembers in similar occupations, but the percentage of private-sector workers that are unionized is much smaller than that found among public-sector workers. When these conditions are combined with the fact that private sector union members tend to have less education and lower wages than those in the public sector, the result is that the political power of the working class as expressed through voting is weakened, making political inequality between the classes greater (Rosenfeld 2010).

In addition to lower voting rates and less participation in political activities, weakness in the political power of the working and lower classes is further indicated by the lack of government responsiveness to the arguments of these classes. An analysis of data from the Senate in the 1980s and 1990s shows that the positions of wealthy constituents were much more likely to be considered by lawmakers than those of poorer constituents, and that those on the bottom were not likely to be considered at all (Bartels 2008).

While class position affects political participation, some have argued that, as a basis for political advocacy, class has been supplanted by "cultural" factors. Prominent issues like gay marriage, abortion, medical malpractice, stem cell research, marijuana usage, and immigration incite groups that are not organized around *class* but around religious and other *cultural* dimensions. *Status*-based politics has moved into the foreground while *class*-based politics has receded. Michael Hechter (2004) observes, "[t]hat status politics may be gaining in recent times is suggested by the increasing political salience of ethnicity, religion, nationalism, gender, and sexual orientation" (p. 404). But while status-based issues may be increasing in prominence, especially within the upper class, economic issues still predominate in the minds of voters. Government spending and income-maintenance programs are more salient among voters than are topics like abortion and gay marriage (Bartels 2008). The 2010 Congressional election would appear to affirm the priority of economic issues like employment and taxes.

Holding Political Office

Holding political office is another and more substantial means by which to wield political power. White males dominate political positions at the federal level. In terms of absolute figures, the number of Black elected officials has gone up dramatically since 1970. In 2001, there were 9,101 Black elected officials, compared to 1,469 in 1970. But Blacks still compose only about 2 percent of all elected officials, even though they make up over 11 percent of the voting-age population. Under 1 percent of these positions are at the federal level. In the 112th House of Representatives, 44 of the 435 members, or 10 percent, were Black, compared to 23 Hispanic, nine Asian American, and one Native American members. The 112th Senate in 2011 had no Black members, compared with two Hispanics and two Asian Americans. At the same time, there was only one openly gay person in the Congress. In total, minority persons made up about 18 percent of the House and 4 percent of the Senate in 2011.

Women in general are underrepresented in elected political positions. Seventy-three (17%) of the 435 members of the 2011 House of Represen-

Women and minorities are underrepresented on Capitol Hill in Washington, D.C. In 2011, only 17 percent of the House of Representatives and 15 percent of Senate members were women. Racial and ethnic minorities composed 18 percent of the House and 4 percent of the Senate. (© Brandon Bourdages/ Shutterstock)

tatives were women; 15 (15%) of the members of the Senate were women. Although the first woman was elected to the House of Representatives in 1916, the influx of women into the Congress is a relatively recent phenomenon. Regular increases in the number of women serving in Congress began in the 1970s. About one-third of all the women ever to have served in Congress were members in 2006 (Palmer and Simon 2006).

Despite the increased movement of women into elected federal positions, gender stereotypes still create obstacles for them. Men have more often held leadership positions and have, consequently, been thought to have stronger leadership qualities. Whereas men are viewed as being more forceful, sure of themselves, and knowledgeable, women are generally seen as being more compassionate, relational, and open to compromise. Stereotypes are also one of the reasons women are less likely than men to consider running for office (Dolan 2005; Palmer and Simon 2006; Carli and Eagly 2007). Counteracting these pressures has been the international women's movement, which has fostered an increase in participation by women

in the political process (Paxton, Hughes, and Green 2006). Internationally, however, women still lag behind men in holding legislative positions. Worldwide in 2009, only 14 heads of government were women, and only one in six cabinet members was a woman. Moreover, in only a small number of countries do women compose more than 30 percent of members of parliament (United Nations 2010).

In addition to gender and race, socioeconomic status has also been tied to holding political office. Historically, most members of Congress not only have been White men, but also members of the middle or upper class, and a majority have been lawyers, bankers, or other businessmen (Matthews 1954). The Congress of 2011 was similarly composed; 80 of the 100 Senators were either lawyers or business people, while only 3 were blue-collar workers. In the House of Representatives, 329 of the 435 members (76%) were in business or law; 13 (3%) were in blue-collar labor (*CQ Roll Call,* November 4, 2010). The overrepresentation of individuals from higher-status backgrounds has clearly continued in Congress.

The executive branch has also contained disproportionate numbers of higher-status individuals. Mintz (1975) and Freitag (1975) researched the class backgrounds of *all* cabinet officers during the period from 1897 to 1973 and found that there were strong ties to the upper class. A full 66 percent of these officers were from upper-class backgrounds and 90 percent had occupied a top corporate position before or after being appointed or had upper-class origins. The particular political party that happened to be in power at the time did not make much difference (Mintz 1975). Freitag's analysis supports Mills's conclusion that there is a clear connection between corporate and political elites and does not support Keller's and other pluralists' arguments about autonomous elites. His study, based on biographical information for all cabinet secretaries from McKinley to Nixon's first term, involving 358 cabinet positions, shows that *at least* 76 percent of cabinet members were tied to the corporate sector by being either corporate executives, officers, or corporate lawyers. Since President Truman's administration, this percent is even higher: 86 percent under Eisenhower, 77 percent under Kennedy, 86 percent under Johnson, and 96 percent under Nixon (Freitag 1975). Freitag concluded that the data do not prove that the corporate and governmental elite sectors are unified in terms of policies, but they do suggest that it is a "serious possibility" that the cabinet may be accountable to large corporations.

A predominance of individuals in Cabinet positions with strong ties to business continued under the Reagan, Clinton, and Bush administrations. During the Reagan administration, the initial secretaries of commerce, health and human services, labor, transportation, and treasury had business backgrounds. Under Clinton, a Democratic president, the first secretaries of state, defense, treasury, agriculture, and energy had been executives, owners, or had other strong ties to business. In the Republican administration of George W. Bush, the vice president, national security advisor, and secretaries of state, defense, treasury, and transportation all had held top executive positions in business (Domhoff 2002).

Top federal officials are not likely to come from working-class or lower-class families. Presidents also tend to come from higher educational and occupational backgrounds, and certain ethnic backgrounds are overrepresented in these positions. For example, 34 of the first 44 presidents (Washington through Obama) had college degrees, and the vast majority of them received their educations at elite schools in the Northeast. Twenty-eight of them were lawyers by occupation.

For over two decades, Dye (2002) has documented the characteristics, backgrounds, and interconnections of the institutional elite in the United States. He included in his definition of elites all those who occupy positions of high authority in the governmental, media, educational, civic/cultural, military, financial, industrial, and legal institutions in the United States. Considering only the governmental elite—that is, those who occupy the top positions in the executive, legislative, and judicial branches—almost 75 percent have law or other advanced degrees. More than 40 percent are graduates of highly prestigious, private universities or

---

MINI-CASE 5.1

States' Rights versus the Federal Government

One of the main reasons for the Civil War was disagreement about the power of individual states versus the power of the central federal government. This issue has not disappeared. States often differ in their laws over fundamental issues such as gun control, Medicaid, and what constitutes a crime or a legitimate marriage. As in the case of the definition of marriage, sometimes these laws clash with federal law. For example, two same-sex individuals who are legitimately married according to their state's law are not recognized as a married couple under the 1996 federal Defense of Marriage Act (DOMA). As a result, from the point of view of the state, individuals may have certain rights, but not according to federal law. When, if ever, should state law take precedence over federal law? ∎

colleges. Women and African Americans, as might be expected, are grossly underrepresented.

What is the meaning of these studies in terms of the perspectives on power presented earlier? If the essence of pluralism is the presence of a rough balance of power between constituencies with different interests, then these data clearly do not support the pluralist position. Some groups—most notably women, racial minorities, and working- or lower-class individuals—are seldom found in national-level offices of political power. To the extent that these offices are a principal means by which to gain and exercise political power, and that incumbents reflect and work for their own interests, then some groups have much less power than others.

INTERLINKAGE OF ECONOMIC AND POLITICAL POWER

As noted in Chapter 1, there has been a long-standing concern for keeping economic power from contaminating the political arena and thereby keeping those who are wealthy from controlling the political process. A recent analysis of data from numerous advanced democratic nations, including the United States, demonstrates the significant relationship between economic inequality and political participation. Greater income inequality reduces interest in political issues, dampens political debate, and lowers voter participation among all citizens except the wealthy (Solt 2008). When compared to past active protests and mass movements against the political power of wealth, "the democratic urge to rein in the dangerous ambitions of privileged elites has grown frail" (Fraser and Gerstle 2005, p. 291). Those who have higher incomes can maintain their interest and involvement in politics because they have an inordinate effect on the political process, shaping policies that fit their own interests rather than those of the majority: "Rarely have elites pioneered on the frontiers of democratic reform" (Fraser and Gerstle 2005, p. 287). This may be a partial explanation for the consistent relationship that has existed between socioeconomic status and voting. In the absence of effective power, the nonwealthy and uneducated

may feel that the political process is out of their hands. These findings give credence to arguments going back to Aristotle, Tocqueville, and others, that contend there is a close tie between economic equality and political democracy. The studies discussed earlier in this chapter show that office incumbents are most likely to come from high social classes. This class connection raises additional questions about the relationship between economic and political power. First, are political action committees (PACs) and lobbying groups so influential in the political process as to suggest dominance by one social class? Does money buy elections and votes? Second, and perhaps most important, is the upper class in general and its ruling "power elite" as united as Domhoff suggests?

Candidate Selection and Campaign Funding

Running for a federal political office is extremely expensive. The 2008 presidential and congressional campaigns, during which $5.3 billion was spent, outdid the 2004 elections by $1.1 billion (Center for Responsive Politics 2008). The 2010 congressional elections cost an estimated $4 billion. Short of actual occupancy in a political office, another substantial manner in which an individual or organization can attempt to have political impact is through direct influence of officeholders. In the recent past, direct lobbying has been carried out by various groups with financial power. Since the 1960s, there has been a significant increase in the number and activity of interest groups, an increased centralization of their headquarters in Washington, D.C., a rise in the number of public-interest and single-issue interest groups, and more "formal penetration" on their part into governmental activities (Cigler and Loomis 1995). The number of PACs has spiraled upward in recent years, reaching 4,611 in 2009. Basically, **political action committees (PACs)** are interest groups that receive money from individuals sympathetic to their cause(s), so they can affect a federal election.

PACs represent many different interest groups. Corporations, labor, assorted trade associations, and nonconnected specific-issues groups are among the organizations with PACs, and each follows different strategies. In 2009–2010, the top 10 PACs spent between $2 and $3.5 million each.

So-called super PACs developed in 2010 as a result of a Supreme Court decision on campaign financing. These groups can raise unlimited amounts of money from organizations and individuals and then spend unlimited amounts in support of specific issues or candidates. The most successful super PAC, American Crossroads, raised about $22 million by July 2010 for the fall congressional elections. But unlike PACs in general, super PACs cannot give funds directly to a candidate (Center for Responsive Politics 2010).

Contributions by PACs are part of the "soft money" candidates receive during their campaigns. Such funds also include money from individuals, unions, and corporations. Loopholes in federal legislation have fostered growth in the amount of soft money in political campaigns. More money has flooded into political campaigns because of recent Court rulings. The Supreme Court's decision in the *Citizens United v. Federal Election Commission* opened the door to unlimited spending by corporations and unions, arguing that these organizations have the same First Amendment rights to free speech as individuals. While they cannot give money directly to individual candidates, these organizations can use their own money to fund federal election campaigns that advocate issues and candidates that they prefer.

The concern over the influence of PACs is based on the assumption that, *as a monolithic group,* contributors disproportionately influence federal policies. But it should be kept in mind that these groups vary widely in their specific interests and are not monolithic in this sense. In fact, the proliferation of varying interest groups might be viewed as an indication of pluralism at work (Alexander 1992). At the same time, however, there is some question about whether the attention paid to *specific* interest groups will hinder the ability of governing officials to effectively address problems that affect the *general* interest of U.S. society (Cigler and Loomis 1995).

Regarding the issue of PACs and their impact, studies suggest that although PACs may increase an individual's access to given members of Congress, they do not systematically affect how these members vote. However, Senator Russell B. Long once said that "the distinction between a large campaign contribution and a bribe is almost a hairline's difference" (quoted in Stern 1988, p. 146). But in a research study on 20 labor-related issues in the U.S. House of Representativ es, Jones and Keiser (1987) found that the amount of contributions from union-approved PACs was related to voting only on issues that had little media attention. In other words, the less visible the issue, the greater the effect of contributions on voting behavior.

An analysis of 120 PACs connected to 10 different organizations examined the effect of PACs on the voting behavior of members of the House of Representatives and no significant influence on voting was found. However, these PACs and the organizations they represent can influence voting to the extent that they can influence the election process in the districts from which these congressional members originate (Grenzke 1989). It is not through the amount of the PAC contribution itself, but through other mechanisms that economically powerful groups can influence voting patterns. Peoples and Gortari (2008) found that U.S. Representatives who received funds from the same *business* groups voted in a similar manner, but did not vote in the same way if they received money from the same *labor* organizations. In a study of Ohio state legislators, Peoples (2008) discovered that contributions affect voting of lawmakers primarily when they are in the same party. The qualifications and varied results in these studies suggest that contributions may have an effect only under certain conditions. The conditions included and methods used in these studies differ, yielding different findings. An overview of 33 research studies on the relationship between monetary contributions and roll call voting found mixed results, with some studies suggesting that contributions have a major impact while others find that they have little or no effect on public voting by congressional members (Baumgartner and Leech 1998).

The impact of money on elections and voting continues as an issue largely because it pits

NUTSHELL 5.1   Money, Politics, and Justice

The infiltration of money into the political process has been an ongoing concern throughout U.S. history. Alexander Hamilton and John Jay, our first chief justice, believed that the people who own the country ought to run it, whereas Thomas Jefferson and Theodore Roosevelt argued against and tried to stem the tendency towards a plutocracy, that is, government by the wealthy. It should come as no surprise then that the issue of unlimited and unrestricted campaign contributions would be a hot-button topic that would rally opposing groups to loudly argue their positions.

On January 21, 2010, these positions intensified when the United States Supreme Court issued a ruling in the case of *Citizens United v. Federal Election Commission*, 130 S. Ct. 876 (2010). Briefly, the 5-4 majority opinion ruled that a section of the Bipartisan Campaign Reform Act (popularly known as the "McCain-Feingold Act"), which prohibited corporations and unions from spending money on media political ads during the final stages of campaigns, violated the First Amendment to the United States Constitution. Citing prior decisions which recognized that corporations have First Amendment rights, the Court concluded that the ban on such corporate spending was an impermissible ban on speech. The decision conflicted with laws in 24 states that banned corporations from using money from their general funds in campaigns. It also further polarized opinions. President Obama saw it as a victory for big companies and interest groups and a setback for ordinary Americans who have little leverage and little money.

The Supreme Court was clearly divided on the issue. Proponents viewed the decision as a victory for the First Amendment that in part says, "Congress shall make no law . . . abridging the freedom of speech." Even though corporations are not flesh-and-blood entities, under the law they have the same rights and responsibilities as persons. Consequently, being allowed to spend one's money the way one wants is one aspect of the individual's (or corporation's) right to free speech. "Political speech is 'indispensable to decision making in a democracy, and this is no less true because the speech comes from a corporation rather than an individual.'" *Citizens United,*

130 S. Ct. at 904 (quoting *First Nat'l Bank v. Bellotti,* 435 U.S. 765, 777 [1978]; footnote omitted). Judges supporting the decision did not believe it would undermine public support for the government: "The appearance of influence or access, furthermore, will not cause the electorate to lose faith in our democracy." *Citizens United,* 130 S. Ct. at 910 (citing *Buckley v. Valeo,* 424 U.S. 1, 46, 96 S. Ct. 612 [1976]).

Opponents of the decision worried about the potential flood of money that may lead to the buying of government positions by those with the most wealth. Former Supreme Court Justice Stevens, dissenting from the majority decision in *Citizens United,* argued that giving corporations the same status as individuals was wrong, that corporations and individuals are not the same. "In the context of election to public office, the distinction between corporate and human speakers is significant. Although they make enormous contributions to our society, corporations are not actually members of it" (*Citizens United,* 130 S. Ct. at 930 [Stevens, J., dissenting]). He also contended that the decision overturns past rulings that limited corporate spending: "The majority's approach to corporate electioneering marks a dramatic break from our past. Congress has placed special limitations on campaign spending by corporations ever since the passage of the Tillman Act in 1907" (*Citizens United,* 130 S. Ct. at 930 [Stevens, J., dissenting]). Finally, Justice Stevens argued that lawmakers have a duty to guard against possibly negative effects of corporate spending in local and national elections. One of these effects, he feared, was a weakened stature for the Court: "The Court's ruling threatens to undermine the integrity of elected institutions across the Nation. The path it has taken to reach its outcome well, I fear, do damage to this institution" (*Citizens United,* 130 S. Ct. at 931 [Stevens, J., dissenting]).

The costs for state and federal elections have skyrocketed. These include spending for supreme court positions in the states' court systems, which more than doubled since the 1990s to $207 million in the 2000–2009 period. The economic tug-of-war for these elections primarily involved powerful interest groups on the right and left who sought to move the justice system in their direction. U.S. Supreme

(*continued*)

NUTSHELL 5.1   *(continued)*

Court Justice Ruth Bader Ginsberg and former U.S. Justice Sandra Day O'Connor worry that this trend can erode the average American's belief in the fairness of the justice system and confirm the belief of those who feel that those with money rule. A central question, of course, is whether the election of a given state court judge means that he or she will always cast decisions favorable to the interests that heavily funded the election. The majority in the *Citizens United* decision apparently would not envision a problem here. "The fact that speakers may

have influence over or access to elected officials does not mean that these officials are corrupt" (*Citizens United*, 130 S. Ct. at 910).

Sources: Neal Peirce, "A Gusher of Campaign Money Infects Judicial Elections," *Akron Beacon Journal*, August 30, 2010, p. A7; Kristin Sullivan, and Terrance Adams, "Summary of *Citizens United v. Federal Election Commission*," *OLR Research Report* 2010-R-0124, March 2, 2010; Adam Liptak, "Justices, 5-4, Reject Corporate Spending Limit," *New York Times*, late edition, January 22, 2010, pp. A1 and A18; and *Citizens United v. Federal Election Commission*, 130 S. Ct. 876 (2010).

those who are concerned about the corruption of politics against those who believe that everyone, including corporations and labor unions, should be allowed to spend their money as they wish. The recent Supreme Court ruling supporting First Amendment rights for corporations and other organizations served to bring this debate more fully into the public consciousness.

RULING-CLASS UNITY

Concerns about soft money and the power of PACs are related to suspicions that those with plentiful resources are unified and will exercise disproportionate control of the political process. Most of the data on elite cohesiveness indicate that the elite are broadly unified because of similarities in class background, membership patterns on corporate boards, and political behavior (Roscigno 1992).

Mills's and Domhoff's descriptions of the social backgrounds of the elite and the historical circumstances in which they rule suggest that they are unified. Domhoff described their common membership in and interaction at exclusive clubs, attendance at elite schools, and frequent listing on the Social Register, while Mills described not only their social-psychological similarities but also the concentration and coalescence that occurred among the major institutions involved in the power elite. Domhoff detailed some evidence of

intermarriages, unique schooling, and common leisure and social activities that point, he argued, to the existence of a cohesive upper class of which the public is conscious.

Ostrander's (1984) and Kendall's (2002) studies of upper-class women suggest that they are highly conscious of their class and their responsibilities in maintaining their social-class position. As supporters of their husbands' economic activities, and as members of voluntary associations and social clubs, upper-class women work to perpetuate their social class. Although there are tensions and individual disagreements within this group, as a whole they are united in defense of their class. This helps to maintain not only their class but also, because it is male dominated, the subordinate position of these women within it (Ostrander 1984).

The studies cited focus on the unity of the upper class as a whole. Other studies reviewed earlier on political activity, however, also imply unification of the elite as a group, many of whom are not of upper-class backgrounds. In his study of elites, involving individuals from a variety of institutional areas, Dye (2002) also concluded that there is general unity of opinion among the elite, even though there is some evidence of rising factionalism within it.

Verba and Orren's study of 2,762 leaders from various institutional areas in the late 1970s also suggests unity on *basic values*. They found that all types of leaders tend to agree, for example, that a fair distribution of economic resources is one in which everyone has equal opportunity to pursue legitimate goals. They do not feel that everyone should have an equal amount, however. This solidarity of opinion included African American, feminist, and labor leaders. However, when it comes to opinions on *specific* matters rather than *general* values, or to descriptions of actual rather than ideal situations, there is disagreement among these leaders. For example, only 9 percent of business leaders view poverty as the result of the workings of the economic system, whereas 86 percent of African American leaders and 76 percent of feminist leaders see it this way (Verba and Orren 1985, p. 74). Seider's (1974) content analysis of the speeches of big-business executives also indicated that although there are differences among them on specifics, there is fundamental unity on beliefs supporting the capitalist economic system that are never challenged.

Even though he has concluded that the elite are generally united on basic values, Dye (2002) argued that a split has developed within the elite between those he labels the "sunbelt cowboys" and the "established yankees." As the labels suggest, the "cowboys" as a group are individualistic, conservative, and often from non-upper-class backgrounds. Their wealth has been recently acquired. In contrast, the "yankees" tend to be more liberal and have established family wealth. They have attended the best Ivy League schools and are also likely to have occupied high positions in prestigious corporate, financial, or legal institutions. Thus, as to the issue of how unified the elite or upper class is, it is important to indicate whether one is speaking of the *general* or *specific* level, in *ideal* or *real-situational* terms, and of *social background* or *behavioral* unity. In some ways, these groups appear unified and in others they do not; the results from attitudinal and positional studies on unity are clearly mixed and one can find statistics to support both positions.

Like Domhoff, Dye, and others, Useem has dissected the capitalist class and its unity in detail. His studies concern the structural texture of that class (cf. 1978, 1979, 1984). Useem defined the capitalist class as "those who own or manage major business firms and their immediate kin" (1980, p. 200). In one analysis, he studied 2,843 officers from 200 corporations that varied in size and sector. The officers also differed in the number of corporations to which they were tied through directorships. Generally, Useem found that members of the capitalist class are not equally powerful. Those from larger firms who were also directors at other corporations were significantly more likely to have served on advisory committees for government at the local, state, and federal levels. They were also more likely to participate in national business groups such as the Business Roundtable, Business Council, Council on Foreign Relations, National Association of Manufacturers, and U.S. Chamber of Commerce and to be involved in significant cultural organizations (elite university boards, and art and research organizations; Useem 1980). Useem, however, did not find significant participation differences between major industrialists and financiers.

In other research, Useem directly addressed the issue of the political unity of what he calls the "inner circle" of business, looking at whether members of this group act on behalf of their own separate corporations or on behalf of the capitalist class as a whole. Useem drew his information and conclusions from a wide variety of data sources, including personal interviews and documentary and survey data. The inner circle he described is a network of leaders from large corporations who serve as top officers at more than one firm, who are politically active, and who serve the interests of the capitalist class as a whole rather than the narrow immediate interests of their individual companies. To be a member of the inner circle, it helps to (1) have been successful in a major corporation, (2) have multiple directorships, (3) have occupied a senior position, (4) be a member of business associations, and (5) have been a consultant or advisor to government. Members of the inner circle are more often members of the upper class than are other business leaders—that is, they are richer, have attended elite prep schools, and are in the Social Register (Useem 1984, pp. 65–69). The circle's political style is to adopt a "posture of compromise" and accommodation rather than to be directly confrontational on any specific issue. Its interests are in the general protection of capitalism as a whole, not in the interests of specific companies.

Useem (1984) viewed capitalism in the United States as having moved from (1) "family capitalism" in which individual upper-class families dominated corporate ownership, through (2) "managerial capitalism" in which managers began to replace the dominance of upper-class owners around the turn of the twentieth century, to (3) "institutional capitalism" in which networks of intercorporate ties characterize the core of capitalism. The increasing control of corporations by their managers rather than owners and the increased concentration and interlocking in the corporate sector during this century have helped lay the basis for the development of this powerful circle.

Indeed, Dye's study (2002) of individuals in top institutional positions revealed that 6,000 individuals have formal control over 50 percent of the country's industrial, banking, communications, insurance, educational, legal, and cultural assets. The top 500 out of 5 million corporations control about 60 percent of all corporate assets. Twenty-five banks out of 12,000 possess over 50 percent of all banking assets in the United States, and 30 of the 2,000 insurance companies control over half of all insurance assets. Some 15 percent of the 7,314 institutional leaders studied by Dye occupied more than one top position (i.e., were interlockers) and a smaller percent held as many as six or more such positions. He viewed this "inner group" as cohesive for a number of reasons, and, like Useem, found that multiple corporate interlockers were more likely than single directors to participate in governmental and other major organizations. Inner-circle members play crucial political roles by directing nonprofit organizations, serving as political fund-raisers, endorsing candidates, giving larger campaign contributions, and influencing media content (Useem 1984, pp. 76–94).

This inner circle is much more politically active than business in general because its members occupy several important positions at once, which (1) creates cohesiveness among its members,

(2) helps mobilize economic and other resources, and (3) provides a powerful platform from which to express political positions. Moreover, its members are also closely tied to the upper class, which increases the circle's influence (Useem 1984). In contrast to other research, Useem found that if members of the upper class are in the business elite, they are more likely than persons from other classes to get into the inner circle. In sum, characteristics of the U.S. political economy create opportunities for the interconnection of political and economic power.

A significant part of the reason for the tie between economic and political power lies in the interlocking between private and corporate wealth and political opportunity. It takes wealth, or at least access to wealth, to run a viable campaign for a major national political office. The connection between economic and political power may be deeper than this suggests, however, and may be based not on the characteristics of particular *individuals* but rather on the *structure and functioning* of the society.

The *structuralist* position suggests that given the structure of a capitalist society such as the United States, the government *must* act in a manner that supports the capitalist class and capitalism in general. This occurs regardless of who is in office. Political and economic institutions are so intertwined that the government, although it may be "relatively autonomous," is constrained to support and pass policies that maintain the capitalist economy. The state needs to provide a hospitable environment for investment and create a stable and smooth-running economy because it relies on the returns from the economy for its revenue. A stable economy also encourages political support for the government. In addition, the state provides programs (e.g., welfare, unemployment compensation) to deal with the fallout that comes from the operation of a capitalist system in which a relatively small number of corporations exercise inordinate influence. Inevitably, the state becomes involved in economic matters (O'Connor 1973; Block 1977). During the 2008–2009 economic crisis, for example, the U.S. government provided hundreds of billions of dollars to large financial institutions—despite widespread public opposition—arguing that such support was needed to strengthen all aspects of the economy.

The preceding studies on campaign financing, holding office, and the capitalist economy indicate that both individuals and structural arrangements foster a relationship between economic and political power. Structural ties among institutions make it possible for some individuals to have access to positions of great power. According to some, however, one of the major problems with both these analyses is that they assume that all major policies are made within the government and, therefore, the focus of both approaches is on the state. In fact, it has been suggested, many major policies are created outside the government, principally by the actions of corporations. Industrial change, for example, to the extent that it can be considered a "policy," has largely been the result of actions by the private sector, not the government (Schwartz 1987).

POWER INEQUALITY IN THE WORK EXPERIENCE

The discussion so far should leave little doubt that, by a variety of measures, there is extensive inequality in power at the national level. The focus in this section will be on power differentials that are experienced by individuals in their everyday work world. Unfortunately, until recently organization-level data have seldom been the focus for studies of inequality (Stainback, Tomaskovic-Devey, and Skaggs 2010). The power differences found in organizations are often related to central characteristics of organizations, as well as to society-wide issues of race, gender, and class. What exists and happens *outside* organizations often infiltrates and affects what happens *within* them. As we will see in Chapter 13, there have been social movements going on for decades based on class, race, and gender that are generally organized attempts to gain greater power in society. The historical conflict between labor and management, for example, was generally one over the relative power and control of each side. In addition, developments in technology have allowed contemporary corporations to expand their monitoring power and control over their employees. With cell phones, BlackBerries, e-mail, texting, and iPads, is it ever possible for a manager to escape from work? Technology has broken down the traditional divide between work and home, the public and private spheres.

The structures and traditions of organizations themselves affect the manner in which power is organized and exercised. Total institutions such as the military and strict religious orders, with their clear, fixed, and legitimate hierarchies and complete control over members, perhaps provide the best expression of the use of power in organizations. Power differentials in organizations can be maintained simply because of the inertia that exists in them (Stainback, Tomaskovic-Devey, and Skaggs 2010). The status quo can be comfortable and inviolate, while change can be threatening and disruptive. Older, smaller organizations with long-standing patrimonial traditions tend to rely upon factors like age, kinship, and seniority rather than a formal hierarchy as bases for the exercise of power. Still other organizations rely on the charisma and normative power of their leaders to control their members.

Power itself can be situational, that is, it may be operative only in particular contexts (e.g., at work but not elsewhere), or it may be trans-situational, that is, apply regardless of the situation (e.g., as against a minority person). Power can also be derived from a number of sources. As the examples above suggest, sometimes power is based on one's formal position in an organization (*legitimate* power). In other situations, power is based on one's knowledge (*expert* power), attractiveness (*referent* power), ability to reward (*reward* power), or ability to punish (*coercive* power) (French and Raven 1959). *Information* can also be a base of power (Raven 1965) as can connections or associations one has with others (*referred* power). In each of these cases, but for different reasons, one person is *dependent* on another, and can be constrained to act in a particular way despite his or her resistance. In their classic study of working-class employees, for example, Sennett and Cobb (1973) found that workers promoted greater independence for their children by encouraging college educations so that they could become professionals rather than manual workers; that is, they wanted their children to have autonomy in their jobs and be able to exercise greater control over their own lives.

The different bases of power conjure up some interesting scenarios about the relationship between power on the one hand, and race, class, and gender on the other. Men, for example, are thought to possess more expert and legitimate power than women, while women are believed to have more referent power, that is, their greater likeability gives them some leverage in relationships (Carli 1999). Individuals in lower-authority positions, secretaries for example, can exercise power through their control or possession of information. Professionals who have a specialized knowledge/experience can exercise power over higher-ranking individuals who are dependent on their expertise. Persons who appear threatening to others, for example, Black males, can exercise control over others with higher status based on their perceived power to coerce. These are just a few of the ways in which bases of power are linked to race, class, and gender in everyday life.

In addition, power relationships are shaped by people's mental biases and beliefs about individuals in other groups. Gender ideology, racism, and class distinctions are frequently implicated in the treatment employees receive from others, including their superiors. Internalized images about the fundamental traits of men versus women, Blacks versus Whites, and professional versus working-class manual workers affect the way members of each group relate to individuals in the other group. Gender and racial stereotypes also have impacts on the kinds of positions for which candidates are deemed suitable, and on the relative power of individuals once they obtain positions in work organizations (Stainback, Tomaskovic-Devey, and Skaggs 2010). Whether a job requires "masculine" or "feminine" abilities, for example, can affect who is hired into the position (Gorman 2005; King and Cornwall 2007). In some cases, beliefs about a lower-status group can even allow a person in a lower position in the organization to dominate a superior, as when, for example, a male subordinate harasses a female supervisor (Rospenda, Richman,

and Nawyn 1998). Thus, power at work and at home are often derived from the dominant society-wide ideologies and policies about gender, sexuality, race, and class.

Bullying is a good example of how cultural ideologies about women and minorities affect power in the workplace. *Bullying* refers to "*repeated* and *persistent negative* acts towards one or more *individual(s),* which involve a *perceived power imbalance* and create a *hostile work environment*" (Salin 2003, pp. 1214–1215; italics in original). While supervisors, who have power because of their formal position, can and sometimes do bully subordinates, bullying can also occur between individuals who are formally equal in their work positions, but who differ in race, class, or gender. In other words, power imbalances between groups in the wider society can infiltrate the work setting. "Thus, for example, power differences associated with traditional gender roles and minority status may also affect bullying behavior, as it can be assumed that women and minorities are perceived to have less power and status" (Salin 2003, p. 1219). The differential status of individuals invites a greater probability of bullying. Employees who are women, lower-paid workers, or members of a minority are more likely to be victims of bullying than their higher-status counterparts, as are temporary employees or those with little job security (Roscigno, Lopez, and Hodson 2009).

Conditions in the work environment, such as a poorly articulated organizational structure, a lack of accountability, and the absence of groups to protect the vulnerable, also enhance the probability of bullying behavior (Roscigno, Lopez, and Hodson 2009). Power and bullying are likely to operate when serious competition exists and significant rewards are at stake. When a company is bought out or merges with another, it becomes apparent how dependent and how powerless employees are. It is often when the economic environment is changing or uncertain, when resources are limited or strained, or when the decision-making process is not fixed that many of the nonlegitimate forms of power cited above become most evident in an organization because battles over turf, position, and rewards become more prominent under these conditions. Battles for power in the workplace often bring racial, gender, and class ideologies and related discourses to the foreground.

Women and members of minorities generally occupy positions of lower authority and greater dependence than White males. Individuals in these positions often complain about the lack of respect they receive (cf., e.g., Johnson 2002). Minorities and women have less power than White men at work, in part because of less education and/or experience. But even if these deficiencies did not exist, women and minorities would still have difficulty gaining power because of racism and gender bias that could be used by White men to keep these groups out of power (Elliott and Smith 2004). Men not only are more likely to dominate positions of high authority, but also to screen potential colleagues so that individuals who are similar to them are admitted into those positions while those who are dissimilar are screened out.

Central characteristics held by those in power become a basis for favorable evaluations while opposite characteristics become a basis for unfavorable evaluations (DiTomaso, Post, and Parks-Yancey 2007). Individuals are more attracted to persons who are like themselves, and are, therefore, more likely to interpret the behaviors of those individuals in a positive manner while interpreting the behavior of dissimilar others in a more negative manner: people who are like us are successful because they work hard and are talented, whereas people who are not like us are successful because they are lucky or were given a break (Stainback, Tomaskovic-Devey, and Skaggs 2010). Because the duties of executive positions tend to be central to organizations, yet broad in scope, it is important to those already at the top that reliable (i.e., similar) persons be brought in when vacancies occur. The result is "homosocial reproduction" in which White men in high-level positions recruit other men similar to themselves (Kanter 1977a).

To move up the authority ladder, one needs a "cognitive map" of the social network at the organization and may have to be a "team player" as well. To be such a player, one has to appear to be similar to colleagues, subscribe to the dominant approach or ideology of the organization, and spend a lot of time at the office. All these qualities make other managers or executives feel comfortable with you (Jackall 1988). It is when people step out of line, violate traditional cultural expectations, or are believed to have a distinct outlook or lifestyle that difficulties arise for them. In their study of sexual harassment, for example, Uggen and Blackstone (2004) found that "women in supervisory positions and men who do more housework are likely to experience the behavioral harassment syndrome" (p. 83).

If a "token" or dissimilar person such as a woman or working-class or minority person does reach a high level in an organization, she or he will be under intense pressure to perform and conform to racial, class, or gender expectations. Research indicates that women, for example, face greater pressure and discrimination as they gain experience and move up the corporate ladder (Kanter 1977b; Carli 1999; Elliott and Smith 2004; Uggen and Blackstone 2004). In part, this is because they are viewed as outsiders to the males who dominate the positions, and because they are expected to conform to mainstream gender expectations about women at the same time that they are also expected to excel at their jobs. This often produces such a high degree of pressure that some women resign their positions. "A woman who behaves in a competent and assertive manner is often less influential, particularly with men, because she lacks legitimacy. At the same time, when a women does not exhibit exceptional ability, her competence is doubted by both genders and she is less able to influence women. These findings underscore the dilemma that women face in the workplace" (Carli 1999, p. 95).

Such pressure and the power used with it can be justified by gender, class, or racial ideologies, or by one's perception of the "target" of the pressure. Bruins (1999) theorizes that "the stronger the means of influence used by the agent [of power], the more the agent [e.g., White male] will tend toward making an internal attribution for the target's [e.g., minority, woman] compliance, in turn leading to a more negative evaluation of the target and a tendency to increase the social distance toward the target" (p. 10). In other words, claims about the basic inferiority or inadequacy of the target will be used as justifications as more force or power is exercised over the subordinate.

Jennifer Pierce's findings (1995) on women lawyers from her research on legal firms demonstrate these pressures, and reveal how "masculine" traits (e.g., aggressiveness, directness, competitiveness) of "Rambo litigators" are thought to be more valuable and effective in the courtroom than "feminine" qualities (e.g., empathy, emotionality, sociability), even though this does not always prove to be the case. Female paralegals in these firms as well were dominated by being expected to defer to and "take care of" their male bosses. In sum, these women were expected to be therapists, mothers, listeners, and supporters for male lawyers. Male paralegals did not have the same expectations placed on them. The result is that women needed to engage in more emotional labor to appear successful to colleagues.

The success or power one has at work affects power relationships at home. Traditionally, husbands' power at home has been tied to their ability to support their families through their occupations. Their work in the public sphere has generally meant, especially in past generations, that their wives' efforts were restricted to the private sphere of family. The balance of power and dependence has shifted as more women have entered the labor force and earn their own salaries. However, this does not always mean that their increased independence is accepted at home, because it violates traditional beliefs about appropriate gender roles. A recent study of U.S.-born Mexican Americans found that the more women earned outside the family and participated in decision making at home, the more spousal abuse they reported (Harris, Firestone, and Vega 2005).

POWER INEQUALITY IN A GLOBAL AND GLOBALIZING CONTEXT

I have noted above that power maneuvers and differences are most likely to become salient when economic conditions are in a state of flux, when one's employment and income are at stake. An unpredictable economy produces a sense of competition among its workers, workers who will use the tools at their disposal to maintain or attain scarce positions. Among these tools are cultural ideologies and policies that privilege some groups over others. Increasingly, the operation of national economies has become less predictable because of their involvement in the worldwide network of economies and states.

Over the last few decades, there has been extensive discussion about the structure of the world economic system, the shifting relationships among nations, and the effects of globalization on the relative power of nations in the international order. In broad terms, the world system is often described as consisting of interdependent core, semiperipheral, and peripheral countries. Each of these types tends to perform particular functions in the world system. Core nations are those that are wealthy, industrialized, and technologically advanced. They hold a privileged position in the world economic system because they possess an inordinate amount of the world's capital and also have strong, stable political systems. Peripheral nations, on the other hand, are described as poor, technologically deficient, generally "underdeveloped," and lacking in political stability. Semiperipheral countries occupy an intermediate position in the system. Because the poor and working classes in peripheral nations are primarily racial minorities and women, economic, political, and immigration relationships with core nations take on racial and gender overtones.

The global power of a nation partly depends upon the **"soft power"** it wields among its international neighbors. In contrast to the hard forms of power like military or economic, a country's soft power is based upon the respect accorded its culture, values, and ideals by other nations. Historically, a significant source of the international influence of the U.S. has been due to its soft power.

For all of the twentieth century, the West, particularly the United States, dominated international politics and economics. In recent years, however, some parts of Asia, especially China, have strengthened their international economic position.

In the next decade or two, China's productivity is expected to increase threefold. It is now a manufacturing giant, producing most of the world's toys, microwave ovens, shoes, and DVD players. In 2004, Wal-Mart alone imported $18 billion in products from China (Zakaria 2005). Its surging economic power and large population have also meant greater political leverage in the world system. With increasing openness in trade and foreign investment across the globe, China's progress suggests that a significant realignment in international power arrangements may be taking place.

Also part of the world's "new geography of power" are (a) transnational corporations that are beyond the full control of any given nation, (b) transnational legal institutions that regulate international economic relationships, and (c) the growth of electronic technology, which makes economic transactions possible independent of space. While these three developments may appear to reduce somewhat the regulatory power of sovereign states, they also mean that the state's role in the world political economy is also changing (Sassen 2000). Evidence indicates that between 1960 and 2000, core nations have strengthened their global power position by increasing their ties to international nongovernmental organizations and creating new ones (Beckfield 2003).

Historically, the economic power and political power of a nation have been intertwined. International economic expansion generally leads to more political power, power which is then used to maintain economic dominance. But today, capital and national governments are bases of international political power that are more autonomous than in the past. As Hanagan puts it, "[i]n an age when capital can electronically flee continents in nanoseconds, can national states resist national markets? Despite the claims of distinguished scholars, most nations simply cannot" (2000, p. 83). The developments mentioned above also have implications for the sources, nature, and extent of immigration to be discussed in subsequent chapters, and the structure of economic inequality within nations.

In addition to effects on its international position, the political structure of a country affects the degree of inequality within it. Numerous studies have found that political democracy is related to less economic inequality. In his study of 50 countries, for example, Muller (1988) found that the longer and more stable the democratic tradition in a country, the less income inequality it experienced. Conversely, when income inequality continues for a number of years, political democracy is undermined. These relationships persist even when a country's level of development is considered. Reuveny and Li's research (2003) using data from 69 developed and less-developed nations also revealed that democratic characteristics reduced income inequality in both types of nations.

Wider political input within a society also promotes less economic inequality. The greater the percentage of individuals who vote and the more wages are determined on a national basis, the lower is earnings inequality. A survey of 84 studies found that democracy indirectly promotes economic growth by fostering increases in human capital, economic freedom, and political stability (Doucouliagos and Ulubasoglu 2008). Increased governmental spending on social programs such as education and health care also encourages greater income equality (Rudra 2004). Greater participation by women in national legislatures, in turn, increases the probability for higher spending in these areas (Bolzendahl and Brooks 2007). Taken together, the results of these studies strongly suggest that policies reached democratically are most likely to benefit all citizens rather than just a privileged segment. This again alerts us to the significance of the democracy–equality connection.

Summary

We began this chapter with a brief discussion on the importance and difficulty of conceptualizing power. We then moved to an analysis of pluralist, power-elite, and ruling-class views of the national power structure, and the data that bear on the validity of each.

There are clear relationships between socio-economic position and voting, holding political office, and other forms of political participation. Those closer to the bottom of the class hierarchy are less likely than those in the middle and upper classes to vote, be elected to office, and be represented in powerful lobbying groups. Research indicates that those from higher socioeconomic levels, especially the upper class, are disproportionately represented in elite positions in a variety of institutional spheres. The tie between economic and political power, however, is more than just individual in nature; it is also structural. The fates of government and economy are linked, each needs the other. Consequently, a government in a society with a capitalist economy, for example, must support capitalism because its revenue and stability heavily depend on the smooth operation of that economy.

In addition to power differences at the national level, power inequality also exists in the workplace. Power has a variety of immediate sources within organizations but can also be rooted in broader cultural ideologies surrounding race, class, and/or gender. To some extent, power differentials are based in features of organizations themselves, including their traditions, the clarity and strength of their structure, and the presence or absence of positions to enforce accountability. They are also determined and maintained by broader ideologies and stereotypes regarding the characteristics of groups distinguished by race, sex, and social class.

Worldwide power differentials also exist between nations, as countries occupy different positions in the world's economic and political system. Throughout most of the twentieth century, the United States was a dominant political player. Transnational corporations and international nongovernmental organizations are part of a broader network that in many cases binds nations together but at the same time can benefit some more than others. Finally, the political structure within nations affects the degree of social inequality within them. Generally democratic characteristics lend themselves to less inequality.

Critical Thinking

1. Are information technology and the World Wide Web creating new bases for power and domination? Is it the corporate rich who will claim these bases or are new, powerful groups being created by these technological developments? Discuss your answer.
2. As globalization continues to open up nations to each other, do you think the soft power of a nation, that is, the respect for its culture, ideals, and values, will increasingly affect power arrangements between nations?
3. If the working and lower classes are underrepresented among those who vote, hold office, donate large sums of money to elections, and have effective lobbying power, how can we ensure representative or democratic government in the United States?
4. What features would you introduce into the design of an organization so that the chances of bullying and inappropriate use of power would be minimized?

Web Connections

The Center for Responsive Politics lists the amount of money spent on federal elections, along with the amounts given by major individual and organizational donors. The center also gives information on the political affiliations of these donors. Visit www.opensecrets.org. Another source, the Joint Center for Political and Economic Studies, presents summary information on Black elected officials at every level of government. Its information also allows you to compare rates for Black men and women as well as differences in rates between states. Where does your state stand on electing Blacks to office? Visit www.jointcenter.org.

CHAPTER 6

Sex and Gender Inequality

A woman can hardly ever choose . . . she is dependent on what happens to her.

GEORGE ELIOT (1819–1880)

Race and sex are ascribed statuses in the sense that there is a physical component to each of them. These physical components are given particular meanings within the context of a culture's values and beliefs, and a society's economic and political arrangements. What is immediately significant about race and sex, therefore, is not the differences in themselves, but the fact that these characteristics are socially defined and have meanings attached to them. These interpretations often result in races and sexes being hierarchically arranged and differentially treated in society. But not all women are in the same social and economic positions. Because the United States is a multicultural, multiracial society, the status of any woman is complicated by her race and class. As we will see, the position of a woman as well as the expectations of and interpretations associated with being a woman often depend on whether a woman is a member of a particular minority or class.

In Chapter 8, we will pursue an analysis of racial inequality and demonstrate how race, gender, sex, and economic inequality are intertwined. In this chapter, we will be surveying the forms and extent of gender inequality, as well as explanations for it. We begin with a brief overview of the historical condition of women in U.S. society.

THE STATUS OF WOMEN IN THE EARLY UNITED STATES

What has it meant to be a woman in the United States? When I was growing up in the 1940s, my parents had a traditional arrangement—my mother was a homemaker and my father "brought home the bacon." Earlier, however, my mother had worked in a hosiery factory. Throughout our nation's history, women have contributed to the economy while still maintaining a family.

In our own agricultural, preindustrial colonial society, women were directly involved in a variety of ways in production. On the one hand, their work contributed significantly to the prosperity of the society, but on the other hand, the nature of the labor was more often than not based on gender (Chafe 1977; Blau 1978; Marshall and Paulin 1987). The cultural norms of that time, as well as for the periods that followed, dictated that first and foremost, women should be good wives and mothers; but, in fact, women were involved in the economy and often had difficult lives. They were involved in raising stock, weaving, gardening, and even running businesses. While some women took over for their deceased or disabled husbands, most of the unmarried and widowed women went on the market as hired domestic workers (Marshall and Paulin 1987).

Although there is some debate about the actual diversity of employment undertaken by women during this period, they made valuable contributions to local economies, but were deprived of many of the political-legal, economic, and personal rights accorded men. They were attached to their families in a literal way, dependent on and subservient to their husbands (Matthaei 1982). A woman's identity was defined by her relationship to her husband and children. Moreover, wife beating was fairly common at this time. "The husband had the right to chastise his wife physically, and he had exclusive rights to any property she might have owned as a single woman, to her dower, and to any wages and property that might come to her while she was his wife. In short, like slave or servant women, married women whether rich or poor were legal non-entities" (Foner 1979, p. 11). Thus, the idealized life of the female as someone removed from the harsh realities of economic life was strongly inconsistent with the actual circumstances of her life.

Through their economic activities, women contributed to the development of the first significant *industrial* organizations in the United States. The first textile factories, built around 1800 in Rhode Island and Massachusetts, recruited unmarried women from the farms of New England. Despite the promises of a proper place to work, conditions at these early factories left much to be desired. Even though the Lowell Corporation in Massachusetts, among the most famous early textile mills, was considered an advanced factory for its time, women worked an average of 13 hours a day, 73 hours a week, including 8 hours on Saturday (Dublin 1979). Working conditions were stifling. Windows in the plant were nailed shut and the air was periodically sprayed with water to keep it humid enough so that the cotton threads would not break. The vapors from whale-oil lamps and floating lint made the air in the shop quite oppressive (Eisler 1977). The Lowell Corporation paid women mill workers $1.85 to $3.00 per week, depending on their abilities, from which $1.25 was deducted for board. Female workers were paid only half of what men were paid, even though they made up approximately 75 percent of the workers at Lowell (Eisler 1977). Neighboring states exhibited similar sex differences in wages (Marshall and Paulin 1987).

Jobs in these early plants were also sex segregated. Men held all supervisory positions as well as jobs in the mill yard, watch force, and repair shop; women were restricted to particular jobs operating equipment such as the looms and dressing machines. The immediate reasons given for this segregation concerned differences in the skills developed and monopolized by men and women over the years, perceived physical strength and dangers associated with various jobs, and the general cultural values prescribing particular roles for men and women (Dublin 1979). Men also were concerned about the entrance of women into the labor market because they felt that it would have a depressing effect on their wages. They fought to keep women out of the craft unions that later developed. Women held strikes in the 1830s and 1840s to protest reductions in wages, speedups in work pace, and increases in working hours (Dublin 1979).

Between the end of the Civil War and 1900, the percentage of females in the workforce increased (U.S. Department of Labor 1947, p. 34). In 1900, just over 20 percent (5,000,000) of all U.S. women 15 years of age and older were employed as breadwinners, but only 15 percent of native White females were, compared to 43 percent of Black females and 25 percent of White females with at least one foreign-born parent (U.S. Department of Commerce and Labor 1911, p. 262). Many young women 10–15 years of age also worked outside the home. In 1900, almost 6 percent of White, native-born females did so, compared to over 30 percent of non-White females 10–15 years old (pp. 256–259).

At the turn of the twentieth century, women made up a disproportionate number of workers in several occupations. For example, in 1900, they constituted 80–90 percent of all boarding and lodging housekeepers, servants, waiters, and paper box makers and over 90 percent of all housekeepers and stewards, nurses and midwives, dress makers, milliners, and seamstresses. Men, on the other hand, dominated agricultural, common labor, bookkeeping, clerk/copyist, watch and shoemaker, printer, dye works, and photography positions (U.S. Census Office 1903, Plate 90). Perhaps surprisingly, women composed over 70 percent of the teachers and professors in colleges and over 50 percent of teachers of music, and men made up the majority of artists and teachers of art (Plate 90). Black females, however, were more likely to be wage earners than either native- or foreign-born White females. Those who were "native White of native parents" dominated the higher status professions, with over 50 percent of college teachers and clergy and about 75 percent of lawyers and physicians coming from this group. In contrast, they made up less than 30 percent of those in servant, tailoring, laundering, and textile mill working positions (Plate 88).

BALANCING WORK AND HOME

The influx of women into the labor force has continued. Over the last several decades, the percentage of employed women in the civilian labor force has increased dramatically, while the percentage of men 16 years of age and older employed in the labor force has consistently declined. In 1973, for example, 42 percent of women 16 years of age and older were employed, compared to 54 percent in 2009. In contrast, the employment of men slid from 76 percent in 1973 to 65 percent in 2009 (U.S. Department of Labor, January 2010). The presence of women in the labor force is expected to increase.

In 2009, Black, Hispanic, and White women participated in the labor force at roughly equal rates, generally between 57 and 60 percent (U.S. Department of Labor, January 2010). While educational and other **human capital** factors help account for slight differences between some groups, other elements such as cohort and cultural differences in the meaning of marriage also appear to be important, especially as immigration creates a more diverse population (Read and Cohen 2007).

Among the most important factors behind the increased participation of women in the labor force are the shift toward a service and information-based economy, increased possibilities for flexibility in work scheduling, lower marital stability, and a greater need for dual-earner families (Gerson 1998; Presser 1998). In working- and lower-class families, the income brought into households by women is a necessity, and makes a major difference in the economic lives of families. In middle-class families, a college-educated wife is likely to work because her education allows her to receive a good salary. Forgoing the opportunity for employment by staying home would cost her family those earnings, so there is an incentive to work outside the home. This has been a primary reason why well-educated women enter the labor force (England 2010). One ironic consequence of highly educated spouses entering the labor force, however, is that parity with her husband's earnings increases the earnings inequality between married-couple families (C. Schwartz 2010).

On average in 2007, wives accounted for 36 percent of their families' incomes. In 2009, married women who worked full-time earned a median weekly salary of $708, significantly higher than that of women who were single, divorced, separated, or widowed. Both the proportion of income that wives contribute and the proportion of wives who earn more than their working husbands have increased in the last few decades. In 2007, for example, over 26 percent of all working wives earned more than their working husbands (U.S. Department of Labor, September 2009; U.S. Department of Labor, June 2010).

But the impact of wives' incomes on family economic status is not equally distributed across the income hierarchy. Rather, the contributions of wives are especially noticeable among lower-income families. Without their incomes, family incomes in the bottom 60 percent would suffer significantly. Wives' incomes make much less of an impact in families with the highest incomes. This suggests that were it not for wives' earnings in middle- and lower-income families, the degree of income inequality between families would be much higher than it is (Mishel, Bernstein, and Shierholz 2009).

The increase in the proportion of family income contributed by working wives since 1970 largely reflects an increase in the number of hours they worked between 1970 and 2000. The increase in hours worked by married women since the late 1970s, in turn, has intensified the struggle to balance home and work responsibilities. The related stresses are greater for women because of traditional gender-role expectations of women's responsibilities to families. Most employed married men and women agree that it is women who end up being most responsible for cooking, cleaning, shopping, and child care. If a child is ill, it is employed mothers rather than fathers who are most likely to miss work because of it (Galinsky and Bond 1996). In the case of dual-career professional families, when the husband works increasingly long hours, the chances of his wife quitting her job increase as well. In the reverse situation, however, the probability that the husband will quit his job does not go up. This increases the likelihood that the traditional gender roles of men at work and women at home will be reinforced (Cha 2010).

Women's contribution to housework does decrease as they earn more and the housework done by husbands increases. Ironically, at the point where wives begin to earn more than their husbands, the latter also reduce their housework, suggesting an attempt by husbands to counter their income dependency on their wives by reinforcing traditional gender roles at home (Bittman et al. 2003; Evertsson and Nermo 2004). But the tendency for men to contribute more to household tasks when they earn less than their spouses appears to be related to how important a society considers the traditional masculine tasks of employment and high earnings. In cultures that rank paid work and high earnings as highly important in life, men who earn less than their spouses contribute less to household chores than comparable men in other societies. Men in the latter societies who are not breadwinners contribute significantly more to household work than do male breadwinners in those societies (Thebaud 2010).

Due to their traditional role as caregivers, "women in the middle" are often expected not only to take care of their children but also an elderly parent as well. And as the U.S. population ages, the need and responsibility for elder care is likely to intensify (Singleton 1998). Opting for contingency or part-time employment, having fewer children, and choosing a nonstandard work schedule are some of the ways women juggle home and work responsibilities (Gerson 1998; Presser 1998; Raabe 1998). More often than not, it is mothers who make the compromise at work and who feel that they are not doing as well as they could in either the family or work spheres. Under these conditions, neither family life nor work is fully satisfying (Galinsky and Bond 1996). Mothers who work full-time value motherhood less than those who do not work, and this may be due to the unfriendly conditions that working mothers encounter in the workplace (McQuillan et al. 2008). This may be especially true for women who work in lower-status service jobs rather than for high-ranking professional women, whose businesses are more likely to make accommodations for their motherhood (Kantor, September 1, 2006). Until a better integration of home and work conditions is reached, stress will remain high for the majority of employed mothers.

SEX SEGREGATION IN OCCUPATIONS

Gender inequities involved in balancing home and employment comprise just one area of the inequalities between employed men and women. Inequalities also extend to the nature of employment. To identify occupational inequalities between men and women in their work experiences, however, it is important to examine how they are distributed (1) across broad occupational categories, (2) among detailed occupations, and (3) among specific occupations within specific organizational contexts. At each of these levels, from the broad to the very specific, there is evidence of sex segregation and inequality. This is despite the apparent liberalizing of attitudes about women's roles that attended women's increased entrance into the labor market over the last 40 years (Carter, Corra, and Carter 2009).

In spite of the increase in labor-force participation by women, occupational distinctions between the sexes remain within *broad occupational* groupings. Analysis of broad occupational categories suggests some recent decline in overall sex segregation. Declines in occupational sex segregation in private firms were more significant between the late 1960s and mid-1980s than they were later (McTague, Stainback, and Tomaskovic-Devey 2009). Changes in the economy's industrial composition were a major reason for the decline. The decrease in some traditionally male occupations such as agricultural, unskilled labor, and self-employment also contributed to those declines (Blau and Ferber 1986). Declines in sex segregation were not uniform across the economy. The degree of sex segregation in firms varies, with larger companies in more concentrated industries having less sex segregation (McTague, Stainback, and Tomaskovic-Devey 2009). Movement of women into management positions has been especially evident in the growing service sector (Stainback and Tomaskovic-Devey 2009).

Table 6.1 presents current information on the distribution of men and women over broad occupational categories. In general, women tend to be concentrated in white-collar and service occupations, while men are more spread out throughout the occupational spectrum. But among women, there are also significant variations. While White women are more likely than Black women to be managers or professionals, Black and Hispanic women are more likely to be found in service and blue-collar production positions.

Although Table 6.1 indicates some gender differences in occupation, as we examine more *detailed occupational* categories, the nature and extent of occupational segregation become clearer. A decline in occupational segregation has occurred in broad occupational categories, largely because of shifts in technology and organizational structures. But despite these general improvements, women still are found disproportionately in particular kinds of occupations. For example, women have increasingly moved into the ranks of managerial and professional occupations, but they tend to be concentrated among sex-typed occupations, such as teaching and nursing, and hold only a small percentage of positions as computer specialists, scientists, and engineers. Similarly, a man and a woman may both be in sales, but the woman is much more likely to be in clothing sales, while the man is involved in the selling of stocks and bonds. Craft occupations (carpentry, electrical contracting) are another group of occupations in which women continue to be significantly underrepresented (Herz and Wootten 1996). Initially moving into traditionally male occupations is easier than sustaining a growth in the percentage of women in those occupations. There appears to be resistance when the number of women grows too high (Krymkowski and Mintz 2008).

TABLE 6.1 Broad Occupational Distribution of Employed Persons 16 Years and Over, by Occupation and Sex: 2009

Occupation	Men	Women
Management, professional, and related	35%	41%
Service	14%	21%
Sales, administrative support, and office	17%	32%
Natural resources, construction, and maintenance	17%	1%
Production, transportation, and moving	17%	5%

Source: U.S. Department of Labor, *Employment & Earnings,* January 2010. Table 10, p. 203.

Despite small movement toward sex deseg-regation, many aspects of current occupational profiles are quite similar to those that existed in earlier years. In 1940, almost all of the servants, stenographers/secretaries, housekeepers, and nurses were women, and they comprised more than half of the teachers (not elsewhere classi-fied), apparel and accessories operators, wait-resses, and bookkeepers. As far back as 1870, women dominated in servant, clothing, certain kinds of teaching, and nursing occupations (cf. U.S. Department of Labor 1947, p. 52).

Table 6.2 suggests that this sex-typing has continued. As one glances over the lists, it is easy to see that the positions in which women domi-nate tend to be those that demand "feminine" or "motherly" characteristics. Being able to work directly with people and to take care of others are qualities that are required in these occupations. In contrast, the positions held mostly by men are characterized by a different set of qualities; they require manual labor or physical attributes, often contain an element of danger, involve work with a product rather than a person, and demand techni-cal or scientific skill. In essence, these two sets of occupations are distinguished by their "femi-nine" or "masculine" character. Why does this sex-typing continue? It is due to a combination of the devaluing of traditionally "female" posi-tions and the continued belief that men and women have different qualities by nature and are, therefore, meant for different jobs. Both of these notions have stalled the movement of women into most "male" blue-collar occupations and the movement of men into "female" occupations (England 2010).

Many of the occupations dominated by women also do not have the protections afforded other positions. For example, nannies and maids often suffer long hours, low pay, few legal pro-tections, and physical harassment. "Nannies are among the most exploited workers in the coun-try. There are almost no legal protections for this relatively new, mostly female class of work-ers that is more than 350,000 strong. Nor are there even social pressures to keep employers from subjecting nannies to abuses—from low wages and long work weeks to sexual harass-ment and physical violence." They are a "dirty little secret in middle- and upper-middle-class

TABLE 6.2 Broad Sample of Occupations in Which Women Represent at Least 90 Percent or Less Than 5 Percent of Employed Labor Force: 2009

Over 90%	Under 5%
Kindergarten teachers	Logging workers
Teacher assistants	Firefighters
Registered nurses	Carpenters
Maids/housekeeping cleaners	Construction laborers
Speech-language pathologists	Electricians
Dental hygienists	Sheet metal workers
Licensed practical nurses	Highway maintenance workers
Medical assistants	Mining machine operators
Hairdressers/cosmetologists	Automotive mechanics
Child care workers	Power-line installers/repairers
Bookkeeping/auditing clerks	Tool and die makers
Receptionists	Pest control workers
Secretaries	Welders
Word processors/typists	Boiler operators

Source: U.S. Department of Labor, *Employment & Earnings,* January 2010, Table 11, pp. 205–211.

America" (Lipman 1993, p. A1). Said one nanny of the family for which she worked, "Their cats were treated better than I was." Another confessed, "I was like a slave" (p. A1). Often these nannies are recent immigrants who are dependent on their employers for fair treatment. Maids often find themselves in a similar position of exploitation and dependence. Mary Romero, a sociologist who has served as a maid, suggests reforms involving higher wages, Social Security benefits, unionization, and, above all, the elimination of the idea that household work should be done primarily by women (Romero 1992).

When we move on to examine specific occupations *within specific organizational contexts* in the private economy, occupational segregation is again magnified. Not only are women found among fewer occupations than men, but within the same occupation they are employed in different kinds of organizations and economic sectors, tend to have less authority and have different job titles, and make less money in their jobs than men do. Just breaking into the authority hierarchy, especially at the lower ranks of management, appears to be very difficult for women regardless of their personal qualifications, resulting in significant gender differences in authority among employees (Baxter and Wright 2000).

Though an increasing number of women have moved into professions that promise high levels of rewards, such as the legal profession, they still do not fare as well as men. The chances of promotion for women already employed in a corporate law firm are lower near the top of the organization (Gorman and Kmec 2009). A recent study of almost 800 lawyers found that even when background, training, experience, seniority, preferences, and personal values are taken into account, female lawyers are less likely than men to practice or become partners in lucrative firms. Women who choose to work fewer hours or leave a high-powered legal firm lower their chances of becoming highly paid partners. This is at least in part due to the fact that difficulties in balancing work and family demands have a negative effect for women (but not for men) on the probability that they will become partners (Hull

and Nelson 2000). Some research even suggests that higher standards and expectations are placed on women in jobs, even when men and women are in the same positions (Catalyst 2007; Gorman and Kmec 2007).

Not only is it difficult for women to obtain positions of authority, which are usually dominated by men, but if they do get such a position, a variety of gender-related pressures make it hard for them to retain or want to stay in the position. The result is that women often move on to other less-prestigious, less-authoritative, and consequently, lower-earning positions in smaller firms. A result is continued sex segregation in occupations. Roth's study (2004a) of securities positions on Wall Street bears out the problems that women face in a male-dominated profession. These women were much more likely than men to leave their positions because of family pressures or outright discrimination. In performance ratings, women were not given the leeway that was allowed for men. Roth (2004b) also found that the belief that securities clients (who are primarily male) preferred to work with male employees further strengthened sex segregation in these occupations.

When women leave positions, they often end up in smaller firms. In general, women are more likely to be found in the *peripheral* than in the *core* sector of the economy. The peripheral sector is largely made up of small, less stable, local, nonunionized organizations that lack a clear career ladder, while the core consists of the larger, stable, multimarket, unionized organizations with career systems. These differences between men and women exist even when experience, education, and other factors are taken into account (Coverdill 1988). Factors that are characteristic of each of these sectors, moreover, appear to contribute to differences in unemployment rates and earnings levels between the sexes (Bibb and Form 1977; Beck, Horan, and Tolbert 1980; Coverdill 1988). Given the organizations in which they tend to find jobs, it should not be surprising that women are more likely than men to be in occupations with short career ladders and, therefore, have comparatively flat career trajectories.

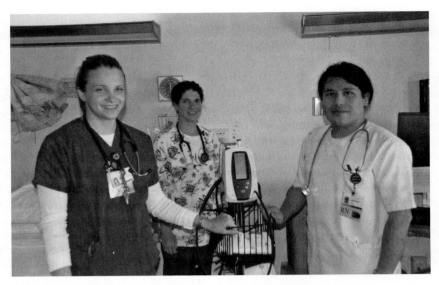

For salary and image reasons, men seldom seek out occupations that have been dominated by women. About 9 out of 10 individuals in nursing are women. (Photo by Brendan R. Hurst.)

Women have been underrepresented in higher posts even in those institutions that have publicly indicated a concern for equality and fairness. In higher education, for example, women are more likely than men to be employed at less-prestigious institutions and at nonresearch universities. They are less likely to be found at the full-professor level or to be among the tenured faculty. Even when men and women are equally productive, they are likely to occupy different ranks (Long and Fox 1995). Women are also much less likely to be found in the leadership positions of unions. Even in occupational areas where they dominate (e.g., elementary education and social work), they are not often found in the decision-making positions of principals or department heads. And, as Kanter's research (1977b) in corporations demonstrates, when women are put in unusual positions of authority, they are watched closely and under great pressure to perform because they are seen as **"tokens."**

Despite all the difficulties discussed above, or perhaps in part because of them, the number of businesses owned by women has increased significantly since the 1970s and so have their revenues. In 2006, there were 7.7 million businesses that were majority-owned by women, accounting for almost 30 percent of all businesses in the United States. About 2 million of them were owned by minority women. These firms employed in excess of 7 million people and had over $1 trillion in annual sales. Over two-thirds of these businesses were in the services area (Center for Women's Business Research 2008).

Accounting for Occupational Sex Segregation

What are the reasons behind the sex segregation in the occupations just discussed? Some have suggested that differences in education and skills, experience, and career aspirations may account for women moving into particular kinds of jobs, but evidence suggests that individual factors such as these do not fully account for differences in occupations and earnings between the sexes (e.g., Blau 1984; England et al. 1988). Gender-role socialization appears to have affected choice of occupation, but differences based on such socialization have declined in recent years. Younger women now plan for more continuous lifetime employment (England and Farkas 1986). Those who argue that gender-role socialization is an important source of sex segregation also overestimate the incompatibility of home and employment responsibilities. Among mothers, valuing motherhood and achievement in work are positively related to each other (McQuillan et al. 2008).

One should keep in mind that the free choice of an occupation takes place within a gendered structure with particular characteristics. In a broad sense, employment is limited by shifts in the types of jobs on the market and by the supply of and demand for qualified workers. This context also includes cultural values into which both employers and employees have been socialized and a historical record, both of which encourage the employment of men and women into certain kinds of occupations. As Risman (2005) argues, "[g]ender itself must be considered a structural property of society. It is not manifested just in our personalities, our cultural rules, or other institutions. Gender is deeply embedded as a basis for stratification, differentiating opportunities, and constraints" (pp. 296–297). Consequently, the choices women make about jobs and their work at home are conditioned by broader labor-market discrimination in the first place. This means that labor-market opportunities affect the role and amount of time spent in home labor by men and women. If women spend more time in the home than men because of fewer opportunities open to them in the market, it seems questionable, at best, to argue that it is their free choice alone that determines the amount of time spent in accumulating the experience and education which in turn affect their occupational positions (Blau 1984, pp. 124–125).

The following are among the more prominent barriers that have prevented women from obtaining more well-paying occupations:

- Less access to training and apprenticeship programs
- Appointment to perceived gender-related tasks ("light" work)
- Nonbureaucratized, patrimonial relationships with males in authority positions

- Less access to information about job openings
- Less fully developed job and contact network
- Seniority systems that limit women
- Protective laws inhibiting women from pursuing certain positions and restricting the number of hours and time of day they could work
- Pressure on women to take on the bulk of family obligations
- Tendency for coworkers or clients to prefer employees of matching sex
- Stereotyping, discrimination, and the consequent crowding of women into certain kinds of positions
- Lack of internal mobility ladder for many so-called female occupations within organizations (i.e., dead-end or flat-career jobs; cf. Roos and Reskin 1984)
- Prevalence of informal recruitment practices (Reskin and McBrier 2000)

Several factors also appear to be at work that specifically limit the number of women in high-level supervisory or executive positions. First, the **social capital** of men and women is different. Because social relationships tend to be dominated by members of the same sex, women receive most of their information about job openings from other women. That is, since men dominate in top positions and tend to share information with other men, women do not have access to as much information as men about high-level positions (McDonald, Lin, and Ao 2009). Second, some organizations are more open to women because they have a "gender logic" that is supportive of qualities that have traditionally been associated with women, such as nurturing, providing personal attention, and so on (King and Cornwall 2007). Other, less supportive organizations are imbued with logics that are more masculine in nature. Third, the few token women who occupy executive or high supervisory positions may feel pressure to be extra tough about letting other women move up so they can show that they "have what it takes" to make hard decisions (Kanter 1977a). That is, they may have to adopt masculine tendencies to maintain credibility among their male colleagues. This encourages a conservative explanation of why more women are not upwardly mobile in an organization. In their research on professional women in the fields of science and technology, for example, Cech and Blair-Loy (2010) found that women who are in very high positions in their organizations were more likely than those in lower positions to argue that women are underrepresented at the top because they lack the human capital to succeed and not because they are discriminated against in some way. Finally, men are more likely than women to perceive support when in positions traditionally dominated by members of the opposite sex. When it comes to support, women tend to feel that they do not receive it when in male-dominated positions (Taylor 2010). Men who are in female-dominated positions like nursing, for example, not only receive frequent support but also can ride a smooth "glass escalator" to higher positions in those fields. This is especially the case for White men (Wingfield 2009). Each of the above elements are often affected by the race and class of the women involved, but all of these factors create conditions and mechanisms that make it difficult for women to assume positions of high authority.

Many of the barriers listed above occur at the job level within the contexts of work organizations. It is, in part, within these concrete settings that gender inequality is reproduced. "All organizations have inequality regimes, defined as loosely interrelated practices, processes, actions, and meanings that result in and maintain class, gender, [sexuality] and racial inequalities within particular organizations" (Acker 2006, p. 443). Formally, these regimes cover a wide variety of interrelated areas including how tasks are organized, access to resources and benefits, promotion opportunities, authority structure, job ladders, and salary scales. Informally, they include the everyday comments, social arrangements, and interactions among employees. All of these may be gendered in ways that perpetuate inequality in jobs and occupations (Acker 2006).

An important source of power and mobility is the size and nature of a person's social network. Social capital can lead to job possibilities and promotions not only for oneself but for members of one's family as well. Being "in the know" has been a significant reason for the power and position of men in economic institutions, although women have increasingly strengthened their social networks in recent years. (© ofoto/Fotolia LLC)

Some factors do appear, however, to contribute to a decline in occupational sex segregation. Organizations that emphasize close camaraderie, a common identity, and limited choices among its members, like the military and military schools, reduce the probability of informal status systems arising and inequalities based on ascriptive qualities (Milner 2004; Lundquist 2008). The development of new forms of work resulting from broad economic changes and white-collar service employment of an unspecialized nature also loosens the grip of sex segregation. Shakeups in the formal division of labor also appear to weaken traditional notions about appropriate roles for men and women. For example, reorganizing positions into work teams that cut across the usual job descriptions not only creates more public visibility for women and minorities, but undermines stereotyping of them, and opens up new work contacts, all of which encourages the breakdown of sex segregation in occupations (Kalev 2009). Greater formalization—that is, increased presence of written rules, tasks, procedures, and so on—has been linked to sex segregation, but also to the greater hiring of women. Research indicates that when organizations use formal, standardized procedures when recruiting rather than an informal network and word of mouth, they hire a greater proportion of women,

including more for managerial positions (Szafran 1982; Reskin and McBrier 2000).

EARNINGS AND GENDER

As in occupational distribution, there are also significant earnings differences between men and women. In 1979, women earned only 63 percent as much as men. Despite a post-1970s decline in the wage gender gap, caused by a combination of reductions in men's wages and a slight rise in the median wages of women (Mishel, Bernstein, and Shierholz 2009), *weekly* earnings continue to differ between men and women, with median earnings for full-time working women in 2009 being about 80 percent those of men ($657 vs. $819). The differences exist across all major occupational groups (see Table 6.3).

The gender differences in wages vary by race and ethnicity, with Black and Hispanic women who worked full-time earning 79 and 71 percent as much per week, respectively, as White women in 2009 (U.S. Department of Labor, June 2010). Increases in earnings among White women have been much higher in the last 20 years than those for minority women. Still the differences between men and women are greater among Whites than among either Blacks or Hispanics. In 2009, within the latter groups,

TABLE 6.3 Median Weekly Earnings of Full-Time Workers Age 16 and Older, by Occupational Category and Sex, Annual Averages: 2009

Occupational Category	Median Earnings		
	Men	Women	Ratio of Women's to Men's Earnings
Managerial and professional	$1,248	$907	0.73
Sales and office	737	590	0.80
Service occupations	524	418	0.80
Natural resources, construction and maintenance	727	542	0.75
Production, transportation, moving	648	472	0.73
Median earnings for all workers	819	657	0.80

Source: U.S. Department of Labor, *Employment & Earnings,* January 2010, Table 39, pp. 246–253.

women earned at least 90 percent of what men earned, compared to 79 percent among Whites (U.S. Department of Labor, September 2007). Greater occupational specialization among Whites has been suggested as one possible reason for this difference (Greenman and Xie 2008).

The information given above is for *weekly* earnings. But we must keep in mind that weekly earnings are the result of *both* the number of hours worked and hourly wage rate. *Hourly* wage rate is often considered a more accurate gauge of earnings because it discounts the role played by hours worked, which is not the case when using weekly earnings as a measure. Just as in weekly earnings, however, women make lower hourly wages than men at every earnings and educational level. In 2009, median hourly wages for women were $11.76 versus $13.76 for men. Even among those in the top 5 percent of wage earners, women's hourly wages were still only 77 percent those of men in 2005. Moreover, in 2007, among full-time workers who were employed year-round, a larger percentage of women than men earned hourly wages that did not put their families above the poverty level (31% vs. 22%; Mishel, Bernstein, and Allegretto 2009). Among hourly workers, 6 percent of women compared to 4 percent of men received wages that were below the federal minimum wage rate (U.S. Department of Labor, June 2010).

How are differences in wages between men and women to be explained? Differences in human capital (experience, skills) may continue to account partly for the earnings gap. But differences in work effort or work interruptions, or attachment to labor force, which can take one away from the job, are not major variables in explaining sex earnings differences (Bielby and Bielby 1988). Even census data indicate clearly that differences in earnings persist even when work interruptions are taken into account. Women earn less than men even when their tenure on the current job is the same (U.S. Bureau of the Census, August 1987, Tables D and F). However, "interruptions" can be of many kinds. A study conducted recently in Indiana suggests that domestic work, especially child care, negatively affects

women's earnings significantly more than men's. This is especially the case for women who are in non-working-class jobs. The earnings of non-working-class men, however, benefit when their wives work only part-time as opposed to full-time (Shirley and Wallace 2004). Women appear to experience domestic and work pressures that men do not, and their earnings suffer as a result.

One structural factor that is clearly important is the distribution among and concentration of men and women in occupational categories. Occupations that are culturally defined as appropriate for women and in which a high proportion of women work tend to have lower earnings attached to them regardless of who occupies them. Jobs of comparable worth do not have equivalent earnings because of the sex compositions (Treiman, Hartmann, and Roos 1984; England and Farkas 1986). Earnings tend to be lower in those jobs in which the sexes are most segregated (Cohen and Huffman 2003; Cotter, Hermsen, and Vanneman 2003). For example, faculty in nursing, library science, and social work positions, all of which contain a high percentage of women, have significantly lower salaries than faculty in male-dominated departments such as engineering, physics, and dentistry (Bellas 1994).

Within occupational categories, women are less likely to be in positions of authority and to be given distinct kinds of tasks—factors that also influence earnings (Wright and Perrone 1977; Blau 1984). A recent study of U.S. companies suggested that most of the differences in compensation that existed between male and female executives were due not only to women being in smaller firms, but also to the fact that they were less likely than high-ranking male executives to be heads of their companies (Bertrand and Hallock 2001). In their study of variations in power at work, Elliott and Smith (2004) conclude that "there are strong findings to indicate that most superiors, regardless of their race and sex, tend to fill power positions they oversee with ascriptively similar others, . . . [and] because there are more white men at higher levels of workplace power than members of other groups, white men have greater opportunities to exercise this self-similar preference and, in the process reproduce their advantage over successive generations of employees" (p. 384).

Another factor in accounting for the earnings gap, the crowding of women into specific kinds of jobs, of course increases the supply of women and thereby reduces the wages associated with those occupations and jobs (Bergmann 1974). Evidence also suggests that female-dominant jobs yield lower earnings, even when men are in those jobs. "Net of human capital, skill demands, and working conditions, those who work in occupations with more females earn less" (U.S. Bureau of the Census, August 1987; England et al. 1988). These jobs frequently have shorter career ladders, which may further affect long-range earnings. Consequently, in addition to differences in characteristics between individuals, occupational, job, and organizational factors play significant roles in explaining earnings discrepancies.

Related to the occupational clustering of women and relegation to positions of lower authority are more subtle stereotypical beliefs about women that also lower their earnings. These include the perception that a woman's earnings are not as important to a family as those of a man, and that she is more committed to her family than to her job. Because salary and wage levels are based in part on subjective assessments of job performance, how bosses interpret worker behavior becomes an important factor in determining the earnings workers receive. The fact that salary and wage differentials between men and women persist even after differences in levels of education, college major, hours worked, family commitments, productivity, occupation, and related factors are taken into account, strongly suggests that subjective evaluations play a role in determining wage differentials (Dey and Hill 2007; Petersen, Snartland, and Milgrom 2007; U.S. Department of Labor, September 2007). The chances of a greater gender wage gap are higher when performance levels are either not clearly verifiable or open to interpretation, allowing biases to enter into the earnings equation (Gorman and Kmec 2007; Castilla 2008). This would suggest that having a greater proportion of women in high positions

who evaluate work performance may result in a lower earnings gap between the genders. Indeed, this appears to be the case (Cohen 2007).

Even women's perceptions of themselves may continue to affect the wage gap. "Women sell themselves cheap—and companies know it. . . . Women tend to be more reluctant than men to talk money" (Krotz 1999, p. 47). This behavior, in turn, may be related to their socialization into the traditional feminine gender role.

Finally, a slightly smaller percentage of employed women than employed men belong to unions, and union members consistently have had higher median earnings than nonunion workers. In 2009, the median weekly earnings of full-time union workers were 22 percent higher than those of nonunion workers (U.S. Department of Labor, January 2010). Part of the reason for women's lower union membership rates relates to their lower percentage in occupations such as protective service and precision craft, where a significant proportion of employees are union members.

While the gender gap in pay remains, there has been a decline in its size in recent years. Two of the immediate factors that have increased annual earnings among women in working-class occupations are an increase in the number of wives who work and an increase in the number of hours worked by women. In contrast to women, however, the slower wage growth for men in working-class occupations since 2000 has been instigated in part by declines in the economic power of unions along with declines in and movement abroad of manufacturing and other jobs. Among women in higher positions, it has been a rise in their real hourly wages relative to men that explains most of their increases since 1979 (Mishel, Bernstein, and Allegretto 2007).

MICROINEQUITIES IN THE TREATMENT OF WOMEN

Beyond the occupational and earnings differentials just discussed, there are other forms of inequalities experienced by women. Sexual harassment on the job is one of the areas that demonstrates this inequitable treatment. While forms of inequity relating to occupation and earnings have been in the public eye for years, microinequities between the genders permeate the everyday world that we take for granted. "**Microinequities** refer collectively to ways in which individuals are either *singled out,* or *overlooked, ignored,* or *otherwise discounted* on the basis of unchangeable characteristics such as sex, race, or age" (Sandler 1986, p. 3). These microinequities generally take the form of different kinds of language, treatment, or behavior exhibited toward women on a regular basis. This brief section merely points to some inequities that appear in everyday language, communication, the media, and education.

As suggested, these inequities are often deeply rooted and seemingly unconscious. Growing up, we seldom sift through the reasons why we think the way we do. For example, young boys rarely think about the everyday difficulties of being a woman and are not fully aware of the consequences that flow from their often unique experiences (Sandler 1986).

Even educated adults often find it difficult to identify with these deep unseen inequities. Reflecting on her work in women's studies, Peggy McIntosh observed that she had "met very few men who are truly distressed about systemic, unearned male advantage and conferred dominance. . . . Many men likewise think that Women's Studies do not bear on their own existences because they are not female; they do not see themselves as having gendered identities" (McIntosh 1988, p. 15). All these experiences and events give evidence to our lack of conscious recognition of many everyday inequities.

Microinequities of a subtle sort permeate our culture. Sexism can sometimes be unnoticed and unintentional, as in instances when a person uses sexist language and does not know it. For example, the pronoun *she* is often used when speaking of occupations in which a majority of persons are women. Nurses, elementary school teachers, and the like are almost always referred to as *she,* whereas mechanics, doctors, and mathematicians are usually spoken of in terms of *he.* Choosing words that assume that only men and not women occupy a particular position

(e.g., "chairman") is another example (Swim, Mallett, and Stangor 2004). While unintentional, the use of such terms subtly reinforces gender stereotypes. Our own names, which are part of our identity, reflect gender inequities. Traditionally, women who marry have been expected to give up their surnames and take on that of their new husbands. Women who are named after their fathers frequently have names that are diminutive versions of their father's first names—for example, Georgina (after George), Paulette (after Paul), and so on. These names "are copies, not originals, and like so many other words applied to women, they can be diminishing" (Miller and Swift 1993, p. 79).

Even the styles of speaking and communication are often different between the genders, reflecting their social positions in society. For example, women's language tends to involve a greater use of qualifiers and to be less direct and forceful than men's language (Parlee 1979). Men also talk more than women, interrupt women more often than they do other men, and are more likely to initiate conversation on a topic that is then carried on by others (Bernard 1972; Zimmerman and West 1975; Eakins and Eakins 1978; Parlee 1979). People in an audience are also more likely to respond in depth to comments made by a man than by a woman, and to be more attentive to a speech by a male (Sandler 1986). It has been suggested that many of these differences are due to inequities in power rather than to the sex of the communicators. Research among undergraduates indicates that when individuals with different levels of formal authority communicate, subordinates are more supportive and cooperative, and speak less than leaders, regardless of the sex involved (Johnson 1994).

In their study of the top 100 U.S. films in 2002, Lauzen and Dozier (2005) also found gender stereotypes to be alive and well. Not only were men much more likely to be the leading characters in the films, they were also more likely to be depicted in positions of leadership and power. A 2001 Gallup poll revealed that both men and women in the United States continue to associate particular characteristics with women rather than men. Consistent with media images, women are much more likely than men to be viewed as emotional, affectionate, talkative, patient, and creative (Newport 2001). As in our earlier history, stereotypes and images have not kept pace with the reality of changes in women's social and economic lives. What is important about these media images of women's appropriate physical and psychological traits is that they help to lock women into traditional roles and reinforce their subservient position in society.

Within schools, sex and gender biases remain significant. In primary and secondary schools, females are more likely than males to be ignored by their teachers and get less attention and encouragement in math and science. Textbooks used are rarely authored by women. "Students sit in classrooms that, day in, day out, deliver the message that women's lives count for less than men's" (cited in Chira 1992, p. A8). The contents of elementary school textbooks continue to portray men as competitive and aggressive while portraying women as characteristically warm, emotional, and nonconfrontational (Evans and Davies 2000). All of these treatments are part of the unofficial hidden curriculum of what schools teach their students.

Inequity problems can even be found in colleges and universities. A glaring example of the sexual objectification of women among students took place in October 2010 at a prestigious Ivy League university. As part of the pledging process, members of a major fraternity were caught marching by a building where first-year women lived yelling out "no means yes, and yes means anal," "sluts," and other similar comments ("Disgusting," October 17, 2010). Among faculty, the comparatively small numbers of women in top positions increase the chances of their being treated differently from men. A review survey by the Project on the Status and Education of Women reported that women are provided with fewer resources and less desirable offices, are not taken as seriously as male colleagues by students or male faculty, are considered less for their scholarly accomplishments than for their feminine characteristics, and are subject to a variety of forms of sexual harassment (Sandler 1986).

A further indication that women's activities in education have not been taken as seriously as men's is evident in the history of women's athletics. Partly as a legislative reaction, Title IX was passed in 1972, which stated that no person can, on the basis of sex, be denied access to, denied benefits of, or discriminated against in any education program that receives federal funding. While the law was not intended specifically for athletics, over the last three decades, a variety of lawsuits have been filed on behalf of female coaches alleging that they had been discriminated against because of their sex (see Nutshell 6.1). These include complaints about unlawful termination, demotion in rank and pay, sexual orientation discrimination, punishment for whistle-blowing, and inequitable distribution of resources within athletic departments. Because of their predicament, female coaches often face a series of dilemmas out of which there is no satisfactory answer. For example, on the one hand, they are expected to produce winning seasons, but on the other, they are sometimes given inadequate resources to do so. In addition, female coaches may be taken advantage of if they exhibit behavior that is consistent with gender traditions, but also be punished if they act in a manner that is considered too masculine, that is, threatening to male colleagues or superiors (Buzuvis 2010).

Problems also occur among academic faculty. Sociologist Theda Skocpol reflected on the significance of gender for her career, noting that in 1984 she "was offered the Harvard tenured professorship that I am convinced would have been mine in 1981 if I had been 'Theodore' rather than 'Theda'" (Skocpol 1988, p. 155). She went on to comment that, in general, "ambitious women are still not accepted at the top and, no matter what their achievements, they still have to endure the worst personal insults and struggle without end against virtually insuperable obstacles to their having real power" (p. 156).

Traditionally appropriate gender roles are further reinforced by many college textbooks. A recent study of texts from several decades in the areas of human sexuality and marriage and the family concluded that traditional photographs of

NUTSHELL 6.1   Retaliatory Cases under Title IX

In the past, coaches and others have complained that they have had their salaries reduced, been demoted, or been fired because they had complained about gender inequality in athletics. In the 2005 case of *Jackson v. Birmingham Board of Education,* the U.S. Supreme Court decided to affirm the right of the individual to sue for retaliatory discrimination under Title IX. Since that time, a number of colleges and universities have been taken to court for allegedly discriminating against female coaches and other athletic administrators. Here are examples of the cases:

Case 1: Despite having a winning record as volleyball coach at Fresno State, Lindy Vivas was fired for not meeting performance standards. She took the school to court, arguing that her firing was not due to her record, but because of her marital status, gender, suspected sexual orientation, and exposure of discrimination in athletics. In July 2007, the court agreed with all except the first of the claims, and awarded her $5.85 million as compensation.

Case 2: Karen Moe Humphreys was swim coach and assistant athletic director for student services at the University of California–Berkeley before her position was eliminated. A new assistant athletic director position was created, but she was passed over for a man who possessed less seniority and experience. Ms. Humphreys filed suit alleging that she had not been kept on because of her protests about the athletic department's hostile atmosphere and poor treatment of female members. She also stated that male employees told her that she was "intimidating" and "too strong for a woman" (Buzuvis 2010,

p. 18). In the court's 2007 decision, Ms. Humphreys was awarded over $3.5 million.

Case 3: At Iowa State University in 2008, softball coach Ruth Crowe was fired allegedly for her poor record and complaints from students and parents. But she argued that the dismissal was really for her complaints about gender discrimination in salaries and inequity in funds available to recruit male and female athletes. The court ruled that the explanations given by the school were only retaliation for her complaints against the school, and awarded her $287,000 in damages.

Case 4: In her 2009 case against the University of Nevada–Reno, the court decided against Terri Patraw's position. Ms. Patraw, who had been the head women's soccer coach, argued that she had been dismissed because of her complaints that the university had violated NCAA rules and that sexual harassment and unfair treatment of women's athletics at the university. In an unusual turn of events, the court dismissed her case because she had not alleged "protected speech within the meaning of the First Amendment" (Buzuvis 2010, p. 21). No other court had used this reasoning and the case may be appealed.

This smattering of cases suggests the variety of conditions that female coaches face in some university athletic departments. Are there any situations in which athletic programs can be treated differently and still fairly?

Source: Erin E. Buzuvis, "Sidelined: Title IX Retaliation Cases and Women's Leadership in College Athletics." *Duke Journal of Gender Law & Policy* 17(2010):1–45.

women's roles are dominant in them. Although the proportion of such images was higher in the 1970s, a large majority of images were still traditional in texts of the 1990s. This is especially disturbing because there was an increase in the number of photographs with women at their center (Low and Sherrard 1999).

These examples suggest the variety of problems that women face in U.S. society. Benokraitis and Feagin (1986) summarized the kinds of subtle sex discrimination that exist. Some are intentional and others are not, but generally they occur on an informal basis. Following are among the types they cited:

- Chivalry, which treats women in an overly protective manner and thereby encourages the image of them as nonadults
- Encouraging women to be ambitious and active but then creating blockages that make it difficult for them to perform effectively
- Forms of humor and suggestion, which on the surface may appear innocuous but are demeaning and embarrassing
- Treating women as objects—that is, as sex symbols or as status objects
- Devaluating the talents and abilities of women and focusing on stereotypical or superficial characteristics to honor them
- Overloading or overburdening women in their tasks or jobs under the guise of allowing them full participation or equality with men
- "Benevolent exploitation" in which women are exploited in an often unnoticed manner—that is, showcasing token women, using their talents and then not giving them appropriate credit
- Portraying dominant males as considerate and concerned with the welfare of women
- Socially and physically isolating women in professional settings

This list should serve as a reminder that sex discrimination can occur in several forms, not only in the formal institutional areas of occupation and earnings. The list also parallels the kinds of subtle discrimination that African Americans have experienced historically under paternalistic treatment of them as simpleminded children and tokens of their group.

GENERAL THEORIES OF SEX AND GENDER INEQUALITY

In addition to specific sources of gender inequality mentioned earlier, several types of general theories of sex inequality (i.e., inequality between males and females) have also been suggested. Because of the broad range of theories available, our discussion will be limited to theories that are more sociological or anthropological in nature. That is, the focus will be on explanations that emphasize the importance of social structure, ecology, or cultural contexts rather than biological or psychological elements. Biological explanations of sex inequality that suggest that basic genetic, hormonal, or physical differences determine sex inequality are inadequate for several reasons. Although there are some hormonal and physical differences between the sexes, they do not mandate that men will dominate women. These differences and any behaviors associated with them still have to be culturally and socially interpreted (i.e., gendered). For example, aggressiveness is related to domination only if it is interpreted in a particular way. In some societies, such behavior may be not only tolerated but also admired; in others, it may be considered deviant and those who engage in it may be assigned low status (Coontz and Henderson 1986).

Largely for the sake of convenience, the theories on sex inequality are divided into four general categories: (1) cultural, (2) social-structural, (3) ecological, and (4) capitalist/patriarchal. This set of categories does not, of course, exhaust all the types of theories of sex inequality that have been developed, nor are they mutually exclusive. The categories in the list overlap to some degree, but they also serve to separate theories whose foci and thrusts differ from each other. One other point should be made. The theories discussed are principally concerned with addressing the *origins* rather than the *maintenance* of sex inequality. Theories involving socialization and the role of education in inequality, on the other hand, shed light on the maintenance of such inequality across generations.

Cultural Values, Sex, and Gender Inequality

Cultures expect different attitudes and behaviors from members of each sex, but those expectations vary among cultures. In some cultures, what we consider masculine behavior is expected of women, and in some cultures, men engage in what we would consider to be feminine (i.e., effeminate in the U.S. value system) behavior. All this is to say that *sex* is a term used to describe a biological constant and *gender* is a term used to describe socially and culturally approved expectations, and these vary among societies. For example, we might argue that being a bouncer at a night club is quintessentially a male role; however, among the Dahomeyan of Africa, rulers used women as bodyguards because they considered women to be excellent fighters (Light, Keller, and Calhoun 1989). Among the Tchambuli of New Guinea, women were the dominant figures, the principal breadwinners, wore no jewelry, and kept their heads shaved. Margaret Mead's research uncovered some societies in which both sexes were expected to be nurturant and gentle, and others where men and women were expected to be aggressive and arrogant (Mead 1963).

Thus, although women are members of the same sex and are therefore biologically the same across cultures, their gender roles may be markedly different and differentially ranked among those same cultures. In the United States, as in other countries, sex is one of the fundamental ways by which we categorize individuals and gender a determinant of how we approach and interact with them. Consequently, our beliefs about the characteristics of each sex and appropriate gender roles help shape the positions individuals occupy in society. In this way, gender and the associated stereotypes serve as a basis for inequality between the sexes (Ridgeway 2006). These become embedded in labor market and organizational structures, and serve to maintain occupational, job, and status differences between men and women (Acker 2006). When women are viewed as too soft, less competent, less competitive, and generally lacking leadership qualities compared to men, it is no wonder that fewer women are found in high-paying, top-level positions.

One of the pitfalls of equating sex with gender has been to define the gender roles given to each sex as "natural," that by their nature men and women perform particular roles and have particular characteristics. The old phrase "men are men and women are women" captures this belief. The heterosexual matrix that holds cultural sway in our society posits direct, inviolate, and *normal* relationships between sex, gender, and sexuality. In this matrix, sex determines gender, and sexuality is a reflection of one's gender. Men are masculine, for example, and masculine men desire women. Violating this set of relationships in U.S.

society creates problems. "[M]ale homosexuality threatens male solidarity and superordination because some men take on what are thought of as female characteristics. Lesbianism is likewise seen as threatening to male superiority because the women who engage in it appear not to need men" (Caplan 1987, p. 2).

In eighteenth- and nineteenth-century Europe, it was common to associate women with nature. Women's nature was thought to reflect natural laws and their behavior to reflect a basic emotionalism and passion. Ortner (1974) has argued that because of women's reproductive role, they have been and still are viewed as being closer to nature than men, who, "lacking natural creative functions, must . . . assert [their] creativity externally, 'artificially,' through the medium of technology and symbols. In doing so [the man creates] relatively lasting, eternal, transcending objects, while the woman creates only perishables— human beings" (p. 75). Women are also seen as mediating between nature and culture, and men are seen as divorced from nature. Since nature is generally interpreted as being lower than culture and subject to the constraints of culture, Ortner argued, men are accorded more prestige and women less. While realizing that not all cultures neatly divide the sexes in terms of nature versus culture, Ortner said that most of the differences between the sexes are seen in dichotomous terms, nature versus culture being one of them. Others of a similar kind involve the notion that women's activities and values are circumscribed by the domestic sphere or self-interests, whereas men's roles are in the public domain or for the social good. Since the public or social sphere of life encompasses the narrowly focused domestic sphere, higher value is attached to it (Ortner and Whitehead 1981, pp. 7–8).

The proposals that these dichotomies are central to the explanation of sex inequality have been severely criticized in recent years. Why are women necessarily seen as more natural than men when the procreative role of men and many of their other activities (eating, sleeping, etc.) are just as natural as those of women? Moreover, many of the forms taken by natural behaviors surrounding reproduction are limited by cultural constraints and are not, therefore, purely natural (MacCormack 1980).

While incorporating the element of cultural beliefs into her theory, Ortner appeared to ignore the structural constraints placed on behavior by the social and natural contexts of the society (Schlegel 1977). Not all cultures devalue what is natural, and the meaning of "natural" changes historically rather than remaining timeless and static as in Ortner's view (Coontz and Henderson 1986; Yanagisako and Collier 1987). Perhaps the most serious deficiency of the nature–culture dichotomy is that it simplifies the complex reality of diverse cultures. Research indicates that even where such a dichotomy can be derived, nature and culture may be defined in a manner different from Western society, or males may be viewed as being closer to nature than females, or the dichotomy may not be associated with the sexes at all (Harris 1980; Strathern 1980).

The cultural variability found in the relationships between gender and sex, sex and nature, and sex and sexuality have instigated questions about the stability of these concepts and their connections. The alleged binary nature of sex, gender, and similar dichotomies has come under attack in the last several decades. So have the beliefs that gender is a *consequent* and *cultural* creation whereas sex is a logically *prior* and *biological* fact, and that one's gender is determined by one's sex. If there is no fixed, necessary tie between gender and sex, then gender can be attached to anyone, male or female (Butler 1999). Gender itself is not an entity or property of the individual, says Judith Butler (1999); rather it is "performative," a set of ritualistic, recurrent acts performed by individuals acting within a cultural and political system.

Borrowing from Foucault and French feminists, Butler argues that concepts like "woman" and "female" are created within a cultural framework that is also a system of power. This framework is one that interprets heterosexuality as normal. Those who act in ways that are inconsistent with this framework are considered unintelligible or not normal (Butler 1999; Lloyd 2007).

Sex is just as culturally constructed as *gender*, contends Butler. Bodies have always been interpreted culturally and do not exist as social objects prior to their naming and interpretation. They appear to do so because culture is capable of producing "frames of reference which are so powerful that they congeal into the invariance and irreducibility of material reality" (Kirby 2006, p. 23). Even the expressions of women, as the traditional subject and object of liberation for feminist theory, sometimes indicate their unwitting adherence to frames of reference that are culturally dominant. In the 2010 congressional elections, for example, female candidates often challenged their opponents to "man up," to have the "cojones" to be tough and strong, thereby reinforcing the traditional sex-gender connection (Hennessey 2010, p. A3). The goal of a genealogy of the concept of gender is to uncover the acts that create and sustain it, and the social and political frameworks that underlie it and "police the social appearance of gender" (Butler 1999, p. 44).

Social-Structural Explanations

Several of the most significant social-structural theories highlight the importance of women's work activities and kinship structure in generating inequality between the sexes (e.g., Rae Blumberg 1978, 1984; Chafetz 1988). They are usually cross-cultural in nature in that they propose to explain the degree of sex inequality in societies that are radically different in technology, size, culture, and so forth. Janet Saltzman Chafetz's explanation is a good example of a social-structural theory.

CHAFETZ'S THEORY OF SEX STRATIFICATION

Chafetz argued that there has never been a situation in which women dominated men on a systematic and long-term basis, so that societies vary "from near equality to radical inequality favoring males" (Chafetz 1988, p. 51). She has tried to explain the "degree of **sex stratification**" in a given society—that is, "the extent to which societal members are unequal in their access to the scarce values of their society" (Chafetz 1984, p. 4). These values include material goods and services, prestigious roles, political power, interpersonal decision making, freedom from unwanted constraints, and educational opportunities. In other words, Chafetz views stratification as multidimensional in nature. Moreover, some of these dimensions may vary independently of each other, causing women's positions to be high on some and lower on others.

Three of the factors most directly related to sex stratification, according to Chafetz, are (1) the nature of the work organization, (2) the type of kinship structure, and (3) the degrees of ideological and stereotyping support for sex inequality in the society. Of these, the most important is the work organization, which includes a number of specific elements (see Figure 6.1). Sex inequality will be high in a society when the following circumstances exist: (1) women do not contribute significantly to highly valued tasks, (2) women are easily replaced, (3) occupational tasks are sex-typed, (4) attention span is an important variable in a valued task, and (5) women do not have ownership and control over the means and products of their production.

The work organization itself is affected by several other independent variables, most of which are directly related to the level and type of technology in the society. Specifically, the more the time women have to spend on child-rearing

activities, the greater the distance between workplace and home, the more the need for physical strength and/or mobility, and the less the emphasis that is placed on subsistence rather than surplus production for exchange, the less women can be meaningfully involved in valued work tasks and, consequently, the higher the degree of sex stratification will be.

In addition to work organization factors, kinship structure also has an impact. When (1) married women live with or in the same places as their husbands' families (patrilocal), (2) a society traces lineage through the male line (patrilineal), and (3) there is a domestic division of labor based on sex, then inequality between the sexes will be high.

Finally, Chafetz included both the degree of ideological/religious support for sex stratification and the degree of gender stereotyping as factors that affect the acceptance of inequality between the sexes. For example, some societies may support the notion that "women's place is in the home" or that a wife must be submissive to her husband, while other societies may emphasize above all the belief in the worth and equality of all individuals as human beings. In addition, cultures usually contain stereotypes of male and female characteristics and appropriate behavior for each sex. According to Chafetz, these factors are more important for sustaining and justifying inequality than they are for generating it.

There have been conflicting reactions to Chafetz's argument. In a discussion of his view of how sociological theory should be structured, Gerhard Lenski (1988) praised Chafetz's model for being presented in a diagrammatic and essentially propositional form. Lenski believed that this makes the theory clearer and more amenable to empirical testing. In sharp contrast to the praise of Lenski, Pierre van den Berghe (1985) was quite critical of Chafetz's formalistic approach to theory, which appears to be becoming more dominant in the field. In assessing her theory, he bluntly stated that "an exercise in loosely linking a grab bag of 'variables' does not constitute anything that a real scientist would recognize as a theory" (p. 1350). However, this is an extreme

(1) *Nature of Work Organization*
(sex division of labor; nature of work contribution; labor substitution; ownership/control of means of production)

(2) *Kinship Structure*
(descent; residence rules; sex division of labor in family)

(3) *Degree of Ideological Support for and Degree of Gender Stereotyping*

SEX STRATIFICATION

FIGURE 6.1 Factors Most Immediately Related to Sex Stratification

Source: Based on Chafetz 1984, pp. 10–22.

reaction to what is a useful predictive model. It brings together variables that have been cited as important by others into a somewhat coherent and testable package. One variable minimized by Chafetz, considered central for Sanday's theory, which is to be discussed next, is the role of cultural factors in explaining and maintaining sex stratification.

Ecological Explanations

The structural theories of Chafetz and others often rely on the cross-cultural evidence and ideas of anthropologists who have developed theories of sex inequality. The latter group's theories usually focus on societies that are simpler technologically, whereas sociological theories usually emphasize complex industrial societies when trying to explain inequality (Chafetz 1988).

SANDAY'S THEORY OF MALE DOMINANCE

Peggy Sanday's (1981) theory is based on her analysis of information from over 150 societies, most of them not known to the average reader and many of them extinct. But they provide clues to the origins of male dominance. Sanday defined male dominance in terms of the "exclusion of women from political and economic decision-making" and "male aggression against women" (p. 164). Her principal question addressed the origins of male dominance: Where does it come from? The basic generating cause for male dominance relates to the nature of the environment in which a society operates. If that environment is one in which risk is great, danger is present, or resources are uncertain or in scarce supply, then the society is more vulnerable to male dominance. For example, when a society's ability to feed itself is dependent on hunting large migrating animals, its continuity is not all that certain. This means that the people's tie to the environment is more negative than positive under these circumstances. Survival is at risk. This contrasts with situations in which the immediate environment supplies abundant food without risk or uncertainty, as, for example, among the Mbuti, an African forest people.

These two different environments generate different stresses for the people exposed to them, their relationships to the environment are defined differently, and the general cultural orientation and consequent sex-role plans they develop also differ as a result (Sanday 1981). In other words, a group develops its sense of peoplehood and cultural orientations as responses to its environmental circumstances. When those circumstances involve risk, uncertainty, and so forth, as in the case of societies that rely heavily on the hunting of large animals, then there is a greater reliance on the aggression of men. These societies, in which animals must be killed, in which death and destruction predominate, develop what Sanday calls an **"outer orientation"** in their worldview. "Men hunt animals, seek to kill other human beings, make weapons for these activities, and pursue power that is *out there*" (p. 5). On the other side are societies whose environments produce abundantly and with certainty, cultures that rely on the surrounding plants for sustenance. Nature is viewed in a friendly manner, as freely satisfying human needs. In many cases where this situation is present, a basic affinity is seen between women and nature. As women produce, so does nature. Women are seen as being more in tune with nature and men are largely extraneous to this relationship. In these cultures, an **inner orientation** is dominant.

The cultural system that develops in a society contains scripts for the relationships not only between humans and the natural environment but also between the sexes. In societies in which the environment is potentially hostile, men spend much of their time in activities in the outer environment, outside the family, wrestling with forces beyond the family. In these kinds of societies, the ultimate source of power is believed to reside either in animals or in a supreme being of some kind who lives in a place beyond human beings. In these societies, because of their hunting activity, men are distant from their children and do not engage much in nurturing activity. The myths surrounding origins of the culture or world are imbued with masculine characteristics. The opposite is the case when a society, especially a technologically simple one, relies on plants in plentiful supply. Here, the earth supplies the food and men are close to their families and children. Growth and life are an inherent part of the culture. Like women, the earth provides and creates life. Tales of life origins have a feminine quality to them. Under both these circumstances, "the phrases 'man the animal' and 'mother earth' make a great deal of sense" (Sanday 1981, p. 73). There is a close connection between the economy of a society and the role of the sexes in myths and child rearing.

A strict sex-based division of labor is more likely when the society depends heavily on hunting as its means of subsistence, whereas a society that depends equally on hunting and gathering or inordinately on the latter for food is more likely to produce a division of labor that is sexually integrated. Cooperation rather than competition is likely to be emphasized. Females *achieve* power when a society has to depend on their economic activity for survival. This makes men more dependent on them. Women are *given* power when they are associated closely with nature and the society's continuity, as in the origin myths just mentioned (Sanday 1981, pp. 89, 114).

With Western colonialism, women lost much of the higher status they held in traditional societies. The infusion of new weapons and new technologies and the increased importance of aggression helped to redefine the roles of the sexes, with male activity becoming more highly valued. In many cases, the increased complexity of economic technology also led to the decline of women's status. In her survey of societies, Sanday concluded that "male dominance is associated with increasing technological complexity, an animal economy, sexual segregation in work, a symbolic orientation to the male creative principle, and stress" (1981, p. 171). Sex inequality is much more likely when the environment is unfavorable and unstable than when the opposite is the case.

To summarize Sanday's explanation, the nature of the surrounding environment gives shape to the economy and the stress in society and determines the relative worth of men's and women's behavior. Cultural orientations, myths, and sex-role plans develop that are consistent with these conditions. When environmental conditions create stress because they involve risk, danger, or uncertainty, greater reliance is placed on the economic efforts of men. An outer cultural orientation develops along with **origin myths** in which men dominate and create, and sex-segregation of roles follows, ultimately leading to male dominance. Sanday's basic model is suggested in Figure 6.2.

Sanday's theory has been criticized for overemphasizing the role of the environment in determining cultural beliefs and for ignoring the internal sources of stress in society. It also does not take into account the fact that different cultures may react differently to similar environmental circumstances (Coontz and Henderson 1986).

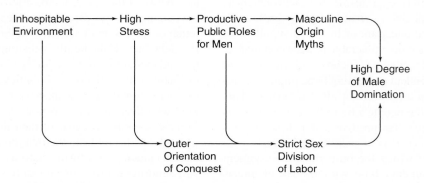

FIGURE 6.2   Sanday's Basic Model of the Genesis of Male Dominance

Source: Based on Sanday 1981, pp. 11–12, 64–75, 163–172ff.

Additionally, her theory neglects the possibility that the difficulties men encounter in dealing with a harsh environment may strengthen them enough to dominate women directly.

Randall Collins has suggested, for example, that the form of the economic system and the habitability of the surrounding natural and political environments influence the extent to which warfare is an important element in the society. Men are generally larger and stronger than women and are therefore more likely to control the fighting that occurs. In such a potentially hostile environment, political alliances become important, and males use the exchange of females through marriage with surrounding groups as a means of establishing political, economic, and social ties. This control of females by males results in separate cultures and roles developing for each of the sexes (Collins 1971, 1986, 1988).

The causal nature of the relationships outlined by Sanday also needs to be more fully examined (England and Dunn 1985). One would suspect, for example, that cultural orientation and beliefs would have an impact on the degree to which the environment is interpreted as being hostile or friendly. In other words, not only can the environment affect the culture, but the culture may affect the definition of the environment as well.

Capitalism, Patriarchy, and Sex Inequality

Generally, structural theorists, as well as many anthropologists, recognize the significance of broadly defined economic factors for sex inequality. Many point to the significance of labor, work organization, and family structure in shaping inequality. In a general way, then, their perspectives have been affected by Marxian thought as well as by perspectives that focus on the family structure and the sex/gender divisions within it. Some explanations, however, explicitly focus on the effects of capitalism and patriarchy on sex inequality. Figure 6.3 gives a basic model showing some of the alleged major impacts of capitalism/class on sex inequality. There are a number of individuals who present such explanations; Lise Vogel is one of them.

VOGEL'S REPRODUCTION THEORY Vogel (1983) began the development of her theoretical framework by reviewing several Marxian concepts: production, reproduction, and labor power. **Labor power** refers to the capacities, mental and physical, an individual exercises whenever he or she produces something of use. *Production* is a result of labor power. But every act of production is also an act of *reproduction,* because whatever is produced lays the basis for its being reproduced later.

Specifically, a society needs a labor force to continue to produce products, and this labor force, in turn, needs food to maintain itself. In other words, part of the reproduction process involves reproducing the laborers who are involved in the labor process. Workers must be maintained and, when necessary, replaced. Sex becomes a significant factor in the generational replacement of bearers of labor power, because it is only women

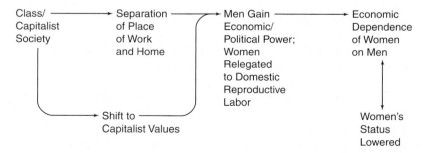

FIGURE 6.3 The Relationship of Class/Capitalism to Sex Inequality

who can perform this function. But regeneration or replenishment of the labor force does not have to occur within the family. Other sources—such as migration, enslavement, and the enlistment of nonworkers within the family—also may serve as potential sources of labor power.

In order for the capitalist system of production to continue, labor power must produce the conditions necessary for the constant renewal of the labor process. The labor needed to reproduce workers and their replacements is **necessary labor**. For example, a certain minimum amount of labor is needed to provide basic subsistence to existing workers and to produce new workers. Part of this necessary labor is done at the workplace and is paid for by wages, with which the worker can buy those necessities needed to support himself or herself and other nonworkers in the working class. As it takes place in the social or public sphere it is the *social* aspect of necessary labor. But as mentioned, biological reproduction and the rearing of children are also needed, and as such constitute a second *domestic* component of necessary labor. In addition to necessary labor, there is **surplus labor**. This is the labor time that is left over after socially necessary labor has been subtracted from the total labor time spent on the job. It provides the profit to the employer.

It is the unavoidable performance of the domestic component of necessary labor by women that creates a basic sex division of labor. But their involvement in reproduction creates a dilemma for capitalists and constitutes an internal contradiction in the capitalist system. On the one hand, this domestic labor reduces any time women can spend in the labor force producing profit for employers. So in the short run, capitalists suffer because of the smaller direct contribution of women to profit. On the other hand, if capitalism is to continue in the long run, replacement and reproduction are necessary. So in these terms, capitalism benefits.

In order to benefit both ways, capitalists try to minimize the amount of necessary domestic time needed for reproduction in order to maximize the surplus value of labor, thereby increasing their profit. Thus, employers may allow maternity leaves for female workers, but the leaves are kept short so as to maximize the work time of new mothers. At the same time, however, male workers try to get the best conditions and wages they can for themselves, their families, and their wives. This may mean more and better-quality domestic time for their wives. So while employers may be trying to enlist wives in the marketplace, husbands are trying to create conditions that will make it more possible for them to stay comfortably at home. This conflict is related to the gender issues involved in the balancing of home and work tasks discussed earlier. In trying to resolve this contradiction, according to Vogel, what almost invariably occurs is the involvement of men in the labor force and the production of surplus labor and profit on the one hand, and the involvement of women in the reproduction of the labor force at home on the other. Accompanying this resolution is a male supremacy based on males as the laborers who produce the means of subsistence and receive a wage.

It is in capitalism that a distinct and strong division is accentuated between the arena in which surplus labor is carried out and that in which domestic labor is performed. In order to increase profit, separate factories in which workers are concentrated that are socially and culturally isolated from the home are needed. "Capitalism's drive to increase surplus . . . forces a severe spatial, temporal, and institutional separation between domestic labor and the capitalist production process. . . . Wage labor comes to have a character that is wholly distinct from the laborer's life away from the job" (Vogel 1983, p. 153). Men are clearly associated with the social, working sphere, whereas women are associated with the domestic sphere. This is a carryover from earlier class societies.

Of course, exceptions exist. Depending on the specific historical circumstances of a given society, either the importance of women's power of reproduction or their involvement in the labor force may be stressed. Migration and natural or other disasters may tip the scales in such a way that the participation of females in the work force is more important than their domestic labor. But the usual division of labor consists of men and women being associated with distinct spheres of labor. This clear division of labor, when accentuated in a situation of male supremacy, is the source for ideologies that serve to explain and maintain the sexual basis of the division of labor. Since this division of labor is so prominent and obvious, it comes to be viewed as natural even though it is rooted in the capitalist mode of production (Vogel 1983, p. 154).

As noted previously, according to Vogel, women's involvement in and relegation to domestic labor is the basic source of their subordination. By working, receiving wages, and supporting women who are bearing and raising children, men gain economic power over women, and women remain in a subordinate position.

Since many of the immediate conflicts take place within the context of the family, it is easy to conclude that it is the sex division of labor within it that is at the source of the problems experienced by women. But Vogel reminds us again that it is the nature of the relationship of men and women to the capitalist system of production and women's role in reproducing it that is the basic cause. As long as capitalism remains unchanged, inequality between the sexes will continue. Figure 6.4 presents the core of Vogel's argument.

One of the problems with Vogel's theory is that she dated the beginning of women's oppression with the advent of class societies. Many would argue that male domination predated class society (Nicholson 1984). Vogel's theory also heavily stressed economic factors to the exclusion of cultural, psychological, and other possible contributors to male domination.

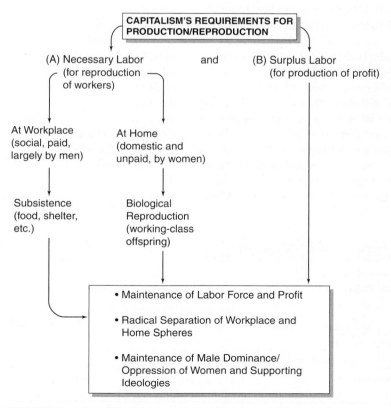

FIGURE 6.4 A Simplified Version of Vogel's Theory of Women's Oppression

THE ROLE OF PATRIARCHY   Vogel acknowledged the division of labor and the inequality that exists between the sexes in capitalist society, but Sacks (1975) noted that in many nonclass societies the sexes were also unequal. This suggests strongly that sex inequality preceded capitalism and indeed is a form of domination distinct from class inequality.

In brief, many feminists argue that patriarchy not only preceded capitalism but also existed even in the earliest societies. The term **patriarchy** has been defined in a variety of ways, but basically it refers to a whole complex of structured interrelationships in which men dominate women. It is a "system of sexual hierarchical relations" (Eisenstein 1981, p. 19). Just as capitalism is based on the relationship between capitalists and workers, so patriarchy is a system based on the unequal relationship of men and women (Phelps 1981). Because of its early appearance, patriarchy is considered by most radical feminists to be the most fundamental of all forms of social inequality, as one in which "men learn how to hold other human beings in contempt, to see them as nonhuman and to control them" (Lengermann and Niebrugge-Brantley 1988, p. 306).

In other words, in this view, sexism and the domination of women did not appear with class societies as some Marxists would have it; rather, it existed long before capitalism came on the historical scene. The roots of patriarchy have been tied to the reproductive function of women in society (Eisenstein 1981; Phelps 1981; Chafetz 1988). "On the basis of this capacity she has been excluded from other human activities and contained within a sphere defined as female" in Western society (Eisenstein 1981, p. 14). The division of labor between the sexes in this respect is ancient: "Where there is society, there is gender, and the gender division of labor is pervasive" (D. E. Smith 1987, p. 4). There was no primordial matriarchal society preceding class society. Table 6.4 suggests some of the basic elements tied to patriarchy and some of the forms it has taken under precapitalist and capitalist societies.

Once men dominate in areas outside the family and gain the economic and political resources attendant with those activities, they can use these resources to maintain patriarchy. The maintenance of patriarchy over generations is clearly in the interests of men. Women serve the material interests of men by serving not only as sexual partners but also as potential laborers, childbearers, ornaments, and status enhancers.

The social institutions dominated by men, then, influence not only the shape of society and relations within it but also the cultural values and ideas that dominate in society. Thus, in present-day society, education and socialization agents instill those values consistent with patriarchal structure. Under capitalism, the culture consists largely of the ideas and values sanctioned by those in power—that is, men. This ruling ideology provides an official version of social reality, including beliefs about the real nature of men and

TABLE 6.4 Patriarchy and Sex Inequality

General Features of Patriarchy	Under Precapitalist Societies	Under Capitalism
1. Power, force of men 2. Control of outer resources by men 3. Separate work spheres 4. Division of labor based on sex 5. Reproductive capacity of women critical	Men engage in status-enhancing hunting; men control domesticated animals; women used as exchange, women are purchased (bride wealth); men control military	Radical separation of home and work; women cheap labor for market, women largely confined to home, women economically dependent on men

women. Eventually, among women living under capitalism, a line of fault or disjuncture occurs between this official version of reality and how the system works and the concrete everyday experiences of women. But this experience is difficult to articulate because the symbols, language, and organization of thought in the society are those of men not women (D. E. Smith 1987).

The separation and inequality of men and women is reflected in dichotomies that go back to ancient times. The distinctions between rationality and passion, city and household, and public and private all derive from a belief in the basic differences and inequality between the sexes. In feudal and in capitalist societies, the public sphere is associated with the male, whereas the private sphere is the designated place for the female. In feudal society, females were considered private property of the male heads of families, and in capitalist society, women are largely relegated to the private sphere of the family. In other words, although the economic system may change, basic patriarchal relationships remain intact and only change form.

One of the difficulties with patriarchal theories is that the original source of patriarchy is not always clearly spelled out. Sometimes it is associated with the differences in the reproductive function between the sexes, sometimes with the physical force of men over women, and other times its source is left undescribed. Collins (1988) argued that the basic problem with theories that propose patriarchy as the fundamental, original cause of sex inequality is that they are merely restating the question using a different label. That is, if "patriarchy" *refers* to male domination of one sort or another, then how can it be used to *explain* male domination? This seems to be too severe a criticism, given that many of those proposing such theories do attempt to locate the sources of patriarchy itself. Since that source is often viewed as being tied to the elemental function of reproduction, the task remains to identify the exact conditions under which such distinctions in the division of labor do *not* lead to patriarchy. For example, can socializing or spreading a large part of the child-rearing function free women to a degree from the destiny of remaining in the domestic sphere, thereby potentially raising their status in society?

SOCIALIST-FEMINIST THEORIES OF SEX INEQUALITY   In contrast to those who would opt for viewing either capitalism *or* patriarchy as the principal cause of women's subordination, there are those who see the two as complementary causes. Women's oppression by men cannot be reduced to a matter of class exploitation, according to these scholars. *Exploitation* of women, Eisenstein (1977/1990) argued, exists when men and women are wage laborers. But women are also in a lower sexual hierarchy in their roles as mothers and housewives. "The study of women's oppression, then, must deal with both sexual and economic material conditions if one is to understand oppression rather than merely understand economic exploitation" (Eisentein 1977/1990, p. 124). As we will see, those who use an internal-colonialism model in explaining Black–White inequality in the United States make a similar argument about understanding racial oppression.

Eisenstein and Hartmann both emphasized the mutual reinforcement between capitalism and patriarchy. Patriarchy supplies capitalism with generations of laborers it needs at minimal costs and with the techniques of control needed to keep oppressed women in their place. All the tasks carried out and raw materials worked on by housewives (e.g., children, husbands) are "future worker-commodities" (Secombe 1973, p. 19). In turn, capitalism reinforces patriarchy by only hiring women for certain low-paying positions, thereby encouraging job segregation, women's relegation to the domestic sphere, and their continued economic dependence on males.

The domestic division of labor is the linchpin that connects capitalism and patriarchy (Philipson and Hansen 1990). Patriarchy defines the role of women as being in the home, whereas capitalism defines men's role as being in the wider economy and women's role as reproducer of workers in the economy. The division of labor, as it were, brings the private-domestic and public-economic spheres into contact. This has raised a number of questions about the nature of the relationship between the marketplace and the home.

One issue pits the obvious contributions of domestic work to the continuance of capitalism against the fact that domestic labor is basically unpaid low-status work outside the economy. If such work contributes to the economy by providing functioning laborers, why is it not paid labor? Because it is not paid, it has lower status in a society in which the amount of money labor brings in is a measure of its status (Benston 1969).

A second issue concerns the basic character of domestic labor. In contrast to work in the marketplace, which is seen by some as being alienating and rationalistic, work in the home is sometimes seen as much less alienating and more leisurely (Sontag 1973; Vogel 1983). The home and family life are viewed as the areas in which love, warmth, spontaneity, cooperation, and fun have a central place. In sharp contrast, the public sphere of paid labor is interpreted as one where work is forced, competitive, and rational. It is, of course, questionable whether those who feel trapped in the home would describe it in the glowing terms just used. But part of our socialization is aimed at fostering the belief that these terms accurately describe family life in modern society.

A third issue among scholars relates to the effects of involvement in the marketplace on women. Engels viewed industrialization as providing women with a means of escape from the drudgery of housework and the oppression of domestic life. Work outside the home was interpreted as a liberating experience. However, if capitalism creates work that is fundamentally alienating, a legitimate question can be raised about how liberating and beneficial such an escape would be for women. Are they not just escaping into work that is also alienating and compounding their alienation by doing not only paid labor but unpaid domestic labor as well?

A final area concerns the family's role in socializing new members of society into a dominant set of values and ideas that perpetuate patriarchy

and capitalism (Hartmann 1981). The traits attributed to the ideal male—competitiveness, rationality, coolness—are those valued in the marketplace, whereas those attributed to the ideal female under capitalism—emotionality, sentimentality, and so on—are those valued in the family. These are values that keep patriarchy and capitalism intact.

The last point demonstrates that the concerns with profit in capitalism and with social control in patriarchy are "inextricably connected" and "cannot be reduced to each other." Capitalism and patriarchy, being mutually reinforcing, become an "integral process" (Eisenstein 1977/1990, p. 134). The conditions in the marketplace affect what goes on in the family in terms of production, reproduction, and consumption; conversely, production, reproduction, and consumption in the family affect the production of commodities in the marketplace.

The centrality of the sexual division of labor in maintaining both patriarchy and capitalism has caused both Eisenstein and Hartmann to call for its elimination. Eisenstein argued forcefully that it is this division of labor that must be changed because it is the principal means by which men maintain control. It suggests that the roles and activities that divide men and women are rooted in nature (Eisenstein 1977/1990). Eisenstein stated that for conditions to change, women must organize and they can do so by becoming conscious of what they have in common with each other. They may differ in their ties to the marketplace, but their "commonality derives from the particular roles women share in patriarchy. From this commonality begins the feminist struggle" (p. 140). Similarly and even more pointedly, Hartmann (1976/1990) believes that both men and women will be better off and more equal only when "we eradicate the socially imposed gender differences between us and, therefore, the very sexual division of labor itself" (p. 169).

One of the great values of seeing capitalism and patriarchy as dual systems is that doing so encourages us to examine the interlinkage between class and sex in trying to understand the relative roles of men and women in society. Clearly, an individual's position in the general system of inequality is an outcome of the confluence of economic, sexual, and racial/ethnic factors. Understanding the nature of this intersection and its origins will provide us with a more comprehensive and exact explanation of sex inequality. There is no question that women as a group are in a unique position in contemporary society.

Multiracial Feminist Theories

All the theories discussed above focus on the position of women in general. In recent years, however, numerous feminist theorists have stressed that (when developing an explanation of women's situation) we need to take into account women's experiences as they have lived them along with their accumulated wisdom. In doing that, it is necessary to recognize that all women do not have the same experiences or live the same kinds of lives. While they may have some experiences in common because they are women, they vary along other dimensions, for example, with regard to race and social class. These dimensions intersect in different ways for different women and affect each other, the particular combination characterizing a given woman and having a unique effect on her life chances. As Browne and Misra (2003) put it in speaking about the relationship of gender and race, "[r]ace is 'gendered' and gender is 'racialized' so that race and gender fuse to create unique experiences and opportunities for all groups—not just women of color" (p. 488). We could add that race and gender are also "classed," and class has been "gendered" and "racialized" as well in our history. That is, the particular pattern *itself* has an impact independent of the separate effects that might flow from one's gender, race, or class. This is what is meant by the importance of **"intersectionality"** and what Patricia Hill Collins (1990) calls "the matrix of domination." Each of these patterns has particular cultural images or stereotypes associated with it. For example, Black, lower-class men are often seen as dangerous, Black women as unusually sexually active, White women as dependent and feminine, and so on (Browne and Misra 2003).

A woman's race, class, and gender may all affect her position in society. As we have seen in several instances, for example, the occupational and earnings positions of women vary with their race. The situation of women also depends on their class. In their study of power at work, Elliott and Smith (2004) found that "men and women of various races and ethnicities experience increasing inequality in workplace power, relative to white men, but they experience it to different degrees and via different mechanisms. . . . Evidence here suggests that a one-size-fits-all explanation hides more than it reveals" (pp. 384–385). Since each group faces problems that are in part unique, the solutions to their domination need to vary as well.

In addition to the intersection of race, class, and gender, recent issues on employment, welfare, and wages surrounding immigration have added *nationality* to the mix. Globalization and the continual movement of people, jobs, and capital across national boundaries associated with it have also had an impact on women's position in our own society and in others. Having examined a variety of general explanations of gender inequality, let us now examine the position of U.S. women in a global context and assess the specific roles played by globalization in determining the status of women around the world.

THE GLOBAL CONTEXT AND THE IMPACT OF GLOBALIZATION

The examination of gender inequality in the United States showed that women are generally below men in their earnings, income, and occupational statuses, and the families that they head are more likely to be poor. However, gender inequality and oppression encompass a broader range of life chances than just narrow economic opportunities. The life conditions for women in many parts of the world often entail subjection to extreme forms of discrimination.

To avoid taking an ethnocentric perspective in determining what conditions and acts constitute gender exploitation, one needs to consider the causes and reasons for specific practices within the cultural context in which the acts occur. This is especially important if one hopes to work for change in such practices (Gruenbaum 2001). One such practice is female circumcision or—as it is often called by Western analysts—genital mutilation. While common in many African countries, it has also been found among some groups in Asia and to a lesser extent in some European countries, and even North America. The operation, which involves surgical removal of segments of a female's sexual anatomy, has been maintained by the myth that such an operation will dampen the female's sexual drive and thereby guarantee chastity. The painful procedure, often performed with unsterile knives, has been done on an estimated 140 million girls and women, mostly in African countries. Girls as young as age 6 have been subjected to the operation (Scott 2000; Smucker 2001).

So-called **honor killings** constitute another form of extreme discrimination against women aimed at controlling their behavior. These killings take place because of alleged disobedience or sexual indiscretions on the part of women. Muslim countries in the Middle East have been among the most cited for this discrimination. Between 1998 and mid-1999, for example, 36 women were killed in Jordan for family honor. Islam is used as justification. The Koran has been interpreted as supporting wife beating and the assignment of much lighter sentences for the murders of women than of men. In the 5,000 cases of honor violence against women recorded in four Pakistani hospitals in the 1990s, 97 percent of the women died but guilty verdicts were reached in only 3 percent of the cases (Ligner 2001). Customs and laws often entrap girls in relationships and make it difficult for them to escape. Marriage to girls under the age of 12 is not uncommon in some Middle Eastern countries, and it is much more difficult for a woman than a man to divorce ("The Women of Islam" 2001).

Finally, in some countries, conditions for women prove so unbearable that many commit suicide. China, for example, has one of the highest suicide rates in the world, and more than half of these suicides are by rural women. This contrasts with most other countries where the male suicide

rate is higher. Each year, approximately 157,000 Chinese women commit suicide. Part of the reason for the higher female suicide rate in China is that women who attempt suicide there are more successful at doing it. More significant, however, is the fact that rural Chinese women are generally not considered as valuable or worthy as their male counterparts and are thought of as the property of males (Fackler, April 28, 2002). Genital mutilation, honor killings, and suicide are all indicators of the extreme gender oppression that women, but not men, face in some cultures. In the small village of Umoja in northern Kenya, a group of women have tried to escape the widespread oppression they have faced from their husbands and men in general by creating a village composed almost entirely of women (Lacey 2004). The leader of the village complained that their only reason for existence had been to give men children and to be treated like property. In this new setting, the women seem to be prospering economically and psychologically.

As these examples suggest, there are great variations between countries in the quality of life experienced by women. In its analysis of international gender inequality, a recent United Nations study took into account women's (1) life expectancies, (2) educational attainment, and (3) incomes in its measure of gender-related development. Results in a 2005 ranking of 157 countries showed that, *compared to men,* women are worst off in Sierra Leone, Guinea-Bissau, Niger, Burkina Faso, and the Central African Republic. Countries ranked best on the index were Iceland, Australia, Norway, Canada, and Sweden. The United States ranked 16th. In an assessment of their political, decision-making power, women were most likely to be in high-level positions in Norway, Sweden, Finland, Denmark, and Iceland, and least likely to have political power in Yemen, Saudi Arabia, Egypt, Turkey, and Kyrgyzstan (United Nations 2007). The United States came in 15th on the UN's gender empowerment measure. Keep in mind that the "gender-related development index" used by the United Nations merely measures the *relative disparity* between men and women on the above three variables; it does not directly tap the level of quality of life in an *absolute* sense.

Save the Children is an independent, nonprofit organization that, for the last several years, has conducted an evaluation of conditions for women across the world. Its 2004 survey of conditions for mothers and children in 119 countries revealed results similar to those of the United Nations. Sweden, Denmark, Finland, Austria, Netherlands, Norway, Australia, Canada, and the United Kingdom ranked highest, respectively, in measures of mothers' well-being. The United States ranked 10th best. The 10 countries with the lowest rankings, starting with the worst, were Niger, Burkina Faso, Mali, Ethiopia, Guinea-Bissau, Yemen, Sierra Leone, Chad, Mauritania, and the Central African Republic. In general, Scandinavian countries, and industrial nations in general, rank highest, while sub-Saharan African countries dominate the lowest rankings on this measure. The measure includes rates of maternal mortality, anemia, use of contraceptives, births by qualified professionals, female literacy, and participation of women in national government (Save the Children 2004). One of the problems of national-level data is that it obscures inequalities between subnational groups in a country. Ethnic cleansing, violence, and oppression in general have targeted some groups of women more than others.

Worldwide, there appears to be some evidence of a decline in gender inequality in a wide variety of areas (Dorius and Firebaugh 2010), but significant discrepancies still exist. As in the United States, the world's employed women are unevenly distributed across occupational categories. Women "are still rarely employed in jobs with status, power and authority or in traditionally male blue-collar occupations" such as craft, trade, and machine operator positions (United Nations 2010, p. ix). About half of employed women are involved in various services (e.g., retail, restaurants, communications, insurance, personal services, etc.) and over one-third are involved in agricultural work. The rest participate in manufacturing (Neft and Levine 1997). Overall, women are heavily represented in professional, sales, clerical, and service

positions. By and large, these patterns follow those found in the United States. In Europe, Latin America, and the Caribbean, women occupy about half of all professional and technical positions and about two-thirds of clerical and service jobs (United Nations 1995).

Among industrial countries, the gender gap in authority in the private economy appears to be lower in the United States than in many other countries. A recent study of employed individuals in Canada, the United Kingdom, Australia, Sweden, Norway, Japan, and the United States revealed that the gap was smallest in the United States and Australia, whereas Japan showed the widest difference in male and female authority. These differences persisted even after variations in characteristics in workplaces, jobs, and individual, were taken into account (Wright, Baxter, and Birkelund 1995).

Earnings constitute another area in which gender inequality is prominent. In none of the 50 countries in which men's and women's earnings have been analyzed are women's earnings equal to those of men. Unfortunately, these studies focus on earnings from manufacturing or nonagricultural occupations. Since many women work in agricultural jobs, especially in developing nations, the picture given of wage discrepancies between the genders in these studies is, at best, incomplete. Those countries in which women receive earnings that are at least 85 percent of what men receive include Norway, Sweden, and Australia among industrial nations, and Tanzania, Vietnam, Sri Lanka, Colombia, Kenya, and Turkey, among developing countries. In 2004, U.S. women earned about 80 percent of what men did, which puts the United States near the middle in terms of earnings differences between men and women. Among industrial countries, the United States lags behind Australia, Norway, Sweden, France, New Zealand, Denmark, Finland, Netherlands, Germany, Belgium, Italy, Portugal, Greece, Austria, and Poland in gender earnings equality. Among the nations with the greatest earnings inequality are Russia, Bangladesh, Japan, and Guam, where women's earnings equal no more than half those of men (United Nations

1995; Neft and Levine 1997). In sum, women's involvement in the economy, occupation segregation by sex, and lower authority for women are common around the world, but when compared to many other industrial countries, earnings differences between men and women have been higher in the United States.

In addition to their involvement in the formal economy, women throughout the world also spend significantly more time than men on unpaid housework. In industrial countries, women spend at least 30 hours per week on housework, compared to 10 to 15 hours for men. In developing countries, the figures are 31 to 42 hours and 5 to 15 hours, respectively. How equally housework is distributed between men and women is affected by *individual-level* variables such as belief in gender inequality and the time that women have for housework, and these factors in turn are affected by *national-level* factors that provide the context in which individual elements operate. Among the national-level variables that are important in this regard are level of economic development, gender ideology, and welfare policies (Fuwa 2004). This research supports several of the general theoretical arguments discussed earlier.

International differences in gender inequality as well as disparities within the United States are affected by globalization. Rather than being gender-neutral or impartial, globalization has profound and unique gender effects, effects that are generally more costly for women than for men (Chow 2003; Mills 2003; Gottfried 2004). This should not be surprising because globalization is simultaneously an economic, cultural, social, and political process; and in each of these spheres there are gender differences. Among the economic costs for women are "feminization of labor in segregated and low-paying work, wage dependency, labor exploitation, economic marginalization, poverty, sex tourism, and international human trafficking of women and young girls" (Chow 2003, p. 454). Economically, global capitalism can enlist sexist ideology to justify and perpetuate lower wages for women in a variety of cultural contexts. Women migrating from poorer to richer countries in search of better lives serve as domestic workers and nannies for two-career families in wealthy countries. As low as their wages may be by Western standards, the conditions and opportunities that immigrants experience in their new countries are often better than those they had in their countries of origin. We need to understand that a group's cultural and social experiences will affect its views of the costs and benefits of globalization. Whether globalization is seen as a largely positive or negative force depends in part on the vantage point from which it is viewed (Kabeer 2004).

The prevalence of women working in the United States along with continued gender inequities in housework and lack of child care support, for example, create a need and opportunity for domestic workers, many of whom are immigrants who expect better economic conditions than in their home countries. In other words, gender inequalities *within* a nation help spur the immigration of women *between* countries. The migration of women as workers is a widespread phenomenon. "In the United States, African-American women, who accounted for 60 percent of domestics in the 1940s, have been largely replaced by Latinas, many of them recent migrants from Mexico and Central America. In England, Asian migrant women have displaced the Irish and Portuguese domestics of the past. In French cities, North African women have replaced rural French girls. In western Germany, Turks and women from the former East Germany have replaced rural native-born women" (Ehrenreich and Hochschild 2005, p. 52). Lacking political, union, and economic power, these workers are open to exploitation by their employers.

Internationally, poverty and gender inequality are linked to the high prevalence of sex and slave trafficking of women and children. Estimates of trafficking range wildly; at least 700,000 victims and perhaps several million are trafficked every year (Troshynski and Blank 2008; Yen 2008). Some 100,000 to 150,000 individuals are believed to be in slavery in the United States. The United States ranks second in the world, behind Germany, as a destination or market for sex slavery. Well over 90 percent of the sexually exploited are women (Schauer and Wheaton 2006). In 2000, the United Nations estimated that sex trafficking yielded $5–$7 billion in profit (Shifman 2003). The technology of the Internet has made the buying and selling of women easier and increased its prevalence. In the demand for sex laborers, gender often intersects with racial, class, and age characteristics in that men may have desires for particular kinds of women. Gendered values in a society may privilege certain qualities: "perhaps some of this demand grows out of the erotic lure of the 'exotic.' Immigrant women may seem desirable sexual partners for the same reason that First World employers believe them to be especially gifted as caregivers: they are thought to embody the traditional feminine qualities of nurturance, docility, and eagerness to please . . . some men seek in the 'exotic Orient' or 'hot-blooded' tropics a woman from the imagined past" (Ehrenreich and Hochschild 2005, pp. 53–54). In this way, globalization activates the use of gendered values in the perpetuation of gender inequality.

While domestic work and sexual labor offer two specific areas in which globalization has an impact, globalization has also had a broader effect on labor-force segregation. It has reinforced and reproduced traditional gender differences in the workplace, relegating women to positions of lower pay and authority than those of men. At the same time, globalization has created some economic independence for some women and encouraged labor activism among them (Mills 2003). Some have even found that greater foreign investment by transnational corporations reduces occupational segregation (Meyer 2003).

How much globalization reproduces sex segregation in occupations within a nation depends in part on the relative position of the country in the world economic system as a whole. Globalization may exacerbate gender occupational inequality in some countries while lessening it in others. For example, Meyer (2003) found that high levels of trade and increased foreign investment have more of a weakening effect on segregation and inequality in the occupational structure in less-developed

countries than in more-developed countries. This results in part from the movement of women into traditional male occupations, such as manufacturing. But she cautions that this lessening of segregation does not reveal many of the qualitative properties of the jobs that women get nor does it take into account the prevalence of women in the underground economy. She also observes that the segregation reductions may be temporary.

Occupational segregation and inequality in industrial countries appear to be much less affected by these globalization processes. From her study of 56 nations, Meyer (2003) contends that "[t]his is likely due to the fact that the economic structures in advanced industrialized nations counteract global forces and societal features . . . thereby promoting nominal segregation through the incorporation of women's traditional tasks into the formal economy" (pp. 270, 272).

While occupational segregation may not be as affected by globalization in industrial countries like the United States as it is in less-industrialized nations, globalization does have other implications for gender inequality in the United States. For example, globalization has created more competition for major stockbroker firms on the international market and, consequently, greater pressure for increased effort and longer work hours for employees, most of whom are men. The result is the perpetuation and even intensification of gender inequity in housework. More time at work means less time for family, and higher pay means less need for spouses to work, thereby solidifying the traditional division of labor between husbands and wives (Blair-Loy and Jacobs 2003). More generally, globalization in the form of increased trade appears to be more likely to reduce gender wage inequality in concentrated than in competitive industries in the United States because it opens up these traditionally sheltered industries to international competition (Black and Brainerd 2004). Thus, as in other areas of inequality, conclusions about the effects of globalization need to take into account the economic and cultural contours of the units being examined.

Summary

This chapter has documented the historical socioeconomic position of women in the United States. Despite having been consistently involved in the economy since colonial times, women have regularly faced sex segregation and relegation to lower statuses in their employment. Occupational conditions today still reveal distinct inequalities between men and women. Women (1) are involved in a smaller range of occupations, (2) are less likely to be in positions of authority, (3) are more likely to work in smaller organizations in the peripheral sector of the economy, (4) are more likely to occupy positions with short career ladders, and (5) make less money than men even when they work full-time, year-round, and have comparable educational levels. A variety of microinequities involving language, popular media and stereotypes, and education also pervade relationships between men and women.

Attempts to account for the inequalities between the sexes suggest that differences in human capital, commitment to the labor force, work effort, and interruptions due to childbearing and rearing do not account substantially for the differences in earnings and occupational placement. The differential arrangement of women and men along the occupational hierarchy is, however, directly related to the discrepancy in earnings between the sexes, especially when we consider the differences in the characteristics of the jobs most often held by men and women.

Broader theories of sex inequality have focused on (1) the cultural underpinnings of gender inequality, (2) the position of women in the work organization of society, (3) the hostile or friendly character of the natural environment, (4) capitalism's requirements and women's role in necessary labor, and (5) early patriarchal structures. Women's roles in the domestic and economic public spheres appear to have direct consequences for their overall position in society. At the same time, we must keep in mind that not all women are in the same position because each one's position is affected by the intersection of her race, class, and gender. Multiracial feminist theories warn us against the dangers of generalizing too broadly.

Oppression against women varies widely around the world. The extent of extreme forms such as female circumcision, honor killings, suicide, and sex trafficking differs among societies. Women also spend significantly more time on housework than men. And there is sex segregation in the occupational structure. Globalization has had an impact on the constraints and opportunities afforded women across the world. Its effects vary among nations depending on the position of the country in the world economic system. For example, the movement of women into careers in the industrial world has fostered a demand for more domestic workers, many of whom are immigrants from technologically less-advanced countries. This creates opportunities for some women but also the possibility for continued oppression.

Critical Thinking

1. Think about a specific occupation and its likely occupant (e.g., police officer, elementary school teacher, home builder). Does a specific sex come to mind? Why?
2. In your own life, how have sex and gender limited you or allowed you to act a certain way or get involved in particular kinds of activities? What was it about your sex or gender that created this effect?
3. In many parts of the world, women are pressed by customs to accept beatings by their male spouses for minor cultural infractions such as talking back and leaving the house without notifying the husband. How can this be changed without showing disrespect for the culture in those countries?
4. As technologies and the bases of the U.S. economy change, will men and women become more equal economically? Support your answer.

Web Connections

The Global Policy Forum is a nonprofit, tax-exempt organization that consults with the United Nations on issues of international law and equity among nations. The section on global inequality, there are recommended articles on gender inequality and comparisons of countries on the gender gap. Visit www.globalpolicy.org/socecon/index.htm.

Film Suggestions

American Women of Achievement (1995). A 10-part series on important women in U.S. history.

Dreamworlds 3: Desire, Sex, and Power in Music Video (2007). Concerns sexual identity, masculinity, and femininity.

Men Are Human, Women Are Buffalo (2008). A documentary about domestic violence in Thailand.

CHAPTER 7

Sexual Orientation, Gender Identity, and Inequality

Out of the crooked timber of humanity no straight thing can ever be made.

IMMANUEL KANT (1724–1804)

In the previous chapter, we focused on sex and gender and discussed a variety of inequalities that exist between males and females as the two traditionally recognized sexes. In this chapter, we will examine status inequality that results from sexual orientation, principally the inequities associated with being gay or lesbian. Unfortunately, sexual orientation has generally been ignored as a basis for inequality. Like gays and lesbians themselves, the study of these groups in the field of inequality has been largely invisible. "With some noticeable exceptions . . . sociologists of race, class, and gender nonetheless tended to treat sexuality as a weakly integrated addendum to the list of intersecting oppressions" (Gamson and Moon 2004, p. 52).

Historically, Western society has viewed the either/or sets of male/female, masculine/feminine, and heterosexuality/homosexuality as exhausting sexual possibilities and as closely interlocked. Men are meant to behave in a masculine manner while women are supposed to perform in a feminine manner, and heterosexuality is considered a part of their masculine and feminine performances. Heterosexuality has been viewed as natural and therefore normal, a view supported by dominant institutions, values, and behaviors. Additional typologies such as public/private, instrumental/expressive, and rational/emotional, have further reinforced the legitimacy of traditional sex/gender dichotomies.

The continued emphasis on these dichotomies as "natural" lends them a seemingly timeless and universal quality. Consequently, individuals who do not fit into such neat categories or do not behave in the culturally prescribed manner have been thought of as deviant. Judeo-Christian dogma views normal, moral, and legitimate sex as having a reproductive function and as belonging in monogamous marriages between men and women, and views same-sex relations as sinful and abnormal (Herdt 1997).

But traditional binary categories of sex and related genders are neither timeless, nor universal, nor natural. They are social constructions found only in some societies during specific periods of time. Katz (2004) observes that " 'homosexual' and 'heterosexual,' the terms we moderns take for granted, are fairly recent creations. Although presented to us as words marking an eternal fact of nature, the terms 'heterosexual' and 'homosexual' constitute a normative sexual ethic, a sexual-political ideology, and one historically specific way of categorizing the relationships of the sexes" (p. 45). How one defines oneself sexually is also not permanent but rather varies according to historical, situational, and cultural circumstances, and can be affected by one's race and class. The meaning of sexuality intersects with cultural images of gender, race, and class, and this intersection helps to reinforce stereotypes and justify oppression and inequality (Gamson and Moon 2004). The meanings of masculinity, femininity, and sexuality in general vary with one's race and class.

THE COMPLEXITY OF SEXUALITY AND GENDER

The fact that some individuals use surgery to cross the lines separating male and female, and engage in behaviors and demeanors that breach gender lines of masculinity and femininity, attests to the fluidity of both sex and gender. In some cases, gender can even be a temporary or situational experience, as when an individual routinely shifts behavior and physical presentation according to desire. "I'm not trying to be permanently that person [i.e., a man or a woman]. I just like [taking] the opportunity to be a man or a woman, if I want" (Irvine, October 2, 2005, p. A5).

The simplistic, traditional, either/or categories of male/female, masculine/feminine, and heterosexuality/homosexuality miss much of the variety of actual human experiences (Lorber 1996). While most Westerners think of man and woman as

mutually exclusive categories, a number of countries around the world recognize more than two sexes, sexualities, and genders. For example, in India, the *hijras,* while male at birth, define themselves as neither men nor women but as a third gender. They wear women's clothing and may marry men. Yet they are not stigmatized, but are thought to exemplify the time-honored Hindu belief that each person possesses both male and female elements. *Hijras* personify this dualism and the valued "ambiguity of in-between sexual categories" (Andersen 1997, pp. 21–22). Another illustration of the complexity of sexuality concerns individuals who have intersexed anatomies. " **'Intersex'** refers to a condition in which a person is born with reproductive or sexual characteristics that do not fit neatly into either the female or male category" (Intersex Society of North America 2011). A person may have some cells that have XX chromosomes while other cells have XY chromosomes. This variation in human anatomy covers a wide array of sex-anatomy combinations, and is thought to occur in about one out of 1,500 children (Blackless et al. 2000).

The traditional and allegedly universal pairs of male/masculine and female/feminine are also undermined by **transgendered** individuals who have the anatomy of one sex but feel like another. For example, a biological male may psychologically identify as a female, or vice versa. Given their emotional identities, transgendered persons may cross-dress or become transsexual by pursuing hormonal or surgical prescriptions to create consistency between their physical bodies and psychological identities (Johnson, Mimiaga, and Bradford 2008).

Individuals who are transsexuals may describe themselves as being heterosexual, bisexual, gay, or lesbian. Ironically, a majority of transsexuals do not challenge the idea that men should be masculine and women should be feminine. That is, they accept the traditional gender categories. However, they define themselves as members of the opposite sex, and therefore adopt many of those roles and attitudes traditionally associated with that sex. Some argue that sexual identity involves a variety of elements and thus their combinations can result in multiple possible sexual identities. Among others, these elements include one's biological sex at birth, self-identity of gender, biological sex of partner, and the distribution of masculine and feminine traits in one's personality (Sedgwick 1998). The wide variety of self-identities, gender practices, and even biological differences found in contemporary society have led a growing number of scholars to urge replacement of the traditional dichotomies of male/female and masculine/feminine with more complex classification systems of sexuality and gender (e.g., Lorber 1996; Andersen 1997; Herdt 1997).

Because of their mixing of gender, sex, and sexuality, the position of transsexuals and bisexuals remains ambiguous within the gay and lesbian community. In other words, transsexuals violate the norms within the homosexual community of what it means to be a "normal" or "good" homosexual. They are not fully accepted and are stigmatized by many "ordinary" homosexuals. The final result is that transsexuals and bisexuals are often relegated to a position of low status within a community that is itself stigmatized by the larger heterosexual society (Phelan 2001, pp. 115–117).

In the discussion that follows, I will concentrate on gay and lesbian groups. It appears that while knowledge of same-sex relations goes far back in history, the technical dichotomy of heterosexuality and homosexuality as we know it today is of nineteenth-century origin; it "is a product of the transition to modernity. . . . This sexual transformation involved such factors as the institutionalization of bourgeois middle-class values, the secularization of social medicine and state discourse on sexuality, the individualized concept of desire and identity, and the premium placed on reproduction within the nuclear family" (Herdt 1997, p. 39). At that time, homosexuality was considered abnormal and a disease, a kind of degeneracy from the healthy condition of heterosexuality. In fact, up until 1973, homosexuality was listed as a mental illness by the American Psychiatric Association (APA). Recent studies indicate that homosexuality *itself* is not a good predictor of mental illness. However, strong and consistent identification with the opposite gender (gender identity disorder) is still listed as a disorder in the *Diagnostic Statistical Manual* (DSM IV).

Despite evidence to the contrary, and even after removal from its list as an illness by the APA, some psychoanalysts and Christian counselors continue to view homosexuality as a pathological condition (Gonsiorek 1996). In large part, this is because the standard heterosexual view of the strict, accepted relationships among sex, gender, and sexuality is not observed by homosexuals. Instead of a female desiring a male, there is sexual inversion in which a female, for example, desires another female. In heterosexual society, this defines homosexuality as an aberration (Phelan 2001). In each of the traditional dichotomies of male/female, masculine/feminine, and heterosexual/homosexual, one category has been given higher social status in the United States over the other. In the case of the last, heterosexuality is valued and honored over homosexuality. This belief was manifested in the recent political controversy surrounding gay marriages, which most opponents viewed as being antithetical to traditional moral values.

PUBLIC OPINIONS ON HOMOSEXUALITY

The preceding comments suggest that many still believe deeply that homosexuality is unnatural and unhealthy, if not immoral. When one adds to this the belief by staunchly religious groups that homosexuality is also sinful, it is not surprising that, up until the early decades of the twentieth century in the United States, gay networks tried to avoid harassment by keeping out of the public eye. In the mid-twentieth century, the anti-alien crusades of Senator Joseph McCarthy and FBI director J. Edgar Hoover as well as city police across the country continued to single out gays and lesbians as targets who were thought to undermine the heterosexual family as a cultural foundation. "Homosexual acts were illegal in most states under existing anti-sodomy statutes. . . . Furthermore, gays and lesbians were specifically excluded from laws and policies regulating fair employment practices, housing discrimination, rights of child custody, immigration, inheritance, security clearances, public accommodations, and police protection" (Button, Rienzo, and Wald 1997, p. 24).

The public's attitudes about the morality of homosexuality have become more positive in recent years. Data from the General Social Survey showed that in 2002, 53 percent of American adults felt that homosexuality was "always wrong." In contrast, a 2008 Gallup poll found people split on the morality of homosexuality, and a 2010 survey found that a slight majority thought that homosexuality was "morally acceptable" (Gallup Poll 2008; Saad, May 5, 2010). Consistent with these polls, a general review of surveys done between 1992 and 2007 revealed a decrease in the percentage of those who believe homosexuality is morally wrong. The reviewers also found that solid majorities would be willing to have gay neighbors, and thought that it was okay to hire homosexuals as elementary or high school teachers (Schafer and Shaw 2009).

However, Americans appear to disagree on whether the trend toward greater acceptance of lesbians and gays is a positive one. Republicans, White evangelical Protestants, less-educated and older adults are more likely than other groups to see the trend in a negative light (Pew Research Center, December 21, 2009). The continuing split in public attitudes is reflected in the fact that, up until very recently, a number of states still had laws against sodomy. Sodomy laws in 18 states were only repealed after 2000, several of these in 2003.

When it comes to gay marriage, several polls indicate that more Americans still disapprove than approve of it despite a decline in opposition in the last few years. In two 2010 polls of over 6,000 people, 42 percent favored same-sex marriage while 48 percent disapproved of it. But this is up from 2008, when 39 percent expressed approval and 51 percent disapproval, and 2001 when 35 percent approved while 57 percent opposed same-sex marriage (Pew Research Center, October 6, 2010). Other polls also show slight movement in the direction of approval (Saad, May 5, 2010). In 2011, same-sex couples could receive marriage licenses in only five states (Massachusetts, Connecticut, Iowa, New Hampshire, New York, and Vermont) and the District of Columbia. Thirty-one states had passed laws banning such marriages (Schwartz,

November 9, 2010). Interestingly, gays and lesbians are about as likely to be partnered together as families as are heterosexual individuals (Black, Sanders, and Taylor 2007). Because they cannot get married in most states, same-sex couples are denied a wide variety of rights that are given to married couples. Among others, these include the right to hospital visitation if the partner is seriously injured, Social Security and pension benefits for a surviving partner, employer health insurance, and family leave if the partner is sick. These rights may be present in some states that permit civil unions but not marriage for same-sex couples. In 2009, a majority of adults reportedly supported civil unions for same-sex partners, allowing gays and lesbians to obtain many of the same rights as married heterosexual couples (Pew Research Center, October 9, 2009).

When specific rights are singled out, the public's attitude often softens or becomes more ambivalent (Gallup Poll 2008; Pew Research Center 2006). For example, when asked about homosexuals' rights to adopt children, the public is almost evenly split. But almost two-thirds consider a gay couple with children to be a family (Pew Research Center, November 18, 2010). About 9 out of 10 adults believe homosexuals should have the same job opportunities as everyone else. A majority also believes that homosexual relations between consenting adults should be legal. By and large, the belief that civil liberties ought to be curtailed among homosexuals has steadily declined since the early 1970s (Gallup Poll 2008; Pew Research Center 2003).

The sharp contrast in Americans' reactions to homosexuals' *morality,* on the one hand, and their rights to *civil liberties,* on the other, may in part be explained by how each of these is interpreted. While *morality* relates to *individual behavior* and activates traditional heterosexual and religious beliefs of Americans, *civil rights* relates to homosexuals as a *group,* does not refer to a specific behavior, and is not as easily linked to religious beliefs. Rather, the civil rights issue is more easily tied to traditional American values of equality and fairness (Loftus 2001). The difference in respondents' attitudes in these two areas exposes contradictions within the value systems of most Americans.

Not all subcategories of adults are equally likely to hold positive or negative attitudes about lesbians and gays, however. Those who believe that homosexuality is something one is born with or cannot be changed are more sympathetic toward homosexuals and are more likely to support homosexual rights and marriage than are those who view it as a chosen lifestyle (Button, Rienzo, and Wald 1997; Pew Research Center, May 14, 2003; Haider-Markel and Joslyn 2008). In 2007–2008, Americans were almost evenly split between those who think homosexuality is something one is born with and those who believe it a result of their environment (Dienstfrey 2007; Gallup Poll 2008).

In general, men appear to be more heterosexist than women on a variety of dimensions. They are more hostile toward (1) homosexuals as *individuals,* especially when this involves gays rather than lesbians; (2) homosexual *behavior*; (3) *civil rights* for gays in traditionally masculine roles such as service in the military; and (4) gay marriage (Kite and Whitley 1998; Pew Research Center 2006; Harris Interactive 2007; Brumbaugh et al. 2008). In addition to gender, education is also related to homophobia, with more education being associated with lower degrees of prejudice. Within educational institutions, students in the arts and social sciences are more positive in their attitudes than are those majoring in business or science (Schellenberg, Hirt, and Sears 1999). Among age groups, a greater proportion of those age 65 and older are prejudiced, compared to those under 30 years of age. This may be partially accounted for by the generally lower education and greater religious traditionalism among older adults. Table 7.1 lists the population categories found by Loftus (2001) to be most negative about the morality of homosexuality and most willing to restrict the civil liberties of homosexuals. Results from a 2006 Pew survey reveal similar results, with those who are male, older, rural, lesser-educated, southern, conservative, and White evangelical Protestant having more negative views of homosexuals. With regard to race, a review of 31 national surveys conducted between 1973 and 2000 indicates that while Blacks are more likely to be against

TABLE 7.1 Demographic Categories Most Negative on Morality and Civil Liberties of Homosexuals

Most likely to view homosexuality as immoral or to believe in restricting civil liberties of homosexuals are those who are:

- Older
- Less educated
- Male
- From the south central part of the United States
- Other than White or Black
- Persons who lived on farm or in country at age 16
- Fundamentalist Protestant in religious affiliation

Source: Loftus 2001.

homosexuality on moral grounds, they are more supportive than Whites of protecting the civil rights of homosexuals (Lewis 2003).

Several studies suggest that the greater hostility of Blacks to homosexuality appears to be directly related to their higher degree of religiousness. There is some evidence that African American undergraduate women have more negative attitudes toward gays and lesbians than their White counterparts. Religious views and perceived threats of AIDS and about the availability of acceptable men for marriage may help account for these racial differences in attitudes (Vincent, Peterson, and Parrott 2009). Other research shows that an estimated 58 percent of Blacks and 59 percent of Hispanic voters in 2008 supported Proposition 8, which banned gay marriage in California. The support of Blacks was linked to their greater religiousness. Seventy percent of voters who attended religious services weekly, along with a greater percentage of politically conservative, Republicans voted for the ban (Egan and Sherrill, January 2009). Finally, a survey of gay rights ordinances in 126 communities identified evangelical, charismatic churches as most likely to oppose gay rights legislation (Button, Rienzo, and Wald 1997).

The attitudes adults hold about homosexuals are at least moderately related to stereotypes held about them. These stereotypes include beliefs about gays' personality traits, behavior, and physical characteristics. Popular stereotypes of gays and lesbians suggest that negative reactions to them are due in part to the fact that they are seen as violating traditional gender rules about behavior and interests. The hostility toward men who violate masculine roles appears to be stronger than that toward women who violate feminine prescriptions (Kite and Whitley 1998; Herek 2002). Parents seem to be concerned that their sons, more so than their daughters, conform to the traditional gender role associated with their sex (Kane 2006). Gay men are more likely than lesbians to be seen by respondents as being mentally ill, as potential child predators, and as less likely to make good parents. These feelings are more prevalent among heterosexual men than women. Although this was found to be true for both, heterosexual men are also more likely than women to feel uncomfortable around a homosexual of the same sex. Herek's 2002 results are also consistent with research that finds victimization to be higher among older gay men than lesbians (D'Augelli and Grossman 2001).

Stereotypes about gay men suggest that they are viewed as being feminine, emotional, security-seeking, neat, interested in fine arts, and creative, with high-pitched voices (see Simon 1998 for a summary). In her multimethod study among Rutgers University students, Stephanie Madon (1997) found that there are also subtypes within stereotypes of gay men. On the one hand, they are generally viewed as possessing some positive feminine personality traits (e.g., compassion, gentleness), while on the other hand, they are seen as violating masculine roles (e.g., "walk like girls," "transvestites"). Of these two components, it is their violation of traditional masculine roles that is more strongly held in popular stereotypes, and it is this dimension of the stereotype that may be most clearly linked to prejudice against gay men. Stereotypes about lesbians, like those of gay men, contain violations of traditional feminine roles in featuring many masculine traits. Lesbians are characterized as being independent

and independently minded, open and loud, stubborn, and not good for children.

Labeling an individual as having the traits of either of these stereotypes, and therefore as being automatically lesbian or gay, can have significant consequences. Consider the case of Sara Harb Quiroz, a permanent and employed U.S. resident who, on her way back into Texas from Juarez, Mexico, was stopped by an immigration agent (Luibheid 1998). Evidence indicated that she was stopped because her appearance revealed several masculine characteristics. She wore pants and a shirt instead of a dress and her hair was cut "abnormally" short for a female. Ms. Quiroz may or may not have been a lesbian.

Since as late as 1990, lesbian immigrants could be refused entry into the United States, and conscious attempts were made by border agents to identify lesbians. They looked for visible cues to the individual's sexual preference. Lesbian immigrants were often aware of this kind of screening, so they dressed and prepared themselves physically so that they would not appear to violate traditional images of what a woman *should* look like. This is known as "straightening up," which "includes practices like growing one's hair and nails, buying a dress, accessorizing, and donning makeup. . . . [The fact that one has to do this only] confirmed the 'bug'-like status of lesbians within the immigration system" (Luibheid 1998, pp. 485–486).

It appears that the stereotyping of gays and lesbians has helped to perpetuate negative attitudes about them. Since stereotyping often develops in the absence of regular contact between the groups involved, it would seem that increased contact and acquaintance with gay and lesbian individuals might decrease prejudice against these groups, and indeed, this is the case. An analysis of 41 studies revealed that contact reduces prejudice toward gays and lesbians. However, contact is more effective in reducing negative attitudes about lesbians than it is in reducing prejudice by heterosexuals against gay men (Smith, Axelton, and Saucier 2009). The positive effect of contact on lowering prejudice has been found for other groups in many other studies as well (Pettigrew and Tropp 2006). This is especially likely if the contact is of an equal status type among individuals pursuing a common goal.

GAYS AND LESBIANS AS STATUS GROUPS

As the surveys just discussed indicate, lesbians and gays, like women and Blacks, form status categories with low prestige or social honor in the United States. As such, they possess all the core attributes of status groups. Most notably, they are viewed by others as sharing certain lifestyle characteristics and being qualitatively different from outsiders. Being gay or lesbian is associated with having certain kinds of occupations (e.g., hairdresser) and dress (high fashion, artsy) (Madon 1997). However, their differences are defined as even deeper. Recall that in his depiction of status groups, Max Weber argued that extreme status separation between groups is most likely if the differences that separate them are thought of as being "ethnic" in nature. Consistent with this conception, gay scholar Stephen Murray has referred to the homosexual community as a "quasi-ethnic group" (1996, p. 4). This suggests that the differences must be viewed as fundamental, almost biological in nature, for castelike arrangements to develop between groups. Indeed, about 8 out of 10 U.S. adults currently believe that homosexuality is either biologically based or something with which one is born that cannot be changed, *or* a product of upbringing (Dienstfrey 2007; Gallup Poll 2008). In their fight for political legitimacy and equal rights, the earliest gay-rights organizations in the United States (e.g., the Mattachine Society) characterized "homosexuals as a sexual minority, similar to other ethnic and cultural minorities" (Button, Rienzo, and Wald 1997, p. 25). Those currently at the forefront of the gay-rights movement also "argue that homosexual orientation is a genetic condition like skin color or gender" (Newport 1998, p. 14).

The latter comment is quite revealing because in the case of each of the three principally involved groups implied in the statement (i.e., homosexuals, Blacks, women), fundamental values are at stake. Specifically, sexual orientation, race, and gender are each controversial and sensitive areas of conflict. They are touchstones for battles in the United States over basic values involving sexual behavior, racial superiority, and appropriate gender roles. Since these are important matters in U.S. society, it should be expected that status boundaries should separate those who fall on different sides of these values. In the case of sexual orientation, gays and lesbians are clearly defined as being on the wrong side regarding moral values. One consequence is their exclusion from full citizenship in U.S. society (Phelan 2001).

In addition to being viewed as qualitatively different in lifestyle, being seen as a different "kind" of people, separated from the rest of society, and occupying a distinctive place on a hierarchy of social honor or prestige, a status group is also perceived as having an internal social cohesion that unites them. That is, they are seen as sticking together and being mutually supportive of each other. As with most status groups, outsiders lump them all together, even though there are sources of internal division, such as race, within the homosexual community. On the other hand, given that the crucial factor of sexual orientation is what divides them from and is the prime basis for conflict with outsiders, it is defense involving this factor that helps to unite them. This has resulted not only in the creation of informal friendship networks among gays and lesbians but also in the development of neighborhoods with high concentrations of lesbians and gays, separate institutions catering to a homosexual clientele, and political-rights organizations.

Finally, what further marks gays and lesbians as negatively defined status groups are fears of contamination and contact on the part of outsiders. Concerns about purity on the part of traditionalists and heterosexuals are indicative of concerted attempts to keep boundaries between heterosexuals and homosexuals intact. Publically known association by a heterosexual with homosexuals, especially of a personal kind, creates the risk that some of the ostracism held for lesbians and gays may "rub off" on the individual. The murder involving guests on a television show is a good example of the stigmatization felt by a man who had been connected to a gay acquaintance. In front of live and national audiences, the gay guest professed his love for the man. The man later killed his gay friend because he felt "humiliated" by this profession of love (Turner, May 17, 1999).

Fear of association is also suggested by polls that indicate that only a small percentage of U.S. adults feel warmhearted about gays and lesbians and only about half feel homosexual couples should be allowed to adopt children (Yang 1997; Pew Research Center, August 21, 2008). This is despite the fact that evidence does not support the conclusion that homosexuals are more likely than heterosexuals to be sexual predators or that children who are raised by gays or lesbians will be damaged or turn out to be homosexuals themselves (Andersen 1997). In the 1960s, gay and lesbian parents who sought custody of their children were frequently denied it because court opinions were dominated by the beliefs that gay men and lesbian women were more likely than heterosexual parents to molest their children and pass on their sexual orientation to their children. These beliefs gradually eroded so that by the mid-1980s, court opinions were shifting (Rivers 2010). Recent research indicates that children who grow up with lesbian or gay parents are not likely to be abused by them, and that most child sexual abuse in homes is done by heterosexual men (Balsam, Rothblum, and Beauchaine 2005; Gartrell, Bos, and Goldberg 2010). Results also show that adolescent children of lesbian mothers appear to be well-adjusted, more socially and academically competent, and less likely to engage in delinquent behavior than children of heterosexual parents (Gartrell and Bos 2010).

Still, negative beliefs persist in part because they are consistent with prevailing stereotypes and help justify hostile treatment of homosexuals. Despite evidence to the contrary, opponents of gay rights often use "lurid stereotypes of gays as child molesters, sources of disease, and an abomination in the eyes of God" (Button, Rienzo, and Wald 1997, p. 195). It is feared that unless gays and lesbians are held in check, traditional morality and family structure as foundations of our society will become contaminated and seriously weakened. In the eyes of these opponents, social, cultural, and moral purity must be maintained, and contamination avoided at all costs.

DISCRIMINATION, LEGAL CONFUSION, AND SEXUAL ORIENTATION

No federal laws explicitly prohibit discrimination based on sexual orientation. For example, Title VII of the 1964 Civil Rights Act prohibits employment discrimination because of an individual's race, color, religion, national origin, or sex, but it offers no such prohibition based on sexual orientation. Arguments in favor of protection for homosexuals under Title VII generally involved reference to the inclusion of "sex" in the law.

The meaning of the phrase "because of sex" has been a subject of debate, and its interpretation has varied between courts and levels of courts. Some judges have argued, for example, that just because a man harasses a woman on the job, this does not mean he does so because of her sex. Others have suggested that simply showing interest in the other sex constitutes discrimination. Many recent courts have argued that harassment is often based on hostility that has nothing to do with the recipient's sex, and, therefore, is not protected under Title VII (Hebert 2001). The confusion over this issue is explored more fully below.

The fate of proposed legislation on sexual orientation is strongly tied to (1) the extent to which it is seen as supporting or undermining traditional values and social order, and (2) how effectively and in what manner the issue is framed by proponents and opponents to the legislation. The 1996 Defense of Marriage Act (DOMA) provides a good example of this process. The subject of DOMA related directly to the moral dimension of public opinions on homosexuality. As we saw earlier, polls often uncover a clear schism in the public's view of the morality of homosexuality on the one hand, and the affording of civil rights to gays and lesbians on the other. While a majority of the public views homosexuality as immoral, a large majority also feel that the economic rights of lesbians and gays should be protected. On a broad level, the conflict experienced by the majority is one that pits religious values against those of a secular democracy, and highlights the issue of separation of church and state.

Traditional U.S. values assign privilege to heterosexual over homosexual relationships, and assume a narrow and clear relationship between one's sex and gender role. Congressional sponsors proposed the DOMA bill "to define and protect the institution of marriage" and "to make explicit what has been understood under federal law for over 200 years; that a marriage is the legal union of a man and a woman as husband and wife, and a spouse is a husband or wife of the opposite sex" (Barr et al. 1996, p. 2). In arguing for its passage, the proponents of DOMA focused on the need to preserve traditional values of family and morality and on alleged attempts by the gay community to undermine "civilized" society. Traditional marriage was praised "as a 'corner-stone,' 'foundation,' 'bedrock,' and 'fundamental pillar' of any civilized society" (Lewis and Edelson 2000, p. 202). In these ways, proponents of DOMA sought to frame the legislation in *moral* rather than *civil rights* terms, knowing the public's perception of homosexuality as immoral.

In contrast, opponents to DOMA—for example, those who wished to extend marriage rights to gays and lesbians—emphasized the need to enforce the *rights* of gays and lesbians as citizens. In this case, the moral framing of the issue won. Because of the public's continued negative reaction to homosexuality as a behavior, interest groups that wish to succeed in getting legislation passed that ensures homosexuals' full citizenship "will be most successful in the states if they can frame the issues in terms of *rights,* effectively mobilize group resources and sympathetic heterosexuals, and demobilize conservative religious groups" (Haider-Markel 2000, p. 314; emphasis added). Historically, success has been more likely in areas such as labor discrimination than on morally tinged issues such as sodomy and same-sex marriages (Lewis and Edelson 2000).

It is estimated that over 3 million people are in same-sex relationships, and that several million

The controversy over same-sex marriage hinges on the conflict between civil rights and moral values. (Photo by Brendan R. Hurst.)

children are being raised in them (Human Rights Campaign 2005a). The DOMA does not recognize same-sex marriages at the federal level, the result being that persons in long-term, same-sex relationships are not protected in the same ways that individuals in traditional marriages are. Proponents of gay marriage argue that same-sex couples are now denied many of the rights afforded persons in traditional marriages. Among others, the rights that are fully or partially denied to lesbians and gays include hospital visitation, Social Security survivor benefits, health insurance for partners, estate taxes, family leaves, pensions to survivors, and living together in nursing homes. As a whole, the federal government offers 1,138 benefits based on marital status, benefits that are not offered to same-sex couples (Human Rights Campaign 2005b; National Gay and Lesbian Task Force 2005).

More inclusive laws on hate crimes, marriage, employment discrimination, and adoption, remain issues in the homosexual community. In viewing the United States as "a heterosexual regime" with its denial of many protections to lesbians and gays, Shane Phelan (2001) argued that gay men and lesbians are not full citizens because "citizenship does not concern only what rights, offices, and duties are to accrue to citizens, but also how the polity decides who is eligible for them; that is, it concerns the structures of acknowledgment that define the class of persons eligible for those rights, offices, and duties" (p. 14). Acknowledgment means recognition and respect for a group's lifestyle and for *being* who one is. Social status is about *being* something, and in this case, being homosexual does not afford the same recognition as being heterosexual.

Fierce opposition is one of the reasons for the paucity of specific laws to protect lesbian women and gay men. In addition, effective and uniform legislation to protect homosexuals has been hampered by the legal profession's lack of clear understanding of basic terms relating to sexuality. Confusion and inconsistency in conceptualizing and defining "sex," "gender," and "sexual orientation" abound in legal venues. The manner in which these have been linked in legal cases reveals the biases in favor of traditional definitions and connections among these terms. Underlying these interpretations is the acceptance of heterosexuality as opposed to any other form. In this view, one's sex (defined biologically in terms of genitalia) is thought to automatically determine one's gender demeanor and role (social) as well as one's sexual orientation (sexual attractions and behavior). For example, males are expected to act in a masculine manner and to be attracted to females. They are not meant to be homosexual in their sexual orientation.

One consequence of these assumed associations is that courts often confuse sex, gender, and sexual orientation, and confuse them in a way that results in denying the rights not only of gays and lesbians, but also of those who do not present themselves or act in a manner traditionally expected of their sex. A man, for example, who acts "effeminately" and who may or may not be gay might not be protected by a court because judges directly link such behavior with being gay. As a consequence, while individuals who bring their complaints to court may argue that they are being discriminated against because they do not act in a "masculine" manner, courts often make decisions in these cases on the basis of sexual orientation, assuming that such behavior *means* that the persons are gay. In this way, gender role and sexual orientation are conflated and incorrectly tied together (Valdes 1995; Nathans 2001). This results in plaintiffs losing because, as noted earlier, Title VII does not cover discrimination based on sexual orientation. An example of the narrow manner in which courts have often interpreted Title VII is revealed explicitly in a 1979 case involving a female employee who was having a sex-change operation. The Ninth Circuit Court judge argued that in including sex as a basis for discrimination in Title VII, "Congress had only the traditional notions of '*sex*' in mind," and that it "applies only to discrimination on the basis of *gender* and should not be judicially extended to include sexual preference such as homosexuality" (quoted in Zimmer et al. 2000, pp. 624–625; italics added).

Ironically, the word *sex* was added to Title VII at the last minute by a powerful anti–civil rights representative who thought that, by adding it, Title VII would be voted down (Eskridge and Frickey 1995). It passed anyway. It is still difficult to know exactly what Congress had in mind, however, since *sex* was added to Title VII only a day after it was presented. Consequently, there was little time for discussion of the meaning of this inclusion (Nathans 2001). Attempts to use other bases, such as the right to privacy, free speech, and equal protection to protect gays and lesbians, have not been particularly successful (Zimmer et al. 2000). The ruling discussed above shows how the court used the terms *sex* and *gender* interchangeably (see also Case 1995). The easy substitution of the terms *sex* and *gender* in legal arguments adds to the confusion concerning the terms' meanings. The case also reveals the narrow manner in which sexuality is framed by the court. Finally, the legal situation is further complicated by the fact that some courts define *sex* according to the biology of the person at birth, while others consider later operations that change an individual's biological makeup (Valdes 1995).

Although Title VII of the 1964 Civil Rights Act prohibits discrimination on the basis of sex, it is not clear what this means. As we have seen, the result has been confusion. Another example will illustrate the confusion of gender and sexual orientation. In the case of *Smith v. Liberty Mutual Insurance Co.,* Smith was not hired as a mail clerk because he was seen as "effeminate" and, consequently, "not too suited for the job" (quoted in Valdes 1995, p. 138). The representative for the Equal Employment Opportunity Commission, which examined the case, reported that Smith liked "playing musical instruments, singing, dancing and sewing." These were viewed as "interests . . . not normally associated with males" (p. 138). Smith argued that he had been denied employment because he had hobbies that were not consistent with the masculine role and, therefore, was a victim of gender stereotyping. That is, his argument had to do with the traditional connection made between sex and gender behavior. In contrast, the employer argued that he had not been hired because Smith was "suspected" of being gay. In other words, the employer drew a conclusion about Smith's sexual orientation based simply on his gender behavior. The court ended up drawing the same connection, noting that Title VII did not cover an individual's sexual orientation. Thus, it ignored the argument of Smith and the fact that the evidence demonstrated that the discrimination had been based, as Smith proposed, upon his *gender behavior* (effeminacy) and not his *sexual orientation.* This shows how the court used the plaintiff's behavior as a measure of his sexual orientation, and how stereotypical misinterpretations can result in legal defeats for lesbians, gays, and others.

Men who exhibit gender behaviors traditionally associated with females are more likely to face defeat in court than women who act in masculine ways. For example, in the famous 1989 case of *Price Waterhouse v. Hopkins,* the U.S. Supreme Court found that Ann Hopkins had been discriminated against because partners refused to propose her as a partner in the firm on the basis of her gender behavior. To them, Ann displayed many of the characteristics traditionally associated with masculinity. She was described by some partners as "macho," as having "overcompensated for being a woman," and in need of "a course at charm school" (*Price Waterhouse v. Hopkins* 1989). In spite of her evidenced abilities and experience, Hopkins was passed over for partnership. In ruling against Price Waterhouse because of sex stereotyping, Justice Brennan stated that:

> [W]e are beyond the day when an employer could evaluate employees by assuming or insisting that they matched the stereotype associated with their group. . . . An employer who objects to aggressiveness in women but whose positions require this trait places women in an intolerable and impermissible catch 22: out of a job if they behave aggressively and out of a job if they do not. Title VII lifts women out of this bind. (490 U.S., p. 251)

The disposition in the Ann Hopkins case was the opposite found in the Smith case discussed earlier. It appears there is less tolerance for "sissies" than for "tomboys" (Valdes 1995, p. 179). "The man who exhibits feminine qualities is doubly despised" (Case 1995, p. 3). This is consistent with public opinion surveys, which find a greater contempt for men who violate their traditional roles than for women who act similarly. Consequently, gay men who act effeminately are likely to bear a disproportionate amount of the discrimination leveled against homosexuals.

While legal protection for those with nontraditional sexual orientations has been weak at best at the federal level, a number of local and state governments have passed laws granting protection. Before 1985, only 2 states and 30 local governments provided protection for private and public employees, but by 1994, 9 states and 81 local governments had done so, and by 2010, over 130 cities and counties had passed laws against employment discrimination because of gender identity (Klawitter and Flatt 1998; Human Rights Campaign 2010). In these statutes, sexual orientation typically includes bisexuality, homosexuality, and heterosexuality (Zimmer et al. 2000). Even in many of these statutes, however, there are limitations to the protection of homosexuals. Some statutes exempt religious organizations, and if it can be proven that one's sexual preference is actually a "bona fide occupational qualification" for a position, then gays and lesbians may be excluded from that job (Zimmer et al., p. 634). Full legal protection for lesbians and gays has a long way to go.

A SOCIOECONOMIC PROFILE OF LESBIANS AND GAYS

Like data on the wealthy, we do not know very much about the actual socioeconomic position, or even the number, of gays and lesbians because many still fear "coming out" and can remain hidden because of the generally lower visibility of sexual orientation compared to one's race and sex. This alone tells us a great deal about the stigma attached to being homosexual. Moreover, the measurements of homosexuality have varied wildly. Persons who have sex with others of the same gender do not necessarily define themselves as lesbian or gay, nor are individuals who have had a homosexual experience at one time or another necessarily thought of as homosexuals.

The *invisibility* of lesbians and gays in society is a key feature differentiating this group from groups based on gender and race. On one hand, it provides a group that the majority may attack without concern regarding damage to family and friends who are unknown members of the group. On the other hand, the invisibility of homosexuals prevents young gays and lesbians from finding local positive role models and supporters. The unique invisibility of homosexuals as a group is revealed by reference to the military's previous "don't ask, don't tell" policy which assumes that gays and lesbians are invisible unless they are purposefully identified as such.

This invisibility has encouraged disagreements about how to measure the gay/lesbian population. Measurement issues have revolved around how to define homosexuality and how to procure a representative sample so as to estimate the size of this population. Some estimates have put the figure as high as 10 percent, but that is considered by some to be too high. A national survey of sexual practices suggested that about 2.4 percent of men and 1.3 percent of women (1) consider themselves homosexual or bisexual, (2) have same-sex partners, and (3) are attracted to homosexuality (Laumann et al. 1994). This may help account for the regional differences in prejudice against homosexuals discussed earlier.

Most recently, three national data sets have been used to determine the gay/lesbian population in the United States. The General Social Survey (GSS), the National Health and Social Life Survey (NHSLS), and the U.S. census provide the most accurate estimates. Each also provides several measures of sexual orientation. Historically and cross-culturally, determining a person's sexual identity on the basis of sexual behavior has been problematic (Badgett 2001).

Not surprisingly, the estimates of this population vary with the measure used. Pooling GSS and NHSLS data from the early and mid-1990s, Black and colleagues (2000) estimated that while 4.7 percent of men have had at least one homosexual experience since age 18, only 2.5 percent had only same-sex partners in the year before the survey, and only 1.8 percent of men defined themselves as gay. The figures for women also vary with the measure. For the same definitions, the percentages for women were 3.6, 1.4, and 0.6, respectively. The authors estimated that about 28 percent of men and 44 percent of women who had only same-sex relationships in the prior year had partners—that is, were living with a person of the same sex with whom they were having sexual relations. Estimates from the census suggest that there were about 777,000 same-sex couples in the United States in 2005, with slightly more male than female couples. About 8 out of 10 couples were White. Individuals in these couples average 40 years of age, younger than the average age (48) of married couples. Over three-quarters were employed in 2005, and approximately 25 percent had children in their households (Romero et al., December 2007; O'Connell and Lofquist 2009).

California, New York, Texas, Florida, and Illinois have the most same-sex couples. According to U.S. census data, the gay and lesbian population tends to be concentrated in larger urban areas. For example, almost 60 percent of gay men reside in 20 cities. While also concentrated, the lesbian population is somewhat more widely dispersed. Among smaller cities, those with universities or colleges are more likely than others to have significant numbers of homosexuals in their populations. But unfortunately, data from these cities are not very reliable (Black et al. 2000). This may reflect regional differences in prejudice against homosexuals discussed earlier.

Education is also related to the incidence of homosexuality, with those in the college ranks being more likely than those with less education to have had homosexual experiences. This relationship is stronger for women than for men, however (Laumann et al. 1994). Educationally, data from the three national surveys show that a greater percentage of lesbians and gay men have higher degrees than other individuals. For example, census data indicates that over 31 percent of lesbian-partnered women have college degrees compared to under 18 percent of married women. About 30 percent of gay-partnered men in the 25–34 age bracket have college degrees compared to under 7 percent of married men. Gay and lesbian partners have more formal education than heterosexual couples (Black, Sanders, and Taylor 2007).

Despite their higher educations, the poverty rate among single and coupled lesbians is higher than the rates among heterosexuals and heterosexual couples. Gay men have slightly higher rates than heterosexual men (Albelda et al., March 2009). They also have lower earnings, despite conclusions of earlier studies that suggested the opposite. The erroneous findings of early studies were based on small samples and tended to include disproportionate numbers of more affluent individuals, so their results did not accurately reflect the situation of the gay/lesbian population as a whole.

National census data from the 1990s and 2000 suggest that the household earnings of gay men who work full-time are significantly lower than those of comparable heterosexual men, while those of lesbians are somewhat higher than the earnings of heterosexual women who work full-time. These differences hold even when age, education, and area of residence are taken into account (Badgett 2001). Similar findings have been uncovered using U.S. census and other data on same-sex and married couples, although much of the difference among women appears due to variations in weeks and hours worked (Klawitter and Flatt 1998; Black et al. 2000; Carpenter 2007). In addition to their higher educations, their greater attachment to the labor force and smaller likelihood of choosing a "female-typed" occupation also help account for the higher earnings of lesbian women over those of heterosexual women. Lesbians also earn more because they are less likely to have enrolled in a traditionally female major in college, investing more in human capital that will prepare them for a career since they do not anticipate having a traditional marriage (Black et al. 2003). They also appear to get an earnings benefit from children that heterosexual women do not receive (Baumle 2009). Gay men, in contrast, are more likely than heterosexual men to have a female-dominated major while in school and to be in a traditionally female occupation. They also tend to work fewer hours per week than employed heterosexual males, whereas lesbians average more hours of employed work per week than their heterosexual counterparts (Black, Sanders, and Taylor 2007).

A review of over 50 studies revealed that between 16 percent and 68 percent of gays and lesbians experienced employment discrimination during the 1980s and 1990s. Most frequently mentioned were physical and verbal abuse, denial of promotion or poor evaluations, firing, and denial of employment (Badgett et al. 2007). There have been some improvements in protections. In 2008, 85 percent of Fortune 500 companies had protections based on sexual orientation, and over half granted benefits to domestic partners. But only 20 states and the District of Columbia had laws prohibiting employment discrimination against gays and lesbians (Human Rights Campaign, February 2009).

Ironically, the presence of state or local laws prohibiting discrimination against homosexuals does not appear to have a significant impact on only their earnings. Rather, the earnings of *both* heterosexuals and homosexuals tend to be higher in places with such laws. Laws of this kind are more likely to be found in more urban areas where populations have higher levels of education (Klawitter and Flatt 1998). These are likely to be areas where gays and lesbians experience lower levels of discrimination and, consequently, prosper more easily.

Occupationally, evidence cited by Hewitt (1995) indicates that gay men are more likely to be self-employed than other men and to be in the labor force, probably because of the greater likelihood that they are younger and single. With respect to the distribution of occupations among gay men, information from different sources reveals several broad patterns. First, gay men are not as broadly distributed along the full range of occupations as are heterosexual men. Like minorities and women, they tend to be concentrated in a smaller number of occupations. Second, the concentration is especially great within white-collar occupations. A much greater proportion of gay men than heterosexual men are in white-collar, higher-status jobs. Well over half of gay men are in managerial, administrative, "artistic-creative," or "nurturant" occupations, the latter category referring to traditionally female jobs in which a customer or client receives a face-to-face service of some kind. Under 10 percent are in blue-collar occupations. Third, within broad white-collar categories, there are concentrations of gay men in specific occupations. Although frequently based on small samples, it has been estimated that a disproportionate number of male artists, hairdressers, librarians, architects, entertainers, and fashion designers are gay. Although gay men are heavily overrepresented in these fields, they appear to be very underrepresented in quintessentially "male" occupations such as business, law, and sports (Hewitt 1995).

The U.S. military is among the most masculine of institutions, yet a significant number of gays and lesbians currently serve. In 2010, over 48,000 lesbians, gay men, and bisexuals were on active duty or in the ready reserve. Among those on active duty, 43 percent were women (Gates, May 2010). Sexual harassment against women has led to a disproportionate number of them being dismissed from the military because of alleged homosexuality (Damiano 1998/1999; Ransom 2001). Two recent cases illustrate the difficulties women encounter when sex, prevailing gender-role definitions, and heterosexual culture intertwine to permit continued discrimination by dominant groups. In the first case, a lesbian cadet resigned from West Point Military Academy because she did not want to continue lying about her sexuality, and because of the antihomosexual attitudes of some cadets. She tired of being "coerced into ignoring derogatory comments towards homosexuals for fear of being alienated for [her] viewpoint," and put up with "sexual harassment for fear of being accused as a lesbian" ("Lesbian Cadet," August 13, 2010, p. B4). In the second instance, a decorated Air Force Major and flight nurse had kept her sexual orientation secret, but was exposed as a lesbian by the husband of a woman with whom she was having an affair. This exposure led to Margaret Witt's discharge by the Air Force in 2007. As a result of her lawsuit to be restored to her position, a federal judge ruled that the Air Force must give back her job. Under the policy of don't ask, don't tell, "you can't be honest" (Dao, September 13, 2010, p. A19).

The pressure to be dishonest is not confined to lesbians and gays, but to transgendered individuals as well. In their social interactions with heterosexuals, especially at work, they need to negotiate the relationships between their biological sex, gender identity, and gender performance. While moving between gendered behaviors, transgendered individuals become highly sensitive to gender discrimination because they experience differences in their treatment as they change their gender performances (Connell 2010). Some give gender performances that are consistent with

NUTSHELL 7.1   "Don't Ask, Don't Tell"

The "don't ask, don't tell" (DADT) policy of the U.S. military required that recruiters not inquire or seek to find out about the sexual orientation of military members, and that gay enlistees not openly admit to or discuss their homosexuality. The law existed from 1994 to December 2010, and, as a result, between 1994 and 2009, 13,389 individuals were discharged from the military.

In December 2010, Congress voted to repeal the law. The repeal came as a result of support from the secretary of defense and some military leaders, and Pentagon survey findings that showed that three-quarters of military members did not think openly admitting gays into the military would negatively affect a unit's effectiveness. Most said that they believe they had served with a gay or lesbian and did not think it affected the morale or effectiveness of their units. Several national surveys of civilians also showed significant majorities supporting repeal of the policy.

Still, there were arguments against repeal. Among the points made were that in a time of war it was dangerous to change the policy, and that soldiers currently in combat had not been adequately canvassed about their opinions. The commandant of the U.S. Marines worried about potential negative effects the repeal would have on unit cohesion because of close sleeping arrangements. Some religious leaders and chaplains were concerned that they would not be able to follow their consciences because they believe homosexuality is a sin.

The points made in favor of repeal included the argument that the policy was discriminatory, unconstitutional, and not based on any hard evidence.

Rather, the policy appeared to be based on stereotypes about gays and lesbians, and required applicants to essentially live a lie about who they were. The Pentagon survey results and results from other countries also gave strong indication of the need to abolish the DADT policy. Currently, many countries, including strong U.S. allies with established militaries, allow gays and lesbians to openly serve in their military. These include Britain, Israel, France, Spain, Italy, Canada, South Africa, and Australia.

Under the new policy, gay sex will no longer be labeled a crime in the military, chaplains will be required to serve gay and lesbian troops like any others, and bathrooms and sleeping arrangements will be shared with others. While some of the benefits that are given to heterosexual married couples might be given to gay partners, others, such as lower-cost housing, will not. Implementation of the new policy will likely be careful and gradual, but it formally removes a stigma and blocked opportunity faced by many U.S. citizens who wish to openly serve their country. The end of the military's "Don't Ask, Don't Tell" policy was officially implemented on September 20, 2011.

Sources: Eve Conant, "What Repeal Will Mean," *Newsweek*, December 13, 2010, p. 15; Elizabeth Bumiller and David M. Herszenhorn, "Repeal of Policy on Gay Service Faces Struggle," *New York Times,* November 9, 2010, pp. A1 and A19; Anne Flaherty and Anne Gearan, "Pentagon Says Openly Gay Troops No Risk," *Akron Beacon Journal,* December 1, 2010, pp. A1 and A8; and David Lightman, "Congress Repeals Military Gay Ban," *Akron Beacon Journal,* December 19, 2010, pp. A1 and A11.

and expected of their biological sex; for example, a male exhibits masculine behavior. He will *do* the gender that is expected of him by heterosexual colleagues, even though it is inconsistent with the gender with which he identifies. Others act with a mix of masculine and feminine behaviors or act openly in a manner consistent with their gender identity (Connell 2010). For example, a "transman," or anatomical female who feels like a man inside, presents a demeanor and acts in a manner that is masculine.

NEGATIVE CONSEQUENCES OF STIGMATIZATION

Despite the higher educations of homosexuals and the higher earnings of lesbians, as ostracized *status* groups, lesbians and gays have historically experienced a wide variety of recurrent stresses and obstacles in the United States, ranging from psychological difficulties, to personal physical attacks, to institutional and legal discrimination. While the extreme eighteenth-century reaction of executing persons because of their homosexuality no longer exists, almost all gay men and lesbians have experienced physical victimization at one time or another (Button, Rienzo, and Wald 1997). In this section, I will touch on some of the significant emotional and physical consequences of the stress placed upon gay and lesbian individuals. A brief discussion of hate crimes is included in Chapter 12.

Minority Stress

The stigma placed on homosexuality exposes gay men and lesbians to a wide array of stresses ranging from everyday microinequities, such as slurs and constant sensitivity to not being too obvious about their identity, to problems in their families, religious practice, and the labor market. In turn, these stresses affect health and feelings of well-being, and have been related to recurrent headaches, depressive moods, and more serious psychological conditions. In the case of women and minorities who are homosexual, these stresses can be intensified because of their status as gender and ethnic/racial minorities (DiPlacido 1998). Indeed, gays and lesbians who experience discrimination because of their gender, race, and sexual orientation are almost four times as likely to have a substance abuse disorder as those who have not been victims of discrimination (McCabe et al. 2010). The negative labeling of same-sex intimacy and the consequent uneasiness among some lesbian women and gay men about their own behavior and feelings can also lead to problems in developing and maintaining intimate relationships, as well as greater stress and adjustment problems in general (Meyer and Dean 1998).

Growing up gay or lesbian in a cultural and social setting in which there are strong expectations of heterosexuality can create deep stresses for an individual. Interviews with gay men from a small working-class town in England bear out the agony felt by many gays in a culturally hostile setting as they realize that they do not fit in: "I knew there was something wrong, something different in my life," commented one

Bullying is a major problem among youth, and it is more likely to occur in schools located in disadvantaged neighborhoods. Gay and lesbian youth are often easy targets. Research has suggested that boys are more likely to be victims of physical bullying while girls are more likely to be victimized by indirect bullying such as teasing. Some data also indicate that victims are likely to be of lower social status in the school (Berger and Rodkin 2009; Carbone-Lopez, Esbensen, and Brick 2010). (© Mandy Godbehear/Shutterstock)

gay man (Flowers and Buston 2001, p. 54). Another remarked, "I remember going home at night and crying myself to sleep because I knew that I was different, and I was terrified of being different" (p. 54). Many of the men in this study kept their feelings to themselves, resulting in a sense of alienation from others: "I never really talked to anyone about my sexual feelings. I used to lay in bed and hide them away thinking about these things and 'I'm not normal'" (p. 56).

During the school years, when boys and girls are culturally expected to date each other, young homosexuals find themselves at a psychological and social disadvantage. A lesbian recalls from her youth: "Love of women was never a possibility that I even realized could be. You loved your mother and your aunts, and you had girlfriends for a while. Someday, though, you would always meet a man" (quoted in Savin-Williams 1996, p. 170). A gay man remembers experiencing a similar plight: "Throughout high school and college I had no way to meet people of the same sex and sexual orientation. These were more years of isolation and secrecy. I saw what other guys my age did, listened to what they said and how they felt. I was expected to be part of a world with which I had nothing in common" (p. 170). Gay youths may experience the stress of their family's bigotry because of their invisibility, unlike Black children whose status is obvious and generally the same as that of their parents and siblings. All of these consequences exist on the personal and interactional levels, but stresses that result from the homosexual label exist on the institutional level as well.

In schools, bullying and harassment is a serious problem, and especially for gay and lesbian students, who are marginalized, stigmatized, and often without support from fellow students (Craig, Tucker, and Wagner 2008). Results from a 2003 national survey indicated that 80 percent of lesbian, gay, bisexual, and transgender students are harassed because of their sexual orientation (Kosciw 2004). Teachers who are gay or lesbian often face psychological dilemmas to which there do not appear to be fully satisfying solutions. If a lesbian teacher, for example, wants to work with students as if they were her peers, she has to struggle to be seen as an effective professional without being seen as a sexual predator of children (McQueeney 2008). Or a gay teacher may have to hide who he is because being a "professional" generally means acting in a masculine manner (Connell 2009, p. 15).

Because many of the occupations and organizations that are most prestigious and offer the highest salaries are also those that embody a masculine ethic and are dominated by a male labor force, they are the same places that can create psychological stresses for gay and lesbian employees. These include, for example, the areas of law, finance, and business.

To avoid verbal and physical assaults in a normatively heterosexual culture, gay and lesbian persons may try to pass as heterosexual by adopting gender-appropriate manners and behaviors. It is a delicate matter for those who walk the tightrope of working to pass as heterosexual in the public realm but to be accepted as homosexual in their private lives. However, while passing may protect the individual, a continuous effort must be put forth to maintain it, and, when successful it also perpetuates the heteronormative culture that demeans homosexuality (Rosenfeld 2009). These are the dilemmas of being a minority in a majority's society.

Suicide

Heterosexism, social isolation, self-blame, and other stresses can have dire consequences for their victims. Reviews of research suggest that gay and lesbian youths are generally two to three times more likely to attempt suicide than their heterosexual counterparts (Suicide Prevention Resource Center 2008). It has been fairly typical for studies of homosexual youths to cite suicide attempt rates of 20–40 percent (Savin-Williams and Cohen 1996; D'Augelli 1998). Adolescence has its own set of stressful events, and when homosexuality is added to these, its problems are intensified.

- A talented 18-year-old freshman at Rutgers University jumped off the George Washington Bridge after his sexual encounter with another male was put on the Internet (Mulvihill and Henry, October 2, 2010).

Boy Scouts and Gay Leaders

The controversy over whether or not the Boy Scouts should permit gays to serve as leaders in their organization came to head in 2000 when the U.S. Supreme Court ruled that, as a private organization, the Boy Scouts had a right to exclude openly gay men from serving as Boy Scout leaders because such inclusion violated the basic message and moral values of the organization. There are many instances, however, where this avowedly *private* organization receives *public* resources. Earlier, a state supreme court had ruled in favor of the plaintiff, arguing that the state must try to eliminate discrimination where it occurs and that the gay leader's presence did not prevent the Boy Scouts from carrying out their mission. The U.S. Supreme Court decision overruled the lower court. How would you resolve this issue? ▪

• A 15-year-old Indiana boy who was gay hung himself because he could not take the constant bullying and taunting he received at school because of his sexual orientation (McKinley, October 4, 2010).

• A 13-year-old Californian hung himself as a result of persistent abuse from his classmates. A friend said: "People would say, 'You should kill yourself,' 'You should go away,' 'You're gay, who cares about you?'" (McKinley, October 4, 2010, p. A9).

However, suicide attempt rates are not spread evenly over this minority population. Gays and lesbians most likely to attempt or seriously think about suicide tend to (1) be younger, (2) be victims of physical assault, (3) feel more confused about sexual identity, (4) have lower self-esteem, (5) have more family problems, and (6) have recently "come out" or been exposed as homosexual (Savin-Williams and Cohen 1996; D'Augelli 1998). It has also been suggested that gays and lesbians who are members of a racial or ethnic minority may be more vulnerable to these problems because of the singular problems they face as both racial/ethnic and sexual minorities (Savin-Williams and Rodriguez 1993; Meyer, Dietrich, and Schwartz 2008). Blacks and Latinos as opposed to Whites who are lesbian, gay, or bisexual experience greater continuing stress over their lifetimes and have fewer resources to help them cope (Meyer, Schwartz, and Frost 2008).

Despite the obvious need among these individuals for various kinds of social support, however, seeking out and obtaining such support is problematic because of the demeaned social status of gays and lesbians in U.S. society. Homosexual youths find themselves between a rock and a hard place. On the one hand, they may be willing to seek out individuals who might be able to help, but on the other hand, they may be unwilling to risk rejection or reveal their situation because of the stigma attached to the homosexual label. Finally, the invisibility of the homosexual group presents a further barrier for youths who are seeking a support network or role model to guide them through a difficult period.

SEXUALITY IN THE GLOBAL CONTEXT

The unequal treatment of gays and lesbians is not exclusive to the United States, of course. In other parts of the world, discrimination against groups that do not fit traditional sex and gender categories is also present. Homosexuals in Hong Kong, for example, often experience workplace discrimination that results in both psychological and financial costs (Lau and Stotzer, June 1, 2010). In Namibia, during the period 1995–2006, masculine-oriented political leaders initiated a campaign against gays and lesbians, broadcasting that "homosexuality was unnatural, evil, a threat to the nation, western, unchristian, unAfrican, colonial residue, and . . . that homosexuality should be eradicated, or at a minimum, rendered publicly invisible" (Currier 2010, p. 112). In some Middle Eastern Muslim countries, homosexuality can be punished by death, and in many Asian countries it carries the threat of imprisonment.

Not only do reactions to homosexuality vary internationally, but so do the very meanings of sex and gender. At the beginning of this chapter, I commented on the subjectivity and variety of sexual classifications across time and cultures. I also mentioned that members of different racial and class groups define and highlight masculinity and femininity in varying ways. In other words, there is no one way to classify sexualities nor is there only one meaning for how one *does* sexuality. "Different cultures and different periods of history construct gender differently. Striking differences exist, for instance, in the relationship of homosexual practice to dominant forms of masculinity" (Connell 2005, p. 37). The complexity of classifications and sexual identities can only be expected to grow in the United States with globalization and the continued immigration of peoples of varying ethnicities and cultural backgrounds (Gamson and Moon 2004). The open borders that accompany these events will have an impact on our views of sexuality and the meanings that we give it. Individuals whose sexual identity is not honored in their own society can immigrate to another, more hospitable society and thereby affect and be affected by that society's cultural views.

Given that societies often differ in their sexual mores, meanings, and classifications, when different cultures meet it should not be surprising that clashes occur over these matters, as a host society seeks to impose its own hegemonic culture on those who immigrate into it. Movements by some rights groups to push for a more positive attitude toward homosexuality can inadvertently lead to backlashes by host governments, which establish policies that reinforce traditional meanings and definitions of sexuality (Massad 2002). Western religious missionary work has reinforced the idea of heterosexual marriage as ideal and

served to denigrate and weaken homosexual and other nontraditional sexual behaviors. Technological innovations have also allowed the mass media to promulgate alternative images of sexuality (Connell 2005).

The effects of globalization on definitions of sexuality and gendered behavior and their acceptance depend in part on the relative positions of countries in the world political-economic system. "The conditions of globalization, which involve the interaction of many local gender orders, certainly multiply the forms of masculinity in the global gender order. At the same time, the specific shape of globalization, concentrating economic and cultural power on an unprecedented scale, provides new resources for the dominance of particular groups of men" (Connell 2005, pp. 41–42). Thus, as groups and individuals flow between countries, there are likely to be changes in and reactions to varying definitions of gender and sexuality, including homosexuality. Which definitions and practices become dominant and accepted depends on relative power in the world order.

Altman (2005) contends that homosexual communities in other industrialized nations model themselves after such communities in the United States. The language used and histories evoked are those that originate not in their own countries, but in the United States. For example, the Stonewall riots that occurred in the United States as a result of police harassment are cited by European gays as giving birth to gay activism even though such activism occurred earlier in their own countries. This suggests the hegemonic position held by the United States in the world community.

Altman's argument that gay culture and identity are becoming homogenized across the world as a result of globalizing forces has been challenged by recent research which describes a much more complicated picture of sexuality in varied settings. The "transmissions" relating to sexuality between globalizing forces and local cultures are complicated and result in sex and gender definitions that are neither fully global nor local (Berry, Martin, and Yue 2003; Boellstorff 2003).

While globalization may help ignite international cultural clashes over the meaning of sexuality, it has also fostered the development of a transnational network of gays and lesbians. Similar movements have been under way to unite transgendered individuals as a means of protecting them against the harassment they regularly experience (Altman 2005).

Summary

This chapter has presented a brief overview of the inequities involved in being homosexual rather than heterosexual in sexual orientation. As a dishonored status group, homosexuals have been singled out and stigmatized as individuals who do not fit dominant cultural ideas about appropriate sexual behavior and lifestyles. Although sympathy and opinions in specific areas of civil rights appear to have improved in recent years, significant proportions and subgroups within the United States continue to be hostile to homosexuality. Stereotypes of both gay men and lesbians persist, and they continue to be a minority with distinct status-group attributes, yet without the legal protections afforded other minority groups.

Because of the difficulties that homosexuals face and the disregard in which they have been held, reliable and thorough statistics on this group are nonexistent. Estimates about the size of the homosexual population and its characteristics vary from study to study. Lack of knowledge about this community only helps to reinforce existing stereotypes. The consequences for individuals in this group are momentous. Few areas of their lives are untouched; psychological, economic, social, legal, and health problems arise from their position as a stigmatized status group. At the same time, however, some homosexuals have prospered despite the difficulties they face, excelling in areas as diverse as sports, entertainment, literature, and politics.

Discrimination against gays and lesbians is widespread globally. Globalization has had an impact on the sex categories used as well as the meanings ascribed to sexuality and masculinity and femininity. In the case of disagreements, which of these categories and meanings is privileged depends in part on the position of a society in the global context. Finally, globalization has helped to unify gay and lesbian groups across national boundaries.

Critical Thinking

1. What would be the social consequences if everyone accepted the belief that sexual variation is a continuum rather than a dichotomy (i.e., if we believed that there are many more than two sexes)?
2. How does the invisibility of being homosexual affect homosexual individuals and the status image of homosexuals as a group?
3. Bullying appears to be a significant problem in many schools. What do you think can be done to curtail it?
4. What do you think should be done about same-sex marriage? Do bans against it discriminate and perpetuate inequality or do they justifiably protect a viable tradition of marriage? How can we reconcile a desire for fairness with a desire for morality on this issue?

Web Connections

For brief discussions of issues of concern to gay, lesbian, bisexual, and transgender groups, see the websites of the Human Rights Campaign (www. hrc.org) and the Williams Institute (www.law.ucla. edu/williamsinstitute/home.html. Visit also www. thetaskforce.org/reslibrary for reports on issues related to same-sex marriage, civil unions, race and same-sex relationships, and related matters.

Film Suggestions

One in 2000 (2006). A discussion of the lives of several intersexed persons and their families.

Men Are Human, Women Are Buffalo (2008). A documentary about domestic violence in Thailand.

Becoming Çhaz (2011). A documentary about Chaz Bono's transition from a woman to a man.

Gender Puzzle (2006). Science is discovering new biological processes that determine one's sex and gender identity.

CHAPTER 8

Racial and Ethnic Inequality

He had but one eye, and the popular prejudice runs in favour of two.

Charles Dickens (1812–1870)

The positions of women and minorities are often thought to have a lot in common. Moreover, as mentioned in Chapter 6, race and sex have both been associated with biological differences that have been given social and cultural meanings. While their specific histories and socioeconomic conditions are different, both women and members of minority groups tend to occupy lower positions than White males in our society. Each group has even been referred to as being in a lower caste when compared to White males. Finally, the terms *sex, gender,* and *race* each have specific meanings that vary with the cultural, historical, and social context in which they are used. Consequently, none of these concepts has a fixed, unvarying definition.

THE MEANING AND CREATION OF RACE

"What is a black person?" This question, posed by a 7-year-old relative of mine, seems pretty straightforward. Bridget is a U.S. citizen who lived abroad for many years; she has spent most of her life in England, not in the United States. Her mother responded to her question by saying that a Black person is a person who is "dark-skinned." Bridget responded: "You mean like Tarush [who is Indian]?" Her mother then went on to explain the traditional racial distinctions, but it was clear that Bridget thought her mother meant that a Black person is distinguished solely by the color of her or his skin. "Color" is an important social and cultural trait, and we know that within "races," individuals can vary in the color of their skin. In our society, individuals with lighter skin generally are accorded higher status than those with darker skin. I will discuss the issue of "colorism" more fully later in this chapter.

The exchange between Bridget and her mother hints at the complexity involved in defining race. Race is a slippery term. There have been past attempts to define it "scientifically" and to develop clear classifications of race, but these have always been found to be faulty for one reason or another, and virtually all have fallen by the wayside. Some of the earliest attempts classified individuals by their ancestry rather than physical features. These classifications tended to conflate ethnicity, nationality, and physical characteristics (e.g., Jewish or Irish "race"). Other classifications tended to identify and rank groups in an ethnocentric fashion, separating the socially dominant group from others and ranking it highest. The features chosen to distinguish the races were those that appeared to separate the dominant from lower-ranking groups, groups which could then be exploited for their alleged inferiority. The attempted annihilation of the "Jewish race" by the "Aryans" is an example of how racial categorizations can be based on and used for political rather than scientific reasons. As the social, economic, and cultural positions of groups changed, so did their race. While we usually think of a person's race as affecting his or her class position, in this case, *class* position helped to determine "*race*." For example, with assimilation, Jewish, Irish, and Italian immigrants, once defined as "non-White," became defined as "White."

The continual changing of racial categories in society and by governmental offices indicates that race is something that is created and anchored in the social, economic, and cultural conditions of the time. In the words of Omi and Winant (2005), it involves "racial formation," which is a "sociohistorical process by which racial categories are created, inhabited, transformed, and destroyed" (p. 195). As historical conditions and contexts change, so do racial classifications. In a real sense, racial classifications reflect the structure of inequality in a society.

We need only to review changes that the U.S. Census Bureau has made since its first census in 1790. Native Americans and Blacks were separated out from others because of their political status, but it was not until 1820 that "race" or color was used in the census (Snipp 2003). Throughout the rest of the nineteenth century, the racial classifications used by the Census Bureau were rooted in cultural, social, and intellectual developments going on in the wider society. The addition of "Chinese" and "Japanese" to the 1890 census racial classifications reflected growing concern on the part of the dominant group about the increasing numbers and potential competition of these groups with native citizens on the West Coast. The added inclusion of "Octoroon" (one-eighth Black) and "Quadroon" (one-fourth Black) to the classifications symbolized the growing interest in and concern about racial purity at the end of the nineteenth century in the United States (Snipp 2003; Schaefer 2006). States often defined a person as Black if they had only one drop of Black blood and used this definition as a means to prevent and outlaw racial intermarriage (Brunsma and Rockquemore 2002). Restrictive definitions of race like this clearly affect who is and who is not a member of a particular racial category. Not only the number of categories then, but the breadth of each category used by the Census Bureau in its classifications of individuals as well can affect the numbers of persons classified as being a member of each racial/ethnic category. Historical records, for example, show significant increases in the number of Puerto Ricans classified as White in early twentieth-century censuses of Puerto Rico's population. In large part, this occurred because of "boundary shifting," that is, changes in the definition of "White" which broadened who could be included (Loveman and Muniz 2007). These changes in turn reflect fluctuations in racial dynamics in the society at large.

Racial categories continued to fluctuate in the twentieth century, reflecting changes in social and cultural conditions. The term *Hispanic* is still used even though Hispanics can be of any race. It is considered more as a description of ethnicity and is separated out because Latinos often do not agree on their race or view themselves as belonging to another race, and because they are considered a minority group by the government (Lee and Bean 2004).

In part because of problems encountered by census workers in accurately classifying a person's race, in 1960 the Census Bureau began to allow individuals to identify their own race (Snipp 2003). In 2000, because of increased recognition of the mixed backgrounds of individuals, the Census Bureau made it possible for people to identify themselves as belonging to more than one race. Tiger Woods helped to call attention to this issue by calling himself a "Cabalinasian" (i.e., part Caucasian, Black, American Indian, Thai, and Chinese; White 1997). Currently, about 2.5 percent of individuals in the United States identify themselves as multiracial.

When we examine historical fluctuations in the definition and meaning of race, it becomes apparent that racial definitions and classifications have served as indicators of which groups have political, economic, and social power and which ones do not. "Throughout the history of racialization, material (economic, social, and political resources) and ideological elements of race have been inextricably linked" (Lewis 2004, p. 625). Moreover, as we will see, high rates of immigration from Hispanic, Asian, and other groups will continue to accelerate the multiracial character of the United States and further complicate the racial/ethnic picture. Finally, the move toward self-identification has further revealed the fluidity and complexity of race as a concept.

Interestingly, most Whites do not think of "White" as a race. Rather, when speaking of race, the tendency is to think of racial "minorities" as belonging to a race. Whiteness is invisible in this sense. "From an early age," observes Rothenberg (2008, p. 2), "race, for white people, is about everyone else." Whiteness is not racialized. The invisibility of whiteness as a racial category fosters the illusion that being "white" is to be normal or the standard by which others are measured. Race is a term ordinarily used only in reference to other, non-White persons (Dye 2008). The claim that Whites are the regular, normal people and, therefore, representative of humanity allows whiteness to be a central basis for power and privilege in society. The racial categories with which people are identified have direct consequences for their lives because society's social structures and the opportunities and blockages they create are shaped in part by the dominant group.

It is clear that the term *white* has various meanings for different people. For some it has a distinct racial connotation, while for others it does not. The same is found for the term *black*. It has even been suggested that research in this area should focus not on "who is black" but "what does 'black' mean?" (Brunsma and Rockquemore 2002, p. 109). This is essentially what Bridget was asking earlier. How one defines oneself or others racially appears to depend on the geographical context, education, age, race of the identifier, and nativity (Farough 2004; Roth 2005). On nativity, for example, Pyke and Dang (2003) found that the adult children of Korean and Vietnamese immigrants thought of themselves as bicultural, but described others in their group as being either "fresh off the boat" or "whitewashed." In using these terms, these children were able to minimize or eliminate the stigma they faced by distancing themselves from their coethnic *others*. Doing this is a response to the racial hierarchy in U.S. society and the desire to maintain a respected position within it.

U.S. RACIAL AND ETHNIC RELATIONS: AN HISTORICAL SKETCH

The unequal treatment of racial minorities in the United States goes back to the early years of colonization. Anglo-Saxon colonists' earliest contact with a visibly different group were with American Indians. Ideas and stereotypes of the "savage" had developed in the sixteenth and seventeenth centuries and provided colonists with a framework within which to interpret American Indians. Rather than color or racial distinction, religious and ethnocentric criteria were used initially to separate groups into superior and inferior categories. Specifically, distinctions were made between "Christians" and "heathens" and between "civilized" and "savage" (Fredrickson 1981). Clearly, the American Indians were placed in the heathen and savage categories. Thus, distinct attitudes about this group were entrenched by the time the American Revolution occurred.

Despite these beliefs, early relations between colonists and American Indians were often cooperative since both groups were interested in trade and barter. In fact, American Indians frequently had quite a bit of power when it came to bargaining because of their prowess in the fur trade (Lurie 1982). But this cooperation was short-lived. Relationships with the British became increasingly belligerent, since the British were farmers and interested in obtaining American Indian land (Garbarino 1976). The American Indians whose economies emphasized agriculture and who were located near the East Coast were the first to be overwhelmed by the colonists (Lurie 1982).

In order for the colonists to spread their civilization, they had to obtain land held by American Indians. Many of the latter resided in villages and cultivated crops in a manner not very different from the traditional European way. But arguments about the savage and heathen way of life of American Indians were used as devices to justify taking over this land. Many of the arguments were similar to those used to justify slavery (Farley 1988). The belief was that such action would rescue the earth from these savages and speed progress and Christianity (Fredrickson 1981). This is an early instance of a group using an ideology to justify the taking of economic resources from another.

In the period roughly between 1880 and 1930, over 65 percent of the 138 million acres that had been held by American Indians moved to White ownership (Carlson and Colburn 1972). By the last decade of the nineteenth century, most American Indians were on reservations where they were forbidden to practice their religions and their children were forced to attend boarding schools run by Whites where they had to speak English (Farley 1988). Much of the policy of this period was aimed at forcing American Indians to assimilate into the dominant White culture (Marden and Meyer 1973). Nevertheless, they were not allowed to vote since they were not considered citizens. The Constitution had never actively incorporated concerns for the rights of these groups, and it was not until the 1920s that American Indians were granted citizenship. Even as late as the 1920s and 1930s, there was a feeling among some influential individuals that American Indians were biologically inferior to White Anglo-Saxons (Carlson and Colburn 1972).

Actions by the federal government further damaged socioeconomic conditions among Indians. The Termination Act of 1954 in Wisconsin, for example, eliminated the sovereign status of the Menominee Nation, reducing it to just another county in the state. While the apparent intent was to aid assimilation of the tribe into the rest of the state, the effect was to destroy Indian institutions that had made the Menominee self-sufficient. In 2008, Menominee County had the highest rates of poverty and health problems in Wisconsin (Dresang 2008). For American Indians in general, ill-advised legislation and prejudice have continued to bear bitter fruit.

In the 2000 census, 2.5 million people, or 0.9 percent, identified themselves as only American Indian or Alaska Native. An additional 2.6 million reported a mixed race identity that included American Indian or Alaska Native (U.S. Census Bureau, February 2002). The West has the largest number of American Indians (43%), followed by the South, Midwest, and Northeast, respectively. New York and Los Angeles were the cities with the highest American Indian populations. About one out of eight American Indians live on reservations.

The economic status of American Indians is well below that of Whites in the United States. In 2004, the median household income for American Indians and Alaska Natives was about $32,000 compared to almost $49,000 for non-Hispanic White households. About 25 percent had incomes below the poverty rate compared to 9 percent of non-Hispanic Whites. The 2004 median value of owner-occupied homes among American Indians was also much lower than that for non-Hispanic White homes ($95,000 vs. $154,000). Finally, American Indian unemployment rates are much higher and rates of health insurance ownership much lower than those found among non-Hispanic Whites. But in the last 20–25 years, there has been a dramatic increase in postsecondary education among American Indians, and in 2007, more than 237,000 businesses owned by American Indians and Alaska Natives brought in $34.5 billion. Members of tribes that have casinos tend to have higher incomes and better health care

(U.S. Census Bureau, May 2007; U.S. Census Bureau 2010; Wolfe et al. 2010).

Historically, the waves of immigrants who arrived in the United States from Europe during the nineteenth and early twentieth centuries were also often victims of economic and social discrimination. Jews, Irish, and immigrants from southern and eastern Europe such as Italians, Poles, and Greeks were initially categorized as non-White and suffered the consequences. Widespread concerns about maintaining purity of the "White race," fascination with eugenics and **Social Darwinism**, and the Red Scare early in the twentieth century, heightened fear of immigrants who were considered alien, and led to the restrictive immigration policies of the 1920s. Eventually, because of assimilation into American culture and economic mobility, many of these groups became classified as "White" (Brodkin 2008; Barrett and Roediger 2008). This shows again how racial classifications, rather than being scientifically based, were closely linked to the power and economic status of the groups involved.

Black–White Relations

Land in early America was plentiful but greater labor power was needed to take full advantage of its resources. The absence of large numbers of willing free laborers led to attempts to obtain forced labor that could be justified on ideological or philosophical grounds. American Indians were difficult to subdue and were a potential major threat because they were familiar with the countryside and could put up fierce resistance. On the other hand, large-scale, prolonged use of indentured White servants was unrealistic because they were freed after a period of servi-

---

NUTSHELL 8.1 Immigrant Hardships of the Past

In 1941, Thomas Bell published his novel *Out of This Furnace*. Like his own family when growing up, the Slovak family in the book faces the hardships that were endured by many Eastern European immigrants who emigrated to the United States in the 1880s and worked in the steel mills of Western Pennsylvania. While the characters in it are fictional, the general social conditions and experiences related in *Out of This Furnace* are typical of those faced by lower-status immigrants during this period. Atrocious working conditions, meager pay, and little power characterized their work-a-day existence. The novel follows three generations of the family as they struggle to improve their lives.

Of course, Eastern European immigrants were not the only nineteenth-century immigrants to face discrimination and violence. Irish immigrants too had to endure grueling work, including work on the emerging railroads. In August 2010, several skulls were found near Philadelphia in what looked like a mass grave. While it was thought that the persons had died of cholera, examination of the remains suggests that they may have been murdered. These persons were part of a group of 57 Irish immigrants who worked on the Philadelphia and Columbia railroad in 1832. All died within weeks of beginning work. After finding traumatic damage and possible bullet holes in the skulls, a primary researcher at the site concluded that "this was much more than a cholera epidemic." Another agreed: "I don't think we need to be so hesitant in coming to the conclusion now that violence was the cause of death and not cholera, although these men might have had cholera in addition . . . They do have indications on their skeletons that life was not a bowl of cherries." No one in their families had been told about the deaths of these men. Prejudice and discrimination against Irish immigrants was common in the nineteenth century, not only because of their lower education and cultural differences, but because of their Catholicism. Anti-Catholic sentiment often led to violence against persons and property.

Source: Associated Press, August 17, 2010. Available at http://history4everyone.wordpress.com/2010/08/21/irish-immigrants-malvern-pa-and-an-1832-murder-mystery.

tude. This made the importation of non-White slave labor attractive. Slavery created a large labor pool of workers who did not know the land, and it helped to elevate all Whites to a higher status (Fredrickson 1981). A major difference in the initial contacts, of course, was that whereas colonists conquered American Indians and annexed their land, in initial Black–White contact, it was a case of involuntary immigration (O'Sullivan and Wilson 1988).

Given English views of Blacks as evil, animalistic, uncivilized, and un-Christian, it is not surprising that the early colonies passed laws banning sexual mixing and intermarriage. Children of mixed parentage were considered Black (Fredrickson 1981). Enslavement was a thorny issue that troubled some of the Founding Fathers (e.g., Washington, Hamilton) more so than others (e.g., Jefferson). The result was that the problem of what to do with slavery after the Revolution was put off again and again. Several thousand African Americans had fought in the Continental Army, but nevertheless at the Constitutional Convention it was decided that a Black man was only three-fifths of a man. Although Thomas Jefferson is associated with the belief that "all men are created equal," he owned 180 slaves when he died and thought of Blacks as inferior to Whites: "I advance it therefore as a suspicion only, that the Blacks, whether originally a distinct race, or made distinct by time and circumstances, are inferior to the Whites, in the endowments both of body and mind" (quoted in Feldstein 1972, pp. 52–53). Beliefs in the different endowments helped to justify slavery. After all, inhuman treatment could be tolerated if the members of a race were not considered fully human.

At the time of the first official census in 1790, the Black population was approximately 757,000, of whom almost 700,000 were slaves. The Black population grew to almost 4.5 million in 1860, of whom 89 percent were slaves. Between 1790 and 1860, about 90 percent of all Blacks in each census were slaves. Even though the slave trade was officially outlawed in 1808, it still flourished along the long East Coast of the country (U.S. Bureau of the Census 1979). In 1790, 23 percent of all families had slaves, whereas in 1850, 10 percent of families owned them. Most of these families owned a small number of slaves, the average being seven to nine per family (U.S. Bureau of the Census 1979).

The system of inequality that developed between the races during the heyday of slavery up to the Civil War was essentially a **caste system**. Laws forbade Blacks to (1) intermarry with Whites, (2) vote, (3) testify against Whites in legal cases, (4) own firearms, (5) use abusive language against Whites, (6) own property unless permitted by a master, (7) leave the plantation without permission or disobey a curfew, (8) make a will or inherit property, and (9) have anyone teach them to read or write, or give them books (Elkins 1959; Franklin 1980; Fredrickson 1981; Blackwell 1985).

The end of the Civil War, Emancipation, and Reconstruction did not end the misery for Blacks, and, in fact, appear to have done little to change their caste relationship with Whites (Turner, Singleton, and Musick 1984). Legal, intellectual, economic, and population changes were occurring that provided support for continued discrimination against Blacks. The Jim Crow laws in the South and beliefs about the inferior nature of Blacks, along with increased labor competition from a continuously rising number of White immigrants from all parts of Europe, conspired to keep Blacks in a lower socioeconomic position. Lynching of Blacks increased in the latter part of the nineteenth century. IQ tests, developed as early as the 1890s, were erroneously used to test native intelligence, and then used to demonstrate the intellectual inferiority of Blacks. This occurred even though some of the early inventors of such measures cautioned against using them for this purpose (Gossett 1963). Migration of Black southerners to the industrializing North during and after World War I resulted in severe clashes between Black and White workers, and in the years from 1917 to 1919, riots broke out in several cities (Brody 1980). Protectionist and nativist feelings ran high as well, and in the 1920s, legislation was passed that restricted immigration.

In the 1920s, anthropologist Franz Boas spoke out forcefully against the racially based theories being propagated at the time, and by the 1930s and 1940s, other important scientists joined him in attacking the idea that Blacks were inferior to Whites (Gossett 1963). Nazi racism also contributed to a reexamination of race domination in this country (Turner, Singleton, and Musick 1984). But discrimination continued, with Blacks still encountering problems within unions and industry. Blacks also were segregated within the military. Riots occurred during World War II, which further demonstrated that the United States still had a long way to go to bring about equity between the races. Increasing organization and political power of African Americans during the late 1940s and 1950s helped to bring about some legislative changes and, eventually, the civil rights movement.

Other Minority Groups in History

The preceding historical sketch reveals how extensive racial inequality has been in U.S. society. In addition to the groups already mentioned, Mexican Americans have been exploited for their land and labor. In the last half of the nineteenth century, Mexican Americans frequently had their land taken away by Anglos. Historically, the use of Mexican workers has waxed and waned, depending on the demand for labor. They were used and then dispensed with when no longer needed. For example, early in the twentieth century, many Mexican immigrants came to the United States as agricultural laborers, only to be deported or repatriated after demand for their services declined. During World War II, Mexican workers were again imported, only to be sent back during the 1950s under "Operation Wetback" as expendable and undesirable. Illegal raids, threats, and expulsions have not been uncommon in our treatment of Mexicans (Farley 1988).

Asian Americans have also suffered the effects of stereotyping and unfair treatment. Near the end of the nineteenth century, Japanese immigrants took laboring jobs but were disliked by unions and other employees. They were lumped in with the Chinese as part of the "yellow peril," the fear that yellow races would overtake the White race. The events at Pearl Harbor, initiating the entry of the United States into World War II, exacerbated negative feelings toward Japanese Americans. Under Executive Order 9066, people on the West Coast with virtually any Japanese ancestry at all were rounded up and moved into concentration camps. This was not done to either German or Italian Americans, even though the United States went to war against Germany and Italy as well as Japan. This strongly suggests a heavy influence of racism. The 113,000 Japanese sent to these camps without the benefit of trial could take only personal items, leaving behind and often losing most of their property. After the war, terrorism and bigotry against Japanese Americans continued, although no instances of espionage by them were ever proved. Even while in the camps, they remained loyal to their adopted country. Today, when we examine the low rates of social problems among Japanese Americans, they appear to be model citizens. They also have achieved levels of earnings and education that are higher than those of Whites.

Hispanic Immigration and Arizona's Law

Immigration of Latinos to the United States, while slowing recently, has been especially heavy over the last couple of decades. Hispanics constitute the largest ethnic minority group in the country, accounting for over 15 percent of the population, and that percentage is expected to increase. Of the roughly 47 million Hispanics in 2008, 38 percent were foreign-born. Almost 9 million of unauthorized immigrants in the United States are Hispanic. Mexico alone accounts for about one-third of all immigrants to the United States, and almost two-thirds of all Hispanic immigrants. In 2009, there were 11.5 million Mexican-born people in the country (Passel and Cohn 2009).

These influxes have undoubtedly helped to complicate the issues surrounding racial classification. A majority of Latino immigrants recognize the value of being labeled as "White," and prefer a White designation when asked about racial identity. But the chance that their preference will result in the inclusion of all Latinos into the White category within current racial classifications is unlikely because of variations in the skin color of Latinos. Darker-skinned Latinos, who experience more discrimination, are especially unlikely to be incorporated into the White category in the near future (Frank, Akresh, and Lu 2010).

Negative attitudes about immigrants and immigration are fairly common across countries, with most natives preferring less immigration (Ceobanu and Escandell 2010). Concerns about increased Hispanic immigration often revolve around wage and job issues, welfare dependency, and ethnic allegiance. Americans appear to be increasingly concerned but divided about immigration (Segovia and Defever 2010). Even Latinos vary in their views. Mexicans, foreign-born, and those who identify more strongly with their own rather than American culture, express more favorable attitudes about immigration than other Latinos (Rouse, Wilkinson, and Garand 2010). Persons with higher educations and social networks that include immigrants are more likely to have positive attitudes about immigration than are those who are older, of lower socioeconomic status, and have social networks that contain no immigrants. The latter groups are more likely to feel threatened by a significant immigrant presence in their communities (Berg 2009; Ceobanu and Escandell 2010). The presence of "foreign" groups in U.S. cities has led to debates about what it means to be an American and about personal safety. These issues crystallized in the arguments for and against a proposal to build a mosque a few blocks away from the site of the 2001 terrorist attack on the World Trade Center in New York City.

Perceived religious and cultural threats are not the only ones currently experienced by a majority of White Americans who feel under assault. At a time when many people are struggling economically, it is not surprising that efforts would be made to identify and deal with perceived sources of their economic problems. One of these perceived sources is illegal immigrants, who many people view as both criminal and economic threats. Some evidence suggests that increased Hispanic immigration has led to severe interethnic competition for low-skill jobs in the agricultural, manufacturing, and construction sectors, instigating increased Black unemployment and violence (Shihadeh and Barranco 2010). Consequently, immigration legislation has been proposed to confront these issues.

The recessionary climate, concerns about illegal immigration, and its extensive border with Mexico led Arizona to pass controversial immigration legislation in 2010. Principally, the "Support Our Law Enforcement and Safe Neighborhoods Act" requires police to question an individual if they suspect that the person is in the United States illegally. Immigrants are expected to carry proper documentation at all times, and if they do not, they will be charged with a misdemeanor. The law also penalizes employers who hire or transport illegal immigrant workers.

Proponents say the states need to monitor their borders, and need to act because the federal government has neglected its duty to protect citizens because of its lax enforcement of current federal law and inability to pass immigration reform. As of late 2010, Arizona's law was being challenged in federal court for a variety of reasons. Opponents, Hispanics among them, argue that immigration is a federal, not a state matter. They also believe that the legislation unlawfully profiles certain kinds of people and thereby violates civil rights law. In addition, they contend that enforcement might undermine any trust minority groups have in the police. Because immigration has racial and ethnic undertones, the legal controversy over Arizona's legislation raises the issue of whether the law racializes immigration by profiling certain ethnic groups, reinforcing ethnic stereotypes, and providing another example of how some ethnic groups enjoy political power over others.

MINI-CASE 8.1

Multiculturalism versus Assimilation

In the United States and many European countries, economic problems have intensified nativist feelings and led to more limitations on and more careful screening of newly entering immigrants. One offshoot of these developments is the issue of whether immigrants should be required to fully adopt their new country's cultural values and social rules or whether they should be allowed to keep their own language and cultural and social customs. The former solution suggests that a country should be a melting pot while the latter preference promotes an image of nations as salad bowls, or patchworks of separate groups. What do you think? Can a nation still cohere if groups retain their separate identities? Can they identify with *both* their own groups and the nation at the same time? What requirements, if any, should be placed on immigrant groups in this regard? ▄

RACIAL AND ETHNIC INEQUALITY TODAY

Despite some advances, Blacks, Hispanics, and Whites continue to have significantly different incomes, occupations, and earnings. The tables to follow include data only on Whites, Hispanics, and Blacks because these groups constitute roughly 95 percent of the U.S. population, and thus provide a broad idea of the extent of inequality involving racial and ethnic groups.

Wealth and Income

As we saw in Chapter 2, there are significant differences in the wealth of Whites, Blacks, and Hispanics, and while the gap between Black and Hispanic groups, on the one hand, and Whites on the other, generally narrowed between 2001 and 2007, it is still large. In 2007, the median net worth of non-Hispanic Whites was almost 16 times as great as the net worth of Blacks and Hispanic families (Wolff, March 2010). More than one-quarter of Blacks and almost one-third of Hispanics have zero or negative net worth, a rate that is more than twice that of non-Hispanic Whites. To a large extent, the wide differences between means and medians with respect to wealth noted in Chapter 2 reflect the extreme variations in wealth within these groups. As mentioned earlier, wealth is much more unequally divided than income, and this is especially true among Blacks and Hispanics.

Historically, inheritance of family wealth, or lack of it, has been a significant factor in the "sedimentation of racial inequality. . . . Between 1987 and 2011 the baby-boom generation stands to inherit approximately $7 trillion. . . . One-third of the worth of all estates will be divided by the richest 1 percent, each legatee receiving an average inheritance of $6 million" (Oliver and Shapiro 1995, p. 6). Wolff's analysis (April 2000) of national data from the Survey of Consumer Finances (SCF) indicates that 24 percent of White households, but only 11 percent of Black households, received an inheritance sometime during their lives. Moreover, the average amount received by Whites was $115,000 compared to only $32,000 for Black inheritors. A review of other studies similarly shows that Whites are about five times as likely to inherit wealth from their parents, and the amounts are significantly larger than those received by Black children. The amounts of income and wealth received from living relatives are also greater among Whites (Shapiro 2004).

The future does not look any brighter for greater equality in wealth. Estimates are that we can also expect racial inheritance differences to increase when the baby-boom generation enters retirement. "The mean white baby boomer's lifetime inheritance will be worth $125,000 in current (2000) dollars at age 55, as compared to only $16,000 for the black baby boomers and around $70,000 for the preceding generations of whites"

(Avery and Rendall 2002). The differences in these amounts indicate the differences in the size of the bases upon which more wealth can be built.

The building of Black wealth for the next generation has been further hindered by discrimination in the mortgage industry. Regardless of credit history and income, Blacks tend to be given less information about loans, be denied loans more often, and be charged higher interest rates (Turner and Skidmore 1999). Loan denials appear to be especially likely when Blacks seek housing in higher-income, predominately White neighborhoods (Holloway and Wyly 2001). These denials help to perpetuate wealth differentials and "sediment" Blacks into lower levels of wealth.

Wealth inequality between Blacks and Whites has been perpetuated since early in U.S. history, beginning with slavery, by governmental policies that prohibited Blacks from beginning certain kinds of businesses or entering particular markets, agencies such as the Federal Housing Authority which made loans and mortgages for Blacks more difficult to obtain, and the lack of opportunity to take advantage of the wealth-accumulation benefits of lower capital gains taxes, home mortgage deductions, and Social Security benefits. White mob violence has also weakened attempts to build up wealth that could be passed on to future generations. Consequently, 75 percent of Black children grow up in families with no wealth assets (Oliver and Shapiro 1995).

Income differences between groups are not as extensive as those in wealth. Between 1980 and 2009, the income gap between Black and non-Hispanic White households closed slightly. In those years, the median incomes of Black households went from 57 percent to 60 percent that of non-Hispanic White households. In 2009, the median income for Black households was $32,584, compared to $54,461 for non-Hispanic White households. In that same period, the gap between the median incomes for Hispanic and non-Hispanic White households increased. In 1980, Hispanic household income was 72 percent that of White households, but dropped to 70 percent in 2009 ($38,039 vs. $54,461; U.S. Census Bureau, September 2010a).

A significant factor in the increase in family incomes among lower-income Blacks has been the increase in their number of hours worked. By the late 1990s, lower- and middle-income Black families were working roughly between 100 and 500 more hours per year than either comparable Hispanic or White families. Among the highest income quintile, Black families put in about 500 more hours than high-income White families (Mishel, Bernstein, and Schmitt 2001). This suggests that Blacks have to work longer to remain in the middle- and upper-income groups. Among families, the contributions of wives' earnings to total family income has increased among all these groups. In addition to lagging behind Whites on median income, as we saw in Chapter 3, Hispanics and Blacks also have poverty levels about three times that of Whites, and they are poorer.

The later part of the 1990s witnessed the most equal income growth in two decades (Mishel, Bernstein, and Schmitt 2001). This is reflected in the closing of the income gap between Whites and others just mentioned. Since 2000, however, things have changed. Incomes for White households and families stagnated between 2000 and 2007, but those for minorities declined. Minority groups were hit especially hard because of a softer labor market and industrial shifts, including losses in the manufacturing sector. The result is that the household income gap between groups that had been closing has grown since 2000.

Table 8.1 shows the trends in household incomes between 1980 and 2009 for different groups. The percentage in households with incomes below $25,000 went down for all groups between 1980 and 2000, and that for households with incomes of at least $75,000 went up for the same period. In 2009, however, there were increases for all groups in the percentages of those with incomes below $25,000, and decreases for all groups in the percentages with incomes of at least $75,000. This very likely reflects the downturn in the economy during this time. Still, the proportion of White households with incomes of $75,000 or more remains significantly higher than those for Blacks and Hispanics. Conversely, the percentage of households with incomes below $25,000 remains noticeably higher for Blacks and Hispanics.

Concentrations in income distribution increased within the Black and Hispanic subpopulations during the 1980–2009 period, while a slight decline in income inequality occurred within the White subpopulation between 2006 and 2009. In all these groups, the proportion of income going to the top 20 percent increased between 1980 and 2009 (see Table 8.2). In 2009, the greatest concentration of income existed among Blacks. The increased polarization of income suggests a growth in class distinctions within these groups. Among Blacks especially, it complicates relative allegiances to class and race.

TABLE 8.1 Percentage of Households with Incomes under $25,000, $25,000–$74,999, and $75,000 or Higher, by Race and Hispanic Origin: 1980–2009

Household Incomes Below $25,000			
	1980	1990	2009
Non-Hispanic Whites	25.2%	22.5%	21.6%
Black	48.4%	44.2%	38.9%
Hispanic	36.9%	36.2%	31.7%

Household Incomes Between $25,000 and $74,999			
	1980	1990	2009
Non-Hispanic Whites	51.0%	46.7%	43.1%
Black	42.0%	42.0%	43.1%
Hispanic	50.4%	48.7%	47.3%

Household Incomes $75,000 or Higher			
	1980	1990	2009
Non-Hispanic Whites	23.9%	29.9%	35.3%
Black	9.6%	13.7%	18.0%
Hispanic	12.9%	15.2%	20.8%

Note: All incomes are in 2009 adjusted dollars.

Source: U.S. Census Bureau, *Income, Poverty, and Health Insurance Coverage in the United States: 2009.* Current Population Reports, Series P-60, No. 238, September 2010, Table A-1, pp. 33–39.

TABLE 8.2 Share of Aggregate Income Received by Bottom 20%, Middle 60%, and Top 20% Within Non-Hispanic White, Black, and Hispanic Populations: 1980-2009

Non-Hispanic Whites			
	1980	1990	2000	2009
Bottom 20%	4.4%	4.2%	3.7%	3.7%
Middle 60%	52.2%	50.0%	47.0%	47.1%
Top 20%	43.4%	45.8%	49.3%	49.2%
Gini Index	.392	.416	.459	.455

Blacks			
	1980	1990	2000	2009
Bottom 20%	3.7%	3.1%	3.2%	2.9%
Middle 60%	49.2%	48.0%	47.8%	46.0%
Top 20%	47.1%	49.0%	49.0%	51.0%
Gini Index	.439	.464	.458	.481

Hispanics			
	1980	1990	2000	2009
Bottom 20%	4.3	4.0%	4.0%	3.7%
Middle 60%	51.1%	49.7%	47.4%	46.8%
Top 20%	44.5%	46.3%	48.5%	49.5%
Gini Index	.405	.425	.444	.456

Source: U.S. Census Bureau, Tables H-2 and H-4, at www.census.gov/hhes/www/income/data/historical/inequality/index.html

The special vulnerability of Blacks to weak labor markets, reductions in manufacturing employment, the decline of union power, and the fact that the richest 25 percent of Blacks possess more than 90 percent of all Black wealth suggest that economic discrepancies will continue to grow within this group. In 2009, only a third of Blacks felt fairly well satisfied with their financial positions (Pew Research Center, May 21, 2009).

Earnings and Occupations

Given the differences in household incomes, it should not be surprising that there are also inequalities in the earnings of these groups. The median *weekly* earnings of Blacks and Hispanics working full-time are lower than those of Whites, among both men and women (see Table 8.3). Differences are also found in *hourly* wages. In 2007, 34 percent of Black workers and 42 percent of Hispanic workers, compared to only 22 percent of White workers, had hourly wages that put them below the poverty level. Within each racial/ethnic category, a greater percentage of women than men have poverty-level wages, that is, wages that even when working full-time do not raise the household above the poverty threshold (Mishel, Bernstein, and Shierholz 2009).

The earnings gap increased dramatically during the 1980s, and while it has slowed since then, significant disparities remain. Interestingly, Black–White wage differentials appear to be greater in high-earnings occupations. Consequently, while occupational mobility may increase Black earnings, it appears to accelerate

TABLE 8.3 Median Weekly Earnings of Full-Time Wage and Salary Workers 16 Years and Older, by Race, Hispanic Origin, and Sex: 2009

	Male	Female
White	$845	$669
Black	$621	$582
Hispanics	$569	$509

Source: U.S. Department of Labor, *Employment & Earnings,* January 2010, Table 37, p. 244.

the inequality between Black and White private-sector employees (Grodsky and Pager 2001). The availability of manufacturing jobs and union membership appear to be especially important for reducing Black–White wage inequality. The movement of industry out of cities and declines in manufacturing jobs have reduced the employment rates and earnings of Blacks, while immigration has had a dampening effect on the earnings of Hispanic workers (Mouw 2000; McCall 2001).

Part of the reason for the differences in earnings between racial and ethnic groups relates to differences in their occupational distributions. There seems to be at least a three-step process involved in producing the earnings discrepancy. First, Blacks are segregated into jobs that are dominated by other Blacks (Huffman and Cohen 2004). A recent study in New York City found that Black and Latino applicants for low-level jobs were less likely than White applicants to receive second interviews or job offers even though their qualifications and experience were basically the same as those of White candidates. Discrimination was not blatant, but took the subtle forms of seeing more potential in the resumes of White applicants, viewing minority Black candidates as a last resort, and shuttling minority candidates into positions with less customer contact and more physical work (Pager, Bonikowski, and Western 2009). Second, jobs in which there is a high concentration of minority employees have lower wages attached to them regardless of the qualifications of the workers or the characteristics of the place of employment. Evidence indicates a causal relationship between racial composition of jobs and their wages (Catanzarite 2003; Kmec 2003). Third, minority workers tend to lose ground in wages to White workers as they get older and move through their careers (Wilson 2003; Maume 2004). The initial lower levels of wages for these workers coupled with their cumulative disadvantage is another factor that makes it difficult to accumulate wealth or develop an inheritance for their children.

Examining broad occupational categories, we find that Blacks, Whites, and Hispanics are variously concentrated among them. There has been some occupational upgrading for Blacks in recent decades, however. A greater percentage of Blacks have moved into white-collar and blue-collar manufacturing positions since World War II, and a smaller percentage are service and farm workers. Areas that contain a high proportion of low-wage labor for Blacks include retail trade, health care, leisure, and other services, areas that contain about one-third of all Black workers. Together, manufacturing, retail trade, and health care employ about 40 percent of all Black workers. Blacks are especially underrepresented in mining, construction, and wholesale trade (Pitts 2007). An analysis of data from the Equal Employment Opportunity Commission indicates that racial integration among occupations increased in the 1960s and 1970s, but stopped after 1980. Interestingly, but perhaps not surprisingly, occupational integration is highest in low-wage industries, for example, retail trade (Tomaskovic-Devy et al. 2006). How smoothly Blacks and other minorities become harmoniously integrated into a business establishment depends in part on the latter's internal structure. Organizations that are larger and more formalized, and contain a smaller proportion of managers but higher percentages of minority managers, engender fewer complaints of racial discrimination (Hirsh and Kornrich 2008).

The evolving distribution of Blacks among occupations also reflects broader changes in the U.S. economy, culture, and polity. Among these have been

- The shift away from agriculture since 1900
- A decline in the centrality of unskilled work
- The movement toward a service-oriented economy
- The movement of industry out of central cities into suburbs, different regions of the country, or even different countries
- Attacks on unions, and the general weakening of the power of labor relative to corporate management
- "Retrenchment of civil rights enforcement" (see also Blau and Ferber 1986; Wacquant and Wilson 1989)

Not only are these macrolevel shifts important for understanding the distribution of occupations among African Americans and Whites but they are also directly tied to unemployment and poverty levels, the **hyperghettoization** of the inner city, and the size of the underclass. The decline in basic blue-collar jobs, especially those requiring little formal education, and the mismatch between the location of jobs and Blacks have intensified the unemployment problems of inner-city Blacks (Lichter 1988; Kasarda 1989). These shifts in the economy, however, do not mean that race itself has become unimportant as a factor in accounting for occupational differences between Blacks and Whites. The relative significance of economic class and race will be discussed shortly.

Table 8.4 presents the current broad occupational distributions for Blacks, Hispanics, and Whites of each sex. The greatest concentration of White males is in the managerial/professional category, while Black males are most often found in production/transportation or managerial/professional occupations, and the highest percentage of Hispanic men occur in the natural resources/construction group. Among women, the greatest concentration of White women is in managerial/professional occupations, while most Black women are in managerial, professional, or office positions. Almost two-thirds of Hispanic women are in office or service positions.

But these general categories mask real discrepancies among more detailed classifications of occupations. As is evident in Table 8.5, Blacks are most underrepresented in certain high-level professional and upper-level skilled white-collar positions involving authority or decision making and they are overrepresented in various private and governmental service and aide occupations. Those positions in which they are typically underrepresented require specialized training or high levels of education. Their overrepresentation lies in certain mid- to lower-level service jobs, such as service station attendants, barbers, and bus drivers. Some of these positions have direct or indirect ties to government, suggesting to many that the government is a significant route to the middle class for Blacks. However, the economic benefits

TABLE 8.4 Occupational Distribution of Employed Civilians Age 16 and Older, by Race, Hispanic Origin, and Sex: 2009 Annual Average*

Occupation	White Male	White Female	Black Male	Black Female	Hispanic Male	Hispanic Female
Managerial/professional	35%	41%	24%	34%	16%	25%
Office/sales/adm. support	17	33	19	31	14	32
Service occupations	13	20	21	29	21	32
Natural resources/construction/ maintenance	18	1	12	1	27	2
Production/transportation/ moving	17	5	24	6	22	10

*All percentages rounded.

Source: U.S. Department of Labor, *Employment & Earnings,* January 2010, Table 10, pp. 203–204.

TABLE 8.5 Sample of Specific Occupations in Which Blacks and Hispanics Are Significantly Over- and Underrepresented: 2009

Blacks

Underrepresented	%	Overrepresented	%
Artists	0.8	Barbers	35.0
Environmental scientists	1.0	Nursing/home health aides	34.0
Farmers and ranchers	1.4	Security guards	28.6
Dentists	1.4	Baggage porters	27.1
News analysts/reporters	1.8	Postal service clerks	28.3
Physical scientists	2.1	Residential advisors	29.6
Millwrights	2.1	Taxi drivers	25.7
Carpet/tile installers	2.3	Bus drivers	24.9
Aircraft pilots	2.3	Mail clerks	24.3
Veterinarians	2.4	Service station attendants	24.4

Hispanics

Underrepresented	%	Overrepresented	%
Editors	1.3	Agricultural graders/sorters	58.0
Environmental scientists	1.2	Cement masons/finishers	51.5
Farmers and ranchers	1.7	Drywall installers	56.6
Millwrights	2.1	Construction helpers	48.6
Occupational therapists	2.6	Roofers	47.7
Lawyers	2.8	Packaging operators	45.1
Chemical engineers	2.6	Carpet/tile installers	44.5

Hispanics			
Underrepresented	%	Overrepresented	%
Surveyors	2.8	Sewing machine operators	41.7
Tax examiners	3.1	Maids and housekeeping cleaners	41.7
Public relations managers	3.3	Dishwashers	39.5

Source: U.S. Department of Labor, *Employment & Earnings,* January 2010, Table 11, pp. 205–211.

for Blacks of working for the government seem to have eroded in the 1980s and 1990s (Zipp 1994).

One explanation for the paucity of Black men in leadership positions is their experience in occupational hierarchies. Even in some feminized occupations, it appears that while White men may be able to move up to supervisory and leadership positions, Black men are less likely to have access to such a "glass escalator." A study of nursing, for example, revealed that black male nurses face hostility with White female colleagues, stereotyping from patients that damages caregiving, and prejudice in promotion assessments (Wingfield 2009). Moreover, even when Blacks do gain high-level positions in the public economy, their positions are tenuous because of the volatility of political conditions (Collins 1993).

Similar to Blacks, Hispanics are underrepresented in many professional, high-authority occupations and overrepresented in manual labor, agricultural, and personal-service positions. Interviews with agricultural employers suggested that they use monolithic cultural reasons to justify hiring Latinos into manual agricultural jobs. They view Hispanics as being meant for this kind of work and that they are more willing to do hard physical labor than White workers who, they say, seldom apply for such jobs. Moreover, employers argue that the working conditions are better than workers would find in their own countries. A steady flow of immigrants and use of race-neutral rhetoric on the part of employers ensures a low-wage ethnic working force, continued profit for White employers, and maintenance of a racialized division of labor (Maldonado 2009).

Blacks, Hispanics, and Whites differ, like males and females generally, with regard to (1) the authority they possess in their jobs, (2) the specific kinds of organizations in which they are employed, and (3) the economic sector in which they work. Similar to the situation for females, human-capital variables do not fully account for these discrepancies. Rather, structural factors, such as place of employment, along with discrimination, appear to be implicated in inequalities in the occupational structure. Evidence gleaned from 15 years of civil rights commission records suggests that Black women experience more job discrimination than White women and that it is most often race-based rather than sex-based (Ortiz and Roscigno 2009). Fear of being accused of reverse racism can even cause employers to hesitate when hiring minority candidates or prompt sensitive employers to fire minority employees who are suspected, sometime erroneously, of acting in a racist manner. Shirley Sherrod, an employee in the U.S. Department of Agriculture (USDA) who was erroneously fired because of allegedly discriminating against White farmers is an example of such sensitivity to race. Having been falsely accused, she was quickly offered a new job in the USDA.

WHITE PRIVILEGE AND THE RELATIONAL NATURE OF RACIAL INEQUALITY

As suggested earlier, "race" has generally been thought to be a characteristic of non-White groups. Whiteness has been thought of as a noncolor and, therefore, invisible to most Whites. Critical race theorists argue that (1) while whiteness is invisible to Whites, it is a position from which Whites view themselves as well as others; (2) it is a privilege of which Whites are unaware; and (3) society and cultural norms are organized in ways that privilege whiteness (Lucal 1996; Frankenberg 1997). That is, racism is rooted in the way institutions work and laws are structured in society, rather than a psychological property of the individual. For example, federal legislation such as the Wagner and Social Security Acts of the New Deal did not afford the same protections to minority groups as others. Federal home loan policy discriminated against members of minorities who were trying to find decent housing. Environmental racism and federal highway projects to accommodate the growth of suburbs destroyed many minority neighborhoods (Lipsitz 2006). During the last 30 years, housing segregation has been heavily influenced by zoning restrictions that make it difficult for the poor and minorities to move to better neighborhoods (Massey, Rothwell, and Domina 2009). Finally, minority groups have also suffered structural disadvantages in the areas of education, employment, and health care.

From a **critical-race perspective**, viewing racism as an individual phenomenon masks its structural nature and prevents its eradication. Moreover, since Whites are generally unaware of how social arrangements benefit them above others, they do not see a reorganization of society as necessary, assume its neutrality, and instead would argue for a color-blind perspective in which all are able to operate freely within the existing structure, thus leaving success solely up to the individual.

Defining racism in individualistic rather than structural terms has allowed traditional views to avoid the institutional context within which individuals of different races are embedded, and to deflect attention from the issue of White privilege. Just as poverty is viewed by most as a problem of the poor, that is, *their* problem, the race problem is one focused on minorities as their problem. The result is that most studies of racism examine the oppression and discrimination minorities encounter and do not include the privileges that dominant groups enjoy and that foster racial inequality. Just as many view poverty as caused by individual deficiencies, traditional perspectives interpret racism as resulting from individual prejudice. The result is that remedies

for racism emphasize enlightenment, education, and training to change the prejudiced individual rather than reorganizing the institutional structures that privilege the dominant group. In their study of how two school districts worked to address racial bias, for example, Vaught and Castagno noted that because school racial problems were interpreted "as the isolated struggles of individual teachers working with 'different' students," workshops focused on raising awareness and changing the perspective of individual administrators and teachers. "The racialized structural barriers that informed, maintained, and entrenched individual practice went unnoticed" (2008, p. 103).

Racism does indeed involve a set of relations between groups that is embedded in the structure of institutions. Just as the position and life conditions of a social class are determined by its structural relationship to other classes, so too the position and life conditions of a racial minority are determined by its structural relationship to the dominant racial group. Thinking about class or race as an individual's property blinds us from seeing how relational ties affect each group. The oppression of one group is related to the privileges of another, but, like being White, those privileges often go unnoticed. As Lucal (1996) has stressed, a relational model of race relations is needed to incorporate all sides of those relations. This means making visible the often unnoticed privileges enjoyed by Whites: "Because of the segregated structure of the material and discursive environments inhabited by most white people, racial privilege is lived but not seen; whites not uncommonly live much of their daily existence without coming into contact with people of color" (Lucal 1996, p. 247). The evidence for arguments of whiteness and critical race theories that Whites are unaware of their race and its privileges, and that the societal structures are biased in their favor, is mixed. Results from a 2003 national survey indicate that while Whites are less likely than non-Whites to view their race as important to them or to interpret racial problems as caused by structural arrangements, these views are not held by all Whites (Hartmann, Gerteis, and Croll 2009).

MICROINEQUITIES AND MICROAGGRESSIONS AGAINST RACIAL AND ETHNIC MINORITIES

In the United States, it is clear that being White does make many of the daily aspects of life less problematic while being a member of a minority often makes everyday living more problematic. Like women, racial and ethnic minorities have been subjected to a host of everyday indignities. These indignities are independent of class position. Language, which reflects cultural values, helps to undergird the system of social inequality as it pertains to minorities, and yet because it is so much a part of our everyday lives, we seldom step back and look at it in any depth. The derogatory terms used to describe different ethnic and racial groups suggest the value placed on these groups, and reinforce this negative imagery when terms referring to these groups are used to describe some disliked or despised behavior (e.g., "an Indian giver," to "Jew down," to "gyp," to "nigger lip," etc.). Language is a powerful tool for shaping the attitudes toward and general beliefs about groups, and what makes it exceptionally influential is the fact that these terms are part of the matrix of everyday life and often used without intentional thought being given to their implications.

Embedded in this language are stereotypes of different racial and ethnic groups. Jokes and humor aimed at labeling and denigrating minorities have a long history in the United States, going back to the early seventeenth century when the first slaves arrived in the country. As new ethnic groups emigrated to the country, jokes that reinforced negative images of them increased. Such jokes helped to justify the stereotypes and poor treatment many immigrant groups received (Hughes 2003).

Stereotypes often have subtle yet negative effects on the groups targeted. For example, a study of Atlanta employers found that many have a negative stereotype of Black women as single mothers who are more concerned about their children than work, and therefore are generally late to work, lack education, and are not good role models for their children. These stereotypes affect the attitudes employers have toward prospective and current employees, and put Black women at a disadvantage (Kennelly 1999).

In the absence of real knowledge about specific groups, stereotypes provide a means by which individuals develop ideas about the characteristics of other groups. Most Americans, for example, have not had personal or extended contact with Native Americans. Yet many school and professional sports teams have adopted names and mascots that are supposed to represent Native American qualities. The Washington Redskins, the Atlanta Braves and the tomahawk chop of their fans, and the Chief Wahoo mascot of the Cleveland Indians are only a few examples of images that reinforce misperceptions about Native Americans. These terms and images are important because they shape our ideas about the supposed distinctiveness of Native Americans (King and Springwood 2001). They also damage the chances of accurately understanding the diversity and real qualities of Native Americans.

One reason for stereotypes is the lack of personal, concrete familiarity that individuals have with persons in other racial or ethnic groups. Lack of familiarity encourages the lumping together of unknown individuals. This happens even among social scientists. White interviewers have been found to view Black respondents as much darker than do Black interviewers, and conversely, Black interviewers perceive White respondents as being much lighter than do White interviewers. In addition, each type of interviewer sees members of the opposite race as having little variation in color, while seeing much more color variation among members of their own race. Familiarity encourages images of variation and individuality, while unfamiliarity fosters images of sameness (Hill 2002).

The media, especially movies and television, also have perpetuated stereotypes of African Americans learned in other contexts. Traditionally, African Americans and other non-White individuals have either been absent from the media or been portrayed in negative terms—for example, the African American as lazy, slow thinking, and subservient, and the American Indian as savage and hostile (Marger 1997). By

Stereotyping a group often results in all its members being thought of as the same and, therefore, deserving of the same treatment by dominant groups. The September 11, 2001, attacks on the Twin Towers of the World Trade Center in New York City provided an impetus to stereotyping and increased attacks on Muslims, as witnessed by the Minneapolis picketer on the 2010 anniversary of 9/11. (© Michael Rubin/Shutterstock)

ignoring heterogeneity among the more than 500 American Indian tribes through its presentation of the generic Indian and suggesting that American Indians are relics of the Old West, the media have contributed to the distortion in White Americans' image of American Indians.

The stereotype of the "drunken Indian" is also found among Whites. American Indians are viewed in the minds of many Whites as lacking a sense of control and responsibility. Such psychological factors are often used by Whites to explain alcoholism rates among American Indians, although the latter more often trace the problem to White invasions into Indian territory and culture. Allegations of psychological and cultural deficiencies are then used by Whites to explain the continued poverty and related problems among American Indians and to justify the paucity of attempts to alleviate these problems. In other words, such explanations continue to be used as part of an ideology to legitimate the inequalities

that exist between Whites and American Indians (Holmes and Antell 2001). Even the image of Asian Americans as a "model minority" (i.e., as educated, family oriented, and successful) glosses over educational and economic distinctions within the Asian American community, and recently has taken on a negative cast as others look for scapegoats for our economic difficulties. Instead of being viewed positively and as consistent with American values, the competitiveness displayed by some of these groups has been seen as a reason for the nation's problems. Just as competitive women are often seen as being unfeminine and aggressive, Blacks who are competitive are often considered pushy and uppity.

There are many additional, subtle, taken-for-granted advantages that are attached to the status of being White. In their everyday experiences in school, Black undergraduates have typically been tokenized, stereotyped, and assumed to have gained college admission through affirmative action rather than through their own efforts. Latinos often have their citizenship questioned and are treated coldly (Rivera, Forquer, and Rangel 2010; Watkins, Labarrie, and Appio 2010). Such unfair treatment often sends coded messages about the perceptions of minorities by persons in the dominant group. For example, a White woman may unintentionally hold on to her purse extra tightly as a Black man passes by, suggesting she thinks that all Black men are criminals (Sue 2010). Indeed, as we will see in Chapter 12, the image of Black men as threatening, dangerous, and violent is a common one. This image often has more impact than the reality. Regardless of the actual incidence of violence and delinquent behavior, for example, public schools with larger percentages of Black students are more likely than others to use punishment in disciplining students, and more drastic forms of punishment as well, again implying that Blacks are seen as a threatening presence even if they follow the rules (Welch and Payne 2010). Even President Barack Obama has been the victim of stereotyping because of his race and ancestry. Despite clear evidence to the contrary, some have made unfounded accusations that he is a Muslim rather than a Christian, and a Kenyan rather than a U.S. citizen.

One of the classic statements about everyday, taken-for-granted White privileges comes from Peggy McIntosh (1988). Among the 46 she lists are how being White allows her to:

- Freely choose a place that she wants and can afford to live in
- Go shopping, feeling secure that she will not be harassed or followed
- See others of her race prevalently displayed in the media
- Be fairly sure that her voice will be heard even in a non-White group
- Rely on her skin color to protect her from being seen as financially unreliable
- Feel that her children will receive an education that acknowledges the contributions of her race and in which teachers treat her children fairly
- Talk with her mouth full and not have people put this down to her color

- Not worry about acknowledging the views of non-White people
- Consider a wide variety of options in her life without worrying about whether her race would be a factor in limiting them
- Select a service or public accommodation without considering whether she will be treated poorly because of her race
- Not worry about her "shape, bearing, or body odor" being seen as a reflection of her race
- Use a flesh-colored bandage and have it blend with her skin

THE INTERSECTION OF CLASS, RACE, SEX, AND GENDER

In the preceding few chapters, we have examined the economic, racial, and gender dimensions of social inequality, and although they have been, to a large extent, treated separately, in the context of a *society* and in the lives of real *individuals,* these dimensions are interconnected. If we wish to understand how the dynamics and effects of each of these dimensions play out in actuality, we need to probe the nature of these interconnections at both the social/societal and individual levels. The significant meaning of these relationships can be uncovered by examining them at both levels.

When we speak of analyzing the interaction of class, race, and gender at the *social/societal level,* we are essentially considering each of these as separate variables that affect each other at the group or aggregate level. For example, consider the discussion of the relationship between the class measures of occupation and earnings on the one hand, and race on the other. Those relationships might be understood using references to racial compositions of occupations, group stereotypes, and interethnic relationships, without ever including the psychological effects or experiences of *individuals*.

The intersection of race and class can also be understood at the *level of individual experience.* Here, we are concerned with how race and class interact in the lives of individuals. How do people *experience* race and class in their lives? In their everyday lives, individuals accumulate *simultaneous* experiences as members of particular races, classes, *and* gender groups. A person is all of these things at the same time. This is the meaning of *intersectionality*. The dimensions are not as readily separable but rather are nested into each other. How do these elements interact *within* the individual? Consider a person who is Black, upper-class, and male—a Black surgeon, for example. What is it like to be him? How do the effects of class and race and gender interact in his life? And, at the same time, what is it like to be poor, White, and female? To address these questions is to examine the intersection of race, class, and gender at the individual level.

The Relative Significance of Race and Class

One of the most controversial and prominent discussions on the intersection of race and class involves arguments about the relative effects of race and class on the life chances of individuals. Scholars differ on which they think is most important. Around the turn of the twentieth century, W. E. B. DuBois suggested in his study of *The Philadelphia Negro* (1973) that not only racial discrimination but economic factors as well affected the everyday living conditions of Blacks. E. Franklin Frazier (1937) also suggested that both race and class play a role in determining what happens to Blacks, but finally felt that economics may be more important than race, an opinion later shared by Oliver Cox. Cox viewed race relations in the United States as stemming from and continuously being conditioned by economic-class relations. Racism exists as one of several devices used by capitalists to control, exploit, and keep workers down. As a result, it is rooted in economic conflict.

William Julius Wilson has argued that class has become more important than race in determining the life chances of Blacks today. This is because even though political and economic changes in society have opened up more potential opportunities for Blacks, these changes have also helped create urban joblessness. Blacks have been particularly affected, for example, by the

shift from a manufacturing to a service economy, by the broadening split between low-wage and high-wage labor markets, and by the movement of industries out of the central cities (Bonacich 1980; Wilson 1987). "The net effect is a growing class division among Blacks, a situation, in other words, in which economic class has been elevated to a position of greater importance than race in determining individual Black opportunities for living conditions and personal life experiences" (Wilson 1982, pp. 399–400). Wilson has not argued that race is irrelevant today but he has said that historically racism has had a major effect on the lives of Blacks that continues today. However, this *historical* discrimination has a more significant impact on Blacks' lives today than does *contemporary* discrimination. Still, it is broader economic and political forces that are most immediately important for understanding events and behaviors within the Black community.

Class differences have been a source of division within racial and ethnic groups, just as racial and ethnic differences have hindered unification of those in the same classes. (Photo by Brendan R. Hurst.)

Earlier in this chapter, I noted the high degree of wealth inequality within the Black population. There has been a long-standing suspicion between Blacks in different social classes. Since 1986, an increasing percentage of Blacks believe that the gap between the values of the middle and poor classes in the Black community has grown. In 2007, more than 60 percent felt this way compared to less than half in 1986. Almost 40 percent feel that the diversity within the Black community is so great that they can no longer be considered a single race. But a majority still feel that both classes have at least some values in common (Pew Research Center 2007). These results suggest that class operates as a divisive force in the Black community, while race still has a cohesive effect. They pull in opposite directions.

In sharp contrast to those who stress the primacy of economic-class factors in explaining the socioeconomic condition of Blacks, others emphasize the greater and, in some cases, increasing significance of race in understanding the economic predicament of Blacks. They suggest that the gains that Blacks have made relative to Whites have been blown out of proportion (Willie 1979).

Analyses of national surveys done from 1972 to 1996 revealed the continuing influence of race on one's quality of life. Over this period, Blacks continued to score lower on measures of happiness, life satisfaction, and health, and were more mistrusting and anomic than Whites. "What is clear is that being black in U.S. society results in a lower quality of life than does being white. Also clear is the substantial degree of racial inequality in U.S. society . . . and the continuing experience of racism in the lives of African Americans. . . . The coexistence of these facts suggests that racial differences in quality of life are produced by racial inequality and the experiences it produces" (Hughes and Thomas 1998, p. 792).

The interaction of race and class factors is certainly complex. We saw that, historically, economic and racial factors interacted in the treatment of American Indians and African Americans. Economic motives played a role in driving American Indians from their land and enslaving African Americans to create an extensive labor force. At the same time, we found that class distinctions existed among African Americans and women that were important for understanding the differences in life conditions. We also found that racism as a fully developed ideology was used to legitimate and sustain the economic systems that were being constructed. In the same way, ideologies about the sexes and their proper roles have helped to keep occupational sex segregation intact. Economic as well as other conditions helped bring about the migration of Blacks to the North and the consequent form of the class structure within the Black population. Evidence presented earlier shows that race affects one's occupation, and the racial composition of an occupation affects the earnings associated with it. Blacks receive less of a return on their educations than Whites, and race and class position both affect one's income (Grodsky and Pager 2001; Catanzarite 2003; Kmec 2003; Pager, Bonikowski, and Western 2009; U.S. Census Bureau, September 2010a).

Class, Color, and Race

Usually we think of race as a biologically fixed category that cannot therefore be affected by class. But as we saw earlier, races are socially constructed, and how one identifies with a given race and is placed in a racial category can depend on one's class position. Recently, Bonilla-Silva (2004) has argued that increased multiethnicity, immigration, and globalization are among the forces leading the United States into a three-tiered racial system. Within the first two of "White" and "Honorary Whites" categories are varieties of ethnic groups that, traditionally, have been thought of as separate from "Whites" (e.g., Japanese Americans, Arab Americans, Asian Indians). The third category, labeled "Collective Black," includes not only African Americans, but newer, generally poorer East Asian immigrants, "dark-skinned and poor Latinos," and "reservation-bound Native Americans" (pp. 225–227). This suggested classification clearly shows the interaction of economic and racial/ethnic forces.

Race and class forces collide in the phenomenon of colorism. "'Colorism' is the discriminatory treatment of individuals falling within the same 'racial' group on the basis of skin color. It operates both intraracially and interracially" (Herring 2004, p. 3). Among Blacks, a greater proportion of those with darker skins have lower educations and incomes, have poorer jobs, and are less likely to own their own homes (Hochschild and Weaver 2007). Tracing the lifetime occupational attainments of several hundred Black men, Hill (2000) found that lighter-skinned Blacks attained higher positions than darker-skinned Blacks, regardless of their social origins. Skin color is also related to how individuals assess candidates for political office (Hochschild and Weaver 2007). In the 2008 election, some Blacks wondered whether the lighter-skinned Barack Obama was "Black enough" because his mother is white and he did not descend from a slave family or grow up in grinding poverty (Staples 2007). Being authentically "Black" in this case means having a certain kind of socioeconomic background. Here again we see the complex effects when race, defined socially, and class mix.

The shading of one's skin is not only significant in the United States; throughout history, it has been socially important in countries around the globe. In her international analysis of what she calls a "yearning for lightness," Evelyn Nakano Glenn (2008) found rising demand for skin lighteners in all parts of the world, including Southeast and East Asia, India, and many countries in Latin America and Africa. In the United States, skin color made a difference early in its history. Slaves with lighter skins were treated better than those with darker skin or full African ancestry, later giving rise to groups such as "blue vein societies," associations of more prosperous freed Blacks whose blue veins could be seen because of their lighter skins. These organizations mirrored the "blue blood" societies among wealthy Whites. Anecdotal evidence suggests that many Black women still prefer to be lighter (Glenn 2008).

The fact that skin color and social class interact may make growing class discrepancies within the Black community even more significant. In her study of women involved in high-society organizations, Diana Kendall (2002) found that colorism operated not only within White organizations, and between White and Black organizations, but within Black "high society" as well. The **brown-bag test** was used to screen potential members of these organizations, meaning that one's skin should not be darker than a brown grocery bag (p. 129). This is significant if only because it is within such organizations that social capital can be developed that may enhance one's socioeconomic position.

Class Divisions among Blacks

Economic dislocations and restructuring along with globalization forces have helped foster class polarization among Blacks. During the past three decades, at least three major classes appear to have developed as a result of broader economic changes: (1) an underclass living below poverty, (2) an above-poverty class just getting by, and (3) a relatively well-to-do class with high education levels and professional occupations (Kendall 2002). However, the class structure among Blacks is more compressed than that among Whites and each class is different from its White counterpart. The position of the Black middle class, for example, is more precarious than that of the White middle class because of the generally lower stability of their jobs and the smaller "nest eggs" available for future expenses. "Wealthy" Blacks are not as rich as wealthy Whites, the white-collar positions held by members of the Black middle class tend to be of lower status than those occupied by middle-class Whites, and poor Blacks are generally poorer than poor Whites. Also, in contrast to the *invisibility* of whiteness as a color and of Whites as a race, consciousness of race is more prominent among Blacks, in part because of the continued segregation and other problems they face regardless of class.

On a day-to-day basis for adults, race often overrides class in its importance for getting along with life (West 1993). A recent longitudinal study of residential migration among Blacks and Whites, for example, suggests that racial factors may be more important than wealth in explaining the rate of Black movement into heavily White neighborhoods (Crowder, South, and Chavez 2006). In other areas, however, changes in class position seem to affect the salience of race. Among Blacks, an increase in class position in some situations can lead to greater racial allegiance. Evidence from voting studies in California suggests that as Blacks move into the middle class, a greater percentage vote in a pro-Black manner and more liberally than other classes on issues of central importance to Blacks. Among Blacks, "class gains appear to reinforce rather than erode race" (Hajnal 2007, p. 574). In contrast to effects in other ethnic groups, increases in class position appear to lead to more liberalism rather than more conservatism. There are other areas in which unity exists among Blacks in general. Regardless of class position, Blacks have a strong positive identity with their race and do not subscribe to negative images held of them by others (Bowman, Muhammad, and Ifatunji 2004; see also Carter 2003).

Despite these similarities among Blacks, class-related pressures still create fissures and disagreements within the Black community. Many of the issues between classes revolve around differences in lifestyles, attitudes, and child rearing. There are even potential divisive forces at work within classes. One of these is the division between the traditional married couple and the increase in the number of single people who live alone as a segment of the Black middle class, individuals who often view marriage as a hindrance to the attainment of middle-class status (Marsh et al. 2007). In her study of a Black middle-class neighborhood on the south side of Chicago, Mary Pattillo-McCoy (1999) found that residents often distinguish area individuals on the basis of whether they are "bourgie" (i.e., have a *bourgeois* lifestyle) or "uppity" (i.e., think they are better than everyone else). The economic middle class consists of both law-abiding and criminal elements. Perhaps most significantly, residents have to negotiate their daily lives using both "street" and "decent" lifestyles (see also Anderson 1999). While the decent lifestyle professes adherence to traditional, more mainstream middle-class values and behaviors, the street lifestyle requires values and behaviors that reflect the street smarts necessary for survival and respect in the neighborhood. The battle to balance these two lifestyles is constant, but especially intense during adolescence (Pattillo-McCoy 1999).

The conflict between traditional dominant lifestyle values and subgroup values also is found in school settings. In the hothouse environment of the elite prep school, all students, regardless of background, are expected to adhere to a given set of principles. But these principles often come into conflict with the values and attitudes that Black, working-class, and poor children have been taught at home. These children are marginalized in the school setting that is structured to prize and honor children from elite backgrounds. Kuriloff and Reichert (2003) found that Black students can effectively combine the methods and lessons taught at home with those taught at school to successfully navigate their way through the elite school. In other school settings, poor and middle-class Black students are often divided in their lifestyle codes, with poor Blacks adopting what they consider an "authentic," "black" code, and middle-class Blacks subscribing to a "minority culture of mobility" that distinguishes them from middle-class Whites and other Blacks (Carter 2003, p. 150).

Annette Lareau (2003) also discovered lifestyle differences among Blacks of different classes. Her interviews and participant observation of Black and White families in different communities revealed that middle-class parents, regardless of race, used a method of child rearing that Lareau dubbed "concerted cultivation." These parents worked hard to provide crucial tools, and intentionally prepared their children for successful adulthoods. This meant greater monitoring and control of the everyday schedule of their children. It also meant that they enrolled their children in numerous activities, nurtured debate abilities and language development, and taught them how to negotiate and compete with adults to accomplish their goals. Not only did this cultivation provide children with advantages that served them later in life, it also fostered a "sense of entitlement" within the middle-class children (Lareau 2003, p. 6).

In sharp contrast, working-class and poor parents, both Black and White, engaged in a "natural growth" form of child rearing. This was a less directive and controlling, in a sense more easy-going, form of child rearing in which children were more likely to be on their own for much of the day. The worlds of adults and children were kept separate. Children were not treated as equals. Parents did not intentionally develop argumentation skills among their children or encourage them to debate with authority figures. Working-class children engaged in fewer formal, scheduled activities. Clearly, the differences uncovered in Lareau's research indicate significant lifestyle and class differences among Blacks. Not only do class and race intersect in interesting ways; gender further complicates the picture.

Gender, Race, and Class

Sex and gender discrimination appears to be an important element in the continuance of occupational segregation, thereby affecting class position. At the same time, class and race divisions among women historically helped to determine the nature of their involvement in the labor market. Almquist (1984) found, for example, that some female minority groups have different occupational patterns than others. The patterns of Asian women approximate those of Anglo women, whereas those of American Indians are closer to the patterns found among African American and Hispanic women. Educational patterns also vary among these groups. Asian Americans and Whites are more likely than other ethnic and racial groups to have completed high school, and Asian Americans have higher rates of college completion than other groups. But *within* these groups, there are also variations. For example, a much higher proportion of Chinese and Asian Indian individuals than Laotian or Vietnamese have college degrees, and Cubans are more likely than Mexican Americans to have finished four years of college (Kao and Thompson 2003). Among Blacks, a greater percentage of women than men have college educations. In essence, we can say that race, sex, and class are

each important and often interact in their influence on the individual.

Census Bureau data on incomes of full-time workers make it evident that race *and* gender have an influence on income, earnings, and the distribution of occupations. Blacks and Whites differ on each of the latter, but within each race males and females are differently situated with respect to income, earnings, and occupation. Census data clearly show that although Blacks and women, in general, have increased their representativeness in professional occupations, they continue to be severely underrepresented in professions dominated by males. Even though the proportion of male professionals declined, males continue to dominate certain high-ranking professions. In fact, their overrepresentation in these professions has increased. Black men are the next group most represented in these professions, followed by White women and Black women, respectively. These findings again suggest the complex interplay of race and gender that affects class position.

Attitude toward the feminist movement is another area that demonstrates the detailed interworking of race, gender, and class. Many African American women do not identify with the movement because they associate it with White, middle-class women, a group whose interests and needs differ in many ways from their own (hooks 1981; Reid 1984; King 1988). Historically, African American women have been suspicious of White women (Chafe 1977). Many view their class and race interests as separating them from the feminist movement that has developed in the United States.

Some argue that the race-versus-gender stance suggested here is unfortunate because it hinders Black women from working against *both* racism and sexism (Reid 1984). The development of Black feminism was one response to these issues raised about traditional feminism.

The influences of race, class, and sex on the life chances of an individual are multiplicative because they interact in complex and different ways depending on the specific sociohistorical and cultural context and the area of life chances in question (King 1988). In this sense, African American women are often in a situation of "multiple jeopardy" because of their racial, sexual, and class positions. It is inappropriate to lump Blacks and women into the same category because their current life experiences and past histories are unique. Whereas the races have been expected to restrict intimacy with each other, men and women have been expected to do the opposite. In this manner, Blacks have occupied a castelike position while women have not (Keller 1987). Even more specifically, Black women are often left to fall between the cracks in discussions of Blacks (usually meaning Black men) and women (usually meaning White women). The lesson here is that even though the histories of the sexes and races have been unique in many ways, the influences of race, sex, and class interweave when affecting individual lives.

THEORIES OF RACIAL AND ETHNIC INEQUALITY

As is the case for sex and gender inequality, there have been a variety of attempts to explain racial inequality, ranging from biological to cultural and structural. Attempts to anchor an adequate explanation in biology have been widely criticized. The work of Herrnstein and Murray (1994) has elicited an avalanche of commentary, most of it negative. Basically, these scholars have argued first that an elite of highly intelligent people has developed that is increasingly separated from the rest of society, socially and economically. The high demands for intelligence and education in our sophisticated economy have funneled these elite into the high-paying, high-prestige occupations and left the rest of the population behind. The result is greater social inequality. The second part of their argument is that intelligence has been shown to be significantly linked to a wide array of social effects, including wages, poverty, crime, dropping out of school, and having an illegitimate child. A highly controversial position follows this discussion in which Herrnstein and Murray suggested that racial groups vary on intelligence, that a large portion of intelligence is very likely genetically based, and that most of those at the bottom of the socioeconomic ladder are also those who score low on intelligence. The society stands to

suffer since this group is also more likely than the more intelligent to have high fertility rates. In essence, their argument appears to be that intelligence has become more significant for the class placement of individuals, that intelligence has a strong genetic component, and that the United States is moving toward a more volatile class-stratified society based on intelligence in which classes are isolated from each other.

Briefly, Herrnstein and Murray's work has been criticized for, among other things, (1) its reliance on intelligence tests given later in life whose results might thus reflect both genetic and environmental influences, (2) the omission of other significant factors that can affect socioeconomic outcomes (e.g., labor-market experience), and (3) the belief in the fixity and rigidity of genetic mechanisms and related social problems (Haynes 1995; Massey 1995; Nielsen 1995). Earlier research by the psychologist Arthur Jensen, who argued that there are significant differences between Blacks and Whites in native intelligence, was also heavily criticized. But even if such differences could be demonstrated, their relevance for social and economic inequality between the races would still be problematic given the fact that numerous studies demonstrate that individual characteristics do not fully explain such inequality. Finally, the whole idea of racial differences in biology is based on the assumption that different races can be accurately, indisputably, and objectively identified. As we have seen, this is not the case.

In the sections that follow, various interpretations of race relations and explanations for racial inequality will be presented. Most will focus on the United States even though they are frequently based on analyses developed for the characterization of intergroup relations in other countries such as India and Third World countries in general.

Domination Theories of Race Relations

A variety of specific theories are included under this general category, but all of them incorporate the historically crucial role of power and/or domination in shaping racial inequality. They do not anticipate the eventual automatic assimilation of minorities, nor do they emphasize the stability of the system of inequality or the active complicity of the minority group. As was noted earlier, critical-race theory posits that the power of whiteness is woven into the structure and hegemonic culture of U.S. society. The effectiveness of dominant values as disseminated by political, economic, educational institutions, and the media helps to make White privilege invisible to most Whites, who are unaware of the everyday benefits that they enjoy because of their whiteness. In addition to critical-race theory, Noel's theory of ethnic stratification, imperialist/colonial models, and class-based theories also emphasize the centrality of power differentials in explaining racial inequality.

NOEL'S THEORY OF ETHNIC STRATIFICATION

Noel (1968) generated a broad theory of the origins of ethnic stratification which he then tested by applying it to the development of slavery in the United States. By ethnic stratification, he means "a system of stratification wherein some relatively fixed group membership (e.g., race, religion, or nationality) is utilized as a major criterion for assigning social positions with their attendant differential rewards" (p. 157). He begins with the assumption that before the possibility of such stratification even exists, there must be a period of prolonged contact between the groups involved. Whether contact results in stratification depends on the existence of (1) ethnocentrism, (2) competition, and (3) differential power. All three of these factors must be present for ethnic stratification to emerge.

Ethnocentrism, of course, refers to the belief that one's culture is the best, the center of the universe so to speak. All others are judged according to it. Cultures that are similar to one's own are ranked high, and those that are radically different are looked down on. Consequently, ethnocentrism fosters an in-group–out-group or us–them orientation toward others. Since people are so classified, double standards may be applied to the groups involved. What one expects of oneself may not be what is expected of others. It is important to note that each group is ethnocentric, thinking of the other in terms of mild or severe disdain. Each group measures the other in terms of its own values and beliefs, and of course, the other group is always found to be wanting to some degree. Each group also remains separate and autonomous from the other.

However, mere ethnocentrism is not enough to create ethnic stratification according to Noel. Groups can remain independent and relatively equal with a mutual and healthy respect for each other even though both are ethnocentric. Thus, it is also crucial that competition exists between the two or more groups in question. *Competition,* as defined by Noel, refers to the interaction between groups who are trying to attain "the same scarce goal." What is important about this interaction is that the goal is the same and that it is scarce. This could be competition over a prime neighborhood area or desirable jobs, for example. If the groups were after different goals, there would be no sense of competition and perhaps even lack of concern over the goals of the other group. If the goal is easily attainable and in abundant supply, there is no reason for one group to try to exploit or stratify the other. There is plenty for all.

If, on the other hand, the desired object or goal is actually or believed to be in scarce supply, then stratification may be seen as functional by each group. The intensity and terms of the competition along with the relative adaptive capacity of each group will affect the probability and form of ethnic stratification. Competition is more likely to be highly intense if there are many valuable, scarce goals that are shared by both groups, and will be less intense if those shared goals are few in number and relatively unimportant. The more intense the competition, the greater the likelihood of ethnic stratification, other factors being equal. The terms of the competition concern the values, rules, and structural opportunities present in the setting. If competition is regulated by agreed-upon rules and some basic human values are shared by the two groups, then ethnic stratification is far less likely to occur than if the competition is essentially a free-for-all and the groups have no values in common. Moreover, if there are few structural outlets in the form of opportunities, then competition is more likely to lead to stratification.

Finally, the adaptive capacity of a group relative to its competitor also has an impact on ethnic stratification. Basically, the group that has more cultural and other internal resources to call on when problems of adaptation and adjustment arise will more likely be able to dominate the other group. The chances of stratification occurring are lower when both groups are equal in their adaptive capabilities.

According to Noel (1968), in addition to ethnocentrism and competition, a third variable, *differential power,* is also necessary for the emergence of ethnic stratification. "Highly ethnocentric groups involved in competition for vital objects will not generate ethnic stratification unless they are of such unequal power that one is able to impose its will upon the other" (p. 112). Ethnic stratification simply will not appear in the absence of differential power. Once the greater power of one group is established, the more powerful group develops measures to subordinate and regulate the other group and to stabilize the current distribution of differential rewards.

In sum, Noel argued for an interactive model in that all three variables—ethnocentrism, competition with particular characteristics, and differential power—are needed to produce ethnic stratification. In applying this theory to the development of slavery in the early English colonies of the United States, Noel concluded that it adequately explains ethnic stratification. "Given ethnocentrism, the Negroes' lack of power, and the dynamic arena of competition in which they were located, their ultimate enslavement was inevitable" (p. 117). Earlier, we saw how these factors also were implicated in the subjugation of American Indians.

In our early contacts with Mexican Americans throughout the Southwest, competition for land, accompanying racial/ethnic stereotyping, and imbalances in numbers and power contributed significantly to the inequality that developed between Whites and Chicanos (Farley 1988). Although Noel's theory does not identify all the specific historical and societal factors that might affect stratification in specific settings, his theory does identify in broad brush strokes three core factors that make it likely.

The next two theories, which also focus on differential power, have a great deal in common. The colonial model of race relations owes a significant amount to the Marxian class framework, and early architects of that model generally acknowledge their debt to Marx (e.g., Fanon 1963; Memmi 1965). In recent years, there has been a lot of cross-fertilization of both the colonial and class perspectives, with each using concepts from the other. But since the primary impetus that gave rise to each was not the same, they will be presented as if they are distinct approaches. However, their overlap in general orientation will become clear as each is discussed.

INTERNAL COLONIALISM AND RACE INEQUALITY   This approach to understanding the domination of Whites over Blacks in the United States is based on discussions and analyses of relationships between colonizing countries in the First World and those who have been colonized in the Third World. In this way, it bears a striking resemblance to world-system and dependency theories. The popularization of the internal-colonial perspective arose during the tumultuous 1960s when the War on Poverty, civil rights movement, and major urban racial confrontations were at their height. Militancy and discussions of "Black power" and "Black nationalism" made the parallel between the Black predicament and that of other oppressed racial groups seem viable. In other words, the times were ripe for a colonial theory of U.S. race relations. Fanon and Memmi, who wrote about colonial relationships in the Third World, had their writings adapted to the U.S. racial setting. Following them, a large number of scholars suggested and elaborated on what they felt was a basic parallelism between the dynamics in those relationships and those that occur in Black–White relations (cf. Carmichael and Hamilton 1967; Allen 1969; Blauner 1972).

One of the noted differences between classic colonial relationships and the internal-colonial relationship said to exist between Blacks and Whites in the United States is that the former generally involves groups from one territory invading and dominating the territory of another group, whereas in the latter case, both groups are from and occupy the same country. What can be said in response to this difference is that it is the character of the relationship rather than the factor of geography that defines a relationship as colonial (Barrera 1979; Bonacich 1980).

While acknowledging that the analogy is not perfect, Carmichael and Hamilton (1967) argued that Blacks in the United States "stand as colonial subjects in relation to the White society. . . . That colonial status operates in three areas—political, economic, social" (pp. 5–6). *Politically,* while Blacks are technically just as free as Whites, Whites dominate the power structure of society, holding the most influential positions. Moreover, they exercise "indirect rule" by co-opting and controlling selected influential Blacks to help maintain the Black community in a subordinate position. *Economically,* Blacks are more likely to be poor and unemployed and to pay exorbitant prices for shoddy goods. In this manner, the Black ghetto is sapped of its resources, which are transferred to the dominant part of society. *Socially,* Blacks are looked down on and demeaned in everyday contacts with Whites. Racial ideologies arguing their basic inferiority and presenting negative stereotypes help justify and maintain control over Blacks. This interpretation presents all Whites as benefiting from the colonial structure.

Perhaps the most often-cited architect of the colonial model of race relations in the United States is the sociologist Robert Blauner. Blauner argued that **assimilationist theories**, which view minority groups as being on a one-way road to blending into the rest of society, do not accurately characterize the historical conditions of African Americans because they draw a false analogy between the present situation of African Americans and that faced by White ethnic immigrants about a century ago. He pointed out that this analogy cannot hold up because the histories and circumstances of their arrival in the United States were qualitatively and significantly different. Not only the slavery experience, but the nonvoluntary nature of their entrance into the country and the more permanent control of their lives by those outside their communities distinguishes African Americans from earlier White-ethnic immigrant groups. African Americans are not merely the latest batch of immigrants who are waiting to be assimilated and upwardly mobile.

Although there are some differences between classic colonialism and **internal colonialism**, Blauner felt that they share several basic characteristics. First, the political domination and advanced technological level of the West was the basis for both slavery of African Americans and the colonization of many countries by Europe. Second, the economic and political superiority of the dominant group encourages a feeling of racial superiority used to justify the exploitation of the other group. In other words, since both types of colonialism have similar roots, Blauner (1972) said that they share "a common process of social oppression" (p. 84).

Blauner (1972) suggested that there are five basic characteristics in the colonization complex:

1. The dominant–subordinate relationship begins with forced, involuntary entry; that is, African Americans were brought here as slaves and ghettos are controlled from the outside by the dominant group. White settlers also, of course, forcibly took over American Indian lands.

2. The indigenous culture and social organization of the dominated group is altered, manipulated, or destroyed; that is, African American culture and institutions are undermined. Native American culture also has been subjugated.

3. Representatives of the dominant group control the subordinate group through their legal and government institutions; that is, White institutions control much of the lives of African Americans. The placement of American Indians on reservations also serves as an example of control by the dominant group.

4. Racism as an ideology is used to justify the oppression of the subordinated group; that is, Blacks and other racially or ethnically distinguishable groups are seen as biologically or otherwise inferior to Whites.

5. The colonizers and colonized occupy different positions in the labor structure and perform different roles; that is, by and large, African Americans are relegated to menial, nonprestigious jobs while Whites dominate in higher-ranking positions. The dual-labor market characterizes the occupational positions of dominant and subordinate groups.

The listed characteristics suggest that the Black ghetto, instead of being isolated from the rest of society in some kind of autonomous culture of poverty, is in fact tied to White society by bonds of exploitation and dependency. The educational, political, economic, and legal institutions of the dominant society infiltrate and permeate the dominated colony. Then racism is used to maintain and justify the lower status of Blacks.

In addition to these structural characteristics, there are also cultural and psychological ramifications to the colonial relationship. In the colony, individuals cannot break through the racial-ethnic barrier. Colonized individuals can move up in class but cannot change their position of being colonized except through successful revolutionary movements that transform the structure of society. They may try to gain entrance into the larger society but "everything is mobilized so that the colonized cannot cross the doorstep, so that [they understand and admit] that this path is dead and assimilation is impossible" (Memmi 1965, p. 125).

In attempting to assimilate, colonized persons may initially admire and even adopt aspects of their oppressors, but when it is realized that full structural assimilation is not possible, they begin to reassert themselves in part through resurrecting old traditions and through the advocacy of violence. "Those who understand their fate become impatient and no longer tolerate colonization" (Memmi 1965, p. 120).

Most of these stages appear to apply to African Americans and their movements in the United States, although some of the protest behaviors of African Americans could be interpreted in ways other than through the colonial model (Omi and Winant 1986). Among the strengths of this model are its historical and comparative dimensions and the fact that it can account for a relatively large number of factors within a fairly straightforward theoretical framework (Barrera 1979). However, a weakness of simply transferring the colonial model intact to the American setting is that it omits consideration of the uniqueness of the American political and social context (Blauner 1972).

To effectively deal with this shortcoming, Blauner suggested that an adequate theory must incorporate elements dealing with characteristics of both colonialism and capitalism. Indeed, several of the attempts to develop a class-based theory of race inequality include references to both of these (e.g., Bonacich 1980; Hunter and Abraham 1987). Omi and Winant (1986) also pointed out that the internal-colonial model does not take into account class differences within the colonized (African American) group or relationships between minority groups. Despite these difficulties, the colonial model probably provides a more accurate analysis of Black–White relations in the United States than either the assimilationist or caste perspective (Wilson 1970; Barrera 1979).

CLASS-BASED EXPLANATIONS OF RACE INEQUALITY Wilson (1970) has argued that economic and class dynamics are becoming more important for determining the life chances of Blacks. But well before Wilson developed his theory, others also argued that economic factors are behind the inequality between Blacks and Whites in the United States. One of the most sophisticated class-based theories of race relations in the United States was developed by Oliver C. Cox in the late 1940s.

Cox viewed race relations and inequality in the United States as a product of economic exploitation. Forcibly bringing slaves to the United States was essentially a way of getting labor to exploit the natural resources of the country. Racial exploitation is only one form of the proletarianization of labor according to Cox. Racism as an ideology was not the root of exploitation; rather, it followed from it and was used to justify economic exploitation of Blacks. Racism, therefore, is a relatively recent phenomenon. Given its character and economic basis, "racial antagonism is essentially political-class conflict." Racial antagonism is used by employers to divide Black and White workers, and racial ghettos are maintained because they facilitate control over Blacks and perpetuate a self-defeating lifestyle. Blacks may want to assimilate but it is not in the interests of dominant Whites for them to do so (Cox 1948, 1976).

What is attractive about Cox's arguments is that he intermingled elements of racism, colonialism, class inequality, and capitalism in a comparative framework. Racial inequality is bound up with the development and expansion of European empires and the rise of capitalism and its labor needs.

Trade is the lifeblood of international capitalism. The need to control potential markets and sources of raw materials strengthens the tendency of capitalism to colonize and exercise political control in the world economic system. Loans, raw materials, markets for manufactured goods, and imperialism each play a part in creating and fastening ties (chains) between dominant and subordinate nations in the worldwide capitalist system (Cox 1959, 1964). Race prejudice is then used to justify imperialism. Much of Cox's later writing anticipated many of the ideas associated with world-system and dependency theory.

One of the thorny areas of disagreement among class-based theorists of race relations concerns who benefits from racism and the nature of the relationship between Blacks and the White working class. From one point of view, racism is used by employers to drive a wedge between Whites and Blacks in the working class, and nationalism is used to divide members of the working class from different ethnic/racial groups in different countries. White workers come to view foreign workers who labor for low wages as unfair competitors, and their racism, which is ultimately rooted in the worldwide development of capitalism, is an attempt to protect their own jobs (Bonacich 1980). Although White or dominant workers may benefit from this racism in the short run, in the long run, the inequality within the working class creates divisions that weaken its collective power against employers. Employers exploit members of the minority for greater profits

and money with which to pay the dominant working class. Accordingly, the principal beneficiaries of racism are employers rather than all Whites (Reich 1977).

In general, having an ethnic/racial working class provides capitalism with a surplus army from which to draw poorly paid workers to perform jobs that are necessary but that no one in the dominant group wants to perform. But as the capitalist economy advances and the revolutionary potential of minority groups grows, many large employers begin to feel that the long-term costs of race inequality may be too high and that it should be eliminated (Baran and Sweezy 1966). One obvious cost of racism to employers is the loss of bright minority members to employers who could use them to increase productivity.

Edna Bonacich (1980) attempted to integrate and synthesize many of the arguments in class-based theories of race inequality. She began by commenting on the motivations for imperialism abroad. One important source for this movement is the desire to find more malleable and cheaper labor because the cost of labor rises as capitalism develops within a country. Wages rise because (1) the absorption of the entire labor supply into the expanding economy creates labor scarcity, (2) workers have a need for higher wages to purchase the increasing number of commodities produced in the economy, (3) large factories create social conditions conducive to the political organization and greater union power among workers, and (4) increased state support of workers cushions them and enables them to hold out for higher wages (see also Piven and Cloward 1982).

Because of these pressures for higher wages by domestic workers, employers look outside national boundaries for new sources of cheap labor. Pick up a piece of clothing from a well-known and expensive brand (e.g., Tommy Hilfiger, Polo, etc.) and notice where the item has been sewn. The labels frequently cite places such as Honduras and the Dominican Republic. The public scandals dealing with the making of celebrity-endorsed clothing in Third World sweatshops is another example of attempts to profit through the use of low-wage workers. Wages are lower in less-developed countries because of the existence of additional sources of subsistence (production for use) and a traditionally lower standard of living. Members of the domestic working class then see themselves as competing with cheap laborers in Third World countries, and may (1) react with nationalist and racist fervor against such groups or (2) see both themselves and other working-class groups from around the world as victims of capitalist development. Which of the two reactions is pursued by the domestic working class depends in part on the extent to which capitalists can control the colonized working class and manipulate the domestic working class, on how imminent the experience of competition with outside cheap labor is in the domestic working class, and on how proletarianized this class is itself (Bonacich 1980).

It should be obvious by now that there are several similarities between the class and colony theories of race inequality. First, both have as a central theme the notion of the exploitation (especially economic) of a lower group—African Americans and/or the working class. Both perspectives view top and bottom positions in relational terms—that is, the position of one group is considered to be inextricably linked to that of the other group. Second, in both models, justifications (ideologies) are crucial for legitimating the power relationships that exist. But in both, the relationship is both "destructive and creative" (Memmi 1965). Third, both perspectives emphasize the polarization of society and the importance of rising consciousness among the exploited. In general theoretical terms, these basic congruencies between internal-colonial and class theories outweigh their differences (Tabb 1970; Wilson 1970; Blauner 1972; Barrera 1979).

THE GLOBAL CONTEXT, IMMIGRATION, AND GLOBALIZATION

Racial and ethnic inequality, a form of what Charles Tilly (1998) calls "categorical inequality," is found throughout the world. Historically, among the most well-known of these systems of inequality were those found in South Africa,

India, and Japan. In each of these societies, a significant axis of the system of inequality was centered around racial/ethnic differences.

Beginning in the late 1940s and lasting until the early 1990s, South Africa had in place a system of apartheid that enforced social, economic, and legal separation between Whites and Blacks. Even though Whites were heavily outnumbered by non-Whites, they dominated the country politically, socially, and economically. Blacks were required to live in certain areas, lacked political rights, had to use separate facilities, were limited in their job prospects, and were closely monitored by authorities. Under apartheid, the poorest 40 percent of the population, who were mostly Black, lived in conditions that were far worse than those of the richest 20 percent, who were mostly White. For example, in 1993, near the end of the apartheid era, among the crowded households of the poorest in South Africa only about one-fifth had electricity, one-quarter had inside water, and less than one-fifth had toilets in their houses (United Nations 1998). A combination of growing Black organization and political power, economic requirements, and international sanctions and developments led to the decline of apartheid. In 1994, Nelson Mandela was chosen as president in the country's first general election.

Since the formal breakdown of apartheid, significant racial differences exist about national priorities in South Africa. Blacks see unemployment and the need for widespread access to basic services like housing and water as critical issues, while Whites are more likely to be concerned with crime and political corruption. Despite these differences and more positively, however, there is a multiracial government and general agreement that democracy is the government of choice (Schaefer 2006).

Parallels have been drawn between apartheid and the Jim Crow system that flourished in the southern United States after the Civil War. As in South Africa, more powerful colonists and settlers pushed native peoples off the land and captured important resources. Also similarly, racist ideologies were used to justify the growing inequality between dominant and dominated groups. The elements of Noel's theory of racial inequality—competition for resources, ethnocentrism, and unequal power—all operated in the U.S. and South African situations.

Similarities have also been suggested between India's traditional, now outlawed, caste system and Black–White relations in the United States. The caste system that was dominant in India provides an example of an extreme case of status stratification in Weber's sense. It had been both a system of inequality and a means of integration for India, with each layer assigned specific and unique functions (Lannoy 1975). The four major castes or **varnas**, beginning with the top, were the Brahmans, Kshatriyas, Vaishyas, and Sudras. Those at the top were assigned to perform the most honorific functions and were considered purer than those below. Legitimation for the caste system was rooted in early Hindu texts in which the four varnas are described and portrayed as metaphorically representing different parts of the Indian social body. A fifth stratum, the Untouchables (Harijans) were not part of the formal caste system itself; they were outside it. The real, everyday structure and operation of the caste system at the village level was much more complex than the four-varnas system would suggest. Although loosely associated by residents with the national caste system, castes or **jati** at the local level vary in number and character (Kolenda 1978).

There is increasing evidence that the Indian caste system is not the monolithic system it is sometimes portrayed to be. While still influential in more rural areas, educated, Westernized Indians are less likely to believe in the purity–pollution theory, and industrialization, trade, and globalization have helped to weaken the hold of the caste system and spurred a growing class system (Lannoy 1975; Sivaramayya 1983; Beteille 1996). There is some evidence of avenues of social mobility, and some lower-caste persons have started their own religious movements, others have married upward, and the relatively new Indian democracy and constitution have formally outlawed the caste system. At the same time, however, as in the United States, old traditions die hard. As Milner (1994) observed, "while the

caste system has undergone great changes over the long period of its existence, it has been relatively stable compared to most human institutions" (p. 56).

Japan provides an interesting variation on the caste system. One of the minority groups discriminated against in Japan is the **burakumin**, or "hamlet people," but in contrast to most minority groups elsewhere, the roughly three million burakumin are physically indistinguishable from other Japanese. Thus, they are sometimes called an "invisible race" (DeVos and Wagatsuma 1966). The only way to really know if a person is a burakumin is to know where he or she lives (DeVos and Wetherall 1983).

Historically, individuals in this group were considered unclean and were forced to live in certain areas. Their invisibility was reinforced by the absence of their village location on maps (Rowley 1990). While some attempts have been made to ban them, prejudice and discrimination against burakumin remain, for example, in the areas of marriage, job application, occupation, and earnings.

As is the case in the United States, South Africa, and India, traditional cultural values and practices retain a grip in Japan even in the face of technological advances and globalizing forces. In many countries, immigrants bring in new ideas, cultural values, and practices that often clash with and foment change in the native culture. Since 1965, when changes took place in U.S. immigration laws that weakened the old quota system and opened the nation more fully to immigration of relatives, the proportion of immigrants coming from Asia and Latin America has grown significantly. Twenty years after passage of the 1965 Immigration and Nationality Act, almost 85 percent of immigrants were from Asia, Latin America, and the Caribbean (Lee and Bean 2004). In 2002, an estimated 1,064,000 individuals immigrated to the United States, including 342,100 from Asia, 219,400 from Mexico, 96,500 from the Caribbean, 74,500 from South America, and 69,000 from Central American countries (U.S. Census Bureau 2005). In 2008, there were more than 38 million immigrants in the United States, comprising almost 13 percent of its population. Immigrants from Latin America account for more than half the total, while immigrants from Asia, Europe, and Africa make up 25 percent, 13 percent, and 4 percent, respectively (Ohlemacher, September 23, 2008).

The manner and extent of adaptation of these U.S. immigrants have varied, and most of the recent Latino immigrants have not found assimilation to be a smooth or easy process. Nor has assimilation followed the same paths or resulted in the same experiences for different groups. Part of the reason for the lack of smooth assimilation of many immigrant groups is that Americans have decidedly mixed feelings about the effect of immigration on society and have varying attitudes about immigrants from different countries ("The People Speak" 2009). The variation between immigrant groups has resulted in "segmented assimilation," in which the quality of adaptation varies depending on the human capital of the immigrant group, the strength of its family structure, and the reception it receives in the host country (Portes and Rumbaut 2005). Some groups, such as Jewish immigrants, form economic enclaves that develop into a source of support and income for new immigrants. Other groups, like Koreans, become prominent as "middlemen," providing services for a variety of clients.

Generally, greater social and economic inequality in a country encourages emigration of poorer residents out of them and into less unequal countries. Thus, the movement is often from less- to more-developed countries like the United States (Hao 2003). These new immigrants have less education and fewer high-level skills than native citizens. In 1990, for example, the average educational attainment of "recent immigrant" men to the United States was 11.8 years, compared to 13.2 years among native U.S. citizens. Well over one-third of male immigrants had dropped out of high school. Their lower educational levels were reflected in the lower earnings they received. In 1990, recent male immigrants from Mexico, for example, had average annual earnings of $14,251, compared to $37,551 for native men. Women who immigrated

from Mexico had annual earnings of $8,738 compared to $20,196 for women born in the United States. Immigrants in general tend to fall near the bottom of the wage hierarchy. Their concentration in certain kinds of jobs like textiles, cooking, tailoring, and other service positions helps account for their lower earnings (Smith and Edmonston 1997).

Recent economic crises and the increased popularity of more conservative political ideologies, have led many countries to become more concerned and restrictive about their immigration policies. France, for example, has attempted to keep the influence of Muslims in check, pressed for removal of outward signs of their religious beliefs, and has expelled many Roma from the country. Even the traditionally more liberal Scandinavian countries have embraced more anti-immigration arguments. The influx of minorities, including Muslims, into these countries has strengthened the hand of conservative parties. In 2010, the leader of a conservative Swedish political party categorized the growth of the Muslim community as the biggest danger to Sweden since the Second World War (Castle 2010).

In the United States, immigration has again become an issue of concern not only because of the shift that has taken place in most immigrants' countries of origin, but also because of the potential effects of immigrants on the employment and earnings of native citizens. The influx of lesser-educated and lower-skilled Hispanic immigrants, for example, has led many to believe that immigrants have damaged the economic positions of native residents by either taking away jobs from them or lowering their wages because of the competition they provide. Evidence regarding the effect of immigrants on job opportunities has been mixed, but generally Blacks appear to be more negative than either Whites or Hispanics. Hispanics, who compose a large proportion of recent immigrants, tend to be more positive in their assessment of immigration's effects (Newport 2007a; Pew Research Center 2007). Somewhat surprisingly, a majority of Blacks and Whites believe that immigrants work harder at low-wage jobs than members of their own races.

While immigration helps to account for an increase in wealth inequality in the United States because of the diversity of newcomers, evidence indicates that immigration has little effect on the wages of native-born employees (Smith and Edmonston 1997; Hao 2003). Earnings made by immigrants and sent back home, however, appear to have a positive impact on economic growth in their countries of origin (Kaupert 2007).

Despite their minimal impact on natives' wages, the increase in Hispanic and Asian immigrants affects the character of the American racial hierarchy. The continuing influx of Mexican immigrants into the United States, for example, intensifies ethnic and racial boundaries through the encouragement of native practices (Jimenez 2008). Continued immigration of poor Hispanics may also contribute to the reformation of racial categories: "At this time, America's shift in color lines points to the emergence of a new split that replaces the old black/white divide and one that separates blacks from nonblacks. . . . In the black/nonblack divide, Latinos and Asians fall into the nonblack category. . . . The birth of a black/nonblack divide could be a disastrous outcome for many African Americans" (Lee and Bean 2004, p. 237). Another possibility is the incorporation of darker-skinned, poorer Hispanics and Asians into a "collective black" category in a new racial hierarchy (Bonilla-Silva 2004).

The concerns about new immigrants as a social and economic threat have raised questions about the need to control immigration. Yet attempts to screen and limit immigrants' entrance into a country fly in the face of the image of globalization as a process that opens the doors to technology, products, influences, and people from abroad. Concerns like this have led Ronen Shamir (2005) to argue that while theorists advocating globalization may see it as a liberalizing, open process, it is also a conservative, limiting, exclusionary process. This paradox arises from the desire for nations to control their borders and maintain their national identity even in the midst of globalization. Globalization produces "closure, entrapment, and containment" through the "prevention of movement and the blocking of access" since some immigrants are seen as potential threats, even terrorists. This produces a "paradigm of suspicion" in which profiling, quarantining, imprisonment, and other forms of containment are put in place to control the mobility of suspect immigrants (pp. 199, 206–206, 210). Most of these "suspects" are from poorer countries. These modes of control are "a structural response to the problem of maintaining high levels of inequality in a relatively normatively homogenized world" in which there is a "tension between universal rights and universal fears" (p. 214). In this manner, globalization helps to maintain racial hierarchies and status exclusion.

Summary

Historical and contemporary evidence documents the inequality that has existed between Whites and various minority groups, including African Americans, American Indians, Asian Americans, and Hispanic Americans. The exploitation of African Americans for their labor and American Indians and Mexican Americans for their land were justified by racist ideologies, stereotypes, and the force of law. Like women, many minority groups have incomes, earnings, and occupational statuses that are lower than those of Whites, and their poverty rates are higher. Differences in family compositions, educational levels, and labor-force participation do not fully account for these economic discrepancies. African Americans and other minorities also experience day-to-day microinequities, frequently of a type similar to those experienced by women. Biases in language, education, and the media constitute many of these, but there are many, such as those noted by McIntosh, that occur in a variety of settings.

A variety of theories have been developed to explain racial and ethnic inequality, ranging from conservative to more critical and radical explanations. In general, the latter are more sophisticated and focus on the centrality of differential power and economic domination in accounting for race inequality. As is the case with some gender inequality theories, several of these theories are couched in a comparative framework and intertwine class and economic processes in their explanation, which lends them some depth.

These theories and research evidence show how the variables discussed in the last several chapters—class, sex, and race—are intertwined and influence each other. Debates in recent years have centered on the relative importance of race, sex, and class in producing these inequalities between groups. Some have argued for the primacy of one of these over others, but it seems clear that all affect the life chances through complex routes. Early racial and ethnic antagonisms helped to justify the economic exploitation of American Indians, Mexican Americans, and African Americans, and sexual stereotypes had the equivalent effect on women. At the same time, class differences within these groups created divisions that are sometimes hard to bridge. Sex and race also interact. For example, women of different races have different occupational and educational patterns. Race has been a source of division within the feminist movement, as well.

Around the globe, most societies struggle with ethnic and racial divisions. Among the most notable of these are South Africa, India, and Japan. Increased Latino and Asian immigration to the United States has reignited concerns about open immigration and its effects on economic inequality. Little support has been found for the argument that such immigration has a depressing effect on the earnings of native workers. Globalization encourages the free flow of material and human resources between countries, which suggests that every country might benefit from the process. But globalization has also renewed attempts by nations to monitor and maintain the security of their boundaries, the integrity of their cultures, and their position in the world economic order. Consequently, globalization also encourages tendencies toward closure and exclusivity at the same time that neoliberals publicize its open and fluid qualities.

In the last seven chapters, we have surveyed the extent of inequality along several axes: economic, status, power, gender, sexual orientation, and race/ethnicity. It is now time to examine in greater detail the most prominent explanations that have been given for social inequality in general. We begin in Chapter 9 with a discussion of classical explanations, and then move on to an analysis of contemporary theories in Chapter 10.

Critical Thinking

1. How do historical events continue to play a role in racial and ethnic inequality today? Can the effects of these events ever be erased? How?
2. Does degree of darkness or shade of color play a role in the inequality between individuals that is independent of race? Explain and give examples.
3. Critical-race theory argues that racism is primarily structural in nature. What does this mean and what kinds of examples can you provide to demonstrate this?
4. Why, and to whom, are Native American names and mascots for sports teams harmful? Who do they benefit? How?

Web Connections

Segregation is still widespread in the United States. To get an idea of how Blacks, Hispanics, and other ethnic groups are distributed within major U.S. cities, and how these distributions are related to the distribution of incomes in the cities, go to www.umich.edu/~lawrace/seg.htm.

Film Suggestions

Race: The Power of an Illusion (2003). A three-part series that analyzes the meaning, nature, and creation of "race."

Irish in America (1997). Explores Irish immigration to America and the conditions these immigrants faced here.

What's Race Got to Do With It? (2006). Depicts the experiences of race relationships on a college campus.

CHAPTER 9

Classical Explanations of Inequality

Society as a whole is more and more splitting up into two great hostile camps, into two great classes directly facing each other.

KARL MARX (1818–1883)

Let the average vitality be diminished by more effectually guarding the weak against adverse conditions, and inevitably there come fresh diseases.

HERBERT SPENCER (1820–1903)

The discussions throughout Part One make it clear that multidimensional inequality is extensive in the United States, and, in a number of ways, it is becoming even more pronounced and disconcerting for many Americans. The widespread nature of social inequality makes explaining it all the more important. Several previous chapters presented explanations of particular forms of inequality. This chapter examines the broad classical explanations of Marx, Weber, Durkheim, and Spencer, from which many modern thinkers have drawn. Karl Marx is discussed first because virtually all of his central ideas were formulated before any of the others and because subsequent theories are often viewed as reactions to Marx's own work.

KARL MARX (1818–1883)

Few social scientists have had as great a political and economic impact as Karl Marx. His perspectives on society have been used by social scientists and ideologues, and his influence on modern sociology, and even society, has been pervasive. The ideas of all scholars are in large part shaped by the historical events and life situations they experience. This appears clearly in the case of Marx. Karl Marx was born on May 5, 1818, in the city of Trier, Prussia (now part of Germany). His family was of Jewish background and provided a bourgeois setting for Marx in his youth. His father and a neighbor, Ludwig von Westphalen, introduced him to the thinkers of the Enlightenment. Ludwig von Westphalen in particular became an intellectual companion with whom Marx discussed philosophy and literature. Marx later married von Westphalen's daughter, Jenny.

While studying at the universities of Bonn and Berlin, Marx became a friend of a group known as the Young Hegelians. Although Hegel was dead, his ideas survived as an intellectual force at Berlin. The Young Hegelians helped to convert Marx from the study of law to the study of philosophy. The increasing radicalism of his ideas encouraged his departure for Paris in late 1843. It was in Paris, a center of invigorating intellectual activity, that Marx began his close association and collaboration with Frederick Engels, the son of a manufacturer who acquainted Marx more fully with the real conditions of the working class. Marx's writing caused his expulsion, and he moved from Paris to Brussels in 1845. By then, Marx already considered himself a socialist and revolutionary. He had aligned himself with several workers' organizations, and in 1848 he and Engels produced the *Manifesto of the Communist Party.*

After some moving around, in 1849 Marx left for London, where he stayed for most of the remainder of his life. It was there that he produced most of his major writing. During his stay, his life and that of his family were marked by poverty, which was relieved only by his occasional employment as a European correspondent for the *New York Daily Tribune* and periodic help from his friend Engels. He became a leader of the International, a radical movement made up of individuals from several European countries, and in 1867 published the first volume of his monumental *Capital.* In the last decade of his life, Marx was already an honored figure among socialists and was able to live somewhat more comfortably than he did during in his early London years. He died on March 14, 1883, only one year after the death of his elder daughter and two years after the death of his wife, Jenny (Coser 1971).

Despite the familiarity of Karl Marx's name to most, some analysts still do not have a proper understanding of many of his ideas. Two of these ideas are especially relevant to his statements concerning class relations. First, Marx did not believe that everything is determined by the economic structure, that all other institutions are merely reflections of the economic system and are without causal influence. Although Marx considered the economic aspect the "ultimately determining element in history" and the "main principle," he did not think it was the only determining one. In a personal letter, while admitting that he and Marx had probably contributed to the confusion on this point, Engels put the matter succinctly: "The economic situation is the basis, but the various elements of the superstructure . . . also exercise their influence upon the course of the historical struggles and in many cases preponderate in determining their *form.* There is an interaction of all these elements in which, amid all the endless host of accidents . . . the economic movement finally asserts itself as necessary" (Marx and Engels 1970, vol. 2, p. 487; emphasis in original). Thus, political, religious, and cultural factors play a role, though the "ultimately decisive" one is economic. A second misconception is that Marx argued that only two classes exist in any society. On the contrary, Marx was aware of the diversity of classes that can exist at any one time, as well as the factions that can be present within a given class.

The Theoretical Context of Marx's Class Analysis

Marx subscribed to a materialist conception of social life. That is, he argued that activities are what characterize and propel human history. History consists of human beings going about producing and reproducing themselves in interaction with nature. Humans are a part of nature, and both nature and humans change as they interact, making both of them a part of human history. History is really a process of "active self-making" (Simon 1994, p. 98). It is *activity,* especially labor, that defines who we are. Consequently, a concentration on economic activity is fundamental for understanding history's process.

Labor is an expression of our nature. When freely engaged in, it allows us to realize our true human nature and satisfy our real basic needs (not manufactured ones). When freely done, labor is also an enjoyment because it is spontaneous. However, when forced or artificial, that is, alienated, it becomes more of a misery than an enjoyment. It twists our human nature. Alienated labor exists when private property and its owners hire or control others and define their labor for them. Instead of being for oneself, labor becomes a task that primarily benefits owners of property. One works to get food, shelter, and so on; that is, labor becomes a *means* to an end rather than an *end* in itself. Under capitalism, as in other class societies, the laborer and her or his labor belong to the capitalist. As a commodity, laborers have been hired at a price to work for the capitalist; for this period, the capitalist owns the workers and exploits them. It is out of the exploitation of the laborer by the capitalist that new value or profit is created because what is needed to reproduce the laborer (i.e., wage) is less than the value of what the laborer produces. It is this difference in value that defines exploitation and generates surplus value or profit for the employer. It is also private property and its control that defines classes and their relationship.

Historically, there have been several types of societies with class systems. According to Marx, the earliest societies were classless, being based on a "common ownership of land" (Marx and Engels 1969, vol. 1, pp. 108–109). But all known subsequent societies have been class societies, and the engine of change in history has been class struggle. Private property spurs the development of classes. Although societies change and the specific names given to the various classes may change, the presence of dominant and subordinate classes remains. The particular form that relations take between the classes depends on the historical epoch and the existing economic mode of production. The **mode of production** refers to the particular type of economic system in operation, such as feudalism, capitalism, and so on. Within every mode of production are (1) means of production and (2) social relations of production. The **means of production** refer to the tools, machines, and other resources used in production, whereas the **social relations of production** refer to the property and power relationships among individuals in the economic system. Marx contended that up to his time there had been four major "epochs in the economic transformation of society" (p. 504). These were the Asiatic, ancient, feudal, and capitalist modes of production. Our primary focus here is on the last of these.

Generally, classes are defined by their relationship to the means of production. Hence, in the capitalist mode of production, "by bourgeoisie is meant the class of modern capitalists, owners of the means of social production and employers of wage-labour. By proletariat, the class of modern wage-labourers who, having no means of production of their own, are reduced to selling labour-power in order to live" (p. 108). But when viewed specifically, Marx's definition of *class* appears loose, and a variety of criteria are used differentially in different places. A full-fledged class that satisfied the criteria suggested by Marx would be one that possessed the following four features:

1. A distinct relationship to and role in the mode of production (in terms of ownership of the means of production, employment of wage labor, and economic interests)
2. A clear consciousness of its existence as a unified class with objective interests that are hostile to those of other classes
3. An organization of the class into a political party aimed at representing and fighting for its interests
4. A distinct set of cultural values and a separate style of life (Ollman 1968)

"The owners of mere labour-power, the owners of capital, and the landowners, whose respective sources of income are wages, profit, and rent of land . . . form the three great classes of modern society based on the capitalist mode of production" (Bottomore and Rubel 1956, p. 178).

Other transition classes exist, such as the petty bourgeoisie and small landowning peasants, but these would disappear as capitalism inexorably reached its peak as a mode of production. Marx believed that in his day of the "two great hostile camps," the "two great classes" that were being polarized were the bourgeoisie and the proletariat (Marx and Engels 1969, vol. 1, p. 109). However, his use of such terms as "strata," "gradation," "middle classes," and "dominated classes" makes it clear that Marx was aware of the complexity that can characterize a concrete system of inequality. What is also apparent is that mere occupation or source of income is not the criterion used by Marx to define a class. Each class has within it a hierarchy of strata. Thus, within the proletariat, for example, individuals vary according to their specific occupations and incomes.

Because of the classes' different relationships to private property (i.e., owners vs. nonowners), conflict is inherent in class society. Class antagonism is built into the very structure of society. Marx's theory is one of class struggle. The existence of a given class always assumes the existence of another hostile class. "'Who is the enemy?' is a question that can be asked whenever Marx uses 'class'" (Ollman 1968, p. 578). When the economic bases for classes are eliminated, classes themselves will disappear since the proletariat will be without the enemy, the capitalist.

Until then, in the process of class struggle the proletariat develops from an incoherent mass (a class in itself) into a more organized and unified political force (a class for itself). The conditions that bring about this change are discussed in detail later.

Maintenance of Class Structure

The system of inequality—class positions, the given relations of production, and the profits of capitalists—is maintained and protected by a variety of mechanisms. The state, of course, is the ultimate arbitrator and represents "the form in which the individuals of a ruling class assert their common interests" (Bottomore and Rubel 1956, p. 223). "The executive of the modern State is but

a committee for managing the common affairs of the whole bourgeoisie" (Marx and Engels 1969, vol. 1, pp. 110–111). The state has used its force and legislation to maintain capitalist class relations (Marx 1967, pp. 734–741). Struggles that do occur within the state are always class struggles.

A second mechanism used to maintain class relations is ideology, and the dominant ideology supports and legitimizes the position of the capitalist. "The ideas of the ruling class are in every epoch the ruling ideas: i.e., the class which is the ruling *material* force of society is at the same time its ruling *intellectual* force." Just as the ruling class has control over "material production," so too does it control "mental production," and the form these ideas take is clear: "The ruling ideas are nothing more than the ideal expression of the dominant material relationships" (Marx and Engels 1969, vol. 1, p. 47). Of course, the ideas generated have been mentally separated in their association with the dominant class and hence can appear as eternal laws (such as the "free market") or rules generated by all of society. Members of the ruling class have themselves believed that. The ideas that support class relations are frequently promoted by bourgeois intellectuals who are often nothing more than "hired prize-fighters" for capitalism (Marx 1967, p. 15). Religion as an ideological institution similarly helps maintain the class system by preventing labor from seeing its real situation.

A third factor serving to bolster the set of economic relations is much less obvious than the two just mentioned. The capitalist structure itself strengthens its seeming inevitability by creating a working class that because of custom and training comes to view "the conditions of that mode of production as self-evident laws of Nature" (Marx 1967, p. 737). The condition of workers freely hiring themselves out to capitalists who freely employ them to work in factories run for maximum efficiency makes capitalism appear as an entirely natural process and creates a dependency of workers on the system that makes it difficult for them to resist or rebel. As Miliband (1977) wrote, "The capitalist mode of production . . . veils and mystifies the exploitative nature of its 'relations of production' by making them appear as a matter of free, unfettered, and equal exchange" (p. 45).

Stages of Capitalism

According to Marx (1967), capitalism as a mode of production has gone through three principal **stages:** (1) cooperation, (2) manufacture, and (3) modern (machine) industry.

COOPERATION   Capitalism begins when a large number of laborers are employed in one place working together to produce a given product. "A greater number of laborers, working together, at the same time, in one place . . . in order to produce the same sort of commodity under the mastership of one capitalist, constitutes, both historically and logically, the starting point of capitalist production" (p. 322). It is when workers are thus brought together that "the collective power of the masses" for the individual capitalist can be realized. Workers become more productive and efficient under these conditions, resulting in greater profit for the capitalist. This and each successive change in the mode of production are motivated by the desire to increase the surplus value of labor power and, therefore, the level of profit.

MANUFACTURE   "While simple cooperation leaves the mode of working by the individual for the most part unchanged, manufacture . . . converts the laborer into a crippled monstrosity, by forcing his detail dexterity at the expense of a world of productive capabilities and instincts" (p. 360). The period of manufacture begins in the sixteenth century and extends to the last part of the eighteenth century. Its characteristic is a strict and detailed division of labor among workers who have been brought together to cooperate in the production of the capitalists' products. Everyone has a specific function to perform; no one carries out all the tasks. Thus, with this change there no longer exists a group of independent artisans cooperating, but rather a group of individuals performing minute tasks dependent on each other. "Its final form is invariably the same—a productive mechanism whose parts are human beings" (p. 338).

Weber's later description of work under rationalized capitalism is strikingly similar, as we shall see. In manufacture, each person performs the same task over and over again until the job becomes routine and the laborer becomes a mere mechanism, but efficiency and perfection in production become reality. Skills that had been learned in apprenticeship become less necessary, and manufacture creates a set of unskilled laborers. The collective laborer, when organized in this fashion, increases production, and as a result, increases the surplus value of his labor power to the capitalist. The profit for the capitalist goes up, and conditions for him could not be better. For the laborers, however, conditions worsen. Under the capitalist mode, their labor is no longer their own, because to increase capital, each worker must be "made poor in productive powers" (Marx 1967, p. 361). They become unfit to produce independently, and their labor power becomes productive only within the factory. They need the factory. Working on minute operations rather than whole products, they become "a never failing instrument," "a mere fragment of his own body . . . a mere appendage" (pp. 349, 360). And the constant regularity and monotony of the task "disturbs the intensity and flow of a man's animal spirits, which find recreation and delight in mere change of activity" (p. 341).

In essence, the workers become alienated from their own labor. The work being done (1) is not an end in itself but a *means* to an end, (2) is not voluntary but *forced,* (3) is not part of human nature (i.e., it is *external*), (4) is not work for the workers but for *someone else,* and (5) is *not spontaneous.* The object of their labor does not belong to the workers even though they have put a part of themselves into it. Rather, the product "becomes an object, takes on its own existence . . . exists outside [them], independently, and alien to [them], and . . . stands opposed to [them] as an autonomous power" (Bottomore and Rubel 1956, p. 170). As appendages, workers become alienated from themselves, each other, and nature.

Under manufacturing, therefore, capitalists prosper as workers' conditions deteriorate, and the real nature of capitalism as a mode of production becomes clear. Capitalists prosper *because* laborers suffer. The two classes are not merely different levels but are inextricably interlinked in the capitalist mode. People and their labor power become commodities, things of use value to the capitalist, who owns and controls the instruments of production, the raw materials—everything. The laborers, in turn, have nothing but their own labor power to sell, and even that becomes twisted into a form suitable for maximum production.

MODERN (MACHINE) INDUSTRY Like other forms of capitalist production, the development and use of machines are aimed at reducing the cost of commodity production for the capitalist by reducing the part of the day when the worker is working for himself or herself, and increasing that part when he or she is working for the capitalist. That is, it is a way of increasing surplus value for labor. "The machine . . . supersedes the workman" (Marx 1967, p. 376). In modern industry, machines are organized into a division of labor similar to that which existed among laborers during the manufacture period. Since machines replace labor power, physical strength becomes less important, and capitalists seek to hire children and women. The result is a decrease in the value of the man's labor power, and a concomitant increase in the general exploitation of the family overall. When the value of the workman's labor power vanishes, laborers flood the market and reduce the price of labor power. Supply then outweighs demand for labor. In effect, machines are a means of controlling the collective laborer. "It is the most powerful weapon for repressing strikes, those periodic revolts of the working class against the autocracy of capital" (pp. 435–436).

With the advance of machines, production becomes more and more centralized, forcing many small bourgeoisie who cannot compete or find little use for their skills into the proletariat (Bottomore and Rubel 1956, p. 188).

Crises in Capitalism and Class Struggle

The increased competition for profit among capitalists generates crises at both the top and the bottom of the class structure, ultimately leading to the polarization of large capitalists and the massive class of the proletariat. The initial result of the introduction of machinery is to increase profit, but problems arise. Employees are thrown out of work, or work for low wages because they are not in demand. The proletariat increases in number and becomes more concentrated, and life conditions among members become equalized at a level of bare subsistence.

Competition among capitalists produces commercial crises, an "epidemic of over-pro-duction" which in turn leads to increased concentration of capital, since many go bankrupt (Marx and Engels 1969, vol. 1, p. 114). A **crisis of overproduction** serves as an indication that the forces of production have become too strong for the property relations by which they are controlled ("fettered"). The capitalist responds by destroying productive forces and by trying to find new markets abroad, but these solutions are, at best, stopgap measures and crises recur, each more serious than the previous. "Modern bourgeois society . . . is like the sorcerer, who is no longer able to control the powers of the nether world whom he has called up by his spells" (p. 113). The means of production that the bourgeoisie originally brought into existence to benefit their own position and that permitted them to supplant feudalism now become the means that destroy them.

Bourgeois society becomes the stage for the impending class struggle between the capitalists and the collective laborer, between the bourgeoisie and the proletariat. As capitalism improved from simple cooperation through modern industry, the bourgeoisie became more powerful and entrenched, their ideology and ideas became dominant, and the organization of the state more evidently reflected their power. But so, too, did the proletariat develop as a class with the progress of capitalism. Initially, struggle against the bourgeoisie takes the form of individual protests, then protests by larger groups—not against the relations of production, but against the forces of production: workers smash tools, machines, and so forth in order to maintain their status as workers. At this point, they are still just a mass rather than an organized whole. But as conditions for them worsen—that is, as they become increasingly massed together on an equal basis in a minute division of labor under conditions of extreme alienation and misery—and as their livelihood becomes more uncertain, their actions become more those of a united class and less those characteristic of individuals competing among themselves. The appalling work conditions experienced by the proletariat forge it into a social class.

During the struggle that has its roots in the domination of the means of production and appropriation of its products (i.e., in a peculiar set of property relations), the proletariat becomes honed as a class, and the struggle takes on a greater political character. Ironically, the bourgeoisie has created the conditions that develop the class that revolts against it. As the decisive hour approaches, and the class and crisis nature of the society becomes increasingly evident, those in the bourgeoisie who see what is happening on the historical level also join the working class (Bottomore and Rubel 1956, pp. 184–188).

Marx argued that a given social order is not replaced until all the forces of production that can be produced under it have been developed, and new relations of production (i.e., new social orders) do not appear until the material basis for their existence has been formed in the old society. This is essentially what happens, according to Marx, when revolution occurs. Revolutions do not take place until the material conditions for their appearance are present. The mode of production shapes all other aspects of social life, and "at a certain stage of their development, the material productive forces of society come in conflict with existing relations of production . . . . From forms of development of the productive forces these relations turn into their fetters" (Marx and Engels 1969, vol. 1, pp. 503–504).

With proletarian revolution, the bases for the class system are removed and the proletariat is emancipated. In the interim, between the capitalist and classless society, a "dictatorship of the proletariat" exists, paving the way for a communistic society and the beginning of truly human

rather than class history. Figure 9.1 summarizes some of the key elements of Marx's model.

Some Comments on Marx

There are few in the social sciences who have not had to confront the work of Marx. The sheer scope of analyses and critiques of Marx's theory of class struggle and capitalism is voluminous (e.g., Dahrendorf 1959; Mills 1962; Bottomore 1966; Giddens 1973; Miliband 1977). Consequently, only a few of the recurrent comments and criticisms about that theory are presented here.

Marx's theory has had a significant impact not only on the contemporary analysis of class structures but also on the study of society in general. His influence has radiated beyond social science to philosophy and the study of morals and to the political arena. That his work continues to generate discussion, as well as explanations and analyses built on his original ideas, is a tribute to the continued cogency and relevance of his theory. Marx's approach allows us to see at once the simultaneous existence of organization and conflict and their historical roots. Individual actions and emotions, as well as organizations and class structure, are analyzed against the backdrop of societal settings and historical change.

Still, his conception of class is often vague and inconsistent, though the main thrust of his criteria—relationship to means of production, employment of labor, and **class consciousness**—is clear. His description of the classless society and the problems associated with the dictatorship of the proletariat as an interim period are not clear and precise. The state and bureaucracy in what are called communist societies have certainly not withered away. On the other hand, it is doubtful that Marx, who believed in uniting theory, practice, and human needs to help bring about a more humane society, would have considered these societies to be the kind he had in mind. Nevertheless, that these societies turned out as they have suggests a basic flaw in Marx's view of how and why societies become structured as they do. Some have traced this fault to Marx's perspective

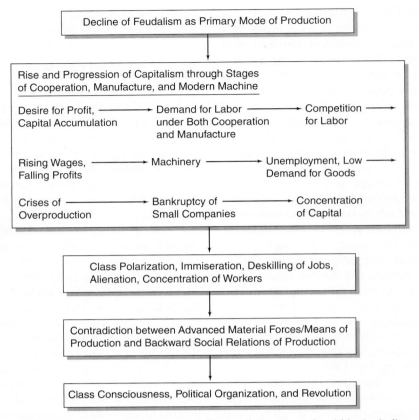

FIGURE 9.1　Core Elements in Marx's Theory of Class Struggle within Capitalism

on human nature which, they argue, is overly optimistic and does not consider the selfishness of people. "The most monumental error in Marx's thought" wrote Lopreato and Hazelrigg (1972), "is his failure to accept the fact . . . that man is by nature a fallible and 'sinful' animal" (pp. 40–41). Moreover, Marx appears to have "seriously underrated" the ability of individuals to adjust to inequality (Duke 1976, p. 34).

It certainly seems true that Marx also underestimated the strength of nationalism as a force inhibiting the international union of classes. Miliband observed that "'nationalism' has proved a much more enduring and therefore a much more difficult problem to confront than early Marxists thought likely" (1977, p. 105).

Another criticism that has some validity is that the extent of pauperization and polarization

of classes that Marx expected to occur in capitalism has not, as yet, occurred. How much one makes of this comment depends heavily on the time frame one selects, because certainly there are indications that the extent of relative economic inequality has not declined and that corporate concentration has increased over the last 100 years. Even during the brief 2008–2011 period, the combined effects of governmental financial support for large corporations and financial institutions alongside little effective policy to reduce high worker unemployment have made many Americans more aware of the economic gap that exists between top capitalists and the average worker.

But capitalism has proved exceptionally resourceful in maintaining itself and forestalling widespread revolution. Being able to internationalize has provided capitalism with a mechanism for obtaining wider and wider markets and, therefore, has put off a crisis caused by its internal contradictions. The capitalist state, in being reformist and offering welfare programs, has alleviated some of its immediate problems. But, according to Marxists, reformism serves only to disguise the real class character of the state, and concrete reforms support the long-term maintenance of the existing economic order and are meant to solve only immediate problems rather than fundamental underlying ones (cf. Piven and Cloward 1971). Moreover, Miliband contended that "capitalism, however many and varied the reforms it can assimilate, is unable to do without exploitation, oppression, and dehumanization" (1977, p. 39).

Marx thought that the members of the working class would be the "gravediggers of capitalism," but, to use Giddens's colorful phrasing (1982, p. 63), "the grave remains undug, a century later; and its prospective incumbent, if no longer in the first flush of youth, does not seem seriously threatened by imminent demise." But the fact that the working class has not revolted is not conclusive proof of the inadequacy of Marx's theory or that capitalism is not a class society. This is because an effective class society, as Marx argued, can have a number of economic, political, and ideological characteristics that encourage false consciousness and minimize the chances for revolt by workers. Sooner or later, however (and Marx believed sooner), workers would become aware of their situation and act accordingly.

Although Marx's main predictions have not turned out exactly as he envisioned, many of the phenomena that he foresaw do exist to a degree. There has been a consistent trend toward more concentration of corporate power. There is also quite a bit of wealth inequality and there are business ups and downs that capitalism follows. Moreover, every capitalist society has "class-based, working-class politics" to a certain degree (Collins 1988). U.S. government responses to the 2008–2009 economic crisis served to crystallize in the public's mind the differences in class interests of the capitalist and working classes. The effects of that crisis were felt worldwide.

The international character of modern capitalism that Marx predicted means that the impact of its internal crises and contradictions reverberate throughout the world.

MAX WEBER (1864–1920)

Many of those who followed Marx, and especially the major social theorists of the period, were engaged in a "debate with Marx's ghost" (Zeitlin 1968). Among those most evidently aware of Marx's work and some of its shortcomings was Max Weber.

Weber is often considered to be the greatest sociologist in history. His "shadow falls long over the intellectual life of our era," wrote Mitzman (1971, p. 3). Much of what he contributed to social science still remains intact, and even those of his ideas that have proved weak or been discarded still provide a foundation from which further analysis can begin. Like Marx and other great theorists whose specific theories fit into a coherent whole, Weber's formulations regarding inequality must be considered in the context of his broader theory of the **rationalization** of the modern world. We will examine what Weber had to say about inequality, how U.S. sociologists have interpreted his work in this area, and if and how he added to Marx's own analysis of class structure.

Max Weber's life was quite different from Marx's, but like Marx's, his life experiences clearly affected the propositions about society that he developed. Weber was born in Erfurt, Germany, in 1864, 16 years after the publication of *Communist Manifesto* and 3 years before the publication of the first volume of *Capital*. His family was upper middle class. His father was a fun-loving conformist who disliked and feared upsetting existing political arrangements. In sharp contrast, Weber's mother was an extremely religious person of Calvinist persuasion, who often suffered the abuses of her much less moralistic husband, a fact that later became central in Max's repudiation of his father.

Despite its drawbacks for Weber, his parents' home was the site of frequent and diverse intellectual discussions featuring many of the well-known academicians of the day. So from the beginning, Max was exposed to a potpourri of ideas. Though he was a sickly child, he was very bright, becoming familiar with the writings of a variety of philosophers before setting off at the age of 18 for the University of Heidelberg, where he studied law, medieval history, economics, and philosophy. At age 19, Weber left for Strasbourg to put in his military service. It was there that he developed a lifelong and deep friendship with his uncle Hermann Baumgarten, an historian, and his aunt, a devout Protestant, who was effective in putting her religious fervor into action. Consequently, Weber developed a greater respect for the religious virtues of his own mother and less of a regard for the worldly and cowardly qualities of his father.

A year later, he returned to live with his parents and to study at the University of Berlin, where he wrote his dissertation on medieval business. Carrying on a strictly disciplined and rigid life, he served as a barrister in the Berlin court system and as an instructor at the university. He wrote several works on agrarian history and agricultural laborers. These investigations included discussions of the social and cultural effects of commercialization and the role of ideas in economic behavior.

After getting married and serving at the age of only 30 as a full professor of economics at the University of Freiburg, Weber and his wife Marianne left for Heidelberg, where he took a professorship, became more politically involved, and quickly developed a close circle of intellectual friends. During this period, Weber suffered a severe emotional breakdown and was able to do little of anything, even reading. He was only 33 years old at the time, and it was a number of years before his energy was restored. The breakdown may have been precipitated by a harsh confrontation with his father, very shortly after which his father died.

In the early 1900s, Weber's health was restored, and it was between this time and his death that Weber produced most of the works for which he is best known. He became enmeshed in German politics and volunteered for service during World War I, but later became disillusioned by the war and the German government's incompetence. Weber, unlike Marx, was accepted in polite society and was not a political radical, but he was generally a liberal and participated in the writing of the Weimar Constitution. There were many occasions when he fought bigotry and close-mindedness. Weber died of pneumonia on June 14, 1920, his broad knowledge leaving an unmistakable mark on social theory (Coser 1971; Mitzman 1971).

Rationalization of the World

Much of what Weber wrote had an undeniably unified theme. His discussions of bureaucracy, the Protestant ethic, authority, and even class, status, and party fit into his overall concern for social change and the direction in which he thought the Western world was moving. Thus, as is the case of Marx and many other nineteenth-century theorists, Weber's work on stratification must be understood within the context of his general perspective.

In contrast to Marx, who believed that capitalism and its accompanying denigration of the human spirit would eventually lead to a communistic and more humane society, Weber contended that alienation, impersonality, bureaucracy, and, in general, rationalization would be permanent societal features. Weber agreed with Marx that modern modes of technology have dehumanizing effects, yet he contended that bureaucracy and alienation are not temporary or peculiar to a passing period, but are instead at the core of an increasingly disenchanted world. What the future promised in Weber's view was not a wonderfully free society in which people are reunited to themselves and nature, but rather an "iron cage"; what we have to look forward to is not "summer's bloom," but rather a "polar night of icy darkness and hardness." Bureaucratization and technical rationality are not likely to decrease but rather to increase under socialism.

A bureaucracy is characterized by its impersonality, hierarchy of rational-legal authority, written system of rules, clear division of labor, and career system. According to Weber, bureaucracy is technically more perfect than other methods of organization and is the most efficient. "Precision, speed, unambiguity, knowledge of the files, continuity, discretion, unity, strict subordination, reduction of friction and of material and personal costs—these are raised to the optimum point in the strictly bureaucratic administration" (Gerth and Mills 1962, p. 214). Bureaucracy is the perfectly rational system. Business is carried out "without regard for persons," under "calculable rules." The lack of regard for persons is a central characteristic of all purely economic transactions. Since status honor and prestige are based on *who* a person is, the domination of the bureaucratic organization and a free market mean "the leveling of status 'honor'" and "the universal domination of the 'class situation'" (p. 215). The leveling of status strengthens the rule of bureaucracy by weakening status as a basis for position and encouraging the equal treatment of all regardless of background.

Capitalism and bureaucracy support each other; both are impersonal. Bureaucracy hastened the destruction of feudal, patrimonial organizations and local privileges. Whereas feudalism was characterized by ties of personal loyalty and was grounded in small local communities, bureaucracy denies or destroys personal loyalty and demands loyalty to position, thereby equalizing individuals. Capitalist production requires it. Conversely, capitalism can supply the money needed to develop bureaucracy in its most rational form (Roth and Wittich 1968, p. 224). Bureaucracy and capitalism are characteristics of the contemporary modern society.

Bureaucracy and capitalism increase the prevalence of authority based on rational-legal, as opposed to charismatic or traditional, grounds. In the rational-legal form, authority is based on the acceptance of rules regarding the right to issue commands as they apply to formal position in the organization. Authority is attached to the office, not the person; it is impersonal.

Putting all of this together, we see that capitalism and the secularized Protestant ethic, class, bureaucracy, and rational-legal authority are mutually supportive and are integral parts of the

increasingly rationalized modern society that Weber saw emerging. They stand in stark contrast to feudalism, the personalism of status honor, tradition and charisma, and premodern forms of organization. An adequate understanding of Weber's perspective on class and status, their relationship, and their distinction can be obtained only if his broader theory of historical development and its associated concepts are incorporated in the analysis. Keeping Weber's broader theory in mind, we turn to discussion of his more specific ideas on inequality.

Tripartite Nature of Inequality

Weber argued that power can take a variety of forms. "Power," in general, refers to "the chance of a man or of a number of men to realize their own will in a communal action even against the resistance of others who are participating in the action" (Gerth and Mills 1962, p. 180). A person's power can be shown in the *social order* through his or her status, in the *economic order* through his or her class, and in the *political order* through his or her party. Thus, class, status, and party are each aspects of the distribution of power within a community. For example, if we think about an individual's chances of realizing his or her own will against someone else's, it is reasonable to believe that the person's social prestige, class position, and membership in a political group will have an effect on these chances.

Social order refers to the arrangement of social honor (prestige) within a society. Different status groups (e.g., professors, construction workers) occupy different places along the prestige continuum. Economic order, in turn, refers to the general distribution of economic goods and services (e.g., owners and nonowners)—that is, to the arrangement of classes within a society. Finally, political order relates to the distribution of power among groups (e.g., political action committees, parties) to influence communal decisions. Weber's general scheme for inequality is presented graphically in Figure 9.2.

Although these are presented as three distinct and separate orders, it is a mistake to see

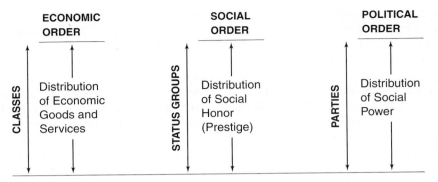

FIGURE 9.2 Weber's View of the General Distribution of Power

them strictly as such. All of them are manifestations of the distribution of power and can and usually do influence each other, often in a quite predictable manner. The inclusion of the social and political dimensions is ordinarily seen as a "rounding out" of the economic determinism of Marx (Gerth and Mills 1962, p. 47). But, as already pointed out, Marx was not a simple economic determinist; he viewed causal relationships in a more complex fashion. Moreover, Weber's own writing suggests that he did not view the three dimensions as being equally salient in capitalist society. Parkin (1971) persuasively argued that neo-Weberians have stressed the independence of these dimensions of stratification and thereby ignored, where Weber did not, the systematic relationship between the dimensions of inequality. Weber did not fully develop his political dimension, and the economic factor, as we shall see, outweighs the status element in the capitalist system of inequality. But at this point, it is necessary to examine each of Weber's three dimensions in greater detail.

CLASS More so than Marx, Weber deliberately set out a number of formal definitions for his concepts (Roth and Wittich 1968). But Weber acknowledged his debt to Marx: "Whoever does not admit that he could not perform the most important parts of his own work without the work that those two [Marx and Nietzsche] have done swindles himself and others" (quoted in Mitzman 1971, p. 182). Weber's own conception of class parallels Marx's in several ways. Class, at its core, is an economic concept; it is the position of individuals in the market that determines their class position. And it is how one is situated in the marketplace that directly affects one's life chances, "a common condition for the individual's fate" (Miller 1963, pp. 44–45). Just as Marx indicated that capital begins when capitalist and laborer meet freely in the market, when the laborer is free to sell his or her labor and form a relationship with the capitalist, Weber pointed out that persons are members of a class only if they have "the chance of using goods or services *for themselves* on the market" (Miller 1963, p. 45; emphasis added). Consequently, slaves are not members of classes.

Weber distinguished three types of classes: property classes, commercial (acquisition) classes, and social classes. Individuals belong to the same class if they are in the same "class situation," which refers to the probability of individuals obtaining goods, position, and satisfactions in life, "a probability which derives from the relative control over goods and skills and from their income-producing uses within a given economic order" (Roth and Wittich 1968, p. 302).

Property classes are "primarily determined by property differences." There are those who monopolize costly foods and status privileges, such as education, and those who control the bulk of wealth, capital, and sales in the society. Such classes usually are composed of "rentiers," who get income from a number of sources, including people, land, factories, and bank securities. Those who are not privileged are those who are unfree or are paupers. Weber stressed the distinction between the top and the bottom classes but did mention that in each set of classes there are "middle classes" (Roth and Wittich 1968, pp. 302–303).

Weber is not clear, but he does not appear to make a complete separation between property and commercial classes. Rather, he has a broad conception of property in terms of ownership, and it is "'property' and 'lack of property'" that are "the basic categories of *all* class situations" (Miller 1963, p. 44; emphasis added). These general categories in turn can be broken down "according to the kind of property that is *usable for returns*; and, on the other hand, according to the kind of *services* that can be offered in the market" (p. 44; emphasis added). In a manner of speaking, one can own and dispose of property as well as skills and services.

Commercial-class position is determined by "the marketability of goods and services," in other words, by the opportunity to exploit the market (Roth and Wittich 1968, p. 302). Commercial classes, then, are determined by the skills and occupational characteristics members bring into the market. Hence, those who are privileged in this regard may monopolize management and exercise influence over government political policies that affect their interests. Merchants, industrial and agricultural employers, bankers, ship owners, professionals, and workers who have cornered certain skills are examples of the entrepreneurs who are members of privileged commercial classes. In contrast, those who are unprivileged are usually laborers (skilled, semiskilled, and unskilled) (Roth and Wittich 1968, p. 304). Again, there are middle classes, but these are treated more as residual categories when compared with the other classes.

Social classes make up all class situations "within which individual and generational mobility is easy and typical" (Roth and Wittich 1968, p. 302). That is, a social-class structure is one in which there is fluidity and movement of individuals between class situations. Upward mobility is most likely, however, between adjacent classes. Examples of such social classes are the "working class as a whole," "the petty bourgeoisie," "the propertyless intelligentsia and specialists," and "the class privileged through property and education" (p. 305).

Class Consciousness and Class Struggle
According to Weber, classes of whatever kind need not be class conscious as Marx conceived them; they are not necessarily unified "communities." Class organization can occur in any one of the three types of classes, but class consciousness and class (communal) action are likely only under certain conditions. Weber argued that just because there are different property classes, for example, does not mean that they will necessarily engage in class struggle, although they may when circumstances are right. And when struggles do occur, they may not be over a basic change in the entire economy but may be more superficially over the distribution of wealth.

Class-conscious action is most likely if, first, "the connections between the causes and consequences of the 'class situation'" are transparent (Gerth and Mills 1962, p. 184). If individuals can plainly see that there is a connection between the structure of the economic system and what happens to them in terms of life chances, class action is more likely. Weber believed this had happened among the proletariat. A second condition for class unification exists if there is an immediate opponent on whom the class can focus. Hence, workers will react against their immediate employers rather than those who are most distantly and perhaps even more profitably involved (such as stockholders). Third, class organization is also more likely if large numbers of individuals are in the same class position. The increasing growth of the proletariat would increase the chances of class action by them. Fourth, if all of the individuals are in one place and therefore are easier to organize, class unity is more probable. Finally, if their goals are directed and interpreted by a group of intelligentsia who are actually outside their class, class organization is more likely (Henderson and Parsons 1947, pp. 427–428; Miller 1963, p. 46; Roth and Wittich 1968, p. 304). These conditions are not inconsistent with those that Marx thought would forge a mass of individuals in the same class situation into a "class for itself." However, Weber cautions us about the belief that fully developed classes are never wrong—that is, "falsely conscious"—about their own interests. They can be.

Class struggles have changed in content throughout history, according to Weber. The focus of conflict has evolved from struggles over debt and credit in antiquity, to struggles over the availability of consumer goods and their prices in the market during the Middle Ages, to struggles over the price of labor in the modern world. Historically, class struggles begin when a credit market exists in which debtors pay high and often increasing rates of interest to the wealthy, who monopolize the credits (Miller 1963, pp. 45, 48). But in each case, by definition, the struggle is of an economic character.

STATUS   Standing in theoretical and practical opposition to the market principle of class, which "knows no personal distinctions" and "knows nothing of 'honor,'" is the principle of status. Traditionally, status groups are ranked in terms of the "*consumption* of goods as represented by special 'styles of life,'" whereas classes are determined by their relations to the production system and acquisition of goods (Miller 1963, p. 56, emphasis in original).

In addition, then, to being ranked in terms of market situation, individuals can be ranked on the basis of honor or prestige. A person's "status situation" consists of all aspects of his or her "life fate" that are determined by a "social estimation of honor" (Miller 1963, pp. 49, 54). Status groups are based on a particular style of life, formal education, and/or inherited or occupational prestige. Certain groups may lay claim to (or, in other words, may usurp) a certain level of honor because of their hereditary background or family tree (such as the "First Families of Virginia"), because of their peculiar lifestyle (such as liberal arts professors, perhaps), or because of their power. The existence of status groups most often shows itself in the form of (1) endogamy or a restricted pattern of social intercourse, (2) sharing of food and other benefits within groups, (3) status

conventions or traditions, and (4) monopolistic acquisition of certain economic opportunities or the avoidance of certain kinds of acquisitions. Thus, because of their formal education and occupational prestige, liberal arts professors might tend to socialize only among themselves and might have certain unwritten rules about how a member of the group should act or what kinds of goods and services are suitable for use in the status group and what kinds are not. The conventions associated with the status group control the kind of lifestyle allowable (Roth and Wittich 1968, pp. 305–306). It is clear that some of the bases of class and status may concern the same factor, such as occupation. However, their characteristics mean that status groups are usually cohesive communities. They tend toward closure—that is, restriction of their memberships (Grabb 1984; Collins 1988).

The stability of status groups is linked to political and economic conditions in a society and is one way in which the latter two aspects of inequality are related to the social dimension. The likelihood of a conventionally recognized status group developing into a "*legal privilege,* positive or negative, is easily traveled as soon as a certain stratification of the *social order* has in fact been 'lived in' and has achieved stability *by virtue* of a stable distribution of *economic power*" (Miller 1963, p. 51; emphasis added). Weber is saying that status groups can be legalized and, therefore, become bases for political power differences when they have been around for some time and are buttressed by parallel differences in the distribution of economic resources. Where such stability exists, *caste groups* develop. Castes become supported by rituals (e.g., of purity), convention, and law. Separate castes may even develop their own religious beliefs. Usually, the status structure approaches this extreme form only when the fundamental differences between the groups are considered ethnic in nature (e.g., Jews). Caste is more than just simple ethnic segregation. The latter still permits each group in question to consider its own values (honor) to be high, but a caste system arranges these groups hierarchically, allotting one more honor than the rest. Any sense of dignity a lower-caste group might have would derive from its belief in a *future* beyond present conditions in which it would have an elevated status. In contrast, the privileged caste groups can and do derive their own sense of dignity from their *present and/or past* situation (Miller 1963, pp. 51–52; emphasis added).

Weber stressed that class, status, and political power can be reciprocally related, with each affecting the others. Status can influence and even determine class (Roth and Wittich 1968, p. 306). However, his writing emphasized the effect of class on status in capitalist society. "Property as such is not always recognized as a status qualification, but in the long run it is, and with extraordinary regularity" (Miller 1963, p. 49). Frequently, the richest person has the greatest prestige, and those in similar economic situations normally socialize with each other rather than with persons from different classes. Equality of status among individuals in unequal classes can "in the long run become quite precarious" (Miller 1963, p. 49). Weber observed that although race, political power, and class have all been bases for status in the past, "today the class situation is by far the predominant factor, for of course the possibility of a style of life expected for members of a status group is usually conditioned economically" (Miller 1963, p. 53).

Despite the controlling importance of the class factor, Weber emphasized that status and class are not necessarily connected. Individuals who are low in class position can be high in prestige and vice versa. Analytically, status is opposed "to a distinction of power which is regulated exclusively through the market" (Miller 1963, p. 54). If individuals who were high in class automatically received high status, "the status order would be threatened at its very root" (Miller 1963, p. 55). Groups who base their high status on their lifestyle rather than crass property are likely to feel threatened when the basis for honor shifts to the economic order.

Weber said very little about the conditions under which stratification by class or status predominate. In fact, his whole definitional classification of class and status is too brief. Parkin (1971) argued that there was greater justification for seeing class and status as distinct and separate orders in the Middle Ages than is the case today, when status seems increasingly to be based on occupational and economic considerations. Weber maintained that "when the bases of the acquisition and distribution of goods are relatively stable, stratification by status is favored" (Miller 1963, p. 56). If a status order is entrenched by virtue of a monopolization of certain goods by particular groups, then the free-market principle is hindered; it cannot operate. Under these conditions, "the power of naked property per se, which gives its stamp to 'class formation,' is pushed into the background." But "every technological repercussion and economic transformation threatens stratification by status and pushes class situation into the foreground" (Miller 1963, pp. 55–56). In contrast to commercial-class societies, which ordinarily operate in market-oriented economies, status societies are economically organized around religious, feudal, and patrimonial factors (Roth and Wittich 1968, p. 306). In capitalist societies, classes play a more important role than status (Giddens 1973).

PARTIES Political power generally is considered to be a third dimension of inequality included by Weber, though some interpret Weber to be saying that class, status, and party are each different forces around which the distribution of power can be organized (Giddens 1973). Although Weber's entire specific treatment of class and status is brief, vague, and sometimes even ambiguous and confusing, his treatment of parties is even briefer.

A **party** is an association that aims to secure "power within an organization [or the state] for its leaders in order to attain ideal or material advantages for its active members" (Roth and Wittich 1968, p. 284). Thus, Weber is not referring narrowly to what we think of as political parties (such as Democrats or Republicans) but to political groups more broadly conceived. Instead of parties being an outgrowth of class struggle, they can represent status groups, classes, or merely their own members and may use a variety of means to attain power. Well-organized interest groups would constitute parties in a Weberian sense.

Since parties aim for such goals as getting their programs developed or accepted and getting positions of influence within organizations, it is clear that they operate only within a rational order in which these goals are possible to attain and only when there is a struggle for power. Parties themselves, however, can be organized around a charismatic or traditional leader as well as being structured in a rational way with formal positions to which members are elected. Formally recognized political parties are not the only kind that exist; parties also can be organized around religious issues or those that concern the traditional rights of a leader in an organization (pp. 285–286).

Marx and Weber

Weber's theory of stratification has traditionally been hailed in U.S. sociology as a major improvement over the perceived narrowness of Marxian theory. Why is this so? To some extent, it reflects the nature of U.S. sociology and the interpretation of Weber by U.S. sociologists. The vagueness in parts of Weber's treatment has encouraged multiple interpretations of what he said on the subject of inequality and the unintentional shaping of what he said to fit the peculiar characteristics of one version of sociology. Weber's incorporation of noneconomic (status, party) and more general economic elements (such as market situation) is more appealing to a U.S. sociology rooted in a society that has been antiradical and staunch in the belief that individuals can distinguish themselves in a variety of ways other than economic. In some societies with long traditions of status ranking, such as Great Britain, the significance of the distinction between class and status in everyday life may be more obvious than in advanced open societies with shorter histories like the United States. Nevertheless, the separate operation of economic and social standings on individuals' situations is always a possibility. Consequently, the need to keep these concepts separate would seem to be important. Unfortunately, the conflation of the separate concepts of class and status into one measure, like socioeconomic status, blurs the real distinction between the concepts and their separate effects on individual lives. While economic class has effects in the areas of employment and income (life chances), the impact of social status is realized more in the area of "cultural consumption" (life choices; Chan and Goldthorpe 2007).

Because they blend economic and social elements, not only do socioeconomic measures fail to separate out social status, they also fail to provide a purely Marxian economic measure of class. Despite superficial measures such as income and occupational status, until recently U.S. sociologists have generally neglected the development of Marxian measures of class and an adequate measure of Weber's market situation. Part of the reason for this appears to lie in the fact that many sociologists have an ideological dislike of purely economic and especially Marxian theory, and that Weber's multidimensional theory offers a more complete portrait of social inequality than does Marx's.

However, it is very easy to exaggerate the differences between these two men. Lopreato and Hazelrigg (1972, p. 90), in fact, argued that Weber added little to what was at least already implicit in Marx's theory. For example, certainly the assignment of prestige (honor) to given positions can be viewed as one way in which the dominant ideology maintains the class system.

There are two basic similarities between Marx and Weber. First, both argued that capitalist society is a class society. Capitalism is characterized by laborers and capitalists meeting freely in the market; it creates a large pool of dehumanized workers of all types and it broadens the market. Second, even though Weber talked about status and party as well as class, he argued that in a rationalized market society, such as capitalism, class becomes predominant, and there is a "leveling of status honor." The distinct separation of status honor from the market principle and property is most characteristic of traditional or premodern societies (Parkin 1971, p. 38). Thus, on the importance of class in capitalist society, Marx and Weber appear to agree.

In light of these core similarities, a good argument can be made that many U.S. sociologists have accepted Weber because they have trivialized his ideas by latching onto the multidimensional aspect of his theory and minimizing the systematic nature of the relationship between those dimensions. Their interpretation of Weber is that class, status, and party are separate and independent dimensions along which each individual can be ranked. By abstracting these concepts while ignoring their systematic interrelationship and the historical context in which they are embedded, Weber's theory becomes seriously distorted.

Of course, there are some basic differences between Marx and Weber. As mentioned earlier, Marx had a more optimistic view of the long-term future than Weber, who believed society would become increasingly rationalized and bureaucratized even under socialism, because bureaucracy once established was virtually "escape proof" (Grabb 1984). Socialism would only intensify the bureaucratic characteristics of the state. Thus, future society would not see the removal of alienation and impersonality but rather their enhancement. A second major difference between the theorists is that because Weber was concerned with status and party and defined class generally in terms of market situation, the system of inequality contained within it many more groups than are suggested by a class society in which only a few groups dominate. Market situation, for example, if defined broadly enough and in detail, could ultimately mean that each individual is in a distinct class position, meaning that there are as many classes as there are persons. Perhaps the greatest weakness in Weber's discussion is the brevity and ambiguity in his treatment of class, status, and party.

ÉMILE DURKHEIM (1858–1917)

In contrast to the theorists we have discussed, Émile Durkheim was not principally concerned with social inequality. Rather, he emphasized establishing sociology as a scientific discipline, uncovering the sources and forms of integration and moral authority, and tracking and understanding the place of individualism in modern industrial society (Giddens 1978). Most of his works revolve around issues of integration and cohesiveness—that is, the question of order in society. Although liberal and reformist in outlook, Durkheim was a central founder of the functionalist school of thought in sociology, which views society as a social system tending toward equilibrium. The organic analogy of society is evident in his writing. Despite his preoccupations with questions of order and the evolutionary growth of societies, however, Durkheim had something to say about social inequality, and it is for that reason that this brief discussion is included here.

Émile Durkheim was born in 1858 in Alsace-Lorraine into a Jewish family, which expected him to become a rabbi. Later, as a young man, he turned away from religion and became an agnostic, even though his study of the "elementary forms of religious life" is one of his major works. Durkheim was a terrific student in his early youth, but was not entirely happy with the lack of scientific and moral emphases at the normal school he attended (Coser 1971). Later, he was to become a highly successful teacher at the high school and university levels.

Durkheim wanted to study a subject that would directly address issues of moral and practical guidance for society, and he wanted to use a scientific approach in the analysis of issues. He turned to sociology as his discipline of choice and, to the disdain of many colleagues, became an imperialistic advocate of sociology rather than the other social sciences (Giddens 1978). It is not surprising that topics related to order, development, and the relationship between the individual and the society would run as a common thread through Durkheim's body of work because of conditions in French society at the time. The early years of the Third Republic in France, when Durkheim was a young man, were marked by instability and conflicts between the political right and left.

Durkheim was actively involved in public affairs, including working toward restructuring the university system and helping early in the

World War I effort by completing articles attacking Nationalist German writing (Coser 1971). Durkheim's major sociological works did not begin to appear until the end of the nineteenth century. *The Division of Labor,* the source we will be concerned with here, was completed in 1893, followed by *The Rules of Sociological Method* in 1895 and *Suicide* in 1897. Later, in 1912, he finished *The Elementary Forms of Religious Life.* Durkheim died in 1917 at the age of 59.

Durkheim and Inequality

In *The Division of Labor,* Durkheim developed his theory of the movement of society from "mechanical" to "organic" solidarity. A society organized on mechanical solidarity is homogeneous, with a simple division of labor, and based on the similarity of the individuals in it. There is a strong collective conscience that serves as a principal source of moral cohesion. The individual ego is not prominent in this kind of society. In sharp contrast, societies organized around the organic form of solidarity are characterized by differences and interdependence in their division of labor. Social uniqueness, along with the increased individualism, can threaten the cohesiveness and stability of society. Corporate groups and the division of labor serve as means for integrating individuals in this kind of society. They stand midway, as it were, between the state and individual.

In a fully developed organic society, characterized by individualism, equal opportunity, specialization, and interdependence, inequality is to be expected because at this point in evolution, Durkheim argued, it is based on differences in the *internal* abilities of individuals. A "normal" division of labor is based on internal differences between individuals, which include differences between men and women. Differences in the division of labor between men and women should persist, but other differences based on *external* qualities (e.g., race, inheritance), including classes, should decline and eventually disappear. As society evolves, differential rewards should, because of equal opportunity, directly reflect

individual differences in abilities and differences in the social value of occupations. In short, Durkheim believed that as time moved on, modern society would be characterized by social inequalities between individuals based on their inner abilities rather than external characteristics. He believed that such internal differences existed between the sexes, and thus justified social inequalities between men and women, but he also argued that class and racial inequalities would diminish. Although there is some ambiguity in his treatment, this is Durkheim's primary position (Lehmann 1995).

Until this point in evolution is reached, however, the division of labor can take on "abnormal" forms that prevent its appropriate and efficient functioning. Durkheim argued that this occurs when individuals' positions in it are forced or determined without moral regulation. Individuals must recognize the rights of others in the division of labor and their duties to society as well as to themselves. Ideally, each person must have the opportunity to occupy the position that fits his or her abilities (Grabb 1984). When these conditions are not present, abnormal forms of the division of labor develop. Two of these are the **anomic** and **forced** forms of the division of labor.

In the first type, relations between people in the workplace are not governed by a generally agreed-on set of values and beliefs. Two of the developments that divided people were the split between "masters and workers" in which the organization is privately owned by the masters and the arrival of large-scale industry in which workers were each given very narrow and different functions to perform. Both of these factors served to drive a wedge between employers and workers. With large industries, "the worker is more completely separated from the employer." And "at the same time that specialization becomes greater, revolts become more frequent" (Durkheim 1933, p. 355). In smaller industries, in contrast, there is "a relative harmony between worker and employer. It is only in large-scale industry that these relations are in a sickly state" (p. 356). Large industry develops as markets grow and encompass groups not in immediate contact with each other. Producers and consumers become increasingly separated from each other. "The producer can no longer embrace the market in a glance, nor even in thought. He can no longer see its limits, since it is, so to speak, limitless. Accordingly, production becomes unbridled and unregulated" (p. 370); that is, a condition of anomie or normlessness exists. Economic crises develop but industry grows as markets grow.

With the growth of industry and an increasingly minute division of labor, the individual worker becomes more "alienated," to use a Marxian term. Like Marx, Durkheim concluded that the worker becomes a "machine," performing mind-numbing, routine, repetitive labor without any sense of the significance of his or her role in the labor process: "Every day he repeats the same movements with monotonous regularity, but without being interested in them, and without understanding them" (p. 371). Although this description may sound intriguingly Marxist, Durkheim's view of the division of labor in modern society was quite different from that of Marx. Because of its nature, Durkheim viewed the division of labor as a central basis for integration in modern industrial society. It is only in certain abnormal forms that it becomes a problem. But basically, a complex division of labor is a necessity in *industrial* society. It is expected that as societies develop they become increasingly complex. In contrast, Marx viewed the division of labor as a source of basic problems in *capitalist* society. Class conflict was over fundamental issues in the property and social relationships involved in the division of labor. For Durkheim, class conflict was a surface symptom of an anomic state in which the employers and workers conflicted because of the absence of a common, agreed-on set of moral rules. The problems of the modern society are not due to contradictions within capitalism, "but derive from the strains inherent in the transition from mechanical to organic solidarity" (Giddens 1978, p. 36). Marx saw regulation in capitalist society as stifling human initiative, whereas Durkheim saw moral regulation as necessary for individual liberty and happiness.

However, the mere presence of rules is not enough to prevent problems in the division of labor because "sometimes the rules themselves are the cause of evil. This is what occurs in class-wars" (Durkheim 1933, p. 374). The problem here is that the rules governing the division of labor do not create a correspondence between individual talents or interests and work functions. The result is that the division of labor creates dissatisfaction and pain instead of integration and cohesiveness. "This is because the distribution of social functions on which [the class structure] rests does not respond, or rather no longer responds, to the distribution of natural talents" (p. 375). When the rules regulating the division of labor no longer correspond to the distribution of true talents among individuals, then the organization of labor becomes *forced* (the second type of division of labor referred to earlier.) Durkheim felt that inequalities that were not based on "internal" differences between individuals were unjust. "External" inequality, which is based on inheritance, nepotism, or simple membership in some biological group, must be eliminated, according to Durkheim, because it threatens the solidarity of society. Superiority that results from differences in the resources of individuals is unjust. "In other words, there cannot be rich and poor at birth without there being unjust contracts" (p. 384). The sense of injustice associated with the significance of external inequalities becomes greater as labor becomes more separated from employers and the collective conscience becomes weaker.

Despite his realization of the injustices suffered by workers in the division of labor, Durkheim was not an advocate of class revolution. As mentioned, he did not feel that there is anything inherently wrong with a complex division of labor and, consequently, believed that only reformist change was needed to eliminate the problems associated with it. Durkheim felt that complete revolution would destroy the delicate and complex membrane that made up society. "I am quite aware when people speak of destroying existing societies, they intend to reconstruct them. But these are the fantasies of children. One cannot in this way rebuild collective life: once our social organization is destroyed, centuries of history will be required to build another" (quoted in Fenton 1984, p. 31). Durkheim felt that deep, lasting change would take place gradually and through ameliorative reform rather than through drastic conflict. In this way also, he differed from Marx. Nor did he agree with Marx that the state was an instrument of oppression, but rather felt it could serve as an instrument of reform for a better society (Giddens 1978). However, like Marx and in contrast to Weber, he had an optimistic view of future society. Fundamental class conflicts would be minimized once problems in the division of labor could be ironed out with appropriate policies and moral regulations over time.

HERBERT SPENCER (1820–1903)

Herbert Spencer's star in social science fell as quickly as it rose. At the turn of the twentieth century, Spencer was highly regarded and popular in academic and public circles. But by the early 1930s, his fame and reputation had suffered greatly. Near the end of the 1930s, Talcott Parsons, who was to become the leading social theorist in the United States, indicated his belief in the irrelevance of Spencer by asking directly: "Who now reads Spencer?" By and large, attitudes have not changed. Spencer does not have the high standing in social theory today that is accorded to Marx, Weber, and Durkheim.

Despite the generally negative reaction to his work by social scientists, I include a brief discussion of Spencer here for three reasons: First, there are some today who argue that Spencer has been inappropriately neglected or ignored despite the value of some of his ideas (e.g., Turner 1985; Adams and Sydie 2002). Second, as we saw in Chapter 3, Spencer's arguments about inequality and its sources, as well as his beliefs about the proper role of the state in addressing poverty and related issues, are reflected in U.S. beliefs about poverty and welfare policies. Third, Spencer's individualistic orientation contrasts significantly and sharply with the more collectivistic views of Marx and Durkheim and, consequently, provides an alternative perspective on inequality. As in

other instances, I will focus only on those ideas of greatest relevance to social inequality.

Herbert Spencer was born in 1820 in England to parents who were religious dissenters and who believed in religious freedom and social egalitarianism. Consequently, he grew to dislike the blind subjugation to authority demanded by traditional religion. His father was an independent, self-employed teacher who encouraged skepticism and freethinking. As a young boy, Spencer loathed formal education, and at 16 quit it for good. His greatest intellectual interests were in pragmatic and hard-scientific areas, such as mathematics and physics. Spencer's interest in concrete practical matters was evident in his inventions of a velocimeter, a fishing-rod joint, and other mechanical devices. He was not a romantic. He cared little for the softer fields of literature and poetry, and consequently, he was rather narrow in his reading. Because of his upbringing and the influence of the Enlightenment, he believed in combining individual reason and the judicious use of scientific method as the means for uncovering social laws. As a young man, Spencer took a job as an engineer with a British railway firm, all the while continuing with his scientific reading.

Spencer was not fully healthy for much of his life, and in later years suffered from what may have been nervous breakdowns. His last years were marked by a bitterness resulting from the lesser publicity given to his later over his earlier works and his distaste for what he saw as England's aggressive militarism against other nations (Ashley and Orenstein 1990; Adams and Sydie 2002). Spencer died in 1903 and is buried in Highgate Cemetery, about 30 feet away and directly across from the tomb of Karl Marx. The worn state of his tombstone may be symbolic of the lack of attention and recognition his theories have received in recent years. In contrast, Marx's gravesite is quite grand and impressive.

Spencer's experiences as an engineer and his expertise in biological and physical/mechanical sciences informed his own interpretations of social evolution and equilibrium, and his work was quite influential in the latter half of the nineteenth century. Indeed, his texts on biology, sociology, and

Just as their views of inequality were opposite each other, so are their tombs. Karl Marx and Herbert Spencer are buried across from each other in Highgate Cemetery in Highgate, England. As the photos show, Marx's tomb is much grander and better kept than is Spencer's. (Photos by Charles E. Hurst.)

psychology were used at prestigious universities in England and the United States. This is despite the fact that Spencer held no higher degrees and never held an academic position. Part of the reason for his popularity was that his views on societal evolution, the state, and the sanctity of the free individual resonated with the ethos of the emerging U.S. capitalist industrial order of that time.

In Spencer's view, inequality originates in militancy, first involving men as a ruling class and women as a subject class. War then creates a slave class of the conquered. The slave class increases when slaves are bought or individuals are brought into slavery because of debt or crime. Serfdom also arises with military conquest and the annexing of land. Male descent rules and kinship with those in power increase men's wealth, as does the possession of slaves. Rank and wealth are tied together. Increases in inequality build on themselves, as more wealth allows for greater accumulation and defense of it. Militancy and regulation in the larger society are reflected in the social structure of the family. Men are dominant in the domicile over women just as they are in the wider society.

The class structure is perpetuated by the abilities and habits developed over time by each respective class. Those on top become adept at control and domination, "an inherited fitness for command," while those below develop "an inherited fitness for obedience." These differences

result in "strengthening the general contrast of nature." Eventually, these class relations are seen by all as "natural" (Spencer 1909, pp. 302, 309).

As a society becomes industrial, original class divisions based on rank, kinship, land, and/ or locality break down. Classes and the distribution of rewards become based more "on differences of aptitude for the various functions which an industrial society needs," that is, on ability and performance in a competitive market (p. 310). Mental habits change as the increased economic exchange required in industrial society cultivates a "growing spirit of equality," that is, individuals become more "habituated to maintain their own claims while respecting the claims of others" (p. 307). Because human attitudes change, class and gender relations become more egalitarian. Industrial societies mean more freedom and greater reverence for the individual.

Drawing on both biological and physical analogies, Spencer viewed society as naturally becoming larger, more complex, integrated, and adaptive. In its free and natural course, societies evolve in a manner that increases their adaptability. He argued that, left to its own devices and like any natural species, a society's best components survive, while its weakest die away. Evolution performs a cleansing function that makes society more adaptive to its environment. In the long run, this makes society stronger.

In the competitive battle of life, winners survive while losers die away. In this sense, inequality is to be expected in society. Spencer coined the phrase "survival of the fittest," which captures the spirit of this social competition. This is a natural process with which there should be no interference from any quarter. "Under the natural course of things each citizen tends towards his fittest function. Those who are competent to the kind of work they undertake succeed, and, in the average of cases, are advanced in proportion to their efficiency; while the incompetent, society soon finds out, ceases to employ, forces to try something easier, and eventually turns to use" (Spencer 1892/1946, p. 138). As humanity evolves, Spencer believed, it develops traits that promote its survival. Unnecessary governmental legislation and other

attempts to modify this process damage the natural evolutionary process. "Let the average vitality be diminished by more effectually guarding the weak against adverse conditions, and inevitably there come fresh diseases" (Spencer 1961, p. 310).

Freedom gives individuals the opportunity to develop their own adaptive traits. If individuals develop positive traits, they can be strengthened and passed on to future generations, making society as a whole much stronger and more adaptive. Even well-intentioned interference in this natural process only weakens the possibility of individuals developing these traits. Overall, it also weakens society's ability to survive since it encourages, or props up, its weakest members at the expense of everyone else. Because weak individuals do not have the properties necessary for survival, their dependence on state aid is "evil" because "all evil results from the non-adaptation of constitution to conditions," and it is in its advance to build its strength that society rids itself of "evil" (Spencer 1897, pp. 28–29).

In modern industrial nations, such as the United States, Spencer envisioned a free-market capitalist economy and a government that performed only basic defensive and protective functions for the nation's citizens. He argued that, by and large, the state should minimize its role in the individual's life. The free individual is a hallmark of an advanced society, and Spencer fiercely believed in the protection of individual rights. As members of society, and at least before marriage, this applies to women as well as to men.

In contrast to Durkheim, Spencer (1897) believed that the state would become smaller and less intrusive and the individual freer as society evolved: "[T]he liberty which a citizen enjoys is to be measured . . . by the relative paucity of the restraints [governmental machinery] imposes on him . . . [especially] such restraints beyond those which are needful for preventing him from directly or indirectly aggressing on his fellows" (p. 19).

State size has implications for both the powerful and the powerless in society. What this means for the powerless and poor is that, in Spencer's view, governmental welfare programs should be eliminated for the good of society as a whole. Such

Regulating Financial Institutions

Each of the theorists discussed in this chapter had distinct views about the role of government in society. Marx saw it as an instrument used by capitalists to maintain and enhance their economic interests. Weber believed government bureaucracy would become increasingly oppressive and intrusive, while Durkheim argued that government served as an effective and positive source of regulation and freedom for individuals. Finally, Spencer viewed the state and individual as being in an adversarial relationship; consequently, the state's functions and size should be kept to a minimum.

One of the alleged causes of the 2008–2010 economic crises in the United States was the failure of government to regulate the operations of financial institutions. The result was that many of these institutions bundled questionable mortgages into securities that were sold worldwide, causing many to lose large amounts of money. Considering the arguments of the classical theorists, should the government regulate financial institutions more rigorously or leave them alone to operate as they see fit? ∎

programs actually weaken the poor and create bitterness among those who must be taxed to support them. In contrast to help given by volunteers to the needy, this aid is not freely given. No one benefits in the long run. It also weakens society because such suffering on the part of the weak must be endured if only to perfect society:

> Blind to the fact that under the natural order of things society is constantly excreting its unhealthy, imbecile, slow, vacillating, faithless members, these unthinking, though well-meaning, men advocate an interference which not only stops the purifying process, but even . . . encourages the multiplication of the reckless and incompetent by offering them an unfailing provision, and discourages the multiplication of the competent and provident by heightening the difficulty of maintaining a family. . . . The process [of natural adaptation] must be undergone and the sufferings must be endured. (Spencer 1897, p. 151)

What smaller government means for the powerful is the creation of fewer opportunities for the rich and powerful to use it for selfish purposes: "It is a tolerably well-ascertained fact that men are still selfish . . . and will employ the power placed in their hands for their own advantage . . .

directly or indirectly, either by hook or by crook, if not open then in secret, their private ends will be served" (Spencer 1897, p. 95). One need only think of recent governmental and corporate scandals to realize the applicability of this observation. In the long run, smaller government benefits all.

Spencer acknowledged the difficulties that the less fortunate face and the indignities and discrimination they suffer at the hands of the higher classes; he admitted that the distribution system gives too much to those on the top. But he contended that the problems that individuals face reflect the limitations of human nature at any given time. Unfortunately, governmental legislation and class organizations hinder this understanding. "[T]he welfare of a society and the justice of its arrangements are at bottom dependent on the character of its members. . . . The defective natures of citizens will show themselves in the bad acting of *whatever* social structure they are arranged into. There is no political alchemy by which you can get golden conduct out of leaden instincts" (Spencer 1892/1946, pp. 52–53; emphasis added).

In criticism, Spencer put too much faith in the natural process of evolution as the proper avenue through which inequality and its ills have to be solved. He appears to have been largely unaware of the negative consequences for many workers of the social-structural arrangements that evolve as a free-market economy "progresses."

To wait for human nature to become less selfish seems like wishful thinking. Outside of voluntary charity and negative regulation that protected the rights of individuals, he left little room for using human activities of any kind as a means of alleviating poverty or inequality. This is because he viewed some inequality as a product of the survival of the fittest. On the positive side, Spencer's arguments call renewed attention to the selfish interests and biases of the powerful that are often present in governmental and other large organizations. As a champion of individual freedom, he also reminds us to be wary of constraints on both the rich and the poor, which may hinder their development as individuals. He reminds us that big government, regardless of its form, is no solution to the problem of social inequality.

MARX, WEBER, AND GLOBALIZATION

During the last three decades, "capitalism has intensified its grasp over the entire world, unleashing processes of economic change that intensify and render increasingly visible the links between the fate of people in the advanced capitalist countries and the rest of the world's population" (Gimenez 2005, p. 11). During this time, many corporations have established plants and markets in foreign countries and have outsourced thousands of jobs. New plants of foreign-owned companies have sprouted up in the United States, at the same time that older companies have left looking for more lucrative foreign markets. Marx's and Weber's analyses of capitalism and inequality provide a framework for understanding many of the processes associated with globalization. From a Marxian perspective, capitalism treats the world as a font of resources, a source of labor, and a large marketplace in which companies can sell their goods and services.

In its constant search for more profit through expanded markets and lower costs through cheaper labor and lower taxes, capitalism has expanded to the most remote parts of the globe. As Marx observed, capitalism is an international force that knows no national boundaries. In seeking economic efficiencies, it has left many unemployed

and harnessed the cheap labor of workers in poor countries. Because it is able to cross national boundaries, capitalists extol the free market as a natural process because it leaves them unencumbered by governmental and other regulation. An unrestrained market allows capitalists to have free rein over its activities. Marx would view free-market arguments as an ideology that helps them maintain their powerful economic position. But what may be of short-term benefit to corporations can be harmful to others. When corporations modernize and introduce new efficiency measures, some workers are left without jobs, and small entrepreneurs who cannot compete are left to find more menial work to make ends meet (Chen et al. 2005).

While the "informal proletariat" composed of self-employed street workers and others like them is not the same group as Marx's factory proletariat, the growth in their numbers is still fostered by the movement of capitalist corporations into these economies (Choi 2006). When individuals are unemployed, their incomes fall, and they are left unable to spend on products being sold by multiple businesses. Their life chances are diminished. The lower demand for goods (e.g., automobiles, televisions) creates more competition among sellers. In the battle for markets and profits, workers and consumers are viewed as commodities that can be manipulated to increase revenue. In this battle, firms jockey for advantageous market position, often evolving through revolutionizing their technology and products. Some firms do not change and remain stagnant. As a result, some go bankrupt, leading to greater concentration in the market.

In the self-interested, rational drive for greater profit, the influence of tradition and social status is weakened. Weber observed that it is in periods of rapid change and tumult that staid beliefs and time-honored positions come under fire. Capitalism and the large state bureaucracy found in most advanced countries are antitraditional, in Weber's view. They operate "without regard for persons." In this climate, economic class position and money become more important as bases of power.

The inequalities created by these international economic processes engender some concerns and pockets of rebellion. But the alienation and false consciousness of many of those who suffer in this system, together with national ideologies that extol individualism and the free market, hold active resistance to a minimum. In Marx's view, conditions would need to get a lot worse before they get better for workers around the world.

NUTSHELL 9.1   Republicans, Democrats, and Economic Crisis

The theorists discussed in this chapter are considered "classical" because many of their ideas live on in the thought processes and policies of contemporary leaders. As President Obama has noted, the basic philosophies of many Republicans and Democrats regarding the role of government and the workings of the economy differ, sometimes resulting in paralysis when policies need to be developed and legislation passed.

These philosophical differences were on ample display in recent Congressional discussions and wrangling over whether to increase the debt limit and how to alleviate the problems in the U.S. economy and restore its health. On the one hand, there are Republicans and conservatives who believe, like Spencer, that government should be small in a modern society and its functions minimal. For these groups, government, ideally, should not intrude in the free-market economy, but should let the market work out its own problems. There should be no "bailout." Like Spencer, they argue that market mechanisms will sort out the strong from the weak, and in the long term leave the economy in a healthier state. If some businesses go bankrupt, so be it. Most Democrats and liberals, on the other hand, believe that government has an important and large role to play in creating a just society and an economy that benefits everyone. Like Durkheim, they believe that government is a positive institution which often is needed to correct problems in the wider society. Consequently, they are less hesitant to suggest grand and sometimes expensive solutions to problems.

Many Democrats—as well as some Republicans—also argue that some financial and corporate capitalists have abused their power, and consequently, should be held accountable for many of the difficulties that individuals and institutions have experienced. "Greed" has often been mentioned as a principal cause of the crisis. As Marx observed, capitalists' primary motivation is to increase profit, and leaders in financial markets tried to do so by creating new mechanisms, such as the bundling of faulty mortgages into securities for sale on the international market. Since individuals are viewed as being basically driven by egoistic motives, Democrats often contend, like Durkheim, that some regulation over individual behavior is advisable.

In dealing with economic crises, members of Congress often take sides when considering what group should be the primary focus in resolving problems. Should it be the banks since they are the source of needed funding and credit for businesses and individuals? Or should it be private businesses since they are the main source of employment in a capitalist economy? Or should it be average members of the public since they are often the first to experience unemployment and declines in their standard of living when crises occur? Like those for other questions, one's answers to these are conditioned by ideological and other beliefs.

Another point of disagreement is whether money should be put in the hands of citizens so they can spend it, or if it should be spent directly by the government to spur the economy. Generally, Republicans stress the conservative position of lowering taxes, providing more money for *individuals* to spend, while Democrats are more likely to value *government* spending as a means to create jobs and stimulate the economy. Ironically, like Marx, although not for the same reason, Republicans are more suspicious than Democrats of government.

Republicans and Democrats, conservatives and liberals, often differ on the thrust of their policy recommendations, but as Marx and Weber argued, the fact that capitalism is an interconnected system in which capitalists and workers, technology and bureaucracy, are all entangled, means that the unique problems of each constituency must be addressed and their real needs accommodated if economic crises are to be attacked effectively.

Summary

It was mentioned at the outset of the chapter that a thorough understanding of what Marx, Weber, Durkheim, and Spencer had to say about inequality depends on seeing and analyzing that work in the context of their broader theories and perspectives on society and human beings. Too often, as a reflection of our specialization and departmentalization, we wrench out only those segments of an individual's theory in which we have an immediate interest. This is not the way in which these theories were developed, and so taking them out of context can lead to distortions and, at best, only superficial understanding. Consequently, the specific observations made by these individuals on inequality should be couched in the broader frameworks of their overall perspectives and life experiences. Hopefully, this leads to a fuller comprehension of what each of these theorists was trying to convey.

It is clear from the discussion in this chapter that these men differed significantly in their views on human nature, the forms that inequality could take, and the bases and future of inequality. Weber saw human beings as self-seeking, whereas Marx viewed them in more selfless terms. Durkheim felt that individuals required regulation and guidance. Spencer believed people were selfish but that their nature would be changed to become moral and respectful of others as industrialism took hold. Marx focused on economic classes, as did Durkheim in *The Division of Labor,* whereas Weber examined economic classes as well as status groups, and to some extent, parties. Spencer analyzed shifts in class, political, and gender inequality as societies moved from **militant** to industrial, and from simple to complex systems. Marx sought the source of inequality in an individual's relationship to the means of production, whereas Weber saw inequality arising from a number of sources, including market situation, lifestyle, and decision-making power. Durkheim argued that although inequality continued to be based on biological and inheritance factors, he assumed that eventually in organic society most social inequality would be founded solely on individual differences in abilities. Spencer placed the sources of the earliest and most rigid forms of inequality in militancy, conquest, and annexation of territory, while later, more

TABLE 9.1 Summary of Basic Ideas on Inequality from Classical Theorists

Theorists' Views on Inequality					
Theorist	**Major Concern**	**Forms**	**Causes**	**Inevitability**	**Future**
Marx	Classes in capitalist society	Historical class structures	Private property	No	Revolution and classless society
Weber	Dimensions of inequality and shifts in their prominence	Class, status, party	Market situation; granting of status honor; political power	Yes	Rationalization of society and growing salience of class
Durkheim	Abnormal forms of division of labor	Masters and workers	Anomic and forced divisions of labor	Mixed	Decline of class conflict in industrial society
Spencer	Evolutionary changes in bases and degree of inequality	Classes and gender relations	Form and evolutionary stage of society	Yes	Greater egalitarian ethos and inequality based on achievement

fluid forms in industrial societies were based on one's function and performance in the economy. Weber, Durkheim, and Spencer did not see inequality as disappearing in the future, but Marx was more optimistic on this point.

Marx and Weber agreed that classes, class struggle, or both are significant elements in societies. Weber and Marx both felt that capitalism has dehumanizing effects and is class structured and that class is a predominant factor in modern society. Their conceptions of the effects of class anticipated many of the specific effects discussed in later chapters on life chances, crime, and protest.

Similar conditions for class consciousness and protest were outlined by Marx and Weber. In contrast to Marx and Weber, Durkheim and Spencer argued that, because of its nature, industrial society contains less alienating and structured forms of inequality.

Table 9.1 highlights the central features of the main theorists covered in this chapter. The theories of Marx, Weber, Durkheim, and Spencer were presented here because their perspectives have helped to shape modern social science. Their impact has not always been obvious, but it has been pervasive.

Critical Thinking

1. Is class or social status more important in understanding the everyday conditions and choices of individuals in the United States?
2. Is a classless society possible or even approachable? If so, what problems, if any, would arise from the classlessness? If not, why not?
3. In light of current trends in poverty, income, and wealth inequality in the United States, which of these theorists seem to make the most sense? Why?
4. Taking into account that the United States is a capitalist society, but also considering Spencer's arguments, do you think the federal government should or should not have a role in reducing inequality and poverty? Why?

Web Connections

Marx, Weber, and Durkheim were among the giants of sociology during its classical period. To find out more about them, and to read interviews that Marx and Engels had with various media representatives, go to the Marxist Archive, which also contains information on writers who followed in their footsteps. Comparisons of Marx with Weber and Durkheim can also be carried out by browsing and reading in these two websites: www.marxists.org/ and http://socserv.mcmaster.ca/w3virtsoclib/theories.htm.

CHAPTER 10

Contemporary Explanations of Inequality

Fortunes . . . come tumbling into some men's laps.

FRANCIS BACON (1561–1626)

This chapter consists of a discussion of some of the more recent explanations of social inequality. Generally, theories of inequality tend to stress either the *structural* or *individual* causes of inequality (Gould 2002). Some explanations incorporate both elements, and try to explain both the *structure of inequality* as well as *individuals' positions within it*. *Structural* explanations focus on the effects of the market's organization, occupational structure, institutional discrimination, and/or the social network of positions on social stratification in a society. Over time, as positions disappear and new ones appear, individuals' class positions also change. Position in the structure affects access, opportunities, and outcomes for individuals. The controversial **functionalist theory** of Davis and Moore and the dual labor market theory in this chapter stress the importance of structure and position within that structure for understanding inequality in rewards. In the last chapter, we saw that Marx's and Durkheim's theories are especially representative of this approach. *Individualist* explanations, on the other hand, emphasize the role of individual differences in qualities (traits, talents, education, etc.) in explaining the inequality among people. In other words, it is because of differences in effort, ability, training, experience, and the like that inequality in rewards emerges. In this chapter, neoclassical economic theories that focus on differences in human capital best exemplify this form of theory, while Herbert Spencer's explanation from the last chapter is also representative of the individualist type. Some explanations to be encountered shortly incorporate both structural and individualist, macro and micro elements. Included in these are certain forms of social constructionist and reproduction explanations. It can be inferred from some of these theories that even though it is helpful to make the analytical distinction between structural and individualist explanations, it is the case that structure and individual factors affect each other reciprocally in complex ways.

This chapter is not an exhaustive treatment of all contemporary theories of inequality. The work of Erik Wright, for example, a prominent American Marxist scholar, is not discussed in this chapter. Wright's principal publications have been concerned with the Marxian conceptualization and measurement of class and their application to understanding the shape of class structure in capitalist societies. As a result, his view of the class concept and class structure was reviewed in Chapter 2, along with other perspectives on class structure.

FUNCTIONALIST THEORY OF STRATIFICATION

Durkheim's belief that inequality in modern society is based primarily on differences in internal talents and the division of labor are echoed in the 1945 theory of Kingsley Davis and Wilbert Moore. Few theories of stratification called forth the attention and criticism that the Davis–Moore theory received.

Like Durkheim's theory, Davis and Moore's theory is based on a functionalist framework. The functional perspective views societies as social systems that have certain basic problems to solve or functions that have to be performed if the society is to survive. One of these problems concerns the motivation of society's members; if that motivation is absent, a society will not survive (Aberle et al. 1950, p. 103). If a society is to continue, important tasks must be specifically delineated and some means for their assignment and accomplishment created; for a society, "activities necessary to its survival must be worked out in predictable, determinate ways, or else apathy or the war of each against all must prevail" (p. 105). And since certain goods of value are scarce (property, wealth, etc.), "some system of differential allocation of the scarce values of a society is essential" (p. 106). The result of this differential allocation (stratification) must be viewed as

being legitimate and "accepted by most of the members—at least by the important ones—of a society if stability is to be attained" (p. 106). Many functional prerequisites are assumed to be necessary for the survival of a society, but it is the assumption of the necessity of stratification that concerns us here.

The arguments in Davis and Moore's functionalist theory are quite easy to grasp and, on the surface, may appear to be commonsensical and even self-evident. One should keep in mind that the kind of thinking that is represented in their theory dominated sociology throughout the 1950s and much of the 1960s in the United States.

Davis and Moore (1945) indicated at the outset of their argument that they were trying to explain (1) the presence of stratification in all societies, and (2) why *positions* are differentially ranked in the system of rewards in a society. Assuming that structure is at least minimally divided into different statuses and roles (i.e., a division of labor), Davis and Moore began by arguing that every society has to have some means to place its members in the social structure. A critical issue is the problem of motivating individuals to occupy certain statuses (full-time occupations) and to make sure that they are motivated to adequately perform the roles once they occupy those positions. Since some tasks are more onerous, more important for the society, and more difficult to perform, a system of rewards (inducements) is needed to ensure that these tasks are performed by the most capable individuals. "The rewards and their distribution become a part of the social order, and thus give rise to stratification" (p. 243). Like Durkheim's view of the ideal industrial society, Davis and Moore assumed that the society will run smoothly because the distribution of rewards to individuals will reflect the "internal inequalities" of their skills and capabilities.

Every society has a variety of rewards that it can use: (1) those "that contribute to sustenance and comfort" (money, goods of different kinds), (2) those related to "humor and diversion" (vacations, leisure plans), and (3) those that enhance "self-respect and ego expansion" (psychological rewards, promotion). Consequently, Davis and

Moore are not simply talking about the distribution and system of economic rewards but all kinds of inducements that can promote motivation to perform tasks in the society. Not all positions have equal rewards attached to them, of course, and since that is the case, "the society must be stratified because that is precisely what stratification means. Social inequality is thus an unconsciously evolved device by which societies ensure that the most important positions are conscientiously filled by the most qualified persons" (p. 243). According to this approach, since every society has tasks that are differentially important to its survival, every society is stratified.

Davis and Moore specified two criteria that determine the amount of rewards that accrue to given positions: (1) functional importance of the task and (2) the "scarcity of personnel" capable of performing the task, or the amount of training required (pp. 243–244). Together these determine the rank of a given position in the system of rewards—that is, in the stratification system. Consequently, "a position does not bring power and privilege because it draws a high income. Rather it draws a high income because it is functionally important and the available personnel is for one reason or another scarce" (pp. 246–247). The exact contribution of each of these criteria, singly and in combination, to the level of rewards is not spelled out, so one can only guess as to how rewards would be affected if one of these criteria ranked high but the other low on a given position (Abrahamson 1973).

Davis and Moore (1945) implied that a third and more radical factor also is involved in deter-mining an *individual's* (as opposed to a position's) rank and reward: economic power or control over resources. They recognized that having a great deal of money can give an individual an advantage in seeking a higher position. Power and prestige can be based on ownership, and "one kind of ownership of production goods consists in rights over the labor of others. . . . Naturally this kind of ownership has the greatest significance for stratification because it necessarily entails an unequal relationship" (p. 247). These comments are repeated in Davis's revised version of the theory (1948–1949). Kemper (1976) stated that it is remarkable that, given all the critics of the theory, none seems to have noticed that economic power also is considered a cause of distribution in the reward system by Davis and Moore. Clearly, however, economic power takes a secondary place alongside functional importance and training or talent, especially since it is more clearly a determinant of why *individuals,* and not *positions,* are distributed as they are in a reward system.

Societies differ in their stratification systems because they contain different conditions that affect either one or both of the principal determinants of ranking—that is, either functional importance or scarcity. The stage of cultural development and their situation with respect to other societies vary between societies, causing certain tasks to be more important in one society than in another, and in personnel being more scarce for certain tasks than for others.

Figure 10.1 outlines the essential argument of the Davis–Moore thesis. Davis and Moore concluded their presentation by noting several

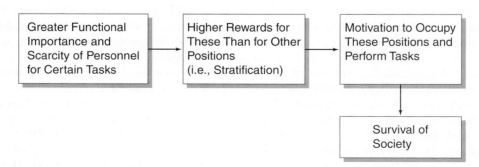

FIGURE 10.1   The Davis–Moore Theory of Stratification

dimensions along which stratification systems in different countries can vary. Among others, these include how fine the gradations are between ranks (specialization), the degree of social distance from the top to the bottom, the extent of mobility in the system, and the extent to which classes are clearly delineated in the society. What could be more logical? Certain tasks are more important than others, and some are more difficult to carry out. In order to make sure they are performed, more rewards are attached to them. Thus, people are motivated to perform them, and the society continues to function.

Critique of the Functionalist Theory of Stratification

For the first 40 years after its publication, Davis and Moore confronted a storm of criticism over their theory. The vehemence with which some of the arguments were made and the endurance of the debate suggest that a number of fundamental issues were involved. Three of these concerned (1) the issue of the differential functional importance of positions, (2) the question of whether the functionalists are addressing real societies, and (3) the neglect of the dysfunctions of stratification.

DIFFERENTIAL FUNCTIONAL IMPORTANCE A central problem of the Davis–Moore theory is how to establish the *functional necessity* of a task for a society. Davis and Moore acknowledged that it is difficult to define functional necessity, but they suggested two indicators of importance: (1) "the degree to which a position is functionally *unique*"— that is, there are no functional alternatives to the position; and (2) "the degree to which other positions are *dependent* on the one in question" (Davis and Moore 1945, p. 244; emphasis added).

It is not clear whether Davis and Moore are speaking of the *subjective evaluation* of positions as being differentially important or of positions being differentially important by some more *objective standard*. In the 1945 version, the indicators for measuring functional importance suggested that they were speaking of functional importance in an objective sense. But in a later

statement, Davis (1948–1949) suggested that it is the *subjective evaluation* of a role's importance which is the significant determinant of its functional importance. And, of course, if this is the case, about whose evaluation is he speaking—all of society or a select few? Moore (1970) also took a more subjective position later when he noted the importance of evaluating performance, qualities, and achievement in determining rewards. The bottom line is that Moore and Davis's criteria for defining *functional importance* are not clear nor are their attempts to measure it adequate (Huaco 1963). Studies attempting to measure the effect of functional importance on reward structures have yielded, at best, mixed results (e.g., Abrahamson 1973; Broom and Cushing 1977; Wallace 1997).

THE ISSUE OF DEALING WITH REAL SOCIETIES Another of the principal criticisms of the functional perspective is that it deals with highly abstract social systems (utopias) and has little to do with the operation of concrete societies (Dahrendorf 1958). As it applies here, the criticism means that if stratification of rewards is the means by which a society ensures that the most qualified people fill the most important positions, then it is crucial that there be a free flow of talent throughout the society. But, in fact, as Tumin (1953) made plain, this is not the case in real societies. People in the lower strata usually have restricted opportunities, societies are not freely competitive, and people probably are not taking full advantage of the talent they may have. The roles of conflict and lack of opportunity must be considered when trying to understand the socioeconomic arrangement of real societies (Dahrendorf 1958), and although Davis and Moore did mention the roles of power and wealth in determining and maintaining positions, they did not stress these as major determinants.

One way in which Davis and Moore tried to handle the criticism that some are hindered from attaining a high position was by reiterating that the theory is about *positions,* not the mobility of *people.* However, even given this insistence on their part, people do, in fact, become important in the theory because of Davis and Moore's belief that "it does make a great deal of difference who gets into which positions, not only because some positions are inherently more agreeable than others but also because some require special talents or training and some have more importance than others" (1945, p. 367). Moreover, differential power, as reflected in variations in resources and advertising, would certainly seem to play a role in determining which positions are defined as important in a society.

NEGLECT OF THE DYSFUNCTIONS OF STRATIFICATION   Tumin (1953) was the first major critic to point out that stratification can have numerous dysfunctions for society and the individual, a point ignored in the original Davis–Moore argument. Among the dysfunctions he noted are that stratification (1) inhibits the discovery of talent, (2) limits the extent to which productive resources can be expanded, (3) provides those at the top with the power to rationalize and justify their high position, (4) weakens the self-images among those at the bottom and thereby hinders their psychological development, (5) can create hostility and disintegration if it is not fully accepted by all in society, and (6) may make some feel that they are not full participants and, therefore, make them feel less loyal to the society.

It is somewhat surprising that the original argument by Davis and Moore would neglect the question of dysfunctions, given their comments about power and wealth affecting the reward system. But, on the other hand, Tumin does not indicate that a condition of full equality may also generate problems of its own, such as lack of motivation and feelings of inequity. Wrong (1959), in fact, has indicated that many critics of the Davis–Moore theory point to the dysfunctions of stratification and the role of power and so forth in determining rank, but they neglect the dysfunctional effects of equality of opportunity. In a society where individuals can freely move up on the basis of their talent, would not the failures they suffer be felt even more acutely, knowing that they and not the system are to blame for their low position in the system of rewards?

THE SOCIAL CONSTRUCTION OF INEQUALITY

Traditionally, most dominant sociological theories have placed social structure, culture, and similar "social facts" at the center of their arguments. That is, they have tended to focus on the larger, macro world around us as the principal source for our individual fates and behaviors. Theorists have also been inclined to look at inequality on a broad social level rather than to focus on a more fine-grained analysis of the changes occurring *within* occupational groups or classes. Reskin (2003) has argued that we need to delineate the specific mechanisms that distribute resources and rewards differently among different types of people. The focus should be on *how* rather than *why* inequality is produced. That is, through what process is inequality created in the first place? As Myles (2003) succinctly puts it: "The aim of the exercise is still to explain who gets what and why" (p. 556) A second related question concerns how individuals produce inequality by their everyday behavior.

Identifying the mechanisms that explain inequality means providing details of the sequential causal process that brings it about (Sampson 2008; Gross 2009; Hedstrom and Ylikoski 2010). A **social constructionist** approach to understanding inequality requires explanations to show how individual actions and relationships in given situations actually generate inequality. That is, knowledge of how and why individuals act (a micro-level phenomenon) is needed to understand the ranking of groups and the distribution of valued resources (a macro-level phenomenon; Ridgeway 1991; Hedstrom and Ylikoski 2010).

Schwalbe (2008) suggests that, when we examine inequality over the long stretch of history, we find that unequal distributions of valuable resources among racial and ethnic groups in the early United States were often the result of "theft, extortion, and exploitation" (pp. 32–33). But it is the placement of groups of people into particular categories (e.g., less than human, biologically distinct) that are different from "us" (human, superior) that initiates and justifies the theft, extortion, and exploitation. In this sense, rather than being a natural inevitability, social inequality is a humanly manufactured "accomplishment" (Schwalbe 2008). Categorizations of individuals such as male/female, Black/White/Hispanic are human creations, and the nominal characteristics of individuals that are developed into salient classifications which, in turn, become the bases of social distinctions, are results of the historical and cultural contexts (Ridgeway et al. 2009). As the shifting racial classifications of the U.S. Census Bureau demonstrate, changing historical and cultural situations produce changing classifications.

But what mechanisms spur the translation of simple nominal classifications like race and gender into subjective rankings that evaluate a given race or gender as higher or lower in status than others? In a structural condition in which there is a perfect match between a socially recognized nominal characteristic like race or gender and the distribution of jobs, creating economic and status inequalities among those jobs through exploitation and hoarding of opportunities by one group is easier (Tilly 1998; Tomaskovic-Devey et al. 2009). That is, when there is a clear and strong correlation between a recognized nominal trait like race or gender and possession of a valued resource (e.g., high salary), the nominal trait takes on a status value and becomes more salient in social situations (Ridgeway 1991).

The status value associated with one's race or gender is further reinforced and becomes broadly accepted when repeated interactions take place among individuals with similar perspectives. (Ridgeway et al. 2009; see also Mark, Smith-Lovin, and Ridgeway 2009). Individual judgments made about the qualities possessed by others are shaped in interaction. This social influence, in turn, magnifies differences in the perceived qualities of individuals, with higher-status persons being "overvalued" and those of lower status "undervalued." Notable public persons receive high status from an individual simply because they get it from everybody else (Gould 2002). Individuals then carry these beliefs into other situations and actions. As a result, status beliefs get disseminated throughout the society (Ridgeway et al. 2009).

This legitimizes and helps to stabilize the different status evaluations individuals receive. At the same time, however, individuals will moderate the status they attribute to others depending on the extent to which they themselves receive attention or status from those others. If the demand for reciprocity in attention is pervasive, status inequality can be minimal.

The classifications that become important and broadly accepted bases for social status are generally invented by those who have economic, political, or social power (Rigney 2001). Consequently, the categories/classifications often reflect their interests and result in dividing up the social world in a manner that privileges them. For example, *intelligence* is generally defined by psychological experts or persons in authority using the "intelligence quotient" or IQ, even though in recent decades this measurement has come under attack from different, often less privileged groups. Using this definition, only certain persons are defined as "intelligent." Through classifications like this (intellectual, racial, status, etc.) we create "others" who simply do not measure up to the standards we have created. This process of "othering" creates and helps reproduce inequality (Schwalbe et al. 2000).

The concept of "homosexuality," as discussed in Chapter 7, provides another example of how classifications are created. The classification of heterosexual/homosexual is historically recent, as is the privileging of heterosexuality over homosexuality, for example, in the interpretation of homosexuality as a form of "deviance." It was not until 1966 that the American Psychiatric Association introduced homosexuality as a form of sexual disorder. Battles with gay groups over this definition and interpretation later led to changes (Spector and Kitsuse 1977).

When their interests are at stake, groups will often compete for acceptance of their definitions or classifications. At different times, different groups may win, and some groups may win almost all of the time. Consequently, classifications may change or they may not. "When one group wins, its vocabulary may be adopted and institutionalized while the concepts of the opposing groups fall into obscurity. . . . The categories and meanings that they have created have direct consequences for the ways such phenomena are conceived, evaluated, and treated" (Spector and Kitsuse 1977, pp. 8, 15).

When one puts together all the accepted terms, definitions, classifications, and so forth that proliferate in society, it is easy to see why social constructionists view society as being made up of symbols and words, since it is these labels that constitute reality for us on a day-to-day basis. Different definitions and classifications suggest different realities. When sociologists, as "professional experts," create measures of social class and, using data on income, education, and so on, define given individuals as "working class" or "middle class" or "upper class," they are, in effect, inventing these classes or "doing class."

Individuals are "doing race" or "doing gender" when they engage in conversations or behaviors that create or reinforce differences between groups. In his engaging recollection about growing up in a poor minority neighborhood in New York, White sociologist Dalton Conley discussed how he had to learn what it means to be White or Black (2000, p. 37): "Learning race is like learning a language. First we try mouthing all sounds. Then we learn which are not words and which have meaning to the people around us." It did not take long for Conley and his sister to learn the meanings and symbols associated with different groups. In their daily school and neighborhood experiences, they learned what it meant to be rich or poor and Black or White.

Similarly, we learn what gender means by how it is done, that is, by how different individuals are defined and treated. It is in this defining and treatment that different genders are created, beginning early in life when boys and girls are treated differently. In this way, gender is socially constructed and is maintained through the recurrence of distinctions made in school, on the job, in the home, and in other institutions. We then define gender differences as inherent in each individual or as natural, and by treating individuals differently, we reproduce gender inequality (Lorber 2001). It is in our daily interactions with others that gender is

invented. Women and men are viewed as being *meant* for different roles and positions. Once constructed, inequalities are then reproduced.

Part of the interest in examining the dynamics of inequality in everyday life is related to a larger concern for understanding the real, active processes by which inequality is generated. A few more recent attempts have tried to tease out more of the "nitty-gritty" processes involved in the development and maintenance of structures of inequality. They resonate with earlier and previously mentioned undertakings to *ground* theory, such as Omi and Winant's (2005) analysis of how racial categories are actually formed in historical context, for example, and West and Zimmerman's (1987) discussion of how individuals "do gender" in their everyday lives.

One of the most detailed and grounded explanations of inequality comes from Charles Tilly. Like Gould and others, he is interested in identifying the explicit mechanisms that generate and maintain structures of inequality. Tilly (1998, 2003) cites two mechanisms that produce "durable" inequality, *exploitation* and *opportunity hoarding*. Inequality becomes established when individuals use their resources to extract something of value (e.g., resources, labor) from others (i.e., exploitation), or when they deprive the access of other groups or categories of people to valued resources (i.e., opportunity hoarding). Among other things, "valued resources" include weapons, labor, land, machines, capital, knowledge, and media control, that is, those items that provide their owner with power over others.

In opportunity hoarding, the categories selected for exclusion may be determined in part by social categories already existing in the wider society, for example, those involving gender or race. These categories may be borrowed for use in specific situations or organizations, as when socially defined gender roles are extended to work positions in a corporation. Means that are effective in maintaining dominance over women at home, for example, may be used in the workplace as well. Or racial categories and meanings associated with them may be used to keep Blacks or other minorities out of certain establishments

One of the reasons some low-income individuals remain poor is that the payday advance loans they take out to support themselves from week to week generally have exorbitant, even usurious, interest rates attached to them. Loans then have to be taken out to pay the interest on earlier loans, resulting in a vicious cycle that reproduces their low-income position. (Photo by Brendan R. Hurst.)

(e.g., Jim Crow laws). This process of borrowing categories from other spheres of life is what Tilly refers to as *emulation.*

Use of such preexisting categories can serve to clarify, justify, and maintain unequal arrangements in the work setting. As with other classifications, social categories of groups simplify relationships among individuals at the same time that they often function to rank them. "Categories matter. . . . [C]ategories facilitate unequal treatment by both members and outsiders. . . . The [c]ategories that matter most for durable inequality, however, involve both mutual awareness and connectedness; we know who they are, they know who we are, on each side of that line people interact with each other, and across the line we interact with them—but differently" (Tilly 2003, p. 33). Categories and the meanings attached to them come and go, as we saw with historical shifts in racial classifications. How they come about and change depends heavily on the nature of the contact and interactions between the groups involved.

Adaptation also aids in the maintenance of inequality (Tilly 2003). For example, in his study

of total institutions, Goffman (1961) noted that one way inmates or residents adjusted to their controlled position was by becoming "model" inmates or residents, that is, by adjusting to and even accepting the role expected of them. Like emulation, such adaptation helps to sustain hierarchical arrangements. The four mechanisms of exploitation, opportunity hoarding, emulation, and adaptation along with the systematic use of social categories aid in the explanation of inequality structures and their durable nature. As a group, the ventures into identifying processes and mechanisms that create and maintain social inequality are all attempts to clarify the specific and concrete forces that underlie systems of inequality.

THEORIES OF SOCIAL REPRODUCTION

While social constructionist theories attempt to explain how social inequality *originates,* **social reproduction** theories examine how inequality is *reproduced* over and over again in our everyday behavior and situations. Social reproduction theories are generally built on a conflict model of society and are often aligned with Marxian views on inequality. Specifically, they are concerned with the question of how the class structure reproduces itself generation after generation. As MacLeod (1987) stated, "Social reproduction theory explains how societal institutions perpetuate (or reproduce) the social relationships and attitudes needed to sustain the existing relations of production in a capitalist society" (p. 9). Thus, even though they are concerned with the reproduction of inequality over time, these theories are in sharp contrast to those that emphasize a culture-of-poverty approach—that is, blaming the perpetuation of inequality on the values and other characteristics of poor individuals and their families.

Needless to say, there are a number of specific theories of reproduction. They variously focus on the role(s) of (1) institutions, (2) culture, and/or (3) the individual in the perpetuation of social inequality. Institutions as social structures create avenues of and barriers to achievement. Societal and subcultural values encourage or discourage attitudes and behaviors that affect achievement. Finally, even though individuals may share values, they may enact them in different ways. Moreover, since each individual's situation is at least a little different, his or her immediate values that are grounded in this situation may also differ, and thus so may the individual's actions/reactions. Examples of arguments that stress each of these follow.

Institutions provide the normative framework that creates the accepted channels through which valuable resources can be obtained and accumulated. That is, they contain the legitimate rules, policies, and procedures that define acceptable (i.e., legal) and unacceptable behavior for individuals. This means that those who control institutions and shape their rules also shape the distribution of resources, and those with greater resources to begin with are in the most advantageous position to create and interpret the rules for a society (Schwalbe 2008). Critical among these institutions is the state, which develops the laws that regulate the economy. These laws concern business and economic behavior such as contracts and transactions, minimum wage rates, tax rates, loan and investment policies, and other regulations that define how wealth can be legitimately accumulated. Since these laws operate continuously and apply to the whole nation, they contribute to the reproduction of economic inequality's structure in a society.

The role of government has always been critical in shaping racial wealth inequality across generations (Oliver and Shapiro 1995). As reviewed in Chapter 8, through mortgage and other programs, governmental agencies have often created opportunities for wealth accumulation for some but not for others. Since degree of access to opportunities affects the growth of wealth for current and future generations, institutional conditions impact the economic gaps between racial groups. Historically, hoarding of

---

NUTSHELL 10.1   An Example of the Roles of Government and Financial Institutions in the Reproduction of Economic Inequality

During the summer and fall of 2008, the U.S. economy suffered a serious downturn. The stock market declined significantly, some high-powered financial institutions collapsed, unemployment rose, rates of home foreclosures skyrocketed, and the value of individuals' stockholdings and retirement savings eroded. This event provides some clues to the roles of government policy and the

activities of financial institutions in the establishment of economic inequality in the United States.

One of the responsibilities of government is to provide conditions and a context in which markets can operate effectively and freely in our capitalist economy. In the United States, this has meant allowing economic activities to operate without heavy interference from the government.

(Continued)

NUTSHELL 10.1 (Continued)

In the current political climate, for businesses this has meant deregulation and minimal monitoring of many financial activities, and favorable tax laws and allowances. For the consumer, this has meant easy access to credit and credit cards, and the freedom to select from a wide range of financial choices.

A central feature of capitalism is the privatization of profit. This provides a strong incentive for businesses and employers to seek out techniques and avenues that maximize their profits. In the absence of vigilant government oversight during 2007–2008, financial institutions were willing to take risks and try novel arrangements to maximize profits and increase the incomes of their top employees. Mortgage loans were given out to individuals who often could not afford them and for homes that were overpriced, because significant profits could be made on the interests being charged. These mortgages were then bundled into securities that were widely sold to other institutions. A relatively new financial device, the credit-default swap, served as a contract between institutions to insure against the possibility of losses on these securities. When the inflated value of these securities collapsed, the financial integrity of many financial institutions was endangered. Millions of consumers who had taken out loans found themselves unable to pay the mortgages on their price-inflated homes, the consequence being that many found themselves in foreclosure. Some consumers went bankrupt. Others sought out payday lenders to get loans that had exorbitant interest rates attached to them. Lower-income individuals have often gotten "refund anticipation loans" from lenders in anticipation of their tax refunds. The interest rates generally range from 70 to 700 percent. Middle- and upper-income persons have access to loans at more competitive rates.

What all this means is that poorer individuals get caught up in seeking out credit and building up a pile of financial debt from which it is difficult to escape. They can do this because some financial institutions and lax government regulation create conditions in which institutions can profit while consumers can too easily lose. Americans in general have, in recent years, been encouraged to spend in order to possess the latest technologies, be competitive with their neighbors, and keep the economy going. One consequence has been that many in the middle class as well as those below them have saved little and accumulated high levels of debt, resulting in little financial security.

Of course, in the 2008 crisis, both financial institutions and ordinary citizens suffered because they were tied together in these economic arrangements. While profits were privatized, the costs of the crisis were socialized, that is, borne primarily by taxpayers. Taxpayer money was used to rescue failing financial institutions and to provide some relief to consumers whose homes were in foreclosure. The consequent unemployment in many industries also put downward pressure on the incomes of many middle- and working-class employees. Profits were made by a few, but many others shared in the cost of the crisis.

The encouragement to spend, to multiply the number of credit cards one has, and to buy on installment in a marketplace with little regulation is seductive, but it has led to a "debt culture" and a debt trap for many of the most vulnerable. For lenders and others, on the other hand, it has led to high incomes and short-term profits. This suggests that the manner in which government policies intersect with the economy shapes conditions that affect the distribution of economic resources, helping to reproduce inequality.

Sources: Steven Lohr, "Wall Street's Extreme Sport," *New York Times,* November 5, 2008, pp. B1 and B5; Children's Defense Fund, *The State of America's Children 2005* (Washington, D.C.: Children's Defense Fund); David Brooks, "Debt, the Great American Seduction," *Akron Beacon Journal,* June 11, 2008, p. A7; Institute for American Values, *For a New Thrift: Confronting the Debt Culture* (New York: Institute for American Values); James O'Connor, *The Fiscal Crisis of the State* (New York: St. Martin's, 1973).

opportunities and exploitation by the White majority were supported by U.S. laws during the period of slavery and Jim Crow, and during the government's treatment of Native Americans over the last two centuries (Massey 2007). In all cases, racist and other ideologies or official arguments were then used to justify the policies and perpetuate the inequality.

In addition to the state, the educational system is another institution that occupies a prominent place in some reproduction theories. Drawing on Marx's work, Bowles and Gintis's theory (1976) addresses how the educational system helps to reproduce class relationships in capitalist society. Rather than simply being an avenue to upward mobility and a means for developing the human personality, Bowles and Gintis view education as a vehicle to perpetuate the capitalist or class system in U.S. society. Even early in its development, education was a means "to help preserve and extend the capitalist order. The function of the school system was to accommodate workers to its most rapid possible development. . . . Since its inception in the United States, the public-school system has been seen as a method of disciplining children in the interest of producing a properly subordinate adult population" (Bowles and Gintis 1976, pp. 29 and 37). A higher level of education for most people has not reduced economic inequality, nor has it developed their full creativity. Its structure rewards those who conform to its rules and obey authority.

As in the workplace, obedience to authority and rules is expected in school. There is a correspondence, Bowles and Gintis argue, between the structure of educational institutions and the workplace. Specifically, there is a similarity between the two spheres in (1) the nature of their authority structures, (2) students' lack of control over their classes and workers' lack of control over the work process, (3) the role of grades and other rewards (e.g., colored stars on papers) in schools and the role of wages in the workplace, as extrinsic motivators, (4) ostensibly free competition among students and similar competition among workers, and (5) the specialization and tracking of courses in school and the narrow functional specialization and career paths in the workplace (Bowles and Gintis 1976; MacLeod 1987). These correspondences between the school and workplace reflect a parallelism between them.

In going through the educational process, individuals are prepared for their respective roles in the economy. In performing this function, "schools are constrained to justify and reproduce inequality rather than correct it" (Bowles and Gintis 1976, p. 102). By providing a setting in which success appears to depend solely on the individual and his or her talent and effort, schools give the appearance of rewarding those who are most meritorious. The school rewards certain attitudes and behaviors, and penalizes others. It rewards those who act and think in a manner that will serve them in the jobs they will perform in the division of labor. Not all who go to school will move on to higher white-collar professional jobs; many will perform the tasks of blue-collar work. As I noted in an earlier discussion of prep schools, education prepares each class differently, depending on the roles they will play when they collectively leave school. This means not only teaching the appropriate skills but also inculcating the appropriate values and demeanor for each class. Schools in different class neighborhoods differ in their organization and value structure.

Parents conspire with the school to sort students into their respective social classes. Parents from the middle class expect a more open school structure in which autonomy and creativity are valued. This reflects their image of what is needed in middle-class jobs. In contrast, working-class parents know from their job experiences that obedience and discipline are important. This is reflected in the organization and value structure of schools that are made up primarily of working-class students (Bowles and Gintis 1976, pp. 131–134). As Rubin (1976) found in her study of the working and middle classes, "for the working-class parent, school is a place where teachers are expected to be tough disciplinarians; where children are expected to behave respectfully and to be punished if they do not; and where one mark of that respect is that they are sent to school neatly dressed in their 'good' clothes and expected to stay that way through the day" (p. 126). In contrast, the professional middle-class parent, who has had a different work experience, expects school "to be relatively loose, free, and fun; to encourage initiative, innovativeness, creativity, and spontaneity; and to provide a place where children . . . will learn social and interpersonal skills" (p. 126).

This one-way form of education serves the interests of those in the dominant group. It is not liberating to those who receive it. Instead, it serves "to minimize or annul the students' creative power and to stimulate their credulity [which in turn] serves the interests of the oppressors, who care neither to have the world revealed nor to see it transformed" (Freire 1986, p. 60). It launches a "cultural invasion" in which "those who are invaded come to see their reality with the outlook of the invaders rather than their own; for the more they mimic the invaders, the more stable the position of the latter becomes" (Freire 1986, p. 151). The educational experience, then, reproduces different workers for the economy and the social relationships on which the economy is based.

In sum, schools are not only interested in producing appropriate laborers for the economy but also serve the long-term goal of perpetuating the institutions and social relationships that will ensure the continued profitability of capitalism. An educational system accomplishes these goals in four ways:

1. It provides some of the skills needed to perform jobs for each class adequately. Curriculum tracking channels individuals from different classes into appropriate courses.
2. Through its structure and curriculum, the educational system helps to justify and legitimate the economic and occupational inequality present in society. It fosters a belief that individuals wind up in different positions solely because of differences in merit.
3. It encourages the development and internalization of attitudes and self-concepts appropriate to the economic roles individuals will perform. Those who conform to prized values (e.g., those of the upper or middle class) are rewarded, while those who do not are negatively labeled.
4. Through the creation of justified status distinctions within the school, education helps to reinforce a taken-for-granted acceptance of social stratification in the wider society (Bowles and Gintis 1976).

MacLeod (1987) has criticized the Bowles–Gintis theory as being too crude and mechanistic because it views individuals simply as outputs of capitalism and the educational system. It does not give adequate attention to the possible individual differences in reactions to structures that constrain a person. Nor does it take into account cultural or subcultural variations in values and lifestyles that may shape unique adaptations to structural barriers. Giroux (1983) has similarly criticized Bowles and Gintis for ignoring the active element in the individual within the structural framework of the school and economy. People *experience* the authority structure of the school and its teachers and react to them, sometimes through acceptance and sometimes through resistance. In Bowles and Gintis's theory, "the subject gets dissolved under the weight of structural constraints that appear to form both the personality and the workplace" (Giroux 1983, p. 85). In other words, attention to the micro processes of individuals' interpretations and interaction, like those specified in social constructionist arguments, are ignored. Structures may provide the broad parameters for behavior, but individuals interpret those structural constraints on their own.

A more culturally oriented theory of class reproduction is suggested by the work of Pierre Bourdieu. In this perspective, culture is a mediating element between class structure/interests and everyday life and behavior. By appearing to be objective and a source of knowledge, schools that produce both successful and failing students can justify the inequality that follows. Since schools represent the interests of the dominant culture, Bourdieu argued, they value the cultural capital of the dominant class more than that of the lower classes. **Cultural capital** refers to all the sets of beliefs, practices, ways of thinking, knowledge, and skills passed on from one class's generation to the next. Schools, especially those in higher education, espouse the cultural capital that is most characteristic of the privileged classes, thereby denigrating that which is characteristic of the working and lower classes (Bourdieu 1977a, 1977b). Since this occurs in the objective setting of the school, those in the latter classes who do

FIGURE 10.2   A General Model of Bourdieu's Explanation of Social Reproduction

not do well in classes develop an attitude in which they blame themselves and "actively participate in their own subjugation" (Giroux 1983, p. 89).

Generally, Bourdieu suggested that individuals compete within different "fields" in a struggle for economic, cultural, and social capital. These fields constitute networks of relationships among positions (Bourdieu and Wacquant 1992). As a result of these struggles, individuals come to occupy different classes that vary in the amounts and forms of their economic, social, and cultural capital. Research does indeed indicate that variations in capital are reflected in positional arrangements within fields (Anheier, Gerhards, and Romo 1995). Respectively, some possess great amounts of wealth, extensive social networks, and fancy tastes and lifestyles (whereas others do not) and can use these resources to justify their possession of capital. Individuals in higher occupational positions tend to have more diverse and extensive social networks that provide them with access to greater social resources. Moreover, since they tend to associate most often with similar kinds of individuals, most of the resources controlled by this group stay within it, helping to reproduce inequality (Erickson and Cote 2009). The presence or absence of these resources forms a large part of the social context in which individuals live, and these objective conditions give rise to particular tastes, lifestyles, and ways of looking at the world. The upper class possesses a "taste of liberty and luxury," whereas the lower has "popular taste." "Distance from necessity" permeates the taste of the upper class, meaning that it is less directly functional and practical compared to the taste of the lower class.

An individual's **habitus**, or system of stable dispositions to view the world in a particular way, is a direct product of the person's structural situation; in fact, it is the psychological embodiment of the objective conditions in which one lives. Thus, different life conditions give rise to different forms of habitus and those exposed to the same conditions will develop the same habitus (Bourdieu 1990). The habitus, in turn, has a direct, constraining effect on the social action of individuals, which, coming full circle, contributes to reproducing the social structure. Figure 10.2 gives a rough outline of Bourdieu's model. For example, an adolescent who lives within a structure with poor job opportunities as evidenced by the experiences of his or her parents will develop a view that chances of success are slight and that school makes no difference. This leads to behavior that accommodates him or her to a menial job, which in turn reinforces the existing job opportunity structure. Nothing changes.

A similar process involving the effect of social structure on outlook and decision making appears to reinforce racial segregation in neighborhoods. Black neighborhoods in Chicago, for example, remain largely Black because Whites and Latino residents tend to move out when neighborhoods are or become disproportionately Black. Blacks, in turn, often remain in their own or similar neighborhoods, not because they do not prefer mixed neighborhoods, but because they find their own neighborhoods more "hospitable" than richer White neighborhoods. Consequently, continued residential segregation and decisions to stay or move in part reflect the perceptions of different racial groups of each other (Sampson 2008; Sampson and Sharkey 2008).

Such an image of reproduction of social structure does not lend itself to reconstructing the social order, nor does it acknowledge the possibility of resistance or rebellion on the part of dominated groups (Giroux 1983). In Bourdieu's theory, the prospect of radically altering educational institutions or the system, in general, seems dim indeed (MacLeod 1987). MacLeod believes that while Bourdieu has incorporated an important cultural element into his theory of reproduction, a necessary corrective to the structural-correspondence theory of Bowles and Gintis, his theory is still too deterministic. To have an adequate theory, "we must appreciate both the importance and the relative autonomy of the cultural level at which individuals, alone or in concert with others, wrest meaning out of the flux of their lives" (MacLeod 1987, p. 139).

Too often, as well, class reproduction theories have ignored the separately lived and varied experiences of women and minority groups, an omission that can seriously limit the theories' ability to understand the habitus of these individuals and the reproduction of their economic situations. One of these lived variations concerns childbearing inside and outside marriage. In her analysis of childbearing outside of marriage, Sara McLanahan (2009) found that unmarried mothers, who often come from economically disadvantaged families and have lower-than-average educations, tend to have less stable partners, and are likely to have weaker social support, more mental stress, and lower incomes than married mothers. The poorer resources and lower stability ultimately reduce their children's life chances and optimize the probability that their children will remain in a low economic position. Thus, low economic status is reproduced between generations.

MacLeod's (1987) case study of the conditions and behavior among two groups of adolescent males in a public housing development reveals much about the process by which social positions are reproduced. The "Brothers" are a Black group and the "Hallway Hangers" are White. Over time, the adolescents in these groups develop lower aspirations about their futures which, in turn, help to reproduce their class positions. MacLeod's research vividly demonstrates the specific and sometimes different factors that produce these leveled aspirations. Among the Brothers, there is some evidence that success is possible when they look at the occupations of their siblings. Their parents also believe that conditions have gotten better for Blacks, and thus they encourage their children

in their schoolwork. They have been exposed to tenement living for a shorter time, on average, than the Hallway Hangers, and they are antagonistic to the views of the latter group, which regard the Blacks with disdain. These conditions lead the Brothers to accept the dominant achievement ideology that opportunity exists for all and success is possible if one puts forth the proper amount of effort. What ultimately leads the members of this group to lower their aspirations is a combination of the devaluing of their cultural capital by school officials, lower teacher expectations, tracking, discrimination, and their own self-blame. The school's treatment of them leads to relatively poor performance, and since they subscribe to the achievement ideology that says it is the individual's own characteristics and efforts that determine how far he or she can get, poor performance leads to self-blame. The combination of self-blame and poor performance results in a lowering of expectations and aspirations. Figure 10.3 outlines the basic processes present in the development of leveled aspirations among the Brothers.

In contrast to the Brothers, the Hallway Hangers do not subscribe to the achievement ideology even though they are White. The conditions of their lives are such that they see little evidence for its validity. Their parents and siblings have not done well even though they are White; their parents believe things are stacked against them; they have lived (or been trapped) in the tenements longer than the Brothers and have a longer history of experience with the welfare system. They have not seen that education produces many successes in their immediate surroundings. These conditions have bred a feeling of cynicism about the achievement ideology. Their own subculture exerts peer pressure that encourages the rejection of raised aspirations. These experiences and feelings lead to leveled aspirations and a negative attitude toward school. The latter, in turn, results in poorly rated performance and tracking, which reinforce the leveled aspirations and result in a negative evaluation of them from others. The lowered self-esteem that derives from this negative evaluation leads these adolescents to turn to their own subculture and its associated values. But that

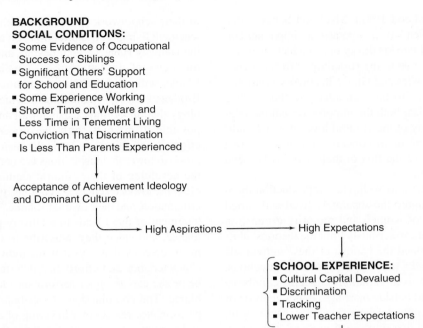

FIGURE 10.3   Basic Dynamics Involved in Lowering of Aspirations among the Brothers

Source: Based on MacLeod (1987), pp. 42ff.

subculture provides only an imperfect haven from the shame of failure in school, shame rooted in the fact that the wider society values success in school. MacLeod (1987) stated that "the mechanisms of social reproduction" are "well hidden," and thus these adolescents partially blame themselves for their predicament. The Hallway Hangers also resort to racism as a convenient scapegoat. Neither of these interpretations by them, however, results in a full and accurate understanding of their situation or in a radical consciousness on the part of the Hangers. In the final analysis, the conditions that perpetuate their lower-class position are repeated. The basic process leading to leveled aspirations among the Hallway Hangers is laid out in Figure 10.4.

LABOR MARKET THEORIES OF EARNINGS INEQUALITY

In contrast to the theories already discussed, labor market theories of inequality are derived principally from economics and focus narrowly on explanations for income and earnings differences. Some of these are based on rather old explanations of the working of the marketplace, while others are quite different. The treatment that follows is general and aimed at drawing out the core elements of the approaches. What is immediately appealing about these theories is that they make the detailed process of inequality more testable. Whereas it might be extremely difficult to satisfactorily test a theory of inequality based on the

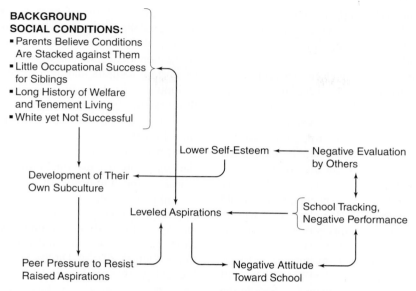

FIGURE 10.4   Basic Dynamics Involved in Leveled Aspirations among the Hallway Hangers

Source: Based on MacLeod (1987), pp. 23ff.

functional necessity of inequality, for example, it is possible to see what the effects of various kinds of human capital investment, such as education and training, are on an individual's earnings.

Neoclassical Labor Market Theory

This theory is based on the assumptions that: (1) a relatively free and open market exists in which individuals compete for positions; (2) position in that market depends heavily on the individual's efforts, abilities, experience, training, or human capital; and (3) there are automatic mechanisms that operate in the marketplace to ensure that imbalances between one's input (human capital) and one's rewards (wages) are corrected in a way that restores balance.

In a society in which free competition exists, persons who contribute equal resources in the society receive a wage commensurate with their contributions. The more resources one offers and the greater one's value to any potential employer, the greater the demand for one's services and the higher the wages (Thurow 1969;

Leftwich 1977). Thus, factors such as one's education, training, skills, and intelligence are productivity components that are crucial in explaining an individual's wages. These are the elements that must be changed if one's wages are to change (Thurow 1969, p. 26). An extreme version of this argument would assume that individuals are free to choose the amounts of their human capital investments such as education, training, and so on, as well as their occupations. Thus, African Americans and women might be considered to have lower levels of income than White men because they have invested less in education and have less or interrupted work experience (Gordon 1972; Mincer and Polachek 1974). The ultimate result is "that you take out what you put in" (Okun 1975, p. 41). Of course, as we have seen, it often does not work that way.

In addition to one's resources, the demand for one's skills is also important and that demand depends on conditions in the marketplace. Demand for individuals, and therefore their wages, depends on the type of skills they possess and how talented they are at using them. In sum, it is the combination of supply and demand in the market and one's resources (human capital investments) that determines one's wages in the open marketplace (Cain 1976).

If an imbalance develops between what individuals contribute and the wages they receive, then supply and demand forces are set in motion to restore equilibrium in the market. For example, if wages for teachers are too low, the job will be viewed as undesirable and the supply of qualified teachers will go down. As the supply of teachers shrinks, demand for teachers increases. If greater demand for quality teachers occurs, there should be an increase in the wages employers are willing to pay these workers. In this way, equilibrium is restored. If the opposite occurs—that is, individuals are paid too much for the resource(s) they offer—a large supply of potential workers will appear, too large for the demand for them in the market. In order to ensure getting jobs, they will lower the wages for which they are willing to work. With the lower wages, employment expands, thus leading to a clearing of the labor market and a balancing between supply and demand. Again, equilibrium is restored (Leftwich 1977, p. 76). So, in addition to assuming a competitive market, this approach assumes that automatic mechanisms operate in the market to regulate it toward equilibrium. This tendency toward equilibrium, according to some critics, implies that there is a basic harmony between employers and employees (Gordon 1972, p. 33). Figure 10.5 summarizes the basic elements in the neoclassical explanation of earnings inequality.

If one accepts this argument, then what must be done to reduce earnings inequities is to attack the problems of human capital investment and the choices and returns associated with such investment. Thus, solutions might stress more education and training opportunities as well as accurate and appropriate assessment of individuals' skills and economic payoffs for those skills.

The pure neoclassical model has some distinct limitations, two of which are noted here. First, it is more concerned with wage differentials than with occupational differences and thus is less equipped to deal with sex segregation, for example (Blau and Jusenius 1976). Second, it presents an image of a U.S. economy that is freely competitive and tending toward equilibrium. Like the scarcity and functional-importance factors of the Davis–Moore theory of inequality, this model argues that the level of one's human capital (i.e., how scarce one's talents are) and the demand for them in the market (i.e., their functional necessity) largely determine differences in earnings. Like the kind of society conjured up in the functional approach, Dahrendorf would consider the open, largely conflict-free society of neoclassical theory to be a utopia. It should be mentioned that most economists are aware that the real marketplace does not operate without flaws and imperfections, and that discrimination does limit the opportunities of some in the market.

Dual Labor Market Thesis

It has become increasingly obvious to some in recent years that explanations of income and earnings distribution which rely on images of the

Open Competitive Market
+
Differential Free Investment in Personal Human Capital
+
Differential Supply of and Demand for Positions

↓

Earnings Inequality

FIGURE 10.5 Basic Elements in the Generation of Earnings Inequality according to Neoclassical Theory

free market and investments in human capital as the primary or sole factors in understanding economic inequalities are inadequate. Critics of the orthodox view assert that the market simply does not work the way that pure traditionalists say it does. Rather, the major reasons for inequality lie deep within the workings and cleavages of the capitalist economy.

A number of observations about continuing difficulties in the market have made many analysts skeptical about the orthodox approach and its potential effectiveness in reducing inequality. Among those observations are (1) the continuation of poverty; (2) continued income inequality; (3) the ineffectiveness of educational and training programs in reducing inequality; (4) discrimination against minorities in the labor market; (5) the power of labor unions, employer monopolies, and government intervention to weaken the competitive market; and (6) extensive alienation among workers, suggesting that the competitive, equilibrating economy is not working as smoothly as the orthodox model suggests (Cain 1976).

In the face of these alleged anomalies in the economy, some have tried to devise alternative explanations for continued poverty and income inequality. One of the more prominent of these is the dual labor market approach. Briefly, this thesis consists of four basic assumptions: (1) the private economy is split into two major sectors; (2) the labor market is similarly divided into two parts; (3) mobility, earnings, and other outcomes for workers are contingent on place in the labor market; and (4) a systematic relationship exists between race/ethnicity, gender, and position in the labor market (Hodson and Kaufman 1982).

On observing labor market processes in the ghetto, a number of economists came to the conclusion that two markets exist which operate by different rules. In one market, the tasks seem to be menial, not intellectually demanding, and are associated with poor working conditions and low wages. The occupations are isolated and have no internal structures or career system. In other words, they appear to be qualitatively distinct from other kinds of jobs in the market.

Because of the poor nature of the work, workers in this **secondary labor market** often quit their jobs, which only encourages the belief that these jobs are unstable, and that performing these types of jobs to the exclusion of others encourages instability in the habits of the workers themselves. This secondary labor market is set off from the **primary labor market** in which jobs are characterized by stability, high wages, good working conditions, greater degree of internal job structure, and unionization (Gordon 1972, pp. 43–48). In the real economy, of course, the labor market is not neatly divided into only two parts. Many jobs possess a mixture of primary and secondary characteristics.

Dual labor market theorists contend that, to a large extent, the primary labor market is limited to a certain sector of the private economy, sometimes called the **core** or **monopoly sector**, whereas the secondary labor market exists primarily within the **peripheral** or **competitive sector** of the private economy. In the monopoly sector, firms tend to be large and capital intensive, with high productivity per worker, and operate in large, often national and international, markets. Examples of firms in this sector would be those in the automobile, railroad, steel, electric, and airlines industries. On the other hand, firms within the competitive sector are much smaller, more labor intensive, and more local in their markets, with low productivity per worker, and not in control of any stable product market (O'Connor 1973, pp. 13–16). Examples of firms in this sector would be local restaurants, gas stations, grocery stores, garages, and clothing stores.

Despite the fact that conditions are generally worse for the workers in the secondary market and competitive sector, the tasks performed, though often irregular, are needed in the economy. Consequently, an effort was made to stabilize this market and sector; employers worked toward creating a separate market for these workers and these kinds of jobs. Some workers are in that sector even though they may have the characteristics that would qualify them for work in the primary market. Blacks and women, for example, have been disproportionately represented in the secondary market because of statistical discrimination and other reasons (Gordon 1972, pp. 46–47). Secondary workers were then left with little alternative but to work as part of the secondary labor market in the competitive sector.

Historically, the movement toward separate markets has been strengthened by (1) the desirability of retaining individuals who have been carefully trained in large established firms, (2) the presence of unions in some and not other industries, and (3) federal legislation. The trends toward greater job specificity, more on-the-job training in the primary job sector, and the power of custom within given firms have tended to increase the structuring of the internal labor markets within the primary job sector, setting it off more from the unstructured, noncareer-patterned secondary job sector (Doeringer and Piori 1971). Recent analysis of multiyear census data suggests that the degree of labor segmentation has increased, but largely due to an influx of immigrant labor, the decline in the influence of unions and an increase in the size of the contingent labor force. These factors have become at least as important, if not more so, than race and sex as determinants of labor market placement. Nonunionized Hispanic immigrant labor and contingent workers have become significant sources of low-wage labor for employers (Hudson 2007).

The existence of segmentation in the U.S. economy, especially in the form of a dual labor market, helps to perpetuate income inequality and poverty. Changes in the occupational structure and a growing immigrant labor force have intensified the dual character of the labor market and the continued tendency for minorities to be overrepresented within the secondary market. Despite conclusions by early architects of dual labor market theory that there is little movement out of the secondary labor market once in it, national data show that between the 1970s and late 1990s, most workers who began their careers in the secondary market had left it by the time they were in their 30s. However, the rate of exodus was much lower for minorities and women than it was for White men. Greater concentration of minorities and women in the secondary job market is a significant source of earnings inequality (Wang 2008).

Figure 10.6 brings together several of the core elements of the dual labor market argument on the factors that produce earnings inequality. Notice that in sharp contrast to the neoclassical explanation which stresses the characteristics of *persons,* the dual labor market theory focuses on the importance of *impersonal* labor markets and economic sectors in producing inequality.

Being in either the secondary or primary labor market has an initial impact on an individual's wages. But once in either the secondary or primary market, the determinants of earnings vary. In the primary market, earnings are affected by seniority and whether a person is in a career job hierarchy. O'Connor (1973) stressed that in the monopoly sector, wages and prices are not primarily determined by market forces; prices are largely administered since the corporations in this sector usually have considerable market power. With respect to wages, when the demand for labor

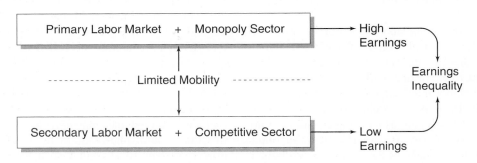

FIGURE 10.6   The Effect of the Dual Private Economy on Earnings

is low and the supply is large, monopoly industries, because of their attractiveness to workers, can choose from the oversupply at the going rate.

In the competitive sector—that is, for most of those in the secondary labor market—wages are largely determined by market forces. Since the workers in this market are generally considered homogeneous in nature and have little, if any, union power, their wages are primarily the product of supply and demand forces. A large supply of lower-skilled immigrants, for example, would depress wages. But if the supply of labor is particularly small and the demand consequently high, workers' earnings are likely to go up because they will work more. Thus, the differences in earnings among those in the secondary labor market are probably due more to differences in the hours worked than to variations in education or experience (Osterman 1975). But because of the homogeneous interchangeable nature of the individuals in this market, wage differences are not likely to be great (Gordon 1972, pp. 50–51). Moreover, in the competitive sector, the raging competition among firms and the poorer and more unstable economic environment in which they operate often mean that they are less able to raise wages compared with the large firms in the monopoly sector that are relatively free from the extremes of competition (Bluestone 1977).

In the higher-ranking jobs in the primary market, education, age, and hours worked are important, whereas in the lower tier in the primary market, education is important although less so than in the higher jobs. Age and hours worked are also significant for the lower-ranking jobs in the primary market, as is race. In sum, the human capital argument seems much more viable in the primary than in the secondary market. Osterman's conclusion (1975) is that "an individual's income is greatly affected by the segment of the labor market in which the individual works" (p. 21).

In applying the dual market theory to poverty, the central conclusion is that many individuals are poor not because they are unemployed or do not participate in the economy but because of the way in which they participate in the economy. Not only are they *excluded* from certain kinds of activities and organizations, they are *included* in the economic structure at particular places because "they have economic value where they are and hence . . . there are groups interested, not only in resisting the elimination of poverty, but in actively seeking its perpetuation" (Piori 1977, pp. 95–96).

Many of the notions of dual market theory have found their way into a radical denunciation of orthodox theory. Basically, the radical argument is that capitalists have found it beneficial to segment the labor market and to stratify the working class so as to prevent its unification and to stabilize the labor market. During the late nineteenth century, the potential threat of a unified working class, and the increasing evidence of their militancy, had to be met by employers. To deal with this problem, argue Reich and associates (1977), employers actively promoted labor market segmentation in order to effectively split up what might otherwise have been a unified workforce. Public prejudices against some groups were one device used to encourage divisiveness within the working class. Those most readily looked down on by unions and the public—namely, women, Blacks, and youth—could more easily be used to fill less-desirable jobs. Stereotypes and dislikes of these groups were used to further segment the labor market (p. 111).

Assessment of Labor Market Theories

In assessing these labor market theories, it is clear that there are inadequacies in the orthodox explanation. Perhaps the most valuable contribution of the dual labor market approach to understanding economic inequality is its emphasis on a textured economy and labor market—that is, on its insistence that these are not homogeneous in nature and that this texture affects rewards for workers (Hodson and Kaufman 1982). The orthodox approach is most likely to be accepted when it incorporates some of the elements of dual labor market theory and information about imperfections in the market. Some evidence appears to support segmentation arguments, as was indicated in our discussion, whereas other critics (e.g., Cain

1976) do not see it as being able to replace orthodox theory.

Dual labor market theory has its evident weaknesses. Within broad sectors, there is a large variety of firms. How are differences among them to be explained? The dual labor market theory does not explain differences and sex segregation within each market and differentiation within the female sector (Blau and Jusenius 1976). Moreover, within each sector of the economy, there are firms that cater to both the primary and secondary labor markets. Evidence suggests that the tight link assumed by the approach between the primary labor market and core sector on the one hand, and the secondary labor market and peripheral sector on the other, is much looser than suggested by the model.

Finally, splitting the private economy into two parts results in too coarse an image of the real economy within which there are continuous variations among organizations along a variety of dimensions (Baron and Bielby 1984; Hodson 1984). It also ignores changes occurring in economies *within* and *between* nations. As U.S. corporations increasingly enter a world market involving highly competitive adversaries who may concurrently enter the U.S. market, they have reacted by downsizing and streamlining, which has lowered job stability for many employees. In a sense, what may have been a monopoly sector becomes more competitive, and those employed in those organizations become more vulnerable to fluctuations in economies. In essence, the primary job market takes on some of the characteristics traditionally associated with the secondary market: lower wages, lower job stability, and less unionization. This blurs the distinctions between monopoly/competitive sectors and primary/secondary markets. In addition, the recent influx of small, entrepreneurial firms into the economy also makes a dual market perspective appear to be too crude to capture the richer and changing texture of the U.S. economy. Despite weaknesses, however, the dual market and radical perspectives have properly forced us to address the role of market and economy variations in generating inequality.

THEORIES OF GLOBAL INEQUALITY

The major explanations that have been given for economic inequality between nations mirror those that have been offered to account for poverty and inequality in general. That is, inequality is said to exist because the parties (1) have simply not had enough time to catch up with each other; (2) differ in motivation and values related to economic success; and/or (3) differ in the chances they have for success, given their different circumstances or places in the social structure. The evolutionary/ stage, psychological/value, and dependency/ world system theories address each of these respective arguments.

Briefly, the older evolutionary perspective contends that economic progress for a nation requires that it pass through a set of stages brought about by processes at work within the society. In other words, progress is largely a matter of time. For example, Rostow (1960) suggested that societies go through five major stages in their movement toward development. In each stage, certain events must occur in order for a society to move on to the next phase. His fifth and final stage, "the age of mass consumption" is clearly modeled after the United States, which is viewed as the most fully developed nation. Cruder versions of this approach are found in earlier evolutionary theories that portray development as an almost automatic and universal process which comes with increasing population and progressive integration within the society. Leaving aside the ideological issues surrounding this perspective, Rostow's theory, like others in this school of thought, has been heavily criticized as being ahistorical, Western-biased, and weak in its consideration of how the ties between countries affect development and inequality.

A second set of theories, which developed during the 1950s to the early 1970s, stresses that a particular set of values has to be present in a significant proportion of the population for economic progress to occur. Countries differ in economic standing because their dominant values and traditions differ. Psychologist David McClelland (1961), for example, emphasized the importance of need-for-achievement as an individual value, and sociologists Inkeles and Smith (1974) argued that several values were important for a "modern man" personality to develop. Among the listed characteristics of a modern man are (1) a readiness for new experience, (2) a democratic orientation, (3) a belief in human efficacy, (4) faith in science and technology, and (5) a disposition to form and hold opinions. Traditional values such as superstition, ethnocentrism, fatalism, pride, dignity, and modesty are viewed as cultural barriers to development (Foster 1973). In these theories, the significance of structure and history for economic development pales next to the importance placed upon personality and values.

Both of the above **modernization theories** assume that there is a fundamental and irreconcilable conflict between tradition and modernity, and that the gap between them must be bridged if development is to occur. The idea that the two can coexist or aid each other is foreign to the logic of these explanations. By and large, these modernization theories also imply a narrow view of development and modernity, often implicitly offering the United States as the model of development. But it is possible that variations in development and national wealth may occur for reasons not suggested by these explanations. Dependency and world system perspectives offer such reasons, and were developed to counter the modernization arguments of evolutionary and psychological theories. Rather than emphasizing *internal* causes of economic development, these perspectives focus on *external* factors, the relative positions of nations in the world economy and polity (Sanderson 2005; Lee, Nielsen, and Alderson 2007; Kaya 2010).

The core arguments of **dependency** and **world system theories** share much in common, and consequently, they will be treated together. Advocates posit that the capitalist world economy forms an expanding network of unequal relations between nations. The most economically advanced countries constitute a "core" that controls the world economy. The "periphery" nations are underdeveloped, and through exploited labor provide natural resources for the core. The third component of the world economy is the "semiperiphery" that structurally lies between the core and periphery and performs a stabilizing function in the world economy (Wallerstein 1974, 1979). These theories state that the principal reason some countries are underdeveloped and unequal to others is because they are linked to major nations through ties of exploitation.

The core dominates the periphery. Historically, core nations became dominant because of their protective trade policies, conquest, and economic support from the state. This allowed the core to siphon off natural and human resources from peripheral nations, many of which had been colonies of core nations. Dominance in the world economy is principally established through state control and legislation, trade policies, and economic penetration of poorer countries. While the periphery provides resources to the core, the core, in turn, uses peripheral nations as markets for its manufactured goods. In other words, each part of the world economy plays a particular role. Since a majority in the periphery nations are non-White while most in the core are White, the economic inequality that results takes on racial overtones.

The dependency and exploitation of peripheral nations goes through several phases during which dependency deepens and exploitative ties strengthen, resulting in a virtually permanent state of underdevelopment and subordinate position in the world economy (Frank 1969). In the first phase of dependency development, core nations return to sell finished products to peripheral nations, discouraging the development of local, indigenous manufacturers. In the second phase, peripheral nations borrow capital from foreign banks and transnational corporations to build capital-intensive factories that produce goods for the local market. To create these factories, heavy machinery must be purchased from core sources. This keeps dependency alive as more capital flows from the periphery to the core. In the third phase, the lower labor costs in peripheral countries attract transnational corporations that use the labor power in less developed nations to assemble products for export to developed nations. Lower labor costs, weaker unions, fewer environmental restrictions, and beneficial tax packages from host governments make movement into peripheral countries attractive to many corporations. Pharmaceuticals, electronic equipment, and clothing are among the products created (Ward 1993). These selective investments foster uneven development and greater income inequality within poorer nations. Because of these relationships, foreign investment is viewed as a drag on the economic growth of peripheral countries. According to this perspective, "these countries are trapped in relations of unequal world-economic exchange and world-political oppression" (Herkenrath, et al. 2005, p. 371). The advance of one set of countries means the decline of others.

Since the 1970s, world system and dependency theorists have had a major impact in many social sciences because their arguments touch on economic, political, and social relationships in the world context (Sanderson 2005). Their roots in Marxian and radical theories made world system and dependency theories popular and compatible with the criticisms hurled at traditional modernization theories. But world system and dependency theories have also been criticized for, among other things, ignoring the role of women and gender inequality (Ward 1993), and assuming that core and peripheral positions are stable and permanent. Many countries that had been in the periphery have moved up into the semiperiphery (Sanderson 2005). This suggests that, in addition, world system theorists have paid too little attention to variations among peripheral nations themselves (Cardoso 1977; Herkenrath et al. 2005). Finally, they have also not given full due to the role of internal factors, such as the state and past

history, when explaining the degree of inequality and development in peripheral countries (Lee, Nielsen, and Alderson 2007; Kaya 2010).

The prominence of world system and dependency theories initiated a wave of studies attempting to test their central propositions. Among the most important of these propositions is that foreign investment and corporate penetration into peripheral nations increases their dependency and income inequality, and slows their economic development. Trade flows and foreign investment are viewed by world system theorists as the most important causes of maintaining inequality in the world economic system (Kaya 2010). And yet, the research on this matter over the last several decades has yielded mixed results, suggesting that the relationships involved are not as simple as the theory argues. Some studies have found that foreign corporate penetration, foreign debt dependence, and export patterns of concentration are related to greater income inequality and slow development in the peripheral nation (e.g., Bornschier and Ballmer-Cao 1979; Stack and Zimmerman 1982; Kentor 1998). Other studies have found that foreign penetration appears to have little, if any, effect on inequality and development, or that its effects depend on the reaction of the peripheral government to it and whether one is considering short-term or long-term effects (cf., Sanderson 2005; Lee, Nielsen, and Alderson 2007; Kaya 2010). These variations in findings also appear to be partially due to the kinds of "foreign-investment" measures used (Bornschier and Chase-Dunn 1985) Needless to say, the argument over the effects of inter-nation economic relationships on income inequality and development needs more careful specification and are far from settled.

Summary

The focus in this and the previous chapter has been on general explanations of inequality. Each of the theories covered views the concept of inequality in a different way and is suggestive of different measures of it. Nevertheless, all of them are concerned with the distribution of scarce resources in society, principally political power, economic power, or both. One of the primary values in looking at the classic theorists is that each of them suggests different ways of viewing inequality and makes us sensitive to different aspects of it.

Several of the theories covered in this and the previous chapter have basic elements in common. Most generally, one can see the influence of Marxian thought in social reproduction theory and dual labor market theory. The role of the social construction of categories in producing inequality resonates with Weber's discussion of status and subjective side of social inequality. On the more conservative side, Durkheim's functionalist tradition has been carried through most fully in neoclassical economic theory and the Davis–Moore theory.

All of these theories organize the phenomenon in diverse ways and evoke different images of how to view society. Some of these, such as the functionalist and labor market theories, assume a society that is largely free, competitive, and lacking in organized constraints and conflict, while others, most notably social reproduction and dual labor market theories, view society as consisting of constraining structures and systemic conflict between groups. Because this is so, each of the theories provides us with alternative tools and concepts with which to approach the study of inequality; together, they anticipate the kinds of questions and issues that significantly can be raised about inequality.

While each of the explanations discussed in this chapter is distinct in many ways, this does not mean that they cannot complement or build on each other. For example, social constructionists suggest how minority and majority groups come to be labeled and evaluated in society. The labels given to groups, in turn, affect their treatment by educational, political, and other institutions. This treatment, as explained by reproduction theories, helps to account for patterns of social and economic capital within groups. Finally, it also serves to solidify inequalities such as those found in neighborhoods, occupations, and labor markets.

Critical Thinking

1. What is wrong, if anything, with an argument which says that rewards are simply a reflection of one's skills and credentials as well as the importance of one's job?

2. Is it possible to categorize people without ranking them? If so, how? If not, why not?

3. What role do you think parent-child relationships play in the reproduction of social and economic inequality?

4. It has been argued that networks of interactions between countries and individuals have become faster, more complex, and widespread (Herkenrath et al. 2005). Will this lead to more or less inequality, or will it have no effect on it?

Web Connections

As suggested in this chapter, Pierre Bourdieu was one of the most influential social reproduction theorists. A summary of his ideas can be found at http://wikipedia.org/wiki/Pierre_Bourdieu.

Immanuel Wallerstein is a principal architect of world systems theory. Read how his ideas developed at http://iwallerstein.com/intellectual-itinerary/.

Film Suggestions

Inside Job (2010) A documentary on the mechanisms in economic, financial and political policies that led to the 2008-2009 economic crisis.

Waiting for Superman (2010) A documentary that follows students through their education and demonstrates failures within the public school system.

CHAPTER 11

The Impact of Inequality on Personal Life Chances

A large income is the best recipe for happiness I ever heard of.

JANE AUSTEN (1775–1817)

There would not be much point in studying inequality if it did not affect individuals and society. Inequality is an important subject because, ultimately, its existence affects the day-to-day lives of people. The social positions that individuals occupy help to determine who they are, what they think and do, where they are going, and what happens to them. Close your eyes for a moment and imagine yourself as a very poor or extremely wealthy person. What do you see? As a person in either position, how do you feel about life in general and yourself in particular? How do you view the future and your prospects?

Most basically, social inequality affects the life chances of individuals. But as Figure 11.1 suggests, its effects are far-reaching, reverberating outward from individuals themselves to their immediate families and the wider society. Chapters 12 and 13 will address some aspects of the *social* effects of inequality, beginning with a discussion of its relationship to the broader issues of crime, and proceeding to examinations of environmental justice, social trust, and social movements. The present chapter will focus on the relationship of inequality to *individuals'* chances for physical and mental health, adequate food, and shelter. More specifically, we will see how socioeconomic status, gender, and/or minority status affect personal lives at the most basic level.

BASIC LIFE CHANCES: PHYSICAL HEALTH

There is nothing more basic to life than physical health, and it is evident that individuals rate their own health status differently, depending on their race and income. Generally, Blacks, Hispanics, and American Indians are more likely than Whites to rate their own health as only fair

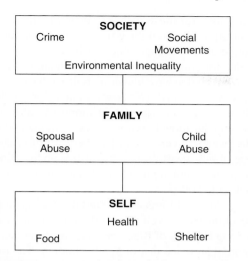

FIGURE 11.1 A Sampling of the Range of Effects of Social Inequality

or poor, and individuals who are poor are more than twice as likely as nonpoor persons to consider their health this way. Similarly, a slightly greater percentage of women than men classify their health as below average (see Figure 11.2).

Interestingly, this self-assessment is a good predictor of a person's actual health, and, indeed, minorities and poor individuals are worse off on a wide variety of health measures (National Center for Health Statistics 2010). The life ex-

pectancies at birth of Blacks and Whites, males and females, have varied historically, and these differences are expected to continue in the twenty-first century. In 2006, average life expectancy for all Americans was almost 78, lower than that of most other industrial countries, including Japan, Australia, Canada, and most western European countries (National Center for Health Statistics 2010). The life expectancy of Whites at birth was 5 years longer than that of Blacks, and within each racial group, those with lower incomes were expected to live a shorter time. Across the country, many counties in Appalachia, the Southeast, and the southern Midwest experienced a decline in life expectancy between 1983 and 1999, while other counties had increases in life expectancy. By and large, the former tend to be poorer and to have higher proportions of Blacks. The divergence in life expectancy is partly a result of "stagnation or increase in mortality among the worst-off segment of the population" (Ezzati et al. 2008, p. 7). Most of the increases in life expectancy during this period were among those with more than a high school education (Meara, Richards, and Cutler 2008). Generally, women live longer than men, but the life expectancy of Black women is closer to that of White men than to White women (Meara, Richards, and Cutler 2008).

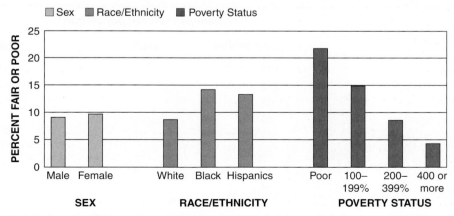

FIGURE 11.2 Percent of Respondents Assessing Health Status as Fair or Poor, by Sex, Race/Ethnicity, and Poverty Status: 2009.

Source: National Center for Health Statistics, *Health, United States, 2010.* Hyattsville, MD. Table 56, p. 225.

Differences in mortality rates parallel the discrepancies in life expectancies, and the differences between socioeconomic groups are especially strong among *urban* residents (Hayward, Pienta, and McLaughlin 1997). Moreover, it is not only differences in income that affect mortality, but the kind and variety in sources of income that have an impact. Individuals with assets and income from a variety of sources have lower mortality risks. This may be due in large part to the greater sense of stability that is gained from having a secure economic base (Krueger et al. 2003).

Mortality rates from different causes also vary by status. As Table 11.1 indicates, death rates in 2007 for major diseases varied by race and ethnicity. With the exception of suicide and respiratory disease, rates were higher for Blacks than for other groups. Homicide and HIV rates were especially high among Blacks compared to other groups. Interestingly, the death rates for heart disease, cancer, respiratory disease, and stroke were lowest among Hispanics.

The years of life lost to these long-term or **chronic illnesses** are also greater for Blacks. Five-year survival rates for cancer in general are higher for Whites than Blacks. Death rates from all causes for those with less than a high school education are about three times higher than those found among higher-educated individuals. This holds for both men and women, although men in general tend to have higher mortality rates regardless of the cause (National Center for Health Statistics 2007). The gap in mortality rates between educational groups increased at the end of the twentieth century, in part because of greater use of new heart disease treatments and declines in smoking among more highly educated individuals (Elo 2009).

Status differences in mortality rates extend to children as well. The infant mortality rate among children of Black mothers, for example, is more than twice that of White children. The rate for Hispanic children is lower than it is for either of these groups. For all groups, children of mothers with lower educations have higher infant mortality rates. In 2004, among the major racial/ethnic groups, the greatest discrepancy in rates existed between White children whose mothers had more than a high school education and Black children whose mothers did not complete a high school education (4.2 vs. 14.4; National Center for Health Statistics 2007).

Table 11.1 Age-Adjusted Death Rates for Major Diseases, Suicide, and Homicide, by Race and Hispanic Origin: 2007

	Rate per 100,000 population*		
	Non-Hispanic Whites	**Blacks**	**Hispanics**
Heart disease	191	247	136
Cancer	182	216	116
Stroke	41	60	33
Respiratory disease	45	28	18
Unintentional injuries	43	37	30
Diabetes	20	43	29
HIV disease	2	17	4
Suicide	14	5	6
Homicide	3	21	7

*All rates rounded to nearest whole.

Source: National Center for Health Statistics, *Health, United States, 2009*. Updated Trend Tables, November 2010. Hyattsville, MD. Table 26.

Health and Status

The social and economic *context* in which lower socioeconomic individuals live has a causal effect on their rates of mortality and morbidity that is independent of the effects of the *personal* status of the individuals. Neighborhoods with high unemployment and poverty, for example, have higher rates of suicide among both Blacks and Whites than more affluent neighborhoods (Kubrin and Wadsworth 2009; Denney et al. 2009). On an individual level, the lower socioeconomic status of individuals also contributes to their earlier mortality and probability of sickness. They tend to have higher rates of victimization and lower rates of preventive care. They also possess less knowledge of and access to newer treatments for HIV/AIDS, helping to account for the higher rates of HIV mortality among Blacks (Rubin, Colen, and Link 2010). The link between status and morbidity is causal; lower status is more likely to lead to sickness than sickness is to lead to a lower status (Warren 2009; National Center for Health Statistics 2010).

Key to understanding this relationship is identifying the significant mechanisms among lower-status groups that lead to illness. Health-related factors such as smoking, poor diets, lack of exercise, and obesity are more prevalent among lower socioeconomic groups (Pampel, Krueger, and Denney 2010). Obesity rates are especially high among minority women, and the rate of smoking is highest among Black men. A variety of explanations, all of which derive from low status position, have been given for the higher rates of these behaviors among lower socioeconomic groups: (1) higher stress leading to smoking, etc. as a means of coping; (2) greater fatalism about their longevity; (3) lifestyle differences between status groups; (4) less knowledge about the health effects of some behaviors; (5) weaker sense of efficacy and self-control; (6) lower incomes creating fewer opportunities for exercise, etc.; (7) poor neighborhood influences; and (8) weaker social networks and support (Elo 2009; Pampel, Krueger, and Denney 2010). Finally, compared to Whites or the nonpoor, minority and lower-status individuals generally experience more traumatic events in their lives that affect their health, and are more likely to be limited in their daily activities because of chronic health problems (Hatch and Dohrenwend 2007).

Differences in health between socioeconomic groups are also affected by variations in the broader historical cultural and social conditions experienced by different generations. Rates of disability, depression, and self-assessed health, as well as changes in them, vary between older and newer cohorts, but the sex and race inequalities in most of these rates persist across cohorts (Yang and Lee 2009). The findings of a study of almost 7,000 adults over a 15-year period show that the health of Blacks deteriorates more rapidly over time than that of Whites, and that Blacks more often than Whites increasingly view their health as poorer as they get older (Ferraro and Farmer 1996; see also Yang and Lee 2009). By both objective and subjective standards, the health of Blacks declines more dramatically with age. A recent study of 8,231 Black and White respondents found that middle-aged Blacks have significantly higher rates than their White counterparts of both fatal chronic (e.g., hypertension, diabetes, stroke) and nonfatal (e.g., asthma, foot/leg, kidney, ulcers, vision, depression) diseases.

The poor health disproportionately experienced by Blacks is a continuation of racial differences in health that exist all through the life cycle. Moreover, it appears that it is mostly these racial groups' differing socioeconomic positions (which are strongly linked to their race) that account for their differences in health (Hayward et al. 2000). Greater rates of single-parent family structures, and the poorer educational and occupational statuses of Black male parents, depress their children's own statuses when they become adults, which in turn, foster their higher mortality rates (Warner and Hayward 2006). Both current low socioeconomic status and poor childhood socioeconomic conditions have a negative effect on being able to physically function as an adult (Haas 2008; Huquet, Kaplan, and Feeny 2008). Continuous **economic hardship** throughout one's life cycle appears to increase the chances for being functionally disabled, having a chronic condition, and experiencing recurrent physical symptoms (Kahn and Pearlin 2006). Proportionately, Blacks lose about twice as many years of life before age 65 as Whites because of chronic conditions. Of those born in 1940, only about 61 percent of Black males were still alive in 1990, compared to 81 percent of White males. Similar discrepancies existed among females.

All these findings make it clear that health is related to *individual* socioeconomic status. But as noted earlier, the health of individuals is also related to the socioeconomic status of the *community* as a whole and to the degree of income inequality in a *society,* independent of the effects of one's individual status. Communities with lower average incomes and higher unemployment rates report higher rates of chronic conditions (Robert 1998). The physical deterioration, environmental problems, and social disorder found in poorer neighborhoods, along with the fear that they create, play significant roles in the poorer self-assessments of health and higher rates of chronic disease conditions found among their residents (Ross and Mirowsky 2001). Frustration as a factor in health may be manifested in the finding that greater income and occupational inequality in a metropolitan area is related to higher suicide rates among Blacks in the United States (Burr, Hartman, and Matteson 1999).

In sum, there have been and continue to be distinct gaps in the health statuses of Blacks and Whites and between those in different socioeconomic groups, and in some areas the gap appears to have widened in recent years. Gender is also related to differences in health, but we know less about the factors related to women's health because most medical research has focused on men (Andersen 1997). In general, women live longer than men but suffer from more illnesses, some of which, such as arthritis, are related to their longer lifetimes (Read and Gorman 2010). Women have higher rates of disability; of acute conditions such as respiratory, infective, and digestive problems; and of most chronic conditions. Women over the age of 70 are more likely than older men to report difficulty in their daily activities. Their rates of acute conditions are typically 20

to 30 percent higher than those of men. Among chronic conditions, the rates for *nonfatal* varieties are especially higher for women. These include various digestive problems, anemias, arthritis, migraine headaches, urinary infections, and varicose veins. The rates for fatal chronic conditions are higher for men.

Verbrugge (1999) suggested that differences in work and leisure risks, consistent health care, lifestyles and role behaviors of the sexes, and proactive health care, are important reasons for these gender discrepancies in health. Riskier behaviors and greater exposure to serious violence contribute to men's lower life expectancy. On the positive side, women tend to engage in healthier lifestyles and seek more preventive care than men. Women are also more attentive to their bodies and therefore more sensitive to symptoms. They take more continuous care of their health problems than men do. Finally, women are better at reporting minor health problems, which might help minimize the seriousness of those problems later in life and help account for their higher life expectancy.

On the other hand, the lower occupational and earnings status of women raises their vulnerability to illness, as do the greater family stresses and intimate violence they face (Read and Gorman 2010). However, even when their initial health is the same, women become healthier and have fewer physical limitations the longer and more continuously they are employed than women who are either intermittently employed or not in the labor force. Those who are recently nonemployed are the least healthy (Anson and Anson 1987; Pavalko and Smith 1999). In addition to employment itself, the number of work hours also affects health among men. Working more than 40 hours per week has a positive impact on their health, but when their wives work longer than 40 hours per week, husbands' health suffers. In contrast, long work hours by their husbands do not harm wives' health, nor does the number of their own work hours affect their health (Stolzenberg 2001).

Finally, increases in earnings are positively related to health, but the effects of increases in *spousal* earnings appear to be different for men and women. A national longitudinal study suggests that, among married couples, an increase in wives' earnings has a positive impact on their health but raises the chances of husbands dying, whereas the reverse was found for wives when husbands' earnings increase (McDonough et al. 1999; Schnittker 2007). These results on the effects of work hours and earnings on health suggest that men are most likely to suffer when their wives become more involved and successful in the world of work, a sphere which, traditionally, has been more of a man's province.

Use of Health Services

Given the differences in health conditions between groups, one would expect to find parallel differences in the preventive use of physicians and other health care providers. There is little disagreement that there are significant differences in the quality of care received by nonpoor Whites on the one hand, and the poor and minorities on the other (Institute of Medicine 2002; Good et al. 2003; Schnittker, Pescosolido, and Croghan 2005). Indeed, Black and Hispanic mothers are less likely to have had a Pap smear in the last year, and less likely to have had prenatal care when pregnant, but more likely to die during pregnancy or while giving birth. Minorities, the poor, and the uninsured are less likely to have a family physician whom they see on a regular basis, and are less likely to have visited a physician's office in the last year. Poor children are also less likely to have received a full set of vaccinations. Unmet dental needs are more likely among the poor and minorities (National Center for Health Statistics 2010). Among the consequences of lower rates of preventive care among the poor and minorities are greater numbers of emergency-room visits and higher rates of hospitalizations that might have been avoided had preventive care been taken.

There is no widespread agreement on a single reason as to why the poor and minorities receive less than adequate health care. Perhaps it is simply that those in lower socioeconomic positions choose not to seek care for their health problems. This does not appear to be the case, however. A national study found that, regardless of income or education, Blacks are no less likely to seek care than Whites, and may be even more inclined to do so. Nor do they expect less benefit from modern medicine. Disparities in care may result from a confluence of patient and physician expectations, beliefs, and behaviors (Schnittker, Pescosolido, and Croghan 2005). In their 2002 review of more than 100 studies, researchers at the Institute of Medicine concluded that while patient attitudes do not appear to be a major factor, "research suggests that healthcare providers' diagnostic and treatment decisions, as well as their feelings about patients, are influenced by patients' race or ethnicity" (Institute of Medicine 2002, p. 4). A 2004 Gallup poll reinforced this position, finding that 38 percent of Blacks felt that they were treated unfairly by physicians and health care facilities. Twenty-eight percent of Hispanics but only 17 percent of Whites agreed (McMurray 2004).

The argument that differences in care may be linked to beliefs and expectations held by health care professionals suggests a need for more research on the "culture of medicine." Most of the attention has been on patients' attitudes rather than on professionals' culture. But service involves both patient and physician. Stereotypes and general beliefs about racial and ethnic minorities and the poor held by physicians can affect diagnosis and treatment of patients. These orientations, in turn, have their source in racist ideologies that are widely dispersed in the larger society (Institute of Medicine 2002; Good et al. 2003). Despite the potential importance of cultural factors, however, it is most likely that a full explanation of disparities in health care service involves multiple causes.

Other explanations offered for disparities in health care treatment include lack of access and affordability. Kirby and Kaneda (2005) found that access to health care was negatively affected by living in a neighborhood where a disproportionate number of residents were poor, unemployed, and poorly educated. They speculate that such neighborhoods may create fear in residents, receive worse city services than others, and not be attractive to health care providers. Access to effective care may also be compromised by the difficulties that minority physicians have in arranging appropriate care for their patients (Hargraves, Stoddard, and Trude 2001).

High health care costs may also make doctor visits and other services too expensive for many, especially if they do not have health insurance. In 2007, almost 11 percent of poor individuals said that they did not get medical care during the previous year because of the cost involved, as did 29 percent of those who were both poor *and* uninsured (National Center for Health Statistics 2010). In 2009, almost 51 million persons, or 17 percent of the U.S. population, were without health insurance coverage of any kind. About one out of seven of these were under 18 years old. Not unexpectedly, minority persons and those lower in socioeconomic status were more likely to be uninsured (see Figure 11.3). Insurance coverage by private employers has declined since 2000, affecting both white-collar and blue-collar workers, and employees from all educational levels.

Between 2000 and 2006, 6.4 million employees lost their employer insurance (Bernstein and Shierholz 2008). But even those with insurance have seen premiums rise and co-payments, especially for prescription drugs, increase. High morbidity and mortality rates for lower socioeconomic groups are, in part, a reflection of the high cost of insurance. Lack of insurance means that a greater proportion of health care costs have to be borne by private individuals. In the late 1990s, for example, it was estimated that low-income elderly Medicare beneficiaries spent about half of their own incomes on health care (Gross et al. 1999). In 2007, 7 percent of adults said they did not get needed prescription drugs because of their high cost. The attempts by some U.S. citizens to get their drugs from Canada because of the lower prices there is one indicator of the financial strain that health care costs place on persons who have chronic problems.

In addition to cost factors, differential treatment is also affected by sex and gender. "When a woman seeks medical care from a physician, there are seventy-eight chances out of one hundred that

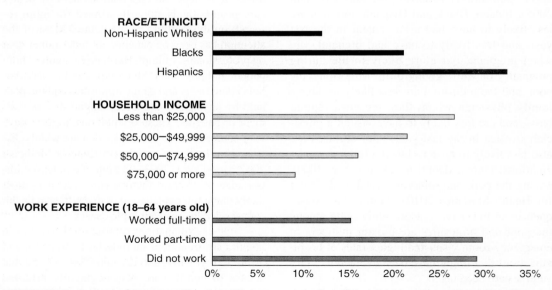

FIGURE 11.3   Percent of Persons without Health Insurance, by Race/Ethnicity, Income, and Work Experience: 2007

Source: U.S. Census Bureau, *Income, Poverty, and Health Insurance Coverage in the United States: 2009,* Current Population Reports, Series P-60, No. 238, September 2010, Table 8, p. 23.

the person she sees will be a man" (Andersen 1997, p. 216). Doctors tend to bring their expectations about gender roles and behaviors into their beliefs about health and illness. Male doctors often see illness and complaints among women as having a psychological rather than physiological origin. This suggests that women are not taken as seriously as men who come in with health problems (Andersen 1997).

The negative image of women's bodies and sexist beliefs about women's nature have a long history. In the nineteenth and early twentieth centuries, the female body was considered abnormal compared to the male body. Pregnancies, menstruation, menopause, and similar natural biological events were considered conditions to be "treated" and physicians generally thought that it was in women's nature to be sick (Ehrenreich and English 1981; Rothman 1984). Many biased attitudes continue to survive. An analysis of 27 general gynecology textbooks published since 1943 in the United States revealed that at least 50 percent of them emphasize that women are "destined to reproduce, nurture, and keep their husbands happy" (Scully and Bart 1981, p. 350). Many of these same texts also stress that women's primary interest in sex is for "procreation" rather than "recreation" and that most females are "frigid." The authors of this study concluded: "Gynecologists, our society's official experts on women, think of themselves as the woman's friend. With friends like that, who needs enemies?" (p. 354).

Class differences also have surfaced in the images of women's health and bodies. Historically, women of the upper class were thought to be more "civilized" and refined than those in the working and lower classes. As a result, they were thought of as more fragile and vulnerable, more susceptible to various maladies. Ehrenreich and English (1981) suggested that much of their sickness may have been due to the "sexuo-economic" relationship in their marriages. Essentially, these women were viewed as providing sexual and reproductive services in exchange for economic support from their working husbands. The ill-fitting, heavy clothes expected to be worn by "ladies" of the upper class were responsible, in fact, for many of the illness symptoms experienced by these women. But as a consequence of these "health" problems, middle- and upper-class women became a "client caste" to physicians, while poor women received virtually no medical attention. African American, American Indian, and working-class women were seen as having hearty constitutions in contrast to their upper-class counterparts and, therefore, in need of less attention. This stereotype provided a convenient rationale for giving medical care to those who had the financial resources to pay for it (Ehrenreich and English 1981; Wertz and Wertz 1981).

BASIC LIFE CHANCES: PSYCHOLOGICAL HEALTH

Consider for a moment how important physical health is in anyone's life. It affects one's chances in employment, social activities, travel, and relationships with others. Psychological health is also a basic element of a meaningful life, but are the chances for such health evenly distributed among groups in U.S. society? In 2009, over 45 million adults in the United States had some diagnosable mental illness, and 11 million of these had serious mental illnesses, disorders that substantially reduced their ability to carry out major activities. Of the latter, only 60 percent received mental health services (Substance Abuse and Mental Health Services Administration 2010). The unemployed, American Indians, and women had the highest rates of mental illness in general and serious mental illness in particular. The unemployed and women were most likely to have had a "major depressive episode" during the last year. Interestingly the rate of mental illness among Whites was higher than those for Blacks and Hispanics. Historically, the vast majority of those admitted to inpatient mental health facilities have been White and disproportionately poor. Men and members of minorities, especially Blacks, have been more likely than White women to be placed in state and county psychiatric facilities than in private or general hospitals.

Class, Race, Gender, and Distress

"Many studies have found a relationship between lower socioeconomic status and poor physical and mental health" (Latkin and Curry 2003, p. 34). But the nature of the relationship is complex and the direction of causality is a source of controversy. One argument is that individuals who become mentally ill lose their jobs and incomes, and are socially selected or "**drift**" into a lower class as a result. The alternative view is that the characteristics of a class position create conditions that foster mental health or illness. This is the **social causation** position. Both positions may apply in different circumstances and the nature of the relationship may vary depending on the specific illness in question (Miech et al. 1999).

But, as with physical health, there appears to be little question that economic conditions affect the degree of an individual's psychological distress and whether they receive treatment for it. To have "serious psychological distress" means that during the year one often had feelings of worthlessness, sadness, nervousness, or hopelessness (National Center for Health Statistics 2007). A 2005–2006 national survey of adults confirmed higher rates of "serious psychological distress" among minorities, women, and the poor. Individuals with incomes below the poverty line had rates that were four times those of persons with incomes that were at least 200 percent above the poverty level. These groups also have higher rates of depression and generalized anxiety. Not surprisingly, low income creates multiple hardships, such as the inability to pay monthly bills, which, in turn, foster depression (Heflin and Iceland 2009).

Similar relationships exist between feelings of distress and lower levels of education (Pleis, Benson, and Schiller 2003). Unemployment increases the amount of distress experienced by individuals, but reduces the rate of hospitalization, perhaps because of inability to meet the costs of treatment (Bye and Partridge 2003). In 2009, almost 43 percent of adults who needed mental health care said they did not seek it because they could not afford it (Substance Abuse and Mental Health Services Administration 2010).

Besides its economic impact on probability of treatment, how does living in poverty contribute to mental distress? We know that lower socioeconomic status contributes to an accumulation of physical health problems in later life, which is linked to depression (Miech and Shanahan 2000). At the individual level, family poverty has a long-term impact on children's later feelings of well-being as adults, because it strains relationships within the family, and depresses children's later educational and economic attainment (Sobolewski and Amato 2005). Living in a poor neighborhood also takes its toll on health. Latkin and Curry's study of over 800 respondents in disadvantaged neighborhoods in Baltimore uncovered a strong correlation between perceptions that a neighborhood had serious trash, theft, and vacancy problems and the degree of depression felt by respondents. They linked this effect to the high levels of stress and powerlessness along with weak networks of social support produced by living in such neighborhoods (Latkin and Curry 2003). The greater stress and lower support in some family types may also account for the higher rates of depression found among young adults who live in single-parent families. A smaller percentage of poor individuals live in two-parent families, and such intact families appear to have salutary effects for both the parents and the children. This may also help account for the higher rate of psychological distress among the poor (Simon 2002; Barrett and Turner 2005).

Race, ethnicity, and socioeconomic status appear to have their own effects on feelings of distress (Hughes and Thomas 1998). There are disagreements about explanations for the different rates between Blacks and Whites. Blacks, for example, are less likely than Whites to accept "genetic" factors or poor "family upbringing" as reasons. Perhaps this is because these explanations resemble past attacks that have been made on Black intelligence and family structure. Rather, Blacks are more likely to accept "chemical imbalances" or "life stresses" as causes of mental illness (Schnittker, Freese, and Powell 2000).

Evidence does indicate that life stresses are implicated in the psychological distress experienced by minorities. Hispanic and Black youth are less likely than Asian Americans or Whites to attend 4-year colleges and to participate fully in school activities. This situation together with their more troubled relationships with parents and/or peers symbolizes the greater difficulty of the route to adulthood that some minorities face. In turn, these conditions contribute to stronger feelings of depression among Hispanics and Blacks (Gore and Aseltine 2003). Indeed, lack of social support has been related to increased psychological distress, especially among Blacks (Lincoln, Chatters, and Taylor 2003). Moving into a middle-class occupation does not necessarily alleviate distress either, since their placement in racially segmented positions creates another source of stress because these individuals compare themselves to others around them who are primarily Whites. Having an occupation that has been labeled as a "Black job" decreases life satisfaction and increases feelings of sadness, hopelessness, and worthlessness (Forman 2003). As Black adults age, they also experience more traumatic losses than Whites, which further enhances the probability of depression (George and Lynch 2003). Data suggest that the relationship between race and feelings of well-being have not changed significantly in recent years (Hughes and Thomas 1998). One of the factors that appears to serve as a buffer against psychological distress for young Black adults is the extent to which they identify with their race. Strong racial identity appears to reduce the distress effects that arise from any racial discrimination young Black adults might experience (Sellers et al. 2003).

Like minorities and the poor, women also experience greater psychological distress when compared to men. Women are more likely to regularly experience feelings of hopelessness and worthlessness, and to report "serious psychological distress" during the previous month (Pleis, Benson, and Schiller 2003; Mandersheid and Henderson 2004). Clinically defined major depression and anxiety have been found to be two to three times more likely among women than among men, although the gap between them may be narrowing because of the recent increase in depression among young men.

It appears that a greater breadth of roles for women may be producing healthy results. There is evidence that individuals with multiple roles display a greater sense of psychological well-being, and that loss of roles is related to increased feelings of distress. People with multiple roles—for example, employee, spouse, and parent—tend to have better health than those with none of these roles (Verbrugge 1983). Sociologically, this makes sense since roles provide people with their identities. "The greater the number of identities held, the stronger one's sense of meaningful, guided existence. The more identities, the more 'existential security,' so to speak. A sense of meaningful existence and purposeful, ordered behavior are crucial to psychological health" (Thoits 1983, p. 175).

On the other hand, involvement and responsibility in *too many* areas can increase a person's feeling of loss of personal control and thereby increase stress and depression symptoms (Cleary and Mechanic 1983; Rosenfield 1989). Another factor probably contributing to the greater distress felt by housewives is their lesser power in the home compared to their employed husbands (Steil 1984). Employment brings power in the family, and distress may be a function of both lack of power and lack of multiple roles outside the family.

Obviously, some conditions and life events may help prepare and strengthen individuals for stressful conditions. Middle-class women who were in or approaching young adulthood during the Great Depression and who suffered serious economic loss because of it are today less likely to feel helpless and are more assertive and in control of their lives than middle-class women who did not experience such losses. Working-class women, on the other hand, who entered the Depression with fewer resources to begin with and experienced serious reductions in economic resources, feel less assertive and have a greater sense of being victimized (Elder and Liker 1982). What this suggests is that life's obstacles are more easily overcome and can even have long-term beneficial effects when those experiencing them have had, at the outset, ample resources on which to build a strong life.

Labeling, Diagnosis, and Inequality

General cultural images and expectations pertaining to different categories of people appear to be important for how mental illness symptoms are interpreted. Blacks are diagnosed most frequently with schizophrenia and at a much higher rate than Whites, whereas Whites are more likely to be labeled as having a bipolar disorder (Good et al. 2003; Neighbors et al. 2003). Some research suggests that cultural differences in language and symptom interpretation as well as physician biases enter into diagnoses of illness, although results about the exact effect of the clinician's race have been mixed (Institute of Medicine 2002). Clearly, interpretations of mental illness interact with racial, gender, and class characteristics of patients. The same symptoms in a White patient tend to be interpreted more negatively when found in a Black patient. Part of the stereotype of Black men is that they are dangerous and potentially violent; this is related to the diagnosis of schizophrenia often given to them (Institute of Medicine 2002; Good et al. 2003).

Stereotypes and gender role expectations may also affect how mental illness in men and women in general is handled. "[I]t is possible that our American culture addresses mental illness differently for women than men, with women seeking treatment when distressed whereas men may be more predisposed to break laws when distressed. There are significantly more men than women incarcerated in the United States . . . many of whom have a mental illness" (Bye and Partridge 2003, p. 44).

Stereotyping and labeling the mentally ill according to traditional gender and racial roles is nothing new, however. In the seventeenth and early eighteenth centuries, the artistic and scientific images of "the mad" were decidedly male in nature, depicting someone who was "aggressive," "muscular," "seminude," and "raving," with "uncivilized animality." By the first half of the nineteenth

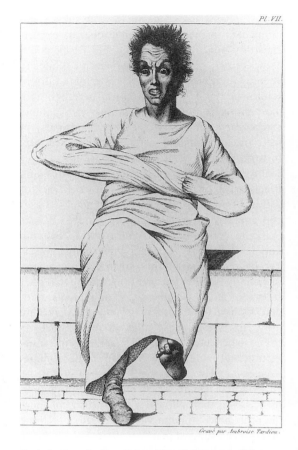

Pl. VII.

Gravé par Ambroise Tardieu.

Early in the nineteenth century, the image of the insane person as female and feminine became established, reflecting concerns about the rising political power of women after the French Revolution.

Source: From Etienne Esquirol's *Des Maladies Mentales*, 1838, courtesy of the National Library of Medicine.

century, the image of madness had changed to a feminine one: "antisocial, violent, unruly, and oversexed. . . . The figure of the sexually aggressive madwoman effectively displaced the previously more common figure of the raving male lunatic" (Kromm 1994, pp. 507–508, 530–531). In part, this shift reflected concerns about the increasing political involvement of women in Europe after the French Revolution. This imagery served to control women's power (Kromm 1994).

Sense of Control, Choice, and Inequality

Mental illness and distress indicate the presence of serious psychological difficulties. But there are other psychological feelings that, while not requiring institutionalization, are indicators of one's general sense of well-being and life satisfaction. Central among these are feelings of control over one's life and that one's actions make a difference. In fact, feelings of control and mastery have been linked to better health (Lachman and Weaver 1998). Those in high-ranking or professional positions are more likely to have such feelings, because those who spend much of their lives in occupations that are characterized by autonomy and decision-making ability are also likely to feel that they are responsible for and can take control of their lives. Moreover, this effect of work on feelings of self-direction is long lasting (Schooler, Mulatu, and Oates 2004).

In contrast, the greater feelings of distress found in the lower socioeconomic groups have been linked to greater feelings of vulnerability, powerlessness, and alienation, while those in higher positions have a greater feeling of mastery and control (Wheaton 1980; Mirowsky and Ross 1983). Women, those in lower-status jobs, and those who are unemployed have less of a sense of control over their lives (Wheaton 1980; Kohn and Schooler 1982; Mirowsky and Ross 1983). Individuals with a sense of powerlessness have feelings of little control over their lives, believing that they cannot master or determine the paths that life will take. Rather, they believe that factors outside the individual—fate or "society," for example—determine what happens to them and that there is little they can do to change that.

Feelings of self-mastery and control over one's life appear to be an important set of mediating influences on mental health. Those in low socioeconomic positions generally have a greater sense than those in higher statuses that their lives are determined by factors beyond their immediate control. A young electrician's apprentice summarized this feeling well: "See, I feel like I'm being held back, like I'm not on top of things. . . . I don't know what you would call it, maybe sort of powerless, but it's a feeling not about any one thing that's gone wrong" (Sennett and Cobb 1973, p. 34). Falling from their comfortable upper-middle-class life, Kerry Russo reflected on the predicament of her newly unemployed husband: "I look at a successful businessman going through this absolute torture. I can hold him. I can tell him it's going to be okay. But it's out of my hands. And that's the frightening part, how little control we have over our lives. . . . It used to be that if you followed the rules, you'd be fine. That doesn't apply anymore. They've changed the rules" (Safran 1992, p. 115).

These feelings, in turn, are related to greater depression and less overall satisfaction with life (Lachman and Weaver 1998). The importance of mastery over one's life for mental health is further implied by findings that show that job restructuring and increased job demands, over which individuals have little control, increase depressive feelings and lower a sense of life satisfaction (Tausig and Fenwick 1999). Of course, those with few resources lack the choices available to others. In a critical sense, lacking a sense of power and control is about lacking choices. The luxury of considering choices is not available to someone who is scrambling to merely stay alive or to have a little bit of comfort.

It should not be surprising that the self-image of individuals with this perspective would differ from those who feel they can and do control their lives. Consistent with this view are the findings of a recent Gallup survey that revealed that groups with more resources were more likely than others to have excellent self-images. Table 11.2 shows that higher proportions of men, generally those who earned higher incomes and felt their health was excellent, classified their self-images as "excellent." The fact that a higher percentage of non-Whites than Whites consider their self-image this way appears to be inconsistent with this argument. However, recent research suggests that strong racial identities and unusual adversity may toughen individuals psychologically, helping to create stronger feelings of mastery and purpose in their lives. This is especially the case for Blacks with more education (Ryff, Keyes, and Hughes 2003). Whites, in contrast, are not as likely to think of their whiteness as a race and are in a weaker

TABLE 11.2 Percentage Rating Personal Self-Image* as Excellent, by Income, Employment Status, Race, and Sex: 2003

Income	% Excellent
Earn less than $20,000 per year	25
Earn $20,000–$29,999 per year	26
Earn $30,000–$49,999 per year	36
Earn $50,000–$74,999 per year	46
Earn $75,000 per year or more	44
Employment Status	
Adults who are not employed	29
Adults employed full- or part-time	40
Race	
Non-Hispanic Whites	34
Non-Whites	43
Sex	
Women	33
Men	38

*Survey question asked was, "How would you describe your self-image; that is, how you generally feel about yourself—excellent, good, just fair, or poor?"

Source: Joseph Carrol, "Health, Age, and Income Factor into Americans' Self-Image." *Gallup Poll Tuesday Briefing,* August 12, 2003.

position to justify their difficulties using external adversities such as discrimination.

Sharply contrasting with the belief that one has little control is traditional American individualism, the belief that individuals are responsible for their own fates. Imagine how you would feel if, on the one hand, you believed in individualism and, on the other hand, had little opportunity to improve your situation. The presence of different opportunities for classes combined with an ingrained belief in individual responsibility can produce self-damaging feelings and doubts among those who are not economically successful, and feelings of self-confidence and entitlement among those in successful families. Sennett and Cobb's (1973) moving study of working-class male Bostonians and their families who sense a lack of control revealed the corrosive psychological effects that the nasty combination of individualism and varying success has on individuals.

Individualism encourages the desire to excel, and some do excel while others do not. Those who *do* excel develop feelings of competence and freedom, while those who *do not* develop feelings of guilt and suspicions of their own inadequacy. For those at the top, individualism reinforces their belief in the deservedness of their position and abilities and reaffirms their high self-worth, while for those at the bottom, especially Whites, individualism has the doubly damaging effect of confirming the deservedness of their lowly position and reinforcing in their minds that they do not have what it takes. Analyses of answers given in 2008 and 2009 by 450,000 respondents revealed that a higher percentage of those with high incomes than those with low incomes were satisfied with where they were in life. However, *increases* in income result in similar increases in life satisfaction for individuals in all income categories (Kahneman

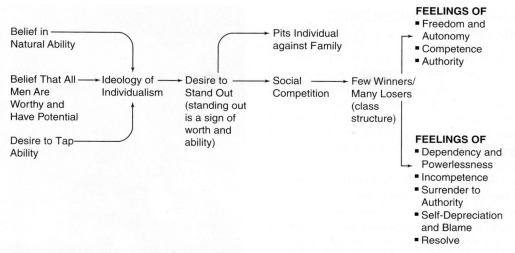

FIGURE 11.4 Ideology, Class Inequality, and Their Effects on Self-Perceptions among Men of Different Classes

Source: Based on Sennett and Cobb (1973).

and Deaton 2010). Figure 11.4 summarizes this process.

Education is often seen as a way to gain control over one's life, to gain autonomy and choices and increase life satisfaction. Indeed, those with lower levels of education are more likely to feel vulnerable and less in control of their lives (Umberson 1993). The working-class respondents in Sennett and Cobb's (1973) study realized the potential of education to give their children independence in their lives, but they also suspected that educated people can get away with things that the average person cannot, and that education drives a wedge between less-educated parents and their children. Thus, education becomes a double-edged sword, serving to grant independence but also creating a seemingly permanent breach in understanding between generations. Richard Rodriguez, who went from knowing little English to earning a Ph.D. and becoming a successful writer and professor, described how he and his family drifted farther apart (1982, p. 190): "Years passed. Silence grew thicker, less penetrable."

To summarize, the conditions and resources with which people live affect their beliefs and outlook. The feelings of lack of control, vulnerability, and powerlessness held by many in lower socioeconomic groups generate higher levels of distress and weaken their ability to cope effectively. In their review of research on the relationship between socioeconomic status, beliefs, and distress, Mirowsky and Ross (1986) concluded that "people in lower socioeconomic positions have a triple burden: They have more problems to deal with; their personal histories are likely to have left them with a deep sense of powerlessness; and that sense of powerlessness discourages them from marshalling whatever energy and resources they do have in order to solve their problems. The result for many is a multiplication of despair" (p. 30).

Their sense of powerlessness stems in part from their inability to leave their poor neighborhoods. This immobility leads to greater feelings of distress. Individuals who live in poor neighborhoods where most people have not moved are more likely than residents of stable nonpoor neighborhoods to experience depression and anxiety; living in a neighborhood where everyone is poor reduces feelings of happiness, regardless of one's personal income (Firebaugh and Schroeder 2009). This is due in part to perceptions that their neighborhood is physically broken down and dangerous: "The stress of living in a place where the streets are dirty, noisy, and dangerous takes its toll in feelings of depression and anxiety" (Ross, Reynolds, and Geis 2000, p. 594).

BASIC LIFE CHANCES: FOOD AND SHELTER

The research on physical and psychological health clearly shows that economic, racial, and gender inequality are deeply implicated in the chances of individuals for a healthy life. It does not warrant belaboring that food and shelter, like health, are basic to a decent life, and it is the poor who are disproportionately found among the hungry and homeless.

According to some, the kind of food one eats has become a status marker for the middle and upper classes in the United States, and as a result, the more nutritious, freshest foods have increased in price at a greater rate than other foods (Miller 2010). But those who are hungry are very likely less concerned about status than they are about survival.

Because of controversies over the definition of *hunger* and the lack of a *consistent national* attempt to assess the magnitude of the problem, there is little agreement on the extent of the problem in the United States. Estimates for 2009 are that at sometime during the year, almost 15 percent of U.S. households did not have regular access to the food necessary for a healthy diet. This is the highest level since 1995. Members in almost all of the 6.8 million households that experienced serious food insecurity worried that they would not have enough money for food, could not afford to eat balanced meals, and would skip meals because of lack of food. More than twice as many households with children as those without children were food-insecure. In 2009, 23 percent of children lived in households that were food-insecure.

Black and Hispanic households had rates of food insecurity that were two to three times higher than those of White households, and, not surprisingly, poor households had rates that were five times higher than those with incomes at least twice that of the poverty level. Low-income, minority, and children-present households also spend much less on food than higher socioeconomic and childless households (Nord et al. 2010). When surveyed, over half of food-insecure households in 2009 indicated that they had participated in a major federal food program during the previous month.

Over the last decade and a half, the proportion of people who are hungry has increased, and many of these individuals are also homeless. While single men are still the modal group, children, women, and minorities are composing a higher percentage of the homeless. Violent crimes against the homeless have also been on the increase. (© Xavier Marchant/ Fotolia LLC)

Major cities have food programs that serve the hungry, but they are not always adequate. In a 2009–2010 survey of 27 cities, need for food increased over the previous year, the result being that almost one-quarter of residents who needed food had to be turned away (U.S. Conference of Mayors 2010). Estimates are that 5.7 million are served each week in Feeding America's food pantries, shelters, and kitchens. This represents an increase of 46 percent over 2006 levels. More than one-third of these clients do not have high school degrees, over three-fourths are unemployed, and 80 percent live in households with incomes below poverty levels (Mabli et al. 2010).

The problem of hunger, of course, is linked to the issue of good health. The Physician Task Force on Hunger in America argued that inadequate diet has an impact on the health of pregnant women and on the children to whom they give birth. Higher infant mortality rates, low birth weight, slower or deficient brain growth, poorer resistance to infection, and general stunting and anemia are among the conditions related to poor nutrition among children. Independent of other factors, children who experience severe hunger have also reported more stress and anxiety than children who are not hungry, and to suffer from more chronic illnesses (Weinreb, Scott, and Gundersen 2002). Thus, the consequences of chronic hunger can be life-long. Other negative effects are found among older persons who are chronically hungry. Many of the health problems among older people—for example, hypertension and weakening of the bone mass (osteoporosis)—require careful attention to quality and quantity of diet, and hunger worsens these maladies (Physician Task Force 1985).

Many of those who are hungry are also homeless, although it is primarily those homeless who have personal health and related problems and who have been consistently homeless who are most likely to experience hunger (Lee and Greif 2008). A 1996 governmental survey of homeless assistance centers found that 20 percent of the homeless eat at most only one meal a day, and 40 percent said that they went at least one day in the last month without food (Hombs 2001).

Determining the extent of homelessness, however, is another difficult matter. Because of methodological differences, national surveys yield wildly different appraisals on the extent of homelessness in the United States, with estimates ranging from several hundred thousand to several million. Indications are that homelessness has increased over the last two decades. Estimates based on single counts at a given time ("point-in-time counts") tend to be lower than estimates based on counts of those who are homeless sometime during a period of time ("period prevalence counts"). One point-in-time study estimated that there were 665,000 homeless during the month of January 2008. A period estimate, on the other hand, showed that almost 1.6 million used a shelter or transitional housing between October 2008 and September 2009 (U.S. Department of Housing and Urban Development 2010).

The homeless population has become much more heterogeneous since the 1980s. Of the approximately 88,000 people reportedly living on the streets, in shelters, or transitional housing on any given night in 26 major cities in 2009–2010, 44 percent of the adults were severely mentally ill or physically disabled, 81 percent were unemployed, 14 percent were victims of domestic violence, and 14 percent were veterans (U.S. Conference of Mayors 2010). Not surprisingly, a higher degree of homelessness is found in urban than in rural areas. While single men are still the modal group, children, women, female-headed families, and minorities (especially Blacks) make up an increasing proportion of the homeless. Generally, the composition of the homeless population in a given area reflects the composition of the local population (Lee, Tyler, and Wright 2010).

What is it like to be homeless? In New York, Frank, a 34-year-old homeless former warehouseman worries about being assaulted while he sleeps, so he does not sleep on his back or stomach because in those positions he feels he would be an easy target. In Houston, Rosa, a 42-year-old homeless woman, has to decide when to join the line at the local soup kitchen. Arriving early means a longer line, but arriving later would mean going without food longer. In Detroit, 33-year-old Arch says he doesn't really have any friends, but has heard murmurs that some don't think he is going to live very long (Sweeney 1993).

These vignettes suggest the unique set of stresses faced by the homeless. Homeless persons suffer greater emotional pressures than those encountered by the housed poor. They have higher levels of depression and are more likely to avoid active confrontation of problems than other members of the poor population (Banyard and Graham-Bermann 1998). Again, the relationship between health and socioeconomic status appears reciprocal. Mental disorder may precipitate homelessness, and homelessness generally intensifies psychological distress. Adding to this distress is the distinct stigma placed on the homeless by the public. National research indicates that the stigma of being homeless adds to the stigma of just being poor. One supported explanation for the stigma is that the homeless "are viewed as dirty, smelly, lice-ridden, or diseased," resulting in a desire on the part of the public to keep from being contaminated by them (Phelan et al. 1997, p. 333). A national telephone survey found that almost two-thirds of respondents felt that "the presence of homeless people threatens the quality of life in America's cities, hurts local businesses, spoils parks for families and children, and makes neighborhoods worse" (Link et al. 1996, p. 145). In the same study, a majority also believed that the homeless were either dangerous, potentially violent, or threatening. Although the public does not fully blame homeless individuals for their plight, these perceptions of the homeless mark them as a negatively evaluated status group, as defined in Chapter 4.

Violent crimes against the homeless have increased in the last decade. Between 1999 and 2007, a total of 774 violent crimes in 235 cities have been committed against them (National Coalition for the Homeless and National Law Center on Homelessness & Poverty 2008). Most of the victims were men and most of the perpetrators were youths under 20 years of age. The stigma and low social status attached to homelessness encourages attacks against them: "Young men see the way we treat homeless people— criminalizing them, shoving them out of sight, and they get a message: These people are less than human and it is OK to attack them" (quoted in Chancellor, May 10, 2008, p. A4).

A number of factors have been linked to the rise in homelessness. Primary among these is the lack of affordable housing. The higher cost of housing is due in large part to declines in the building of affordable private homes and in public housing. In addition, the decline in value of the minimum wage has made decent housing difficult to obtain for low-wage workers, most of whom are adults. This has left a larger poor population competing for smaller numbers of affordable residences. Increased demand has pushed rents up (Koegel, Burnam, and Baumohl 1996). The destruction or conversion of housing units for other purposes, along with gentrification, has worsened the problem. Most of the homeless also list unemployment and poverty as major causes of their homelessness (U.S. Conference of Mayors 2010).

Health difficulties and the associated lack of services available to the homeless have also helped maintain homelessness. Deinstitutionalization of those with mental problems, recessions, the declining value of public assistance benefits, no-fault divorces and increasing numbers of no-children rental rules, the net migration to metropolitan areas, and tighter governmental rules about disabilities have all had an effect on this problem (Hope and Young 1986; Hoch 1987; Wright and Lam 1987). Thus, many of the elements that affect the extent of homelessness are "macroprocesses" related to the government and market economy (Rossi and Wright 1989). And it is the poor who are especially vulnerable to shifts in these processes. "As long as the distribution of shelter security remains tied to income and social class the poor will bear the burden of going homeless" (Hoch 1987, p. 29).

NUTSHELL 11.1   The Stresses of Too Much Versus Too Little

Throughout the text, there are numerous discussions of the negative effects of being on the bottom of the socioeconomic ladder. The poor are worse off when it comes to basic life chances such as health, hunger, and homelessness. They also have less social status and political power than others. Does this mean that the very wealthy are without significant problems? After all, they can afford the homes, vacations, and life styles they want. Money can provide the physical comforts and much of the security that everyone desires.

But what are the stresses, if any, associated with being wealthy? Many religious groups consider too much wealth to be dangerous because it can potentially weaken a sense of community and increase egoism. I found this to be the case among the Amish

NUTSHELL 11.1   (Continued)

(Hurst and McConnell 2010). Wealth is seductive but it holds hidden dangers: "It's just like eating," one Amish businessman told me, "we have to eat but it we don't discipline ourselves we become gluttons."

In their interviews with 130 millionaires, some of whom had inherited their wealth while others were self-made millionaires, Schervish and his colleagues found that most felt that a lot of money does not guarantee happiness or that one will be taken seriously (Schervish, Coutsoukis, and Lewis 1994). One millionaire entrepreneur, for example, admits that while she has been very successful, she also believes that she is often not taken seriously because she is a woman. In effect, her wealth does not save her from being a victim of

prejudice. Some of the interviewed wealthy wish they had spent more time with their children. Guilt about having inherited wealth is also a recurrent theme in the self-told stories of many of these millionaires. It is a feeling that makes many want to prove their worth by their own achievements and contributions. Wealth also draws the jealousy and envy of others, and the sense that one was just lucky or more ruthless than others.

The lesson here is that while wealth may allow one to have more possessions, better health care, and a fancier life style, it has its own attendant pressures and stresses. A question for you to consider is how much wealth is enough to live a happy, meaningful life. What do you think?

LIFE CHANCES IN A GLOBAL CONTEXT

So far our discussion has focused on relationships between inequality and life chances in the United States. But connections between economic inequality, on the one hand, and health and sustenance, on the other, exist in the international setting as well. The United States spends a much higher percentage of its gross domestic product on health care compared to other industrial nations. In comparison to the United States spending 16 percent of its gross domestic product on health care, for example, Canada, United Kingdom, and Sweden, which have national health plans, spend 8–10 percent (National Center for Health Statistics 2007). In 2007, U.S. health care spending at $6,697 per capita was the highest in the world (Begley 2008).

When compared to other wealthy nations, however, the United States does not fare very well on some morbidity rates and life expectancy and infant mortality measures. Survival rates for several types of cancer are higher in most other industrial nations (Begley 2008). In a comparison of 35 major countries in 2005, the United States ranked 30th in life expectancy for women and 27th for men. The life expectancy for women in Japan, which ranked first, was more than 5 years longer,

and the life expectancy for men in Hong Kong, which ranked first for men, was about 4 years longer than in the United States. In 2006, among this same group of nations, the United States also ranked among the worst in infant mortality rate, ahead of just Costa Rica, Cuba, Romania, and the Russian Federation (National Center for Health Statistics 2010). Of course, when compared to individuals in low-income countries, persons in wealthier nations can expect to live much longer. In 2006, the average life expectancy for low-income nations was only 59, compared to 80 for high-income countries (World Health Organization 2008). Since 1980, life expectancies have risen in parts of Asia, the Middle East, and North Africa, but have declined in sub-Saharan Africa, where the average life expectancy in 2005 was only 47. That decline is due largely to the HIV/AIDS epidemic (Goesling and Baker 2008).

High-income countries also have five to six times the number of physicians per capita than poor countries (World Health Organization 2008). The distribution of psychiatrists and psychologists is even more unequal. High-income countries have a median 10 psychiatrists per 100,000 persons, while the median for low-income countries is almost zero (0.05). The discrepancy is similar for psychologists (World Health Organization 2005). The lack of access to mental

Access to basic needs such as food and water is severely limited in many African nations. The women in this Kenyan village are preparing to walk 5 miles to retrieve water for bathing, drinking, and cooking. (Photo by Susan L. Tipton.)

health professionals and other widespread deprivations in poor countries coincides with higher rates of major depression found in countries that rank low on the UN's Human Development Index (HDI). Among high HDI countries, a higher degree of income inequality is associated with higher rates of depression episodes (Cifuentes et al. 2008). Depression rates in industrial countries tend to be higher among women than men, especially poor women. "Frequent exposure of low-income women to uncontrollable life events such as illness and death of children or of husbands, imprisonment, job insecurity, dangerous neighborhoods, [sexual abuse], and hazardous workplaces places them at a significantly higher risk of depression than men" (World Health Organization, June 2002). Not only individuals' income relative to that of others, but the amount of *absolute* income possessed by individuals also appears to be related to a sense of well-being and happiness. A 2008 study of numerous countries revealed that higher incomes lead to greater satisfaction (Stevenson and Wolfers, August 19, 2008).

A lack of adequate food also haunts poorer countries. Estimates are that 820 million of the 854 million who are undernourished live in developing countries. Malnutrition may very well contribute to the higher infant mortality rates and illness among children (World Hunger Education Service 2008). Slow growths in food supply, use of grains for biofuel rather than the food market, and higher food prices have all contributed to hunger and malnutrition problems (Von Braun, December 2007).

Summary

This chapter has focused on a variety of areas concerning personal life chances in different racial, gender, and socioeconomic status (SES) groups. It appears clear that the latter factors are related to physical and mental health in several ways. Moreover, these groups also tend to use health services in different ways, to contact doctors and dentists at different rates, and to differ in the likelihood of possessing health insurance and taking preventive health measures. Inequality also is related to the problems of hunger and homelessness.

Two points should be made about the research conducted on these relationships. First, frequently different measures of SES have been used in studies on the same issue, and, for the sake of convenience, the term *social class* has been used in this chapter as if it were synonymous with SES measures. Second, although significant relationships have been found between race, gender, and SES, on the one hand, and health, on the other hand, I do not want to suggest that these are the only variables or always the most important variables in explaining variations. Rather, the question of interest has been whether inequality in its various forms plays any role in producing various personal life chances. It

seems apparent that it does. Indirectly, the organization of a competitive capitalist society and, more directly, the system of inequality that it creates, results in individuals and families being placed in different positions regarding access to and possibilities of gaining the "good things" in life. The role of poverty and inequality in affecting life chances extends beyond U.S. borders into the world as a whole. Income inequality and poverty are implicated in physical and mental health and food inequalities between nations. In many ways, then, the effects of inequality reach inside the intimate lives of individuals in the United States and elsewhere. In Chapter 12, we turn from these personal effects of inequality to more society-wide effects—crime, environmental justice, and social trust.

Critical Thinking

1. Imagine your starting point in life as a young child and the path you are likely to follow to adulthood. If you were born into a poor family in the United States, what barriers and detours would you be likely to encounter while traveling on this path? Would your race or gender make a difference? Compare those to the obstacles likely to be encountered by a person born into a wealthy family.
2. To what extent should individuals be held responsible for their health and actions if these are shaped by their opportunities and circumstances?
3. Why do research results regularly show that women have higher rates of mental illness and distress than men in the United States?
4. What effect do you think a requirement for everyone to have health insurance will have on the health of the U.S. population? Will it reduce, increase, or simply maintain the overall level of health in the country? Why?

Web Connections

Health, United States, a volume published yearly by the National Center for Health Statistics, contains a wealth of longitudinal and cross-sectional information on the life expectancy, mortality, and health conditions of the U.S. population, including information on all the states. Check it to see how your income, age and educational group compare on health measures, as well as how your state compares to others. Go to http://www.cdc.gov/nchs/hus.htm.

Film Suggestions

African-American Women: Where They Stand: Healthcare (2007) Part of a 5-part series on the status of African-American women produced by NBC News.

Deadly Deception (1993). The story of the infamous Tuskegee experiment.

Unnatural Causes: Is Inequality Making Us Sick? (2008) A seven-part series on socioeconomic status, race, and health.

Waging A Living (2005). Follows four working-class individuals facing numerous problems and struggling to make a living.

CHAPTER 12

Social Consequences of Inequality

Laws grind the poor, and rich men rule the law.

OLIVER GOLDSMITH (1730–1774)

The previous chapter focused on how position in the system of social inequality affects an individual's *personal* life, that is, its impact on physical and mental health, access to food, and chances of homelessness. In addition to affecting the personal life chances of individuals, social inequality has broader effects on the quality of life and stability of society as a whole. Through its impact on different forms of crime, environmental degradation, and general trust, inequality creates a problematic context in which we must all live. In the long run, inequality affects all of us.

INEQUALITY AND THE MEASUREMENT OF CRIME

The quality of life in any society is affected by the amount of crime within it, and many aspects of crime and its consequences appear to be closely related to social inequality. Inequality has been connected to the nature and collection of crime statistics, the likelihood of arrest, the social production of crime, and sentencing. In other words, its effect appears to permeate most phases of the criminal justice process. Unfortunately, discussions about the relationship between inequality and crime are mired in disagreements about the definition of *crime* and the varying statistics about it.

Clearly, labels applied to persons and actions have an impact on what behaviors are defined as criminal, how much laws are enforced, and how the behavior of individuals is interpreted. Because of this, the definition of the "crime problem" is a social construction, and the definitions given by some groups may be favored over those of others. Perhaps you consider the crime problem to consist mainly of street crimes such as rape, robbery, murder, and the like, but others may feel that the real crime problem is found in white-collar crime that costs billions of dollars every year and yet receives less attention in the popular press. In the small city in which I live, it is now illegal to "cruise" the downtown in the evenings, a pastime previously engaged in by many youths. What defines *cruising* is rather arbitrary, however. *Loitering* is another rather vaguely defined illegal act. The more one examines various "crimes," the more it becomes evident that they are defined into existence.

Similarly, once laws and crimes are defined, their enforcement may also be uneven. Several scholars have suggested that the police are biased against those in the lower class and, thus, are more likely to arrest them than individuals in higher classes who commit the same offenses (Turk 1969). In sum, these and similar observations should make us wary in drawing conclusions about crime because statistics about it have several shortcomings.

Because (1) "crimes" are the result of only certain behaviors, being defined as illegal, and because (2) police actions appear to be affected by the socioeconomic and racial characteristics of citizens, many have questioned the fairness of the criminal justice system. A 2007 national survey found that half of all Blacks and those with incomes below $20,000 had very little or no confidence in the criminal justice system (Pastore and Maguire 2008). An examination of 110 men whose guilty verdicts were later thrown out as a result of DNA tests seems to give credence to these feelings. Most were either working class or poor, and two-thirds were either Hispanic or Black (Cohen and Hastings 2002). The discussion that follows of the relationship between inequality and crime covers street, white-collar, corporate, and hate crimes. Included are discussions of phases of the criminal justice process, starting with arrests and the commission of crime and ending with sentencing.

STREET CRIME AND INEQUALITY

Crime rates are ordinarily determined by using the FBI's Crime Index, which includes both property crimes (burglary, larceny-theft, motor vehicle theft, arson) and violent crimes (murder, forcible rape, robbery, and aggravated assault). One of the problems with this list of **street crimes** is that it does not include any serious, very costly white-collar, corporate, or "suite" crimes, as they are

sometimes called. Since the latter are largely crimes perpetrated by middle- or upper-class individuals, it would be a mistake to look only at the index crimes to reach a conclusion about the relationship between race, sex, socioeconomic status, and crime. To do so would bias the conclusion against individuals in lower social and economic rankings.

Another point to keep in mind is how perceptions about racial groups affect individuals' fears and views of crime rates. Racial stereotypes and fears may be reinforced by crime reporting by the media that, evidence shows, overrepresent Blacks in their stories of criminal perpetrators and that minimize their portrayal as victims of crime. If Whites rather than Blacks are continuously portrayed as the victims, Whites may begin to be more fearful of crime than warranted by the facts, and the lack of attention paid to groups that are the most victimized may result in less public support for policies that would lessen their rate of victimization (Bjornstrom et al. 2010).

Evidence from several cities also indicates that respondents' perceptions of the extent of the crime rate in a neighborhood is affected by the percentage of residents who are Black. The greater the percentage of Blacks in an area, the more likely is the perception of a high crime rate. In fact, the racial makeup of a neighborhood actually has a stronger impact on perceptions of high crime rates *than does the actual crime rate*. This provides ample evidence that racial stereotypes are at work in labeling neighborhoods (Quillian and Pager 2001). Feelings that one might be a victim of crime are also affected by neighborhood racial composition (Chiricos, McEntire, and Gertz 2001).

This stereotyping of neighborhoods as dangerous according to their racial composition appears evident also in research on police interpretations and actions. A study in Washington, D.C., found that in contrast to Blacks residing in a middle-class neighborhood, Blacks who live in a poor neighborhood are likely to feel they are treated unfairly compared to those who live in White and higher socioeconomic neighborhoods. Blacks in middle-class neighborhoods do not

Minorities who live in poor neighborhoods are more likely than others to view police and other governmental authorities with suspicion and to feel that they are treated unfairly in the justice system. Evidence shows that the racial composition of police forces affects the rate of arrests among racial groups. (Photo by Brendan R. Hurst.)

believe that *their* neighborhood is treated any differently by police than White neighborhoods. This suggests the importance that differences in class have for perceptions among Blacks. But even individuals from middle-class neighborhoods believe police generally treat Blacks and Whites differently. Whites are most likely to use the perceived rate of crime among Blacks as the reason for this disparate treatment (Weitzer 2000).

Most Whites believe that police treat people impartially. Minorities, however, tend to see law enforcement as another institution that maintains their subordination (Weitzer and Tuch 2005). These views may be shaped by greater negative experiences with police and more exposure to media accounts of police abuse (Weitzer and Tuch 2004).

Part of the reason for differences in treatment may also be related to the racial composition of police forces. Evidence suggests that increases in the proportion of minority police lead to more arrests of Whites but not non-Whites, and conversely, increases in the number of White police results in more arrests of non-Whites but not Whites (Donohue and Levitt 2001). The racial characteristics of the victim also seem to make a difference in arrest rates. A South Carolina study showed that when the rate of Black crimes against *Whites* increased, the rate at which Blacks were arrested also increased. When the rate at which Blacks committing crimes against other *Blacks* went up, however, the arrest rate did not increase. This may mean that when Blacks are perceived as a criminal threat against the White majority by authorities, arrest activity intensifies (Eitle, D'Alessio, and Stolzenberg 2002).

Whether or not youth have actual encounters with police or are arrested also appears to be related to the socioeconomic status of the persons involved. Police generally have particular images of delinquents, stereotypes that result in lower-class persons being arrested more often (Sampson 1986). In essence, police have certain expectations of the criminal behavior of youths, and these images lead them to more frequently monitor and arrest youths in the lower class, regardless of the frequency of their actual criminal behavior (Irwin 1985). Research in Seattle, using multiple data sources, supports the conclusion that racial differences in drug arrest rates are not primarily caused by actual differences in drug usage and the violence associated with it. Rather, arrest rates are strongly tied to police perceptions of the "drug problem" as a "black" problem, and to "crack" rather than "powder" cocaine as the more dangerous drug (Beckett et al. 2005). Historically, sentencing for crack cocaine crimes was significantly more severe than that for powder cocaine convictions, which primarily involved Whites. Recently, however, the states and federal government have moved to reduce that discrepancy ("Law Evens Penalty" 2010).

Their negative perceptions of lower-class youths lead police to label whole neighborhoods as being contaminated because they are made up of individuals who are considered undesirable

(Irwin 1985; Sampson 1986). The result is that the general socioeconomic status of a neighborhood can influence the attention paid to it and its inhabitants by authorities. A study by Sampson (1986), using data from the Seattle Youth Study, found that the number of contacts and reports by police is strongly and inversely related to a neighborhood's general SES, independent of the actual extent of criminal and delinquent behavior in the area. He concluded that "for the bulk of offenses typically committed by juveniles (e.g., larceny, fighting, vandalism, burglary, drug violations) official police records and referrals to court are structured not simply by the act itself but by socioeconomic and situational context (e.g., delinquency of friends) as well, a process which may in turn amplify the effect of prior record in later decisions concerning official delinquents" (p. 884).

This research strongly suggests that the ecological area and perceptions of law enforcement officials affect the relationship between official rates of crime/delinquency and social class. These additional limitations of official statistics should be kept in mind when viewing the information in Table 12.1, which presents the arrest distributions for FBI Crime Index offenses by race and sex of those arrested. In 2009, there were 2,310,050 arrests made for such crimes, and almost three-fourths of those arrested were men. The highest arrest rate for women was for larceny-theft (44%). In recent years, the arrest rates for women have increased. While most of those arrested in 2009, with the exception of robbery, were Whites, Blacks were disproportionately represented in the arrest rates for all index crimes. In total, 39 percent of all those arrested for violent crimes and 30 percent of those arrested for property crimes were Black. A small percentage of arrests, generally 2–3 percent, involved American Indians, Alaskan Natives, Asians, or Pacific Islanders.

TABLE 12.1 Arrests by FBI Crime Index Offense Charged, Estimated Distributions by Sex and Race: 2009

Offense Charged	Arrest Distribution				
	% Male	% Female	% White	% Black	% Other[a]
Murder and nonnegligent manslaughter	90	10	49	49	2
Forcible rape	99	1	65	33	2
Robbery	88	12	43	56	2
Aggravated assault	78	22	64	34	3
Burglary	85	15	67	32	2
Larceny-theft	56	44	68	29	3
Motor vehicle theft	82	18	61	36	3
Arson	83	17	75	23	2
Violent crime[b]	81	19	59	39	2
Property crime[c]	63	37	68	30	3
Total Index arrests = 2,310,050					

Note: Totals may not add up to 100 percent because of rounding.

[a] American Indian, Alaskan Native, Asian, or Pacific Islander.

[b] Violent crimes are murder and nonnegligent manslaughter, forcible rape, robbery, and aggravated assault.

[c] Property crimes are burglary, larceny-theft, motor vehicle theft, and arson.

Source: Crime in the United States 2009 (Washington, D.C.: Federal Bureau of Investigation, 2009).

Social Class and the Commission of Crime

These statistics suggest strongly that Blacks and males are more likely to commit crimes than their counterparts, and that the differences in arrest rates are too large to believe otherwise (LaFree 1995). However, as you will see in the next section, the differences in rates between Blacks and Whites are not due primarily to cultural differences between these groups, but to differences in the structural contexts in which they live. That is to say the causes of Black crime are similar to the causes of crime by any group, but Blacks are exposed more forcefully and thoroughly to social contexts that encourage criminal behavior. Much of this context involves elements related to inequality such as poverty, economic discrepancies, social isolation, poor jobs, and unemployment. For example, one of the arguments used to explain the economic stress faced by minorities has emphasized the role played by the decline of manufacturing and the deindustrialization of cities, leaving only low-wage employment or high rates of unemployment in their wake. Researchers of 683 U.S. metropolitan areas discovered that such "employment volatility" promotes a higher property-crime rate (Bausman and Goe 2004).

In contrast to the apparently clear relationships between race, sex, and arrests, the relationship between social class and actual *commission* of crime/delinquency has been a source of great controversy. Certainly there are arguments that suggest that the definition of crime, the enforcement of laws, and the judicial and sentencing procedures work against the lower classes, which are reflected in higher crime rates and more severe sentencing for those groups.

Past overviews of studies done on the relationship between social class/socioeconomic status and crime/delinquency have yielded inconsistent conclusions (Tittle, Villemez, and Smith 1978; Braithwaite 1981). A large part of the explanation for discrepancies in findings on this relationship appears to relate to the measures used for social class and crime. Virtually all of the studies in recent years have used occupational prestige, income, or educational hierarchies as measures of class, rather than Marxian measures (e.g., ownership, control over labor, etc.). Hagan and his colleagues (1985, 1987) suggested that differences in power ought to be more fully incorporated into studies of class and crime. When one considers that power differences exist between races, classes, and frequently between men and women in families, and may be directly linked to the probability of white-collar crime, the request for other measures of class seems more than reasonable.

To test their ideas about the importance of power differences in producing delinquency, Hagan and his associates (1985, 1987) collected data from students in Toronto and used a measure of authority and ownership to determine the position of men and women in the households. The authors hypothesized that in families in which wives and daughters have little power, there is less freedom and risk taking on the part of women. Hence, they will be significantly less likely than the sons to commit delinquent acts. It is in these types of families that gender differences in delinquency will be most pronounced. On the other hand, in those families in which females have some freedom and can take risks, there will be little difference between the sexes in their delinquency rates. Analyses by Hagan and his colleagues supported these hypotheses and also revealed that the gender differences in delinquency declined as one went down the class hierarchy. Gender differences were largest in the employer class. A large part of the reason for this gender difference seems to be that sons in this class have greater power relative to their mothers and are not taking as great a risk in being punished as are daughters. In other words, the authors pointed out again that gender differences in delinquency are linked to power differences in the family, which in turn are a reflection of power differences in the workplace.

The Structure of Inequality and the Social Production of Crime

When it comes to the commission of crime, an analysis of its relationship to inequality involves more than just examining the connection between the statuses of individuals and criminal acts. At the social-structural level, or macro level, the system of inequality itself may be related to crime rates. Unemployment, employment in unstable jobs, gender and racial inequality, poverty rates, and economic deprivation have all been found to be positively related to crime rates (e.g., Blau and Blau 1982; Williams 1984; Williams and Flewelling 1988; Crutchfield 1995; Kposowa, Breault, and Harrison 1995). Extensive reviews of studies suggest strongly that unemployment and property crime are positively related (Chiricos 1987; Devine, Sheley, and Smith 1988). In a longitudinal study, Cantor and Land (1985) examined rates for seven Crime Index offenses from 1946 to 1982. Their results are valuable because they indicate that unemployment can have both positive and negative effects on crime, depending on the particular crime in question. Specifically, unemployment can have a dampening effect on the crime rate because it means in part that the opportunity to be a victim of a property or violent crime is lower. When people are unemployed, they are at home, among friends and relatives, "guarding" property more often. This means that they are less likely to be victims of crimes by a stranger. On the other hand, unemployment has a positive effect on criminal motivation, thereby increasing the probability of crime, especially property crime.

At the individual level, employment has been found to be related to a lower probability of committing a crime. An experimental study of over 2,000 ex-offenders in Texas and Georgia revealed that those who were given employment were less likely to commit a crime after being released than those who were not given employment (Berk, Lenihan, and Rossi 1980). Moreover, those who were given some money in the form of transfer payments, which in effect reduced their poverty, were less likely to commit a crime. The latter suggests that there may be a trade-off between unemployment/poverty and crime. Among African American teenagers, employment and criminal behavior do appear to be used as substitutes. Both are viewed as income-producing activities. African American teenagers who are employed engage in fewer criminal behaviors and vice versa. Involvement in criminal activity, in turn, results in less employment (Good and Pirog-Good 1987; Freeman 1989).

In addition to property crime, violent crime is also related to inequality of different types. An analysis of 2,462 U.S. counties suggests that even less than full-time, year round employment can lower violent crime rates (Lee and Slack 2008). Gender inequality has also been linked to homicide rates in developed countries. Child homicide rates are higher in developed countries in which there is (1) high female labor-force participation but (2) little child support for them and (3) low female status in the society (Fiala and LaFree 1988). This combination creates greater economic stress that heightens the likelihood for child abuse and homicide. Nations that provide more public assistance to mothers in the form of family allowances or social assistance programs have lower rates of such homicide. It has been argued elsewhere that not alleviating this kind of stress among women in families increases child abuse and is part of the reason why the United States has a higher rate of abuse than many other developed countries (Kamerman 1980; Zigler and Muenchow 1983).

The Blau and Blau study (1982) of inequality and violent crime rates in metropolitan areas used official crime statistics from 125 largest metropolitan areas in the United States to find out if the crime rates varied with the extent of socioeconomic inequality in the area. Theoretically, they reasoned that in a democracy, inequalities based on skill or other achieved qualities are perceived as justifiable, while those based on ascribed characteristics such as race or sex are not. When a nominal or horizontal trait like race is closely connected to the vertical structure of economic inequality, racial and class differences become consolidated, and conflict between groups results in the society. One result of this situation is higher violent crime rates. Their findings bear out this theory. Economic inequality generally, and socioeconomic inequality *within* racial groups in particular, is related to the production of violent crimes (Hipp 2007).

Indeed, homicide rates in democratic societies, including the United States, are related to the degree of economic inequality and the relative deprivation that accompanies moderate levels of inequality. When inequality is moderate so that individuals in the lower ranks can see and compare their own circumstances with others who are better off, feelings of relative deprivation are more frequent, and result in higher rates of violence. As the Blau theory suggests, the most volatile combination is when the existing inequality is highly related to ascriptive qualities such as race, and when, at the same time, the society is based on meritocratic principles (Messner 1989). In these societies, where economic differences are closely tied to race, the inequality is seen as illegitimate and more likely to result in violence. Crime rates are positively related to income inequality, especially in situations where individuals in different classes interact and where the inequality is not seen as based on merit, for example, on educational differences. Such inequality fosters a sense of injustice that can instigate criminal behavior among some individuals (McVeigh 2006).

However, high homicide rates are less likely in polar situations where there is either little inequality or extreme inequality. In the latter instance, comparisons that generate feelings of relative deprivation are less probable because of the presence of segregation that eliminates most contact and visibility between higher- and lower-status groups. "Resentment is more likely among the relatively deprived in an affluent society than it is among the absolutely deprived in an impoverished society" (Jacobs and Richardson 2008, p. 31). Given that economic inequality is higher in the United States than in other democratic, industrial nations, it should not be surprising that its homicide rates are noticeably higher as well (Jacobs and Richardson 2008; Pryor 2010).

A reanalysis of the Blau data by Williams (1984) suggested that the level of poverty may also be related to homicide rates, especially in areas outside the South. This supports the findings of other studies (e.g., Danziger and Wheeler 1975; Williams and Flewelling 1988). Resource deprivation is related to higher rates of violent crime (Lee and Slack 2008). As Williams and Flewelling (1988) stated, "It is reasonable to assume that when people live under conditions of extreme scarcity, the struggle for survival is intensified. Such conditions are often accompanied by a host of agitating psychological manifestations, ranging from a deep sense of powerlessness and brutalization to anger, anxiety, and alienation. Such manifestations can provoke physical aggression in conflict situations" (p. 423).

Given this rationale, let us consider the situation of Blacks living in an inner city. Residential segregation of Blacks has been highly intransigent but has declined somewhat since 1980. It continues to be extensive, especially in the East and Midwest. Many of these cities remain "hypersegregated"—"a black core surrounded by a white ring" (Massey and Denton 1993, p. 67). Segregation of Asian and Hispanic immigrants is moderate at worst, although it is increasing as their immigration into the United States has increased. Movement into the suburbs has been marked by the same patterning of racial and ethnic concentration (Charles 2003).

Such residential segregation itself is largely a result of inequality processes. Early in the twentieth century, Blacks moved in large numbers from the South to the North, frequently recruited by employers who were fighting unions and who wished to use Blacks as strikebreakers. This only intensified racist feelings among Whites. Fear by Whites led to "restrictive covenants" in neighborhoods and blockbusting by real estate dealers who hoped to profit from the Black migration. Later, movement of industry out of cities and increasingly poor opportunities for stable employment impoverished these areas. These developments led to the consequent concentration of Blacks into isolated, overcrowded, poor neighborhoods or ghettos.

The current extreme segregation experienced by Blacks is not one of choice; in contrast to Whites, most prefer a decidedly mixed neighborhood. Rather, it has been the actions of government, real estate agencies, banks, and the construction industry that have shaped and maintained segregation through their loan and mortgage policies, gatekeeping of neighborhoods, and construction requirements. Sometimes the stereotypes are evident but the style of discrimination is soft and nuanced as found in these comments by real estate agents who guide Whites away from certain areas:

> "Black people do live around here, but it has not gotten bad yet"; [or] "That area is full of Hispanics and blacks that don't know how to keep clean"; or "(This area) is very mixed. You probably wouldn't like it because of the income you and your husband make. I don't want to sound prejudiced." (Farley and Squires 2005, p. 36; see also Charles 2003)

What is important about such segregation is that it "is not a neutral fact. . . . Because of racial segregation, a significant share of black America is condemned to experience a social environment where poverty and joblessness are the norm, where a majority of children are born out of wedlock, where most families are on welfare, where educational failure prevails, and where social and physical deterioration abound. Through prolonged exposure to such an environment, black chances for social and economic success are drastically reduced" (Massey and Denton 1993, pp. 2–3). The tools and avenues needed to succeed are largely out of reach; access to decent education, health care, and employment is severely limited. The possibility of investing in a desirable home that would increase in value over time, laying a foundation for future wealth, is also almost nonexistent. These conditions perpetuate the low socioeconomic position of residents and freeze the positions of those middle-class persons who live there. As a structural fact, these conditions are beyond the power of any person to change them (Massey and Denton 1993; Farley and Squires 2005). Figure 12.1 captures much of the context in which ghetto residents live and the factors that have created it.

The concentration of poverty and unemployment in these isolated and highly dense areas of cities has led to a stable underclass, the collapse

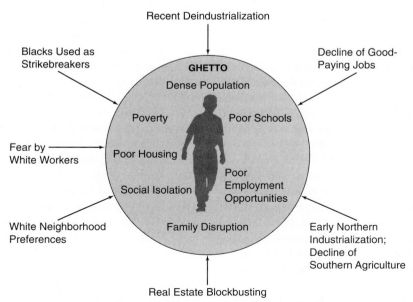

FIGURE 12.1 Causes and Characteristics of the Social Context in Which Ghetto Residents Live

Source: Based on Massey and Denton 1993.

of effective institutions (leading to family disorganization, poor housing, poor employment opportunities), and the development of cultural adaptations that undermine mainstream values. There is little to bind individuals to the community. Consequently, social controls to minimize crime are not in place; neither institutions nor cultural values are effective in controlling crime in this context. Segregation and Black isolation from Whites are highly and directly related to higher rates of violence (Olzak, Shanahan, and McEneaney 1996; Shihadeh and Flynn 1996). This setting results in fewer opportunities and less attachment of Blacks to the wider society and its values. Higher crime rates follow, as do victimization rates, and since it is Blacks who are concentrated in these areas, it is their rates that spiral upward. In 2009, for example, 48 percent of murder victims were Black, even though they compose only about 11 percent of the population. The victimization rates of Blacks and low-income individuals for other kinds of violent crimes are also disproportionately higher than those of Whites and higher-income persons (see Table 12.2). They are also higher for urban dwellers.

What is clear from research is that the causes of crime and victimization among Blacks are not unique. Any individual exposed to this environment over time is vulnerable to criminal behavior and victimization (Kposowa, Breault, and Harrison 1995; Sampson and Wilson 1995). Conditions in the wider community are also important. Living in a poor family or neighborhood that is located in a community which is also suffering economically intensifies the effects of family and neighborhood disadvantage on crime. Thus, it is not just one's immediate poverty but the surrounding context that contribute to violent and other crime rates (Hay et al. 2007; Peterson and Krivo 2009). Thus, to understand differences in crime and victimization rates between rich and poor, Blacks and Whites, we need to appreciate the social context that generates such differences.

All of these results suggest that changes in the structure of inequality would result in changes in crime rates. Danziger and Wheeler's research (1975) suggested that income distribution affects crime rates and that reduced inequality is related to reduced crime rates. They contend, as others have, that inequality generates crime both of the street and suite variety. They concluded from their analysis of 57 large metropolitan areas that "levels of criminal activity are responsive to changes in the distribution of income . . . a one percent reduction in . . . inequality was shown to reduce crime to a larger extent than a one percent increase in deterrence" (pp. 126–127).

Inequality and Criminal Sentencing

Criminal justice is a process with several stages, beginning with the definition of crime, and continuing with labeling of individuals as potential criminals, arrest procedures, court procedures, and sentencing. "At all stages of the system—beginning with arrest and proceeding through imprisonment and parole—substantial racial and ethnic disparities are found in virtually all jurisdictions in the United States" (Sentencing Project 2003, p. 1). Data from the most heavily populated counties in the United States, for example, reveal that even before trial, men, Blacks, and Hispanics are less likely to receive pretrial releases, a major reason being their inability to pay bail. Another factor may be that "judges and other court actors develop 'patterned responses' that express both gender and race-ethnicity assessments relative to blameworthiness, dangerousness, risk of recidivism or flight" (Demuth and Steffensmeier 2004).

If convicted, sentencing is the next stage. Sentencing goes to the heart of questions about the fairness of the criminal justice system. As is the case with likelihood of arrest and conviction, those who are lower in status do worse than others when it comes to sentencing. Even when the type of offense and previous criminal record are taken into account, lower-income individuals have been found to receive longer sentences. Some studies, however, find that this relationship occurs for some crimes but not for others (D'Alessio and Stolzenberg 1993). In their study of burglary and larceny crimes, Clarke and Koch (1976) argued that lower-income persons have less of a chance for pretrial release on bail and for a private rather than a court-appointed attorney.

TABLE 12.2 Estimated Rates of Victimization in Violent and Property Crimes, by Race, Ethnicity, Sex, Income, and Residence: 2005

Victim/Household Characteristics	Violent Crime Victimization Rate*	Property Crime Victimization Rate*
Race		
White	21	156
Black	29	145
Other	14	123
Ethnicity		
Hispanic	26	210
Non-Hispanic	22	148
Sex		
Male	26	——
Female	18	——
Household Income		
Under $7,500	38	201
$7,500–$14,999	27	174
$15,000–$24,999	30	170
$25,000–$34,999	26	174
$35,000–$49,999	22	160
$50,000–$74,999	21	156
$75,000 and over	16	171
Residence		
Urban	30	200
Suburban	19	141
Rural	16	125
Home Ownership		
Owned	——	137
Rented	——	192

*Rates for violent crime are per 1,000 persons age 12 and older and do not include murder or manslaughter; rates for property crime are per 1,000 households. All rates rounded.

Source: Kathleen Maguire and Ann L. Pastore (Eds.), *Sourcebook of Criminal Justice Statistics—2008*, U.S. Department of Justice, Bureau of Justice Statistics (Washington, D.C.: U.S. Government Printing Office, 2008), Tables 3.21, 3.22, 3.23, 3.4, 3.5, 3.8, and 3.9. Online at www.albany.edu/sourcebook. Accessed on October 6, 2008.

This may explain why they found that low-income defendants received harsher punishment. After examining results from many studies, Jeffrey Reiman (2004) concluded that, generally, *"for the same crime,* the system is more likely to investigate and detect, arrest and charge, convict and sentence, sentence to prison and for a longer time, a lower-class individual than a middle- or upper-class individual" (p. 146).

A review of studies conducted between 1980 and early 2003 indicates that young, unemployed Black or Hispanic men are especially likely to

Turnips and Jail Time

Should individuals be put in jail or prison if they cannot afford to pay a monetary penalty? This question came up in a 2011 case involving a South Carolina father who did not make his required $50 per week child support payments. He spent 1 year in jail because he could not pay the child-support money he owed. Since he faced a jail term, he said that a public attorney should have been provided to him so he could have more effectively argued his case. South Carolina is one of four states that do not provide attorneys for indigent defendants involved in child support cases. Poor defendants who cannot make child-support payments because they simply do not have the money have been referred to as "turnips" (as in the phrase *you can't get blood out of a turnip*; Mincy and Sorenson 1998). The case has been referred to the U.S. Supreme Court. How would you decide and defend this case? Should the person be sent to jail or not? ▪

receive lengthy sentences compared to their White counterparts. Often, although not always, this relationship is found even when other relevant factors such as previous record are taken into account. Harsher penalties are also meted out if the victim of the crime is White and the perpetrator is Black. In cases of murder, the death penalty is more likely to be given to Blacks who have been convicted of killing Whites (Sentencing Project 2005b). In his analysis of 7 years of data from Harris County, Texas, Scott Phillips (2009) found that the probability of receiving the death penalty would be 20 times greater for a poor Black person who murdered a respected, culturally and socially involved, high-status person than if a White high status person killed a low-status, unsophisticated, marginal individual. Between 1995 and 2000, 72 percent of the 159 cases recommended for the death penalty in the federal judicial system included minority defendants. Plea agreements waiving the death penalty were twice as likely to occur if the defendant was White, and prosecuting attorneys were about twice as likely to seek the death penalty in cases with a Black defendant and a non-Black victim. A survey of 28 studies involving cases in state judicial systems revealed the same relationship between defendant/victim characteristics and receipt of the death penalty (Sentencing Project 2005b). Moreover, some research suggests that darker-skinned Blacks are more likely than lighter-skinned Blacks to receive the death penalty (Trei 2006). In January 2010, 41 percent of the 3,261 prisoners under a death sentence were Black, 44 percent were White, and 12 percent were Hispanic. In 2006, slightly more than half of death-row prisoners possessed less than a high school education; only 9 percent had any college education at all. Almost all (98 percent) were male (Pastore and Maguire 2008).

While most of those given a death sentence are actually executed, the probability of being executed is higher for Black inmates convicted of killing Whites than it is for other death row inmates (Jacobs et al. 2007). Not surprisingly, a significantly larger percentage of Blacks than Whites are against the death penalty, in part because they believe the criminal justice system is biased against them. Rather than attributing Black incarceration to bias, Whites, on the other hand, are more likely to believe that Blacks simply commit more crimes (Peffley and Hurwitz 2007).

In addition to the death penalty, length of sentence is also related to race. Research on the judicial systems in seven states found that Blacks and males are more likely to be sentenced for longer terms than Whites or females if the jurisdiction involved is conservative and subscribes to a "law-and-order" perspective (Helms and Jacobs 2002). Longer sentences are given also, in part, because crime in general is considered "a black phenomenon" (Chiricos, Welch, and Gertz 2004, p. 380). Some crimes in particular, for example drug offenses, are considered minority crimes, and consequently result in stiffer punishment for Blacks and Hispanics (Steffensmeier and Demuth 2000). A national survey in 2002 suggested that there is a "conflation of race and crime" in the minds of many Americans, part of a broad brush that paints Blacks as bad in general and as a "social threat" in particular (Chiricos, Welch, and Gertz 2004, p. 380). This is consistent with the earlier discussion regarding the image and classification of young, mentally ill Black men as dangerous, paranoid, and schizophrenic.

In some cases, however, Blacks may receive more lenient sentences than Whites for the same crimes if (1) the victim involved was Black, (2) White paternalism toward or guilt about Blacks is present, and/or (3) Blacks are perceived as being less responsible because they are exposed to more stressful living conditions than Whites (Kleck 1981).

The concern for crime and punishment in the United States is reflected in its rapidly growing jail and prison populations. Since 1980, the number of individuals in federal and state prisons in the United States has increased more than fourfold to reach almost 1.6 million persons in 2006, giving this nation the largest rate of incarceration in the world (Sabol 2007). *Jail* inmates totaled more than 766,000 in 2006. Table 12.3 profiles the populations for jails and state prisons. Compared to the outside population, inmates have lower levels of education. Jail inmates are also 8 to 11 times and prison inmates 4 to 6 times more likely than individuals in the general population to have been homeless at least sometime during the year before their incarceration (Greenberg and Rosenheck 2008a, 2008b). Minorities in general, with a disproportionate number of Blacks, compose the majority of those populations. In fact, almost 13 percent of Black men aged 25–29 were in jail or prison in 2004 ("Nation's Inmate," April 25, 2005).

The impact of such high rates of minority incarceration reaches beyond prison walls to affect inmates' future employment and present political power. Recent research in Milwaukee found

TABLE 12.3 Percent Distribution of Jail Inmates and State Prison Inmates

	Jail Inmates (2009)	State Prison Inmates (2004)*
Sex		
Male	88	93
Female	12	7
Race, Hispanic Origin		
White, non-Hispanic	43	35
Black, non-Hispanic	39	39
Hispanic	16	19
Other	2	2
Education	*(1996)*	*(1997)*
8th grade or less	13	14
Some high school	33	26
GED	14	29
High school graduate	26	21
Some college	10	9
College graduate or more	3	2

*Includes only those sentenced for 1 year or more.

Source: Kathleen Maguire and Ann L. Pastore (Eds.), *Sourcebook of Criminal Justice Statistics,* U.S. Department of Justice, Bureau of Justice Statistics (Washington, D.C.: U.S. Government Printing Office), Tables 6.0001, 6.17, and 6.45. Online at www.albany.edu/sourcebook.

that even with identical résumés, not only were job applicants with criminal records less likely than noncriminals to be called back for interviews, but Black *noncriminals* even got fewer callbacks than Whites with *criminal* records. Whether Black or White, having a criminal record decreases the chances for employment. This is especially true for Blacks (Pager 2003). Imprisonment also erodes the employment skills and related human capital of inmates, making them less likely and less eager to seek employment after being in prison (Apel and Sweeten 2010). It should not be surprising, therefore, to find that criminal conviction also reduces one's future income, especially if the conviction happens when one is young (Kerley, Benson, and Lee 2004). The loss of an inmate's income while in prison, the lower earnings after release, the cost of visiting inmates, and the high probability that the conviction carried monetary fines which need to be paid, all exacerbate the already low incomes of most inmates and their families (Western and Wildeman 2009; Harris, Evans, and Beckett 2010; Wakefield and Uggen 2010; Wildeman and Western 2010). These effects further reduce the chances of building up wealth for the next generation and help reproduce inequality.

Prison incarceration also reduces a person's political power because 48 out of 50 states in the United States do not allow prison inmates to vote. Many states also severely limit the chances of individuals voting even after they have served their sentences. About 4.7 million citizens, including 1.4 million Black men, do not have voting rights as a result (Sentencing Project, 2005a). A recent telephone survey of adults indicated that a large majority of citizens favor restoring voting rights to ex-felons, but only about one-third believe that felons currently in prison should be allowed to vote (Manza, Brooks, and Uggen 2002). Many of the disenfranchisement rules were passed after the Civil War during Reconstruction, when Blacks were a potential political force. States in which non-Whites make up a large percentage of the prison population are those most likely to have the most restrictive disenfranchisement laws (Behrens, Uggen, and

Manza 2003). Beyond simply forbidding prisoners to vote, strict disenfranchisement rules may also have a dampening effect on voting rates of Blacks and lower socioeconomic groups in general, further weakening the impact of these groups on political outcomes and policies (Bowers and Preuhs 2009). Such laws can and do affect who gets elected to the U.S. Congress and the presidency (Uggen and Manza 2002). Whether intentional or not, both imprisonment and disenfranchisement serve as means of controlling and disempowering Black men.

In contrast to the correlations of race and socioeconomic status with sentencing, the relationship between gender and sentencing is more complicated. Recent studies are more mixed in their results than earlier ones that suggested a paternalistic or chivalric reaction to female offenders. Nagel and Weitzman's often-cited study (1971) of national data concerning over 11,000 criminal cases revealed that while the poor and

The negative effects of imprisonment go far beyond the isolation, monotony, and regimentation experienced by inmates. They also include strained family relationships, disenfranchisement, and dampening of future economic prospects. (© Dan Bannister/Shutterstock)

Blacks received less favorable treatment than well-off Whites, women were treated more leniently. They were less likely to be held in jail before the trial and to be sentenced to prison. The analysis focused on the crimes of grand larceny and assault. A study by Curran (1983) in Florida supported the leniency argument. She found that at the sentencing stage of the criminal process women received lighter sentences even when relevant legal (e.g., prior arrests, etc.) and other nonlegal (race, age, occupational status) factors were taken into account. Whether female defendants are treated more leniently may depend on the crime and circumstances involved. Ragatz and Russell (2009) found that heterosexual women involved in a love triangle and arrested for homicide were seen as less guilty and given shorter sentences than others arrested for the same crime.

Whether a judge is male or female also affects the probability of incarceration and length of sentence. In contrast to the image of women as more lenient, female judges tend to be harsher in their sentencing. They are more likely than male judges to incarcerate an offender and for a longer period of time. Judges of both genders are less likely to incarcerate White, older, and female offenders, but this is especially the case for female judges. Female judges are significantly more likely than their male counterparts to give longer sentences to Black repeat offenders. In other words, offender characteristics affect the decisions of women on the bench more so than those of male judges (Steffensmeier and Hebert 1999).

WHITE-COLLAR CRIME, CORPORATE CRIME, AND PUNISHMENT

All the adult crimes discussed thus far involve those listed on the FBI's Crime Index. **White-collar** or **suite crimes** are not part of the FBI's Crime Index, which raises further questions about equity in the treatment of types of crime generally associated with different segments of the population. Generally, though not always, white-collar crime refers to crimes committed by white-collar persons in the course of their occupations. It is the latter part of the definition that is critical; thus,

blue-collar workers who steal or defraud in the course of their jobs might be considered guilty of similar crimes, but ordinarily the focus has been on those in the higher-status occupations.

Since the crime occurs in the context of a job, white-collar crime usually involves a violation of trust. Thus, such acts as misadvertising, price fixing, identity theft, computer scams, insurance fraud, and other kinds of duplicities and misrepresentations are a part of white-collar crime. Losses to the victims of white-collar crime are estimated to be over $250 billion annually, compared to estimates of $18 billion for ordinary street crimes, which receive more publicity (Holtfreter et al. 2008).

More recently, larger-scale corporate scandals have involved alleged insider trading, and accounting irregularities and misrepresentation of company assets that have bilked stockholders and drained the retirement packages of thousands of average employees. Investigations of criminality have included large corporations integral to the U.S. economy: Enron, WorldCom, Xerox, Tyco International, Adelphia, Global Crossing, Kmart, Columbia/HCA, and Sunbeam, for example. These acts constitute "corporate crimes," which are crimes committed by businesses or by high-level officials acting in their capacity as representatives of given corporations. Billions of dollars are involved in these cases alone. As of 2008, the savings-and-loans scandals of the 1980s is estimated to have cost taxpayers about $160 billion. A more current example is Medicare fraud by health care professionals and fake clinics that falsify billings in order to get large sums of money from the government. In many cases, the alleged procedures were never performed. In 2011, it was estimated that Medicare fraud costs taxpayers billions of dollars every year ("100 Accused" 2011).

Corporate crime appears to be extensive and it is expensive. As only one example, an analysis of 959 cases of occupational fraud committed between 2006 and 2008 estimated that organizations lose over $900 billion each year to crimes involving bribery, kickbacks, extortion, deceitful billing, and related offenses. Owners, executives, or managers are the offenders in more than half of the cases, with other employees accounting for the remainder (Association of Certified Fraud Examiners 2008). But white-collar crime is not a new phenomenon. A study of white-collar crime during World War II uncovered well over 300,000 violations of the price and rationing rules of the Office of Price Administration in 1944 alone (Clinard 1946).

Generally, individual white-collar crimes involve many more than one victim. When safety-code violations or price fixing occur, for example, many are harmed or seriously injured. In fact, although one ordinarily does not think of white-collar crime as violent, "there is considerable evidence that so-called 'nonviolent' white-collar criminals kill and maim more people each year in the United States than do violent street criminals" (Messner and Rosenfeld 1994, p. 32). An average of 6,000 workers die from occupational injuries every year, and roughly 50,000 are killed by occupational illnesses such as brown lung, asbestosis, and different forms of cancer connected to their work (Loeb, February 19, 2003). An additional heavy cost of white-collar crime is the erosion of faith in social institutions that occurs when such crime takes place. Trust is a basis of solidarity and when it is damaged, society as a whole suffers. Thus, the damage resulting from white-collar crime radiates from the immediate victims to include many more.

At the beginning of this chapter, I noted how crime is often "defined" into existence. The terms used to describe street crime—robbery, theft, murder, and so on—leave little doubt of the nature of the behavior involved. In contrast, white-collar crimes are often described in more ambiguous and softer terms like financial "malfeasance," book-keeping "irregularities," and "misconduct." "Misconduct" does not seem quite as criminal as "theft," even though *stealing* may be what is involved in both cases. This terminology and the complicated nature of these cases, along with the physical appearance and self-definition of white-collar defendants as upstanding citizens, encourages a different treatment of white-collar defendants. Some argue that the terminology has to become more straightforward: "you've got to boil it down to lying, cheating, and

stealing," says a securities board commissioner (Leaf 2002, p. 76).

Corporate officials who commit **corporate crimes** are also usually subject to civil rather than to criminal law, and such violations are handled by agencies rather than by the criminal courts. This is because "corporations" have not, traditionally, been considered "persons" who commit criminal acts with "intent" (Reid 1988). The manner in which white-collar crime is treated—namely, the special kind of legislation, the special kind of enforcement groups used, and the generally minimal types of punishment meted out—indicates that white-collar crime is treated differently than street crime in the U.S. justice system, even though its cost to victims is much greater.

Wheeler, Weisburd and Bode's early study (1982) of several white-collar crimes over a 3-year period in seven federal districts suggests that socioeconomic status is positively related to being incarcerated and to the length of sentence given those convicted of these crimes. The crimes included in the study were eight federal crimes: "antitrust offenses, securities and exchange fraud, postal and wire fraud, false claims and statements, credit and lending institution fraud, bank embezzlement, IRS fraud, and bribery" (p. 642). Paradoxically, the authors found that not only were those with occupations of higher prestige more likely to be imprisoned and given longer sentences but the same was also true for those with less impeccable past lives. They suggested that a "paradox of leniency and severity" runs through a judge's decisions on these matters, impeccability and SES pulling in opposite directions. Men were much more likely than women to be sent to prison: "There is something about the specter of women behind the bars and walls of the prison that leads many judges to a kind of protective paternalism" (p. 656).

Following up on Wheeler and colleagues' model of sentencing, Benson and Walker (1988) studied sentencing for a sample of white-collar criminals in one federal court over a 10-year period. In contrast to the Wheeler study, Benson and Walker found that SES and impeccability had little to do with the decision to send an offender to prison. They also found that non-Whites were more likely than Whites to be imprisoned even after SES was taken into account. In essence, most of their results contradict those of Wheeler and associates. They attribute much of this variation to differences in the distribution of crimes among the sample, the differences in the districts studied, and perhaps different values among judges in large urban settings and those in smaller rural areas.

As illuminating as these studies may be, they do not address the issues of what percentage of alleged white-collar crimes are actually brought to court, or the length of sentences perpetrators receive. In these areas, there appears to be a greater discrepancy between white-collar and street crimes. This is especially the case for high-level crimes: "The U.S. regulatory and judiciary systems . . . do little if anything to deter the most damaging Wall Street crimes" (Leaf 2002, p. 64). White-collar criminals convicted of massive fraud in the 1980s savings-and-loan crisis served an average of just over 3 years in prison, while common burglars (usually stealing $300 or less) received sentences of 4.5 years, and first-time drug criminals got about 5.4 years (Leaf 2002).

In 2000, 8,766 individual were charged with white-collar crimes and 6,876 (78 percent) were convicted. Of these, almost 4,000 were sent to prison (Leaf 2002). On closer examination, however, we find that all kinds of crimes, including welfare fraud, are included in the "white-collar" category, and that only 226 of these cases are for securities or commodities fraud. The high-level, "*starched*-collar criminals" are generally not in this group (Leaf 2002, p. 68). These starched-collar criminals are often guilty of corporate crimes since they were committing crimes to benefit their companies and as acting officials of their companies. In contrast, white-collar crime like embezzlement, for example, is a crime committed by an employee for his or her own gain.

Of the 156,238 people in federal prisons in late 2001, only 1,021 were white-collar criminals, and less than 10 percent of these were starched-collar criminals. Moreover, over half of the white-collar inmates are in minimum rather than "medium" or "maximum" security prisons (Leaf 2002).

Since 2002, there have been several high-profile convictions of corporate executives for fraud, grand larceny, conspiracy, obstruction of justice, and/or money laundering. These include CEOs at WorldCom, Tyco International, and Adelphia Communications. Because of the publicity given major corporate scandals recently, a majority of citizens consider white-collar crime serious, and public opinion about punishment for white-collar criminals has become harsher (Holtfreter, Piquero, and Piquero 2008). In this climate so have some of the punishments. Former CEOs of Enron and WorldCom were sentenced to 24 to 25 years, for example; a former stock analyst at Goldman Sachs & Co. was sentenced to almost 5 years for his role in a $6.7 million fraud, and British Petroleum (BP) was fined $20 million for its oil spill in Prudhoe Bay, which was a violation of the Clean Water Act (Podgor 2007; "BP Pleads Guilty" 2008; "Former Stock Analyst" 2008). In 2009, a sentence of 150 years was given to stockbroker and investment advisor Bernie Madoff for a **Ponzi scheme** that defrauded thousands of investors of $50–$65 billion. The Great Recession of 2009–2010 exposed a variety of financial crimes that contributed to the financial crisis, creating an incentive for officials to pay closer attention to white-collar crimes and their punishment. Some of these, such as mortgage fraud, appear to have been perpetrated disproportionately on those living in poorer socioeconomic neighborhoods (Carswell and Bachtel 2009).

The Roots of White-Collar and Corporate Crime

The lower probability that white-collar or corporate crimes will result in convictions and incarceration reflects difficulties and deficiencies in the system of justice: case overloads, ambiguous and vague regulatory laws, powerful law teams at the disposal of some but not others, and the complexity of the cases themselves. These deficiencies help to account for the commission of these types of crime.

But there are other proposed explanations. One argument focuses on the greed and immorality of individual perpetrators. In this view, white-collar crime is the result of a few "bad apples" with character flaws. A second view emphasizes the role that U.S. and corporate cultures play in encouraging this type of crime. U.S. culture encourages free enterprise and open competition, honors economic winners rather than losers, and winks at those clever people who are able to "pull the wool" over others' eyes. Similarly, and over other values, corporate culture sometimes encourages success and profit making and taking full advantage of opportunities to maximize the bottom line. This may even involve intentionally protecting valuable executives from accusations of criminality (Lyons 2002).

A third, and potentially more perceptive, view involves the political structure and economic context within which corporations operate. This is especially relevant for corporate rather than simple white-collar crime. A significant part of the structure that affects corporations is the federal regulation to which they are subject. In this case, regulations are often vague and ambiguous, leaving room for multiple interpretations. They are also complex: "[J]uries have a hard time grasping abstract financial concepts, and well-counseled executives have plenty of tricks for distancing themselves from responsibility" (France and Carney 2002, p. 35). The broadness of the regulations means that while a given activity might be considered immoral, it is not necessarily illegal. Sometimes changes in rules create opportunities for crime. Banking deregulation in the 1980s, for example, made it possible for savings and loans associations to engage in fraudulent actions because deregulation removed many of the controls that held these institutions in check. Repeal of earlier laws such as the Glass-Steagall Act removed central limitations that had been placed on banks. Deregulation created an economic climate in which greed, risk taking, and corporate crime were encouraged. In addition to lack of effective regulations and lax monitoring of financial transactions, resource inadequacies and case overloads in enforcement agencies encourage illicit and unethical activity by lessening the chances of getting caught or being indicted. Large, complicated cases are costly, and indictment rates are low (Tillman, Calavita, and Pontell 1997). Finally, corporate lobbying for favorable legislation facilitates regulations that are pro-business. The result is that, while the average person may consider certain legal behaviors to be unethical and even "criminal," they may be allowable under law. For example, the "business-judgment rule" permits business executives to carry out almost any transaction as long as it could be interpreted as economically sound and is not clearly illegal. The broadness of this rule has resulted in executives being protected from many legal actions against them. Rules allowing corporations to export earnings to avoid taxation, allowing stock options to be left undefined as company costs, and allowing executives but not other employees to sell company stock during certain times reveal the corporate bias in many regulatory laws. In Charles Derber's opinion (2000, p. 148), "[T]he business-judgment rule and the growing set of constitutional rights vested in the corporation have created an unaccountable entity with sovereign powers far greater than natural entity theorists of the Gilded Age could ever have imagined." Favorable rules and laws, when combined with the lobbying power of corporations, optimize the opportunity to *define* what is legal and what is not. In a broad sense, these conditions demonstrate the role of economic power in directing operations within the criminal justice system.

With respect to corporate crime, a capitalist society in which corporations must successfully compete to survive creates pressures to violate the law. The uncertainties in the social, political, and economic environments in which corporate profits must be obtained make success problematic (Box 1983). Corporations, like other large organizations, try to control their environments in order to create a level of certainty in their operations, and they are powerful actors in their own right. One of the means to create predictability in the resource and consumer markets is to behave in an illegal manner. When legitimate means to obtaining organizational goals are either difficult to use or unavailable, pressure exists to obtain legitimate goals such as profit by illegitimate means. This suggests that capitalism itself helps to generate corporate and white-collar crimes.

HATE CRIMES AND INEQUALITY

Social conditions also affect the number of crimes committed against members of demeaned status groups. **Hate crimes** are violent or property crimes against someone or some group primarily because of the victim's race, religion, disability [mental or physical], gender, sexual orientation, gender identity, or ethnicity/national origin. One characteristic that distinguishes them from other crimes is the nature of the motivation. Hate crimes have a symbolic function in that they are directed as a *warning* against groups of low status. Consequently, who the specific victims are may be irrelevant to the perpetrator(s) since they serve only as a representative of the group. As warnings, hate crimes are aimed at reinforcing the existing social hierarchies and keeping groups in their place. Thus, their effects of intimidation and fear reach into the entire group, not just the individual victim. Expectations are that hate crimes will not only continue but also increase in the future as the United States becomes more diversified and as pressures mount for dominant groups to share scarce economic, political, and other resources (Perry 2001; Craig 2002).

Knowledge about the extent, causes, and consequences of hate crimes is incomplete for several reasons. First, there has been little systematic research on hate crimes. "The empirical investigation of the causes of hate crime remains a science in its infancy" (Green, McFalls, and Smith 2001, p. 490). Second, states vary in the groups that they include as potential victims, making rate comparisons difficult and conclusions about total numbers suspect. Moreover, some states do not provide any information. Third, hate crimes are underreported; enforcement of hate crime laws is particularly lax in states with a history of lynching and large Black populations (King, Messner, and Baller 2009).

Despite deficiencies, the FBI data are generally used to reach conclusions about hate crimes in the United States as a whole. The gathering of these data began as a result of the Hate Crimes Statistics Act in 1990. In 2009, according to FBI statistics, 6,604 hate crime incidents were reported, involving 8,336 victims. Just over half were racially motivated, followed by biases based on religion, sexual orientation, ethnicity/nationality, and disability, respectively (see Table 12.4). About 59 percent of the perpetrators were White; one-third of the victims were targets of anti-Black feelings.

Extreme concerns about racial and ethnic purity, continued immigration, job competition, residential infiltration, and the sanctity of marriage and Christianity most often lie behind these biases. Target groups are viewed as threats to the living standards of perpetrators, who see their own way of life as under siege from contaminating elements.

Biases against particular groups are long-standing. As we saw in Chapter 8, abusive acts against Blacks were permitted during slavery, and the creation of the Ku Klux Klan (KKK) after the Civil War helped keep racist fires burning. Current White separatist groups in the United States include the various segments of the KKK, neo-Nazi and skinhead groups, and some extreme Christian groups such as Christian Identity and the Christian Defense League. Estimates in the mid-1990s put the number of members and supporters of these groups at 200,000 (Dobratz and Shanks-Meile 1997).

One of the more publicized instances of a racial hate crime was committed on June 7, 1998, against 49-year-old James Byrd, Jr., a Black man, in Jasper, Texas. Byrd was picked up, beaten, chained to the bumper of a pickup truck, and dragged three miles until his head, shoulder, and other body parts were severed from each other. Showing no remorse and only contempt for Byrd and his family, John William King, a White supremacist and one of three White men arrested for the murder, was sentenced to death (Lyman 1999).

A second widely publicized case occurred the fall of 1998. Matthew Shepard, a 21-year-old gay college student, was kidnapped, robbed,

TABLE 12.4 Number of Incidents and Victims of Hate Crimes by Bias Motivation: 2009

Motivation	No. of Incidents	No. of Victims
Race	*3,199*	*4,057*
Anti-White	545	668
Anti-Black	2,284	2,902
Other	370	487
Religion	*1,303*	*1,575*
Anti-Jewish	931	1,132
Other	372	443
Sexual Orientation	*1,223*	*1,482*
Anti-male homosexual	682	817
Anti-female homosexual	185	227
Anti-homosexual	312	391
Ethnicity/National Origin	*777*	*1,109*
Anti-Hispanic	483	692
Other	294	417
Disability	*96*	*99*
Anti-physical	25	25
Anti-mental	71	74
Multiple-Bias Incidents	*6*	*14*
Total	6,604	8,336

Source: Federal Bureau of Investigation, *Hate Crime Statistics 2009,* November 2010. Washington, D.C.: U.S. Department of Justice.

beaten, and tied to a fence in Laramie, Wyoming. Shepard died from his ordeal less than a week later (Brooke 1998). Individuals who are openly gay and have public associations with gay organizations and activities are especially vulnerable to hate crimes because they are more easily identified as homosexuals, a group that has had a denigrated status in our society (Waldner and Berg 2008).

Like racism, prejudice against homosexuals has deep historical roots, principally highlighted by laws against sodomy, which were in place as early as the 1600s in the United States, and which required the death penalty or severe mutilation as punishment. Such laws continued in many states until 2003, when the U.S. Supreme Court

declared them unconstitutional. Among other elements, feelings of superiority and concerns about competition over resources demonstrate the role of status inequality in the production of hate crimes.

SOCIAL INEQUALITY AND ENVIRONMENTAL EQUITY

Criminal justice is an issue closely linked to conditions of social inequality, and it affects the community at large. **Environmental equity** is another social problem that has been tied to social, especially racial, inequality. This problem principally concerns the unequal access to land resources and variations in proximity to dangerous environmental hazards. Generally, environmental equity has not been considered a part of the area of social inequality, and consequently, few social-inequality researchers have addressed this issue. Indeed, the first serious studies of environmental equity go back only to the early 1980s.

Since it is reasonable to hypothesize that in the competition for a decent and healthy life, those with fewer resources and less power will lose out to those with more, and since the accessibility of attractive land and geographic location of potentially dangerous wastes likely affect the chances citizens have for a healthy life, the study of environmental equity legitimately belongs in the field of social inequality. Whatever the effects of accessibility and location are, "those impacts will fall unevenly, along existing divisions of wealth/poverty, power/powerlessness; the transformations of nature will tend to occur in a way that reproduces and exacerbates existing social inequalities. In effect, environmental inequality is one facet or moment of social inequality. . . . [It is] a necessary and inevitable facet of social inequalities, embedded in the very fabric of modern societies" (Szasz and Meuser 1997, pp. 116–117).

The last several decades have witnessed increased competition over land as developers have sought to purchase prime settings, gentrify poor urban neighborhoods, construct gated communities, and gain access to publicly owned areas. The more economically and politically powerful are better positioned to win this competition. As scenic shore land is bought up by those who can afford it, for example, access to some of the country's most beautiful sites becomes restricted. Even access to national parks is limited to those who can afford it because of the need to pay fees.

In addition to battles over owning or controlling access to desirable tracts of land, another component of the conflicts over land is what has been called "environmental racism." This conflict involves the claim that the poor and/or minorities are disproportionately exposed to various kinds of dangerous waste sites and to hazardous chemical contamination. It is to this debate that we will now briefly turn.

Two major events helped give impetus to the "environmental justice movement" in the 1980s. One was a protest. Poor citizens had organized and successfully fought off the building of an industrial-waste landfill in their North Carolina county. A second event involved the publication of three studies which provided evidence that hazardous waste facilities tended to be located in areas with heavy Black populations (Bullard 1983; U.S. General Accounting Office 1983; United Church of Christ 1987).

Most current environmental-racism research examines either (1) the differential location of commercial treatment, storage, and disposal of hazardous waste facilities (TSDFs) or (2) the degree of exposure to toxic chemical releases as measured by the U.S. Environmental Protection Agency's (EPA) Toxic Release Inventory (TRI). We will discuss examples of each of these types of studies in turn to arrive at a conclusion about the existence of environmental inequity. Anderton and colleagues (1994) examined government census-tract data to analyze the relationship between the location of minority populations and the presence of commercial TSDFs. Rather than race or ethnicity, they found that the most consistent predictors of TSDF location were a lower percentage of males employed and a higher percentage of employment in precision manufacturing. That is, TSDFs tend to be found in industrial areas.

The authors cautioned that their results do not mean that environmental *racism* does not exist, but only that, with their measures and sampling method, they did not find a relationship. In fact, even though their results yielded no evidence of environmental racism, they concluded that "[r]acism is a continuing, pervasive problem in our society; it would be surprising to find that environmental matters were somehow immune to this problem" (Anderton et al. 1994, p. 244). One significant limitation of this and other studies using commercial TSDFs as a measure is that the latter compose less than 10 percent of all

Toxic waste sites, which can be significant health hazards, are more likely to be located in areas populated by minorities and those of lower socioeconomic status. Home property values near these sites suffer making it more likely for those with little capital to be able to afford homes there, but also making it less likely for residents to move from there. (© deserttrends/Fotolia LLC)

hazardous waste facilities and handle less than 5 percent of all U.S. hazardous waste material (Ringquist 2000). Estimates suggest that there are several hundred thousand unregistered waste sites in the United States that may contain toxic chemicals (Szasz and Meuser 1997). In addition to these sites, there are nonhazardous waste landfills for which there is no national database as well as other unregulated dumping sites. Moreover, "commercial" TSDFs only *take in* material produced elsewhere; they do not produce their own hazardous waste.

Another investigation of environmental equity using TSDFs as a dependent variable examined the location of all 82 TSDFs in Los Angeles County (Boer et al. 1997). Because it involves only the Los Angeles area, generalizations from this case study should be made with great caution. Nevertheless, the results support the thesis of environmental racism: TSDFs are more likely to be located in areas with high minority populations. Interestingly, like Anderton and colleagues, researchers found that Hispanics were more likely than Blacks to be residing near a

TSDF. The authors suggested that the relationship may, in part, be related to the fact that Anderton and colleagues' sample was drawn from the Southwest, a region where Hispanics are prominent.

In addition to race and ethnicity, like Anderton and colleagues, this study found that TSDFs were more likely to be sited in areas of industrial use and high employment in manufacturing. Finally, income also was found to be related to TSDF location, but not in a linear manner. Both poor and wealthy areas were less likely than working-class sections to contain TSDFs. The authors suggested that this may be because, on the one hand, poor areas have little employment of any kind (even in TSDFs), and on the other, wealthier neighborhoods can more easily fight off those who would want to build a TSDF in their area. The basic conclusion is that TSDFs are most likely to be located in industrial areas that have a high percentage of minority working-class residents. The largest hazardous waste landfill in the United States is located in a poor, rural, overwhelmingly Black town in Alabama. The operation receives waste from 48 states and some foreign nations (Herbert, October 5, 2006).

General reviews of past TSDF studies concluded that race is a significant predictor of TSDF location, even though these studies have methodological limitations (Ringquist 2000; Lester, Allen, and Hill 2001). Research utilizing exposure to pollutants rather than TSDFs as a measure also tended to find a relationship between minority populations and toxic pollution. Some research has found that poor, working class, and Black individuals are more likely than other groups to live near environmental hazards or facilities that emit polluting chemicals (Mohai et al. 2008; Scanlan 2009). Daniels and Friedman (1999) examined aerial release of more than 300 toxic chemicals over all U.S. counties, as recorded by the TRI. Despite its deficiencies, "the TRI is currently—and will likely continue to be—the most consistent and comprehensive source of information on environmental contaminant releases" (p. 252). The results showed a positive relationship between the proportion of the population that was Black and the emission of toxic chemicals, even when controls such as urbanization and presence of manufacturing were considered. Researchers found that income was curvilinearly related to the amount of chemical releases. Poor and wealthy areas had lower emissions than moderate-income or working-class counties.

Similar findings were uncovered by Ringquist (1997) in his study of the location of TRI facilities across the country. Briefly, he found that zip codes that had disproportionate numbers of Blacks and Hispanics were also more likely to have TRI facilities. This was also the case for working-class, older, urban, industrial areas. However, somewhat paradoxically, Ringquist also found that even though wealthy areas are less likely to contain any TRI facility at all, when they do they are more likely to have multiple facilities. That is, income is positively related to the *density* of TRI facilities.

The fairly consistent research finding that minority populations are more likely to live near TSDFs or be exposed to toxic chemical releases from manufacturing plants raises the question of causality. How do minority populations come to be at higher environmental risk? Is it pure racism? What were these areas like when plants first decided to move into them? Were they disproportionately composed of minorities? Do such plants intentionally locate in these areas because of the high minority population or for other reasons? Or do minority populations move into these areas because of the greater affordability of homes and availability of industrial jobs? And if they do move into these areas, is it by choice or because they are constrained to do so? The process by which the relationship between minority residence and concentration of environmental risks comes about needs to be identified to reach a fully satisfactory conclusion about the existence and nature of environmental racism.

Some of the described research does suggest that racism may be involved because housing segregation may indirectly contribute to the disproportionate exposure that Blacks receive. That is, because Blacks are more limited than Whites in where they can live, they are more often funneled into living in urban industrial areas where manufacturers emit toxic chemicals (Boer et al. 1997; Daniels and Friedman 1999). Another potential reason for the relationship is that some areas may have been zoned or targeted for industrial development by local officials, and TSDF plants, for example, may locate in a particular area because of these regulations (Boone and Modarres 1999). On this level, if racism is present, it may have resulted from the actual zoning or local planning process rather than from policies of company plants.

The research on environmental racism is growing and the issue of environmental equity in general will become more salient as competition for land use and population diversity increase across the United States. At the present time, while the bulk of the research suggests that minorities and members of the working class are more exposed to potential toxic chemicals, the research methodologies need to be improved. More information on the location of *all* toxic hazards, more agreement on which is the best unit of analysis to use in studies, and more historical examinations to identify the causal processes involved in explaining exposure levels are required.

INEQUALITY, TRUST, AND SOCIETAL WELL-BEING

Like the effects of a stone thrown on the water, the effects of inequality ripple outward from the individual, to groups and neighborhoods, and ultimately to the society as a whole. Moreover, its negative effects do not simply impact the unfortunate and minorities. *Everyone's* quality of life is damaged by high levels of inequality. In their review of evidence from dozens of studies, Wilkinson and Pickett (2009) found that greater income inequality was related to higher rates of violent crime, including homicide, obesity, poor educational achievement, mental illness, racism, hostility, morbidity, teenage births, imprisonment, and drug overdose. Inequality also helps generate governmental corruption, a greater sense of injustice among citizens, more political activism outside the voting booth, and less participation and charity-giving in the community. In a broad sense, it creates what Rory McVeigh refers to as a "social structure of discontent" (McVeigh 2006; see also Rothstein and Uslaner 2005; Uslaner and Brown 2005). Times of economic difficulty further weaken civic participation because people in tough financial straits "lose some of their trust in society" (McManus 2010, p. A11).

Within the structure of inequality in which we all live out our lives, social relationships are more tenuous and more restrictive. At the same time, in a democracy like the United States, increased contact between individuals from different income classes can intensify feelings of relative deprivation among those in the lower ranks, and magnify perceptions of the degree of economic difference between themselves and others. Inequality weakens the belief that we are all in this together; rather, it "draws attention to conflicting interests between the haves and the have-nots" (McVeigh 2006, p. 521). Social solidarity is especially weakened when inequality is tightly linked to religious and racial heterogeneity in society. This is because social ties *within* each racial, religious, and economic group will be stronger than those *between* different groups. The implication here is that societies which have less inequality will create stronger feelings of trust among its citizens as well as a sense of a common fate (Jordahl 2007).

Indeed, in cross-cultural studies and in research in the United States, the degree of economic inequality is inversely related to the degree of trust among populations. Greater inequality means less trust (Rothstein and Uslaner 2005; Jordahl 2007; Wilkinson and Pickett 2009; Elgar 2010). Multiyear data from the General Social Survey indicate that states with less inequality and more racial/ethnic homogeneity have higher levels of trust. States in the North and Northwest (North Dakota, Montana, Minnesota, South Dakota, and Wyoming) are relatively more homogeneous, have more income equality than other states, and are highest in trust. In contrast, states in the South and Southeast (Mississippi, Alabama, Arkansas, and North Carolina), which have more racially mixed citizenries and significantly more income inequality, exhibit less trust within their populations (Alesina and La Ferrara 2002).

If one thinks of a civil society as one in which most individuals are fully and cooperatively joined with others in a common enterprise that benefits all of society, that is, one in which social capital is widely and deeply spread, and one in which civility, diversity, and justice are respected (Persell 1997), then it is clear that economic inequalities weaken our civic life as a society. One of the central casualties of income inequality and inequality of opportunity is a decline in social trust within the population. This decline is significant because increases in distrust weaken faith in governmental institutions, involvement in civic activities, tolerance toward those who are different, personal happiness, and feelings of control over one's life. Trust in others implies that there is some underlying agreed-upon morality which knits different groups of society together in basic ways (Rothstein and Uslaner 2005; Zmerli and Newton 2008). The absence of such a common moral standard makes it less likely that all groups can work together effectively in the common cause that is the whole society.

Trust is especially critical in large, complex, increasingly heterogeneous societies like the United States in which virtual strangers with frequently conflicting interests must interact with each other. The instability, unpredictability, and openness of social relationships make trust a valuable commodity in part because it lowers the psychological, social, and economic prices we pay for monitoring others' behavior and enforcing rules (Jordahl 2007). "Generalized trust links us to people who are different from ourselves . . . [and it] depends upon a foundation of economic and social equality" (Rothstein and Uslaner 2005, p. 45). When inequality is high, trust is low, and in this context, the probability is low that the government will successfully enact social programs in which all groups are seen to benefit. Ultimately, inequality makes it difficult to find widespread acceptance for broad public policies that would address inequality. Thus, inequality is related to trust both as a cause and as a consequence, the result being that some countries find themselves in a repeating cycle of inequality and distrust (Rothstein and Uslaner 2005).

The fact that inequality increases distrust suggests that groups having varying positions of advantage in the income and status hierarchies will display different levels of trust—and they do. Compared to other groups, greater percentages of Blacks and those with lower incomes and educations have little trust in others (Alesina and La Ferrara 2002; Taylor, Funk, and Clark 2007; Smith 2010). The reasons for these relationships appear to be relatively straightforward. Individuals from these groups are more likely to have experienced some recent traumatic event in their lives (e.g., unemployment, hunger, prejudice), and to have experienced discrimination or mistreatment historically. They are also less likely to have been materially successful. Blacks and other minorities, for example, distrust more often because they believe that they have been treated unfairly, compared to other groups. Living in neighborhoods that suffer from high rates of unemployment,

poverty, and violent crime exacerbate feelings of fear and distrust, feelings that can be passed on to the next generation (Alesina and La Ferrara 2002; Smith 2010).

In her excellent study of intergenerational poverty in Mississippi Delta and Appalachian communities, Cynthia Duncan found that historical structures of racial and class oppression created situations in which gaps between the privileged and impoverished remained intact over time. Biased structures of opportunity, patronage, stereotyping, and segregation were among the mechanisms that served to perpetuate class and racial inequalities. These, in turn, heightened distrust between groups and strengthened attitudes of self-interest and weakened feelings of obligation to the community (Duncan 1999). The end result was a poor civic culture, an absence of investment in the community as a whole, and a perpetuation of poverty. In short, economic and social inequality harms the whole community.

SOCIAL CONSEQUENCES ON A GLOBAL SCALE

Just as distrust is greater in countries with higher degrees of inequality, so too are problems like crime and environmental degradation. Pratt and Godsey's study (2003) of 47 countries revealed that income inequality in a country was positively related to its homicide rate. Its effect was especially noticeable when the amount of social support provided for the population by the government was low. The percentage of a country's gross domestic product used in public spending on health care was how the authors measured the degree of "social support." This suggests that the civic and political framework within which citizens live has an impact on the role that inequality plays in generating violent crime. If not paid by the government, health care costs can place an economic strain on individuals, a strain that may, together with other economic needs, instigate property crime. Indeed, economic difficulties accelerate robbery rates by Blacks in racially heterogeneous cities, which, in turn, increase interracial homicides by them (Wadsworth and

Kubrin 2004). In sum, societies with high degrees of income inequality create pressures that generate both property and violent crime.

A recent global study of white-collar corporate crime involving 5,500 corporations examined the extent of economic crimes against them, and how they address these crimes and plan to control their commission (Bussmann and Werle 2006). The crimes studied included embezzlement, insider trading, bribery, kickbacks, accounting fraud, money laundering, and similar violations. Almost half of the companies had experienced at least one of these crimes. Rates were highest in Africa, Australia, and the United States, and lowest in Asian countries like Hong Kong and Japan. The differences in rates are probably due to a variety of factors, for example, methods of crime control, willingness to report crimes or to deal with them informally, and differences in definitions of crime. However, a disproportionate number of the offenders have high social statuses in their companies. Over 40 percent occupy positions in middle management or higher. They also have educations that are above average. Financial and reputational losses to companies tend to be greater when the crimes are committed by high-level employees.

Finally, an examination of relationships between countries also uncovers abuses against the environment. More than half of the 370 million pieces of electronic equipment waste that U.S. citizens disposed of in 2007 were shipped to developing countries such as Pakistan, China, and India. While the European Union has had tougher waste disposal regulations, Nigeria and Ghana still receive a significant portion of their electronic trash (Young 2009). The higher energy consumption of industrial nations like the United States results in a high level of carbon dioxide and other gas emissions, ozone depletion, deforestation, and resource consumption. In the first major global study to estimate the costs of rich countries' ecological impact, researchers examined human activities during the period 1961–2000, and estimated that the cost of the damage brought about by practices in wealthy countries totals well over $2 trillion. "The imbalance of activity and harm is most pronounced for low-income countries. . . . Our analysis highlights the ecological harm poor countries bear to indirectly enable the living standards of wealthier countries" (Srinivasan et al. 2008, p. 1771). The authors suggest that continued globalization and economic development may even widen the gap in ecological harm borne by poor and rich countries. Given the worldwide movement of capital, finances, and resources, it should not be surprising that the ill effects of inequality spread beyond national boundaries. Many of the same processes evident in the United States are manifested on the global stage.

Summary

Inequality can affect behavior and social events in several ways. At the outset it was stated that not only individual position in the system of inequality but also the system as a whole can have such effects, and in this chapter concern was expressed for both aspects. We looked at the relationship between class, race, sex, and crime rates, as well as the relationship between capitalism/inequality and crime rates in general, and found that in each case inequality is implicated in the incidence of crime. Official statistics reveal a relationship between being Black and of low income and the probability of being arrested.

The bulk of the studies on sentencing suggests a bias against groups of lower socioeconomic standing. A variety of data, then, raise questions about the fairness of the criminal justice system. The definition of the crime problem in terms of FBI Crime Index offenses, the special treatment given to white-collar crime, the frequent discovery that SES is related to likelihood of arrests, official reporting of crimes, and type of punishment strongly suggest that justice is not evenly meted out in U.S. society. Moreover, the findings of a relationship between income inequality and property crime rates further suggest that inequality helps produce crime and that reductions in inequality may produce reductions in property crime. Hate crimes, motivated by biases against particular demeaned status groups, also reflect the social inequalities perceived by different clusters of people.

Recent evidence has also raised the possibility of environmental racism. There appears to be a relationship between the presence of minority and working-class populations and the location of hazardous waste facilities and chemical pollution. The social consequence of this inequity is that these populations are disproportionately exposed to potential health hazards. Issues of environmental equity and competition over land will become only more prominent as the U.S. population grows and diversifies.

Finally, it was stressed that inequality has negative implications for the whole society because it creates an environment that lowers the quality of life for everyone. In fomenting distrust between individuals and groups, inequality stalls the development of a vibrant civic culture in which community interest takes precedence over self-interest. In an increasingly heterogeneous society, social and economic inequality becomes an even stronger predictor of division and separation.

Critical Thinking

1. What must be done to change the living conditions in inner-city and low-income neighborhoods that help generate crime?
2. Historically, why has ordinary street crime received more attention from authorities than white-collar and corporate crimes when evidence suggests they result in greater costs for individual victims and society than street crime?
3. How can trust between individuals be increased, given that the United States is a religiously, ethnically, and racially heterogeneous society? Is complete equality necessary for this to happen?
4. As competition for them increases, how can access to desirable spaces and land be made equitable? What role, if any, should the government play in this process?

Web Connections

The Sentencing Project regularly collects and reviews information on prison populations, state laws, sentencing issues, and criminal justice in general. It is a good place to find data summaries on a variety of law enforcement topics. Go to www.sentencingproject.org.

Film Suggestions

Ask Not (2008). Explores the causes of the military's don't ask don't tell policy and its effects on gay and lesbian service members.

Question of Racial Profiling (2004). Does it happen?

CHAPTER 13

Social Inequality and Social Movements

A little rebellion now and then is a good thing.

Thomas Jefferson (1743–1826)

In societies where extensive social inequality not only exists but is also perceived as being unjust, it is not unusual for people to demonstrate their feelings against it. The large-scale street protests on New York's Wall Street in 2011 are a good example. Systems of inequality instigate social movements aimed at altering them, and conversely, the degree of ultimate success of social movements is measured in terms of their impacts on those systems. The extent to which either of these relationships is actualized, as you will see, depends on structural, cultural, and historical conditions in the society at the time. Economic shifts, prevalent ideologies, political policies, and unique historical events all impress themselves on the shapes of inequality and social movements.

Consistent with the multidimensional focus of treatment, this chapter will explore three social movements related to class, race, and gender that were explicitly aimed at reducing inequality and improving the life chances of the groups in question. The early labor movement of the latter part of the nineteenth century and the first decades of the twentieth century in the United States, the civil rights movement of the 1950s and 1960s, and the women's movement of recent decades are examples of concerted efforts to change social and economic conditions for their constituencies. The purpose here is not to provide an exhaustive history of these movements, but rather to demonstrate systematically how each of them grew out of conditions relating to the structure of social inequality at the time, and how that structure affected the ebb and flow, goals, and tactics of those movements.

THE LABOR MOVEMENT

One of the first things to understand when examining any social movement is that the wider social, historical, and cultural context in which it takes place has an impact on the development, shape, and ultimate fate of the movement. John Godard contends that the viability of a continuously strong labor movement has been made problematic in the United States by cultural values associated with the founding of the country. Beliefs in individualism, small government, a Protestant ethic, the sanctity of private property, free markets and free labor, have made it difficult for the labor movement to prosper on a consistent basis (Godard 2009).

Obviously, the poor conditions and deprivations experienced by industrial workers in the latter part of the nineteenth and early part of the twentieth centuries created dissatisfaction and feelings of hostility. Even though there was some improvement in wages after 1880, hours were long, wages remained low, and working conditions were dangerous. There were few, if any, protections against the hazards of chemicals, machinery, and inhalants from work in the mines and mills. Laborers on the railroads and in construction and logging industries also were exposed to extreme dangers. There was little concern for safety, and many of the wildcat strikes of this time were related to safety issues.

Writing of the period between 1865 and 1917, Asher (1986) observed that "industrial workers have been victimized by low wages, company stores, blacklisting, arbitrary dismissals, forced overtime, sexual exploitation, company spies, police brutality, and a host of other ills" (p. 115). Some of the dangers were inherent to the nature of the work and the technology used, and the fear of competition and concern for profit kept employers preoccupied with matters other than safety (Asher 1986). The early scientific-management movement among employers sought to organize, systematize, and thoroughly gain control of the workplace for management. In order to keep production and efficiency up in the early twentieth century, the pace of work in many plants was accelerated, stopwatches were used, and work was constantly checked by inspectors. This created further alienation among workers.

Living conditions in most instances also left much to be desired. Dubofsky (1975) described a typical immigrant residential area in Pittsburgh: "Situated in what is known as the Dump of Schoenville runs a narrow dirt road. Frequently strewn with tin cans and debris, it is bereft of trees and the glaring sun shines pitilessly down on hundreds of ragged, unkempt, and poorly fed children" (p. 23). The company towns and cramped urban ghettos made for dreary living conditions. In his study of "How the Other Half Lives," Riis (1890) described the conditions in which New York City workers lived. He found "an urban jungle of exploitation, family disintegration, crime, and human degradation" (quoted in Green 1980, p. 20). Even as late as the 1920s, living conditions for most workers were still poor. During these years, although some improvements had been made, work was hard, hours were long, and the level of wages left little money for leisure and recreational activities. In 1929, 42 percent of families had incomes below $1,500, which was barely enough to keep a four-person family going (Zieger 1986). In sharp contrast, the richest 1 percent held almost one-third of all the nation's private wealth. Economic inequality was obvious and extensive.

Despite the awful circumstances of the lives of most industrial workers, however, more is needed to explain the development and continuation of the labor movement over time. The growth of the labor movement was affected by a combination of external and internal factors. Externally, the strength of workers tended to be greater when there was a tight labor market; this gave them greater bargaining power. Strength also grew when economic opportunities were plentiful. The chances of a labor movement being successful also were enhanced when society allowed a variety of political and legal expressions and permitted greater access to resources (Jenkins 1983). This occurred, for example, during the 1930s after Franklin Roosevelt's election and passage of the Wagner Act, which legalized the right to unionize. These events created alternate sources of power, and when the potential for political and economic power of labor was high, so was the solidarity of workers. The belief by workers that they would be spending a large part of their lives in their jobs and that they could make a political difference in society also increased their solidarity and the probability of a labor movement.

Sources of Control over Workers

Not surprisingly, employers were interested in keeping the power of labor to a minimum, and used a variety of techniques to divide and control workers (Griffin, Wallace, and Rubin 1986). With their superior political resources and generally better organization, employers fought workers in bloody battles in the latter part of the nineteenth century and well into the twentieth century. To weaken worker solidarity, employers replaced native workers with unskilled immigrants, and used them and Blacks as strikebreakers. This created animosity and weakened the cohesiveness of labor in general.

A second technique that created divisions within the ranks of labor involved reorganizing the division of labor. For much of the nineteenth century, craftsworkers had exercised a great deal of control over their work and occupied indispensable positions in the iron, steel, and machinery industries (Dubofsky 1975). Nevertheless, employers and their foremen controlled the workers through direct personal control, "intervening in the labor process often to exhort workers, bully and threaten them, reward good performance, hire and fire on the spot, favor loyal workers, and generally act as despots, benevolent or otherwise" (Edwards 1979, p. 19).

The scientific-management movement further strengthened the power of supervisors over workers by taking away control of the work process from the worker. **Scientific management** divided the work process into its smallest components in order to increase efficiency and output. But in so doing, it also introduced extreme specialization and monotonous work on the shop floor. Tasks were divided into such small parts that even completely unskilled individuals could perform them. Numerous early confrontations occurred over the question of who should direct the pace of work tasks (Dubofsky 1975; Piven and Cloward 1977; Edwards 1979; Stephenson and Asher 1986).

The techniques for controlling the work process changed as technology transformed capitalism. Improved manufacturing techniques such as the assembly line created technical controls. "*Technical control* involves designing machinery and planning the flow of work to minimize the problem of transforming labor power into labor as well as to maximize the purely physically based possibilities for achieving efficiencies" (Edwards 1979, p. 112). Later, control was achieved through the widespread implementation of bureaucratic structure, which consolidates control into formal sets of rules, positions, and authority hierarchies. Both technical and bureaucratic methods build control into the very fiber of the organization, replacing the personal control of the manager or foreman, which was often perceived as being arbitrary. The evolution of different forms of control can be legitimately viewed as a series of attempts by industrialists to increase efficiency, production, and profit.

The use of foreign and African American labor along with changes in the mechanisms of control were only two of the techniques used to weaken labor. Industrial management also used **welfare capitalism** to minimize solidarity among workers. Briefly, welfare capitalism included special savings plans and bonuses, homeownership aid programs, stock-purchasing options, and group insurance plans. Most significant among the programs offered were employee representation plans or work councils and company unions. The latter plans presumably gave workers a meaningful voice in the operation of the organization. Around the time of World War I, the concept of "industrial democracy" had become quite popular. Clearly, these employee representation plans, while suggesting a democratic and more equal relationship between employer and employee, were aimed at reducing worker allegiance to outside unions and slowing their attempts to organize themselves (Brody 1980; Griffin, Wallace, and Rubin 1986). The motivation for these programs was very likely a combination of paternalistic concern for workers, the belief that a more satisfied workforce would increase productivity and efficiency, and a desire on the part of employers to control labor. The latter function, however, appears to have been the most important (Brody 1980; Griffin, Wallace, and Rubin 1986).

Employers also opposed the organized labor movement by fighting against closed or union shops, advocating open shops in their place. In the latter, employees need not be members of unions to remain employed. This push for open shops under the "American Plan" label was especially dominant during the first decade of the twentieth century. The National Association of Manufacturers launched a campaign for open shops across industries, while other business-oriented groups (e.g., National Civic Foundation) argued that if unions were to exist and be acceptable, they had to be "responsible" in nature. In response to business attacks on union shops, some trade unions began to take in more unskilled workers as members (Green 1980). The conservative trade unionism of the American Federation of Labor (AFL) was preferred by business over the more militant and revolutionary approach of the International Workers of the World (IWW; Griffin, Wallace, and Rubin 1986). The espousal of welfare capitalism and a conservative brand of labor organization helped employers appear as being reasonable and fair. But neither of these enhanced the ability of labor to organize effectively in its own interests.

Employers had, of course, other resources by which to resist encroachment by labor. Spies were employed to monitor labor activities; legal actions were encouraged against militant workers and organizations; and the power of police, state militia, and federal troops also were used to quell labor unrest. Some states had laws specifically outlawing unions that were considered to be revolutionary or that openly advocated the taking over of industries by workers (syndicalism). Leaders of such unions could be and were put in prison or deported (Perlman and Taft 1935; Griffin, Wallace, and Rubin 1986). The informal political alliance between business and government was reflected in the frequent use of police or military might in putting down worker protests.

In the late nineteenth century, workers often had the support of local officials, so industries had to get help from state and federal sources (Dubofsky 1975; Green 1980). In numerous strike actions between 1890 and 1920, state militia and federal troops were used against workers. The 1892 steel plant conflict at Homestead, Pennsylvania, and the Pullman railroad boycott of 1894 are only two instances in which soldiers were used against strikers. In Lawrence, Massachusetts, in 1912, the American Woolen mill employed roughly 40,000 individuals, about half the city's population. About half of the employees were young women and most were foreign born. But when a group of young Polish women were given reduced wages for no explicit reason, a strike was organized and spread to other mills. In this case, too, police and militia were used against strikers, but after a couple of months, the workers in the "Bread and Roses" strike, as it was called, won wage gains (Green 1980). In 1914, militia in Colorado waged a violent attack on coal miners, shooting strikers and burning their families out of homes. Their violence across the southern part of the state reminded some of the tactics that had been used in the earlier Indian Wars (Zieger 1986). Many other labor–employer confrontations occurred during this period. Throughout World War I and up to 1920, large strikes by rail, meat-packing, and steelworkers occurred. In 1919 alone, there were 3,600 strikes (Zieger 1986). But in most cases, employers emerged as the victors (Piven and Cloward 1977; Brody 1980).

In the last years of the nineteenth century and the early years of the twentieth century, workers simply did not have the political or organizational power to be consistently successful against industrial owners. The only effective legal control on the contract imposed by the employer at the turn of the century was the condition of the labor market. As long as employers had government, the press, and the market behind them and a large number of immigrant workers available, there was little that could get employers to voluntarily improve their contracts with workers (Ginzberg and Berman 1963).

Internal Divisions in the Labor Movement

The particular directions taken by the labor movement have been explained in a variety of ways, but not altogether successfully (cf. Laslett 1987).

The varying images of the roles of unions, industrial changes, and social and cultural heterogeneity within the working class and disagreements on the goals of unions all helped to shape the differentiation within the movement. An early approach of the 1880s emphasized the educational function of unions. These organizations were seen as educators of immigrants, proponents of public schools, and often supporters of the socialization of private industry. Thus, in this approach, unions were not seen as being preoccupied with wages and job conditions alone, but with broader issues. The actions and goals of several early unions (Knights of Labor, IWW, Congress of Industrial Organizations [CIO]) make that clear. Another approach to understanding unions saw them as organizations created to buffer the effect of the ill fit between humans who desired to be free and the controls inherent in modern mechanization. The Marxian approach viewed unions as being rooted in class struggle over control of the means of production.

A final and most influential view of labor unions in early America was as tools for increasing the economic benefits of workers. Perlman (1928) argued that workers had become reconciled to their positions as employees in businesses owned by others and realized there was not a great deal they could do to change the way things were. Given this situation, workers could hardly be expected to be revolutionary; they were only willing to fight for better wages and job conditions.

There is no question that some of these frequently conflicting emphases were reflected in the internal structure of the organized labor movement of the early twentieth century. The forms the labor movement took in the United States were also conditioned by industrial changes. In the waning decades of the nineteenth century, the social organization of the economy was undergoing rapid change, and these changes had implications for both employers and employees. For example, the period beginning with the late 1880s was one in which economic enterprises dramatically increased in size and frequently merged with each other. In other words, it was a period in which economic power became more consolidated and concentrated (Edwards 1979). Even though in most of the nineteenth-century factories authority was decentralized among foremen and various craftsworkers, industrialization brought in its wake a more simplified, detailed division of labor, increasing the need for less-skilled laborers.

Machines often fomented dissatisfaction among skilled craftsworkers and encouraged antagonism between the unskilled industrial workers, who could do simple work and operate basic machines, and those who were skilled craftsworkers before machines became dominant (Stephenson and Asher 1986). Machines rapidly took the place of workers, and control over the workplace more frequently fell into the hands of owners and their foremen. These shifts in technology helped to drive wedges between unskilled and skilled workers, thereby stimulating the different directions in which the organized labor movement would go.

Along with technological changes, productivity rose rapidly, but so did the demand for labor. Immigrants flooded into the United States from a variety of countries. Consequently, the late nineteenth century was also a period in which the size of company workforces increased. The industrial working class grew significantly, but it was composed of individuals from sharply contrasting social and cultural backgrounds. The industrial working class for much of the latter half of the nineteenth century was a conglomeration of native-born craftsworkers, farmers who had left the land to come to the cities of New York and New England, skilled immigrants from Britain and western Europe, Irish who came to the United States after the potato famine in their native land, and Chinese who became employed primarily in the railroad industry.

After 1880, immigrants from eastern and southern Europe joined the ranks of the less skilled in industry and became an increasingly large part of the industrial working class (Aronowitz 1973). As the demand for labor grew and these immigrants flooded into the country to take lower positions in the mines, mills, and factories, the labor force in the North was almost as segregated by nationality in 1900 as the southern market was by race (Green 1980). Moreover, as the century came to an end, the proportion of women and African Americans involved in industry also increased. In 1900, almost a quarter of all women were in the labor force. The point of all this is that the heterogeneous nature of the working class at this time created divisions that often hindered the solidarity of workers when conflict arose with their employers. As noted earlier, this heterogeneity was exploited by employers to minimize worker cohesion.

The racial and ethnic differences within the working class meant language, skill, and religious differences as well, making control of working-class militancy easier. So these internal divisions had direct implications for both the working class and its employers. Some labor leaders had no wish at all to bring non-Whites into the organized labor movement, but rather were primarily interested in advancing the interests of White, skilled craftsworkers. Exclusionary practices, including explicit policies prohibiting admission of non-Whites, were not uncommon among many AFL unions (Green 1980). This was to be a bitter source of antagonism within the labor movement. Samuel Gompers, who founded the American Federation of Labor in 1881, was against the inclusion of non-White, nonskilled workers. In 1905, Gompers proclaimed to a group of union members in Minneapolis that "caucasians" were "not going to let their standard of living be destroyed by Negroes, Chinamen, Japs, or any others" (quoted in Green 1980, p. 46). The miscellaneous category of "others" referred to people from what were considered at that time the less desirable regions of Europe, such as the Slavic countries and Italy. Keep in mind that ideas about the biological inferiority of different groups were still circulating at this time (see Chapter 8).

In contrast to the American Federation of Labor, which sought to unionize skilled White craftsworkers, other organizers felt that it was crucial to organize all industrial workers. Among those groups that supported the organization of all workers, some had socialist or communist leanings. The Knights of Labor, briefly popular in the 1880s, was among those groups that argued that

all workers should be included in the organized labor movement. Rather than advocating the homogeneous composition found in the trade and crafts unions of the AFL, the Knights preferred mixed groupings of workers. The Socialist Party of America, founded in 1901 and under the leadership of the charismatic Eugene Debs, also favored an organizational umbrella that would cover the mass of workers in industry. A few years later, the Industrial Workers of the World, and several decades later, the CIO also actively sought the membership of Blacks and all industrial workers.

As their views about the compositions of labor organizations varied, so did labor leaders' views on the appropriate goals for the labor movement. The goals of the Knights of Labor were broad and involved the reorganization of the industrial order to create a more just society. These utopian goals were eschewed by the newer AFL trade unions that sought more immediate narrow rewards for their members, such as higher wages and better working conditions. This "pure-and-simple" or "business" unionism was more consistent with native American values according to some interpreters. A large part of the reason for this orientation, argued Lipset (1971), is related to the openness of the class structure, and the values of materialism, egalitarianism, and individual opportunity. Individuals in this context see themselves more as individuals than as members of a class, and see social change as resulting more from individual efforts than from mass organization or social structure. The American values of work, social and geographic mobility, comfort, and common sense also lie behind the belief that individuals do and should determine their own economic fates (Dunlop 1987).

The AFL's trade unionism has aimed at working within the present economic system rather than trying to change it. The emphasis on increasing labor's power has been for the purpose of more effective collective bargaining than for political reasons. Early AFL leaders felt that government should not interfere in labor matters. It should be up to labor to chart its own course and make its own gains (Brody 1971). Gompers's "voluntarism" perspective underscored the belief that labor should not solicit aid from the government for those goals it can accomplish by itself (Green 1980). Paradoxically, this stance helped to create a bond between the AFL and establishment forces, fostering increased cooperation between the union, management, and the government (Rogin 1971; Brody 1980).

In this interpretation, U.S. workers were not as interested as their European counterparts in a basic change *of* the economic system as much as they were in changing their individual positions *within* the system. "Most men and women live in a real world," wrote Dubofsky (1975), "a world of simple, everyday happenings, small pleasures and recurrent sufferings, which shape their attitudes as much as abstract principles" (p. 48). Brody (1980) concluded that in the waning years of the nineteenth century, the labor movement was (1) practical rather than utopian or theoretical, (2) nonrevolutionary with narrow material interests, and (3) impatient with intellectuals and academicians who had theories about the direction the labor movement should pursue.

Despite the narrow orientation of many workers, however, one should not conclude that there has been no revolutionary fervor or concerns within labor. "Such an approach has always been unfair, especially during the heyday of the IWW between 1905 and 1917, and in the early years of the history of the CIO. It was especially untrue during the period of the Knights of Labor . . . which . . . upheld producer's and consumer's cooperation, equal pay for women, and a 'proper share of the wealth that they (the workers) create'" (quoted in Laslett 1987, p. 362). Organized labor has not been a uniform homogeneous mass.

Just prior to World War I, then, organized labor contained several different types of organizations and orientations. The trade-union wing, exemplified by the AFL, was solidly on its way but did not incorporate most unskilled and semiskilled industrial workers. The Socialists had political influence on many workers even though the latter's trade-union orientation remained intact. The IWW organized those left out by the more conservative AFL affiliates, was active and militant, and was led by the imposing Big Bill Haywood (Brody 1980).

The Russian Revolution, America's involvement in World War I, and the accompanying patriotic fervor that swept the nation legitimated political and coercive attacks on Socialist organizations and the IWW. As a result, the power of the left in organized labor declined. "The labor hopes of the American left, hitherto bright, died in World War I and its aftermath" (Brody 1980, p. 41). In the patriotic context of the postwar period, organized labor, in general, was a victim of attacks from industry. The "American Plan" of business proclaimed the consistency of the open shop with U.S. values. In this hostile atmosphere, the AFL became more cooperative with industry and government. With the restrictive immigration laws of the 1920s reducing the inflow of unskilled labor from culturally undesirable countries, industry's source of fresh workers was weakened. By the late 1920s, labor unrest had calmed down even though the cost of living was increasing, erasing many of the gains that had been made by some workers (Zieger 1986).

From the Depression to the Present

On the whole, the 1920s and the early 1930s were not kind to U.S. workers. "The symbol of the twenties is gold . . . the twenties were, indeed, golden, but only for a privileged segment of the American population. For the great mass of people—workers and their families—the appropriate symbol may be nickel or copper or perhaps even tin, but certainly not gold" (Bernstein 1960, p. 47). Bernstein labeled the 1920 to 1933 period as "the lean years" for the worker (p. 47). A litany of the problems for workers would include the stagnation of the union movement during the period (union membership fell from 5 million in 1920 to 3.5 million in 1929) and the absence of any effective industry-wide collective-bargaining tools. Employers could hire who they wanted and workers had little recourse in the matter. Older workers found it more and more difficult to hold on to their jobs, as farm migrants and women increasingly entered the urban labor force. Mechanization displaced workers. Between 1920 and 1929, it is estimated that about one-third of those displaced by machines in the manufacturing, coal mining, and railways industries remained unemployed (Bernstein 1960). Moreover, the shift to more mechanized professional positions did not help many workers, who did not have the qualifications for such positions. Income inequality was also extensive in the society. The combined incomes of the top 0.1 percent of families were as great as those of the bottom 42 percent of the population. Within the working class there were also divisions in wages based on regional, ethnic, racial, skill, union membership, sex, and residential differences. Irish, Italian, Jewish, African American, and Mexican workers were generally worse off than native White workers (Bernstein 1960).

The effects of the Great Depression on employment were disastrous. In the middle of 1930, almost 4.5 million were without jobs. Shanty areas cropped up in and around cities, places of makeshift residences sometimes called "Hoovervilles." Hunger also rose dramatically. By early 1931, an estimated 8.3 million were unemployed, but the number was to rise even further to 13.6 million by the end of that year, and to 15 million by early 1933. At that time, about one-third of all wage/salary workers were completely out of work. Many others were only working on a part-time basis (Bernstein 1960).

Needless to say, the Depression in the early 1930s changed political dynamics inside and outside the labor movement. The AFL had successfully cultivated close relationships with industrial management and government forces. It stressed union–management harmony and fought against leftist elements in the labor movement. The Depression made many workers and unions recognize the need for state help and intervention. It spurred questions among the unemployed about the ability of the present economic and political systems to deal with catastrophic problems, especially as it became clear over the bitter years of the 1930s that it was not the lack of individual efforts but rather broader social forces that were behind much of the misery being experienced (Piven and Cloward 1977). At the same time, however, the vast majority of citizens still had faith in the U.S. system and did not see socialism or

communism as a viable alternative. Nor did they think of themselves as a cohesive working class fighting capitalism (Aronowitz 1973; Zieger 1986).

In the early part of the twentieth century, labor had received little help from the federal government, especially during the Republican administrations of the 1920s. Several critical events strengthened labor's hand during the 1930s, in addition to the political-administration changes that had occurred. One was the rising prospect of war in Europe. U.S. companies that had armament contracts with European countries could not afford major labor unrest to disrupt production. A second event was the passage of the Wagner Act in 1935, which legalized the right of workers to organize and bargain collectively under the protection of the National Labor

Historically, unions have been a major source of organized strength for workers, helping to improve wages, benefits, and working conditions. (Photo by Brendan R. Hurst.)

Relations Board, which could monitor business compliance with the law. This law, bitterly fought by business, resulted in a rapid upsurge in union membership. In the mid- and late 1930s, union membership tripled, reaching about 9 million in 1939 (Zieger 1986). A third event that increased the power of labor was the creation of the CIO in 1935. The CIO unionized many of the previously unorganized mass-production industrial workers. Unlike the AFL, it aimed at being a union for all workers. Its leader, John L. Lewis, also realized that the CIO had to recruit skeptical Blacks to prevent their being used as strikebreakers. In 1937, the CIO had about 4 million members. The New Deal and events during the 1930s left in their wake a triumvirate of power: big government, big business, and big labor. During and after World War II, union membership was still high and growing, and unions were an effective force for improving working conditions for their members.

Despite this growth in union power, the ideological tide had already begun to shift against organized labor by the end of the 1930s. The recession of 1938–1939, which led to a weakening of federal recovery programs, factionalism within the CIO (which many suspected had communist leanings), the growing patriotism during the early years of World War II, and the impatience of many with the increased militancy of workers immediately after the war strengthened conservative forces against unions (Zieger 1986). The increased bureaucratization and job consciousness of unions over the years and the routinization of formal contracts and the "rule of law" in industry also helped to institutionalize labor–industry conflict. Employers were more willing to buy off workers with higher wages than to relinquish control of the production process (Brody 1980; Zieger 1986). The Taft–Hartley Act of 1947 renewed many of the powers that had been lost to business by the Wagner Act. It also curbed the power of unions to strike, required an anti-Communist pledge from workers, and redefined labor's rights in much narrower terms (Piven and Cloward 1977; Zieger 1986).

The increased conservatism and narrowness of unions meant that workers often fought against the wishes of union leadership. The interests of workers and those of the union leadership did not always coincide. This internal division within the labor movement has continued. Although union membership generally grew during the 1950s and 1960s, and more public employees initiated unionization drives, differences of opinion within the labor community surfaced over Vietnam and the civil rights and women's movements of the 1960s. During the conservative 1980s and early 1990s, unions were again under attack, membership declined, and union leadership appeared weaker than in the earlier heyday of organized labor. More specifically, the breach of traditional understandings between unions and management, coupled with vigorous business attacks on unions since the 1970s, helped to weaken unions. In addition, globalization, and the rapid employment growth in new areas coupled with higher unemployment in traditional occupations, the lack of national unity among unions, and a hostile political climate have certainly contributed to the decline of union power (Western 1993; Clawson and Clawson 1999). Elements internal to labor unions themselves have also contributed to their decline. Publicized corruption, ethnic and gender biases within unions, and a lack of union democracy for rank-and-file workers have weakened their moral authority (Kallick 1994). In 2010, only 11.9 percent of wage and salary workers in the United States were union members. The rate among public employees was much higher than that found among workers in the private sector (36 versus 7 percent), and it is much higher in traditionally more liberal regions like the Northeast, Midwest, and Pacific West, than in more conservative areas like the South and Mountain West (Francia 2007; U.S. Bureau of Labor Statistics, January 21, 2011).

It must be recognized that labor is not a monolithic force. Different unions continue to react differently to the challenges their workers face, with some more willing than others to adopt nontraditional tactics to increase their influence (Martin 2008; Martin and Dixon 2010). The current splintering and weakness of unions is reminiscent of the labor movement of the 1920s, and these developments come in a 3-decade period marked by relatively stagnant wages and significant economic uncertainty for many in the middle and working classes. Nonunion employees are suffering disproportionately. Workers who are not union members have pensions and insurance benefits valued at less than half those of union workers. Retirement and health insurance benefits have been significantly curtailed by many corporations. In fact, in 2009, almost 51 million Americans were without health insurance.

Historically, union membership has meant significantly higher wages and better benefits.

Importantly but not surprisingly, the decline of union membership is occurring at a time of conservativism, increasing globalization, and open markets, when transnational corporations have

---

NUTSHELL 13.1 Collective Bargaining: A Dying Species?

The power of labor unions in the private sector has been in steady decline since the passage of the Taft-Hartley Act in 1947 that weakened worker rights. The trend to weaken unions has coexisted with a corresponding rise in political conservatism and the increased lobbying and economic power of business. In 2010, 22 states, mostly in the South and Midwest, had right-to-work laws prohibiting closed-shop employment. In early 2011, a proposal for a "National Right to Work Act" was submitted in Congress to eliminate the right of unions to collect dues and fees from nonunion workers. With economic deficits and the 2010 election of more conservative state governors, labor unions in the public sector have also come under attack.

Ohio and Indiana two states engaged in the contest over worker rights between public employees and state government. But Wisconsin has been the lightening-rod for the recent debate about collective bargaining by public employees. Battles between legislators, union members, and sympathizers on both sides in Wisconsin provide a vivid example of the attempts to balance state budgets by stripping union members of some of their historically hard-won rights to strike and collectively bargain for better wages and benefits. In March 2011, the Wisconsin governor signed a bill increasing the amount of health care and pension contributions by state employees, and eliminated virtually all of their collective bargaining rights. Because of a political maneuver, Republican senators were able to pass the bill without the presence of 14 Democratic senators who had left the state because of disagreement over the proposed bill. Mass protests by public employees and members of other unions did not sway the governor, who argued that the bill not only would help balance Wisconsin's budget but also attract business to the state and create 250,000 jobs. Senate Democrats viewed the bill as an assault on workers, with one Senator saying that "in 30 minutes, 18 state

senators undid 50 years of civil rights in Wisconsin" (Davey, March 10, 2011, p. A3).

The bill has deepened splits among workers at a time when unity would strengthen the working class. A 2011 national poll revealed that most Americans opposed the weakening of collective bargaining rights of public employees, and did not think states budgets should be balanced by reducing their pay or benefits (Cooper and Thee-Brenan, March 1, 2011, p. A1). Many workers in the private sector who have lost wages and benefits, however, feel that public sector workers should also have to share the burden of the recent economic downturn. "Everyone else needs to pinch pennies and give more money to health insurance companies and pay for their own retirement," claimed one private sector worker. "I don't get to bargain in my job, either," argued another (Sulzberger and Davey, February 22, 2011, p. A17). At the same time, the leader of the Wisconsin State Employees Union believes that "public employees did not create the recession and the deficit here in Wisconsin. It was Wall Street" (Greenhouse, February 23, 2011, p. A12).

At a time when income and wealth differences are higher than they have been in decades, a reasonable question to ask is how these legislative acts will affect economic inequality. Will these laws actually result in more employment and higher incomes for some or just exacerbate the growing divide between top and bottom?

Sources: Monica Davey, "Wisconsin G.O.P. Ends Stalemate with Maneuver," *New York Times,* March 10, 2011, pp. A1 and A3; Michael Cooper and Megan Thee-Brenan, "Majority in Poll Back Employees in Public Unions," *New York Times,* March 1, 2011, pp. A1 and A16; Steven Greenhouse, "Wisconsin Union Leader Minces No Words When Labor Issues Are at Stake," *New York Times,* February 23, 2011, p. A12; A. G. Sulzberger and Monica Davey, "Union Bonds in Wisconsin Begin to Fray," *New York Times,* February 22, 2011, pp. A1 and A17.

gained more economic and political leverage (Faux 2003). The weakness of labor against business does not bode well for a decline in economic inequality. Perhaps the labor movement has come full circle and will again mobilize its constituencies to restore labor's power, but to do this in an international marketplace it may have to embrace not only differences in class, race, and gender, but those of nationality as well. There is some evidence that unions realize this need and are actively trying to organize the growing number of immigrant workers. Union influence in the Democratic Party has remained strong (Francia 2007). Most of the public are also sympathetic. Perhaps because of high corporate bonuses and the infamous financial scandals of the 1990s and 2000s, a variety of recent polls show that a majority of the public view unions in a positive light and as helpful to workers. The public is also much more likely to see big business and big government as threats to the nation than they are to see big labor as a threat (Panagopoulos and Francia 2008). At the same time, most do not feel that union members who work in the public sphere such as teachers, policemen, and firemen, should be allowed to strike. Indeed, in light of local and state budgetary problems, unionization and collective bargaining by public employees has become a hot issue (see Nutshell 13.1).

THE CIVIL RIGHTS MOVEMENT

Although it often discriminated against both Blacks and women, the labor movement was driven by

concerns over inequities in political and economic power, and historical, cultural, and social conditions shaped its development and form. In general terms, the same can be said of the civil rights movement of the mid-1950s and 1960s. Although an indisputable specific date for its beginning cannot be given, there is general agreement that it began in the period between 1953 and 1955 during which the Supreme Court's historic *Brown v. Board of Education* decision was made, and systematic bus boycotts had occurred in Baton Rouge, Louisiana, and Montgomery, Alabama. The nonviolent movement extended into the mid-1960s up to the point when other, more radical, Black power elements were becoming increasingly important.

As was the case in the labor movement, there had been many instances of protest by African Americans against Whites before the civil rights movement. Revolts by slaves against their masters, the Underground Railroad, the massive growth of the National Association for the Advancement of Colored People (NAACP) membership to almost half a million during World War II, the demands that led Roosevelt to establish a Fair Employment Practices Committee, and A. Philip Randolph's political activity in Washington and before Congress in the 1940s all provide evidence of racial protest and a push for racial equality before the civil rights movement (Morris 1984). Thus, the movements of the 1950s and 1960s did not suddenly appear out of nowhere. Consequently, what may appear to be the beginning of a social movement may only be a resurgence of activism

MINI-CASE 13.1

Affirmative Action: Yes or No?

As we have seen, significant racial inequality continues to exist in the United States, and the question continually arises about what to do about it, if anything. Two approaches to affirmative action have been implemented, one stressing the need for "equal opportunity" for all (e.g., as in the Equal Employment Opportunity Commission), and the other, assuming that there is racial bias built into our institutions, emphasizing "equal representation" of racial and ethnic groups (e.g., as in the Office of

Federal Contract Compliance). The arguments in favor of affirmative action cite past wrongs and continued discrimination as well as success in reducing racial discrepancies and increasing diversity, while those who oppose it argue that it constitutes reverse discrimination, lowers the self-esteem of minorities, and reinforces stereotypes of minorities. What do you think? Should some form of affirmative action be continued or should it be eliminated entirely? ■

that had been kept in abeyance because of lack of opportunity structures in the social context (Taylor 1989a). As was evident in the labor movement's history, particular historical, political, economic, and social conditions created a context in which effective mass protest could be initiated, and the civil rights movement could be nurtured.

In the late nineteenth and early twentieth centuries, African Americans had few resources with which to launch a massive civil rights campaign. First of all, racist ideologies discouraged support from Whites. Second, most African Americans were fully but exploitatively integrated into the Southern economic and political structure. There were few economic opportunities open to them and Jim Crow laws kept them in their assigned place. In other words, the social context offered few political and economic opportunities or alternatives. Third, the federal government did little to alleviate the oppressive conditions under which Blacks lived. Earlier, national leaders had written into the Constitution that Black men, who were unfree, were to be considered only three-fifths persons. Now Congress stood by as Blacks were disenfranchised and treated violently in the South.

The North and the federal government did little while Black subjugation and White supremacy were being systematically institutionalized in the South. This structured inequality was especially evident in the political realm. Blacks were effectively prevented from voting through the use of various devices, including poll taxes, tests of literacy and "good character," grandfather requirements, and primaries limited to Whites. Laws in the South prohibited the integration of Blacks and Whites in schools, hospitals, motels, places of recreation, and even funeral homes and cemeteries. These Jim Crow laws made it legal to spend less public money on Black than on White institutions (Sitkoff 1981).

The Changing Context of Racial Inequality

After World War I, it was clear that changing economic and political conditions would strengthen the power position of African Americans in the United States. Among these economic changes was a decline in the centrality of agriculture in the Southern economy coupled with increasing industrialization of the urban South. This agrarian decline was fostered, in part, by declines in immigration and agricultural exports during the war. Accompanying the decline in immigration was an increase in the demand by northern industry for laborers from the South. Both "King Cotton" and industry needed workers, but changing circumstances created a shift in demand from agriculture to industry. Before and after World War I, there was massive African American migration to the North and to cities to seek employment in industries (Piven and Cloward 1977; Sitkoff 1981; McAdam 1982). Southern agriculture suffered again during the Great Depression of the early 1930s. An overproduction of cotton due to decreased demand led to a drastic decline in its price, which spelled disaster for many Southern farmers. In Mississippi, at that time perhaps the greatest stronghold of White supremacy, farmers lost their land at about twice the national rate (Bloom 1987). Later, during the 1940s, as mechanization also became more and more essential in agriculture, some farmers left agriculture behind, and the average size of landholdings increased. This meant that more Black as well as White farmworkers were economically displaced and needed to seek employment in the industries of Northern and Southern cities (Piven and Cloward 1977). Southern agriculture also had to diversify its products to feed the soldiers in military camps during World War II (Bloom 1987). All of these circumstances served to shake up the foundations of the traditional economy in the South.

The changed geographic and economic base of Blacks helped to develop their voting power and the indigenous institutional bases needed for the civil rights movement (McAdam 1982). Cities provided greater opportunities for Blacks to get organized, to receive more education, and to lay the basis for an expanded Black middle class. The growth of these basic strengths within the Black community was important in the genesis of the civil rights movement. There is good evidence that, despite the importance of external resources to the movement, its origins and development can be traced to reliance on institutions indigenous to the Black community (Oberschall 1973; McAdam 1982; Morris 1984; Jenkins and Eckert 1986).

African American colleges, churches, and civic and fraternal institutions provided not only economic resources but also the communication network and most of the leaders needed to organize the movement. Martin Luther King Jr., for example, was influential as a movement leader not only because of his charisma but also, crucially, because of the personal and organizational backing he received. The influence of the Southern Christian Leadership Conference during most of the movement's career suggests the relevance of religious institutions. Local colleges also provided most of the students who, early in the 1960s, were involved in the civil disobedience actions that helped bring about legislative changes.

External support of protests generally comes after the protests themselves. These additional resources are a *product* rather than a *cause* of protest (McAdam 1982). The patronage that did come later from outsiders appears to have been given less out of feelings of conscience and injustice than out of concern to keep the movement moderate and weaken the radical element— that is, to exercise some control over the direction of the movement (Jenkins and Eckert 1986). The nonviolent sit-ins of college students and others in the South in the early 1960s, for example, brought much financial and other support from outside, northern groups. The violent protests later in the 1960s in northern and western cities, on the other hand, produced a White backlash, partly because of the violence, but also because of the switch in focus of problems from the rural South to the urban ghettos of the North.

The economic and attending geographic shifts that were occurring in the South, then, provided African Americans with the opportunity to "construct the occupational and institutional foundation from which to mount resistance to White oppression" (Piven and Cloward 1977, p. 205). On the other side, changing economic and social conditions also created a split in the "Solid South" between the interests of business and agriculture.

Establishment forces were further weakened by the increased stridence and militancy of the reaction against African American protests for equality, which helped to isolate the South, especially the Deep South, from the rest of the nation. The traditional social and political structure had been grounded in a particular kind of economy. A weakening in the basis of that agricultural economy threatened the survival of sociopolitical arrangements that primarily benefited the rich landowner and discriminated against African Americans. "Racial patterns and racial consciousness have as their foundation particular class structures, and they develop and change as these structures themselves change" (Bloom 1987, p. 3).

This last point is very important. Class and economic factors were implicated in the shifting allegiances to racial inequality. However, *racist ideology* was still an underlying element in accounting for not only social and economic inequality in the South but also reactions to Black attempts to eliminate it. Recall that in the latter part of the nineteenth and well into the twentieth centuries, there were a variety of established racial ideologies justifying unequal treatment of Blacks. Beliefs about the inferiority of Blacks go back even further than that to the early founding of the United States (see Chapter 8). The continued significance of racism itself was manifested in the support given by lower-class as well as upper-class White Southerners to the discriminatory treatment of Blacks. Upper-class White Southerners who had vested local economic interests fought the hardest against voting rights for Blacks because to afford this right would have been tantamount to surrendering power to them.

Although the voting regulations effectively prohibited many lower-class Whites as well as Blacks from voting, the former went along with their upper-class brethren in supporting the laws. The Southern aristocracy played on racist images of Blacks and used the image of competition between Blacks and Whites as a means to obtain the support of lower-class Whites (Piven and Cloward 1977). In addition, not only Southern agricultural aristocrats but also local town and city business people fought against those who pushed for integration into local restaurants, motels, and so on. In essence, both economic factors and racism played roles in the dynamics of racial inequality and reactions to it.

Other cultural events and employment issues also gave strength to the Black effort to confront both racial and economic inequality. During the 1920s, the Harlem Renaissance encouraged Blacks to take pride in themselves and their cultural and literary heritage. Most of the Blacks who had jobs in northern industrial cities during the 1930s and 1940s were working class, and consequently, fought not only against racism, but also for better working conditions and economic fairness (Isaac 2008). The civil rights activists of the late 1920s and 1930s often fought alongside White radical unionists who were pushing the New Deal policies (Sitkoff 1981). Radical union leaders, it will be recalled, wanted to include not only Whites and skilled workers but also Blacks and unskilled industrial workers as well. Both radical unions and Black organizations, however, were often labeled as communist. This would become a familiar theme again after World War II, especially with the rise of McCarthyism.

In addition to the changes in the U.S. economy and social-cultural factors that strengthened Black unity, other historical events and conditions also helped to lay the groundwork for the civil rights movement that was to come in the 1950s. Migration to the North not only meant a greater probability of voting but also led to Blacks holding political office in several major cities (Sitkoff 1981; Bloom 1987). "Estimates of voting strength in 1948 saw Blacks holding the balance of power in sixteen states with a total of 278 electoral votes, compared to 127 electoral votes controlled by the South" (Bloom 1987, p. 76). Politicians with presidential aspirations became increasingly concerned about potential Black political defections and, as a result, often courted the Black vote.

Despite this courtship, governmental policies continued to underrepresent the interests of Blacks. But they also, perhaps inadvertently,

strengthened the position of Blacks. As we saw in the history of the labor struggles, the New Deal's policies had an impact on the fate of the labor movement. Similarly, the public works programs of the New Deal provided Blacks with an alternate source of income outside the relatively narrow range of private positions open to them. Having another source of income, which meant less dependence, created a source of power with which to fight oppression (Piven and Cloward 1971, 1982; Bloom 1987). This federal source of work and the increased demand for labor in industry helped to drive wages up—wages that dominant agricultural groups were increasingly hesitant to pay (Bloom 1987). Federal loans also became available as a substitute for local ones, again making Blacks less dependent on local White funding institutions.

World War II brought further changes to the situation of Blacks. Unionization of Blacks was less difficult than had been the case only a decade earlier. Employment conditions had improved, especially with the wartime economy. But national unity was the preferred emphasis and most Blacks did not favor protest in these circumstances (Sitkoff 1981). Despite continued demands by Black groups, any serious attempts to deal with racial problems took a backseat to dealing with the Axis powers. Although the war brought some positive changes, Blacks were still much worse off than Whites politically and economically, and discrimination was still prevalent.

After the war, several political events occurred that affected efforts for racial equality. The liberation struggles abroad against colonialism heartened many Black leaders who became convinced that change was possible (Rollins 1986). These events, coupled with the racist overtones of Nazism, against which the United States had fought, meant that continued racial inequality at home could prove to be an embarrassment. Harry Truman, in running for the presidency in 1948, had to present a platform that showed a strong desire for civil rights if he was to defeat opponents who also were courting the vote of those Blacks who had migrated to the cities of the North. He also ordered the desegregation of the military. The economic and political context had shifted to the extent that Truman was advised to court Blacks even at the risk of turning away Southern Democrats (Piven and Cloward 1977).

A final political element in the late 1940s that affected civil rights efforts came out of the developing "cold war" with the former Soviet Union. "Red-baiting" was fashionable, and civil rights groups and leaders were not immune to accusations of being communist. White supremacists argued that communists were behind the movement for Black equality. It will be recalled that similar accusations had been made about unions and their leadership when they also pushed for greater economic and political power. McCarthyism frightened Blacks, and the majority of Black leaders took a gradual and calm approach. "The NAACP became less a protest organization and more an agency of litigation and lobbying after World War II" (Sitkoff 1981, p. 18). All of the conditions discussed thus far comprise the context in which the Supreme Court made its momentous *Brown v. Board of Education* decision in 1954.

A Brief History

The *Brown v. Board of Education* decision was a true watershed in the effort for civil rights. It declared segregation in education to be unconstitutional. In concluding his argument, Chief Justice Earl Warren stated simply, "We conclude that in the field of public education the doctrine of 'separate but equal' has no place. Separate educational facilities are inherently unequal" (quoted in Sitkoff 1981, p. 22). This decision had a powerful effect on both Blacks and Southern Whites. The Black movement for equality was given a boost, but at the same time a White countermovement was established to fight these advances. While Blacks were jubilant about the decision, the South's White elite were not about to accept it without a fight. Many said unequivocally that they would not comply with the law in this case. "The prospect of desegregating public schools was fundamentally appalling to the average White Southerner. The thought of young 'niggers' mixing

in school with little White children jarred the sensibilities of Southern Whites, whether poor farmers or highly placed government officials" (Morris 1984, p. 27). Even though the decision by the Court to segregate had been unanimous, it had not come to this decision easily. In order to get the unanimous ruling, Warren had to agree on a policy of gradual implementation of the desegregation policy. The qualification of gradualism left room for Southern dissenters to fight enforcement, and it led to frustration on the part of Blacks who wished speedy implementation of the law.

There was no strong push on the part of the government for swift implementation of the law; the dominance by conservative elements of the major political parties in Congress meant no rapid enforcement would be forthcoming. The FBI's J. Edgar Hoover still saw racial unrest as being communist inspired (Bloom 1987). In the South, White churches and the press generally opposed the ruling, and local White Citizens' Councils were set up to fight desegregation (Sitkoff 1981). In 1956, the membership in these councils approached 250,000 (Piven and Cloward 1977).

In the mid-1950s, notable bus boycotts by Blacks occurred in Baton Rouge, Montgomery, and Tallahassee. Perhaps the most famous of these was initiated by Rosa Parks in Montgomery in December of 1955. Mrs. Parks, who was an active NAACP participant and had been put off a bus previously for refusing to move to the back, had gotten on a crowded bus and refused to surrender her seat to a White male adult. At the next bus stop, Mrs. Parks was taken off the bus and arrested for violating the local bus ordinance (Sitkoff 1981). News of her arrest spread, and a bus boycott was organized by a group of local Black leaders. Assuming that it would be best to appoint an outsider as its leader, they appointed a hesitant, young, middle-class, nonviolent, and intellectually sophisticated Black minister to lead the boycott.

The Reverend Martin Luther King Jr. was well educated, a newcomer to the area, and had attended theological school in the North. He was stunned by the blatant racism that seemed to be so out of place in a period when Blacks had become more educated and urbanized (Sitkoff 1981). Given his background and training, King assumed initially that Whites would respect logic and listen to reason, but he was wrong. "He now realized that the matter was one of power, not reason, that 'no one gives up his privileges without strong resistance'" (Sitkoff 1981, p. 51). Under his new organization, dubbed the Montgomery Improvement Association, King led a nonviolent boycott of the bus system. Local Black churches provided sites for meetings and arranged for alternative modes of transportation. The boycott went on for over a year, and during that time, White resistance tried a range of tactics to bring it to an end. Legal tactics such as arrests and jailings for minor or fictitious infractions of local laws were used. Economic sanctions also were tried; some deeply involved in the boycott lost their jobs. Finally, violent tactics were used: Many beatings occurred, and four Black churches and the homes of King, his associate Ralph Abernathy, and another supporter were bombed. In the last analysis, however, the nonviolent boycott prevailed and the U.S. Supreme Court declared Alabama's bus segregation laws unconstitutional.

The nonviolent, long-suffering, patient approach of the boycott contrasted in the national media with the harsh White reaction. Many outside the South were appalled at the tactics used by the White resistance. In contrast, King's "neo-Gandhian persuasion" seemed reasonable and acceptable as a means for obtaining equal rights. Above all, it was nonviolent and embraced the Christian beliefs of turning the other cheek and not condemning individual racists. It blamed the system of segregation rather than the individuals who enforced it (King 1958; Sitkoff 1981). As a result of the boycott, King and his approach to injustice gained worldwide attention. Out of the boycott, other civil rights groups were organized, most notably the Southern Christian Leadership Conference (SCLC) under King's leadership.

A familiar pattern of Black–White confrontation began to develop as a result of the early boycotts. Basically, the sequence would begin with nonviolent Black protests, followed by a militant White response, which in turn often led to federal intervention. It did not take long for Black leaders to figure out how to get the attention of federal officials who had been unreliable and largely unresponsive in the past in enforcing rights that were theirs under the Constitution.

The violent repressive tactics of Whites against nonviolent protestors angered many in the Black community and some of them were not altogether happy with King's patient, nonmilitant approach. This was especially the case as hostile White resistance intensified during the late 1950s and early 1960s. However, many young college-educated Blacks had had their resolve stiffened by the growing number of successes from King's approach. Beside boycotts and marches, additional nonviolent tactics were used. Among these was the sit-in, which also had been used effectively in the past in union strikes.

In the early 1960s, sit-ins were held throughout the South as a way of protesting segregation of public facilities. Similar protests were held in northern cities to demonstrate sympathetic support of the civil rights protestors. These protests involved thousands of individuals, many of them college students. One of the most famous of the sit-ins occurred in early February 1960 in Greensboro, North Carolina. Four Black students sat down at a Woolworth's lunch counter and asked for coffee and donuts. When refused, they kept their seats until the store closed. The next day, more students did the same thing, but White officials remained implacable, and it was only after repeated sit-ins that Greensboro allowed such service 6 months later. This sit-in inspired similar protests throughout the South and afforded a means by which college students could become meaningfully involved in the civil rights movement. Adults also joined in these protests. Within a year and a half of the Greensboro sit-in, demonstrations had been carried out in over 100 cities and towns in all the Southern states (Rhoda Blumberg 1984). Not only sit-ins at lunch counters, but sleep-ins in the lobbies of motels, swim-ins at pools, play-ins at recreational areas, kneel-ins at churches, and read-ins at libraries followed. Boycotts also were carried out against merchants who refused desegregation (Sitkoff

Victims of the HIV/AIDS pandemic and supporters of HIV/AIDS awareness unite and march near the shores of Lake Victoria in Kisumu, Kenya, with the goal of ending the stigma associated with the virus and promoting education and prevention. (Photo by Susan L. Tipton.)

1981). Local White reactions were often swift and violent. Floggings, kickings, pistol whippings, dog attacks, jailings, and even acid throwings were among the repressive means used against the protestors. But still the sit-ins continued.

One result of these demonstrations was that they showed Southerners the depth of Black feelings about these matters. They were also powerful in bringing to the attention of the nation the injustice of widespread legal segregation practices. Largely as a result of the active concern of Black college youths, their impatience with years of waiting, and the seemingly futile legal maneuverings of the more conservative approaches in the civil rights movement as typified by the NAACP, other, more militant types of organizations (such as the Student Nonviolent Coordinating Committee [SNCC]) began appearing in the early 1960s (Sitkoff 1981; Rhoda Blumberg 1984).

In 1961, the Congress of Racial Equality (CORE), which had been founded in 1942 and

had advocated direct nonviolent means of protest, organized a "freedom ride" from Washington, D.C., to New Orleans to see if states and municipalities were complying with the federal law against discrimination in interstate bus terminals. These rides went into the Deep South where White resistance was strongest. As with other peaceful protests, these rides too evoked violent White resistance. Beatings and deaths of protestors, for example, took place in several Alabama cities, including Birmingham and Montgomery. Again, much of the violence was broadcast through the media.

It was only when waves of public sympathy came that the federal government acted to protect the protestors and enforce the law. When there was no publicity, little was done; violations of the law were left unpunished. It became clear to protestors that they apparently had to elicit a violent response to receive public attention and sympathy, and to prod the government to act. When the White resistance reacted with legal nonviolent measures, such publicity and sympathy were not as likely, nor, as a result, was governmental intervention. Barkan (1984) suggested that had Whites used these means more often, the results may have been different. Examining the confrontations in Montgomery, Selma, Birmingham, Albany (Georgia), and Danville (Virginia), he concluded that in those cities where legal means such as arrests, high bails, court proceedings, and injunctions had been used, protestors were less successful (see also Sitkoff 1981).

One of the most brutal reactions to the nonviolent demonstrations of King and the SCLC occurred in Birmingham in the spring of 1963. Sit-ins, marches, and similar techniques had been used to protest local segregation. After these had been going on for a time, the local police commissioner, Eugene "Bull" Connor, came down violently on the protestors. His violent response was seen by millions on television. Officials used dogs, high-pressure hoses, cattle prods, clubs, and even a police tank to beat down the protestors. President Kennedy and his brother Robert, who had wanted "cooling-down" periods by Blacks and a more gradual approach to desegregation, sent federal representatives to help reach a compromise between King and local officials. But the protestors would not back down. Finally, the SCLC obtained desegregation of some public facilities, a promise of nondiscriminatory hiring, and the formation of a biracial committee in Birmingham (Sitkoff 1981).

As successful protests became more frequent, more working-class Blacks were drawn into the movement. Greater competition among the major Black organizations (SCLC, SNCC, CORE, NAACP) occurred with each group vying for the dominant position. They sponsored massive demonstrations throughout the country. A national March on Washington occurred in August 1963, sponsored by numerous civil rights, union, and church organizations and involving well over 200,000 individuals. During the summer of 1964, hundreds of individuals worked in Mississippi to increase voter registration, and three workers were brutally murdered. The government asked workers to remain calm, but this request only deepened their distrust of administration policies and motives. Riots broke out in several cities. President Kennedy began to press for a civil rights law in 1963, and shortly thereafter the Civil Rights and Voting Rights Acts were passed under President Johnson. This national legislative response to the basic problems of Blacks, particularly in the South, helped to delegitimize the need for protest, especially in the eyes of northern Whites.

Despite the passage of these laws, several other changes had occurred that helped alter the nature of the Black movement from the nonviolent protest tactics of King to cries for "Black power" and Black "liberation." First, the slow, compromising approach of the federal government to the problems experienced by Blacks on a day-to-day basis, coupled with the patient nonviolent method of King, convinced some in the civil rights movement of the need for more drastic action on their own behalf. The consistently violent reactions by Whites to the nonviolent protests of Blacks over the years widened the gap between factions within the civil rights movement in the early 1960s.

Second, the focus of the civil rights movement had been on the South, but the migration of many Blacks into the cities of the North and West led to a shift in goal emphasis within the movement. The problems of Black city dwellers became the focus: poverty, employment, housing, poor schools, and so on. The civil rights movement has been interpreted by some as largely a movement by and for middle-class individuals, while the focus of the Black movement on problems of city residents appeared to demonstrate a greater concern for the Black working and lower classes (Oberschall 1973; Rhoda Blumberg 1984; Bloom 1987). In total, the shift in the movement was from an emphasis on integration, political and social rights, and nonviolence to one on Black separatism, economic needs, and more militant tactics (Rhoda Blumberg 1984; Bloom 1987). Different segments stressed the importance of cultural and Black nationalism, while others spoke of Black power. Despite their dissimilarities, all of these more militant perspectives betrayed a basic distrust of White institutions, the need for Blacks to develop their own institutions or identities, and the need for stronger reactions to discrimination against Blacks. Stokely Carmichael's statement about the need for Black power suggests the feelings that some were having: "Power is the only thing respected in this world, and we must get it at any cost" (quoted in Sitkoff 1981, p. 214).

Violent riots occurred during the "long hot summers" of the 1960s in many major cities, including Chicago, Cleveland, Milwaukee, Dayton, San Francisco, Detroit, Newark, New Haven, Boston, Buffalo, and others. During 1967 alone, there were 150 such outbreaks (Sitkoff 1981). Certainly with this turn of events, it was clear that by the mid-1960s, while the Black push for equality was continuing, the nonviolent civil rights movement phase had passed.

There is evidence that the shift in focus from the South to the North during the 1960s weakened support for the movement and encouraged its decline. The strength of the civil rights movement was also sapped by declines in other movements, such as the antiwar movement against the Vietnam War. The vitality of the civil rights movement appears to have been tied to the vigor of other protest movements (Martin et al. 2009). In addition, shifts in the economy, greater political conservatism and complacency, the rise of Hispanics and concerns about new immigrants, and growing economic inequality outside and inside the Black community over the last couple of decades have softened the national focus on Blacks' living conditions and created divisions among Blacks themselves. There have even been attempts to eliminate affirmative action policies originally aimed at equalizing opportunities for all groups.. Despite the fact that Blacks continue to be worse off than Whites on many socioeconomic and life-chance measures, the broad-based, national sense of urgency to the plight of Blacks appears to have been muted in recent years.

Although the civil rights movement has moved into a quiescent phase, it has left its imprint on a variety of social and cultural changes in U.S. society. It helped to break down Jim Crow and segregation laws, sparked programs to help the disadvantaged, and inspired hope for social progress. It certainly stimulated and provided major parts of the strategic and tactical frameworks for other rights movements such as those on behalf of women, gays, and lesbians. Perhaps most significantly, the battles for civil rights in the 1950s and 1960s changed American culture by fostering more liberal and fair-minded attitudes among those who have clear memories of those days. In this way, the civil rights movement has continued to influence most Americans as we move further into the twenty-first century (Griffin and Bollen 2009; see also Isaac 2008; Martin et al. 2009).

THE WOMEN'S MOVEMENT

In both the civil rights and early labor movements, women had been victims of discrimination and inequality. Women needed their own movement to advance their interests. Like the civil rights movement, the women's movement has had an uneven history. Its unevenness is reflected in the fact that some scholars suggest that there were two or three separate such movements in history, yet others suggest that a single women's movement went through several phases. Freeman (1975b), for example, stated that "sometime during the 1920s, feminism died in the United States" (p. 448). But as is the case in the other movements, the push for political, economic, and other rights for women never completely "died." Rather, during the natural history of the women's movement, there were times when the movement was widely and publicly active, and other times when those in the movement were retrenching and the movement was, so to speak, being held in suspension or in abeyance (Taylor 1989a). As was the case with the other movements we have surveyed, internal conditions interacted with external circumstances to determine the nature of the movement.

Many of those conditions were related to structures of economic, racial, and sexual inequality in the society.

The women's movement in the United States began in the late 1700s and early 1800s and has continued, although not always actively and publicly, to this day (Hole and Levine 1975; Chafe 1977; Snyder 1979). Throughout its history, feminism has incorporated two seemingly paradoxical general goals. One is the belief that since women are, in most respects, the *same* as men in their potential and abilities, they are deserving of the *same* rights as men. The other is the belief that since women are *different* from men and encounter different life experiences, they deserve special protections. At different times and by different groups, each of these positions has been emphasized. Women's rights, then, are defined according to which of these two sets of beliefs and goals is stressed (Cott 1986).

The earliest organized efforts by women involved attempts to increase their educational rights and to fight for the abolition of slavery, and it was during involvement in the abolitionist movement of the 1830s that some women became acutely aware of their own low political status. As proved to be the case with their involvement in other historical movements, women were not given significant status or voice in the abolitionist movement. Indeed, while this movement was fighting for an end to slavery, women were being prevented from joining some abolitionist organizations and were being muzzled in their attempt to speak in public on the issues. Women had to create their own antislavery organizations because they were being excluded from many of the men's organizations (Hole and Levine 1975). Women had had a similar experience in the early labor union movement. While demanding rights and social justice for workers, many unions were at the same time barring women from membership. In those cases where women were members, few held leadership positions.

In 1840, a world antislavery meeting was held in London. Men at the meeting, including so-called radicals, were shocked to see women present, and so had them put in galleries where they could not participate effectively in the meeting. Later, in 1867, Sojourner Truth, a crusader for both women's and African Americans' rights, wrote of the neglect of women's rights among those who advocated such fights for African Americans: "There is a great stir about colored men getting their rights, but not a word about colored women; and if colored men get their rights and not colored women theirs, you see the colored men will be masters over the women, and it will be just as bad as it was before" (quoted in Ferree and Hess 1985, p. 32). Time and again, it became clear to many women that they would have to have their own organizations and movement if equal rights were ever to be achieved (Hole and Levine 1975; Snyder 1979).

Two of the women who had attended the antislavery convention in London were Elizabeth Cady Stanton and Lucretia Mott. Convinced of the need for an organization exclusively for women's rights, these women organized a meeting that was held in Seneca Falls, New York, in July of 1848. About 300 men and women attended, including Frederick Douglass and Susan B. Anthony. The attendees approved a "Declaration of Sentiments" based loosely on the wording of the Declaration of Independence. Among other things, this document argued for the basic equality of men and women and stressed that historically men had dominated over women in religious institutions, employment opportunities, and family and political life. Included among the declarations made was a demand for the right to vote. Although this latter demand has been said to signal the beginning of the suffrage movement, most of the women at the Seneca Falls meeting were more concerned with issues in their immediate experience: control of property and earnings, rights over children, rights to divorce, and so forth. From 1848 to the Civil War, women's conventions were held almost every year in different cities of the East and Midwest (Hole and Levine 1975).

The Early Social Context and Directions

The social environment within which women were advocating greater freedoms and rights was not hospitable. This was reflected not only in women's imposed marginal status in male abolitionist and labor organizations but also in the reactions within other dominant institutions. Religious institutions and the media railed against the embryonic women's movement. It was as if natural and supernatural orders were being violated by the attempts to gain women rights equal to those of men. In order to spread the word, women had to rely on some abolitionist papers and their own journals. Late in the nineteenth century, Stanton and others produced *The Woman's Bible,* a systematic critique to demonstrate that the traditional Bible was a major source of the subjugation of women.

The early formation of the movement also was affected by the forces of early industrialization. Not being allowed to learn skills, women who needed to work were relegated to either household or low-paying work (Huber 1982). Women who were from the middle or upper class, on the other hand, were not expected to work but rather to appear and act as "ladies." "The nineteenth-century concept of a lady was that of a fragile, idle, pure creature, submissive and subservient to her husband and to domestic needs. Her worth was based on her decorative value, a quality that embraced her beauty, her character, and her temperament. She was certainly not a paid employee" (Fox and Hesse-Biber 1984, p. 19). Not only working-class women but also Black women especially were not in a social and economic position to live up to the ideals of this image. They had to work, and in places and ways that did not foster an image of them as "ladies." If a woman was lacking in the qualities expected of a "lady," it "meant a woman was unnatural, unfeminine, and thus a species of a different—if not lower—female order. . . . Women who worked outside the home, or whose race had a history of sexual exploitation, were outside the realm of 'womanhood'

and its prerogatives" (Giddings 1984, pp. 48–49). Thus, race as well as class circumstances divided women.

This class division among women had an impact on the membership and goals of the early women's organizations. It was largely middle- and upper-class women who initiated the early movement and who fashioned its goals to fit their problems and desires, such as the desire for education in the professions and civil service, and property and voting rights. At the same time, they pushed for lower numbers of hours for female factory workers (Huber 1982). Although the latter appeared as a form of protection for women, it also was seen by many men as a way to minimize work competition from women. This suggests, as discussed earlier, the varying emphases on women as being different as well as the same as men. A desire for protection implies that women are different and more vulnerable than men, whereas the desire on the part of some women for equal employment opportunities implies that they are the equals of men. In sum, the religious and cultural milieu, along with the conditions of industrialization and slavery, helped to shape the form of the early women's movement as well as reactions to it.

After the Civil War, when the Fourteenth and Fifteenth Amendments on Black rights were being debated, women were told that attempts to include women in these amendments would only diffuse the focus that was being placed on rights for Blacks alone. The incorporation of women as well as men into the amendments, they were told, would hinder their passage (Hole and Levine 1975; Snyder 1979). The thrust for a separate women's movement accelerated, and basically two strands developed. One, under Elizabeth Cady Stanton and Susan B. Anthony, formed the National Woman Suffrage Association. It emphasized a variety of rights for women and viewed the vote as a means to obtaining them. The other, exemplified by the American Woman Suffrage Association under Lucy Stone and others, focused only on the vote. Eventually, the emphasis on the vote won out in the movement and the two organizations merged into the National American Woman Suffrage Association (Hole and Levine 1975). "By the decade beginning in 1910 the demand for woman suffrage was a capacious umbrella under which a large diversity of beliefs and organizations could shelter, or . . . an expansive platform on which they could all comfortably, if temporarily, stand" (Cott 1986, p. 52). It is during this period that the term *feminism* came on to the public scene. It would have been unthinkable to use such a term during the "woman movement" of the nineteenth century. Feminism suggested a radical change in all relations with men and also attracted smaller numbers of followers than the earlier "woman movement" (Cott 1987).

In this *first wave* of the feminist movement, two of the most militantly active groups pushing for the enfranchisement of women were the Congressional Union and the group derived from it, the National Woman's Party (NWP). Both were at the forefront of the movement between 1910 and 1920. Their intellectual leaders, Alice Paul and Lucy Burns, were both highly educated, militant, and single-minded in their pursuit of enfranchisement. By all accounts, Paul was a highly charismatic and enthusiastic individual who was an ardent advocate of single-issue politics (Cott 1987). Apparently, she also practiced a dictatorial style of leadership in the National Woman's Party, which drove some women from the group (Taylor 1989a). The militancy of the party was evident in mass protests, picketing and marches on Woodrow Wilson's White House, hunger strikes, and even jailings (Hole and Levine 1975; Cott 1987).

The NWP was viewed as having a single objective and any diversion from its pursuit was considered harmful. The rigid adherence to this philosophy resulted in insensitivity to the unique goals and problems of subgroups within the female population. "Only women holding culturally hegemonic values and positions—that is, in the United States, women who are White, heterosexual, middle class, politically midstream— have the privilege (or deception) of seeing their condition as that of 'woman,' glossing over their other characteristics," observed Cott perceptively (1986, p. 58). For example, some Blacks felt that the NWP was basically racist and did not care about the rights of Blacks. Most suffragist groups of the time were imbued with the racism of the broader culture and did little to combat it. Black women's concerns were considered by Paul to be racial rather than feminist problems (Cott 1987). This initial wave of the movement has been criticized for its narrow focus on the vote and absence of a broader consciousness of women's issues (Nachescu 2008).

In 1919, shortly before the passage of the Nineteenth Amendment enfranchising women, Walter White, leader of the NAACP, remarked about the NWP and its leadership: "If they could get the Suffrage Amendment through without enfranchising colored women, they would do it in a moment" (quoted in Cott 1987, p. 69). Just as women had been marginalized in the abolitionist movement by those fighting for Black rights, the specific problems of Blacks were now being put aside to focus on those of women only. In the same vein, some educated women were fighting for the same right to vote that "drunken male immigrant layabouts" possessed. This implied a kind of elitism among some segments of the suffrage movement (Ferree and Hess 1985). But it also reflected a class and race elitism present in the wider society in the early 1900s, a division whose implications for the suffrage movement were not fully understood by its leaders. Those in the movement "profoundly misread the degree to which ethnic, class, and family allegiances undermined the prospect of sex-based political behavior" (Chafe 1977, p. 118).

After the enfranchisement of women was accomplished in 1920, the movement for women's rights changed drastically. Rather than completely dying, the movement fractured internally, in large part because the attainment of the franchise had meant different things to different organizations and individuals. In essence, some women saw enfranchisement as an end in itself, while others viewed it as a means to reach more important goals, such as an equal rights amendment (ERA) for women.

The latter was now the goal of the National Woman's Party, while the more conservative National American Woman Suffrage Association fought against the ERA, formed the League of Women Voters, and worked for the active citizenship of women. The idea of universalistic legislation covering women's rights also was opposed by the Women's Bureau of the Department of Labor and a number of voluntary women's organizations. They feared that the legalization of equality with men would remove the shelters women received under the protectionist legislation of the 1920s, which limited women's involvement in the labor force. Some of the motivation on the part of the government for passing protective legislation was concern over the declining fertility rate early in the twentieth century. Officials feared that too drastic a decline would have harmful effects on the size of the defense forces and on the growth of the economy. It was believed that encouraging women to remain at home might stem the tide toward a lower birthrate.

At the bottom of everything, what divided women was the question of the priority of women's maternal roles compared to their employment opportunities. Protectionist legislation was interpreted by its adherents as conserving the maternal role of women (Huber 1982). Those pressing for an ERA, on the other hand, expressed an interest in the full potentiality of women, not merely their roles in the family. In a real sense, this difference of opinion on ERA resurrected the old question about the natures of men and women. Those who were in favor of the ERA were saying that women and men were basically the same, whereas those opposed to it and in support of protective legislation were saying that the two groups were basically different. Although both groups believed that sex inequality existed, the first group saw it as unnecessary and undesirable, whereas the second saw it as a given and, therefore, women needed protection. This division in position was duplicated in England (Cott 1986).

The movement also was splintered by the multiple ties of many women to other social movements. Once the Nineteenth Amendment had passed, many women moved on to other causes, such as temperance, birth control, union organizing, and poverty (Ferree and Hess 1985). Black women and working women had concerns other than those held by educated middle- or upper-class women, and some eventually formed their own organizations. Black women, for example, did not put the passage of the ERA and goals of the birth control movement anywhere near the top of their agenda: "For them, racial concerns overwhelmed those of sex" (Giddings 1984, p. 183). Lynching was a problem that hit much closer to home for them.

From Limbo to Resurgence

From 1945 to the 1960s, the women's movement was in limbo. In the years immediately after World War II, the social and cultural environment was not hospitable to protest from any minority group. The "feminine mystique" perception of the perfect woman was dominant. This woman was expected to be married, have children, be a helpmate to her husband and his career, and be happy in her domestic life. In other words, it was a conservative cultural period—one that sanctified the traditional male and female roles. Women who protested or sought "masculine" roles were considered not only unstable and possibly neurotic but also deviant (Rupp 1985; Taylor 1989a). Thus, even if some women wanted to protest, there were few effective avenues through which to do so, and their protests would not have had the support of the federal government. The media ridiculed feminism and reinforced traditional husband and wife roles (Taylor 1989a). It will be recalled that during this postwar expansion period, social inequality, in general, was an issue that was minimized.

Adding to the inhospitality of the social and cultural context, support for feminism also dwindled and extant women's groups had little mass power. The Women's Bureau of the Department of Labor had little influence and was anti-ERA anyway, and the National Woman's Party had been reduced to a relatively small number of faithful followers. Most of the women still present in this organization after World War II were

White, middle or upper class, employed, well educated, unmarried, and older than 50 years of age (Rupp 1985; Taylor 1989a). The Alva Belmont House, which served as the national headquarters of the NWP in Washington, D.C., had its own set of hired cooks and servants, suggesting the privileges of class. Moreover, the high and almost exclusive commitment demanded of members and their need to travel to meetings in various cities made it difficult for working-class women or those with major family obligations to become involved (Rupp 1985). None of these groups made much progress during this period, although they kept the movement for women's rights alive.

In light of its persistence through the difficult climate of the postwar period, the National Woman's Party served as the organization of abeyance for the women's movement. It provided tactics, social networks, and an identity to spur the resurgence of the activist phase of the *second wave* of feminism in the 1960s and 1970s. The National Organization for Women (NOW), which was founded in 1966, used many of the tactics of the NWP, such as political pressure and lobbying. NWP activists kept pressure on the government, thereby encouraging President Kennedy's decision to form a Presidential Commission on the Status of Women, and to include "sex" in Title VII of the 1964 Civil Rights Act. The NWP, then, served as a link between the past and the present in the women's movement, and its internal solidarity allowed it to serve as a source for the upsurge in feminist activity in the 1960s.

Although the 1945–1960 period was not marked by significant advances in the women's movement, several other social, cultural, and economic changes were occurring that created the structure necessary for a resurgence of the movement in the 1960s. In the period after World War II, an increasing number of women were obtaining educational degrees and participating in the labor force. Opportunities to work, coupled with a trend toward smaller families and a desire for more consumer goods on the part of families who could go on the installment plan, encouraged more women to enter the market. More children were moving on to attend college, which further increased the

need in most families for added income. The contours of the female labor force changed from one that had been primarily composed of single women in 1940 to one that consisted mainly of married women and mothers in 1950. But women also experienced significant job segregation following their removal from jobs after the war and the return of more men to the labor force (Freeman 1975a; Huber 1982). Nevertheless, successful participation in traditionally male positions during the war convinced many women that they could do the same jobs as men in most cases. Moreover, their increasing participation in the labor market was at odds with the vision of the perfect family in which the wife/mother stays at home to perform domestic and wifely chores.

In other words, by the time the 1960s arrived, women were more educated and had more earnings, and many had had significant experience in the labor force. This experience brought women face-to-face with their limited occupational opportunities. This is important because continuous labor-force experience appears to have a positive impact on feminist attitudes (Plutzer 1988). Added to this was the fact that the civil rights movement was peaking in the early 1960s and ideas about equality and personal intimacy were becoming more popular. The "sexual revolution" of the mid-1960s, which encouraged control of one's own body and tolerance of different sexual practices, also was consistent with feminist goals (Chafe 1977). All these events and conditions made the context ripe for a resurgence of the women's movement.

It should be kept in mind that this resurgence took place at a time and at the partial expense of the civil rights movement. Despite the occurrence of all the racial incidents in the South during this time, sudden concern was deflected from racial issues and focused on the problems of women, especially, it appeared, those of White middle-class women. The concerns that Betty Friedan expressed in *The Feminine Mystique,* those of the bored suburban housewife, seemed far removed from the real everyday problems of Black women. The issues posed clearly described a kind of woman unfamiliar to the average Black woman. Many Black women considered White women to be simply another part of the White enemy, and considered their own problems to be both more serious and qualitatively different from those of White women. They resented White feminists' equating sexism with racism, and promoting the idea that Blacks and women experience a "common oppression" (Nachescu 2008, p. 47). Consequently, during this period most activist Black women did not identify with the priorities of the White women's movement, and did not join it (Breines 2007). Further souring feelings between Black and White women was the fact that the women's movement was seen as having benefited from the earlier and heavily paid for efforts of the civil rights movement (Giddings 1984).

In 1961, after pleas from Esther Petersen of the Labor Department's Women's Bureau, President Kennedy created the President's Commission on the Status of Women, which, although of short duration, was able to thoroughly document the poor status of women relative to men in the United States. One of the most significant outcomes of the commission's work was the proliferation of state-level commissions on the status of women. In turn, an important consequence of these state commissions was the sharing of information and the generation of a network of activists who were cognizant of the problems faced by women and convinced of the urgency of change (Freeman 1975a; Ferree and Hess 1985).

It was at a June 1966 meeting of such state commissions in Washington, D.C., that the National Organization for Women was created, largely because of the belief that the Equal Employment Opportunity Commission, which had developed out of the Civil Rights Act of 1964 and was supposed to deal with sex discrimination, was doing little about the problems of women in the labor market. Race and sex again appeared to be working at cross purposes. NOW's early emphasis on equal rights, which was attractive to many middle- and upper-class women, turned off Black women and those who were members of unions (Giddings 1984). Conversely, when NOW leaders desired membership in the Leadership Conference on Civil Rights, they were denied with

the argument that women's problems did not constitute a civil rights issue (Ferree and Hess 1985).

The civil rights movement and the newly resurgent women's movement of the 1960s intertwined race and sex issues in other ways as well. Experience in civil rights activities provided many women with knowledge about tactics and organizing problems and gave them a sense of their own capabilities. At the same time, however, their participation made it clear, as it had been made clear to women involved in the abolitionist movement, that they needed to develop their own organizations and movement. Women, Black and White, were not accorded high status in the civil rights movement, especially in the later Black power stage. This is despite the fact that, though largely unrecognized, Black women had performed many varied leadership roles in the civil rights movement (Barnett 1993). Black men in the late civil rights movement often thought of White women as conquests. "Women were sexual conquests, supportive workers behind the scenes, effective organizers on a local level; only in these secondary roles were they welcome in the cause. When women questioned their limited power within the movement, and ultimately in the society, they were ridiculed, abused, and excluded" (Ferree and Hess 1985, p. 47). The perception by many young Black leaders and most Whites who identified with them was that it was the Black male who suffered most from discrimination and poverty because his self-esteem, his "manhood" was being attacked (Ferree and Hess 1985).

Young women's experiences in the student New Left movement also left much to be desired. While the movement preached fewer restrictions on sexuality, the men generally treated the movement women as objects available for the taking. Women did not have positions of power in the New Left. The experiences of many younger women in both the Black power and New Left movements helped motivate them to create a network of feminists committed to their own unique cause. Thus, another less formal branch of the women's network developed alongside the more centralized and national-level organizations of the women's movement. In contrast to the older, more bureaucratic sector of the feminist movement that sought equality through formal institutional channels, this strand of the second wave of the movement consisted of more informal, locally based groupings composed primarily of younger women. They were not well organized, nor were they intended to be, and they had no central leadership. While the formal national organizations stressed legislation and lobbying as routes to women's rights, the younger, less formal, and more radical strand emphasized the importance of education, consciousness-raising, and "rapping" as means to personal power and women's liberation. These groups arose all over, in Chicago, Toronto, Detroit, Seattle, Gainesville, and other places.

The diversity hinted at should suggest the level of richness and depth of the current women's movement. But its complexity, broadness of constituency, and decentralized organization is only one of the ways in which it differs from the earlier suffrage phase of the women's movement. A second difference lies in the fact that its development during the 1960s was more in tune with broader changes in the society at large, as well as more in touch with the real experiences of many women. The cultural contexts during the suffrage and abolitionist movements, it will be recalled, were much more hostile to a woman's movement for equal rights or liberation. Third, in contrast to the earlier active phases of the movement, the goals became much more diverse during the second wave. The suffrage movement concentrated on a single issue—the vote (Chafe 1977). Similarly, the abolitionist movement concentrated on a single problem—slavery.

Despite its successes, the women's movement has continued to encounter an array of fearsome obstacles. The political, economic, and social conditions of the 1980s generated a strong antifeminist countermovement. By the end of the 1970s, many average citizens had been told by the media that women had reached their goals. Added to this message was another that portrayed "feminists as antimale, lesbian, humorless, and politically correct ideologues" (Andersen 1997, p. 313). In 1980, Republicans dropped advocacy of the ERA from their platform after 40 years of supporting it. The New Right began to flower in the late

1970s and has consistently attacked the feminist agenda. This movement is composed of professionals, ministers, and politicians who subscribe to a combination of fundamentalist religious dogma and conservative politics antagonistic to feminism. Since 2000, an increasing number of women have been drawn into right-wing movements.

Nevertheless, a *third wave* of feminism, dominated by younger women, continued into the 1980s and 1990s, and emphasized women pursuing a variety of experiences, basically "having it all"—career, sexuality, and motherhood, often outside the confines of the traditional family. Instead of pursuing equality through political action, third-wave feminists often focus on personal empowerment in the cultural sphere, through music, fashion, transgender behaviors, and other multiple identities (Aronson 2003; Diamond 2009; Wrye 2009). Some suggest that in the early years of the twenty-first century, a *fourth wave* of feminism is emerging that reaches outward to others, stressing the importance of an "internal sense of gender inequality," a spirituality that views all humans as part of one community, and actions that aid the whole world and its downtrodden populations (Diamond 2009, p. 218; Wrye 2009).

At this time, the vast majority of Americans appear to support many of the specific ideas associated with the equality of men and women, even though for most, women's rights is an issue of only moderate importance. A review of surveys from the 1980s and 1990s reveals significant splits in support for the movement (Huddy, Neely, and Lafay 2000). While at least two-thirds of Americans are sympathetic with the "women's movement," there is significantly less support for "feminism." Most women do not identify themselves as "feminists" probably in part because of the media's negative image discussed earlier. Nor are most women meaningfully involved in the movement. About one-third of U.S. adults view the women's movement as either unnecessary, too powerful, or irrelevant to the lives of some women. They see it as having helped middle-class professional women, but as having yielded few benefits for working-class women, homemakers, or poor women (Huddy, Neely, and Lafay 2000).

The ambivalence and divisions in perceptions of feminism are reflected in a recent survey of young women who differ in the ways they define "feminism" and vary in their identification with feminism. The priorities given to life's issues depend heavily on the everyday experiences and the racial and class backgrounds of these women. Most of the women interviewed were ambivalent, supporting some feminist ideals but not others, and were hesitant to define themselves as feminists (Aronson 2003). In light of the historical divisions within the women's movement and the conflicting social and cultural forces currently at work in society that were noted earlier, it is perhaps not surprising to find that many young women have ambiguous and ambivalent feelings about feminism.

Although Blacks and working-class women have been recruited and attempts have been made to integrate issues of concern to them, the women's movement has traditionally been a White middle-class one and complete integration of these groups has not yet occurred (Ferree and Hess 1985; Taylor 1989b). One veteran feminist observes that most of the achievements of the women's movement have not really affected poor women: "I think living in poverty is an unresolved problem of the women's movement" (Bolgar 2009, p. 198). The diversity within the movement with respect to race, class-specific goals, and assumptions about the nature of men and women has provided a source of strength. But under the pressures of a countermovement against feminism, these divisions could widen and splinter the movement. What can be a source of strength can also be a source of damaging division. Like the labor movement, the women's movement has yet to bring everyone under its umbrella.

Summary

All of the social movements discussed were focused on reducing social inequalities of one sort or another. But as has been noted before, such grievances are not sufficient for either the development or continuance of a social movement. The surrounding social structure must generate openings and opportunities for movements to develop and prosper. Conditions such as social unrest and economic upheaval create potential economic and political opportunities that lead to the appearance of social movements.

The cultural context also affects the life and structure of a social movement. You have seen how a variety of societal values and ideologies have been reflected in the character of labor, women's, and civil rights movements. Racist, sexist, and class values and their intersection deeply influenced the shape of and membership in each movement, creating internal divisions and pressures toward homogeneous organizations.

In addition to structural opportunities and cultural milieu, the resources available to a group affect the development of a movement. Of course, whether an aggrieved group can obtain such resources also depends on the structure of opportunities and the cultural milieu.

Finally, the presence of opportunities, resources, and a favorable cultural milieu fosters the development of power and a sense of a *cognitive liberation* in which groups of aggrieved individuals redefine their situation and their potential for successful solutions (McAdam 1982). On the other hand, when groups have few opportunities and no resources, and the culture is adverse, the chances of a new revolutionary consciousness and a successful social movement are slim, indeed. Until equity is achieved, however, movements for class, racial, and gender equality are likely to continue in the United States, if only sporadically.

Critical Thinking

1. Given current economic difficulties in the United States at large, what do you think the prospects are for a resurgence of a vibrant labor movement? Explain your answer.
2. What effect, if any, do you think the conservative movements that have arisen in the United States since the early 1980s will have on inequality in the country?
3. What kinds of new inequalities are emerging from which movements might develop? What conditions might maximize or minimize the chances for these movements?
4. Why has it been difficult for those in the labor, civil rights, and women's movements to join forces?

Web Connections

Visit the AFL-CIO's website at www.aflcio.org to learn about issues of importance to unions. To read about the goals of the feminist movement in the 1960s and 1970s, go to http://womenshistory. about.com/od/feminism. The story of the civil rights movement as told by its veterans can be read at www.crmvet.org.

Film Suggestions

Democracy in America: #05 Civil Rights: Demanding Equality (2003). This film examines guarantees of equality and the roles played by government and individuals in ensuring these guarantees for vulnerable groups in society.

Matewan (1987). John Sayles's recounting of the union–coal company battle in West Virginia in the 1020s.

American Women of Achievement (1995). This series looks at the lives of 10 notable American women from Abigail Adams to Wilma Rudolph to Sandra Day O'Connor.

CHAPTER 14

Social Mobility and Status Attainment

A man must make his opportunity, as oft as find it.

FRANCIS BACON (1561–1626)

The United States as a storied land of opportunity and freedom is chronicled in many myths and fables about how the individual, no matter how humble and lowly, can succeed. Children in U.S. society often are told that if they work hard enough and want something badly enough, they will obtain it. They are taught that opportunities are there to be grasped, if a person just has the aspirations and perseverance required to take advantage of them. Americans tend to have a rosy view of the opportunities and prospects attainable in their country. A 2009 Pew survey found that about three out of four believe that it is possible for people to get ahead in a difficult economy and believe that their economic situation will improve over the next decade. In 2010, while more people felt that their economic situation had gotten worse rather than better over the last few years, a majority still believed they were better off than their parents, and that their children will be better off than they are (Smith, March 2011). As in past surveys, more than 8 out of 10 believe that hard work, ambition, a good education, and being healthy are crucial for economic mobility. In other words, it is the attributes of the person rather than outside forces that are most important for advancement. Having little education, too much debt, and making poor choices are the factors most often mentioned for why some persons are downwardly mobile (Economic Mobility Project, March 12, 2009).

In light of these values about the individual and achievement, it is not surprising that a central question raised in the study of inequality has concerned the extent to which the United States is an open society. The issue of openness raises a number of questions:

- In terms of sheer amount, how much mobility has there been and is there now in the United States? How does the United States compare with other countries on mobility?
- What is the nature of the mobility that has occurred? Is it more often long-distance or short-range mobility?

- What have been the trends in intergenerational inheritance? Are individuals more or less likely to have the same socioeconomic status as their parents?
- What roles do socioeconomic background and individual qualities play in determining an individual's present status? To what extent is social mobility determined by forces beyond individuals' control rather than by their own actions?
- What conditions in the economic, social, and cultural structures affect the chances for and levels of attainment by individuals?

Each of these questions concerns a separate issue, but all of them are relevant to the general question of how open U.S. society is, and each of them has been addressed in research. The first three questions have been the concern of traditional mobility studies, whereas the last two have been a main focus of status attainment research.

U.S. MOBILITY OVER TIME

Serious mobility research began in the 1940s, and even then there was concern about what the future held. Changes in mobility studies since the 1940s have been driven by changes in the databases used and increases in the sophistication of techniques for analyzing them.

Estimates of Mobility Trends from World War II to the 1980s

One of the first attempts to arrive at some conclusions regarding post–World War II mobility trends using national sample data was carried out by Jackson and Crockett (1964). The authors compared data for **intergenerational mobility** between father and son collected in 1957 by the Survey Research Center at the University of Michigan with national data collected in 1945, 1947, and 1952 to determine trends in mobility from 1945 to 1957. The results suggested that greater mobility occurred in 1952 and 1957 than in 1947. Some mobility would have occurred simply because of changes in the occupational structure between generations. The amount and

type of social mobility that occurs in a society is in part affected by the opportunities that are created, changed, or eliminated by the structure within which individuals operate. For example, World War II veterans often received occupational training while in the military; they were also able to take advantage of the educational opportunities afforded by the GI bill. Taking advantage of these opportunities allowed veterans to strengthen their human capital and later attain higher wages and more prestigious occupations (Teachman and Tedrow 2004). The structure of opportunities had broadened because new avenues for social mobility had opened up. Indeed, many veterans were able to go to college using the GI bill. The character and composition of the occupational structure at any given point in time also make up part—a very important part—of the **opportunity structure** within which individuals may be able to move. The structure places limits on the possibility and degree of occupational mobility in a society. Increases in the white-collar governmental sector after World War II, for example, even encouraged working-class and middle-class youths to leave high school or college to get jobs in the expanding economy (Shanahan, Miech, and Elder 1998).

In other words, between any two periods of time, some mobility is bound to occur if the occupational distributions in the two generations in question are different. The difference between that minimum amount of *expected* mobility and what *actually* occurs is often referred to as the amount of social fluidity or **circulation mobility**. Most consider this to be a better measure of the openness of a system than the total amount of mobility because it allegedly has already taken into account changes that have occurred because of alterations in the occupational structure. Circulation mobility is also a more direct measure of the impact of family background on an individual's mobility. Greater openness suggests a weaker tie between background and mobility. A greater proportion of the total mobility in 1947 appears to have been due to circulation than to structural conditions or **structural mobility**, whereas in 1952 and 1957, the reverse is the case.

Blau and Duncan (1967) added 1962 national data to that used by Jackson and Crockett. Blau and Duncan's data suggested that circulation increased between 1957 and 1962 and that the son's occupation was less dependent on that of the father. In other words, the system of inequality appears to have been more open in 1962 than in the earlier years.

Some of the principal findings from Blau and Duncan (1967) revealed clear patterns:

1. Despite a good deal of mobility, especially of the short-range variety, occupational inheritance was higher than would be expected if no relationship existed between the father's status and the son's 1962 occupational status.
2. Upward mobility was much more prevalent than downward mobility, most of it being structurally induced.
3. The highest rates of *inflow* into an occupational category from other categories occurred among the lower white-collar and lower blue-collar occupations. That is, they recruited individuals from a wide variety of occupational backgrounds.
4. The highest rates of *outflow* from an occupational category occurred among the two lowest white-collar groups and the blue-collar and farm groupings. That is, a greater proportion of these sons went to other occupations, suggesting that they had greater chances for mobility. In the salaried professions, on the other hand, just the opposite situation occurred. The sons were much less likely to outflow to other occupations, suggesting a high degree of inheritance.
5. An increasing proportion of men with non-farm/manual origins moved up into the white-collar occupations. But men who started their own careers in a blue-collar occupation were less likely to be mobile than those who began their careers as white-collar workers or farmers (pp. 28–41).

In the 1970s, Featherman and Hauser (1978) replicated Blau and Duncan's study and found some similar results. There was a great deal of intra- and intergenerational mobility, most of it

short-distance, and there was more upward than downward mobility. More mobility took place than would be expected by only changes in the occupational structure. Most of the mobility took place in the middle of the occupational hierarchy, for example, in upper blue-collar positions. The top and bottom were fairly closed, suggesting "barriers to movement across class boundaries" (p. 180). Still there was a decline in the relationship between occupational origins and destinations and between fathers' and sons' occupations. Featherman and Hauser concluded that "among American men a reduction of obstacles to occupational change appears to be a long-term and continuing tendency" (p. 136). At least for men, background seemed to have become less important in determining occupational position. This has been substantiated for the period from 1972 to 1985 as well. "Socioeconomic status has become less important for men's and women's occupational mobility since 1972" (Hout 1988, p. 1389). The decline in the association between an individual's social background and where he or she ends up occupationally appears to be linked to the rise in the proportion of workers who have higher education. This is the case for both men and women (Hout 1988).

Race, farm background, and paternal occupation were still important predictors of occupational status and mobility, but contemporary changes moderated their impact. On the one hand, the educational level of Blacks increased. Black fathers were more able to pass on their status to sons, and the growing "rationality" of the economy created pressures to reduce discrimination. But discrimination did not appear to be any less significant than in the 1960s, racial differences in returns to human-capital investments still remained, and the likelihood of young Blacks being in the labor force was smaller in the 1970s than in the 1960s. Stratification within the Black community became more visible and clear. Blacks became more differentiated with respect to socioeconomic status, creating more distinct classes and greater inequalities among them.

With respect to the last point, results from the analysis of several national surveys conducted between 1972 and 1985 indicate that the openness of the U.S. occupational structure may have increased, whereas changes in the composition of the occupational structure may have slowed. This means that, overall, the extent of observed mobility remains unchanged because the increase in openness has been offset by a reduction in mobility resulting from changes in the occupational structure. In the 1980s, women were more likely to have had parents with similar occupational status than was the case even as recently as 1970. The same was true for men. For example, the share of men and women whose origins are upper middle class has grown, whereas the proportion with farm backgrounds has declined. For most of the twentieth century, the extent of mobility in the United States was due primarily to changes in the occupational structure between generations. From the late 1960s into the 1980s, however, mobility shifts may have been due especially to increases in openness and related factors.

Current U.S. Mobility Patterns

In contrast to the Blau and Duncan and Featherman and Hauser studies, which projected a society with increased openness and decreasing inheritance of occupation, recent evidence suggests that occupational mobility slowed and perhaps even declined in the last decade of the twentieth century. Intergenerational mobility in income also appears to have declined since 1980. The amount of social fluidity or openness for men born since the mid-1960s appears to be lower than that for children born earlier in the twentieth century, in part because of the stronger relationship between mothers' class and sons' occupational status (Aaronson and Mazumder 2008; Beller 2009). Intergenerational mobility at the top and bottom of the economic hierarchy remains fairly restricted. There is a distinct persistence in the tendency for individuals born into a high- or low-status family to remain in that position (Hertz 2005; Mazumder 2005). For example, it is estimated that a son born into the top 10 percent of the income hierarchy has at least a 1 in 5 chance of attaining the same position, but that one born

into the bottom 10 percent has only a 1 in 100 chance of moving up into the top income decile. The chances are much greater that the latter will remain at the bottom (Bowles and Gintis 2002). Nam's (2004) study of sons from low-income and high-income backgrounds confirmed this conclusion, finding that intergenerational transmission for those in the high-income group increased over time, but that the chances of low-income persons moving up from their poorer position did not change significantly. "These findings imply that America is not becoming more equal for its children" (p. 202).

The increase in income inequality may have entrenched advantages at the upper end and disadvantages at the lower end of the economic hierarchy, lowering equality of opportunity and circulation mobility. The current increase in income inequality has made intergenerational income mobility less likely (Beller 2009). The paradoxical facts that, on the one hand, most citizens believe in the openness of U.S. society, but on the other hand, the family one is born into has a significant effect on one's **status attainment**, reflect a conflict between a value that extols openness for all, and one that exhorts parents and families to do the best they can for their children. These values clash in struggles over issues of equal opportunity and inheritance (McNamee and Miller, Jr. 2004; Bowles, Gintis, and Groves 2005).

Tracking trends from 1968 to 1986 within a national sample of almost 5,000 families suggest that income mobility has declined whereas the extent of income inequality has increased since 1980. Thus, individuals have less chance to improve their income positions than they did in the late 1960s (Veum 1992). Rytina's longitudinal study of occupational mobility (2000) revealed that the relationship between fathers' and sons' specific occupations may be strengthening. Using data from a national sample of families that have been tracked for 36 years since the late 1960s, a recent study compared parents' 1968 family incomes with those of their children in the late 1990s and early 2000s. While most children have incomes higher than their parents,

This mural in a poor urban neighborhood shows the importance of "choosing the right path" to leave behind the darkness of poverty and crime and to move toward a brighter future. (Photo by Brendan R. Hurst.)

children's income is strongly influenced by those of their parents. Parental influence on children's *wealth* also is present, although not as strong as the impact on *income*. About one-third of children from the top and bottom wealth quintiles remain in those wealth groups as adults, meaning that most possess levels of wealth that are different from those of their parents (Isaacs, Sawhill, and Haskins 2008). On the other hand, forty-two percent of children born into families that were in the bottom income quintile in 1968 are also at the bottom 36 years later, and 39 percent of children from the richest 20 percent of families have stayed in the top. About one-third of children have incomes lower than those of their parents. Only 6 percent of children from the poorest group of families have moved into the top. Americans greatly overestimate their chances of becoming rich; rags-to-riches mobility is very unusual in the United States (DiPrete 2007; Kotkin 2010). The chances of becoming wealthy by being a Horatio Alger-type entrepreneur are much less for those from poor backgrounds than they are for individuals who come from middle- or upper-class families (Hundley 2008).

A smaller percentage of poor children in the United States have incomes greater than their parents than is found in Denmark, Finland, Sweden, Norway, and the United Kingdom (Isaacs, Sawhill, and Haskins 2008). The effects of being raised in a poor family are cumulative. Poor children tend to have poorer health, which, in turn, lowers educational attainment, occupational status, earnings, and subsequent adult health (Haas 2006). Children in persistently poor families are less likely than others to graduate from high school and to be employed at age 25 (Wagmiller et al. 2006). This raises the issue of the extent to which attainment at the top is due to meritocratic rather than ascribed or subjective factors. Both quantitative and qualitative studies of mobility in the higher ranks of organization suggest the importance of subjective criteria in promotion (e.g., Jackall 1988; Bowles and Gintis 2002).

In addition to the importance of the relationship between parents' and children's economic status, the amount of social mobility in a society depends heavily on the combination of social structural conditions and the degree of access to positions in the structure. Historically, upward mobility has been heavily attributed to shifts in the occupational structure. The influx of new jobs and restructuring of old jobs due to advances in information technologies such as the Internet have profound implications for mobility patterns now and in the future. On the access side, changes in the extent of racial/ethnic discrimination also affect mobility patterns. For instance, between 1940 and 1990, the occupational disadvantages of being Japanese or Chinese American appear to have declined, especially in the white-collar sector (Sakamoto, Liu, and Tzeng 1998).

Mobility toward and at the Bottom

Evidence of growing numbers of poor people, rising income/earnings inequality, and speculation about a declining middle class have spurred questions about whether downward mobility has increased in the United States in recent years. Research suggests that in some respects it has, but that conclusions depend on whether such mobility is measured in absolute or relative terms. **Absolute downward mobility** refers to a downward shift in economic resources without a simultaneous change in an individual's position relative to others. For example, one's income may decline, but because the income of others is also declining or because those below are much poorer, one may still remain in the same place on the income ladder. **Relative downward mobility**, on the other hand, refers to an actual shift in position on the ladder, a switching of position with others. So, for example, one may start out in the third quintile in the income distribution, but then fall into the fourth because of declines in income. Evidence from large nationally representative samples suggests that absolute downward mobility increased during the mid-1980s, but that relative downward mobility did not. Moreover, larger amounts of downward mobility came from the middle and lower quintiles than from the upper quintiles. The chances of falling into poverty are much greater for Blacks and those who are **near poor** (Rodgers 1995); they are also greater for women than for men. Together with evidence cited earlier about growing

economic inequality, these trends fit the saying that the "rich get richer and the poor get poorer."

Regardless of similarity in experience, credentials, and human capital, Blacks in high-status occupations early in their careers are more likely than Whites to face downward mobility during their first 4 years in their occupations. This is especially the case in the private sector. This downward movement has negative repercussions for occupational experiences later in their careers. Human capital and other predictors of occupational status appear to be more predictive and protective of high-status White than Black employees. Decisions for Black displacement are "broadly based" and less affected by standard, expected factors like education and background (Wilson and Roscigno 2010, p. 69). Blacks in lower middle-class positions are also more apt than Whites to suffer downward mobility. Blacks who are relatively new to a middle-class status are more vulnerable than their White counterparts to falling in class position because they often lag behind Whites in education and wealth (Hardaway and McLoyd 2009).

Mobility at the bottom of the economic ladder has become a growing concern as questions about the underclass and possible intergenerational transmission of poverty have arisen. National data suggest that the chances of upward mobility of both White and Black children are reduced when raised in a poor family. Being from a Black family increases the negative effects of poverty. Generally, about 25 percent of Blacks who were raised in poor families stay poor in early adulthood, compared to about 10 percent of Whites who were raised poor. In other words, most will move out of poverty, but a minority will be poor like their parents, and the chances of being poor increase significantly for those raised in families in which the parents were poor most of the time (Corcoran 1995). Almost two-thirds of Black children grew up in the bottom 20 percent of families in the nation, compared to only 13 percent of White children, and when they become adults, Black children, especially those in the middle class, are much less likely than White children to have incomes that exceed those of their parents. Close to one-half of Black children compared to only 16 percent of White children with middle-class parents wind up falling into the bottom income quintile when they are adults (Isaacs, Sawhill, and Haskins 2008).

Children who are raised poor are significantly more likely to be poor when they are adults than children brought up in nonpoor families. Compared to poor children, those brought up in wealthy families are more likely to inherit large amounts of wealth, obtain it earlier, attain high levels of education, and develop patterns of consumption and methods of asset allocation that will maintain and even enhance their wealth (Isaacs, Sawhill, and Haskins 2008). In contrast, even if poor children move out of poverty as adults, having come from a poor family negatively and significantly affects children's future education, working hours, earnings, and incomes. "Children's futures are clearly constrained by a lack of economic resources. . . . Being poor matters a lot" (Isaacs, Sawhill, and Haskins 2008, pp. 249, 261). *Why* these effects occur has been a subject of debate. The mechanisms linking background to future poverty are multiple. Lack of economic resources may affect the economic futures of poor children through their negative effects on intellectual development, stress, job networking, and lifestyle choices (Wilson 1987). Children raised in lower-income families are less likely to complete their schooling and more likely to have children out of wedlock (Duncan et al. 1998)—two conditions that would seem to increase the chances of poverty. Not having a high school education, having fewer parental resources, being raised in a troubled family, and not feeling connected to school increase the chances for unemployment among young adults (Caspi et al. 1998). Unemployment, in turn, increases risks for poverty. Evidence also strongly suggests that employment opportunities and neighborhood conditions are important. The number and nature of economic opportunities in an area also affect poverty risks (Haynie and Gorman 1999). Poor neighborhoods then become socially isolated from nonpoor areas as economic and employment flight from them occurs (Wilson 1987).

It should not be surprising, then, that elderly *urban* residents are also less likely than elderly *rural* residents to become poor since the presence of economic opportunities are probably greater in metropolitan areas than in rural places. As is the case for children, the chances of falling into poverty when one is nearing retirement are similarly affected by the work histories of adults and their educations. A study of persons 55 and older found that men who have less than a high school education and were employed in a nonunion, manual job were 16 times more likely to fall into poverty in old age than men who had more education and had been employed in a unionized, or higher-status white-collar job (McLaughlin and Jensen 2000).

COMPARATIVE STUDIES OF MOBILITY

How does the rate of social mobility in the United States compare to rates in other industrial countries? One argument is that all rates are similar. The **industrialism thesis** contends that "industrialization, directly or indirectly, demolishes old barriers, opens new avenues for ascendance, and shifts the basis of status attainment from ascription to achievement. It, therefore, loosens the dependence of destinations on origins and generates a gradual openness in the mobility structure, in addition to transforming the occupational structure and promoting structural mobility" (Wong 1994, p. 122). According to this argument, industrialism has an "inner logic" that, when introduced into countries, overshadows the distinctive cultural and social characteristics of industrial nations.

The argument that industrialization inevitably increases upward social mobility in a similar manner in all industrial countries has come under severe attack, however (van Leeuwen and Maas 2010). In the United States, for instance, income inequality has increased as has the proportion who are poor or near poor. Concerns about increased downward mobility have also intensified in this highly advanced nation. Moreover, as education becomes more important, lack of it gives those at the bottom a smaller chance of moving up.

Many recent studies also indicate that industrial countries vary in their *rates* and *patterns* of mobility. Comparative studies suggest that *overall* observed mobility rates in Western industrial nations are not that similar (e.g., Grusky and Hauser 1984; Kurz and Muller 1987; van Leeuwen and Maas 2010). Roughly, the same can be said for upward social mobility rates in industrialized nations; in fact, social mobility does not seem to have changed in many such nations since World War II (Wong 1994).

What this suggests is that the industrialism thesis is flawed because it ignores the central role of the often unique historical, cultural, and institutional context of countries in which mobility does or does not occur. The patterns of mobility vary between countries because of differences in their contexts. First of all, the process of industrialization does not follow the same route in all countries. Historical and political conditions help shape the occupational structure and mobility within the country (Hauser and Grusky 1988). Second, varying characteristics of educational institutions affect access to quality education and the connection between education and employment. Thus, the pathways to mobility vary between countries (Kerckhoff 1995). Think about this: Every society provides institutional pathways through which a citizen needs to move if he or she is to be mobile. These pathways differ not only in their structure but also, because of the culture, in terms of who is eligible to use them and when they can use them. Between one's origin and one's destination lies a patterned structure through which one must pass to be socially mobile. What did your parents have to go through to get where they are? How about your grandparents? The pathways to mobility for different generations vary to the extent that economic, social, political, and cultural structures also change between generations, creating new opportunities while eliminating or altering old ones.

In comparisons with other industrial countries, the association between sons' and fathers' earnings is stronger in the United States and the United Kingdom than in Canada and some European countries, suggesting less *intergenerational* mobility in those countries. For example, it is estimated that 40 percent of the earnings advantage of high-status fathers is passed on to their sons in the United Kingdom, Italy, France, and the United States, compared to less than 20 percent in Australia, Canada, and Scandinavian countries (Organization for Economic Cooperation and Development 2010; see also Hirvonen 2008). This means that earnings mobility is lower in the first set of countries. Rates of mobility may be even lower in some developing countries like Ecuador, Peru, and Brazil, however, where the relationship between fathers' and sons' income appears even stronger. The United States is in the middle, however, when the U.S. rate of mobility during individuals' own lifetimes (i.e., *intra*generational mobility) is compared to those of other industrial countries (Isaacs, Sawhill, and Haskins 2008).

STATUS ATTAINMENT: WHAT DETERMINES HOW FAR ONE GOES?

Most mobility studies have not provided us with a systematic picture of the *process* through which mobility occurs. That is, they do not lay out the mechanisms and pathways that explain the connection between the positions of parents and their adult children. Status attainment studies attempt to identify the factors that are primarily responsible for this connection by focusing on *how* individual parental status affects the status of offspring. These studies provide us with another way to measure a society's openness. A society is considered open to the extent that the economic statuses of children are not dependent on those of their parents. It is the extent of this dependence and how it is maintained that has been the focus of status attainment research.

The first large-scale set of national data specifically collected for the study of intergenerational mobility in the United States became available with the study of Occupational Changes in a Generation (OCG), later published by Blau and Duncan under the title *The American Occupational Structure*. The data were obtained as part of the Current Population Survey (CPS) of the Bureau of the Census in March 1962. Over 20,000 men formed the basic sample for the OCG study by

Blau and Duncan. This sample represents about 45 million men between 20 and 64 years of age who were in the civilian, noninstitutionalized population in March 1962 (Blau and Duncan 1967, pp. 10–19). Thus, this study said nothing about changing economic conditions among women, youths, or the elderly. Nevertheless, the data were considered to be of unusual reliability and completeness because they were collected by trained individuals using established techniques and working for an institution that had been carrying out such surveys for decades.

Blau and Duncan's basic attainment model is presented in Figure 14.1. They were concerned with the relative role of socioeconomic origins in the determination of the son's occupational status. From the diagram, it can be observed that the greatest direct effects on the occupational status of the son in 1962 came from education. A father's education had an indirect effect on 1962 status through its effect on education, whereas a father's occupation had a direct as well as an indirect effect through its connections with the son's first job and education.

In summarizing the findings of Blau and Duncan, social origin, education, and first job accounted for less than 50 percent of the variation that occurred in 1962 occupational attainments.

The lower the position from which a person begins, argued Blau and Duncan, the greater the probability that he or she will be upwardly mobile, if only because there are more occupational categories above the individual than below. But as men get older and move through their careers, their social origins appear to have less effect on their attainment than past experience and career accomplishments.

The Blau–Duncan findings also suggest that having a stable family life, having fewer siblings, and being the youngest or oldest male are positively related to occupational success. But those who come from large families *and* overcome obstacles are also likely to move up occupationally more readily than others who have not had such challenges. Moreover, evidence suggested that the role of education, which Blau and Duncan viewed as an achievement variable, had become increasingly important to occupational attainment. They suggested that this indicated an increase in the importance of universalistic factors in attainment.

While it only focused on men and did not include housework as a form of occupation, *The American Occupational Structure* opened the door to a whole new way of examining the problem of the openness of the system of inequality,

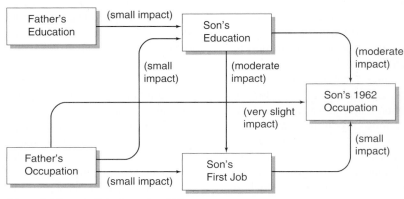

"Very slight" = coefficients under .200
"Small" = coefficients of .200–.325
"Moderate" = coefficients of .326–.440

FIGURE 14.1 Effects of Father's Status on Occupational Status of Son

Source: Based on Blau and Duncan (1967).

gave impetus to scores of studies, and made some valuable contributions to our understanding of movement in the occupational hierarchy.

Explanations of Status Attainment

Basically, the Blau–Duncan model relies on *structural* factors as explanatory variables. It is clear that this model does not consider social-psychological factors, such as aspirations and the influences of parents and peers, that may have a significant effect on attainment. That is, it does not lay out "the finer mechanisms through which status attainment takes place" (Haller and Portes 1973, p. 58).

To deal with the issue of the effect of varied social-psychological factors on educational and occupational attainment, Sewell and others developed what is known as the **Wisconsin model** of socioeconomic attainment (e.g., Sewell and Shah 1967; Sewell, Haller, and Ohlendorf 1970). The large volume of studies of this model grew out of an initial survey in 1957 of over 10,000 high school seniors in Wisconsin. Most of the early research was devoted to studying the influence of socioeconomic background and social-psychological factors on aspirations. Follow-up surveys were done in 1964 and later decades.

WISCONSIN MODEL   A basic version of the Wisconsin model of early occupational achievement is presented in Figure 14.2. Essentially, it shows that socioeconomic background (father's and mother's education, father's occupational status, and parental income) does not affect grades and is independent of academic ability. However, it does have a sizable ultimate effect on educational and occupational attainment through its influence on the mediating variables of significant others' influences and educational and occupational aspirations. Overall, the model explains about 57 percent of the variation in educational attainment and about 40 percent of the variation in early occupational attainment for the men in the sample. The percentages are somewhat smaller for women (Sewell and Hauser 1976). The model has been applied to individuals from both rural and urban backgrounds, although it was first applied to a sample of farm residents and then later applied to groups from a variety of residential backgrounds.

The Wisconsin model is more effective in explaining the variation in educational and occupational attainment than the basic Blau–Duncan model. The earlier structural model accounts for 26 percent and 33 percent in educational and occupational attainment, respectively. It seems clear from the Wisconsin model that a variety of social-psychological factors play mediating roles linking socioeconomic background and ability to attainment (Haller and Portes 1973, p. 68).

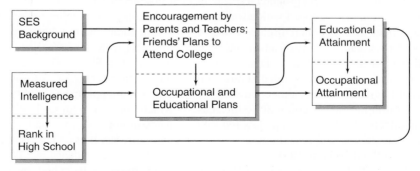

FIGURE 14.2   A Simplified Version of the Wisconsin Model Showing the Mediating Role of Social-Psychological Factors in Individual Attainment

Source: Adapted from Sewell, Haller, and Ohlendorf (1970), p. 1023.

Studies conducted after the development of the Wisconsin model and using national longitudinal samples tended to support the general arguments of the model. What is revealing in the other findings, however, is that none of these models explains a great deal of the variation that exists among individuals in earnings and income, and what small proportion they do explain (under 20 percent) is due primarily to the effect of objective factors, such as SES, rather than to social-psychological variables.

The Role of Education in Attainment

The discovery that neither the Blau–Duncan nor the Wisconsin model of attainment accounts for very much of the variation in earnings and income has given rise to a variety of speculations about what the really significant factors might be. The connection between education and economic achievement, while not always strong, has been among the most important predictors included in past achievement models. In considering the role that education plays in future occupational and earnings attainment, it must be kept in mind that the timing of education during one's life cycle has an impact on future earnings. Generally, those who go smoothly through high school, college, and professional training early in their careers do better than those who stop going to school and then either resume their educations later in life or do not return at all. Needless to say, those who come from higher-status backgrounds, especially White males, are more equipped with advantages that allow them to attain their highest level of education early, creating a further advantage over others that increases with time. "The enduring effects of social origins and ascribed statuses on educational transitions into adulthood are starkly evident. Childhood socioeconomic status has long-term effects that are not completely reduced by adult strategies to improve human capital" (Elman and O'Rand 2004, p. 154).

Background clearly has an impact on the probability of attending college. About twice as high a percentage of students from the top income quintile as those from the bottom quintile are enrolled in some kind of higher education program, and most of them attend highly ranked schools (Smeeding 2009). Two of the reasons for this discrepancy between income groups are the greater economic resources and kinds of skills and abilities that are nurtured in high-status families, which increase the likelihood of acceptance into higher-ranked schools (Jonsson et al. 2009). Moreover, children of professional and other high-status parents are more likely to have grown up with the expectation that they will attend college and their parents prepare and reinforce them accordingly. In contrast, children from poor families grow up with expectations as well, but those expectations do not include college educations (Bozick et al. 2010). Highly educated mothers, for example, are more likely than others to have their children placed in early child care programs that lay a foundation for later school success (Augustine, Cavanagh, and Crosnoe 2009). When they are 3–5 years old, a greater percentage of children of highly educated parents recognize all the letters of the alphabet, can write their first names, can count to 20, and are read to every day (College Board 2010). Statistics support these arguments. In 2008, 80 percent of high school graduates from families in the highest income quintile enrolled in college, compared to 55 percent from the lowest quintile. A greater percentage of high-income than low-income students graduate within 6 years of having entered (College Board 2010).

In addition to family background characteristics, another factor affecting the chances of children going on to college concerns the increasing competition among schools for the best students. Students from lower socioeconomic groups not only are less likely to be accepted at colleges and universities, but they also are at a distinct disadvantage when applying to highly selective colleges which compete with each other for the best students in hopes of maintaining their high ranking and attractiveness. The higher qualifications required for attendance that is an outcome of this competition results in high-resource families being better able than other families to provide the kinds of benefits that will increase the probability of their children being admitted into prestigious schools

(Alon 2009). In other words, affluent parents are capable of making all the investments necessary so that their children succeed throughout their educational careers (Smeeding 2009).

The cumulative advantages or disadvantages that accrue to different individuals over time are matched by the inequalities found within the different educational systems attended by individuals. Moving from the state level to the classroom level, inequalities abound. Within the public school system, states vary in their economic support of education and students, and within states, school districts vary in quality. Schools within districts are often unequal, as are classes within schools, and students within classes. Generally, schools in poor areas do not have the resources available to schools in more advantaged neighborhoods, and consequently, are not as able to prepare their students for successful college entrance (Smeeding 2009). Not surprisingly, across the world, students tend to do better if they are from higher-status families and attend schools in which there are high amounts of varied resources (Chiu 2010). Schools that are predominately White are more likely than predominately Black and Latino schools to have multiple resources. Consequently, regardless of socioeconomic background, students who attend predominately White high schools are more likely to graduate and to get a college degree (Goldsmith 2009). All-White schools have been associated with better student performances, regardless of student racial composition (Condron 2009; Herman 2009). At the same time, however, minorities and students from low socioeconomic backgrounds who attend high schools dominated by higher-income students face problems because of their disadvantages relative to better off students. Crosnoe (2009) found that the greater the proportion of high-income students in the school, the lower the scores in math and science were for disadvantaged students, even though they might have been higher than those they would have received at schools that had predominately minority or low-status student bodies. These students also experienced higher levels of psychosocial problems.

This set of telescoping, **nested inequalities** creates different levels of opportunities and cumulative advantages or disadvantages for students in different educational systems (Hochschild 2003). Being a student in a low-level track, in a poor school, in a weak school district, and in a state that provides minimal support for education has long-term effects for that student. The generally greater deficiencies of poor children in terms of preschool attendance, high school preparation, and college education lower their incomes as adults and reduce the chances of escaping the poverty of the family in which they were raised (Isaacs, Sawhill, and Haskins 2008).

Table 14.1 makes it clear that having a higher education is associated with economic and

TABLE 14.1 Education and Its Economic and Personal Benefits: 2008

	Less Than High School	High School Graduate	Bachelor's Degree Or Higher
After tax earnings	$19,600	$26,700	$42,700–$74,400
Lifetime earnings ratio	0.71	1.00	1.66–2.74
Very satisfied with job	40%	50%	58%
Sense of accomplishment and high importance of job (2006)	21%	36%	59%
Poverty rate of individuals 25 or older	26%	12%	4%
Obesity rate of children 6–11 years of age	29%	22%	14%
Vigorous exercise of those 55–64	13%	23%	47%

Source: From College Board (2010).

personal benefits. In addition to the educational advantages listed there, research also indicates that higher-educated persons have a greater sense of personal control in their lives. This follows from their jobs, which are generally more challenging, interesting, enriching, economically rewarding, and controlled more fully by them than is the case with lower status occupations (Schieman and Plickert 2008).

Even though education is a predictor of first occupation, earnings, and other benefits, the explanation for its importance has been a source of controversy. The traditional argument has been that advances in technology and upgrading of the occupational structure have created a need for the greater skills and training that education is supposed to supply. Others have argued that the importance of education for attainment does not lie primarily in the cognitive skills it imparts to students. In their survey of findings from other studies, for example, Bowles and Gintis (2002) found that other skills—such as communication ability, attitude, work habits, and other personal characteristics that may be affected by the education experience—affect occupational success independently of any cognitive skills a person may possess. College major, which may serve as a proxy for some of these skills, does have an impact on occupational status and economic mobility (Wolniak et al. 2008).

Collins (1971) also challenged the technical skill argument, saying there is evidence that what is important about education is not the training it provides but the fact that it represents an introduction into a particular "status culture." Many individuals, argued Collins, are overeducated for their jobs, and those who are better educated do not necessarily perform better than the less educated. In fact, Collins stated, U.S. schools generally are not very good at providing students with the vocational skills they need to be successful in the performance of their jobs. What is important about schools for early occupational achievement is that they teach students a particular set of values and ways of acting and defining things. Employers then select those who will fit into the status culture of the elite and those who might be

willing to serve under them because of their adherence to the prescriptions of a particular status culture. In this manner, schools can be used to control membership in economic institutions.

While education has an impact on economic status for perhaps a variety of reasons, it does not explain all of the variations in individuals' earnings and income. Sex, race, labor market, industry, economic conditions, and economic sector of employment are all involved. For example, sex segregation in occupation affects the chances for increases in earnings and joblessness. Working in a male-dominated occupation increases the likelihood for wage promotion for men, but also increases the odds that women will be pushed out of jobs. Since male-typed occupations generally have higher earnings than female-typed jobs, access to such positions would seem to be necessary for women to significantly increase their earnings, but the pressures they encounter from resentful men only increase the probability that they will not last in these positions (Maume 1999). Mothers, then, disproportionately enter female-dominated occupations, which, in turn, raises the chances that their daughters will follow a similar path (Khazzoom 1997). Another suggestion is that factors associated with an individual's current experiences may be better predictors of earnings. These might include on-the-job training, job performance and satisfaction, and the nature of the job and labor markets (Sewell and Hauser 1976). The amount of time spent in the labor force also affects an individual's earnings (Spaeth 1976). But as already noted, the length of time spent in a high-paying position depends in part on the pressures to which one is subjected.

In addition to these factors, networking and connections may play important roles in the explanation of earnings and income. Research suggests that individuals who get jobs through personal contacts are more likely to get wage increases and promotion opportunities than those who secure jobs without such contacts. By providing positive information and optimizing the chances of good matches between individuals and jobs, contacts can help create work environments for their acquaintances that are favorable for promotions

NUTSHELL 14.1   Being a First-Generation College Student

In the early 1990s, I researched faculty at eight selective liberal arts colleges, aiming to explore the relationships between their socioeconomic backgrounds and the degree of comfort they felt on their campuses and among their colleagues. I wondered if those from working-class families would feel comfortable or out of place in their elite, high-priced colleges where many of the faculty have upper-middle-class origins. I found that some of the working-class faculty sensed a lack of fit between themselves and the college setting in which they worked, while others had accommodated themselves easily to their surroundings.

Like some working-class faculty, first-generation college students also face challenges when entering the alien environment of higher education, although some experience a sense of alienation more strongly than others. Some schools have offices and programs to assist first-generation students, while others do not. It is often hard for a well-educated faculty member from an upper-middle-class family to fully understand the unique personal issues that first-generation students face, and the feelings they experience as they move through the alien environment of the college campus (Merullo 2002).

What *are* these feelings? Bobby Allyn, a first-generation university student from a working-class family engages in a kind of impostor behavior, not wanting his fellow students to know that he is from a lower class than they are. While he has a

sense of satisfaction because he is effective in masking his class identity, he knows inside that he is still an outsider (Allyn 2009). Another who was attending a prestigious prep school sensed that he was "trying to find a way to weld two very different worlds," but it is often difficult to articulate what the problem is (Merullo 2002). For many students from impoverished backgrounds, there is "a shadow" over the achievement of getting into college because they feel they are on their own without the benefit or support of friends who had been to college who can guide them (Merullo 2002).

Because many of these students are white, they are invisible on campus, and must deal with their unique problems on their own. Bobby Allyn laments the absence of a meeting ground for students in a similar situation (Allyn 2009). But he does not know if such students are present because they are invisible. Most colleges and universities have offices to assist minorities and women, but have not created support programs for students from poor or working-class backgrounds. What, if anything, do you think should be done to support these students?

Sources: Bobby Allyn, "Among Privileged Classmates, I'm an Outsider," *Chronicle of Higher Education,* October 11, 2009; and Roland Merullo, "The Challenge of First-Generation College Students," *Chronicle of Higher Education,* June 14, 2002.

and pay raises (Coverdill 1998). These networks appear to be especially important for women (Aguilera 2008).

Finally, some people just happen to be in the right spot at the appropriate time. For example, you happen to be in a community that has a greater range of jobs than others, or the weather may destroy your jobs in construction, or you happen to be in a city where a new plant locates (Jencks et al. 1973, p. 227). Some of these kinds of events may be appropriately labeled as luck, but others are factors that are systematically related to earnings but have not yet been incorporated into attainment models.

Structures in the Process of Attainment

The notion that luck or being in the right place at the right time may play a role in attainment suggests that one's position in a broader social structure is significant for mobility. Most of the early research on the process of occupational and income attainment focused on characteristics of the individuals involved (i.e., their educations, parents, attitudes, etc.). In questioning what determines how far people get, especially when compared to their parents, U.S. sociology trained its eye almost solely on human capital factors and the peculiarities of people's backgrounds. This was one of the primary limitations of early research.

Especially since the mid-1980s, however, there has been an emphasis on structural factors in status attainment. When one looks outside the individual for reasons for success or failure, one finds that structures in society and in organizations play a significant role in the chances for upward or downward movement. Moreover, while earlier research was concerned primarily with accounting for socioeconomic attainment *in general,* many post-1990 investigations examined the attainment process as it is played out within the structural context of a given economic sector or organization. Attainment always takes place within a concrete organizational or economic context, and variations in the structural networks, hierarchies, and career pathways between organizations can help account for differences in attainment processes and outcomes. This latter realization has led to a focus on **intragenerational mobility** rather than on differences between parents and children.

How, specifically, is structure involved in the attainment process? At a broad level, shifts in the national occupational structure obviously create openings and closures in positions. They create new occupations and eliminate others. For example, there has been a lot of discussion of the United States moving rapidly from a manufacturing to a service-based economy, causing layoffs in one area and creating new openings in the expanding service sector. Over the long run, occupations rise and fall in their dominance of a nation's employment structure. These national economic changes are in turn rooted in technology changes, international competition, and the movement of capital between and within nations. Attendant streamlining, downsizing, and actual closures also affect the alternatives available for attainment.

So-called **vacancy-driven mobility** models stress the fact "that mobility depends on the availability of empty positions and that the filling of jobs is interdependent. One person's move to a new job or out of a job system creates an opening to be filled" (Rosenfeld 1992, p. 41). For example, historically, many immigrants have dominated

certain types of lower-status positions as natives have moved on to the greener pastures of more prestigious jobs. At the national level, attainment is also affected by legislative changes. Affirmative action and equal employment opportunity policies are aimed at broadening the opportunity structures of women and racial/ethnic minorities (Rosenfeld 1992).

Below the national level, attainment is also tied to the structure of opportunities within different economic sectors and organizations. Within large formal organizations of the core economic sector, for example, jobs are more likely than in the peripheral sector to be part of a career ladder (i.e., an internal occupational hierarchy along which an individual can move). Frequently, the ladder may be multifaceted or have multiple branches, or an organization may have several job ladders of varying heights, widths, and connections. The relative location of a person in that structure affects the criteria needed and the chances for advancement. Upward mobility is generally slower if one is in a job that is close to the top of a ladder. The pathways to advancement also can vary within the same structure (DiPrete and Krecker 1991; Rosenfeld 1992). The presence of this treelike structure creates opportunities for differential attainment that are independent of the characteristics of individuals.

Some mobility is not vacancy driven, however. For example, in some unionized plants, one's time-in-grade or seniority affects economic advancement, and in colleges and universities, time-in-rank affects promotion up the professorial hierarchy (Rosenfeld 1992). Knowledge about and access to information about the various avenues to advancement within an organization also are important, and may vary with one's position in the organization and the internal network of which one is a part. Being an insider, having connections, and being "in the know" affect one's chances for attainment, especially within an organization whose opportunity ladder is open solely or primarily only to current employees (DiPrete and Krecker 1991).

Robert Jackall's intensive study of corporations (1988) reveals how critical social skills and personality characteristics are and how they can become more important and eventually displace hard work, education, and other achievement-based factors in moving up the corporate ladder. He found that "managers rarely speak of objective criteria for achieving success because once certain crucial points in one's career are passed, success and failure seem to have little to do with one's accomplishments" (p. 41). One manager observed that once a high administrative level is reached, "all have similar levels of ability, drive, competence, and so on. What happens is that people perceive in others *what they like*—operating styles, personalities, ability to get along. Now these are all very subjective judgments" (p. 45; emphasis in original). Having the appropriate mentor and sponsor helps one's chances for upward mobility. Being in a structural location where one knows who is thinking and doing what enhances the probability that one can tailor oneself accordingly.

MOBILITY AND THE ATTAINMENT PROCESS AMONG AFRICAN AMERICANS

The experience of mobility and the process of attainment vary between races. In their landmark study of U.S. men in the early 1960s, Blau and Duncan (1967) argued that Blacks generally start out from a lower position, but instead of moving up in a manner commensurate with their education and other human capital, they become involved in a vicious circle in which they are hindered at each step along the way in the attainment process. That is, their disadvantages are *cumulative*. They have a hard time getting a higher education, and when they do, the occupational returns for that education are less than those received by Whites. In 2008, the economic payoff for a bachelor's degree was $12,500 less for Black men than for White men (College Board 2010). Knowledge of this fact may lower the incentive of Blacks to obtain such education, and thereby reinforce the negative stereotype of Blacks as unwilling to be educated.

The replication of the Blau–Duncan study in the 1970s found that both Blacks and Whites

gained in educational attainment, but the gains in the later years were greatest for Blacks and the economic returns to their educations increased. While smaller percentages of Blacks and Hispanics than Whites graduate from high school and obtain bachelor's degrees, the rates of increase in these groups in the last 30–40 years has been greater than that for Whites. The National Center for Educational Statistics reported, for example, that while under 7 percent of Blacks and 5 percent of Hispanics obtained bachelor's degrees in 1971, the rate almost tripled for Blacks in 2009 to 19 percent, and more than doubled for Hispanics in 2009 to over 12 percent. The comparable figures for Whites were 19 percent in 1971 and 37 percent in 2009.

Regardless of those apparent improvements, there has been no significant reduction in the income gap between White and Black families since the mid-1970s. Moreover, Black children in middle- and upper-middle class families experience lower incomes than their parents, while White children generally attain higher income levels than their parents (Isaacs, Sawhill, and Haskins 2008).

In terms of class distribution, most Black men are still in the working class in part because their fathers were more likely than White fathers to have been absent or be in low-status occupations, and because the chances of their being upwardly mobile are lower than they are for working-class White men even when their educations are the same (Yamaguchi 2009). The lower probability of upward mobility for Blacks from working-class backgrounds may contribute to the significant earnings difference between Black and White workers (Pais 2011).

Movement from the peripheral to the core sector of the economy is especially difficult for Blacks. Mobility into the higher-paying core sector or into a higher status occupation may be hindered by residential segregation which limits access and opportunities to move up, especially in the private sector (Hirschman and Wong 1984; Hout 1986). If Blacks do move up, it is most likely to an adjacent category rather than to an upper nonmanual position. Blacks seldom advance to managerial positions, and in contrast to Whites, most of the movement into the "mainstream" is in the public rather than private sector. Combined with the greater inheritance of occupational status between upper-level white-collar Black fathers and sons, these processes have helped to create greater economic inequality and accentuated class differences within the Black community that have been noticeable since slavery (Featherman and Hauser 1978; Hout 1984; Cole and Omari 2003).

Nevertheless, though still a minority, the Black middle class has grown in recent decades. Using occupational status, homeownership, income, and education as criteria, a recent study estimated that, in 2000, 10 percent of Black households headed by persons aged 25–54 were middle class, and an increasing number of these households consisted of single persons living alone (Marsh et al. 2007).

A variety of factors have been linked to the middle-class growth, including industrialization, urbanization, increased education and collective action, and occupational differentiation. However, much of the growth of the Black middle class can be attributed to the appreciable number who have assumed public or governmental white-collar jobs, rather than managerial or upper-level technical positions in the private sector (Collins 1983; Hout 1984). This makes the Black middle class potentially more vulnerable to shifts within government and its budget.

The instability in the position of Blacks who are in white-collar positions is further indicated by analyses of mobility in earnings using census data from 1967 to 1991 (Gittleman and Joyce 1995). Blacks, especially Black women, who are in the upper quintile of earnings are much less likely than Whites to maintain that position for at least one year. Part of the reason for this earnings instability is related to the fact that White men are more likely to occupy professional and managerial occupations, and Black men are more likely to be found in sales and clerical jobs, positions associated with greater fluctuations in earnings. Finally, like that of other employees, the vulnerability of the Black

middle class may be higher due to corporations seeking cheaper labor forces and better tax rates abroad (Bowser 2007).

At the top of the Black class ladder, research on eminent Black Americans listed in *Who's Who Among Black Americans* has found that they are more likely to come from privileged backgrounds. Specifically, they are more likely than the average Black person to have had parents who are professionals and are highly educated. Further back in their lineage, their ancestors were more likely to have been "free" Blacks with lighter skin (Mullins and Sites 1984). However, the paths to eminence and the occupations that characterize eminent Black Americans have differed historically from those that distinguish eminent White Americans (Lieberson and Carter 1979). Of course, the impact of class origins among Blacks does not necessarily mean that race has become *less* significant in their lives. Although this research may *suggest* that class is becoming more important than race in determining occupational attainment, Blacks do not perceive it this way.

Race and the Status Attainment Process

Research has been done to determine if the models that have been developed to explain educational and occupational attainment apply to Blacks as well as they do to Whites. Since race has an effect on a variety of areas in U.S. life, we might suspect that what applies to Whites does not apply to Blacks. Since race is an ascribed characteristic, a model based on achievement norms may not fit Blacks as well as Whites. Also, race affects mobility, and the relationship between many of the variables that are included in these standard models differ from one race to another. Finally, the nature of the socialization process in the two races may be different (Porter 1974).

An early study by Portes and Wilson (1976) suggested that the process of educational attainment does differ among Blacks. Analyzing a nationwide sample of boys surveyed over a period of several years, and using a variant of the Wisconsin model of status attainment (described earlier), they found several differences between Blacks and Whites:

1. The variables in the model are better at explaining attainment among Whites than among Blacks, which suggests that factors not traditionally considered are more important for Blacks.
2. The more objective factors of socioeconomic background, mental ability, and academic performance are more important for White attainment, whereas among Blacks, the later and more subjective variables of self-esteem and educational aspirations are the significant ones.
    a. There is a much stronger connection between mental ability and academic performance and between academic performance and educational attainment among Whites than among Blacks. Among Blacks, there is no significant direct connection between academic performance and attainment.
    b. Conversely, the ties of mental ability to self-esteem and the ties of self-esteem to attainment are much stronger among Blacks than Whites.

In summarizing their findings, Portes and Wilson suggested that the results imply a distinction among Whites and Blacks as insiders and outsiders in the U.S. achievement system. In an open society, one would expect that performance and ability would be quite important, and they are for Whites. But for Blacks, educational attainment is more dependent on self-reliance and ambition. In a manner of speaking, then, while Blacks have had to rely on these qualities, Whites "have at their disposal an additional set of institutional 'machinery' which can, in effect, carry them along to higher levels of attainment" (p. 430).

Porter (1974) examined early occupational as well as educational achievement among Blacks and Whites and also found significant racial differences in the processes involved. His study of a large sample of males suggests that among Blacks, grades are largely a function of personality factors, such as conformity and ambition, whereas among Whites, both personality and intelligence play roles. As in the Portes and Wilson (1976) findings, subjective rather than objective conditions appear to play a greater part in the attainment process for Blacks. "It would appear that the official sanctions of the school system operate primarily with reference to the visible being of the pupil, and only secondarily, and on the condition that he is White, with reference to academic ability" (Porter 1974, p. 311). Another interesting finding of this study is that in contrast to the results among Whites, grades have no direct effect on either educational or occupational attainment. This seems to reinforce Wilson and Roscigno's (2010) finding that factors other than expected predictors like education and experience are more significant predictors of downward mobility among Blacks.

Confirming the significance of nonrational, subjective factors in the attainment process of Blacks is the fact that "color" also has an impact on the socioeconomic attainment of African Americans. Simply put, Blacks whose physical appearance more closely approximates the European/U.S. ideal of beauty do better socioeconomically than others (Hill 2000). The importance of "colorism" has been found in other national studies as well (e.g., Hughes and Hertel 1990; Keith and Herring 1991).

Blacks themselves feel that their path to occupational attainment is made more difficult by the lack of decent available jobs for which they are qualified, the concentrated poverty of their neighborhoods, and their lack of social contacts in the inner city. They believe that luck, connections, education, help from those who have made it, and being from the right neighborhood make all the difference (Venkatesh 1994).

These beliefs suggest the importance of the context in which people live as an explanation for why some get ahead while others remain stuck. In her longitudinal study of women's changing economic fortunes over a 30-year period, Andrea Willson (2003) found that Black women were much more likely than White women to be at financial risk in their old age. White women who were married benefited financially from their marriages;

MINI-CASE 14.1

Educational Choice versus the Law

In January 2011, a woman in Akron, Ohio, was arrested and convicted of falsifying records about her residency. She lived in Akron with her two school-age daughters. Her grandfather lived in a smaller suburb known for its better schools. The woman's Akron home had recently been burglarized, and because she worked as a teaching assistant and was pursuing a teaching degree, she was not always at home. Consequently, she worried about the safety of her daughters. Residency laws require that students attend the school district in which they are living. The mother recorded her grandfather's home as her daughters' residence so they could attend schools in that district even though, the court says, her legal residence was still in Akron. She says her reason for putting the girls in the suburban school was safety, but the school also has a fine reputation and is funded heavily by property taxes paid by local residents. So some felt that the mother had also defrauded the school system by sending her children to a school for which she had not contributed taxes. Others sympathized, arguing that the mother's desire to send her children to a safer and better school was praiseworthy since it demonstrated that she only had her daughters' future in mind. Who would you side with in this case and why? ■

---

this was not the case for Black women. Poor health, especially that on the part of the husband, significantly reduced household income among married couples. Continuous employment benefited both Black and White women, although unmarried Black women did not get the same income returns from their employment as White women in part because of their generally lower levels of education and lower-status occupations. The higher economic benefit of marriage and continuous employment for White women meant that they lost more than Black women in old age due to widowhood and loss of employment. On the whole, Black women had flatter and lower earnings trajectories over their lifetimes than White women. Consequently, they did not have as far to fall, experiencing smaller declines. This study demonstrated not only the relevance of marital status for some women but also the significance of the availability and quality of jobs, and indirectly the importance of education for women's long-term income. The job labor market and education are parts of the varying contexts within which women of different races must navigate their careers.

PATTERNS OF MOBILITY AND ATTAINMENT AMONG WOMEN

The major national studies done on intergenerational mobility during the 1960s and 1970s concentrated on the occupational statuses of *men*. Part of the reason for the omission of women in these studies is that they were based on the assumption that women's positions, especially those among women who are married, are dependent on those of their husbands or fathers, and that to know the mobility patterns of men is, therefore, to know the patterns for the entire society. The central problem with all this is that women are not considered as independent persons, even though many married and unmarried women have their own occupational, educational, and income resources. From discussions earlier in this book, you know that sex and gender inequality exists along a variety of dimensions, and yet people's concepts (like class position) reflect a concern primarily for the attributes of males.

While they were divided in the *general* belief that college opportunities were equally available to all, most of the low-income women participating in a vocational program in Bullock and Limbert's (2003) study believed that *they*, personally, would move up in society. They expected to be socially mobile as a result of their training and hard work, and expected to have the opportunities to become successful. How well do these beliefs mesh with reality? Economically, women have experienced *absolute* intergenerational upward mobility in terms of income. Women currently in their 30s have higher incomes than their mothers when they were at a similar age, while the incomes of men in the same age group are not much different from those of their fathers when they were in their 30s. However, a greater percentage of women than men who were born into families in the bottom income quintile are likely to remain at the bottom, and women are slightly more likely than men to experience downward mobility in income (Isaacs, Sawhill, and Haskins 2008).

Certainly, along the road to adulthood, whether people receive encouragement, help, and access to opportunities plays a role in their status attainment. For those at the top, the appropriate resources, values, credentials, and connections are not as problematic as they are for those below them in the socioeconomic hierarchy. In her study of "unequal childhoods," for example, Annette Lareau (2003) found that middle-class parents provided their children with more of the social capital and nurtured linguistic and negotiating skills necessary to compete successfully and attain their goals when reaching adulthood. In contrast to working- and lower-class parents who did not intentionally groom their children to be successful professionals, middle-class parents consciously structured the lives of their children to prepare them for their futures. Lareau pointed out that while every child-rearing approach has weaknesses and costs, that of the middle class smoothes the pathway to occupational success.

The importance of encouragement and help is perhaps most critical for those at the bottom of the socioeconomic hierarchy. Monthly interviews with low-income minority women in 2000 and 2001 demonstrated the role of social capital in affecting upward mobility for these women (Dominguez and Watkins 2003). Strong kin groups can either aid or hinder mobility through their expectations and demands. Sometimes "[s]upport networks can exert a pull away from social mobility ties that is difficult to resist. They enforce kin-scripts that levy time-consuming and professionally limiting expectations on women" (p. 131). On the other hand, an employment situation can create access to social networks of different people who may have resources or information

that open up new possibilities for mobility. "Heterogeneous networks may encourage low-income women to look beyond their present circumstances and learn from those who are more upwardly mobile" (p. 131).

In the past and in general, women have tended to move into clerical, low-status professional, and service occupations, whereas men have gone into professional and production occupations. This has been the case not only in the United States but in many other industrial countries as well (Roos 1985). Among those with salaries or wages, women are *more* likely than men to be and remain at the bottom of the earnings ladder, but are *less* likely than men to be or remain at the top (Gittleman and Joyce 1995). When compared to their parents, sons are somewhat more likely than daughters to have attained incomes higher than their parents. Women raised in low-income families are also more likely than men to remain at the bottom. Almost one-half are in this position (Isaacs, Sawhill, and Haskins 2008).

The likelihood of working in a professional occupation is greatest for daughters from professional or managerial backgrounds, and lowest for those who have fathers who are in farm or production work. This suggests that most of the mobility is short-range in nature. At the same time, however, women who have parents with service occupations are more likely to move into white-collar than blue-collar jobs. While parental occupations affect the attainment of their children, it is the mothers' occupations that appear to have more impact on the destination of their daughters (Khazzoom 1997).

The occupational attainment of women who are employed is affected by a pattern of factors that is different from the pattern that affects the attainment path of men. Thus, the attainment process of employed women is quite different from that of married, unemployed women, whose attainment path is directly tied to that of their husbands. The differences are largely due to the features of the opportunity structure that women encounter when they move into the labor force—features that frequently involve curves, bumps, and walls not often encountered by men. Think of the road to attainment as akin to a maze, and some mazes are more complex and difficult than others. How successful one is in getting through it may depend partially on individual attributes, but it also depends heavily on the structure of the maze itself.

Obstacles and Pathways in Status Attainment for Women

To fully understand the process of status attainment, it is important to remember that such mobility always takes place within a given social and cultural context. This context helps define the ease with which attainment can occur. Some pathways make attainment much easier than others. The shape, smoothness, and contours of the opportunity structure for men make attainment a less troublesome process than is the case for women. The opportunity structure for women is replete with narrow passageways, dead ends, obstacles, steep hills, shaky bridges, and guarded gates that make the process more problematic (Tolbert 1982; DiPrete and Soule 1988).

By and large, status attainment in the United States for both men and women occurs within a culture in which there are different beliefs about and expectations for men and women that affect their role prospects. It should not be surprising, then, that women are more affected by household-related variables than are men. The presence of a child, for example, has a dampening effect on the upward mobility of women, but it has no similar effect for men (Waddoups and Assane 1993). Indeed, motherhood exacts a price of lower mobility and earnings for women when they return to work. In the United States, strong attachment to work is expected and valued, and so the price paid by a new mother for taking even a short time-out can be significant. Many American women are aware of this and, thus, are more attached to the marketplace, taking as little time off as possible (Aisenbrey, Evertsson, and Grunow 2009; Gangl and Ziefle 2009). But when mothers are successful in higher managerial positions, they are often criticized as not being "feminine" by being less warm and interpersonal, and this affects how

they are evaluated. Since most high-level executive positions are assumed to require "masculine" qualities, men are not as subjected to these criticisms (Benard and Correll 2010).

Attainment takes place within a private economic structure in which firms are differentiated in terms of formalization, complexity, size, market, and other characteristics. This structure contains both stable and powerful, and unstable and less-powerful sectors. It also contains a wide variety of occupations and positions, some more autonomous and specialized than others. Within the economy, each organization or industry has an internal labor market that constitutes a pathway for mobility. For women there are broad occupational divides that are difficult to cross. For example, it is harder for women than for men to move from the secondary labor market or lower rungs of the primary market into the well-paying, stable professional, managerial, and craft positions at the top of the primary labor market (Waddoups and Assane 1993).

In the absence of knowledge about a person, external characteristics such as sex and/or race are used to provide clues to what might be expected (Berger, Cohen, and Zelditch 1972; Berger et al. 1977). Sex segregation and the level of earnings associated with it are affected by what Petersen and Saporta (2004) called "the opportunity structure for discrimination" (p. 852). This refers to the variety of opportunities available to employers to discriminate against given categories of individuals. Using data collected over a 9 year period, Petersen and Saporta's research on a large service-producing organization revealed that employers were most likely to discriminate against women at the point of hiring, rather than during their job tenure, because discrimination is less detectable and costly at this juncture. When hired, women were more often placed in lower-level jobs and received lower wages than men even though their educational levels were roughly similar. Thus, women went through a gatekeeping or filtering process that resulted in their being relegated to specific kinds of positions. This was a feature of the opportunity structure within which women had to operate.

Interestingly, the authors found that women were more likely to be promoted and received higher salary raises than men. Possible reasons for this included the company's desire to change its sexist image and concerns about lawsuits alleging discrimination, which is more detectable and measurable at this point of employment. But while women were more likely to be promoted once in a job, women were not likely to occupy the highest positions because (1) they were unlikely to be placed in these positions when hired and (2) there was only a small pool of women with seniority who were eligible to be promoted into the top echelons of the organization.

In her early study of an industrial corporation, Kanter (1977a) found that at the top is an inner circle of individuals who have to be counted on to share a similar view of the organization and to behave in a manner consistent with that view. There are distinct pressures for homogeneity and conformity at the managerial level. A large part of the reason for this pressure to conform arises from the open nature of organizations and the managerial positions within them. Since position tasks are not well defined at that level and the organization operates in a "turbulent" environment with other organizations, the conclusion is that executives have to be able to trust one another and see one another's behavior as predictable. "Women were decidedly placed in the category of the incomprehensible and unpredictable" (p. 58).

Research in corporate law firms by Gorman and Kmec (2009) confirms Kanter's arguments. Their findings showed that women face a disadvantage when promotions near the top are being considered, and similar to Kanter, they attribute this disadvantage to an interaction of gender stereotyping and job characteristics. Specifically, they argue that assumptions about women's competence and appropriateness for particular tasks, together with the uncertainty and variety of the job itself and male dominance at the top, lead to lower chances for upward mobility for female members of law firms. This experience can further dampen the ambition and skills of women colleagues, further reinforcing low mobility rates.

Consistent with such conclusions, additional research has found that middle-level managers *believe* that upwardly mobile men are more likely to be promoted because of greater support and sponsorship within the organization, and that men's future power and mobility would be greater because of this support and sponsorship. The managers also thought that promoted men would be considered to be more successful than women who had been promoted, even if their performances were not any better (Wiley and Eskilson 1983). What all this research suggests is that sex is used as a criterion to conclude that it may be too much of a risk to have women and other "unpredictable" individuals within management. By continually recruiting men into those positions, the inequality in occupational positions between the sexes is perpetuated.

One of the difficult dilemmas for women's mobility concerns the fact that the hiring and promoting of women at given managerial levels may depend on the proportion of women already present in an organization at or below those levels. A study of managerial positions in 333 savings and loan associations suggests that the chances for hiring and promotion into a managerial position are increased as the proportion of women in or below that position goes up. They are also optimized when a solid proportion, though not a majority, of those in higher decision-making positions are also women. Thus, women appear to have to be present in relatively high percentages before women are hired or promoted in good numbers. But the question remains: "Although having women present in managerial positions is crucial to bringing more women into management, it remains unclear how women initially attain managerial positions" (Cohen, Broschak, and Haveman 1998, p. 723).

Women, of course, have traditionally been socialized into the same general beliefs about the sexes as men, and their beliefs can have an impact on the probability of their being upwardly mobile. For example, in their study of white-collar employees in a federal agency, Markham and his colleagues (1983) found that regardless of their education and other factors, women express less desire to move. Part of the reason may be that women see more family conflict arising as a result of moving. Perhaps this sensitivity is due to the socialization among women to have the family as a central focus of their lives. A significant factor in the reluctance to move is that most men consider themselves to be the "primary providers," and most women do not. Women who *do* see themselves in these terms are just as willing to move as men in similar circumstances (Markham et al. 1983).

These self-definitions and expectations combine with occupational segregation and the internal market structure of organizations to limit mobility by women. When women are in a position that is part of an internal labor market, they benefit less from that position than men do, in large part because a majority of them do not make job changes within a firm but move to other employers. Thus, women do not participate as fully as men in the career ladders available in many organizations, and this contributes heavily to the wage differences between the sexes (Felmlee 1982). In any case, "women's" positions are less likely to be linked to apprenticeships and career ladders and more likely to be surrounded by "dead space"—that is, not

connected to a distinct career-promotion ladder (Seidman 1978). Moreover, when women are in "female" white-collar positions, such as that of secretary, and perform admirably because of their accumulated but very specific job expertise, they may have less chance to be occupationally mobile within an organization (Kanter 1977a).

In other words, the entry-level jobs and job families are structured, often even in large firms, to maintain sex segregation. Moreover, if a position is a dead end, it will have consequences on the behavior and demeanor of the individual in that position. While individuals in positions that allow great mobility develop positive attitudes that motivate them, those in dead-end positions tend to develop an apathetic, more fatalistic attitude that, in turn, serves as evidence to others that they are in the position that they deserve (Kanter 1977a).

Once in a low-status, "female" job, it is difficult to move out. This result only reconfirms the position as a "female" one and, therefore, one with certain characteristics. "It may be because the jobs are done by women that they are viewed as unskilled and are lower paid, not just that low-wage (low-skills) jobs are created and women are channeled into them" (Hartmann 1987, p. 63).

Summary

This chapter surveyed some of the research that has dealt with trends in the openness of industrial societies, especially the United States. Generally, study findings suggest that the trend in mobility has not been altogether uniform in U.S. society. Most of the mobility that occurred in the twentieth century appears to have been brought about by changes in the occupational structure over time rather than through greater democracy and freedom in the society. The United States has more upward than downward mobility, but most of the upward mobility is of short distance. There does not appear to have been much significant

change through most of the twentieth century in the extent to which the occupational status of the son is dependent on that of the father, and in general, the last couple of decades have witnessed at least a stabilization, if not a decline, in overall occupational mobility in the United States. Some broad socioeconomic advances have occurred for Blacks and women in recent years, but they still lag significantly behind White males.

Status attainment research reshaped the study of mobility. Two basic models of status attainment surfaced early: the Blau–Duncan model, which emphasizes the importance of structural factors for attainment, and the Wisconsin model, which incorporates social-psychological elements. Both models explain occupational and educational attainment better than they account for differences in earnings and income. In addition to education and family background, other factors in attainment include economic and organizational opportunity structures and one's place in them. The process of attainment among African Americans and females varies from that found among White males. Both experience nonrational barriers not faced by White males. Traditional status attainment studies often neglected discrimination as a significant factor in mobility, instead focusing on individuals' personal characteristics and backgrounds as predictors. This made attainment models less effective in explaining the attainment processes of minorities and women. Discrimination, along with the varying opportunity structures available to different groups, can help us understand why some are rich and others poor, or why some occupy positions of high status or power while others are stuck farther down the social ladder. The continued presence of these inequalities raises the possibility that many may consider them unjust.

Critical Thinking

1. The United States is often thought of as a land of opportunity, one in which there are few obstacles in the path of anyone who wants to move up. What do you think most accounts for this image?
2. Trace your own social mobility or that of your parents. What best explains the degree of attainment and its route?
3. Mobility of children is affected by the socioeconomic status of their parents, putting poorer children at a disadvantage. Does this mean that to eliminate this disadvantage we need to eliminate wealth inheritance between children and parents?
4. Do you think objective criteria to evaluate individuals can be established and agreed upon so that evaluations of the educational and job performances of minorities and women, especially mothers, can be fairer and not reflect prejudices about these groups? Explain your answer.

Web Connections

Change in the occupational structure was the primary factor behind social mobility for most of the twentieth century. What occupations are growing the fastest? Which are declining in employment? What trends exist in wages for specific occupations? How do these vary by state? Visit www.acinet.org/acinet/ to search your state for trends in occupations and wages.

Film Suggestion

Country Boys (2006) A three-part PBS series about two Appalachian youths trying to move up in the face of great odds.

CHAPTER 15

Justice and Legitimacy

Assessments of the Structure of Inequality

Money is like muck, not good except it be spread.

FRANCIS BACON (1561–1626)

Think about situations when you were rewarded differently from someone else. If the situations were important to you, undoubtedly you had feelings about whether such treatment was or was not justified. These feelings become issues and problems when you feel that your treatment was unjustified. What made the difference in whether you felt you were treated fairly or unfairly, and why are some unequal distributions of rewards considered just while others are thought of as unjust?

Virtually every chapter in this book so far has provided evidence of extensive economic, political, gender, and racial inequality in U.S. society. There is no denying that this inequality is present, but is it unfair? It is difficult, if not impossible, to avoid the question of fairness in the presence of such pervasive inequality. Increases in income and wealth inequality since 1980 and recent revelations about excessive executive compensation, golden parachutes, and corporate bailouts while employees are downsized or asked to work for lower wages have helped to stimulate questions about fairness and inequities in earnings and wealth. As Paul Kingston (2006) observes, "Explicitly or implicitly, this normative question animates the sociological study of inequality" (p. 111).

Is it fair that, in 2007, the average chief executive officer (CEO) at a major corporation received almost as much pay for working less than one day than an average worker got for working 50 weeks? Or that in the top 500 U.S. corporations, on average, CEOs' pay was 263 times that of the average worker in 2009 (Anderson et al. 2010)? Or that the richest 1 percent in the United States holds one-third of all wealth while the bottom 40 percent own well under 1 percent? Recent surveys suggest that about half of Americans feel they are underpaid for the work they do and that the rich should be taxed more heavily to redistribute wealth (Jacobe 2008b; Newport 2008a).

What is fair? Who considers it fair? What determines whether individuals think the present distribution of resources is just or not? What criteria do people use before reaching a conclusion about the fairness of inequality? These are the empirical questions to be addressed in this brief chapter.

How people evaluate the inequality around them depends on what they think is primarily responsible for it, on the criteria they use when making their evaluative assessment about the extent of inequality, and on the effectiveness of national ideologies and institutions in justifying extensive inequality. When individuals come to the conclusion that a given distribution of rewards is fair, they also tend to believe that it is legitimate. Beliefs in the fairness and legitimacy of the structure of inequality in a society are two elements that contribute to its stability and continuity over time. Thus, when trying to account for its perpetuation, it is important to know how people feel about inequality and what factors underlie its legitimacy.

U.S. ATTITUDES ABOUT THE DISTRIBUTION OF INCOME AND WEALTH

Americans often have ambivalent attitudes about social and economic inequality because the issues surrounding it touch on different, often conflicting, values held dear by most Americans.

There is still widespread support, even among underdogs, for a system of inequality. A majority of adults believe that "people should be allowed to accumulate as much wealth as they can even if some make millions while others live in poverty," and that inequalities in earnings are required to motivate workers to take on extra responsibilities (Davis and Smith 1996). An analysis of large national samples in nine industrial countries, including the United States, revealed that the United States was among those favoring a higher degree of income inequality between top and bottom occupations (Kelley and Evans 1993). But Americans also appear to believe there should be a limit on the amount of inequality. About two-thirds of Americans think that the amount of income inequality is too large, and most Americans believe wealth and income should be more equally distributed. However, they are more concerned with people at the top getting too much than people at the bottom not getting enough (Osberg and Smeeding 2006). At the same time, however, they are split on whether the government should do more, and more than 8 out of 10 believe that the government should focus on improving the economy in general rather than trying to redistribute wealth (Jacobe 2008a; Newport 2007).

How much credence to put into individuals' judgments about whether an economic distribution is fair, however, depends on whether those people have an accurate grasp of the *actual* extent of economic inequality upon which to base their judgments. Compared to those found in most other industrial countries, individuals' *perceptions* of inequality in the United States tend to understate the *actual* discrepancies in earnings that exist. How people feel about existing inequalities also depends on what they think created them. Inequalities are viewed as justified or unjustified, depending on their perceived sources. Even a majority of Blacks believe that inequality can be just in principle, especially if it is based more on differences in skills than on need (Kluegel and Smith 1986).

The international survey of nine countries mentioned earlier confirmed that citizens feel that those in the highest-ranking occupations should be paid, on average, three to five times the salary of those in the lowest-ranking positions (Kelley and Evans 1993). More so than their citizen counterparts, older persons with higher education, incomes, and self-identified social classes favor greater pay for individuals in high-ranking occupations. For example, a conservative, high-income, 60-year-old man with a college education who identifies with the upper class, and who is also a supervising manager of his own company, feels that those in high-prestige positions should be paid seven times the minimum wage. In contrast, an individual with the opposite characteristics believes that a person in that kind of occupation should receive a salary of only three times the minimum wage. These preferences certainly understate the pay discrepancy noted earlier between CEOs and average workers. When it comes to the lowest-status jobs, however, the results are distinctly different. There is general consensus across groups about the appropriate wages for unskilled workers. Surprisingly, the single difference shows those with higher incomes favoring higher pay for those at the bottom. In essence, then, the only major disagreement among individuals revolves around the size and legitimacy of the salaries accorded high-prestige occupations. At the same time, however, virtually no one in these countries is in favor of a completely egalitarian distribution of income. Nor, argues Adam Swift, would completely open mobility be a sufficient criterion for defining fairness since it alone ignores the rights and duties of parents to help their children, ignores issues related to different rewards for positions, and sidesteps the role of luck in attainment (Swift 2004).

Almost two-thirds of Americans believe that inequality continues because it helps the rich and powerful (Davis and Smith 1996). Perhaps the cynical attitude expressed by a majority of

adults about why inequality continues is related to their belief in a link between wealth and corruption. Jong-sung and Khagram's study (2005) of the relationship between inequality and beliefs about corruption in 129 countries revealed that higher degrees of inequality are associated with stronger beliefs in the presence of corruption. "Inequality increases corruption, especially in democracies, and corruption produces policy outcomes closer to those preferred by the rich than those favored by the median voter" (p. 154). Compared to the United States, however, much higher percentages of individuals in postcommunist societies like Russia, Hungary, and the Czech Republic believe wealth is obtained by dishonest means or because of problems in the economic system. U.S. respondents are more likely to stress hard work as a source of wealth (Kreidl 2000). Recent disclosures of high-level fraud on the part of some extremely wealthy individuals like

NUTSHELL 15.1 Our Values and Fairness in Policy

Sharon Hays spent 3 years talking to welfare recipients and visiting two welfare offices in different-sized cities. Her study, *Flat Broke with Children,* examined the cultural values underlying welfare reform and the effects of reform policy on the poor. Oftentimes, controversies involving fairness or justice are based in allegiances to different and seemingly contradictory values. Current welfare policies reflect these contradictions, which are in turn visited upon the poor who must adhere to the policies. Hays says that while support for dependent women and adequate wages for men who are supporting families were expected under the New Deal established under President Franklin Roosevelt in 1935, neither the government nor free-market processes have resulted in such support.

To back up historical principles of support realistically, Hays argues that we need to provide more economic aid for caregivers through tax credits and supplemental income so that dependents like children and stay-at-home mothers can be effectively supported. National standards also need to be set for caregivers so that the quality of care is uniform and high. Conditions at work should also

be tailored to demonstrate that employers value the work of caregivers. This can take the form of good family leave policies and availability of flexible work hours. Such support would create the opportunity for employees with families to act effectively and consistently on their responsibilities at home.

To further ensure economic independence for all adults, Hays feels that minimum wages need to be raised to help keep families together and keep individuals off welfare rolls who would prefer not to be on. Governmentally supported job training programs and even public employment opportunities would further promote financial independence for those in the working and lower classes. Finally, Hays notes that many of the economic problems faced by the disadvantaged are mirrored in the high degree of income inequality between those on the top and those on the bottom. To address this issue, Hays suggests a more progressive tax policy and a reduction in the various subsidies that favor the well-to-do.

Do any or all of Hays' ideas seem fair or just to you?

Source: Sharon Hays, *Flat Broke with Children* (New York: Oxford, 2003), pp. 235–236.

Bernard Madoff, however, may cause a shift in these attitudes.

In sum, a majority of Americans appear to support the *principle* of income inequality as being fair, but they do not see the present system as necessarily equitable. They also underestimate the extent of economic inequality in the country, and they are decidedly split on whether the government should do something about income inequality. In sum, Americans' attitudes about inequality are complex and often contradictory.

WHAT IS A JUST DISTRIBUTION?

The question of what constitutes a just distribution of scarce and desired goods is an issue that people have wrestled with for centuries. There seem to be two broad principles used to define a just distribution, but each of these is more complex than it first appears. One principle argues that a just or equitable distribution exists when equal people are treated equally and unequal people are treated unequally. It assumes that people (1) start out with different abilities and traits, (2) are free to realize their potentials, and (3) are therefore entitled to make different claims on scarce resources and rewards. This is what Hochschild (1981) called the **"principle of differentiation"** and it approximates what Ryan (1981) called the principle of "fair play." Given that individuals vary in their talents, abilities, and interests, it is predictable that they also will and should vary in their socioeconomic success, and that those with high levels of appropriate talents will assume higher positions in the hierarchy of inequality (Ryan 1981). If persons of *unequal* talent and ability are given *equal* rewards, then this must be justified (Hochschild 1981). While this position is consistent with a belief in meritocracy, one complication is that one's competencies and motivations may be due to luck related to biology or environment, factors over which one may have little control. So if people are not fully responsible for their competencies or motivations, a question can be raised as to whether they really *merit* what they get (Marshall, Swift, and Roberts 1997). Generally speaking, this position is consistent with conservative theories such as functionalism and human-capital theory,

both of which imply that one should get out of a system what one puts into it. Findings from the international study cited earlier are broadly consistent with this view.

A second broad principle, the **"principle of equality,"** argues that people are of "equal value and can make equal claims on society. Differences in treatment must be justified" (Hochschild 1981, p. 51). This conception approximates Ryan's notion (1981) of "fair shares" as a basis for a just distribution. People ought to have equal rights and equal access to society's resources in order to live decent lives. This principle is consistent with more radical, Marxian views of inequality and its roots, such as those that consider private property to be a major source of explanation. Although

Distributive justice is often seen as giving people what they deserve, for example, blaming those who are viewed as causing a problem and not blaming those who view themselves as the victims of the problem. (Photo by Brendan R. Hurst.)

there are a number of variations on these two principles, none of which are agreed on by all, we cannot pursue them here. While the principle of differentiation and the principle of equality appear to be incompatible, there is some evidence that people's perceptions of the fairness of inequality are affected by the arguments of both these criteria, that is, on their personal assessment of both the distributive *outcome* of rewards as well as the *process* that led to it. Moreover, how people feel about the process is related to their feelings about the outcome, and vice versa (Törnblom and Vermunt 1999).

Causal Attributions for Inequality

How do Americans define a just distribution of economic rewards in society? This partly depends on their characteristics and history, the criteria suggested by the society's dominant ideology, and their beliefs about the causes of economic inequality (Shepelak and Alwin 1986; Stolte 1987). With respect to the latter, Americans appear to give mixed messages when asked what they believe determines an individual's economic position.

Generally, most people attribute poverty and wealth to either *individualistic* or *structural* factors. "Individual" arguments include beliefs that poverty or wealth is due to personal qualities such as effort, ability, and ambition, while those who take a "structural" position argue that one's economic status is due to factors beyond the individual's control, such as inheritance, government policy, wage rates, discrimination, and availability of work. Historically, Americans have more often aligned themselves with the individualistic position, believing that hard work, ambition, personal investment in education, and natural ability are critical for economic success (Hanson and Zogby 2010). The widespread endorsement of this position is consistent with the belief that the United States is a free and open society in which anyone can succeed. Most Americans subscribe to the dominant ideology that (1) opportunity for economic mobility is prevalent; (2) each individual is personally responsible for the extent of his or her own economic success; and (3) in general, therefore, the system of inequality is fair (Kluegel

and Smith 1986). "In . . . the United States, principles of justice are based on the assumption that the playing field is level and that opportunities to succeed are the same for everyone" (Flanagan et al. 2003, p. 717). However, a review of recent surveys suggests that an increasing percentage of Americans are not satisfied with the degree of opportunity available for working-class people to succeed even if they work hard, and believe that the American Dream will be harder for the next generation to obtain (Hanson and Zogby 2010).

Not everyone, of course, is equally likely to subscribe to the belief that individuals are primarily responsible for where they wind up. Social class affects one's perceptions. Generally, greater proportions of individuals in high-status positions subscribe to individualistic rather than structural explanations of inequality. The possible exception is individuals with high education, who are less likely to attribute poverty to lack of effort or low morality (Kreidl 2000; see also Hunt 2007). In Bullock and Limbert's study (2003), for example, when low-income women were asked what they believed were the principal causes of poverty, structural explanations were favored over individualistic ones (see also Hunt 2004). Inheritance and being able to go the best schools, that is, being privileged, were the most frequently given explanations for why some people are wealthy (Bullock and Limbert 2003).

Another indication that the disadvantaged often see success as out of their personal control is the finding that Blacks and Latinos consider genetics more important for success in life than do more advantaged groups (Shostak et al. 2009). Among Blacks and Hispanics, working-class are also more likely than middle-class persons to argue that discrimination is an important cause of racial inequality. Paradoxically, higher-educated Blacks are more likely than their less-educated counterparts to believe that discrimination is a significant reason for inequality between the races (Hunt 2007; see also Pew Research Center 2007). These results were consistent with earlier findings (Kluegel and Smith 1986). In another study comparing teens from "security" societies (e.g., Russia, Bulgaria) with those from "opportunity" countries (Australia, United States), Flanagan and colleagues found that working-class teens in the United States were more likely than middle-class youth (especially girls) to endorse the individualistic argument, that is, to believe that this nation is a meritocracy (Flanagan et al. 2003). Working-class adolescents may endorse the meritocratic perspective because "self reliance and hard work for the working class is indispensable. There is no other way for people 'like them' to make it." They do not have the resources and opportunities that middle- and upper-class youth have at their disposal (2003, p. 727). Males, especially White males, are more likely than females to believe in individualistic causes. White women are more likely than men to take a structural position and to believe that the government should help care for the poor (see also Kluegel and Smith 1986). Among Blacks and Hispanics, gender has less of a differentiating role (Hunt 2007).

Race and ethnicity are also significant predictors of beliefs about the sources of poverty and wealth. Interviews in 2000 with over 1,000 White and minority individuals in Los Angeles revealed that, as a group, respondents were more likely to attribute wealth to individualistic causes such as ambition, effort, and talent, but attribute poverty to structural causes such as inheritance, connections, dishonesty, or the economy. In other words, most believe that the "sky is the limit" for most people, but that those at the bottom are held down by factors beyond their control (Hunt 2004). Hunt found that Whites, Blacks, and Latinos were equally likely to attribute wealth to individualistic causes, but Blacks and Latinos were more likely than Whites to also attribute wealth to structuralist sources. Interestingly, Blacks and Latinos are more structuralist but *also* more individualist than Whites in their beliefs about what causes poverty. This "dual consciousness" is more prevalent among minorities (Hunt 2004, p. 845). In recent years, while race differences still exist, an increasing percentage of Blacks and Hispanics are attributing racial inequality to differences in motivation and willpower, and are less willing to cite discrimination as the principal explanation. This "conservative" trend has reduced the racial gap in explanations for inequality (Hunt 2007).

What Americans believe the determinants of income *are,* of course, may be different from what they believe the determinants *should* be. Thinking of a system of inequality as legitimate helps to reduce uncertainty and makes persons feel better and more relaxed. Justification is easier in the United States than in some other countries because in this country there is a strong association between what people believe the determinants of wealth/income distribution actually *are* and what they think they *should be*. As a society with a capitalist, competitive, market-driven economy, personal attributes like ambition, hard work, and ability *should* and *do* operate as the primary bases for success according to most Americans. Individuals who exhibit these qualities to a higher degree merit higher rewards than others (van der Toorn, Berkics, and Jost 2010).

Performance and effort are widely believed to be appropriate bases for rewarding employees. Data from 31 countries indicate that an average of almost three-fourths of the persons in each of the countries considered performance and effort as legitimate determinants of pay. There is much more disagreement about need and education as bases for wages and salaries, however. Women, churchgoers, and individuals in lower socioeconomic positions are more likely to subscribe to "welfare/needs" as an acceptable basis for pay (Evans, Kelley, and Peoples 2010).

Another study presented hypothetical vignettes to a sample of 200 White adults (Jasso and Rossi 1977). The individuals in these vignettes varied in sex, marital status, number of children, educational attainment, occupation, and earnings. Respondents were asked if the fictitious person in each of a limited number of vignettes presented to them was (1) overpaid, (2) fairly paid, or (3) underpaid. There was a 9-point rating scale ranging from "extremely underpaid" to "fairly paid" to "extremely overpaid." The results revealed some interesting patterns. Single females were more likely than married females to be seen as being overpaid. Those with higher education and occupational status (especially males) and those with a greater number of children who are married and male were more likely than opposite groups to be viewed as underpaid.

These findings indicate that people use a mixture of achievement-related and -unrelated criteria to

MINI-CASE 15.1

Equality and Equity

Findings from a number of studies cited in previous chapters indicate that socioeconomic background has an impact on one's life chances. This suggests that the socioeconomic condition of a person's family can affect how far he or she can get in life. At the same time, numerous surveys have shown that Americans' idea of fairness is defined not in terms of equal family conditions, but primarily in terms of equal opportunity. That is, a system of inequality can be seen as fair if it is one in which everyone has an equal opportunity to succeed. Americans are much less inclined to believe in equality of condition, that is, an equal distribution of income, and so on. The question is, Can equality of opportunity exist without equality in socioeconomic conditions of families? Are equal starting conditions needed to achieve equality of opportunity? How would you reconcile these two principles to achieve a fair and equitable society? ▪

---

make decisions about what is fair. While occupation and education are used to make judgments, so are sex and marital status. Indeed, a review of research on the matter suggests that the actual attainment of economic position is due to a combination of achievement and ascribed elements, with achievement or meritocratic factors being more decisive (Kingston 2006). A direct implication of all these findings is that an equal distribution of income among the individuals in the Jasso and Rossi study (1977) vignettes would be considered unfair, although respondents were not in favor of the range of incomes that presently exists. When respondents in that study were asked study to attribute a fair income to each of the fictitious individuals, the responses ranged from just over $7,000 for a single female with 7 years of education and a low-status job, to about $34,500 for a college-educated married couple with high-status professional jobs. This suggested that a preferred fair range in earnings is much smaller than the range that actually exists in the labor market. Thus, Americans have identifiable opinions not only about the factors on which individuals' incomes should be based but also about the overall fairness of the current extent of economic inequality.

BASES FOR THE LEGITIMATION OF STRUCTURED INEQUALITY

The preceding studies indicate that most people in the United States believe that it is the individual

more than anything else that determines upward mobility in the socioeconomic hierarchy. In other words, most people use the "principle of differentiation" in defining a just distribution. It is the *process* that must be seen as being just. The evidence also suggests that criteria over which the individual presumably has great control, such as effort and skills, *should be* used more than other kinds of factors to determine income. These beliefs obviously fit into the dominant American ideology that if people invest in themselves, they can improve their economic fate in life. Yet, as mentioned earlier, the evidence suggests that there are obstacles to equal opportunity for certain categories of individuals, and that not everyone with the same kind of job and education earns the same amount of income.

The question, then, is how do individuals come to accept a belief system even though there is evidence that it is not completely fair? How is an ideology internalized so that Americans come to believe that inequality is legitimate and justified? Mechanisms to assist internalization exist on the micro level of *individuals* in their everyday experiences as well as on the *institutional* macro level, working through the family, the education system, and other institutions.

Legitimation at the Level of the Individual

How do ideologies become internalized by people? This is a question addressed by Della Fave (1980), who tried to describe how individuals develop self-evaluations and judgments about the fairness of inequality. Interaction seems to be critical. To begin with, individuals are social beings—that is, they develop only in relationship with each other. As individuals grow and develop, they come into contact with greater numbers of people who react to them in a variety of ways. Individuals learn the expectations others have of them by noticing how others behave toward them. This combination of the expectations and reactions of others toward us makes up what Mead called the "generalized other" (Della Fave 1980). It is through relationships with the generalized other that individuals develop a definition and image of themselves. Seeing how others react to us leads to the development of a particular self-image. By viewing ourselves as others see us, we come to a conclusion about our own worth and our contributions to society. A consistent self-image over time requires the social support of others. "A person who maintains a self-definition with no social support is mad; with minimum support, a pioneer; and with broad support, a lemming. Most of us are lemmings" (Huber 1988, p. 92).

The generalized other helps us understand why we evaluate *ourselves* as we do. How we evaluate the quality of *others* also depends on interaction. When individuals with different *amounts* of money or other resources *and* different *kinds* of noticeable nominal characteristics (e.g., race, sex, age) interact, each person draws associations between those characteristics, competence, and the differential amount of resources. Eventually, there develops a belief in the greater competence of those with more resources. One result is that better-off individuals can and are expected to present their opinions more forcefully and effectively, resulting in higher esteem for them and lower esteem for the less well-off. To the extent that the better-off tend to be male or White, beliefs in the greater quality of these types of people develop and are accepted by both parties in these interactions. "In effect, double dissimilar encounters [i.e., those in which individuals differ in resources and nominal characteristics] become beacons that continually broadcast support for status beliefs about the nominal distinction, encouraging and under-

pinning their diffusion and eventually their consensuality as well" (Ridgeway et al. 1998, p. 334).

Further strengthening of beliefs in the legitimacy of "who has how much" occurs because people believe that hard work and ambition are critical and justifiable reasons for wealth. Thus, the wealthy are viewed as deserving of their high positions. This positive assessment of the wealthy influences not only individual images of them but people's own self-images.

But how does the individual reach the conclusion that those who are wealthy work harder, contribute more to society, and therefore deserve more than others? Briefly, Della Fave (1980) argued that individuals reach conclusions about the reasonableness of their beliefs from what they consider to be an "objective outside observer." In other words, it is from this observer that individuals develop ideas about what reality is and how it operates, and it is this observer whose judgments are internalized. It is the generalized other who fulfills the role of this observer, and it is the reactions of the generalized other to others that individuals internalize. Since a wide variety of people subscribe to a dominant ideology that emphasizes hard work and talent as the main reasons for success, they react to the wealthy as being deserving. The old saying "If you're so smart, why aren't you rich" captures this belief that wealth is a product of one's intelligence and talent. This appears to be an objective evaluation, and so they come to interpret others, and themselves, accordingly. Those who are reacted to favorably or treated as if they were important by almost everyone, including other important people, develop a very positive self-image, whereas others develop self-evaluations that are not quite as positive. "It is from the generalized other that individuals form an evaluation of self and, thus, of the worth of their 'contributions.' It is upon these evaluations, in turn, that judgments of equity are made in accordance with the principle of distributive justice" (Della Fave 1980, p. 961).

Those who are successful also develop feelings of self-efficacy; that is, they believe that their own actions can bring about successful rewards. This is largely because of positive reactions to their success by others, which then encourage them to do more and reinforce their high self-efficacy. Viewing their own success as being a result of their own actions, they come to define it as legitimate and deserving (Stolte 1983).

Individuals who possess very positive self-evaluations, in turn, come to view their own high level of rewards as being deserved relative to others, whereas those with more negative self-images see themselves as being worthy of fewer rewards. In a large complex society, individuals generally have to piece together broad images of what others are like and what their contributions are on the basis of the limited information to which they have access. Thus, individuals make conclusions about the contributions of others based on the information that shows on the surface—namely, their wealth and income. Those with high incomes, in turn, can use their resources to manage the impressions that others have of them—that is, manipulate the interpretations of others in such a way that the latter develop a positive image of them (Goffman 1959). Moreover, their ability to maintain high positions in educational, economic, and other institutions reinforces the image of their greater contributions and worthiness for higher rewards. Those with greater amounts are viewed as making greater contributions, and, therefore, as deserving of their economic resources. Essentially, the process of legitimation in this case is circular: Those with greater rewards elicit greater respect and the feeling from others that they deserve what they have, which in turn reinforces the inequality found in the hierarchy of rewards (Della Fave 1980). A skeletal interpretation of this process is presented in Figure 15.1.

According to Della Fave (1980), the entire internalization and social process—the **legitimation process**—just described bears directly on the extent to which the system of inequality is legitimated. The greater the degree to which the distribution of self-evaluations in society matches the distribution of rewards, the more legitimate the system of inequality will be considered and the more stable the society's structure of inequality will be. Conversely, if the two sets of distributions are not matched, then the stratification system is less likely to be defined as legitimate. This is consistent with Durkheim's views on the importance of the match between internal differences and rewards. More exposure and

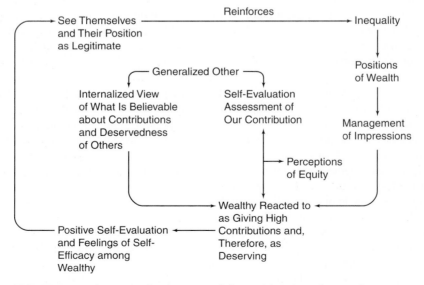

FIGURE 15.1 The Internalized Process of the Legitimation of Inequality

Source: Based on Della Fave (1980), pp. 955–958.

media coverage of corruption among individuals of high status and wealth, however, may increasingly counteract the power of personal resources to justify the level of rewards upper-class individuals receive.

Several of the relationships suggested have been tested recently. Following Della Fave's theory, Shepelak (1987) tested relationships among income, self-evaluations, and the belief in individual responsibility for a person's position. Her interviews with over 300 Indianapolis residents revealed that those with higher incomes did indeed have more favorable self-evaluations than those with low incomes, and that those with better self-evaluations were more likely than others to attribute their incomes to their own effort. However, the latter explanations were not related either to family income or estimates of equity/fairness. Family income and self-appraisals were both found to be positively related to the feeling that an individual's income was fair. Conversely, those with low incomes were more likely to say that they were being underrewarded. In other words, contrary to Della Fave's self-evaluation theory, those with lower incomes do not feel that they deserve less than those above them. In fact, family income is more strongly linked to beliefs in the fairness of one's family income than are either self-evaluations or explanations of income level. "These findings fail to substantiate the view that disadvantaged persons believe they deserve less" (Shepelak 1987, p. 501). Rather, they provide support for those who found that income is inversely related to the belief that the system of inequality is legitimate (e.g., Robinson and Bell 1978). On the other hand, support was found for the conclusions that a person's income standing and explanation of present position do affect feelings of self-worth. Figure 15.2 shows the interrelationships found among self-evaluations, income, perceptions of fairness, and perceived causes of income.

As a further test, experiments on university students examined the relationships among position, rewards, self-evaluation, and views of the fairness and structure of rewards. Sutphin and Simpson (2009) found that higher-positioned individuals who earned higher rewards also developed more positive self-evaluations, and also viewed the

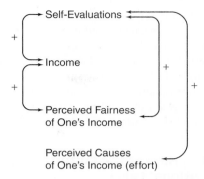

FIGURE 15.2   Relationships between Self-Evaluations, Income, and Fairness

Source: Based on Shepelak (1987), pp. 500–501.

system of unequal rewards as legitimate and their own rewards as fair. Individuals in less advantaged positions, however, varied in their conclusions about the fairness of the system. Those who had high evaluations of themselves were more likely than those with low self-evaluations to see their rewards as unfair.

In addition to the self-evaluation process just discussed, there are other elements in the everyday lives of individuals that promote feelings of system legitimacy. Most people, perhaps especially those who have to scramble to eke out a living, are too wrapped up in their daily lives and personal troubles to give much thought to the broad public issues of legitimacy and stability. Some research studies show that the social activities of those in the working and lower classes are usually limited to those involving friends and relatives; exposure to a wide range of types of people and geographic areas is restricted. The value and belief system that develops out of involvement in this immediate environment is basically accommodative in nature, helping individuals to make sense out of their everyday situation. Thus, it also tends to be parochial—tailored to explain or deal with the specific and immediate context in which these individuals live (Parkin 1971). As it concerns social inequality, part of the accommodation in this value system is to accept inequality but also to try to improve one's position within it. Thus, the value system generated in the local neighborhood does not ordinarily lead to a basic questioning of the system of inequality and its bases or to development of a radical ideology. Rather, people accept it in the abstract and then try to concretely adjust to it. So, "dominant values are not so much rejected or opposed as modified by the subordinate class as a result of their social circumstances and restricted opportunities" (Parkin 1971, p. 92).

Legitimation at the Cultural/ Institutional Level

Although it is clear that self-evaluation and similar social-psychological processes are involved in legitimating social inequality, a society's culture and its social institutions are also directly implicated in the legitimation process. After all, during most of their routine activities, individuals are embedded in institutions. As in the case of self-evaluation's role, the basic question is how institutions and cultural values operate in ways that justify and maintain the hierarchy of social inequality.

It has been noted that Americans have ambivalent feelings about inequality. A large part of the reason for this ambivalence lies in the frequently inconsistent values that make up U.S. culture. At the abstract level, a core value in the culture is the belief in equal opportunity or fair play. But, in addition, Americans also tend to believe in competition, achievement, success, work or activity, efficiency, individual personality, freedom, nationalism, humanitarianism, and morality (Williams 1970). We have seen that differential rewards are more often believed to be the result of variations in effort or work by individuals striving to achieve success in a context of free, open competition with others. To attack capitalism or the structure of inequality that has existed for generations would be, for many, not only unfair but also unpatriotic. So these values, by and large, push people in the direction of supporting the existing system, while other values such as humanitarianism and moralism may suggest that inequality is inequitable.

The impact of values is often reflected in stereotypes that are held about different groups, and these stereotypes, in turn, often help to justify and

sustain social inequalities. For example, images of what are appropriate attitudes and behavior for women have discouraged their movement into high-level corporate executive positions. As recently as 1989, male management students still believed that the qualities necessary to be a successful manager are more likely to be found in men than women. Consequently, these students were less likely to view women as being qualified for such positions. This is essentially the same belief as was held by male managers in the 1970s (Schein, Mueller, and Jacobson 1989). Part of the reason for this mistaken belief is probably the conviction that women are not as serious about their jobs as men and do not really work as hard at them.

Even when in the labor force, as an increasing number of women are, traditional beliefs regarding appropriate roles for women affect attitudes about their behavior. Employed mothers are seen as being more masculine, less feminine, and less desirable than other kinds of mothers (Benard and Correll 2010). Women who are physically attractive are also thought to be less qualified than unattractive ones for managerial positions, and, when they are in such positions, their performance is unjustifiably rated as being of less quality. Interestingly, attractiveness is considered a disadvantage for females in high positions, but it is considered an asset for them in clerical positions, a traditionally "female" occupation (Spencer and Taylor 1988). When in high positions that historically have been dominated by males, women are often pressured to adopt traditional feminine attitudes and behaviors, and if they don't, they suffer the consequences. "Women who do not wish to be classified . . . as deviant . . . must persist in playing the 'proper' role by following the interpersonal behavior pattern prescribed for them. Followed repeatedly, these patterns function as a means of control" (Henley and Freeman 1984, p. 475; see also Pierce 1995). In sum, images and stereotypes function to justify and maintain occupational inequality between men and women. Obviously, negative stereotypes of racial or ethnic minority groups perform a similar function. Perceiving Blacks, for example, as being less intelligent, less interested in education, and having less work incentive than Whites also serves to legitimize the economic and political inequalities that exist between the races. The power of these beliefs persists even when the evidence in each of these cases does not warrant such beliefs.

The beliefs and values that individuals endorse derive, in large part, from the broader institutional and cultural framework in which they operate. The task now is to describe how the system of inequality and the supporting values infiltrate the social institutions so that institutions foster activities and reinforce beliefs that legitimate inequality. How do institutions help to maintain the hierarchy of social inequality?

Institutions consist of rules and structures that define what is permissible and what is not, what is a legitimate issue or problem and what is not. Smith (1987) related how her research on mothering and education, which might help parents organize their collective interests in the schools, was controlled by the local school system. All research in the schools has to be cleared by the school board, and because of this, it has to be organized, proposed, and conducted in a manner that is consistent with the perspective of professional educators, not parents. *Professionalism* defines what is allowable and professionalism is defined by those most esteemed and dominant in the profession (generally White, higher status males). This creates limits on what information can be collected and what can be done with it.

The preceding example suggests that one of the tools used by institutions to legitimate the social structure, including the system of inequality, is to frame the image of that structure and the processes associated with it in a particular way with the use of certain kinds of concepts and terms. Language can greatly influence the interpretations placed on issues such as poverty, welfare, and political participation. The terms used to describe what is defined as a social problem also can influence how people react to them. There is no more apt example than the government's recent intervention into the shaky economic market through its subsidization of private corporations. The program was initially termed a "bail-out," with some calling it "corporate welfare." Given the high value that a "free" market has in our society, the negative reaction to the government "bailout" was understandable. So the terminology was changed to describe it as a "rescue plan" rather than a "bailout" in an attempt to legitimize the plan and make it more palatable to the public. Governments can affect the extent to which citizens interpret "poverty" as legitimate by using particular symbols to describe it. To most Americans, to indicate that some people are "on welfare" suggests something about the character of these individuals and their responsibility for their own fates. Someone who is considered a "welfare case" by an outsider is usually thought to be a person who does not work and probably does not want to work, one who is "living off" the rest of society. The term *welfare* itself evokes an image quite different from the term *poor.*

Similarly, referring to income as "rewards" or "earnings" plants the belief that the money is earned and thus deserved. Attributing the high rewards of a position to its "functional importance" to society helps to legitimize differential rewards. People have been socialized to react positively to the needs of society, the national interest, and earnings. Terms such as these encourage the acceptance and legitimation of "material sacrifices, constricted roles, political weakness, existing power hierarchies, and unfulfilled lives" (Edelman 1977, pp. 153–154).

Institutions of all types use language and symbols to create an image that legitimates the existing social reality. The use of certain terms to evoke specific images, and thus to encourage the acceptance of inequalities between individuals, applies to economic differences not only between rich and poor but also between men and women and Blacks and Whites. Because of the symbolic power of the concepts used by institutions and because of the intrusion of major institutions into most corners of their lives, people develop certain interpretations about society and other people, including those who are meritorious and deserving and those who are not. The institutions of family, education, and religion all contain elements that encourage acceptance of inequality.

FAMILY   Because they differ in resources and structure, it is clear that families contribute to the reproduction of economic, racial, and gender inequalities. Poor parents do not have the material resources to support and pass on to their children that wealthier parents possess. Wage inequalities between races create an incentive for minority women to postpone or eliminate marriage as an attractive option because the low wages paid to male minority members reduces the availability of appealing marriage partners. For poor women, this increases the likelihood that they will have children before marrying, since there are few opportunity costs for them and welfare is available. Moreover, in the absence of alternative sources of fulfillment available to higher-status women, motherhood is a principle source of identity for less-advantaged women. This is especially true for single-parent families, which are found in greater proportions among minority and poor populations. Single mothers bear a wage penalty that single father do not, and carry out most of the child rearing, further exacerbating economic and status inequalities between the sexes (McLanahan and Percheski 2008; Swartz 2009).

The differences in structures and resources between families means that the benefits and experiences of children in families also differ. This has implications for the kind of socialization that occurs between parents and children. The family has always been considered a major instrument of socialization. For example, it is within the domestic sphere that men and women learn much about how they should define themselves, their proper roles, and what they can expect from each other and society. Women are associated traditionally with an *expressive* role in the family; their primary responsibility is for nurturing and addressing the emotional needs of family members. From a conservative perspective, tampering with this prescribed, established gender role would upset stability in society. If most women pursued careers outside the family, there would have to be "profound alterations in the structure of the family" (Parsons 1964, p. 95).

Men, on the other hand, have been expected to perform an *instrumental* role, which means that while the women's focus is on the internal life of the family, men's concerns are with adapting to the outside world, primarily in making a living to support the family. Functionalists such as Parsons have viewed this role differentiation as a source of complementarity and efficiency. Women have a central role in reproduction and, since this occurs in the domestic sphere, it is more efficient and more natural to have them be responsible for the expressive role in the family. The whole trend in social evolution, in this view, has been toward increased specialization and differentiation of function, which further legitimizes the role specialization of the two sexes.

Over generations, the continual socialization of men and women into these roles leads them eventually to be thought of as natural. The fact that this role differentiation has generally been thought of in the past as ideal by many Americans and that most women have adopted the role indicates how powerful this ideology has been (Bem and Bem 1970). The balance that comes from the complementarity of these roles in the traditional functionalist view has integrative consequences for the society; it keeps society functioning smoothly. Of course, the behavior of others outside the family—such as nurses at the hospital when the child is born, babysitters, teachers, and relatives—further reinforces the gender-role distinctions considered appropriate for the sexes (Bernard 1981). The personality stereotypes of the sexes are consistent with their traditional roles. Men are still thought of favorably as being basically competitive, ambitious, independent, and logical, and women are well thought of for having good manners and being gentle, warm, softhearted, and affectionate (Werner and LaRussa 1985).

Although it may appear to be reasonable to view these personality traits and roles as merely complementary, as different but equal, the status and the power connected with each of them are quite different. As was pointed out earlier, capitalism and its values have shaped major institutions in modern society. This means that the social statuses attributed to families by individuals outside the family are based on what the occupational statuses of breadwinners are and how much income they bring home. As was noted in Chapter 6, the differences in status and power between the sexes are linked to the division of labor between them.

EDUCATION   Schools perpetuate and legitimize inequality between the sexes, races, and classes through a variety of mechanisms. In education, individuals with varying abilities and levels of effort are channeled into appropriate levels of the occupational structure. The school appears as a forum in which students openly compete with each other and then are objectively evaluated by the experts. Skills and abilities are often measured through the use of standardized tests; differences in scores are seen as differences in abilities. Of course, performance on such tests depends in part on the learning opportunities that have been afforded students, and these vary by socioeconomic status. The expectation is that students who have had more of these opportunities will do better on tests than other students (Grodsky, Warren, and Felts 2008). Still, different scores are seen as objective measures of the different levels of ability existing between students. "The educational system fosters and reinforces the belief that economic success depends essentially on the possession of technical and cognitive skills—skills which it is organized to provide in an efficient, equitable, and unbiased manner on the basis of meritocratic principle" (Bowles and Gintis 1976, p. 103). Consequently, schools are in the business of preparing students to be funneled into work roles at appropriate status levels.

At another level, various aspects of teacher–student relations encourage acceptance of an individual's traditional place in the structure of inequality. By teaching students about the nature of social reality, such as the values of the free market, intellectuals help to support the status quo. In Gramsci's phrase (1971), intellectuals often have been "managers of legitimation." This includes members of the helping professions, such as social workers, psychiatrists, and teachers. Although educators often have encouraged happiness through adjustment to the status quo, those involved in these professions "have reinforced inequality by

equating adjustment to existing social, economic, and political institutions with psychological health" (Edelman 1977, p. 152). People who deviate from their expected roles or who criticize the social structure are defined as "deviant" and are dealt with accordingly (Mills 1959).

Some of the teacher behaviors that encourage adjustment also reinforce traditional gender roles in U.S. society. Teachers in elementary schools pay more attention to males when they fight, suggesting that boys are more prone to aggression. At the same time, they pay more attention to the needs of girls by giving them more assistance than boys, thereby inadvertently encouraging their dependence on authority figures (Serbin et al. 1973; Fagot 1977). Since men are more likely to be in positions of authority (e.g., as principals in schools), children learn that it is normal for men rather than women to have power. What children read and how men and women are portrayed pictorially in textbooks also have an impact. When children act in a way that violates traditional sex-role expectations, they are usually ridiculed by their peers (Lamb, Easterbrooks, and Holden 1980).

In their social relationships at school, boys and girls themselves frequently reinforce gender distinctions by engaging in "borderwork." This refers to "forms of cross-sex interaction which are based upon and reaffirm boundaries and asymmetries between girls' and boys' groups" (p. 76). Types of borderwork include various contests inside and outside the classroom in which the sexes are pitted against each other. Another form is chasing, in which boys and girls tease and try to elude each other on the playground. Invasions also occur in which members of one sex will "invade" the game being played by the other sex. These activities and what is said while each is going on legitimize traditional ideas about what is appropriate for each sex. The dominance of boys in this informal world is demonstrated by (1) the greater playground space that they control, (2) the greater probability of invasion by boys in girls' games, and (3) the association of greater pollution (e.g., "cooties") with girls.

Along with gender roles, traditional images of minorities are also reinforced. By and large, the information presented in classrooms and textbooks usually offers a favorable interpretation of the United States and its history. Children have seldom been told in detail about unethical acts by national leaders or of the brutalization of such groups as American Indians. "None of this is very surprising. . . . Throughout history all children have been socialized to accept the dominant values and institutions of their society" (Kerbo 1983, p. 388).

Teacher expectations of Blacks and Whites and students from higher and lower classes also have been shown to be different. The images teachers have of lower-status groups influence their expectations of them. Less is expected from them, which ultimately affects how well they do in school. Their lower performance only reinforces the initial negative image held by teachers, resulting in a self-fulfilling prophecy. Their lower performance also appears to justify their lower attainment, further strengthening the belief that attainment is linked to merit. The lower expectations by teachers of lower-status individuals influence the teachers to place these students in lower non-college-oriented tracks. Their placement in these tracks helps to ensure their lower educational attainment.

What is important about all these mechanisms is that their effects are largely unrecognized. The overriding belief is that in schools teachers are the objective experts, and that students study and take valid tests, are judged on the basis of their performance, and end up at a place in the attainment hierarchy that reflects their performance. What level they attain appears to be solely up to them. This reinforces and legitimates the belief that inequality in society is largely the result of differences in individual efforts and abilities.

RELIGION French sociologist Émile Durkheim argued that, for society, religion is integrative for society because its beliefs and rituals take individuals out of their secular private lives and bring them together to form a community. It is out of the social gathering of individuals in a religious setting that feelings of a superior force or power outside individuals first arise. Thus, Durkheim argued that the worship of supernatural forces in religious

rituals is really an adoration of the powers in society. "In the divine, men realize to themselves the moral authority of society, the discipline beyond themselves to which they submit, which constrains their behavior even in spite of themselves, contradicts their impulses, rewards their compliance, and so renders them dependent and grateful for it" (Sahlins 1968, pp. 96–97).

Given this description, it should come as no surprise that images of the supernatural world often mirror the social structure of society. Swanson (1974) showed concretely in his study of non-Western societies that a social hierarchy on earth is reflected in a social hierarchy in the supernatural realm. In societies in which older people occupied positions of importance, ancestors were a subject of worship, and in societies in which there was a great deal of social inequality, religion helped to legitimate the differences between the top and the bottom. A good example of this legitimation occurs in Hinduism in which the concepts of karma, dharma, and samsara combine to explain and justify the continuous inequality generation after generation. *Karma* indicates the belief that a person's present situation is the result of his or her actions in a previous life, and *dharma* refers to the duties and norms attached to each caste. Finally, *samsara* refers to the continual birth and rebirth of life. In other words, central beliefs in Hinduism absolve society or others from responsibility for social inequality. It is the result of individual actions (B. Turner 1986).

Particular branches of Christianity have also legitimated people's beliefs about inequality, for example, in their dictum that self-denial, continuous effort, and hard work result in success. This kind of spirit is what is embodied in Weber's concept of the "Protestant ethic." Hard work and religious beliefs were intermingled by many famous preachers early in U.S. history. Cotton Mather, a charismatic Puritan preacher of the late seventeenth century, lectured that business and people's occupations were "callings" and not to be ignored. If individuals do not engage in their occupations, but rather remain idle (slothful), poverty will befall them. Riches are the result of industry, and poverty is the result of individual laziness. Those who are poor should expect no help from others since it is their own behavior that has resulted in their dismal situation. By engaging in business, people are doing what God intended: "Yea a *calling* is not only our *Duty,* but also our *Safety.* Men will ordinarily fall into horrible *Snares,* and infinite *Sins,* if they have not a *Calling,* to be their preservative. . . . If the Lord Jesus Christ might find thee, in thy *Store House,* in thy *Shop,* or in thy *Ship,* or in thy *Field,* or where thy *Business* lies, who knows, what *Blessings* He might bestow upon thee?" (cited in Rischin 1965, pp. 24, 26). It is only a short jump from this statement to the belief that those who are successful are so because of their own efforts and are among the favored of God, while those on the bottom do not work and are sinful.

Advocates of Dutch Calvinism justified slavery by viewing Blacks as sinners and slavery as a just condition for their sins and inferiority in the eyes of God. The legacy of these beliefs can be found in the contemporary dilemmas of inequality in South Africa (B. Turner 1986). In the United States, a slave catechism was used in many churches during the period of slavery to justify domination by masters, to encourage work, and to attribute lack of work to personal laziness. White pastors told Blacks that God created the masters over them and that the Bible tells them that they must obey their White masters (Fishel and Quarles 1967). There are additional elements in Christianity that have been used to support continual subordination of women to men, including the biblical argument about the origins of woman out of man and the injunctions to obey one's husband in marriage. The impact of religion on beliefs about inequality has continued. Members of dominant religions, especially Whites who espouse Protestantism and Catholicism are more likely than members of minority religions such as Judaism to support the inequality status quo, believing that poverty is a result of individuals' flaws rather than a consequence of luck or structural defects (Hunt 2002).

Civil religion is used to justify the "American way of life." It is a mixture of religious and political ideology in which the U.S. social structure and culture are seen as favored by God. God and Americanism go hand in hand in this ideology. This is a nation "under God" and its institutions are sanctified by the Almighty. At civil ceremonies and during certain public occasions, such as the opening of Congress, presidential inaugurations, and the Pledge of Allegiance, it is suggested that God is the benefactor of the United States. Even most elementary school children believe that the United States "has been placed on this earth for a special purpose," that it has a "chosen" status with God, and that it is successful because it is morally good (Smidt 1980). The "American way" that is so blessed incorporates the values of individualism, freedom, capitalism, and equality of opportunity, which make up a core part of the ideology supporting inequality. Some televangelists conjoin Christianity and Americanism in a manner that makes them not only mutually supportive but almost indistinguishable. In this ideology, to attack Americanism becomes tantamount to committing a serious sin. Americanism is supposed to be accepted, not criticized or undermined.

Karl Marx viewed religion under capitalism as having many of the effects on inequality just discussed. People are expected to put up with inequality; religion lulls them into a false sense of complacency. That is, it makes them *falsely conscious* of their real situation. It blinds them to the real causes of their predicament (i.e., class exploitation, not personal sin). In this way, socioeconomic inequality is seen as legitimate by those who blame only themselves or look forward to another life when conditions will be better for them.

Of course, Marx realized that historically, before capitalism, religion had been used to support the oppressed; even in our own time, religions have not always supported the status quo. Martin Luther King Jr. and the Southern Christian Leadership Conference used religious ideas to try to improve conditions of Blacks in the United States, and Catholic bishops have fought on the side of the poor against many Latin American dictatorships (Hehir 1981; Light, Keller, and Calhoun 1989). Catholicism also has been a force for change in communist Eastern Europe (Parkin 1971). Despite these instances in which religion has opposed inequality, historically it has been more closely associated with its legitimation and maintenance. This has been the case with each of the social insti-tutions we have discussed. By and large, each has served to support the dominant value system as it pertains to inequality, and it is through each of them that individuals come to believe that the social inequality around them is legitimate.

Summary

The principal focus of this chapter has been on examining the assessments of the fairness of so-cial and economic inequality and the criteria that define such fairness, and exploring the factors that contribute to the legitimation and, therefore, the stability of inequality in the United States. Americans are clearly torn on the fairness issue. On the one hand, they believe that hard work, ed-ucation, and similar personal investments are im-portant for economic achievement and believe that they should be important. On the other hand, most feel that the extent of inequality is too great; on the other hand, they do not think that full equality of income or wealth would be fair either. Moreover, when asked what they think deter-mines success, they tend to overestimate the sig-nificance of some factors and underestimate the impact of others, most notably race and sex. Attributing poverty and wealth to individualistic and/or structuralist causes varies with one's class, gender, and minority status. In their assessments of the criteria to be used in determining a fair in-come, Americans tend to use a mixture of achieve-ment and other factors (e.g., education, marital status, sex, occupational status).

The system of inequality itself is legitimated at the individual and institutional levels. Individuals develop interpretations of their own and others' rewards and contributions from the reactions of oth-ers to inequality. Their position in the rewards hier-archy affects their own self-evaluations and their appraisal of the fairness of their own incomes. At the same time, those with positive self-evaluations inter-pret their own incomes as being the result of their own efforts.

Through its culture and institutions, society helps to encourage traditional beliefs about the causes of inequality, thereby maintaining the structure of inequality. Generally, the values impressed on members and clients of those institu-tions are those of individualism and capitalism. Through the language and symbols used and their rules of knowledge, institutions define what is real and proper. In the case of the family and educa-tion, institutions shape beliefs and roles for those in different positions of the system of inequality and encourage a belief in the legitimacy of their positions. Religion also has used its resources on many occasions to legitimate the socioeconomic inequality that surrounds individuals.

Critical Thinking

1. If wealthy individuals are more likely than others to consider the system of inequality fair, what are the chances that the system will ever change?

2. Is it possible to develop a formula for the fair distri-bution of resources that is objective and generally agreed on by most in society? Explain your answer. If you agree that it could be developed, what might go into such a formula?

3. Is there such a thing as *too much* inequality if that inequality is the result of free-market forces and individual differences in effort and talent? How could one determine if there is *too much* inequality?

4. The family, educational institutions, and religion have often perpetuated and justified inequality. Are there any aspects of these institutions that undermine inequality or encourage its decrease?

Web Connections

In considering how wealth might be distributed and whether we should help the poor of the world, consider the arguments at www.sevenoaksphilosophy. org/ethics/distribution-of-wealth.html.

Film Suggestions

Income Inequality (2007). In this episode of the PBS program *NOW,* two authors discuss inequality in the United States and who it is helping and who it is hurting.

Bread and Roses (2000). Janitorial workers fight for better working conditions and unionization.

GLOSSARY OF BASIC TERMS

absolute downward mobility a downward shift in economic resources without a simultaneous change in an individual's position relative to others.

anomic division of labor an abnormal condition in which the rules of relationships among those in the production process and limits in the marketplace are unclear.

assimilationist theory an explanation of race relations that views minority groups as being on a one-way road to blending in with the rest of society.

brown-bag test criterion used to screen individuals from membership in a group or organization if their skin color is darker than a brown grocery bag.

burakumin a minority outcaste group in Japan distinguished and discriminated against on the basis of the impurity of their occupations and place of residence.

capitalism an economic system based on private ownership, competition, and open markets.

caste system a closed social ranking system dividing categories of individuals in which position is ascribed and which is legitimated by cultural and/or religious institutions.

chronic illness health problems that continue over a long period of time.

circulation mobility mobility that reflects the cultural and social openness of a society.

class defined variously as individuals or groups who (1) occupy the same position on hierarchies of occupational prestige, income, and education; (2) are in the same relation to the system of production; or (3) are in the same relation to the system of production and are also class conscious.

class consciousness the full awareness within a group of its class position and relationship with other classes, along with action based on this awareness.

core economic sector the section of the private economy occupied by large, capital-intensive, highly productive firms with large, sometimes international, markets (also called **monopoly sector**).

corporate crime crime generally committed by corporate officials for the immediate benefit of their corporation rather than themselves.

crises of overproduction the inability of capitalism to sell all that it produces, largely because of the inconsistency between low, impoverished wages and advanced technology.

critical-race perspective views racism and race relations as rooted and hidden in the structure and historical social arrangements of society rather than issues of individual prejudice.

cultural capital a group's cultural values, experiences, knowledge, and skills passed on from one generation to the next.

dependency theory argues that international inequality is due to relationships of dependency and exploitation between strong and weaker nations.

digital divide inequality between social classes in technology ownership and use.

drift hypothesis in the study of the relationship between mental illness and social class, the argument that illness causes one's downward mobility through the class system.

dual labor market the view of the market as being split between a primary market with better jobs and a secondary market characterized by lower-paying and less stable jobs.

economic hardship spending more than 40 percent of one's income on debt payment.

embourgeoisement the taking on by the working class of middle-class cultural and social characteristics.

environmental equity/justice concerns the extent to which groups have equal access to public land resources and equal exposure to environmental hazards.

ethnic group a group distinguished on the basis of its native cultural and linguistic characteristics.

ethnocentrism belief that one's culture is the best and should be used as a standard to rate other cultures.

financial wealth those forms of wealth that can be easily and quickly converted to cash.

forced division of labor an abnormal condition in which the distribution of accorded positions and occupations is inconsistent with the distribution of talents and skills among individuals.

functionalist theory of stratification the argument that stratification is a necessary device for motivating talented people to perform society's most difficult and important tasks, and that it arises from scarcity of talent and the differential social necessity of tasks.

gender a set of attitudinal, role, and behavior expectations, which are socially and culturally defined, associated with each sex.

globalization *economically,* the acceleration of international trade and flow of financial capital; *politically,* the opening of national borders to foreign goods and services; and *socially,* the free flow and exchange of cultural ideas and structural arrangements among nations.

habitus Bourdieu's term for a system of stable dispositions to view the world in a particular way.

hate crime a violent or property crime that is motivated at least in part by a bias against the victim's race, religion, disability, sexual orientation, ethnicity, or national origin.

honor killing an extreme form of discrimination in which the person, usually a minority or female individual, is killed for ostensibly violating a cultural norm or tradition related to that person's behavior.

human capital the investments one makes in oneself (i.e., education, acquisition of skills, and experience).

hyperghettoization the extreme concentration of underprivileged groups in the inner city.

income deficit how far below the poverty level one's income falls.

Index of Income Concentration a measure of how far the actual distribution of income is from perfect equality (also called the Gini coefficient).

industrialism thesis the argument that, regardless of the country, industrialization breaks down barriers to social mobility and results in an emphasis on achievement rather than ascription as a basis for vertical mobility.

in-kind benefits noncash outlays given to recipients of government programs, such as food stamps, medical assistance, and job training.

inner circle a network of leaders from large corporations who serve as top officers at more than one firm, who are politically active, and who serve the interests of the capitalist class as a whole.

inner/outer orientation a view of the environment as hospitable, fruitful, and freely giving (inner) or as one in which the environment is alien and hostile, and must be conquered (outer).

institutional view of social welfare belief that since poverty is often beyond the control of individuals, and one of government's legitimate roles is to help those in need, welfare should be available to help people out of poverty.

intergenerational mobility a change in economic or social hierarchical position between generations.

internal colonialism a situation in which a minority group is culturally, socially, and politically dominated as if it were a colony of the majority group.

intersex term used to describe a variety of conditions in which a person is born with a reproductive or sexual anatomy that does not seem to fit the typical definitions of female or male.

intersectionality the idea that one's race, sex, ethnicity, and social class, when combined, create distinctive social positions that have effects that are independent of the separate effects of each component taken separately.

intragenerational mobility vertical economic or social movement within one's own lifetime.

jati the complex system of local castes found in Indian villages.

labor power the mental and physical capacities exercised by individuals when they produce something of use.

legacy college and university preferences given to the sons and daughters of alumni.

legitimation process the means and manner by which social inequality is explained and justified.

mass society a society in which the vast majority of the population is unorganized, largely powerless, and manipulated by those at the distant top.

means of production the material (e.g., machines) and nonmaterial (e.g., lectures) techniques used to produce goods and services in an economy.

microinequities everyday ways in which, because of their social ranking, individuals are ignored, put down, highlighted, or demeaned.

militant societies societies in which there is heavy regulation of individuals and groups; the regulatory system is the dominant institution in the society; contrasted with industrial societies and associated with Spencer.

mode of production the particular type of economic system in a society, including its means of production (e.g., technology) and social/authority relations among workers and between workers and owners. Capitalism and feudalism are two modes of production.

modernization theory assumes that there is a fundamental and irreconcilable conflict between tradition and modernity in "underdeveloped" countries, and that the gap must be eliminated for development to occur.

near poor those whose total incomes fall between 100 percent and 125 percent of their poverty thresholds

necessary labor the labor needed to reproduce workers and their replacements.

neoliberalism a theory that views globalization as an opening up of opportunities and boundaries that results in greater benefits for all countries.

nested inequalities inequalities existing at various levels within a given institutional sphere that have a cumulative or layered effect.

net worth one's wealth minus one's debts.

opportunity structure characteristics of the cultural, social, political, legal, occupational, economic, and other institutions that affect chances of social mobility either positively or negatively.

origin myths in this context, the view of the world's origin as being due to either masculine or feminine forces.

party an association aimed at or specifically organized for gaining political power in an organization or society (Weber).

patriarchy a complex of structured interrelationships in which men dominate women.

peripheral economic sector part of the private economy occupied by small, local, labor-intensive, less productive, and less stable economic organizations (also called **competitive sector**).

phantom welfare government cash, tax, and in-kind programs and policies that largely benefit the non-poor.

pluralism the view stressing that power is distributed throughout society among various groups rather than concentrated.

political action committee (PAC) a group that organizes around a broad or narrow common interest to influence political policy in its favor.

Ponzi scheme economic fraud in which investment money is manipulated to make illegal profit.

power elite a small group or set of groups that dominate the political process and masses in a society.

prestige the social ranking accorded a position or occupation; a synonym for status honor.

primary labor market the labor market associated with jobs that are stable, good paying, and unionized; have good working conditions; and in which there is an internal job structure through which one can move.

principle of differentiation the belief that it is fair that those with unequal talents should receive unequal rewards.

principle of equality the belief that since all people are ultimately of equal value, they should therefore receive equal consideration or treatment.

proletarianization the conversion of white-collar and middle-class occupations into occupations with traditional working-class characteristics (i.e., boring, routine, etc.).

public assistance programs cash and in-kind government programs for the poor that are means tested (i.e., require that individuals prove their eligibility) and to which there is a social stigma attached.

racialization social and psychological process by which poverty and welfare are defined as Black issues.

rationalization the increasing bureaucratic, technological, and impersonal character of the modern world (Weber).

relative downward mobility a shift in one's position on the economic ladder to a lower position and involving a switch in place with another person or group.

residual view of social welfare the belief that since poverty is caused by personal flaws, welfare programs should be minimal, with low benefits and strict eligibility requirements to discourage their use.

ruling class the broad Marxian view that the upper class, or an active arm of it, generally dominates the political process in society to protect its interests.

scientific management a system of control used by management in which labor tasks are simplified and standardized by being broken down into their smallest elements.

secondary labor market the labor market associated with poor, unstable, low-paying, and often dead-end jobs.

sedimentation the reproduction and perpetuation of lower levels of wealth over generations for given groups.

sex stratification the degree to which access to valued resources is restricted because of sex.

social capital the size and nature of networks of social relationships possessed by a person or group.

social causation thesis in the study of the relationship between mental illness and social class, the argument that social class position is causally related to the probability of mental illness.

social constructionism a perspective that explains how social phenomena are socially created through definitions, classifications, and categorizations used by individuals.

Social Darwinism a social philosophy stressing perfection of society through a natural, unfettered process of survival of the fittest.

social insurance government programs, such as Social Security, for which individuals who have worked for a certain period of time are automatically eligible and seen as deserving of aid.

social relations of production the nature of property and power relationships among workers, between workers and managers/supervisors, and between owners and nonowners in an economic system.

social reproduction the process by which structural conditions reproduce themselves.

social stratification a condition in which the ranking system among groups or categories of individuals is firmly established, resulting in a set of social layers separated by impermeable boundaries.

socioeconomic status a person's position on several continuous social and economic hierarchies, such as education, income, occupation, and wealth.

soft power national power that is based on a country's values, cultural traditions, ideas, and foreign policy rather than on its physical might.

stages of capitalism capitalism's movement through phases of cooperation, manufacture, and modern industry (Marx).

status the ranking of individuals and groups on the basis of *social* and evaluated characteristics; contrasts with **class,** which is largely an *economic* ranking.

status attainment the study of the factors and processes that account for the educational, occupational, and economic attainment of individuals.

street crimes crimes listed by the FBI's Crime Index, including burglary, larceny-theft, motor vehicle theft, arson, murder, forcible rape, robbery, and aggravated assault.

structural mobility mobility that is due to shifts in the occupational distribution or changes in technology.

suite crime a synonym for **white-collar crime**.

surplus labor labor time that is left over after socially necessary labor has been subtracted from the total labor time spent on the job. It produces profit for the employer.

tokens individuals who are the only persons seen as representing a distinct minority within a group

transgendered referring to individuals who deviate from traditional gender binaries of Western society and who sometimes define themselves as belonging to a third gender.

underclass a small, urban, largely unemployed, chronically poor, welfare-dependent group of individuals living in impoverished neighborhoods, whose children often wind up in the same position.

vacancy-driven mobility mobility that depends on the availability and distribution of open positions.

varna a major ritual caste in India, such as the Brahmins.

welfare capitalism special benefits used by management to minimize solidarity among workers.

white-collar crime crimes committed by individuals of high status or corporations using their powerful positions for personal gain.

Wisconsin model a model of status attainment that stresses the impact of social-psychological as well as structural factors on attainment.

world inequality the total amount of inequality between nations and the average of amount of inequality within nations combined.

world system theory posits that the world economy is composed of core, semiperipheral, and peripheral nations, which determines each nation's function and place in the world system.

REFERENCES

Aaronson, Daniel, and Bhashkar Mazumder. 2008. "Intergenerational Economic Mobility in the United States." *Journal of Human Resources* 43:139–172.

Aaronson, Daniel, and Daniel G. Sullivan. 1998. "The Decline of Job Security in the 1990s: Displacement, Anxiety, and Their Effect on Wage Growth." *Economic Perspectives* 22:17–43.

Aberle, D. F., A. K. Cohen, A. D. Davis, M. J. Levy, and F. X. Sutton. 1950. "The Functional Prerequisites of a Society." *Ethics* 60:100–111.

Abrahamson, Mark. 1973. "Functionalism and the Functional Theory of Stratification: An Empirical Assessment." *American Journal of Sociology* 78:1236–1246.

Abramovitz, Mimi. 2001. "Everyone Is Still on Welfare: The Role of Redistribution in Social Policy." *Social Work* 46:297–308.

Acker, Joan. 2006. "Inequality Regimes: Gender, Class, and Race in Organizations." *Gender & Society* 20:441–464.

Ackerman, Bruce, and Ann Alstott. 1999. *The Stakeholder Society.* New Haven, CT: Yale University Press.

Adams, Bert N., and R. A. Sydie. 2002. *Classical Sociological Theory.* Thousand Oaks, CA: Pine Forge Press.

Adams, Charles Francis, ed. 1969. *The Works of John Adams,* vol. IX. Freeport, NY: Books for Libraries Press.

Adler, Patricia A., and Peter Adler. 1998. *Peer Power.* New Brunswick, NJ: Rutgers University Press.

Aguilera, Michael Bernabe. 2008. "Personal Networks and the Incomes of Men and Women in the United States: Do Personal Networks Provide Higher Returns for Men or Women?" *Research in Social Stratification and Mobility* 26:221–233.

Aisenbrey, Silke, Marie Evertsson, and Daniela Grunow. 2009. "Is There a Career Penalty for Mothers' Time Out? A Comparison of Germany, Sweden and the United States." *Social Forces* 88:573–605.

Albelda, Randy. 2001. "Fallacies of Welfare-to-Work Policies." *Annals of the American Academy of Political and Social Science* 577:66–77.

Albelda, Randy, M. V. Lee Badgett, Alyssa Schneebaum, and Gary J. Gates. March 2009. *Poverty in the Lesbian, Gay, and Bisexual Community.* Los Angeles: Williams Institute.

Alderson, Arthur S., and Francois Nielsen. 2002. "Globalization and the Great U-Turn: Income Inequality Trends in 16 OECD Countries." *American Journal of Sociology* 107:1244–1299.

Alesina, Alberto, and Eliana La Ferrara. 2002. "Who Trusts Others?" *Journal of Public Economics* 85:207–234.

Alexander, Herbert E. 1992. "The PAC Phenomenon." Pp. ix–xv in *Almanac of Federal PACs: 1992,* edited by E. Zuckerman. Washington, D.C.: Amward.

Allard, Scott W. 2009. *Out of Reach.* New Haven, CT: Yale University Press.

Allen, Michael Patrick. 1987. *The Founding Fortunes: A New Anatomy of the Super-Rich Families in America.* New York: Truman Talley Books.

Allen, Robert L. 1969. *Black Awakening in Capitalist America.* Garden City, NY: Anchor.

Almond, Gabriel A. September 1991. "Capitalism and Democracy." *PS: Political Science & Politics* 24:467–474.

Almquist, Elizabeth McTaggart. 1984. "Race and Ethnicity in the Lives of Minority Women." Pp. 423–453 in *Women: A Feminist Perspective,* edited by J. Freeman. Palo Alto, CA: Mayfield.

Alon, Sigal. 2009. "The Evolution of Class Inequality in Higher Education: Competition, Exclusion, and Adaptation." *American Sociological Review* 74:731–755.

Altman, Dennis. 2005. "The Globalization of Sexual Identities." Pp. 216–226 in *Gender Through the Prism of Difference,* edited by M. B. Zinn, P. Hondagneu-Sotelo, and M. A. Messner. New York: Oxford.

American Society of Plastic Surgeons. 2010. *2009 Quick Facts.* Arlington Heights, IL: American Society of Plastic Surgeons.

Andersen, Margaret L. 1997. *Thinking about Women.* Boston: Allyn & Bacon.

Anderson, Elijah. 1999. *Code of the Street.* New York: Norton.

Anderson, Sarah, Chuck Collins, Sam Pizzigati, and Kevin Shih. 2010. *CEO Pay and the Great*

Recession. Washington, D.C.: Institute for Policy Studies.

Anderton, Douglas L., Andy B. Anderson, John Michael Oakes, and Michael R. Fraser. 1994. "Environmental Equity: The Demographics of Dumping." *Demography* 31:229–248.

Anheier, Helmut K., Jurgen Gerhards, and Frank P. Romo. 1995. "Forms of Capital and Social Structure in Cultural Fields: Examining Bourdieu's Social Topography." *American Journal of Sociology* 100:859–903.

Anson, Ofra, and Jon Anson. 1987. "Women's Health and Labour Force Status: An Enquiry Using a Multi-Point Measure of Labor Force Participation." *Social Science & Medicine* 25:57–63.

Apel, Robert, and Gary Sweeten. 2010. "The Impact of Incarceration on Employment During the Transition to Adulthood." *Social Problems* 57:448–479.

Appalachian Regional Commission. 1985. *Appalachia: Twenty Years of Progress.* Washington, D.C.: Author.

Aronowitz, Stanley. 1973. *False Promises: The Shaping of American Working Class Consciousness.* New York: McGraw-Hill.

Aronson, Pamela. 2003. "Feminists or 'Postfeminists'?" *Gender & Society* 17:903–922.

Asher, Robert. 1986. "Industrial Safety and Labor Relations in the United States, 1865–1917." Pp. 115–130 in *Life and Labor: Dimensions of American Working-Class History,* edited by C. Stephenson and R. Asher. Albany: State University of New York Press.

Ashley, David, and David Michael Orenstein. 1990. *Sociological Theory: Classical Statements.* Needham Heights, MA: Allyn & Bacon.

Association of Certified Fraud Examiners. 2008. *2008 Report to the Nation on Occupational Fraud & Abuse.* Austin, TX: Association of Certified Fraud Examiners.

Augustine, Jennifer March, Shannon E. Cavanagh, and Robert Crosnoe. 2009. "Maternal Education, Early Child Care and the Reproduction of Advantage." *Social Forces* 88:1–30.

Autor, David H., Lawrence F. Katz, and Melissa S. Kearney. 2008. "Trends in U.S. Wage Inequality: Revising the Revisionists." *Review of Economic & Statistics[L1]* 90:300–323.

Avery, Robert B., and Michael S. Rendall. 2002. "Lifetime Inheritance of Three Generations of Whites and Blacks." *American Journal of Sociology* 107:1300–1346.

Bachrach, Peter, and Morton S. Baratz. 1962. "Two Faces of Power." *American Political Science Review* 56:947–952.

Badgett, M. V. Lee. 2001. *Money, Myths, and Change: The Economic Lives of Lesbians and Gay Men.* Chicago: University of Chicago.

Badgett, M. V. Lee, and Holning Lau, Brad Sears, and Deborah Ho. 2007. *Bias in the Workplace: Consistent Evidence of Sexual Orientation and Gender Identity Discrimination.* Los Angeles: Williams Institute.

Baker-Sperry, Lori, and Liz Grauerholz. 2003. "The Pervasiveness and Persistence of the Feminine Beauty Ideal in Children's Fairy Tales." *Gender & Society* 15:711–726.

Balsam, K. F., E. D. Rothblum, and T. P. Beauchaine. 2005. "Victimization over the Lifespan: A Comparison of Lesbian, Gay, Bisexual, and Heterosexual Siblings." *Journal of Consulting and Clinical Psychology* 78:477–487.

Baltzell, E. Digby. 1958. *Philadelphia Gentleman: The Making of a National Upper Class.* Glencoe, IL: The Free Press.

Banyard, Victoria L., and Sandra A. Graham-Bermann. 1998. "Surviving Poverty: Stress and Coping in the Lives of Housed and Homeless Mothers." *American Journal of Orthopsychiatry* 68:479–489.

Baran, Paul, and Paul Sweezy. 1966. *Monopoly Capital.* New York: Monthly Review Press.

Barkan, Steven E. 1984. "Legal Control of the Southern Civil Rights Movement." *American Sociological Review* 49:552–565.

Barnett, Bernice McNair. 1993. "Invisible Southern Black Women Leaders in the Civil Rights Movement." *Gender & Society* 7:162–182.

Baron, James N., and William T. Bielby. 1984. "The Organization of Work in a Segmented Economy." *American Sociological Review* 49:454–473.

Barr, Bob, Steve Largent, Jim Sensenbrenner, Sue Myrick, Ed Bryant, Bill Emerson, Harold Volkmer, and Ike Skelton. 1996. *Defense of Marriage Act. 5/96 H.R. 3396 Summary/Analysis.* Available at www.lectlaw.com/files/leg-23.htm.

Barrera, Mario. 1979. *Race and Class in the Southwest: A Theory of Racial Inequality.* Notre Dame, IN: University of Notre Dame Press.

Barrett, Anne E., and R. Jay Turner. 2005. "Family Structure and Mental Health: The Mediating Effects of Socioeconomic Status, Family Process, and Social Stress." *Journal of Health and Social Behavior* 46:156–169.

Barrett, James E., and David Roediger. 2008. "How White People Became White." Pp. 35–40 in *White Privilege,* edited by R. Rothenberg. New York: Worth.

Barringer, Felicity. January 11, 1990. "The Dress for Success: A Second Time Around." *New York Times,* A18.

Barry, John S. 2002. "Corporate Inversions: An Introduction to the Issue and FAQ." *Fiscal Policy Memo. Tax Bites,* May 30. The Tax Foundation.

Bartels, Larry M. 2008. *Unequal Democracy: The Political Economy of the New Gilded Age.* New York: Russell Sage Foundation; Princeton, NJ: Princeton University Press.

Bartels, Larry M. February 2004. "Partisan Politics and the U.S. Income Distribution." Department of Politics and Woodrow Wilson School of Public and International Affairs, Princeton University.

Batteau, Allen. 1984. "The Sacrifice of Nature: A Study in the Social Production of Consciousness." Pp. 94–106 in *Cultural Adaptation to Mountain Environments,* edited by P. D. Beaver and B. L. Purrington. Athens: University of Georgia Press.

Baumann, Robert. 2006. "Changes in the Appalachian Wage Gap, 1970 to 2000." *Growth and Change* 37:416–443.

Baumgartner, Frank R., and Beth L. Leech. 1998. *Basic Interests: The Importance of Groups in Politics and in Political Science.* Princeton, NJ: Princeton University Press.

Baumle, Amanda K. 2009. "The Cost of Parenthood: Unraveling the Effects of Sexual Orientation and Gender on Income." *Social Science Quarterly* 90:983–1002.

Bausman, Kent, and W. Richard Goe. 2004. "An Examination of the Link Between Employment Volatility and the Spatial Distribution of Property Crime Rates." *American Journal of Economics and Sociology* 63:665–695.

Bavier, Richard. July 2001. "Welfare Reform Data from the Survey of Income and Program Participation." *Monthly Labor Review,* 13–24.

Baxter, Janeen, and Erik Olin Wright. 2000. "The Glass Ceiling Hypothesis: A Comparative Study of the United States, Sweden, and Australia." *Gender & Society* 14:275–294.

Beaver, Patricia D. 1984. "Appalachian Cultural Adaptations: An Overview." Pp. 73–93 in *Cultural Adaptation to Mountain Environments,* edited by P. D. Beaver and B. L. Purrington. Athens: University of Georgia Press.

Beck, E. M., Patrick M. Horan, and Charles M. Tolbert, II. 1980. "Industrial Segmentation and Labor Market Discrimination." *Social Problems* 28:113–130.

Beckett, Katherine, Kris Nyrop, Lori Pfingst, and Melissa Bowen. 2005. "Drug Use, Drug Possession Arrests, and the Question of Race: Lessons from Seattle." *Social Problems* 52:419–441.

Beckfield, Jason. 2003. "Inequality in the World Polity: The Structure of International Organization." *American Sociological Review* 68:401–424.

Begley, Sharon. 2008. "The Myth of 'Best in the World.'" *Newsweek,* March 31, 47.

Behrens, Angela, Christopher Uggen, and Jeff Manza. 2003. "Ballot Manipulation and the 'Menace of Negro Domination': Racial Threat and Felon Disenfranchisement in the United States, 1850–2002." *American Journal of Sociology* 109:559–605.

Beland, Daniel. 2008. *States of Global Insecurity.* New York: Worth.

Bell, Winifred. 1987. *Contemporary Social Welfare.* New York: Macmillan.

Bellas, Marcia L. 1994. "Comparable Worth in Academia: The Effects of Faculty Salaries of the Sex Composition and Labor-Market Conditions of Academic Disciplines." *American Sociological Review* 59:807–821.

Beller, Emily. 2009. "Bringing Intergenerational Social Mobility Research into the Twenty-First Century: Why Mothers Matter." *American Sociological Review* 74:507–528.

Bem, Sandra L., and Daryl J. Bem. 1970. "Case Study of a Nonconscious Ideology: Training the Woman to Know Her Place." Pp. 89–99 in *Beliefs, Attitudes and Human Affairs,* edited by D. J. Bem. Belmont, CA: Brooks/Cole.

Benard, Stephen, and Shelley J. Correll. 2010. "Normative Discrimination and the Motherhood Penalty." *Gender & Society* 24:616–646.

Benokraitis, Nijole V., and Joe R. Feagin. 1986. *Modern Sexism.* Englewood Cliffs, NJ: Prentice Hall.

Bensman, Joseph. 1972. "Status Communities in an Urban Society: The Musical Community." Pp. 113–130 in *Status Communities in Modern Society,* edited by H. R. Stub. Hinsdale, IL: Dryden.

Benson, Michael L., and Esteban Walker. 1988. "Sentencing the White-Collar Offender." *American Sociological Review* 53:294–302.

Benston, Margaret. 1969. "The Political Economy of Women's Liberation." *Monthly Review* 21:15–16.

Berg, Justin Allen. 2009. "Core Networks and Whites' Attitudes Toward Immigrants and Immigration Policy." *Public Opinion Quarterly* 73:7–31.

Berger, Christian, and Philip Rodkin. 2009. "Male and Female Victims of Male Bullies: Social Status Differences by Gender and Informant Source." *Sex Roles* 61:72–84.

Berger, J., P. Cohen, and M. Zelditch, Jr. 1972. "Status Characteristics and Social Interaction." *American Sociological Review* 37:241–255.

Berger, Joseph, and M. Hamit Fisek. 2006. "Diffuse Status Characteristics and the Spread of Status Value: A Formal Theory." *American Journal of Sociology* 111:1038–1079.

Berger, J[oseph]., M. H[amit]. Fisek, R. Z. Norman, and M. Zelditch, Jr. 1977. *Status Characteristics and Social Interaction: An Expectation States Approach.* New York: Elsevier.

Bergmann, Barbara R. 1974. "Occupational Segregation, Wages and Profits When Employers Discriminate by Race or Sex." *Eastern Economic Journal* 1:103–110.

Bergmann, Barbara R. 2006. "Reducing Inequality: Merit Goods vs. Income Grants." *Dissent,* Winter:67–72.

Berk, Richard A., Kenneth J. Lenihan, and Peter H. Rossi. 1980. "Crime and Poverty: Some Experimental Evidence from Ex-Offenders." *American Sociological Review* 45:766–786.

Bernard, Jessie. 1972. *The Sex Game.* New York: Atheneum.

Bernstein, Aaron. February 26, 1996. "Is America Becoming More of a Class Society?" *BusinessWeek,* 86–96.

Bernstein, Irving. 1960. *The Lean Years: A History of the American Worker 1920–1933.* Boston: Houghton Mifflin.

Bernstein, Jared, Elizabeth McNichol, and Andrew Nicholas. April 2008. *Pulling Apart: A State-by-State Analysis of Income Trends.* Washington, D.C.: Center on Budget and Policy Priorities.

Bernstein, Jared, and Heidi Shierholz. 2008. "A Decade of Decline: The Erosion of Employer-Provided Health Care in the United States and California, 1995–2006." *EPI Briefing Paper* No. 209. Washington, D.C.: Economic Policy Institute.

Berry, Chris, Fran Martin, and Audrey Yue, eds., 2003. "Introduction: Beep-Click-Link." Pp. 1–18 in *Mobile Cultures: New Media in Queer Asia,* edited by C. Berry, F. Martin, and A. Yue. Durham, NC: Duke University Press.

Bertrand, Marianne, and Kevin F. Hallock. 2001. "The Gender Gap in Top Corporate Jobs." *Industrial and Labor Relations Review* 55:3–21.

Beteille, Andre. 1996. *Caste, Class, and Power: Changing Patterns of Stratification in a Tanjore Village,* 2nd ed. New Delhi: Oxford University Press.

Bibb, Robert, and William H. Form. 1977. "The Effects of Industrial, Occupational, and Sex Stratification on Wages in Blue-Collar Markets." *Social Forces* 55:974–996.

Biddle, Jeff E., and Daniel S. Hamermesh. 1998. "Beauty, Productivity, and Discrimination: Lawyers' Looks and Lucre." *Journal of Labor Economics* 16:172–201.

Bielby, Denise D., and William T. Bielby. 1988. "She Works Hard for the Money: Household Responsibilities and the Allocation of Work Effort." *American Journal of Sociology* 93:1031–1059.

Billings, Dwight B., and Kathleen M. Blee. 2000. *The Road to Poverty.* Cambridge: Cambridge University Press.

Birchfield, Vicki L. 2008. *Income Inequality in Capitalist Democracies.* University Park: Pennsylvania State University Press.

Bishop, Bill. 2008. *The Big Sort: Why the Clustering of Like-Minded America is Tearing Us Apart.* Boston: Houghton Mifflin.

Bittman, Michael, Paula England, Nancy Folbre, Liana Sayer, and George Matheson. 2003. "When Does Gender Trump Money? Bargaining and Time in Household Work." *American Journal of Sociology* 109:186–214.

Bjornstrom, Eileen E. S., Robert L. Kaufman, Ruth D. Peterson, and Michael D. Slater. 2010. "Race and Ethnic Representations of Lawbreakers and Victims in Crime News: A National Stud of Television Coverage." *Social Problems* 57:269–293.

Black, Dan, Gary Gates, Seth Sanders, and Lowell Taylor. 2000. "Demographics of the Gay and

Lesbian Population in the United States: Evidence from Available Systematic Data Sources." *Demography* 37:139–154.

Black, Dan A., Seth G. Sanders, and Lowell J. Taylor. 2007. "The Economics of Lesbian and Gay Families." *Journal of Economic Perspectives* 21(2):53–70.

Black, Sandra E., and Elizabeth Brainerd. 2004. "Importing Equality? The Impact of Globalization on Gender Discrimination." *Industrial and Labor Relations Review* 57:540–559.

Blackless, M., A. Charuvastra, A. Derryck, A. Fausto-Sterling, K. Lauzanne, and E. Lee. "How Sexually Dimorphic Are We? Review and Synthesis." *American Journal of Human Biology* 12:151–166.

Blackwell, James E. 1985. *The Black Community: Diversity and Unity.* New York: Harper & Row.

Blair-Loy, Mary, and Jerry A. Jacobs. 2003. "Globalization, Work Hours, and the Care Deficit Among Stockbrokers." *Gender & Society* 17:230–249.

Blau, Francine D. 1978. "The Data on Women Workers, Past, Present, and Future." Pp. 29–62 in *Women Working,* edited by A. H. Stromberg and S. Harkess. Palo Alto, CA: Mayfield.

Blau, Francine D. 1984. "Occupational Segregation and Labor Market Discrimination." Pp. 117–143 in *Sex Segregation in the Workplace,* edited by B. F. Reskin. Washington, D.C.: National Academy Press.

Blau, Francine D., and Marianne A. Ferber. 1986. *The Economics of Women, Men, and Work.* Englewood Cliffs, NJ: Prentice Hall.

Blau, Francine D., and Carol L. Jusenius. 1976. "Economists' Approaches to Sex Segregation in the Labor Market: An Appraisal." *Signs: Journal of Women in Culture and Society* 1:181–199.

Blau, Judith R., and Peter M. Blau. 1982. "The Cost of Inequality: Metropolitan Structure and Violent Crime." *American Sociological Review* 47:114–129.

Blau, Peter M., and Otis Dudley Duncan. 1967. *The American Occupational Structure.* New York: Wiley.

Blauner, Robert. 1972. *Racial Oppression in America.* New York: Harper & Row.

Block, Fred. 1977. "The Ruling Class Does Not Rule: Notes on the Marxist Theory of the State." *Socialist Revolution* 7:6–28.

Bloom, Jack M. 1987. *Class, Race & the Civil Rights Movement.* Bloomington: Indiana University Press.

Bluestone, Barry. 1977. "The Characteristics of Marginal Industries." Pp. 97–102 in *Problems in Political Economy: An Urban Perspective,* edited by D. M. Gordon. Lexington, MA: D. C. Heath.

Blumberg, Rae Lesser. 1978. *Stratification: Socioeconomic and Sexual Inequality.* Dubuque, IA: William C. Brown.

Blumberg, Rae Lesser. 1984. "A General Theory of Gender Stratification." Pp. 23–101 in *Sociological Theory,* edited by R. Collins. San Francisco: Jossey-Bass.

Blumberg, Rhoda Lois. 1984. *Civil Rights: The 1960s Freedom Struggle.* Boston: Twayne.

Boellstorff, Tom. 2003. "I Knew It was Me: Mass Media, 'Globalization,' and Lesbian and Gay Indonesia." Pp. 19–51 in *Mobile Cultures: New Media in Queer Asia,* edited by C. Berry, F. Martin, and A. Yue. Durham, NC: Duke University Press.

Boer, J. Tom, Manuel Pastor, Jr., James L. Sadd, and Lori D. Snyder. 1997. "Is There Environmental Racism? The Demographics of Hazardous Waste in Los Angeles County." *Social Science Quarterly* 78:793–810.

Bolgar, Hedda. 2009. "A Century of Essential Feminism." *Studies in Gender and Sexuality* 10:195–199.

Bolzendahl, Catherine, and Clem Brooks. 2007. "Women's Political Representation and Welfare State Spending in 12 Capitalist Democracies." *Social Forces* 85:1509–1534.

Bonacich, Edna. 1980. "Class Approaches to Ethnicity and Race." *Insurgent Sociologist* 10(2).

Bonilla-Silva, Eduardo. 2004. "From Bi-Racial to Tri-Racial: The Emergence of A New Racial Stratification System in the United States." Pp. 224–239 in *Skin Deep: How Race and Complexion Matter in the "Color-Blind" Era,* edited by C. Herring, V. Keith, and H. D. Horton. Chicago: University of Illinois.

Boone, Christopher G., and Ali Modarres. 1999. "Creating a Toxic Neighborhood in Los Angeles County." *Urban Affairs Review* 35:163–187.

Boorstin, Daniel J. 1967. *The Americans.* New York: Vintage.

Bornschier, Volker, and C. Chase-Dunn. 1985. *Transnational Corporations and Underdevelopment.* New York: Praeger.

Bornschier, Volker, and Thanh-Huyen Ballmer-Cao. 1979. "Income Inequality: A Cross-National Study of the Relationship between MNC-Penetration, Dimensions of the Power Structure and Income Distribution." *American Sociological Review* 44:487–506.

Bositis, David A. 2007. "Black Political Power in the New Century." Pp. 221–242 in *The Black Metropolis in the Twenty-First Century,* edited by R. D. Bullard. Lanham, MD: Rowman & Littlefield.

Bottomore, Tom B. 1964. *Elites and Society.* Baltimore: Penguin.

Bottomore, Tom B. 1966. *Classes in Modern Society.* New York: Pantheon.

Bottomore, Tom B., and Maximilien Rubel, eds. 1956. *Karl Marx: Selected Writings in Sociology and Social Philosophy.* New York: McGraw-Hill.

Bourdieu, Pierre. 1977a. "Cultural Reproduction and Social Reproduction." Pp. 487–510 in *Power and Ideology in Education,* edited by J. Karabel and A. H. Halsey. New York: Oxford University Press.

Bourdieu, Pierre. 1977b. *Outline of a Theory of Practice.* Cambridge: Cambridge University Press.

Bourdieu, Pierre. 1990. *The Logic of Practice.* Stanford, CA: Stanford University Press.

Bourdieu, Pierre, and Loic J. C. Wacquant. 1992. *An Invitation to Reflexive Sociology.* Cambridge, MA: Polity Press.

Bowers, Melanie, and Robert R. Preuhs. 2009. "Collateral Consequences of a Collateral Penalty: The Negative Effect of Felon Disenfranchisement Laws on the Political Participation of Nonfelons." *Social Science Quarterly* 90:722–743.

Bowles, Samuel, and Herbert Gintis. 1976. *Schooling in Capitalist America.* New York: Basic Books.

Bowles, Samuel, and Herbert Gintis. 2002. "*Schooling in Capitalist America* Revisited." *Sociology of Education* 75:1–18.

Bowles, Samuel, Herbert Gintis, and Melissa Osborne Groves, eds. 2005. *Unequal Chances: Family Background and Economic Success.* Princeton, NJ: Princeton University Press.

Bowman, Phillip J., Ray Muhammad, and Mosi Ifatunji. 2004. "Skin Tone, Class, and Racial Attitudes Among African Americans." Pp. 128–58 in *Skin Deep: How Race and Complexion Matter in the "Color-Blind" Era,* edited by C. Herring, V. Keith, and H. D. Horton. Chicago: University of Illinois.

Bowser, Benjamin P. 2007. *The Black Middle Class: Social Mobility—and Vulnerability.* Boulder, CO: Lynne Rienner Publishers.

Box, Steven. 1983. *Power, Crime, and Mystification.* London: Tavistock.

Bozick, Robert, Karl Alexander, Doris Entwisle, Susan Dauber, and Kerri Kerr. 2010. "Framing the Future: Revisiting the Place of Educational Expectations in Status Attainment." *Social Forces* 88:2027–2052.

"BP Pleads Guilty, Will Pay $20 Million Penalty for Oil Spill." 2008. *White-Collar Crime* 22:12–13.

Brady, David. 2009. *Rich Democracies, Poor People.* New York: Oxford University Press.

Brady, David, Andrew S. Fullerton, and Jennifer Moren Cross. 2009. "Putting Poverty in Political Context: A Multi-Level Analysis of Adult Poverty Across 18 Affluent Democracies." *Social Forces* 88:271–300.

Brady, David, and Kevin T. Leicht. 2008. "Party to Inequality: Right Party Power and Income Inequality in Affluent Western Democracies." *Research in Social Stratification and Mobility* 26:77–106.

Braithwaite, John. 1981. "The Myth of Social Class and Criminality Reconsidered." *American Sociological Review* 46:36–57.

Breines, Winifred. 2007. "Struggling to Connect: White and Black Feminism in the Movement Years." *Contexts* 6:18–24.

Bremner, Robert H. 1956. *From the Depths: The Discovery of Poverty in the United States.* New York: New York University Press.

Brett, Regina. February 5, 1989. "Myths Disguise Extent, Severity of Problem." *Akron Beacon Journal,* A7.

Brett, Regina. June 8, 1999. "Cliques Draw Clear Lines." *Akron Beacon Journal,* A1 and A6.

Bricker, Jesse, Brian Bucks, Arthur Kennickell, Traci Mach, and Kevin Moore. 2011. *Surveying the Aftermath of the Storm: Changes in Family Finances from 2007 to 2009.* Washington, D.C.: Federal Reserve Board.

Brimeyer, Ted M. 2008. "Research Note: Religious Affiliation and Poverty Explanations: Individual, Structural, and Divine." *Sociological Focus* 41:226–237.

Brodkin, Karen. 2008. "How Jews Became White Folks." Pp. 41–53 in *White Privilege,* edited by R. Rothenberg. New York: Worth.

Brody, David, ed. 1971. *The American Labor Movement.* New York: Harper & Row.

Brody, David. 1980. *Workers in Industrial America: Essays on the Twentieth Century Struggle.* New York: Oxford University Press.

Brooke, James. October 13, 1998. "Gay Man Dies from Attack, Fanning Outrage and Debate." *New York Times,* A1, A17.

Brooks, Clem. 1994. "Class Consciousness and Politics in Comparative Perspective." *Social Science Research* 23:167–195.

Brooks, John. 1979. *Showing Off in America.* Boston: Little, Brown.

Broom, Leonard , and Robert G. Cushing. 1977. "A Modest Test of an Immodest Theory." *American Sociological Review* 42:157–169.

Brown, B. Bradford, and Mary Jane Lohr. 1987. "Peer-Group Affiliation and Adolescent Self-Esteem: An Integration of Ego-Identity and Symbolic-Interaction Theories." *Journal of Personality and Social Psychology* 52:47–55.

Browne, Irene, and Joya Misra. 2003. "The Intersection of Gender and Race in the Labor Market." *Annual Review of Sociology* 29:487–513.

Bruins, Jan. 1999. "Social Power and Influence Tactics: A Theoretical Introduction." *Journal of Social Issues* 55:7–14.

Brumbaugh, Stagey M., Laura A. Sanchez, Steven L. Nock, and James D. Wright. 2008. "Attitudes Toward Gay Marriage in States Undergoing Marriage Law Transformation." *Journal of Marriage & Family* 70:345–359.

Brunsma, David L., and Kerry Ann Rockquemore. 2002. "What Does 'Black' Mean? Exploring the Epistemological Stranglehold of Racial Categorization." *Critical Sociology* 28:101–121.

Bucks, Brian K., Arthur B. Kennickell, Traci L. Mach, and Kevin B. Moore. 2009. "Changes in U.S. Family Finances from 2004 to 2007: Evidence from the Survey of Consumer Finances." *Federal Reserve Bulletin,* February:A12–A52.

Bucks, Brian K., Arthur B. Kennickell, and Kevin B. Moore. 2006. "Recent Changes in U.S. Family Finances: Evidence from the 2001 and 2004 Survey of Consumer Finances." *Federal Reserve Bulletin,* March 22:A1–A38.

Bullard, Robert D. 1983. "Solid Waste Sites and the Black Houston Community." *Sociological Inquiry* 53:273–288.

Bullock, Heather E., and Wendy M. Limbert. 2003. "Scaling the Socioeconomic Ladder: Low-Income Women's Perceptions of Class Status and Opportunity." *Journal of Social Issues* 59:693–709.

Burr, Jeffrey A., John T. Hartman, and Donald W. Matteson. 1999. "Black Suicide in the U.S. Metropolitan Areas: An Examination of the Racial Inequality and Social Integration-Regulation Hypotheses." *Social Forces* 77:1049–1081.

Burri, Regula Valerie. 2008. "Doing Distinctions: Boundary Work and Symbolic Capital in Radiology." *Social Studies of Science* 38:37–64.

Bussmann, Kai-D, and Markus M. Werle. 2006. "Addressing Crime in Companies." *British Journal of Criminology* 46:1128–1144.

Butler, Judith. 1999. *Gender Trouble.* New York: Routledge.

Butler, Sandra S., Janine Corbett, Crystal Bond, and Chris Hastedt. 2008. "Long-Term TANF Participants and Barriers to Employment: A Qualitative Study in Maine." *Journal of Sociology & Social Welfare* 35:49–69.

Button, James W., Barbara A. Rienzo, and Kenneth D. Wald. 1997. *Private Lives, Public Conflicts.* Washington, D.C.: Congressional Quarterly Press.

Buzuvis, Erin E. 2010. "Sidelined: Title IX Retaliation Cases and Women's Leadership in College Athletics." *Duke Journal of Gender Law & Policy* 17:1–45.

Bye, Lynn, and Jamie Partridge. 2003. "Factors Affecting Mental Illness Hospitalization Rates: Analysis of State-Level Panel Data." *The Social Science Journal* 40:33–47.

Cain, Glen G. December 1976. "The Challenge of Segmented Labor Market Theories to Orthodox Theory." *Journal of Economic Literature* 14: 1215–1257.

Cairns, Robert B., and Beverley D. Cairns. 1994. *Lifelines and Risks: Pathways of Youth in Our Time.* Cambridge: Cambridge University Press.

Campbell, Andrea Louise. 2007. "Parties, Electoral Participation, and Shifting Voting Blocs." Pp. 68–102 in *The Transformation of American Politics,* edited by P. Pierson and T. Skocpol. Princeton, NJ: Princeton University Press.

Campbell, Lori Ann, and Robert L. Kaufman. 2006. "Racial Differences in Household Wealth: Beyond Black and White." *Research in Social Stratification and Mobility* 24:131–152.

Campo-Flores, and Howard Fineman. 2005. "A Latin Power Surge." *Newsweek,* May 30, 25–31.

Cancian, Maria. 2001. "Rhetoric and Reality of Work-Based Welfare Reform." *Social Work* 46:309–314.

Cancian, Maria, and Daniel R. Meyer. 2004. "Alternative Measures of Economic Success among TANF Participants: Avoiding Poverty, Hardship, and Dependence on Public Assistance." *Journal of Policy Analysis and Management* 23:531–548.

Cantor, David, and Kenneth C. Land. 1985. "Unemployment and Crime Rates in the Post–World War II United States: A Theoretical and Empirical Analysis." *American Sociological Review* 50:317–332.

Caplan, Pat, ed. 1987. *The Cultural Construction of Sexuality.* London: Tavistock.

Carawan, Guy, and Candie Carawan. 1975. *Voices from the Mountains.* New York: Knopf.

Carbone-Lopez, Kristin, Finn-Aage Esbensen, and Bradley T. Brick. 2010. "Correlates and Consequences of Peer Victimization: Gender Differences in Direct and Indirect Forms of Bullying." *Youth Violence and Juvenile Justice* 8:332–350.

Cardiff, Patrick. 1999. "Profiles of Poor Counties: Some Empirical Evidence." HHES/SAIPE FB3-1065. Washington, D.C.: U.S. Census Bureau.

Cardoso, F. H. 1977. "The Consumption of Dependency Theory in the United States." *Latin American Research Review* 12:7–24.

Carli, Linda L. 1999. "Gender, Interpersonal Power, and Social Influence." *Journal of Social Issues* 55:81–99.

Carli, Linda L., and Alice H. Eagly. 2007. "Overcoming Resistance to Women Leaders." Pp. 127–148 in *Women and Leadership: The State of Play and Strategies for Change,* edited by B. Kellerman and D. L. Rhode. San Francisco: Wiley.

Carlson, Lewis H., and George A. Colburn. 1972. *In Their Place: White America Defines Her Minorities 1850–1950.* New York: Wiley.

Carmichael, Stokely, and Charles V. Hamilton. 1967. *Black Power.* New York: Vintage.

Carpenter, Christopher S. 2007. "Revisiting the Income Penalty for Behaviorally Gay Men: Evidence from NHANES III." *Labor Economics* 14:25–34.

Carr, Deborah. 2005. "Political Polls." *Contexts* 4:32.

Carswell, Andrew T., and Douglas C. Bachtel. 2009. "Mortgage Fraud: A Risk Factor Analysis of Affected Communities." *Crime, Law, and Social Change* 52:347–364.

Carter, Prudence L. 2003. "'Black' Cultural Capital, Status Positioning, and Schooling Conflicts for Low-Income African American Youth." *Social Problems* 50:136–155.

Carter, Scott J., Mamadi Corra, and Shannon Carter. 2009. "The Interaction of Race and Gender: Changing Gender-Role Attitudes, 1974–2006." *Social Science Quarterly* 90:196–211.

Case, Mary Anne C. 1995. "Disaggregating Gender from Sex and Sexual Orientation: The Effeminate Man in the Law and Feminist Jurisprudence." *Yale Law Journal* 105:2–3.

Cash, Thomas F., and Patricia E. Henry. 1995. "Women's Body Images: The Results of a National Survey in the U.S.A." *Sex Roles* 33:19–28.

Caspi, Avshalom, Terrie E. Moffitt, Bradley E. Entner Wright, and Phil A. Silva. 1998. "Early Failure in the Labor Market: Childhood and Adolescent Predictors of Unemployment in the Transition to Adulthood." *American Sociological Review* 63:424–451.

Castilla, Emilio J. 2008. "Gender, Race, and Meritocracy in Organizational Careers." *American Journal of Sociology* 113:1479–1526.

Castle, Stephen. September 20, 2010. "Anti-Immigration Party Wins First Seats in Swedish Parliament." *New York Times,* A5.

Catalyst. 2007. *The Double-Bind Dilemma for Women in Leadership: Damned If You Do, Doomed If You Don't.* New York: Catalyst.

Catanzarite, Lisa. 2003. "Race-Gender Composition and Occupational Pay Degradation." *Social Problems* 50:14–37.

Cauthen, Kenneth. 1987. *The Passion for Equality.* Totowa, NJ: Rowman & Littlefield.

Cech, Erin A., and Mary Blair-Loy. 2010. "Perceiving Glass Ceilings? Meritocratic versus Structural Explanations of Gender Inequality among Women in Science and Technology." *Social Problems* 57:371–397.

Center for Responsive Politics. 2008. "U.S. Election Will Cost $5.3 Billion, Center for Responsive Politics Predicts." Available at www.opensecrets.org/news/2008/10/us-election-will-cost-53-billi.html.

Center for Responsive Politics. 2010. "Super PACS." Available at www.opensecrets.org/pacs/superpacs.php?cycle=2010.

Center for Women's Business Research. Accessed on September 1, 2008, at www.nfwbo.org.

Ceobanu, Alin M., and Xavier Escandell. 2010. "Comparative Analyses of Public Attitudes Toward Immigrants and Immigration Using Multinational Survey Data: A Review of Theories and Research." *Annual Review of Sociology* 36:309–328.

Cha, Youngjoo. 2010. "Reinforcing Separate Spheres." *American Sociological Review* 75:303–329.

Chafe, William H. 1977. *Women and Equality: Changing Patterns in American Culture.* New York: Oxford University Press.

Chafetz, Janet Saltzman. 1984. *Sex and Advantage: A Comparative, Macro-Structural Theory of Sex Stratification.* Totowa, NJ: Rowman & Allanheld.

Chafetz, Janet Saltzman. 1988. *Feminist Sociology: An Overview of Contemporary Theories.* Itasca, IL: F. E. Peacock.

Chan, Tak Wing, and John H. Goldthorpe. 2004. "Is There a Status Order in Contemporary British Society?" *European Sociological Review* 20:383–401.

Chan, Tak Wing, and John H. Goldthorpe. 2007. "Class and Status: The Conceptual Distinction and its Empirical Relevance." *American Sociological Review* 72:512–532.

Chancellor, Carl. May 10, 2008. "Violent Attacks Plague the Homeless." *Akron Beacon Journal,* A1–A4.

Charles, Camille Zubrinsky. 2003. "The Dynamics of Racial Residential Segregation." *Annual Review of Sociology* 29:167–207.

Chen, Martha, Joann Vanek, Francie Lund, James Heintz, Renana Jhabvala, and Christine Bonner. 2005. *Progress of the World's Women 2005: Women, Work & Poverty.* New York: United Nations Development Fund for Women.

Chinn, Menzie D., and Robert W. Fairlie. 2005. "Assessing the Global Digital Divide." *La Follette Policy Report* 15:1–2, 10–14.

Chira, Susan. February 12, 1992. "Bias against Girls Is Found Rife in Schools, with Lasting Damage." *New York Times,* A1, B6.

Chiricos, T. G. 1987. "Rates of Crime and Unemployment: An Analysis of Aggregate Research Evidence." *Social Problems* 34:187–212.

Chiricos, Ted, Ranee McEntire, and Marc Gertz. 2001. "Perceived Racial and Ethnic Composition of Neighborhood and Perceived Risk of Crime." *Social Problems* 48:322–340.

Chiricos, Ted, Kelly Welch, and Marc Gertz. 2004. "Racial Typification of Crime and Support for Punitive Measures." *Criminology* 42:359–389.

Chiu, Ming Ming. 2010. "Effects of Inequality, Family and School on Mathematics Achievement: Country and Student Differences." *Social Forces* 88:1645–1676.

Choi, Wai Kit. 2006. "Proletarianization, the Informal Proletariat, and 'Marx' in the Era of Globalization." Paper presented at Annual Meeting of American Sociological Association, Montreal, August 10.

Chow, Esther Ngan-ling. 2003. "Gender Matters: Studying Globalization and Social Change in the 21st Century." *International Sociology* 18:443–460.

Chura, Hillary. April 28, 2009. "People with Service Jobs Feel Economic Pain Early." *New York Times,* B5.

Cifuentes, Manuel, Grace Sembajwe, SangWoo Tak, Rebecca Gore, David Kriebel, and Laura Punnett. 2008. "The Association of Major Depressive Episodes with Income Inequality and the Human Development Index." *Social Science & Medicine* 67:529–539.

Cigler, Allan J., and Burdett A. Loomis, eds. 1995. *Interest Group Politics.* Washington, D.C.: Congressional Quarterly.

Clarke, Stevens H., and Gary G. Koch. 1976. "The Influence of Income and Other Factors on Whether Criminal Defendants Go to Prison." *Law and Society Review* 11:57–92.

Clawson, Dan, and Mary Ann Clawson. 1999. "What Has Happened to the U.S. Labor Movement? Union Decline and Renewal." *Annual Review of Sociology* 25:95–119.

Clawson, Rosalee A., and Rakuya Trice. 2000. "Poverty as We Know It: Media Portrayals of the Poor." *Public Opinion Quarterly* 64:53–64.

Cleary, Paul D., and David Mechanic. 1983. "Sex Differences in Psychological Distress among Married People." *Journal of Health and Social Behavior* 24:111–121.

Cleaveland, Carol. 2008. "'A Black Benefit': Racial Prejudice Among White Welfare Recipients in a Low-Income Neighborhood." *Journal of Progressive Human Services* 19:71–90.

Clinard, Marshall B. 1946. "Criminological Theories of Violations of Wartime Regulations." *American Sociological Review* 11:258–270.

Cohen, Lisa E., Joseph P. Broschak, and Heather A. Haveman. 1998. "And Then There Were More? The Effect of Organizational Sex Composition on the Hiring and Promotion of Managers." *American Sociological Review* 63:711–727.

Cohen, Philip N. 2007. "Working for the Woman? Female Managers and the Gender Wage Gap." *American Sociological Review* 72:681–704.

Cohen, Philip N., and Matt L. Huffman. 2003. "Occupational Segregation and the Devaluation of Women's Work Across U.S. Labor Markets." *Social Forces* 81:881–908.

Cohen, Sharon, and Deborah Hastings. June 2, 2002. "Exonerated, 110 Inmates Unprepared." *Akron Beacon Journal,* A1, A10.

Cole, Elizabeth R., and Safiya R. Omari. 2003. "Race, Class and the Dilemmas of Upward Mobility for African Americans." *Journal of Social Issues* 59:785–802.

College Board. 2010. *Education Pays 2010.* New York: College Board.

Collins, Patricia Hill. 1990. *Black Feminist Theory.* Boston: Unwin Hyman.

Collins, Randall. 1971. "Functional and Conflict Theories of Educational Stratification." *American Sociological Review* 36:1002–1019.

Collins, Randall. 1986. *Weberian Sociological Theory.* Cambridge: Cambridge University Press.

Collins, Randall. 1988. *Theoretical Sociology.* New York: Harcourt Brace Jovanovich.

Collins, Sharon. 1983. "The Making of the Black Middle Class." *Social Problems* 30:369–381.

Collins, Sharon. 1993. "Blacks on the Bubble." *The Sociological Quarterly* 34:429–447.

Condron, Dennis J. 2009. "Social Class, School and Non-School Environments, and Black/White Inequalities in Children's Learning." *American Sociological Review* 74:683–708.

Conley, Dalton. 2000. *Honky.* Berkeley: University of California Press.

Connell, Catherine. 2009. "Dangerous Disclosures: How Occupational Context Shapes LGB Teachers' Presentations of Self." Paper presented at the annual meeting of the American Sociological Association, San Francisco, August 8.

Connell, Catherine. 2010. *"Doing, Undoing, and Redoing Gender?" Gender & Society* 24:31–55.

Connell, R. W. 2005. "Masculinities and Globalization." Pp. 36–48 in *Gender Through the Prism of Difference,* edited by M. B. Zinn, P. Hondagneu-Sotelo, and M. A. Messner. New York: Oxford University Press.

Connolly, William E. 1969. *The Bias of Pluralism.* New York: Lieber-Atherton.

Cookson, Peter W., Jr., and Caroline Hodges Persell. 1985. *Preparing for Power: America's Elite Boarding Schools.* New York: Basic Books.

Coontz, Stephanie, and Peta Henderson, eds. 1986. *Women's Work, Men's Property: The Origins of Gender and Class.* London: Verso.

Corcoran, M. 1995. "Rags to Rags: Poverty and Mobility in the United States." *Annual Review of Sociology* 21:237–267.

Corcoran, Mary, Sandra K. Danziger, Ariel Kalil, and Kristin S. Seefeldt. 2000. "How Welfare Reform Is Affecting Women's Work." *Annual Review of Sociology* 26:241–269.

Coreil, Jeannine, and Patricia A. Marshall. 1982. "Locus of Illness Control: A Cross Cultural Study." *Human Organizations* 41:131–138.

Coser, Lewis A. 1971. *Masters of Sociological Thought.* New York: Harcourt Brace Jovanovich.

Cott, Nancy F. 1986. "Feminist Theory and Feminist Movements: The Past Before Us." Pp. 49–62 in *What Is Feminism?* edited by J. Mitchell and A. Oakley. New York: Pantheon.

Cott, Nancy F. 1987. *The Grounding of Modern Feminism.* New Haven, CT: Yale University Press.

Cotter, David A., Joan M. Hermsen, and Reeve Vanneman. 2003. "The Effects of Occupational Gender Segregation Across Race." *Sociological Quarterly* 44:17–36.

Coverdill, James E. 1988. "The Dual Economy and Size Differences in Earnings." *Social Forces* 66:970–993.

Coverdill, James E. 1998. "Personal Contacts and Post-Hire Job Outcomes: Theoretical and Empirical Notes on the Significance of Matching Methods." *Research in Social Stratification and Mobility* 16:247–269.

Cox, Oliver C. 1948. *Caste, Class and Race.* New York: Monthly Review Press.

Cox, Oliver C. 1959. *The Foundations of Capitalism.* New York: Philosophical Library.

Cox, Oliver C. 1964. *Capitalism as a System.* New York: Monthly Review Press.

Cox, Oliver C. 1976. *Race Relations: Elements and Social Dynamics.* Detroit: Wayne State University Press.

CQ Roll Call. November 4, 2010. "Guide to the New Congress." Washington, D.C.: Roll Call, Inc.

Craig, Kellina M. 2002. "Examining Hate-Motivated Aggression: A Review of the Social Psychological Literature on Hate Crimes as a Distinct Form of Aggression." *Aggression and Violent Behavior* 7:85–101.

Craig, Shelley L., Edmon W. Tucker, and Eric F. Wagner. 2008. "Empowering Lesbian, Gay, Bisexual, and Transgender Youth: Lessons Learned From a Safe Schools Summit." *Journal of Gay & Lesbian Social Services* 20:237–252.

Crandell, N. Fredric, and Marc J. Wallace, Jr. 1998. *Work & Rewards in the Virtual Workplace.* New York: American Management Association.

Crane, Diane. 2000. *Fashion and Its Social Agendas.* Chicago: University of Chicago.

Critelli, Filomena, and Marsha Schwam-Harris. 2010. "'In a Bind': Foster Mothers' Experiences with Welfare Reform." *Journal of Children & Poverty* 16:123–143.

Crompton, Rosemary, and Gareth Jones. 1984. *White Collar Proletariat: Deskilling and Gender in Clerical Work.* Philadelphia: Temple University Press.

Crosnoe, Robert. 2009. "Low-Income Students and the Socioeconomic Composition of Public High Schools." *American Sociological Review* 74:709–730.

Crosnoe, Robert, Kenneth Frank, and Anna Strassmann Mueller. 2008. "Gender, Body Size and Social Relations in American High Schools." *Social Forces* 86:1189–1216.

Crowder, Kyle, Scott J. South, and Erick Chavez. 2006. "Wealth, Race, and Inter-Neighborhood Migration." *American Sociological Review* 71:72–94.

Crutchfield, Robert D. 1995. "Ethnicity, Labor Markets, and Crime." Pp. 194–211 in *Ethnicity, Race, and Crime,* edited by D. F. Hawkins. Albany: State University of New York Press.

Crutchfield, Robert D., and David Pettinicchio. 2009. "'Cultures of Inequality': Ethnicity, Immigration, Social Welfare, and Imprisonment." *Annals of the American Academy of Political and Social Science* 623:134–147.

Curran, Debra A. 1983. "Judicial Discretion and Defendant's Sex." *Criminology* 21:41–58.

Currier, Ashley. 2010. "Political Homophobia in Postcolonial Namibia." *Gender & Society* 24:110–129.

D'Alessio, Stewart J., and Lisa Stolzenberg. 1993. "Socioeconomic Status and the Sentencing of the Traditional Offender." *Journal of Criminal Justice* 21:71–74.

D'Augelli, A. R., and A. H. Grossman. 2001. "Disclosure of Sexual Orientation, Victimization, and Mental Health among Lesbian, Gay, and Bisexual Older Adults." *Journal of Interpersonal Violence* 16:1008–1027.

D'Augelli, Anthony R. 1998. "Developmental Implications of Victimization of Lesbian, Gay, and Bisexual Youths." Pp. 187–210 in *Stigma and Sexual Orientation,* edited by G. M. Herek. Thousand Oaks, CA: Sage.

Dahrendorf, Ralf. 1958. "Out of Utopia: Toward a Reorientation of Sociological Analysis." *American Journal of Sociology* 64:115–127.

Dahrendorf, Ralf. 1959. *Class and Class Conflict in Industrial Society.* Stanford, CA: Stanford University Press.

Dahrendorf, Ralf. 1970. "On the Origin of Inequality Among Men." Pp. 3–30 in *The Logic of Social Hierarchies,* edited by E. O. Laumann, P. M. Siegel, and R. W. Hodge. Chicago: Markham.

Dale, Maryclaire. May 13, 2005. "Pension Cuts Hit Many Retirees." *Akron Beacon Journal,* D1–D2.

Damiano, Christin M. 1998/1999. "Lesbian Baiting in the Military: Institutionalized Sexual Harassment Under 'Don't Ask, Don't Tell, Don't Pursue.'" *American University Journal of Gender, Social Policy & the Law* 7:499–522.

Daniels, Glynis, and Samantha Friedman. 1999. "Spatial Inequality and the Distribution of Industrial Toxic Releases: Evidence from the 1990 TRI." *Social Science Quarterly* 80:244–262.

Danziger, Sandra K. 2010. "The Decline of Cash Welfare and Implications for Social Policy and Poverty." *Annual Review of Sociology* 36:523–545.

Danziger, Sheldon, and Sandra K. Danziger. 2006. "Poverty, Race, and Antipoverty Policy Before and After Hurricane Katrina." *Du Bois Review* 3:23–36.

Danziger, Sheldon H., Robert H. Haveman, and Robert D. Plotnick. 1986. "Antipoverty Policy: Effects on the Poor and the Nonpoor." Pp. 50–77 in *Fighting Poverty: What Works and What Doesn't,* edited by S. H. Danziger and D. H. Weinberg. Cambridge, MA: Harvard University Press.

Danziger, Sheldon, and David Wheeler. 1975. "The Economics of Crime: Punishment or Income Distribution." *Review of Social Economy* 33:113–131.

Dao, James. September 13, 2010. "Days After 'Don't Ask, Don't Tell' Ruling, Another Challenge Heads to Court." *New York Times,* A19–A20.

Davidson, Chandler, and Charles M. Gaitz. 1974. "Are the Poor Different? A Comparison of Work Behavior and Attitude among the Urban Poor and Nonpoor." *Social Problems* 22:229–245.

Davies, James B., Susanna Sandstrom, Anthony Shorrocks, and Edward N. Wolff. 2008. *The World Distribution of Household Wealth.* Discussion Paper No. 2008/03. United Nations University–World Institute for Development Economics Research.

Davis, James Allan, and Tom W. Smith. 1989. *General Social Surveys, 1972–1989.* Principal Investigator, James A. Davis; Director and Co-Principal Investigator, Tom W. Smith. NORC ed. Chicago: National Opinion Research Center, producer; Storrs, CT: Roper Center for Public Opinion Research, University of Connecticut, distributor.

Davis, James Allan, and Tom W. Smith. 1996. *General Social Surveys, 1972–1996.* Principal Investigator, James A. Davis; Co-Principal Investigator, Tom W. Smith. NORC ed. Chicago: National Opinion Research Center, producer; Storrs, CT: Roper Center for Public Opinion Research, University of Connecticut, distributor.

Davis, Kingsley. 1948–1949. *Human Society.* New York: Macmillan.

Davis, Kingsley, and Wilbert E. Moore. 1945. "Some Principles of Stratification." *American Sociological Review* 10:242–249.

Davis, Mike. 1992. *City of Quartz.* New York: Vintage.

De Jong, Gordon F., Deborah Roempke Graefe, and Tanja St. Pierre. 2005. "Welfare Reform and Interstate Migration of Poor Families." *Demography* 42:469–496.

Defina, Robert H., and Kishor Thanawala. 2004. "International Evidence on the Impact of Transfers and Taxes on Alternative Poverty Indexes." *Social Science Research* 33:322–338.

Della Fave, Richard. 1980. "The Meek Shall Not Inherit the Earth: Self-Evaluation and the Legitimacy of Stratification." *American Sociological Review* 45:955–971.

Demuth, Stephen, and Darrell Steffensmeier. 2004. "The Impact of Gender and Race-Ethnicity in the Pretrial Release Process." *Social Problems* 51:222–242.

Denney, Justin T., Richard B. Rogers, Patrick M. Krueger, and Tim Wadsworth. 2009. "Adult Suicide Mortality in the United States: Marital Status, Family Size, Socioeconomic Status, and Differences by Sex." *Social Science Quarterly* 90:1167–1185.

Department of Workforce Development. June 22, 1999. *Wisconsin Works Overview.* Madison, WI: Author.

Derber, Charles. 2000. *Corporation Nation.* New York: St. Martin's Griffin.

Devine, Joel A., Joseph F. Sheley, and M. Dwayne Smith. 1988. "Macroeconomic and Social-Control Policy Influences on Crime Rate Changes. 1948–1985." *American Sociological Review* 53:407–420.

DeVos, George A., and Hiroshi Wagatsuma, eds. 1966. *Japan's Invisible Race: Caste in Culture and Personality.* Berkeley: University of California Press.

DeVos, George A., and William O. Wetherall. 1983. *Japan's Minorities: Burakumin, Koreans, Ainu and Okinawans.* London: Minority Rights Group.

Dey, Judy Goldberg, and Catherine Hill. 2007. *Behind the Pay Gap.* Washington, D.C.: American Association of University Women Educational Foundation.

Diamond, Diana. 2009. "The Fourth Wave of Feminism: Psychoanalytic Perspectives." *Studies in Gender and Sexuality* 10:213–223.

Dienstfrey, Eric. 2007. *Poll:CNN Homosexuality.* Accessed on September 7, 2008, at www.pollster.com/blogs/poll_cnn_homosexuality.php.

DiMaggio, Paul, and Bart Bonikowski. 2008. "Make Money Surfing the Web? The Impact of Internet Use on the Earnings of U.S. Workers." *American Sociological Review* 73:227–250.

Dionne, E. J. June 13, 2004. "'E Pluribus Unum'?" *Akron Beacon Journal,* B2.

DiPlacido, Joanne. 1998. "Minority Stress among Lesbians, Gay Men, and Bisexuals." Pp. 138–159 in *Stigma and Sexual Orientation,* edited by G. M. Herek. Thousand Oaks, CA: Sage.

DiPrete, Thomas A. 2007. "Is This a Great Country? Upward Mobility and the Chance for Riches in Contemporary America." *Research in Social Stratification and Mobility* 25:89–95.

DiPrete, Thomas, and Margaret L. Krecker. 1991. "Occupational Linkages and Job Mobility within and across Organizations." *Research in Social Stratification and Mobility* 20:91–131.

DiPrete, Thomas A., and Whitman T. Soule. 1988. "Gender and Promotion in Segmented Job Ladder Systems." *American Sociological Review* 53:26–40.

"Disgusting: Yale Frat Caught on Tape Chanting About Rape 'No Means Yes', 'Yes Means Anal' and 'F**ching Sluts'." October 17, 2010. Available at www.alternet.org.

DiTomaso, N., C. Post, and R. Parks-Yancey. 2007. "Workforce Diversity and Inequality: Power, Status, and Numbers." *Annual Review of Sociology* 33:473–501.

Dobratz, Betty A., and Stephanie L. Shanks-Meile. 1997. *White Power, White Pride.* New York: Twayne.

Doeringer, Peter B., and Michael J. Piori. 1971. *Internal Labor Markets and Manpower Analysis.* Lexington, MA: D. C. Heath.

Dohm, Arlene, and Lynn Shniper. 2007. "Occupational Employment Projections to 2016." *Monthly Labor Review,* November:86–88.

Dolan, Kathleen. 2005. "How the Public Views Women Candidates." Pp. 41–59 in *Women and Elective Office,* edited by S. Thomas and C. Wilcox. New York: Oxford.

Dolgoff, Ralph, and Donald Feldstein. 1984. *Understanding Social Welfare.* New York: Longman.

Dollar, David, and Aart Kraay. 2004. "Trade, Growth, and Poverty." *The Economic Journal* 114: F22–F49.

Domhoff, G. William. 1971. *The Higher Circles.* New York: Vintage.

Domhoff, G. William. 1998. *Who Rules America?* Mountain View, CA: Mayfield.

Domhoff, G. William. 2006. "Mills's *The Power Elite* 50 Years Later." *Contemporary Sociology* 35:547–550.

Dominguez, Silvia, and Celeste Watkins. 2003. "Creating Networks for Survival and Mobility: Social Capital among African-American and Latin-American Low-Income Mothers." *Social Problems* 50:111–135.

Donohue, John J. III, and Steven D. Levitt. 2001. "The Impact of Race on Policing and Arrest." *Journal of Law and Economics* 44:367–394.

Dorius, Shawn F., and Glenn Firebaugh. 2010. "Trends in Global Gender Inequality." *Social Forces* 88:1941–1968.

Doucouliagos, Hristos, and Mehmet Ali Ulubasoglu. 2008. "Democracy and Economic Growth: A Meta Analysis." *American Journal of Political Science* 52:61–83.

Dowd, Maureen. May 5, 2005. "Ugly Duckling Has No Chance." *Akron Beacon Journal,* B2.

Dresang, Dennis. 2008. "Menominee Nation Assessment Project." *La Follette Policy Report,* Fall: 25–27.

Drori, Gili S. 2006. *Global E-Litism.* New York: Worth.

Dublin, Thomas. 1979. *Women at Work.* New York: Columbia University Press.

Dubofsky, Melvyn. 1975. *Industrialism and the American Workers, 1865–1920.* Arlington Heights, IL: AHM Publishing.

DuBois, W. E. B. 1973. *The Philadelphia Negro.* Millwood, NY: Kraus-Thompson.

Dugger, Celia W. September 27, 2010. "Efforts Meant to Help Workers Squeeze South Africa's Poorest? *New York Times,* A1, A8.

Duke, James T. 1976. *Conflict and Power in Social Life.* Provo, UT: Brigham Young University Press.

Duncan, Cynthia M. 1999. *Worlds Apart.* New Haven, CT: Yale University Press.

Duncan, Greg J., Jeanne Brooks-Gunn, W. Jean Yeung, and Judith R. Smith. 1998. "How Much Does Childhood Poverty Affect the Life Chances of Children?" *American Sociological Review* 63:406–423.

Dunlop, John T. 1987. "The Development of Labor Organization: A Theoretical Framework." Pp. 12–22 in *Theories of the Labor Movement,* edited by S. Larson and B. Nissen. Detroit: Wayne State University Press.

Durkheim, Émile. 1933. *The Division of Labor in Society.* New York: The Free Press.

Dyck, Joshua, and Laura S. Hussey. 2008. "The End of Welfare as We Know It? Durable Attitudes in a Changing Information Environment." *Public Opinion Quarterly* 72:589–618.

Dye, Thomas R. 2002. *Who's Running America? The Bush Restoration.* Upper Saddle River, NJ: Prentice Hall.

Eakins, Barbara W., and R. Gene Eakins. 1978. *Sex Differences in Human Communication.* Boston: Houghton Mifflin.

Eckholm, Erik. January 16, 2008a. "Blue-Collar Jobs Disappear, Taking Families' Way of Life Along." *New York Times,* A12.

Eckholm, Erik. March 31, 2008b. "As Jobs Vanish and Prices Rise, Food Stamp Use Nears Record." *New York Times,* A1, A16.

Economic Mobility Project. March 12, 2009. *Findings from a National Survey & Focus Groups on Economic Mobility.* Washington, D.C.: Pew Charitable Trusts.

Edelman, Murray, 1977. *Political Language: Words That Succeed and Policies That Fail.* New York: Academic Press.

Eder, Donna. 1995. *School Talk: Gender and Adolescent School Culture.* New Brunswick, NJ: Rutgers University Press.

Edwards, Richard. 1979. *Contested Terrain: The Transformation of the Workplace in the Twentieth Century.* New York: Basic Books.

Egan, Patrick J., and Kenneth Sherrill. January 2009. *California's Proposition 8: What Happened, and What Does the Future Hold?* Washington, D.C.: National Gay and Lesbian Task Force.

Ehrenreich, Barbara, and Arlie Russell Hochschild. 2005. "Global Woman." Pp. 49–55 in *Gender Through the Prism of Difference,* edited by M. B. Zinn, P. Hondagneu-Sotelo, and M. A. Messner. New York: Oxford University Press.

Ehrenreich, Barbara, and Deirdre English. 1981. "The Sexual Politics of Sickness." Pp. 327–350 in *The Sociology of Health and Illness: Critical Perspectives.* New York: St. Martin's Press.

Eisenstein, Hester. 2001. "The Broader Picture." *Monthly Review* 53(5):49–52.

Eisenstein, Zillah. 1977/1990. "Constructing a Theory of Capitalist Patriarchy and Socialist Feminism." *Insurgent Sociologist* 7:3–17. Reprinted on pp. 114–145 in W*omen, Class, and the Feminist Imagination: A Socialist-Feminist Reader,* edited by K. V. Hansen and I. J. Philipson. Philadelphia: Temple University Press.

Eisenstein, Zillah. 1981. *The Radical Future of Liberal Feminism.* New York: Longman.

Eisler, Benita, ed. 1977. *The Lowell Offering.* Philadelphia: J. B. Lippincott.

Eitle, David, Steward J. D'Alessio, and Lisa Stolzenberg. 2002. "Racial Threat and Social Control: A Test of the Political, Economic, and Threat of Black Crime Hypotheses." *Social Forces* 81:557–576.

Elder, Glen H., and Jeffrey K. Liker. 1982. "Hard Times in Women's Lives: Historical Influences across Forty Years." *American Journal of Sociology* 88:241–269.

Elgar, Frank J. 2010. "Income Inequality, Trust, and Population Health in 33 Countries." *American Journal of Public Health* 100:2311–2315.

Elkins, Stanley. 1959. *Slavery: A Problem in American Institutional and Intellectual Life.* Chicago: University of Chicago Press.

Eller, Ronald D. 1982. *Miners, Millhands, and Mountaineers: Industrialization of the Appalachian South, 1880–1930.* Knoxville: University of Tennessee Press.

Elliott, James R., and Ryan Smith. 2004. "Race, Gender, and Workplace Power." *American Sociological Review* 69:365–386.

Ellwood, David T., and Mary Jo Bane. 1984. "The Impact of AFDC on Family Structure and Living Arrangements." Working paper prepared for the U.S. Department of Health and Human Services under grant no. 92A-82.

Ellwood, David T., and Lawrence H. Summers. 1986. "Poverty in America: Is Welfare the Answer or the Problem?" Pp. 78–105 in *Fighting Poverty: What Works and What Doesn't,* edited by S. H. Danziger and D. H. Weinberg. Cambridge, MA: Harvard University Press.

Elman, Cheryl, and Angela M. O'Rand. 2004. "The Race Is to the Swift: Socioeconomic Origins, Adult Education, and Wage Attainment." *American Journal of Sociology* 110:123–160.

Elo, Irma T. 2009. "Social Class Differentials in Health and Mortality: Patterns and Explanations in Comparative Perspective." *Annual Review of Sociology* 35:553–572.

England, Paula. 2010. "The Gender Revolution: Uneven and Stalled." *Gender & Society* 24:149–166.

England, Paula, and Dana Dunn. 1985. "Why Men Dominate." *The Women's Review of Books* 2:14–15.

England, Paula, and George Farkas. 1986. *Households, Employment, and Gender: A Social, Economic and Demographic View.* New York: Aldine de Gruyter.

England, Paula, George Farkas, Barbara Kilbourne, and Thomas Dou. 1988. "Explaining Occupational Sex Segregation and Wages: Findings from a Model with Fixed Effects." *American Sociological Review* 53:544–558.

Erickson, Bonnie H., and Rochelle R. Cote. 2009. "Social Capitals and Inequality: The Reproduction of Gender and Occupational Prestige Differences Through Individual Social Networks." Paper presented at annual meeting of American Sociological Association. August 7–11, San Francisco.

Erikson, Kai T. 1976. *Everything in Its Path.* New York: Simon & Schuster.

Eskridge, William N., Jr., and Philip P. Frickey. 1995. *Cases and Materials on Legislation: Statutes and the Creation of Public Policy.* St. Paul, MN: West Publishing.

Evans, Lorraine, and Kimberly Davies. 2000. "No Sissy Boys Here: A Content Analysis of the Representation of Masculinity in Elementary School Reading Textbooks." *Sex Roles* 42:255–270.

Evans, M. D. R., Jonathan Kelley, and Clayton D. Peoples. 2010. "Justifications of Inequality: The Normative Basis of Pay Differentials in 31 Nations." *Social Science Quarterly* 91:1405–1431.

Evertsson, Marie, and Magnus Nermo. 2004. "Dependence within Families and the Division of Labor: Comparing Sweden and the United States." *Journal of Marriage and Family* 66:1272–1286.

Ezzati, Majid, Ari B. Friedman, Sandeep C. Kulkarni, and Christopher J. L. Murray. 2008. "The Reversal of Fortunes: Trends in County Mortality and Cross-County Mortality Disparities in the United States." PLOS Medicine. Volume 5, Issue 4. Accessed online on October 1, 2008, at www.plosmedicine.org.

Fackler, Martin. April 28, 2002. "Chinese Women in Suicide Crisis: Rural Females in China Kill Themselves at an Extremely High Rate." *Los Angeles Times,* p. A8.

Fagot, Beverly I. 1977. "Consequences of Moderate Cross-Gender Behavior in Preschool Children." *Child Development* 48:902–907.

Fanon, Frantz. 1963. *The Wretched of the Earth.* New York: Grove Press.

Farley, John E. 1988. *Majority-Minority Relations.* Englewood Cliffs, NJ: Prentice Hall.

Farley, John E., and Gregory D. Squires. 2005. "Fences and Neighbors: Segregation in 21st Century America." *Contexts* 4:33–39.

Farough, Steven D. 2004. "The Social Geographies of White Masculinities." *Critical Sociology* 30:241–264.

Faux, Jeff. January 2003. "Corporate Control of North America." *The American Prospect,* 24–28.

Featherman David L., and Robert M. Hauser. 1978. *Opportunity and Change.* New York: Academic Press.

Feldstein, Stanley, ed. 1972. *The Poisoned Tongue: A Documentary History of American Racism and Prejudice.* New York: William Morrow.

Felmlee, Diane H. 1982. "Women's Job Mobility Processes within and between Employers." *American Sociological Review* 43:142–151.

Fenton, Steve. 1984. *Durkheim and Modern Sociology.* Cambridge: Cambridge University Press.

Ferraro, Kenneth F., and Melissa M. Farmer. 1996. "Double Jeopardy to Health Hypothesis for African Americans: Analysis and Critique." *Journal of Health and Social Behavior* 37:27–43.

Ferree, Myra Marx, and Beth B. Hess. 1985. *Controversy and Coalition: The New Feminist Movement.* Boston: Twayne.

Fiala, Robert, and Gary LaFree. 1988. "Cross-National Determinants of Child Homicide." *American Sociological Review* 53:432–445.

Firebaugh, Glenn. 1999. "Empirics of World Income Inequality." *American Journal of Sociology* 104:1597–1630.

Firebaugh, Glenn. 2000. "The Trend in Between-Nation Income Inequality." *Annual Review of Sociology* 26:323–339.

Firebaugh, Glenn, and Brian Goesling. 2004. "Accounting for the Recent Decline in Global Income Inequality." *American Journal of Sociology* 110:283–312.

Firebaugh, Glenn, and Matthew B. Schroeder. 2009. "Does Your Neighbor's Income Affect Your Happiness?" *American Journal of Sociology* 115:805–831.

Fishel, Leslie, Jr., and Benjamin Quarles. 1967. *The Negro American: A Documentary History.* Glenview, IL: Scott, Foresman.

Flanagan, Constance A., Bernadette Campbell, Luba Botcheva, Jennifer Bowes, Beno Csapo, Petr Macek, and Elena Sheblanova. 2003. "Social Class and Adolescents' Beliefs about Justice in Different Social Orders." *Journal of Social Issues* 59:711–732.

Flowers, Paul, and Katie Buston. 2001. "'I Was Terrified of Being Different': Exploring Gay Men's Accounts of Growing-Up in a Heterosexist Society." *Journal of Adolescence* 24:51–65.

Foner, Philip S. 1979. *Women and the American Labor Movement,* vol. 1. New York: The Free Press.

Form, M. H., and G. P. Stone. 1957. "Urbanism, Anonymity, and Status Symbolism." *American Journal of Sociology* 62:504–514.

Forman, Tyrone A. 2003. "The Social Psychological Costs of Racial Segmentation in the Workplace: A Study of African Americans' Well-Being."

Journal of Health and Social Behavior 44:332–352.

"Former Stock Analyst Gets 57-Month Sentence for $6.7 Million Fraud." 2008. *White-Collar Crime* 22:13.

Foster, George M. 1973. *Traditional Societies in Technological Change*. New York: Harper & Row.

Foster, Lucia. 2003. "Establishment and Employment Dynamics in Appalachia: Evidence from the Longitudinal Business Database." CES 03–19. December. Center for Economic Studies, U.S. Census Bureau.

Fox, Mary Frank, and Sharlone Hesse-Biber. 1984. *Women at Work*. Palo Alto, CA: Mayfield.

Fraley, Jill M. 2007. "Walk Along my Mind: Space, Mobility, and the Significance of Place." *Humanity & Society* 31:248–259.

France, Mike, and Dan Carney. July 2002. "Why Corporate Crooks Are Tough to Nail." *BusinessWeek*, 35–38.

Francia, Peter L. 2007. "Wither Labor? Reassessing Organized Labor's Political Power." *International Journal of Organization Theory and Behavior* 10:188–212.

Frank, Andre Gunder. 1969. *Latin America: Underdevelopment or Revolution*. New York: Monthly Review Press.

Frank, Reanne, Ilana Redstone Akresh, and Bo Lu. 2010. "Latino Immigrants and the U.S. Racial Order: How and Where Do They Fit In?" *American Sociological Review* 75:378–402.

Frank, Robert. May 20, 2005. "In Palm Beach, The Old Money Isn't Having a Ball." *New York Times*, A1, A11.

Frankenberg, Ruth. 1997. *Displacing Whiteness*. Durham, NC: Duke University Press.

Franklin, John Hope. 1980. *From Slavery to Freedom: A History of Negro Americans*. New York: Knopf.

Fraser, Steve, and Gary Gerstle. 2005. "Coda: Democracy in America." Pp. 286–292 in *Ruling America: A History of Wealth and Power in a Democracy*, edited by S. Fraser and G. Gerstle. Cambridge, MA: Harvard University Press.

Frazier, E. Franklin. 1937. "Negro Harlem: An Ecological Study." *American Journal of Sociology* 43:72–88.

Fredrickson, George M. 1981. *White Supremacy: A Comparative Study in American and South African History*. New York: Oxford University Press.

Freeman, Jo, ed. 1975a. *Women: A Feminist Perspective*. Palo Alto, CA: Mayfield.

Freeman, Jo. 1975b. "The Women's Liberation Movement: Its Origins, Structures, Impact, and Ideas." Pp. 448–460 in *Women: A Feminist Perspective*, edited by J. Freeman. Palo Alto, CA: Mayfield.

Freeman, Richard B. 1989. "The Relation of Criminal Activity to Black Youth Employment." *Review of Black Political Economy* 16:99–107.

Freire, Paulo. 1986. *Pedagogy of the Oppressed*. New York: Continuum.

Freitag, Peter J. 1975. "The Cabinet and Big Business: A Study of Interlocks." *Social Problems* 23:137–152.

French, John R. Jr., and Bertram H. Raven. 1959. "The Bases of Social Power." Pp. 150–167 in *Studies in Social Power*, edited by D. Cartwright. Ann Arbor, MI: Institute for Social Research.

Frith, Katherine, Ping Shaw, and Hong Cheng. 2005. "The Construction of Beauty: A Cross-Cultural Analysis of Women's Magazine Advertising." *Journal of Communication* 35(1):56–70.

Fullerton, Andrew S., and Jeffrey C. Dixon. 2009. "Racialization, Asymmetry, and the Context of Welfare Attitudes in the American States." *Journal of Political and Military Sociology* 37:95–120.

Fuwa, Makiko. 2004. "Gender and Housework in 22 Countries." *American Sociological Review* 69:751–767.

Galbraith, John Kenneth. 1952. *American Capitalism: The Concept of Countervailing Power*. Boston: Houghton Mifflin.

Galinsky, Ellen, and James T. Bond. 1996. "Work and Family: The Experiences of Mothers and Fathers in the U.S. Labor Force." Pp. 79–103 in *The American Woman 1996–97*, edited by C. Costello and B. K. Krimgold. New York: Norton.

Gallup Poll. 2008. *Homosexual Relations: Gallup's Pulse of Democracy*. Accessed on September 7, 2008, at www.gallup.com/poll/1651.

Galster, George, Jackie Cutsinger, and Jason C. Booza. 2006. *Where Did They Go? The Decline of Middle-Income Neighborhoods in Metropolitan America*. June. Washington, D.C.: Brookings Institution.

Gamson, Joshua, and Dawne Moon. 2004. "The Sociology of Sexualities: Queer and Beyond." *Annual Review of Sociology* 30:47–64.

Gangl, Markus, and Andrea Ziefle. 2009. "Motherhood, Labor Force Behavior, and Women's Careers: An Empirical Assessment of the Wage Penalty for Motherhood in Britain, Germany, and the United States." *Demography* 46:341–369.

Gans, Herbert J. 1995. *The War against the Poor.* New York: Basic Books.

Garbarino, Merwyn S. 1976. *American Indian Heritage.* Boston: Little, Brown.

Gartrell, Nanette, and Henny Bos. 2010. "U.S. National Longitudinal Lesbian Family Study: Psychological Adjustment of 17-Year-Old Adolescents." *Pediatrics* 126:28–36.

Gartrell, Nanette K., Henny M. W. Bos, and Naomi G. Goldberg. 2010. "Adolescents of the U.S. National Longitudinal Lesbian Family Study: Sexual Orientation, Sexual Behavior, and Sexual Risk Exposure." *Archives of Sexual Behavior, Online First.* Available online at www.springerlink.com.

Gates, Gary J. May 2010. *Lesbian, Gay, and Bisexual Men and Women in the U.S. Military.* Updated Estimates. Los Angeles: Williams Institute.

Gaventa, John. 1980. *Power and Powerlessness: Quiescence and Rebellion in an Appalachian Valley.* Urbana: University of Illinois Press.

Gaventa, John. 1984. "Land Ownership, Power, and Powerlessness in the Appalachian Highlands." Pp. 142–155 in *Cultural Adaptation to Mountain Environments,* edited by P. D. Beaver and B. L. Purington. Athens: University of Georgia Press.

General Social Survey. 2006. Accessed on November 3, 2008, at www.norc.org/GSS+Website/Browse+GSS+Variables/Subject+Index/.

Gensler, H. 1997. "Welfare and the Family Size Decision of Low-Income, Two-Parent Families." *Applied Economic Letters* 4:607–610.

George, Linda K., and Scott M. Lynch. 2003. "Race Differences in Depressive Symptoms: A Dynamic Perspective on Stress Exposure and Vulnerability." *Journal of Health and Social Behavior* 44:353–369.

Gerson, Kathleen. 1998. "Gender and the Future of the Family." Pp. 11–12 in *Challenges for Work and Family in the Twenty-First Century,* edited by D. Vannoy and P. J. Dubeck. New York: Aldine de Gruyter.

Gerth, Hans H., and C. Wright Mills, eds. 1962. *From Max Weber: Essays in Sociology.* New York: Oxford University Press.

Giddens, Anthony. 1973. *The Class Structure of the Advanced Societies.* New York: Harper & Row.

Giddens, Anthony. 1978. *Emile Durkheim.* New York: Penguin.

Giddens, Anthony. 1982. *Sociology: A Brief but Critical Introduction.* New York: Harcourt Brace Jovanovich.

Giddings, Paula. 1984. *When and Where I Enter: The Impact of Black Women on Race and Sex in America.* New York: Bantam.

Gilbert, Dennis. 2003. *The American Class Structure.* Belmont, CA: Wadsworth.

Gimenez, Martha E. 2005. "Capitalism and the Oppression of Women: Marx Revisited." *Science & Society* 69:11–32.

Ginzberg, Eli, and Hyman Berman. 1963. *The American Worker in the Twentieth Century.* New York: The Free Press.

Giroux, Henry A. 1983. *Theory & Resistance in Education: A Pedagogy for the Opposition.* South Hadley, MA: Bergin & Garvey.

Gittleman, Maury, and Mary Joyce. September 1995. "Earnings Mobility in the United States, 1967–91." *Monthly Labor Review,* 3–11.

Gladstone, Rick. May 9, 1988. "Despite Crash Executive Salaries Keep Rising." *Wooster Daily Record,* 34.

Glenn, Evelyn Nakano. 2008. "Yearning for Lightness: Transnational Circuits in the Marketing and Consumption of Skin Lighteners." *Gender & Society* 22:281–302.

Godard, John. 2009. "The Exceptional Decline of the American Labor Movement." *Industrial and Labor Relations Review* 63:82–108.

Goesling, Brian. 2001. "Changing Income Inequalities within and between Nations: New Evidence." *American Sociological Review* 66:745–761.

Goesling, Brian, and David P. Baker. 2008. "Three Faces of International Inequality." *Research in Social Stratification and Mobility* 26:183–198.

Goffman, Erving. 1959. *The Presentation of Self in Everyday Life.* Garden City, NY: Doubleday.

Goffman, Erving. 1961. *Asylums.* Garden City, NY: Doubleday Anchor Books.

Goffman, Erving. 1967. *Interaction Ritual.* Garden City, NY: Anchor Books, Doubleday.

Goldberg, Steven. 1973. *The Inevitability of Patriarchy.* New York: Morrow.

Goldsmith, Pat Rubio. 2009. "Schools or Neighborhoods or Both? Race and Ethnic Segregation and Educational Attainment." *Social Forces* 87:1913–1942.

Goldthorpe, John H. 2002. "Globalisation and Social Class." *West European Politics* 25:1–28.

Gonsiorek, John C. 1996. "Mental Health and Sexual Orientation." Pp. 462–478 in *The Lives of Lesbians, Gays, and Bisexuals,* edited by R. C. Savin-Williams and K. M. Cohen. Fort Worth, TX: Harcourt Brace.

Good, David H., and Maureen A. Pirog-Good. 1987. "A Simultaneous Probit Model of Crime and Employment for Black and White Teenage Males." *Review of Black Political Economy* 16:109–127.

Good, Mary-Jo DelVecchio, Cara James, Byron J. Good, and Anne E. Becker. 2003. "The Culture of Medicine and Racial, Ethnic, and Class Disparities in Healthcare." Pp. 594–625 in *Unequal Treatment: Confronting Racial and Ethnic Disparities in Health Care,* edited by B. D. Smedley, A. Y. Stith, and A. R. Nelson. Washington, D.C.: National Academies Press.

Goodman, William C., and Timothy D. Consedine. 1999. "Job Growth Slows during Crises Overseas." *Monthly Labor Review* 122:3–23.

Gordon, David M. 1972. *Theories of Poverty and Underemployment.* Lexington, MA: D. C. Heath.

Gordon, Milton M. 1949. "Social Class in American Sociology." *American Journal of Sociology* 55:262–268.

Gore, Susan, and Robert H. Aseltine, Jr. 2003. "Race and Ethnic Differences in Depressed Mood Following the Transition from High School." *Journal of Health and Social Behavior* 44:370–389.

Gorman, E. H. 2005. "Gender Stereotypes, Same-Gender Preferences, and Organizational Variation in the Hiring of Women: Evidence from Law Firms." *American Sociological Review* 70:702–728.

Gorman, Elizabeth H., and Julie A. Kmec. 2007. "We (Have to) Try Harder: Gender and Required Work Effort in Britain and the United States." *Gender & Society* 21:828–856.

Gorman, Elizabeth H., and Julie A. Kmec. 2009. "Hierarchical Rank and Women's Organizational Mobility: Glass Ceilings in Corporate Law Firms." *American Journal of Sociology* 114:1428–1474.

Gossett, Thomas F. 1963. *Race: The History of an Idea in America.* Dallas, TX: Southern Methodist University Press.

Gottfried, Heidi. 2004. "Gendering Globalization Discourses." *Critical Sociology* 30:9–15.

Gould, Roger V. 2002. "The Origins of Status Hierarchies: A Formal Theory and Empirical Test." *American Journal of Sociology* 107:1143–1178.

Grabb, Edward G. 1984. *Social Inequality: Classical and Contemporary Theorists.* Toronto: Holt, Rinehart and Winston of Canada.

Gramsci, Antonio. 1971. *Selections from the Prison Notebooks.* London: Lawrence and Wishart.

Green, Donald P., Laurence H. McFalls, and Jennifer K. Smith. 2001. "Hate Crime: An Emergent Research Agenda." *Annual Review of Sociology* 27:479–504.

Green, James R. 1980. *The World of the Worker: Labor in Twentieth-Century America.* New York: Hill and Wang.

Greenberg, Greg A. and Robert A. Rosenheck. 2008a. "Homelessness in the State and Federal Prison Population." *Criminal Behaviour and Mental Health* 18:88–103.

Greenberg, Greg A., and Robert A. Rosenheck. 2008b. "Jail Incarceration, Homelessness, and Mental Health: A National Study." *Psychiatric Services* 59:170–177.

Greenberg, Mark, and Jared Bernstein. December 6, 2004. "Holes Starting to Open in Welfare Reform." *Akron Beacon Journal,* B2.

Greenman, Emily, and Yu Xie. 2008. "Double Jeopardy? The Interaction of Gender and Race on Earnings in the United States." *Social Forces* 86:1217–1239.

Greenstein, Robert. March 1985. "Losing Faith in 'Losing Ground.'" *The New Republic* 25:12–17.

Grenzke, Janet M. 1989. "PACs and the Congressional Supermarket: The Currency Is Complex." *American Journal of Political Science* 33:1–24.

Griffin, Larry J., and Kenneth A. Bollen. 2009. "What Do These Memories Do? Civil Rights Remembrance and Racial Attitudes." *American Sociological Review* 74:594–614.

Griffin, Larry J., Michael E. Wallace, and Beth A. Rubin. 1986. "Capitalist Resistance to the Organization of Labor before the New Deal: Why? How? Success?" *American Sociological Review* 51:147–167.

Grodsky, Eric, and Devah Pager. 2001. "The Structure of Disadvantage: Individual and Occupational Determinants of the Black-White Wage Gap." *American Sociological Review* 66:542–567.

Grodsky, Eric, John Robert Warren, and Erika Felts. 2008. "Testing and Social Stratification in American Education." *Annual Review of Sociology* 34:385–404.

Gross, David, Lisa Alecxih, Mary Jo Gibson, John Corea, Craig Caplan, and Normandy Brangan. 1999. "Out-of-Pocket Health Spending by Poor and Near-Poor Elderly Medicare Beneficiaries." *Health Services Research* 34:241–254.

Gross, Neil. 2009. "A Pragmatist Theory of Social Mechanisms." *American Sociological Review* 74:358–379.

Gruenbaum, Ellen. 2001. *The Female Circumcision Controversy.* Philadelphia: University of Pennsylvania.

Grusky, David B., and Robert M. Hauser. 1984. "Comparative Social Mobility Revisited; Models of Convergence and Divergence in 16 Countries." *American Sociological Review* 49:19–38.

Guetzkow, Joshua. 2010. "Beyond Deservingness: Congressional Discourse on Poverty, 1964–1996." *Annals of the American Academy of Political and Social Science* 629:173–197.

Guillen, Mauro F. 2001. "Is Globalization Civilizing, Destructive, or Feeble? A Critique of Five Key Debates in the Social Science Literature." *Annual Review of Sociology* 27:235–260.

Haas, Steven. 2008. "Trajectories of Functional Health: The 'Long Arm' of Childhood Health and Socioeconomic Factors." *Social Science & Medicine* 66:849–861.

Haas, Steven A. 2006. "Health Selection and the Process of Social Stratification: The Effect of Childhood Health on Socioeconomic Attainment." *Journal of Health and Social Behavior* 47:339–354.

Hagan, John, A. R. Gillis, and John Simpson. 1985. "The Class Structure of Gender and Delinquency: Toward a Power-Control Theory of Common Delinquent Behavior." *American Journal of Sociology* 90:1151–1178.

Hagan, John, John Simpson, and A. R. Gillis. 1987. "Class in the Household; A Power-Control Theory of Gender and Delinquency." *American Journal of Sociology* 92:788–816.

Haider-Markel, Donald P. 2000. "Lesbian and Gay Politics in the States: Interest Groups, Electoral Politics, and Policy." Pp. 290–346 in *The Politics of Gay Rights,* edited by C. A. Rimmerman, K. D. Wald, and C. Wilcox. Chicago: University of Chicago.

Haider-Markel, Donald P., and Mark R. Joslyn. 2008. "Beliefs about the Origins of Homosexuality and Support for Gay Rights." *Public Opinion Quarterly* 72:291–310.

Hajnal, Zoltan L. 2007. "Black Class Exceptionalism: Insights from Direct Democracy on the Race Versus Class Debate." *Public Opinion Quarterly* 71:560–587.

Haller, Archibald O., and Alejandro Portes. 1973. "Status Attainment Processes." *Sociology of Education* 46:51–91.

Hamermesh, Daniel S., and Jeff E. Biddle. 1994. "Beauty and the Labor Market." *American Economic Review* 84:1174–1194.

Hanagan, Michael. 2000. "States and Capital: Globalizations Past and Present." Pp. 67–86 in *The Ends of Globalization,* edited by D. Kalb, M. van der Land, R. Staring, B. van Steenbergen, and N. Wilterdink. Lanham, MD: Rowman & Littlefield.

Hanson, Sandra L., and John Zogby. 2010. "The Polls—Trends: Attitudes about the American Dream." *Public Opinion Quarterly* 74:570–584.

Hao, Lingxin. 2003. *Immigration and Wealth Inequality in the U.S.* Russell Sage Foundation Working Paper #202.

Hardaway, Cecily R., and Vonnie C. McLoyd. 2009. "Escaping Poverty and Securing Middle Class Status: How Race and Socioeconomic Status Shape Mobilit Prospects for African Americans During the Transition to Adulthood." *Journal of Youth and Adolescence* 38:242–256.

Hargraves, J. L., J. J. Stoddard, and S. Trude. 2001. "Minority Physicians' Experiences Obtaining Referrals to Specialists and Hospital Admissions." *Medscape General Medicine.* Available at www.medscape.com/Medscape/GeneralMedicine/journal/2001.

Harris, Richard J., Juanita M. Firestone, and William A. Vega. 2005. "The Interaction of Country of Origin, Acculturation, and Gender Role Ideology on Wife Abuse." *Social Science Quarterly* 86:463–483.

Harris Interactive. 2007. "Almost Half Oppose the 'Don't Ask, Don't Tell' Policy." *Harris Poll* #9, February 5. Accessed on September 7, 2008, at www.harrisinteractive.com/harris_poll.

Harris Poll. September 8, 2005. "Firemen, Doctors, Scientists, Nurses and Teachers Top List as 'Most Prestigious Occupations,' According to Latest Harris Poll." *The Harris Poll #69.*

Harris, Alexes, Heather Evans, and Katherine Beckett. 2010. "Drawing Blood from Stones: Legal Debt and Social Inequality in the Contemporary United States." *American Journal of Sociology* 115:1753–1799.

Harris, Olivia. 1980. "The Power of Signs: Gender, Culture and the Wild in the Bolivian Andes." Pp. 70–94 in *Nature, Culture and Gender,* edited by C. MacCormack and M. Strathem. Cambridge: Cambridge University Press.

Hartmann, Douglas, Joseph Gerteis, and Paul R. Croll. 2009. "An Empirical Assessment of Whiteness Theory: Hidden from How Many?" *Social Problems* 56:403–424.

Hartmann, Heidi. 1976. "Capitalism, Patriarchy, and Job Segregation by Sex." *Signs: A Journal of Women in Culture and Society* 1:137–169.

Hartmann, Heidi. 1981. "The Unhappy Marriage of Marxism and Feminism." Pp. 15–29 in *Women and Revolution,* edited by L. Sargent. Boston: South End Press.

Hartmann, Heidi. 1987. "Internal Labor Markets and Gender: A Case Study of Promotion." Pp. 59–92 in *Gender in the Workplace,* edited by C. Brown and J. A. Pechman. Washington, D.C.: Brookings Institution.

Harvey, David. 1989. The *Condition of Postmodernity.* Oxford: Blackwell.

Hatch, Stephani L., and Bruce P. Dohrenwend. 2007. "Distribution of Traumatic and Other Stressful Life Events by Race/Ethnicity, Gender, SES and Age: A Review of the Research." *American Journal of Community Psychology* 40:313–332.

Hauser, Robert M., and David B. Grusky. 1988. "Cross-National Variation in Occupational Distribution, Relative Mobility Chances, and Intergenerational Shifts in Occupational Distributions." *American Sociological Review* 53:723–741.

Hay, Carter, Edward N. Fortson, Dusten R. Hollist, Irshad Altheimer, and Lonnie M. Schaible. 2007. "Compounded Risk: The Implications for Delinquency of Coming from a Poor Family that Lives in a Poor Community." *Journal of Youth & Adolescence* 36:593–605.

Haynes, Norris. 1995. "How Skewed Is the Bell Curve?" *Journal of Black Psychology* 21:275–292.

Haynie, Dana L., and Bridget K. Gorman. 1999. "A Gendered Context of Opportunity: Determinants of Poverty across Urban and Rural Labor Markets." *Sociological Quarterly* 40:177–197.

Hays, Sharon. October 17, 2003. "Studying the Quagmire of Welfare Reform." *Chronicle of Higher Education,* B7–B9.

Hayward, Mark D., Eileen M. Crimmins, Toni P. Miles, and Yu Yang. 2000. "The Significance of Socioeconomic Status in Explaining the Racial Gap in Chronic Health Conditions." *American Sociological Review* 65:910–930.

Hayward, Mark D., Amy M. Pienta, and Diane K. McLaughlin. 1997. "Inequality in Men's Mortality: The Socioeconomic Status Gradient and Geographic Context." *Journal of Health and Social Behavior* 38:313–330.

Hechter, Michael. 2004. "From Class to Culture." *American Journal of Sociology* 110:400–445.

Hedstrom, P. and P. Ylikoski. 2010. "Causal Mechanisms in the Social Sciences." *Annual Review of Sociology* 36:49–67.

Heflin, Colleen M., and John Iceland. 2009. "Poverty, Material Hardship, and Depression." *Social Science Quarterly* 90:1051–1071.

Hehir, J. Bryan. April 10, 1981. "The Bishops Speak on El Salvador." *Commonwealth,* 199, 223.

Helms, Ronald, and David Jacobs. 2002. "The Political Context of Sentencing: An Analysis of Community and Individual Determinants." *Social Forces* 81:577–604.

Henderson, A. M., and Talcott Parsons, trans. 1947. *Max Weber: The Theory of Social and Economic Organization.* New York: The Free Press.

Henderson, Debra A., and Ann R. Tickameyer. 2008. "Lost in Appalachia: The Unexpected Impact of Welfare Reform on Older Women in Rural Communities." *Journal of Sociology & Social Welfare* 35:153–171.

Henley, Nancy, and Jo Freeman. 1984. "The Sexual Politics of Interpersonal Behavior." Pp. 465–477 in *Women: A Feminist Perspective,* edited by J. Freeman. Palo Alto, CA: Mayfield.

Hennessey, Kathleen. November 17, 2010. "Tough-talking Candidates Using Sexual Stereotypes." *Akron Beacon Journal,* A3.

Hennessy, Judith. 2009. "Morality and Work-Family Conflict in the Lives of Poor and Low-Income Women." *The Sociological Quarterly* 50:557–580.

Henry, P. J., Christine Reyna, and Bernard Weiner. 2004. "Hate Welfare But Help the Poor: How the Attributional Content of Stereotypes Explains the Paradox of Reactions to the Destitute in America." *Journal of Applied Social Psychology* 34:34–58.

Herbert, Bob. October 5, 2006. "Poor, Black and Dumped On." *New York Times,* A31.

Herdt, Gilbert. 1997. *Same Sex, Different Cultures.* Boulder, CO: Westview Press.

Herek. Gregory M. 2002. "Gender Gaps in Public Opinion about Lesbians and Gay Men." *Public Opinion Quarterly* 66:40–66.

Herkenrath, Mark, Claudia Konig, Hanno Scholtz, and Thomas Volken. 2005. "Convergence and Divergence in the Contemporary World System: An Introduction." *International Journal of Comparative Sociology* 46:363–382.

Herman, Melissa R. 2009. "The Black-White-Other Achievement Gap: Testing Theories of Academic Performance Among Multiracial and Monoracial Adolescents." *Sociology of Education* 82:20–46.

Herring, Cedric. 2004. "Skin Deep: Race and Complexion in the 'Color-Blind' Era." Pp. 1–21 in *Skin Deep: How Race and Complexion Matter in the "Color-Blind" Era,* edited by C. Herring, V. Keith, and H. D. Horton. Chicago: University of Illinois.

Herrnstein, Richard J., and Charles Murray. 1994. *The Bell Curve: Intelligence and Class Structure in American Life.* New York: The Free Press.

Hertz, Tom. 2005. "Rags, Riches, and Race: The Intergenerational Economic Mobility of Black and White Families in the United States." Pp. 165–191 in *Unequal Chances,* edited by S. Bowles, H. Gintis, and M. O. Groves. New York: Sage; Princeton, NJ: Princeton University Press.

Herz, Diane E., and Barbara H. Wootten. 1996. "Women in the Workforce: An Overview." Pp. 44–78 in *The American Woman 1996–97,* edited by C. Costello and B. K. Krimgold. New York: Norton.

Hewitt, Christopher. 1995. "The Socioeconomic Position of Gay Men: A Review of the Evidence." *American Journal of Economics and Sociology* 54:461–479.

Higley, John, and Given Moore. 1981. "Elite Integration in the United States and Australia." *American Political Science Review* 75:581–597.

Higley, Stephen Richard. 1995. *Privilege, Power, and Place.* Lanham, MD: Rowman & Littlefield.

Hill, Mark E. 2000. "Color Differences in the Socioeconomic Status of African American Men: Results of a Longitudinal Study." *Social Forces* 78:1437–1460.

Hill, Mark E. 2002. "Race of the Interviewer and Perception of Skin Color: Evidence from the Multi-City Study of Urban Inequality." *American Sociological Review* 67:99–108.

Hipp, John R. 2007. "Income Inequality, Race, and Place: Does the Distribution of Race and Class Within Neighborhoods Affect Crime Rates?" *Criminology* 45:665–691.

Hirschman, Charles, and Morrison G. Wong. 1984. "Socioeconomic Gains of Asian Americans, Blacks, and Hispanics: 1960–1976." *American Journal of Sociology* 90:584–606.

Hirsh, C. Elizabeth, and Sabino Kornrich. 2008. "The Context of Discrimination: Workplace Conditions, Institutional Environments, and Sex and Race Discrimination Charges." *American Journal of Sociology* 113:1394–1432.

Hirvonen, Lalaina H. 2008. "Intergenerational Earnings Mobility Among Daughters and Sons." *American Journal of Economics and Sociology* 67:777–826.

Hoch, Charles. 1987. "A Brief History of the Homeless Problem in the United States." Pp. 16–32 in *The Homeless in Contemporary Society,* edited by R. D. Bingham, R. E. Green, and S. B. White. Newbury Park, CA: Sage.

Hochschild, Jennifer. 1981. *What's Fair: American Beliefs about Distributive Justice.* Cambridge, MA: Harvard University Press.

Hochschild, Jennifer L. 2003. "Social Class in Public Schools." *Journal of Social Issues* 59:821–840.

Hochschild, Jennifer L., and Vesla Weaver. 2007. "The Skin Color Paradox and the American Racial Order." *Social Forces* 86:643–670.

Hodge, Robert W., Paul Siegel, and Peter H. Rossi. 1964. "Occupational Prestige in the United States. 1925–1963." *American Journal of Sociology* 70:286–302.

Hodson, Randy. 1984. "Companies, Industries, and the Measurement of Economic Segmentation." *American Sociological Review* 49:335–348.

Hodson, Randy, and Robert L. Kaufman. 1982. "Economic Dualism: A Critical Review" *American Sociological Review* 47:727–739.

Hole, Judith, and Ellen Levine. 1975. "The First Feminists." Pp. 436–447 in *Women: A Feminist Perspective,* edited by J. Freeman. Palo Alto, CA: Mayfield.

Hollingshead, August B., and Fredrick Redlich. 1958. *Social Class and Mental Illness.* New York: Wiley.

Holloway, Steven R., and Elvin K. Wyly. 2001. "'The Color of Money' Expanded: Geographically Contingent Mortgage Lending in Atlanta." *Journal of Housing Research* 12:55–90.

Holmes, Malcolm D., and Judith A. Antell. 2001. "The Social Construction of American Indian Drinking: Perceptions of American Indian and White Officials." *Sociological Quarterly* 42:151–173.

Holtfreter, Kristy, Nicole Leeper Piquero, and Alex R. Piquero. 2008. "And Justice for All? Investigators' Perceptions of Punishment for Fraud Perpetrators." *Crime, Law and Social Change* 49:397–412.

Holtfreter, Kristy, Shanna Van Slyke, Jason Bratton, and Marc Gertz. 2008. "Public Perceptions of White-Collar Crime and Punishment." *Journal of Criminal Justice* 36:50–60.

Hombs, Mary Ellen. 2001. *American Homelessness.* Santa Barbara, CA: ABC-CLIO.

hooks, Bell. 1981. *Ain't I a Woman: Black Women and Feminism.* Boston: South End Press.

Hope, Marjorie, and James Young. 1986. *The Faces of Homelessness.* Lexington, MA: Lexington Books.

Hopkins, Daniel J. 2009. "Partisan Reinforcement and the Poor: The Impact of Context on Explanations for Poverty." *Social Science Quarterly* 90:744–764.

Horrigan, M. W., and S. E. Haugen. 1988. "The Declining Middle-Class Thesis: A Sensitivity Analysis." *Monthly Labor Review* 111:3–13.

Hout, Michael. 1984. "Occupational Mobility of Black Men: 1962 to 1973." *American Sociological Review* 49:308–322.

Hout, Michael. 1986. "Opportunity and the Minority Middle Class: A Comparison of Blacks in the United States and Catholics in Northern Ireland." *American Sociological Review* 51:214–223.

Hout, Michael. 1988. "More Universalism, Less Structural Mobility: The American Occupational Structure in the 1980s." *American Journal of Sociology* 93:1358–1400.

Huaco, George A. 1963. "A Logical Analysis of the Davis-Moore Theory of Stratification." *American Sociological Review* 28:801–804.

Huber, Joan. 1982. "Toward a Sociotechnological Theory of the Women's Movement." Pp. 24–38 in *Women and Work: Problems and Perspectives,* edited by R. Kahn-Hut, A. K. Daniels, and R. Colvard. New York: Oxford University Press.

Huber, Joan. 1988. "From Sugar and Spice to Professor." Pp. 92–101 in *Down to Earth Sociology: Introductory Readings,* edited by J. M. Henslin. New York: The Free Press.

Huddy, Leonie, Francis K. Neely, and Marilyn R. Lafay. 2000. "The Polls—Trends: Support for the Women's Movement." *Public Opinion Quarterly* 64:309–350.

Hudson, Kenneth. 2007. "The New Labor Market Segmentation: Labor Market Dualism n the New Economy." *Social Science Research* 36:286–312.

Huff, Daniel D., and David A. Johnson. 1993. "Phantom Welfare: Public Relief for Corporate America." *Social Work* 38:311–316.

Huffman, Matt L., and Philip N. Cohen. 2004. "Racial Wage Inequality: Job Segregation and Devaluation across U.S. Labor Markets." *American Journal of Sociology* 109:902–936.

Hughes, Melissa K. 2003. "Through the Looking Glass: Racial Jokes, Social Context, and the Reasonable Person in Hostile Work Environment Analysis." *Southern California Law Review* 76:1437–1482.

Hughes, Michael, and Bradley R. Hertel. 1990. "The Significance of Color Remains: A Study of Life Chances, Mate Selection, and Ethnic Consciousness Among Black Americans." *Social Forces* 68:1105–1120.

Hughes, Michael, and Melvin E. Thomas. 1998. "The Continuing Significance of Race Revisited: A Study of Race, Class, and Quality of Life in America, 1972 to 1996." *American Sociological Review* 63:785–795.

Hull, Kathleen E., and Robert L. Nelson. 2000. "Assimilation, Choice, or Constraint? Testing Theories of Gender Differences in the Careers of Lawyers." *Social Forces* 79:229–264.

Human Rights Campaign. 2005a. *Answers to Questions About Marriage Equality.* Washington, D.C.: Human Rights Campaign.

Human Rights Campaign. 2005b. *Marriage/ Relationship Laws: State by State.* Available at www.hrc.org/Template.cfm?Section=Laws_ Legal_

Human Rights Campaign. February 2009. *The State of the Workplace for Lesbian, Gay, Bisexual and Transgender Americans 2007–2008.* Washington, D.C.: Human Rights Campaign Foundation.

Human Rights Campaign. 2010. "Cities and Counties with Non-Discrimination Ordinances that Include Gender Identity." Available at www.hrc. org/issues/workplace/equal_opportunity/gender-identity-city-county-laws.htm.

Human Rights Watch. 2010. *"Criminalizing Identity."* Available at www.hrw.org/en/home.

Hundley, Greg. 2008. "Assessing the Horatio Alger Myth: Is Self-Employment Especially Beneficial for Those From Less-Advantaged Family Backgrounds?" *Research in Social Stratification and Mobility* 26:307–322.

Hunt, Matthew O. 2002. "Religion, Race/Ethnicity, and Beliefs about Poverty." *Social Science Quarterly* 83:810–831.

Hunt, Matthew O. 2004. "Race/Ethnicity and Beliefs about Wealth and Poverty." *Social Science Quarterly* 85:827–853.

Hunt, Matthew O. 2007. "African American, Hispanic, and White Beliefs About Black/White Inequality, 1977–2004." *American Sociological Review* 72:390–415.

Hunter, Herbert M., and Sameer Y. Abraham, eds. 1987. *Race, Class, and the World System: The Sociology of Oliver C. Cox.* New York: Monthly Review Press.

Huquet, Nathalie, Mark S. Kaplan, and David Feeny. 2008. "Socioeconomic Status and Health-Related Quality of Life Among Elderly People: Results from the Joint Canada/United States Survey of Health." *Social Science & Medicine* 66:803–810.

Hurst, Charles E., and David L. McConnell. 2010. *An Amish Paradox: Diversity and Change in the World's Largest Amish Community.* Baltimore: The Johns Hopkins University Press.

Ibarra, Peter R., and John I. Kitsuse. 2003. "Claims-Making Discourse and Vernacular Resources." Pp. 17–50 in *Challenges & Choices,* edited by J. A. Hostein and G. Miller. Hawthorne, NY: Aldine de Gruyter.

Inkeles, Alex, and David H. Smith. 1974. *Becoming Modern: Individual Change in Six Developing Countries.* Cambridge, MA: Harvard University Press.

Institute of Medicine. 2002. *Unequal Treatment.* Washington, D.C.: National Academies Press.

Intersex Society of North America. Available at www.isna.org/faq/what_is_intersex.

Irvine, Martha. October 2, 2005. "Youth Still Pushing Boundaries of Gender." *Akron Beacon Journal,* A5.

Irwin, John. 1985. *The Jail: Managing the Underclass in American Society.* Berkeley: University of California Press.

Isaac, Larry. 2008. "Movement of Movements: Culture Moves in the Long Civil Rights Struggle." *Social Forces* 87:33–63.

Isaacs, Julia B., Isabel V. Sawhill, and Ron Haskins. 2008. *Getting Ahead or Losing Ground: Economic Mobility in America.* Washington, D.C.: Pew Charitable Trusts.

Jackall, Robert. 1988. *Moral Mazes: The World of Corporate Managers.* New York: Oxford.

Jackman, Mary R., and Robert W. Jackman. 1983. *Class Awareness in the United States.* Berkeley: University of California Press.

Jackson, Elton F., and Harry J. Crockett, Jr. 1964. "Occupational Mobility in the United States: A Point Estimate and Trend Comparison." *American Sociological Review* 29:5–15.

Jacobe, Dennis. 2008a. "Americans Oppose Income Redistribution to Fix Economy." *Gallup Poll Briefing,* June 27, 1.

Jacobe, Dennis. 2008b. "Half of Americans Say They are Underpaid." *Gallup Poll Briefing,* August 18, 1.

Jacobs, David, and Amber M. Richardson. 2008. "Economic Inequality and Homicide in the Developed Nations from 1975 to 1995." *Homicide Studies* 12:28–45.

Jacobs, David, Zhenchao Qian, Jason T. Carmichael, and Stephanie L. Kent. 2007. "Who Survives on Death Row? An Individual and Contextual Analysis." *American Sociological Review* 72:610–632.

Jasso, Guillermina, and Peter Rossi. 1977. "Distributive Justice and Earned Income." *American Sociological Review* 42:639–651.

Jencks, Christopher. 1992. *Rethinking Social Policy.* New York: HarperCollins.

Jencks, Christopher, Marshall Smith, Henry Acland, Mary Jo Bane, David Cohen, Herbert Gintis, Barbara Heyns, and Stephen Michelson. 1973. *Inequality: A Reassessment of the Effect of Family and Schooling in America.* New York: Colophon Books.

Jenkins, J. Craig. 1983. "Resource Mobilization Theory and the Study of Social Movements." *Annual Review of Sociology* 9:527–553

Jenkins, J. Craig, and Craig M. Eckert. 1986. "Channeling Black Insurgency: Elite Patronage and Professional Social Movement Organizations in the Development of the Black Movement." *American Sociological Review* 51:812–829.

Jenness, Valerie, David A. Smith, and Judith Stepan-Norris. 2006. "Pioneer Public Sociologist C. Wright Mills, 50 Years Later." *Contemporary Sociology* 35:7–8.

Jimenez, Tomas R. 2008. "Mexican Immigrant Replenishment and the Continuing Significance of Ethnicity and Race." *American Journal of Sociology* 113:1527–1567.

Johnson, Carey V., Matthew J. Mimiaga, and Judith Bradford. 2008. "Health Care Issues Among Lesbian, Gay, Bisexual, Transgender and Intersex (LGBTI) Populations in the United States: Introduction." *Journal of Homosexuality* 54:213–224.

Johnson, Cathryn. 1994. "Gender, Legitimate Authority, and Leader-Subordinate Conversations." *American Sociological Review* 59:122–135.

Johnson, Jennifer. 2002. *Getting By On the Minimum*. New York: Routledge.

Johnston, David Cay. April 7, 2002. "Wealthy More Likely to Escape Tax Audit, IRS Data Show." *The Columbus Dispatch*, A7.

Jones, Woodrow, Jr., and K. Robert Keiser. 1987. "Issue Visibility and the Effects of PAC Money." *Social Science Quarterly* 68:170–176.

Jong-sung, You, and Sanjeev Khagram. 2005. "A Comparative Study of Inequality and Corruption." *American Sociological Review* 70:136–157.

Jonsson, Jan O., David B. Grusky, Matthew Di Carlo, Reinhard Pollak, and Mary C. Brinton. 2009. "Microclass Mobility: Social Reproduction in Four Countries." *American Journal of Sociology* 114:977–1036.

Jordahl. Henrik. 2007. *Inequality and Trust*. IFN Working Paper No. 715. Stockholm: Research Institute of Industrial Economics.

Kabeer, Naila. 2004. "Globalization, Labor Standards, and Women's Rights: Dilemmas of Collective (In)Action in an Interdependent World." *Feminist Economics* 10:3–35.

Kahlenberg, Richard D. September 30, 2010. "Elite Colleges, or Colleges for the Elite?" *New York Times*, A39.

Kahn, Joan R., and Leonard I. Pearlin. 2006. "Financial Strain over the Life Course and Health Among Older Adults." *Journal of Health and Social Behavior* 47:17–31.

Kahneman, Daniel, and Angus Deaton. 2010. "High Income Improves Evaluation of Life But Not Emotional Well-Being." *PNAS Early Edition*. Available at www.pnas.org/cgi/doi/10.1073/pnas.1011492107.

Kaiser, S. 1985. *The Social Psychology of Clothing and Personal Adornment*. New York: Macmillan.

Kalev, Alexandra. 2009. "Cracking the Glass Cages? Restructuring and Ascriptive Inequality at Work." *American Journal of Sociology* 114:1591–1643.

Kallick, David. 1994. "Toward a New Unionism." *Social Policy* 25:2–6.

Kamerman, Sheila B. 1980. *Parenting in an Unresponsive Society: Managing Work and Family Life*. New York: The Free Press.

Kane, Emily W. 2006. "'No Way My Boys are Going to be Like That!': Parents' Responses to Children's Gender Nonconformity." *Gender & Society* 20:149–176.

Kang, Miliann. 2006. "Hooked on Nails: Competing Constructions of Beauty by Black and White Women." Paper presented at Annual Meeting of American Sociological Association, Montreal, August.

Kanter, Rosabeth Moss. 1977a. *Men and Women of the Corporation*. New York: Basic Books.

Kanter, Rosabeth Moss. 1977b. "Some Effects of Proportions on Group Life: Skewed Sex Ratios and Responses to Token Women." *American Journal of Sociology* 82:965–990.

Kantor, Jodi. September 1, 2006. "On the Job, Nursing Mothers are Finding a 2-Class System." *New York Times*, A1, A14.

Kao, Grace, and Jennifer S. Thompson. 2003. "Racial and Ethnic Stratification in Educational Achievement and Attainment." *Annual Review of Sociology* 29:417–442.

Kasarda, John D. 1989. "Urban Industrial Transition and the Underclass." *Annals of the American Academy of Political and Social Science* 501:26–47.

Katz, Jonathan Ned. 2004. "'Homosexual' and 'Heterosexual'." Pp. 44–46 in *Sexualities: Identities, Behaviors, and Society,* edited by M. S. Kimmel and R. F. Plante. New York: Oxford University Press.

Katz, Michael B. 1986. *In the Shadow of the Poorhouse: A Social History of Welfare in America*. New York: Basic Books.

Katz-Gerro, Tally. 2002. "Highbrow Cultural Consumption and Class Distinction in Italy, Israel, West Germany, Sweden, and the United States." *Social Forces* 81:207–229.

Kaupert, Christy Woodward. 2007. "Migrants Bearing Economic Gifts: Measuring Remittance Use in Developing Countries." Paper presented at the Annual Meeting of the American Sociological Association, New York, August 1.

Kaushal, Neeraj, and Robert Kaestner. 2001. "From Welfare to Work: Has Welfare Reform Worked?" *Journal of Policy Analysis and Management* 20:699–719.

Kaya, Yunus. 2010. "Globalization and Industrialization in 64 Developing Countries, 1980–2003." *Social Forces* 88:1153–1182.

Keister, Lisa A., and Stephanie Moller. 2000. "Wealth Inequality in the United States." *Annual Review of Sociology* 26:63–81.

Keith, Verna M., and Cedric Herring. 1991. "Skin Tone and Stratification in the Black Community." *American Journal of Sociology* 97:760–778.

Keller, Suzanne. 1969. "Beyond the Ruling Class-Strategic Elites." Pp. 520–524 in *Structured Social Inequality,* edited by C. S. Heller. New York: Macmillan.

Keller, Suzanne. 1987. "Social Differentiation and Social Stratification: The Special Case of Gender." Pp. 329–349 in *Structured Social Inequality,* edited by Celia S. Heller. New York: Macmillan.

Kelley, Jonathan, and M. D. R. Evans. 1993. "The Legitimation of Inequality: Occupational Earnings in Nine Nations." *American Journal of Sociology* 99:75–125.

Kelly, Maura. 2010. "Regulating the Reproduction and Mothering of Poor Women: The Controlling Image of the Welfare Mother in Television News Coverage of Welfare Reform." *Journal of Poverty* 14:76–96.

Kemper, Theodore D. 1976. "Marxist and Functionalist Theories in the Study of Stratification: Common Elements That Lead to a Test." *Social Forces* 54:559–578.

Kendall, Diana. 2002. *The Power of Good Deeds.* Lanham, MD: Rowman & Littlefield.

Kendall, Diana. 2005. *Framing Class: Media Representations of Wealth and Poverty in America.* Lanham, MD: Rowman & Littlefield.

Kennelly, Ivy. 1999. "'That Single-Mother Element': How White Employers Typify Black Women." *Gender & Society* 13:168–192.

Kentor, J. 1998. "The Long-Term Effects of Foreign Investment Dependence on Economic Growth, 1940–1990." *American Journal of Sociology* 103:1024–1046.

Kenworthy, Lane. 1999. "Do Social-Welfare Policies Reduce Poverty? A Cross-National Assessment." *Social Forces* 77:1119–1139.

Kenworthy, Lane. 2009. "Tax Myths." *Contexts* 8:28–32.

Kephart, William M. 1950. "Status after Death." *American Sociological Review* 15:635–643.

Kerbo, Ronald R. 1983. *Social Stratification and Inequality: Class Conflict in the United States.* New York: McGraw-Hill.

Kerckhoff, Alan C. 1995. "Institutional Arrangements and Stratification Processes of Industrial Societies." *Annual Review of Sociology* 21:323–347.

Kerley, Kent R., Michael L. Benson, and Matthew R. Lee. 2004. "Race, Criminal Justice Contact, and Adult Position in the Social Stratification System." *Social Problems* 51:549–568.

Khazzoom, Aziza. 1997. "The Impact of Mothers' Occupations on Children's Occupational Destinations." *Research in Stratification and Mobility* 15:57–89.

Kiely, Ray. 2004. "The World Bank and 'Global Poverty Reduction': Good Policies or Bad Data?" *Journal of Contemporary Asia* 34:3–20.

King, Brayden G., and Marie Cornwall. 2007. "The Gender Logic of Executive Compensation." Paper presented at Annual Meeting of American Sociological Association, August 11–14, New York.

King, C. Richard, and Charles Fruehling Springwood, eds. 2001. *Team Spirits.* Lincoln: University of Nebraska Press.

King, Deborah K. 1988. "Multiple Jeopardy, Multiple Consciousness: The Context of a Black Feminist Ideology." *Signs* 14:42–72.

King, Martin Luther. 1958. *Stride toward Freedom.* New York: Harper & Row.

King, Ryan D., Steven F. Messner, and Robert D. Baller. 2009. "Contemporary Hate Crimes, Law Enforcement, and the Legacy of Racial Violence." *American Sociological Review* 74:291–315.

King, C. Richard, and Charles Fruehling Springwood, eds. 2001. *Team Spirits.* Lincoln, NE: University of Nebraska Press.

Kingston, Paul W. 2006. "How Meritocratic is the United States?" *Research in Social Stratification and Mobility* 24:111–130.

Kirby, James B., and Toshiko Kaneda. 2005. "Neighborhood Socioeconomic Disadvantage and Access to Health Care." *Journal of Health and Social Behavior* 46:15–31.

Kirby, Vicki. 2006. *Judith Butler: Live Theory.* New York: Continuum.

Kite, Mary E., and Bernard E. Whitley, Jr. 1998. "Do Heterosexual Women and Men Differ in Their Attitudes toward Homosexuality?" Pp. 39–61 in

Stigma and Sexual Orientation, edited by G. M. Herek. Thousand Oaks, CA: Sage.

Klawitter, Marieka M., and Victor Flatt. 1998. "The Effects of State and Local Antidiscrimination Policies on Earnings for Gays and Lesbians." *Journal of Policy Analysis and Management* 17:658–686.

Kleck, Gary. 1981. "Racial Discrimination in Criminal Sentencing: A Critical Evaluation of the Evidence with Additional Evidence on the Death Penalty." *American Sociological Review* 46:783–805.

Kluegel, James R., and Eliot R. Smith. 1986. *Beliefs about Inequality: Americans' Views of What Is and What Ought to Be.* New York: Aldine de Gruyter.

Kmec, Julie A. 2003. "Minority Job Concentration and Wages." *Social Problems* 50:38–59.

Koegel, Paul, M. Audrey Burnam, and Jim Baumohl. 1996. "The Causes of Homelessness." Pp. 24–33 in *Homelessness in America,* edited by J. Baumohl. Phoenix, AZ: Oryx Press.

Kohn, Melvin L., and Carmi Schooler. 1982. "Job Conditions and Personality: A Longitudinal Assessment of Their Reciprocal Effects." *American Journal of Sociology* 87:1257–1286.

Kolenda, Pauline. 1978. *Caste in Contemporary India.* Prospect Heights, IL: Waveland Press.

Kosciw. J. G., 2004. *The 2003 National School Climate Survey: The School-Related Experiences of our Nation's Lesbian, Gay, Bisexual and Transgender Youth.* New York: GLSEN.

Kotkin, Joel. 2010. "Ready Set Grow." *Smithsonian Magazine,* July/August, 61–67.

Kotlowitz, Alex. 1991. *There Are No Children Here.* New York: Doubleday.

Kposowa, Augustine J., Kevin D. Breault, and Beatrice M. Harrison. 1995. "Reassessing the Structural Covariates of Violent and Property Crimes in the USA: A County Level Analysis." *British Journal of Sociology* 46:79–105.

Kreidl, Martin. 2000. "What Makes *Inequalities* Legitimate? An International Comparison." *Czech Sociological Review* 8:255–255.

Kriesberg, Louis. 1979. *Social Inequality.* Englewood Cliffs, NJ: Prentice Hall.

Kromm, Jane E. 1994. "The Feminization of Madness in Visual Representation." *Feminist Studies* 20:507–535.

Krotz, Joanna L. July/August 1999. "Getting Even." *Working Woman,* 42–50.

Krueger, Patrick M., Richard G. Rogers, Robert A. Hummer, Felicia B. LeClere, and Stephanie A. Bond Huie. 2003. "Socioeconomic Status and Age: The Effect of Income Sources and Portfolios on U.S. Adult Mortality." *Sociological Forum* 18:465–482.

Krugman, Paul, and Anthony J. Venables. 1995. "Globalization and the Inequality of Nations." *Quarterly Journal of Economics* 110:857–877.

Krymkowski, Daniel H., and Beth Mintz. 2008. "What Types of Occupations are Women Entering?" *Research in Social Stratification and Mobility* 26:1–14.

Kubrin, Charis E., and Tim Wadsworth. 2009. "Explaining Suicide Among Blacks and Whites: How Socioeconomic Factors and Gun Availability Affect Race-Specific Suicide Rates." *Social Science Quarterly* 90:1203–1227.

Kuriloff, Peter, and Michael C. Reichert. 2003. "Boys of Class, Boys of Color: Negotiating the Academic and Social Geography of an Elite Independent School." *Journal of Social Issues* 59:751–769.

Kurz, Karin, and Walter Muller. 1987. "Class Mobility in the Industrial World." *Annual Review of Sociology* 13:417–442.

Labich, Kenneth. March 8, 1993. "The New Unemployed." *Fortune,* 40–49.

Lacey, Marc. December 7, 2004. "From Broken Lives, Kenyan Women Build Place of Unity." *New York Times.*

Lachman, Margie E., and Suzanne L. Weaver. 1998. "The Sense of Control as a Moderator of Social Class Differences in Health and Well-Being." *Journal of Personality and Social Psychology* 74:763–773.

LaFree, Gary. 1995. "Race and Crime Trends in the United States: 1946–1990." Pp. 169–193 in *Ethnicity, Race, and Crime,* edited by D. F. Hawkins. Albany: State University of New York Press.

Lamb, Michael E., M. Ann Easterbrooks, and George W. Holden. 1980. "Reinforcement and Punishment among Preschoolers: Characteristics, Effects, and Correlates." *Child Development* 51:1230–1236.

Lamont, Michèle. 2000. *The Dignity of Working Men.* Cambridge, MA: Harvard.

Landers, Susan. March 1993. "Family Leave Ushers in New Era." *NASW News* 38:1, 8.

Lannoy, Richard. 1975. *The Speaking Tree: A Study of Indian Culture and Society.* New York: Oxford University Press.

Lapham, Lewis H. 1988. *Money and Class in America.* New York: Weidenfeld & Nicolson.

Lareau, Annette. 2003. *Unequal Childhoods.* Berkeley: University of California Press.

Laslett, John H. M. 1987. "The American Tradition of Labor Theory and Its Relevance to the Contemporary Working Class." Pp. 359–378 in *Theories of the Labor Movement,* edited by S. Larson and B. Nissen. Detroit: Wayne State University Press.

Latkin, Carl A., and Aaron D. Curry. 2003. "Stressful Neighborhoods and Depression: A Prospective Study of the Impact of Neighborhood Disorder." *Journal of Health and Social Behavior* 44:34–44.

Latimer, Melissa. 2008. "A View from the Bottom: Former Welfare Recipients Evaluate the System." *Journal of Poverty* 12:77–98.

Lau, Holning, and Rebecca L. Stotzer. June 1, 2010. *Employment Discrimination Based on Sexual Orientation: A Hong Kong Study.* Los Angeles: Williams Institute.

Laumann, Edward O., John H. Gagnon, Robert T. Michael, and Stuart Michaels. 1994. *The Social Organization of Sexuality.* Chicago: University of Chicago Press.

Lauzen, Martha M., and David M. Dozier. 2005. "Maintaining the Double Standard: Portrayals of Age and Gender in Popular Films." *Sex Roles* 52:437–446.

"Law Evens Penalty for Crack, Powder." 2010. *The Columbus Dispatch,* August 4, A6.

Leaf, Clifton. March 18, 2002. "White-Collar Criminals: They Lie, They Cheat, They Steal, and They've Been Getting Away with It for Too Long." *Fortune,* 61–76.

Lee, Barrett A., and Meredith J. Greif. 2008. "Homelessness and Hunger." *Journal of Health & Social Behavior* 49:3–19.

Lee, Barrett A., Kimberly A. Tyler, and James D. Wright. 2010. "The New Homelessness Revisited." *Annual Review of Sociology* 36:501–521.

Lee, Cheol-Sung, Francois Nielsen, and Arthur S. Alderson. 2007. "Income Inequality, Global Economy and the State." *Social Forces* 86:77–112.

Lee, Jennifer, and Frank D. Bean. 2004. "America's Changing Color Lines: Immigration, Race/Ethnicity, and Multiracial Identification." *Annual Review of Sociology* 30:221–242.

Lee, Matthew R., and Tim Slack. 2008. "Labor Market Conditions and Violent Crime Across the Metro-Nonmetro Divide." *Social Science Research* 37:753–768.

Leftwich, Richard H. 1977. "Personal Income and Marginal Productivity." Pp. 78–81 in *Problems in Political Economy: An Urban Perspective,* edited by D. M. Gordon. Lexington, MA: D. C. Heath.

Lehmann, Jennifer M. 1995. "The Question of Caste in Modern Society: Durkheim's Contradictory Theories of Race, Class, and Sex." *American Sociological Review* 60:566–585.

Leicht, Kevin T., and Scott T. Fitzgerald. 2007. *Postindustrial Peasants.* New York: Worth.

Lengermann, Patricia Madoo, and Jill Niebrugge-Brantley. 1988. "Contemporary Feminist Theory." Pp. 282–325 in *Contemporary Sociological Theory,* edited by George Ritzer. New York: Knopf.

Lens, Vicki. 2002. "TANF: What Went Wrong and What to Do Next." *Social Work* 47:279–290.

Lenski, Gerhard. 1988. "Rethinking Macrosociological Theory." *American Sociological Review* 53:163–171.

Lerman, Robert I., and Caroline Ratcliffe. July, 2001. "Are Single Mothers Finding Jobs Without Displacing Other Workers?" *Monthly Labor Review,* 3–12.

"Lesbian Cadet Asks to Resign from West Point." August 13, 2010. *Akron Beacon Journal,* B4.

Lester, James P., David W. Allen, and Kelly M. Hill. 2001. *Environmental Injustice in the United States: Myths and Realities.* Boulder, CO: Westview Press.

Levine, Steven B. 1980. "The Rise of American Boarding Schools and the Development of a National Upper Class." *Social Problems* 28:63–94.

Levitan, Sar A. 1985. *Programs in Aid of the Poor.* Baltimore: Johns Hopkins University Press.

Lewis, Amanda E. 2004. "'What Group?' Studying Whites and Whiteness in the Era of 'Color Blindness.'" *Sociological Theory* 22:623–646.

Lewis, Gregory B. 2003. "Black-White Differences in Attitudes toward Homosexuality and Gay Rights." *Public Opinion Quarterly* 67:59–78.

Lewis, Gregory B., and Jonathan L. Edelson. 2000. "DOMA and ENDA: Congress Votes on Gay Rights." Pp. 193–216 in *The Politics of Gay Rights,* edited by C. A. Rimmerman, K. D. Wald, and C. Wilcox. Chicago: University of Chicago.

Lewis, Helen. 1974. "Fatalism or the Coal Industry." P. 222 in *Appalachia: Its People, Heritage, and Problems,* edited by Frank S. Riddel. Dubuque, IA: Kendall/Hunt.

Lichter, Daniel T. 1988. "Racial Differences in Underemployment in American Cities." *American Journal of Sociology* 93:771–792.

Lichter, Daniel T., and Rukamalie Jayakody. 2002. "Welfare Reform: How Do We Measure Success?" *Annual Review of Sociology* 28:117–141.

Lieberson, Stanley, and Donna K. Carter. 1979. "Making It in America: Differences between Eminent Blacks and White Ethnic Groups." *American Sociological Review* 44:347–366.

Light, Donald, Susanne Keller, and Craig Calhoun. 1989. *Sociology.* New York: Knopf.

Ligner, Isabelle. December 14, 2001. "Pakistan Women Targeted by 'Crimes of Honour.'" *Agence France Presse,* International News Section.

Lincoln, Karen D., Linda M. Chatters, and Robert Joseph Taylor. 2003. "Psychological Distress among Black and White Americans: Differential Effects of Social Support, Negative Interaction and Personal Control." *Journal of Health and Social Behavior* 44:390–407.

Lindert, Peter, and Jeffrey G. Williamson. 1976. "Three Centuries of American Inequality." Institute for Research on Poverty Discussion Paper No. 333–76. Madison: University of Wisconsin, Madison.

Link, Bruce G., Jo C. Phelan, Ann Stueve, Robert E. Moore, Michaeline Bresnahan, and Elmer L. Struening. 1996. "Public Attitudes and Beliefs about Homeless People." Pp. 143–148 in *Homelessness in America,* edited by J. Baumohl. Phoenix, AZ: Oryx Press.

Lipman, Joanne. April 14, 1993. "The Nanny Trap: The Dark Side of Child Care Is How Poorly Workers Are Sometimes Treated." *Wall Street Journal,* A1, A8.

Lipset, Seymour Martin. 1971. "Trade Unionism and the American Social Order." Pp. 7–29 in *The American Labor Movement,* edited by D. Brody. New York: Harper & Row.

Lipsitz, George. 2006. *The Possessive Investment in Whiteness.* Philadelphia: Temple University Press.

Lloyd, Moya. 2007. *Judith Butler.* Malden, MA: Polity Press.

Lobao, Linda M., Gregory Hooks, and Ann R. Tickameyer, eds. 2007. *The Sociology of Spatial Inequality.* Albany: State University of New York Press.

Loeb, Paul Rogat. February 19, 2003. "Those We Mourn and Those We Ignore." *Seattle Times.* Accessed online on October 8, 2008, at http://seattletimes.nwsource.com.

Loftus, Jeni. 2001. "America's Liberalization in Attitudes toward Homosexuality, 1973 to 1998." *American Sociological Review* 66:762–782.

Long, J. Scott, and Mary Frank Fox. 1995. "Scientific Careers: Universalism and Particularism." *Annual Review of Sociology* 21:45–71.

Lopreato, Joseph, and Lawrence E. Hazelrigg. 1972. *Class, Conflict, and Mobility.* Corte Madera, CA: Chandler & Sharp.

Lorber, Judith. 2001. *Gender Inequality.* Los Angeles: Roxbury.

Lorber, Judith. 1996. "Beyond the Binaries: Depolarizing the Categories of Sex. Sexuality, and Gender." *Sociological Inquiry* 66:143–159.

Loveman, Mara, and Jeronimo O. Muniz. 2007. "How Puerto Rico Became White: Boundary Dynamics and Intercensus Racial Reclassification." *American Sociological Review* 72:915–939.

Low, Jason, and Peter Sherrard. 1999. "Portrayal of Women in Sexuality and Marriage and Family Textbooks: A Content Analysis of Photographs from the 1970s to the 1990s." *Sex Roles* 40:309–318.

Lucal, Betsy. 1996. "Oppression *and* Privilege: Toward a Relational Conceptualization of Race. ' *Teaching Sociology* 24:245–255.

Ludwig, Jack. 2003. "Is America Divided into 'Haves' and 'Have-Nots'?" *Gallup Poll Tuesday Briefing,* May 1, 1–4.

Luibheid, Eithne. 1998. "'Looking Like a Lesbian': The Organization of Sexual Monitoring at the United States-Mexican Border." *Journal of the History of Sexuality* 8:477–506.

Lundquist, Jennifer H. 2008. "Ethnic and Gender Satisfaction in the Military: The Effect of a Meritocratic Institution." *American Sociological Review* 73:477–496.

Lurie, Alison. 1987. "Fashion and Status." Pp. 124–130 in *The Social World,* 3rd ed., edited by Ian Robertson. New York: Worth.

Lurie, Nancy Oestreich. 1982. "The American Indian: Historical Background." Pp. 131–144 in *Majority & Minority: The Dynamics of Race and Ethnicity in American Life,* 3rd ed., edited by N. R. Yetman and C. H. Steele. Boston: Allyn & Bacon.

Lyman, Rick. February 24, 1999. "Man Guilty of Murder in Texas Dragging Death." *New York Times,* A1, A12.

Lyons, Daniel. July 22, 2002. "Bad Boys." *Forbes,* 99–104.

Mabli, James, Rhoda Cohen, Frank Potter, and Zhanyun Zhao. 2010. *Hunger in America 2010.* Princeton, NJ: Mathematica Policy Research.

MacCormack, Carol P. 1980. "Nature, Culture and Gender: A Critique." Pp. 1–24 in *Nature, Culture and Gender,* edited by C. MacCormack and M. Strathern. Cambridge: Cambridge University Press.

MacLeod, Jay. 1987. *Ain't No Makin' It: Leveled Aspirations in a Low-Income Neighborhood.* Boulder, CO: Westview Press.

Madon, Stephanie. 1997. "What Do People Believe about Gay Males? A Study of Stereotype Content and Strength." *Sex Roles* 37:663–685.

Mahler, Vincent A. 2004. "Economic Globalization, Domestic Politics, and Income Inequality in the Developed Countries." *Comparative Political Studies* 37:1025–1053.

Makoba, Johnson W. 2002. "Globalization and Marginalization of Labor in the Third World." Paper delivered at Pacific Sociological Association Meeting, April 18–21, Vancouver, Canada.

Maldonado, Marta Maria. 2009. "'It is Their Nature to do Menial Labor': The Racialization of 'Latino/a Workers' by Agricultural Employers." *Ethnic & Racial Studies* 32:1017–1036.

Manderscheid, R. W., and M. J. Henderson, eds. 2004. *Mental Health, United States 2002.* Rockville, MD: Center for Mental Health Services, U.S. Department of Health and Human Services.

Manley, John F. 1983. "Neo-Pluralism: A Class Analysis of Pluralism I and Pluralism II." *American Political Science Review* 77:368–383.

Mantsios, Gregory. 2004. "Class in America—2003." Pp. 193–207 in *Race, Class, and Gender in the United States,* edited by P. S. Rothenberg. New York: Worth.

Manza, Jeff, Clem Brooks, and Christopher Uggen. 2002. "Public Attitudes towards Felon Disenfranchisement in the United States." *Harris Interactive Survey,* July 2002.

Marden, Charles F., and Gladys Meyer. 1973. *Minorities in American Society.* New York: Van Nostrand.

Marger, Martin. 1997. *Race and Ethnic Relations.* Belmont, CA: Wadsworth.

Mark, Noah P., Lynn Smith-Lovin, and Cecilia L. Ridgeway. 2009. "Why Do Nominal Characteristics Acquire Status Value? A Minimal Explanation for Status Construction." *American Journal of Sociology* 115:832–862.

Markham, William T., Patrick O. Macken, Charles M. Bonjean, and Judy Corder. 1983. "A Note on Sex, Geographic Mobility, and Career Advancement." *Social Forces* 61:1138–1146.

Marsh, Kris, William A. Darity Jr., Philip N. Cohen, Lynne M. Casper, and Danielle Salters. 2007. "The Emerging Black Middle Class: Single and Living Alone." *Social Forces* 86:735–762.

Marshall, Gordon, Adam Swift, and Stephen Roberts. 1997. *Against the Odds? Social Class and Social Justice in Industrial Societies.* New York: Oxford University Press.

Marshall, Ray, and Beth Paulin. 1987. "Employment and Earnings of Women: Historical Perspective." Pp. 1–36 in *Working Women: Past, Present, Future,* edited by K. S. Koziara, M. H. Moskow, and L. D. Tanner. Washington, D.C.: Bureau of National Affairs.

Martin, Andrew, Thomas Maher, Lisa Williams, and John McCarthy. 2009. *Whither the Civil Rights Movement? Towards an Empirical Model of Movement Decline.* Paper delivered at Meeting of American Sociological Association, August 8, San Francisco.

Martin, Andrew W. 2008. "Resources for Success: Social Movements, Strategic Resource Allocation, and Union Organizing Outcomes." *Social Problems* 55:501–524.

Martin, Andrew W., and Marc Dixon. 2010. "Changing to Win? Threat, Resistance, and the Role of Unions in Strikes, 1984–2002." *American Journal of Sociology* 116:93–129.

Marx, Karl. 1967. *Capital,* vol. I. New York: International Publishers.

Marx, Karl, and Frederick Engels. 1969 and 1970. *Selected Works,* vols. 1, 2, 3. Moscow: Progress Publishers.

Massad, J. 2002. "Re-orienting Desire: The Gay International and the Arab World." *Public Culture* 14:361–385.

Massey, Douglas S. 1995. "Review of the Bell Curve." *American Journal of Sociology* 101:747–753.

Massey, Douglas S. 2007. *Categorically Unequal.* New York: Russell Sage Foundation.

Massey, Douglas S. 2009. "Globalization and Inequality: Explaining American Exceptionalism." *European Sociological Review* 25:99–23.

Massey, Douglas S., and Nancy A. Denton. 1993. *American Apartheid.* Cambridge, MA: Harvard University Press.

Massey, Douglas S., Jonathan Rothwell, and Thurston Domina. 2009. "The Changing Bases of Segregation in the United States." *Annals of the American Academy of Political and Social Science* 626:74–90.

Matthaei, Julie A. 1982. *An Economic History of Women in America.* New York: Schocken Books.

Matthews, Donald R. 1954. "United States Senators and the Class Structure." *Public Opinion Quarterly* 18:5–22. Reprinted on pp. 331–42 in *Social Stratification: A Reader,* edited by J. Lopreato and L. S. Lewis. New York: Harper & Row.

Maume, David J., Jr. 1999. "Occupational Segregation and the Career Mobility of White Men and Women." *Social Forces* 77:1433–1459.

Maume, David J., Jr. 2004. "Wage Discrimination over the Life Course: A Comparison of Explanations." *Social Problems* 51:505–527.

Maynard, Micheline. May 11, 2005. "United Air Wins Right to Default on Its Pensions." *New York Times,* A1, C2.

Mazumder, Bhashkar. 2005. "Fortunate Sons: New Estimates of Intergenerational Mobility in the United States Using Social Security Earnings Data." *Review of Economics and Statistics* 87:235–255.

McAdam, Doug. 1982. *Political Process and the Development of Black Insurgency, 1930–1970.* Chicago: University of Chicago Press.

McCabe, Sean Esteban, Wendy B. Bostwick, Tonda L. Hughes, Brady T. West, and Carol J. Boyd. 2010. "The Relationship Between Discrimination and Substance Use Disorders Among Lesbian, Gay, and Bisexual Adults in the United States." *American Journal of Public Health* 100:1946–1952.

McCall, Leslie. 2001. "Sources of Racial Wage Inequality in Metropolitan Labor Markets: Racial, Ethnic, and Gender Differences." *American Sociological Review* 66:520–541.

McCall, Leslie, and Christine Percheski. 2010. "Income Inequality: New Trends and Research Directions." *Annual Review of Sociology* 36:329–347.

McCall, Phil. 2008. "'We Had to Stick Together': Individual Preferences, Collective Struggle, and the Formation of Social Consciousness." *Science & Society* 72:147–181.

McClelland, David C. 1961. *The Achieving Society.* New York: The Free Press.

McDonald, Steve, Nan Lin, and Dan Ao. 2009. "Networks of Opportunity: Gender, Race, and Job Leads." *Social Problems* 56:385–402.

McDonough, Peggy, David R. Williams, James S. House, and Greg J. Duncan. 1999. "Gender and the Socioeconomic Gradient in Mortality." *Journal of Health and Social Behavior* 40:17–31.

McFate, Katherine. June 1987. "Defining the Underclass." *Focus,* 8–12.

McIntosh, Peggy. 1988. "White Privilege and Male Privilege: A Personal Account of Coming to See Correspondences through Work in Women's Studies." Center for Research on Women Working Paper No. 189. Wellesley, MA: Wellesley College.

McKinley, Jesse. October 4, 2010. "Several Recent Suicides Put Light on Pressures Facing Gay Teenagers." *New York Times,* A9.

McLanahan, Sara. 2009. "Fragile Families and the Reproduction of Poverty." *Annals of the American Academy of Political and Social Science* 621:111–131.

McLanahan, Sara, and Christine Percheski. 2008. "Family Structure and the Reproduction of Inequalities." *Annual Review of Sociology* 34:257–276.

McLaughlin, Diane K., and Leif Jensen. 2000. "Work History and U.S. Elders' Transitions into Poverty." *The Gerontologist* 40:469–479.

McManus, Doyle. July 18, 2010. "The Long Shadow of a Great Recession." *Akron Beacon Journal,* A11.

McMurray, Coleen. 2004. "Do Blacks Receive Second-Class Healthcare?" *Gallup Poll Tuesday Briefing,* July 20.

McNamee, Stephen J., and Robert K. Miller, Jr. 2004. *The Meritocracy Myth.* Lanham, MD: Rowman & Littlefield.

McQueeney, Krista. 2008. "True Confessions and their Consequences: Dilemmas of Gender and Sexual Identity in Navigating the Professor-as-Peer

Role." Paper presented at the annual meeting of the American Sociological Association, Boston, July 31.

McQuillan, Julia, Arthur L. Greil, Karina M. Shreffler, and Veronica Tichenor. 2008. "The Importance of Motherhood Among Women in the Contemporary United States." *Gender & Society* 22:477–496.

McTague, Tricia, Kevin Stainback, and Donald Tomaskovic-Devey. 2009. "An Organizational Approach to Understanding Sex and Race Segregation in U.S. Workplaces." *Social Forces* 87:1499–1527.

McVeigh, Rory. 2006. "Structural Influences on Activism and Crime: Identifying the Social Structure of Discontent." *American Journal of Sociology* 112:510–566.

Mead, Margaret. 1963. *Sex and Temperament in Three Primitive Societies.* New York: William Morrow.

Meara, Ellen R., Seth Richards, and David M. Cutler. 2008. "The Gap Gets Bigger: Changes in Mortality and Life Expectancy, by Education, 1981–2000." *Health Affairs* 27:350–360.

Meiksins, Peter F. 1988. "A Critique of Wright's Theory of Contradictory Class Locations." *Critical Sociology* 15:73–82.

Memmi, Albert. 1965. *The Colonizer and the Colonized.* New York: Orion.

Merten, Don E. 1997. "The Meaning of Meanness: Popularity, Competition, and Conflict among Junior High School Girls." *Sociology of Education* 70:175–191.

Messner, Steven F. 1989. "Economic Discrimination and Societal Homicide Rates: Further Evidence on the Cost of Inequality." *American Sociological Review* 54:597–611.

Messner, Steven F., and Richard Rosenfeld. 1994. *Crime and the American Dream.* Belmont, CA: Wadsworth.

Meyer, Ilan H., and Laura Dean. 1998. "Internalized Homophobia, Intimacy, and Sexual Behavior among Gay and Bisexual Men." Pp. 160–86 in *Stigma and Sexual Orientation,* edited by G. M. Herek. Thousand Oaks, CA: Sage.

Meyer, Ilan H., Jessica Dietrich, and Sharon Schwartz. 2008. "Lifetime Prevalence of Mental Disorders and Suicide Attempts in Diverse Lesbian, Gay, and Bisexual Populations." *American Journal of Public Health* 98:1004–1006.

Meyer, Lisa B. 2003. "Economic Globalization and Women's Status in the Labor Market." *Sociological Quarterly* 44:351–383.

Miech, Richard A., Avshalom Caspi, Terrie E. Moffitt, Bradley R. Entner Wright, and Phil A. Silva. 1999. "Low Socioeconomic Status and Mental Disorders: A Longitudinal Study of Selection and Causation during Young Adulthood." *American Journal of Sociology* 104:1096–1131.

Miech, Richard Allen, and Michael J. Shanahan. 2000. "Socioeconomic Status and Depression over the Life Course." *Journal of Health and Social Behavior* 41:162–176.

Miliband, Ralph. 1977. *Marxism and Politics.* New York: Oxford University Press.

Miller, Casey, and Kate Swift. 1993. "Women and Names." Pp. 77–84 in *Experiencing Race, Class, and Gender in the United States,* edited by Virginia Cyrus. Mountain View, CA: Mayfield.

Miller, Lisa. 2010. "Divided We Eat." *Newsweek,* November 29, 43–48.

Miller, S. M. 1963. *Max Weber: Selections from His Work.* New York: Thomas Y. Crowell.

Miller, William Lee. 1977. *Welfare and Values in America: A Review of Attitudes toward Welfare Policies in Light of American History and Culture.* Durham, NC: Welfare Policy Project. Institute of Policy Sciences and Public Affairs of Duke University, The Ford Foundation.

Mills, C. Wright. 1956. *The Power Elite.* New York: Oxford University Press.

Mills, C. Wright. 1959. *The Sociological Imagination.* New York: Oxford University Press.

Mills, C. Wright. 1962. *The Marxists.* New York: Dell.

Mills, Mary Beth. 2003. "Gender and Inequality in the Global Labor Force." Pp. 41–62 in *Annual Review of Anthropology,* edited by W. H. Durham, J. Comaroff, and J. Hill. Palo Alto, CA: Annual Reviews.

Mills, Melinda. 2009. "Globalization and Inequality." *European Sociological Review* 25:1–8.

Milner, Murray, Jr. 1994. *Status and Sacredness.* New York: Oxford University Press.

Milner, Murray, Jr. 2004. *Freaks, Greeks, and Cool Kids.* New York: Routledge.

Mincy, Ronald B., and Elaine J. Sorensen. 1998. "Deadbeats and Turnips in Child Support Reform." *Journal of Policy Analysis and Management* 17:44–51.

Minnich, Daniel J. 2003. "Corporatism and Income Inequality in the Global Economy: A Panel Study of 17 OECD Countries." *European Journal of Political Research* 42:23–53.

Mintz, Beth. 1975. "The President's Cabinet, 1897–1972: A Contribution to the Power Structure Debate." *Insurgent Sociologist* 5:131–148.

Mirowsky, John, and Catherine E. Ross. 1983. "Paranoia and the Structure of Powerlessness." *American Sociological Review* 48:228–239.

Mirowsky, John, and Catherine E. Ross. 1986. "Social Patterns of Distress." *Annual Review of Sociology* 12:23–45.

Mishel, Lawrence, Jared Bernstein, and Sylvia Allegretto. 2005. *The State of Working America 2004/2005.* Ithaca, NY: Cornell University.

Mishel, Lawrence, Jared Bernstein, and Sylvia Allegretto. 2007. *The State of Working America 2006/2007.* Ithaca, NY: Cornell University Press.

Mishel, Lawrence, Jared Bernstein, and John Schmitt. 2001. *The State of Working America 2000–2001.* Ithaca, NY: Cornell University.

Mishel, Lawrence, Jared Bernstein, and Heidi Shierholz. 2009. *The State of Working America 2008/2009.* Ithaca, NY: ILR Press.

Mitzman, Arthur. 1971. *The Iron Cage: An Historical Interpretation of Max Weber.* New York: Grosset & Dunlap.

Mohai, Paul, Paula M. Lantz, Jeffrey Morenoff, James S. House, and Richard P. Mero. 2008. "Racial and Socioeconomic Disparities in Residential Proximity to Polluting Industrial Facilities: Evidence from the Americans Changing Lives Study." Paper delivered at Annual Meeting of American Sociological Association, August 2008.

Moore, Mark P., and Priya Ranjan. 2005. "Globalisation vs. Skill-Biased Technological Change: Implications for Unemployment and Wage Inequality." *The Economic Journal* 115:391–422.

Moore, Wilbert E. 1970. "But Some Are More Equal Than Others." Pp. 143–148 in *The Logic of Social Hierarchies,* edited by E. O. Laumann, P. M. Siegel, and R. W. Hodge. Skokie, IL: Markham.

Morris, Aldon D. 1984. *The Origins of the Civil Rights Movement: Black Communities Organizing for Change.* New York: The Free Press.

Morris, Michael, and John B. Williamson. 1986. *Poverty and Public Policy: An Analysis of Federal Intervention Efforts.* New York: Greenwood Press.

"Most Firms in U.S. Pay No Federal Income Tax." August 12, 2008. *Akron Beacon Journal,* A5.

Mouw, Ted. 2000. "Job Relocation and the Racial Gap in Unemployment in Detroit and Chicago, 1980 to 1990." *American Sociological Review* 65:730–753.

Mouw, Ted, and Arne L. Kalleberg. 2010. "Occupations and the Structure of Wage Inequality in the United States, 1980s to 2000s." *American Sociological Review* 75:402–430.

Muller, Edward. 1988. "Democracy, Economic Development, and Income Inequality." *American Sociological Review* 53:50–68.

Mullins, Elizabeth I., and Paul Sites. 1984. "The Origins of Contemporary Eminent Black Americans: A Three-Generation Analysis of Social Origins." *American Sociological Review* 49:672–685.

Mulvihill, Geoff, and Samantha Henry. October 2, 2010. "Activists Rallying After N.J. Student's Suicide." *Akron Beacon Journal,* A1, A4.

Murray, Charles. 1984. *Losing Ground: American Social Policy 1950–1980.* New York: Basic Books.

Murray, Stephen O. 1996. *American Gay.* Chicago: University of Chicago Press.

Myles, John. 2003. "Where Have All the Sociologists Gone? Explaining Economic Inequality." *Canadian Journal of Sociology* 28:551–559.

Nachescu, Voichita. 2008. "Radical Feminism and the Nation." *Journal for the Study of Radicalism* 3:29–54.

Nagel, S. S., and L. J. Weitzman. 1971. "Women as Litigants." *Hastings Law Journal* 23:171–198.

Nam, Yunju. 2004. "Is America Becoming More Equal for Children? Changes in the Intergenerational Transmission of Low- and High-Income Status." *Social Science Research* 33:187–205.

Nasar, Sylvia. August 16, 1992. "The Rich Get Richer, But Never the Same Way Twice." *New York Times,* E3.

Nathans, Stephen J. 2001. "Twelve Years after Price Waterhouse and Still No Success for 'Hopkins in Drag.'" *Villanova Law Review* 46:713–743.

National Center for Health Statistics. 2007. *Health, United States, 2007.* Hyattsville, MD: U.S. Department of Health and Human Services.

National Center for Health Statistics. 2010. *Health United States, 2009.* Hyattsville, MD: U.S. Department of Health and Human Services.

National Coalition for the Homeless and National Law Center on Homelessness & Poverty. 2008. *Hate, Violence and Death on Main Street USA.* Accessed online on October 1, 2008, at www.nationalhomeless.org/getinvolved/projects/hatecrimes/executive_summary.html.

National Gay and Lesbian Task Force. 2005. *How Unequal Are Civil Unions?* Los Angeles: National Gay and Lesbian Task Force.

National Governors' Association Center for Best Practices. 1999. *Round Two Summary of Selected Elements of State Programs for Temporary Assistance for Needy Families.* Washington, D.C.: National Governors' Association.

"Nation's Inmate Population Increased 2.3 Percent Last Year." April 25, 2005. *New York Times,* A14.

Neft, Naomi, and Ann D. Levine. 1997. *Where Women Stand.* New York: Random House.

Neighbors, Harold W., Steven J. Trierweiler, Briggett C. Ford, and Jordana R. Muroff. 2003. "Racial Differences in DSM Diagnosis Using a Semi-Structured Instrument: The Importance of Clinical Judgment in the Diagnosis of African Americans." *Journal of Health and Social Behavior* 43:237–256.

Newman, Katherine S., and Margaret M. Chin. 2003. "High Stakes: Time Poverty, Testing, and the Children of the Working Poor." *Qualitative Sociology* 26:3–34.

Newport, Frank. July 1998. "Americans Remain More Likely to Believe Sexual Orientation Due to Environment, Not Genetics." *The Gallup Poll Monthly,* 14–16.

Newport, Frank. February 2001. "Americans See Women as Emotional and Affectionate, Men as More Aggressive." *The Gallup Poll Monthly,* 34–38.

Newport, Frank. 2007a. "Americans Have Become More Negative on Impact of Immigrants." *Gallup Poll Briefing,* July 13.

Newport, Frank. 2007b. "Americans More in Favor of Heavily Taxing Rich Now than in 1939." *Gallup Poll Briefing,* April 16, 1–5.

Newport, Frank. 2008a. "Americans Split on Redistributing Wealth by Taxing the Rich." *Gallup Poll Briefing,* October 30, 3.

Newport, Frank. 2008b. "Many Americans OK with Increasing Taxes on Rich." *Gallup Poll Briefing,* April 25, 1.

Nicholson, Linda J. 1984. "Making Our Marx." *The Women's Review of Books* 1:8–9.

Nielsen, Francois. 1995. Review of the Bell Curve. *Social Forces* 74:337–341.

Noel, Donald L. 1968. "A Theory of the Origin of Ethnic Stratification." *Social Problems* 16:157–172. Reprinted on pp. 109–120 in *Majority and Minority: The Dynamics of Race and Ethnicity in American Life,* edited by N. R. Yetman, 1985. Boston: Allyn & Bacon.

Nord, Mark, Alisha Coleman-Jensen, Margaret Andrews, and Steven Carlson. 2010. *Household Food Security in the United States, 2009.* EER-108. Washington, D.C.: U.S. Department of Agriculture.

Norton, Michael I., and Dan Ariely. 2011. "Building a Better America—One Wealth Quintile at a Time." *Perspectives on Psychological Science* 6:9–12.

O'Connell, Martin, and Daphne Lofquist. 2009. "Counting Same-Sex Couples: Official Estimates and Unofficial Guesses." Paper presented at annual meeting of Population Association of America, Detroit, MI, April 30–May 2.

O'Connor, James. 1973. *The Fiscal Crisis of the State.* New York: St. Martin's Press.

O'Hare, William P. 1987. *America's Welfare Population: Who Gets What?* Publication No. 13. Washington, D.C.: Population Reference Bureau.

O'Sullivan, Katherine, and William J. Wilson. 1988. "Race and Ethnicity." Pp. 223–242 in *Handbook of Sociology,* edited by N. J. Smelser. Newbury Park, CA: Sage.

Oberschall, Anthony. 1973. *Social Conflict and Social Movements.* Englewood Cliffs, NJ: Prentice Hall.

Ohlemacher, Stephen. February 26, 2007. "Welfare Numbers Growing, Despite Efforts." *Akron Beacon Journal,* A1, A3.

Ohlemacher, Stephen. September 23, 2008. "Immigration Boom Slows as U.S. Economy Falters." *Akron Beacon Journal,* A6.

Ohlemacher, Stephen. April 18, 2011. "IRS Deadline Becomes Less Taxing for Super Rich." *Akron Beacon Journal,* A1, A4.

Okun, Arthur. 1975. *Equality and Efficiency: The Big Tradeoff.* Washington, D.C.: Brookings Institution.

Oliver, Melvin, and Thomas Shapiro. 1995. *Black Wealth and White Wealth: A New Perspective on Racial Inequality.* New York: Routledge.

Ollman, Bertell. 1968. "Marx's Use of Class." *American Journal of Sociology* 73:573–580.

Ollman, Bertell. 1987. "How to Study Class Consciousness and Why We Should." *The Insurgent Sociologist* 14:57–96.

Olzak, Susan, Suzanne Shanahan, and Elizabeth H. McEneaney. 1996. "Poverty, Segregation, and Race Riots: 1960 to 1993." *American Sociological Review* 61:590–613.

Omi, Michael, and Howard Winant. 1986. *Racial Formation in the United States: From the 1960s to the 1980s.* New York: Routledge, Kegan and Paul.

Omi, Michael, and Howard Winant. 2005. "Racial Formation." Pp. 193–199 in *Great Divides,* edited by T. M. Shapiro. Boston: McGraw-Hill.

"100 Accused of Medicare Fraud." February 18, 2011. *Akron Beacon Journal,* A2.

Organization for Economic Cooperation and Development (OECD). 2010. "Social Mobility is Weak in France, Britain, and U.S., OECD Says." Accessed on March 22, 2011, at www.earthtimes.org/articles/news/308530,social-mobility-is-weak-in-france-britain-and-us-oecd-says.html.

Orlans, Harold, and June O'Neill. 1992. "Preface." *The Annals of the American Academy of Political and Social Science* 523:7–9.

Orr, Andrea. 2010. *At the Top: Soaring Incomes, Falling Tax Rates.* Washington, D.C.: Economic Policy Institute.

Ortiz, Susan Y., and Vincent J. Roscigno. "Discrimination, Women, and Work: Processes and Variations by Race and Class." *Sociological Quarterly* 50:336–359.

Ortner, Sherry B. 1974. "Is Female to Male as Nature Is to Culture?" Pp. 67–87 in *Woman, Culture & Society,* edited by M. Z. Rosaldo and L. Lamphere. Stanford, CA: Stanford University Press.

Ortner, Sherry B., and Harriet Whitehead, eds. 1981. *Sexual Meanings: The Cultural Construction of Gender and Sexuality.* Cambridge: Cambridge University Press.

Osberg, Lars, and Timothy Smeeding. 2006. "'Fair' Inequality? Attitudes Toward Pay Differentials: The United States in Comparative Perspective." *American Sociological Review* 71:450–473.

Ossowski, Stanislaw. 1963. *Class Structure in the Social Consciousness.* New York: The Free Press.

Osterman, Paul. 1975. "An Empirical Study of Labor Market Segmentation." *Industrial and Labor Relations Review* 28:508–523.

Ostrander, Susan. 1984. *Women of the Upper Class.* Philadelphia: Temple University Press.

Page, Benjamin I., and Lawrence R. Jacobs. 2009. *Class War?* Chicago: University of Chicago Press.

Pager, Devah. 2003. "The Mark of a Criminal Record." *American Journal of Sociology* 108:937–975.

Pager, Devah, Bart Bonikowski, and Bruce Western. 2009. "Discrimination in a Low-Wage Labor Market: A Field Experiment." *American Sociological Review* 74:777–799.

Pais, Jeremy. 2011. "Socioeconomic Background and Racial Earnings Inequality: A Propensity Score Analysis." *Social Science Research* 40:37–49.

Palmer, Barbara, and Dennis Simon. 2006. *Breaking the Political Glass Ceiling.* New York: Routledge.

Pampel, Fred C., Patrick M. Krueger, and Justin T. Denney. 2010. "Socioeconomic Disparities in Health Behaviors." *Annual Review of Sociology* 36:349–370.

Panagopoulos, Costas, and Peter L. Francia. 2008. "The Polls—Trends: Labor Unions in the United States." *Public Opinion Quarterly* 72:134–159.

Parenti, Michael. 1970. "Power and Pluralism: A View from the Bottom." *The Journal of Politics* 32:501–530.

Parkin, Frank. 1971. *Class Inequality and Political Order.* New York: Praeger.

Parkin, Frank. 1979. *Marxism and Class Theory: A Bourgeois Critique.* London: Tavistock.

Parlee, Mary Brown. 1979. "Conversational Politics." *Psychology Today* 12:48–91.

Parsons, Talcott. 1964. *Essays in Sociological Theory,* rev. ed. New York: The Free Press.

Passel, Jeffrey, and D'Vera Cohn. 2009. *Mexican Immigrants: How Many Come? How Many Leave?* Washington, D.C.: Pew Hispanic Center.

Pastore, Ann L. and Kathleen Maguire, eds. 2008. *Sourcebook of Criminal Justice Statistics.* Washington, D.C.: Bureau of Justice Statistics. Accessed online on October 8, 2008, at www.albany.edu/sourcebook.

Pattillo-McCoy, Mary. 1999. *Black Picket Fences.* Chicago: University of Chicago.

Pavalko, Eliza K., and Brad Smith. 1999. "The Rhythm of Work: Health Effects of Women's Work Dynamics." *Social Forces* 77:1141–1162.

Pavetti, LaDonna, and Gregory Acs. 2001. "Moving Up, Moving Out, or Going Nowhere? A Study of the Employment Patterns of Young Women and the Implications for Welfare Mothers." *Journal of Policy Analysis and Management* 20:721–736.

Paxton, Pamela, Melanie M. Hughes, and Jennifer L. Green. 2006. "The International Women's Movement and Women's Political Representation, 1893–2003." *American Sociological Review* 71:898–920.

Peffley, Mark, and Jon Hurwitz. 2007. "Persuasion and Resistance: Race and the Death Penalty in America." *American Journal of Political Science* 51:996–1012.

"The People Speak: 'Yes, He Can.'" 2009. *Newsweek,* January 26, 43.

Peoples, Clayton D. 2008. "Uncovering Political Influence by Using Network Analyses and Exploring Contributions/Party Interactions: The Case of Ohio Legislative Voting." *Sociological Focus* 41:300–318.

Peoples, Clayton D., and Michael Gortari. 2008. "The Impact of Contributions on Policymaking in the U.S. and Canada: Theoretical and Public Policy Implications." *Research in Political Sociology* 17:43–64.

Perlman, Selig, and Philip Taft. 1935. *History of Labor in the United States, 1896–1932. Volume IV: Labor Movements.* New York: Macmillan.

Perlman, Selig. 1928. *A Theory of the Labor Movement.* New York: Macmillan.

Perry, Barbara. 2001. *In the Name of Hate.* New York: Routledge.

Persell, Caroline Hodges. 1997. "The Interdependence of Social Justice and Civil Society." *Sociological Forum* 12:150.

Pessen, Edward. 1973. *Riches, Class and Power before the Civil War.* Lexington, MA: D. C. Heath.

Petersen, Trond, and Ishak Saporta. 2004. "The Opportunity Structure for Discrimination." *American Journal of Sociology* 109:852–901.

Petersen, Trond, Vemund Snartland, and Eva M. Meyersson Milgrom. 2007. "Are Female Workers Less Productive than Male Workers?" *Research in Social Stratification and Mobility* 25:13–37.

Peterson, Richard A., and Albert Simkus. 1992. "How Musical Tastes Mark Occupational Status Groups." Pp. 152–186 in *Cultivating Differences: Symbolic Boundaries and the Making of Inequality,* edited by M. Lamont and M. Fournier. Chicago: University of Chicago Press.

Peterson, Ruth D., and Lauren J. Krivo. 2009. "Segregated Spatial Locations, Race-Ethnic Composition, and Neighborhood Violent Crime." *Annals of the American Academy of Political and Social Science* 623:93–107.

Pettigrew, T. F. and L. R. Tropp. 2006. "A Meta-Analytic Test of Intergroup Contact Theory." *Journal of Personality and Social Psychology* 90:751–83.

Pew Research Center. 2003. *Republicans Unified, Democrats Spilt on Gay Marriage.* Washington, D.C.: Pew Research Center for the People & the Press.

Pew Research Center. 2006. *Less Opposition to Gay Marriage, Adoption and Military Service.* Accessed on September 7, 2008, at http://people-press.org/report/273.

Pew Research Center. November 13, 2007. *Blacks See Growing Values Gap Between Poor and Middle Class.* Washington, D.C.: Pew Research Center for the People & the Press.

Pew Research Center. February 14, 2008. *Economic Discontent Deepens as Inflation ConcernsRise.* Washington, D.C.: Pew Research Center for the People & the Press.

Pew Research Center. May 21, 2009. *Independents Take Center Stage in Obama Era.* Washington, D.C.: Pew Research Center for the People & the Press

Pew Research Center. October 9, 2009. *Majority Continues to Support Civil Unions.* Washington, D.C.: Pew Research Center for the People & the Press.

Pew Research Center. December 21, 2009. *Current Decade Rates as Worst in 50 Years.* Washington, D.C.: Pew Research Center for the People & the Press.

Pew Research Center. June 22, 2010. *Public Sees a Future Full of Promise and Peril.* Washington, D.C.: Pew Research Center for the People & the Press.

Pew Research Center. October 6, 2010. *Support for Same-Sex Marriage Edges Upward.* Washington, D.C.: Pew Research Center for the People & the Press.

Pew Research Center. November 18, 2010. *The Decline of Marriage and Rise of New Families.* Washington, D.C.: Pew Research Center for the People & the Press.

Phelan, Jo, Bruce G. Link, Robert E. Moore, and Ann Stueve. 1997. "The Stigma of Homelessness: The Impact of the Label 'Homeless' on Attitudes toward Poor Persons." *Social Psychology Quarterly* 60:323–337.

Phelan, Shane. 2001. *Sexual Strangers: Gays, Lesbians, and Dilemmas of Citizenship.* Philadelphia: Temple University Press.

Phelps, Linda. 1981. "Patriarchy and Capitalism." Pp. 161–173 in *Building Feminist Theory: Essays from Quest.* New York: Longman.

Philipson, Ilene J., and Karen V. Hansen. 1990. "Women, Class, and the Feminist Imagination: An Introduction." Pp. 3–40 in *Women, Class, and the Feminist Imagination: A Socialist-Feminist Reader,* edited by K. V. Hansen and I. J. Philipson, Philadelphia: Temple University Press.

Phillips, Scott. 2009. "Status Disparities in the Capital of Capital Punishment." *Law & Society Review* 43:807–838.

Physician Task Force on Hunger in America. 1985. *Hunger in America: The Growing Epidemic.* Middletown, CT: Wesleyan University Press.

Pierce, Jennifer L. 1995. *Gender Trials.* Berkeley: University of California Press.

Piori, Michael J. 1977. "The Dual Labor Market: Theory and Implications." Pp. 93–97 in *Problems in Political Economy: An Urban Perspective,* edited by D. M. Gordon. Lexington, MA: D. C. Heath.

Pitts, Steven C. 2007. *Job Quality and Black Workers: An Examination of the Bay Area, Los Angeles, Chicago, and New York.* Berkeley: Center for Labor Research and Education, University of California.

Piven, Frances Fox, and Richard A. Cloward. 1971. *Regulating the Poor: The Functions of Public Welfare.* New York: Random House.

Piven, Frances Fox, and Richard A. Cloward. 1977. *Poor People's Movements: Why They Succeed, How They Fail.* New York: Pantheon.

Piven, Frances Fox, and Richard A. Cloward. 1982. *The New Class War.* New York: Pantheon.

Pleis, J. R., V. Benson, and J. S. Schiller. 2003. *Summary Health Statistics for U.S. Adults: National Health Interview Survey, 2000.* Hyattsville, MD: National Center for Health Statistics.

Plutzer, Eric. 1988. "Work Life, Family Life, and Women's Support of Feminism." *American Sociological Review* 53:640–649.

Podgor, Ellen S. 2007. "The Challenge of White Collar Sentencing." *The Journal of Criminal Law & Criminology* 97:731–759.

Pogash, Carol. March 1, 2008. "Free Lunch Isn't Cool, So Some Students Go Hungry." *New York Times,* Section A, 1.

Porter, James N. 1974. "Race, Socialization, and Mobility in Educational and Early Occupational Attainment." *American Sociological Review* 39:303–316.

Portes, Alejandro, and Ruben G. Rumbaut. 2005. "Not Everyone Is Chosen." Pp. 271–283 in *Great Divides,* edited by T. M. Shapiro. Boston: McGraw-Hill.

Portes, Alejandro, and Kenneth L. Wilson. 1976. "Black-White Differences in Educational Attainment." *American Sociological Review* 41:414–431.

Powell, G. Bingham, Jr. 1986. "American Voter Turnout in Comparative Perspective." *American Political Science Review* 80:17–43.

Prabhakar, A. C. 2003. "A Critical Reflection on Globalisation and Inequality: A New Approach to the Development of the South." *African and Asian Studies* 2:307–345.

Pratt, Travis C., and Timothy W. Godsey. 2003. "Social Support, Inequality, and Homicide: A Cross-National Test of An Integrated Theoretical Model." *Criminology* 41:611–643.

Presser, Harriet B. 1998. "Toward a 24 Hour Economy: The U.S. Experience and Implications for the Family." Pp. 39–47 in *Challenges for Work and Family in the Twenty-First Century,* edited by D. Vannoy and P. J. Dubeck. New York: Aldine de Gruyter.

Pressman, Steven. 2007. "The Decline of the Middle Class: An International Perspective." *Journal of Economic Issues* 41:181–197.

Presthus, Robert. 1962. *The Organizational Society.* New York: Vintage Books.

Prewitt, Kenneth, and Alan Stone. 1973. *The Ruling Elites.* New York: Harper & Row.

Price Waterhouse v. Hopkins. 1989. No. 87–1167. Supreme Court of the United States. 490 U.S. 228:231–295.

Pryor, Frederic. 2010. "American Crime from an International Perspective." *Society* 47:175–177.

Pyke, Karen, and Tran Dang. 2003. "'FOB' and 'Whitewashed': Identity and Internalized Racism among Second Generation Asian Americans." *Qualitative Sociology* 26:147–172.

Quadagno, Jill. 1994. *The Color of Welfare: How Racism Undermined the War on Poverty.* New York: Oxford University Press.

Quillian, Lincoln, and Devah Pager. 2001. "Black Neighbors, Higher Crime? The Role of Racial Stereotypes in Evaluations of Neighborhood

Crime." *American Journal of Sociology* 107:717–767.

Raabe, Phyllis Hutton. 1998. "Being a Part-Time Manager: One Way to Combine Family and Career." Pp. 81–91 in *Challenges for Work and Family in the Twenty-First Century,* edited by D. Vannoy and P. J. Dubeck. New York: Aldine de Gruyter.

Ragatz, Laurie L., and Brenda Russell. 2010. "Sex, Sexual Orientation, and Sexism: What Influence Do These Factors Have on Verdicts in a Crime-of-Passion Case?" *Journal of Social Psychology* 150:341–360.

Ramsey, P. G. 1991. "Young Children's Awareness and Understanding of Social Class Differences." *Journal of Genetic Psychology* 152:71–82.

Ransom, Montrece McNeill. 2001. "The Boy's Club: How 'Don't Ask, Don't Tell' Creates a Double-Bind for Women." *Law and Psychology Review* 25:161–177.

Raphael, Dennis. 2009. "Reducing Social and Health Inequalities Requires Building Social and Political Movements." *Humanity & Society* 33:145–165.

Raven, Bertram H. 1965. "Social Influence and Power." Pp. 399–444 in *Current Studies in Social Psychology,* edited by I. D. Steiner and M. Fishbein. New York: Wiley.

Read, Jen'nan Ghazal, and Philip N. Cohen. 2007. "One Size Fits All? Explaining U.S.-Born and Immigrant Women's Employment across 12 Ethnic Groups." *Social Forces* 85:1713–1734.

Read, Jen'nan Ghazal, and Bridget K. Gorman. 2010. "Gender and Health Inequality." *Annual Review of Sociology* 36:371–386.

Reich, Michael. 1977. "The Economics of Racism." Pp. 183–188 in *Problems in Political Economy: An Urban Perspective,* edited by D. M. Gordon. Lexington, MA: D. C. Heath.

Reich, Michael, David M. Gordon, and Richard C. Edwards. 1977. "A Theory of Labor Market Segmentation." Pp. 108–113 in *Problems in Political Economy: An Urban Perspective,* edited by D. M. Gordon. Lexington, MA: D. C. Heath.

Reid, Pamela Trotman. 1984. "Feminism versus Minority Group Identity: Not for Black Women Only." *Sex Roles* 10:247–255.

Reid, Sue Titus. 1988. *Crime and Criminology.* New York: Holt, Rinehart and Winston.

Reiman, Jeffrey. 2004. *The Rich Get Richer and the Poor Get Prison.* Boston: Allyn & Bacon.

Reskin, Barbara F. 2003. "Including Mechanisms in Our Models of Ascriptive Inequality." *American Sociological Review* 68:1–21.

Reskin, Barbara F., and Debra Branch McBrier. 2000. "Why Not Ascription? Organizations' Employment of Male and Female Managers." *American Sociological Review* 65:210–233.

Resnick, Stephen, and Richard Wolff. 2003. "The Diversity of Class Analyses: A Critique of Erik Olin Wright and Beyond." *Critical Sociology* 29:7–27.

Reuveny, Rafael, and Quan Li. 2003. "Economic Openness, Democracy, and Income Inequality." *Comparative Political Studies* 36:575–601.

Rhode, Deborah L. 2010. *The Beauty Bias.* New York: Oxford University Press.

Ridgeway, Cecilia. 1991. "The Social Construction of Status Value: Gender and Other Nominal Characteristics." *Social Forces* 70:367–386.

Ridgeway, Cecilia L. 2006. "Gender as an Organizing Force in Social Relations: Implications for the Future of Inequality." Pp. 265–287 in *The Declining Significance of Gender?* edited by F. D. Blau, M. C. Brinton, and D. B. Grusky. New York: Russell Sage Foundation.

Ridgeway, Cecilia L., Kristen Backor, Yan E. Li, Justine E. Tinkler, and Kristan G. Erickson. 2009. "How Easily Does a Social Difference Become a Status Distinction? Gender Matters." *American Sociological Review* 74:44–62.

Ridgeway, Cecilia L., Elizabeth Heger Boyle, Kathy J. Kuipers, and Dawn T. Robinson. 1998. "How Do Status Beliefs Develop? The Role of Resources and Interactional Experience." *American Sociological Review* 63:331–350.

Riesman, David, with Reuel Denney and Nathan Glazer. 1950. *The Lonely Crowd.* New Haven, CT: Yale University Press.

Rigney, Daniel. 2001. *The Metaphorical Society.* Lanham, MD: Rowman & Littlefield.

Riis, Jacob. 1890. *How the Other Half Lives.* Williamstown, MA: Corner House.

Ringquist, Evan J. 1997. "Equity and the Distribution of Environmental Risk: The Case of TRI Facilities." *Social Science Quarterly* 78:811–829.

Ringquist, Evan J. 2000. "Environmental Justice: Normative Concerns and Empirical Evidence." Pp. 232–256 in *Environmental Policy,* edited by N. J. Vig and M. E. Kraft. Washington, D.C.: CQ Press.

Rischin, Moses, ed. 1965. *The American Gospel of Success.* New York: Quadrangle/The New York Times Books.

Risman, Barbara J. 2005. "Gender as Structure." Pp. 292–299 in *Great Divides,* edited by T. M. Shapiro. Boston: McGraw-Hill.

Rivera, David P., Erin E. Forquer, and Rebecca Rangel. 2010. "Microaggressions and the Life Experience of Latina/o Americans." Pp. 59–83 in *Microaggressions and Marginality,* edited by D. W. Sue. Hoboken, NJ: Wiley.

Rivers, Daniel. 2010. "'In the Best Interests of the Child'": Lesbian and Gay Parenting Custody Cases, 1967–1985." *Journal of Social History,* Summer:917–936.

Robbins, Alexandra. 2004. *Pledged: The Secret Life of Sororities.* New York: Hyperion.

Robert, Stephanie A. 1998. "Community-Level Socioeconomic Status Effects on Adult Health." *Journal of Health and Social Behavior* 39:18–37.

Robinson, James W. 2009. "American Poverty Cause Beliefs and Structured Inequality Legitimation." *Sociological Spectrum* 29:489–518.

Robinson, Robert, and Wendell Bell. 1978. "Equality, Success and Social Justice in England and the United States." *American Sociological Review* 43:125–143.

Robison, Jennifer. 2003. "Social Classes in U.S., Britain, and Canada." *Gallup Poll Tuesday Briefing,* August 6, 1–3.

Rodgers, Joan R. 1995. "An Empirical Study of Intergenerational Transmission of Poverty in the United States." *Social Science Quarterly* 76:178–194.

Rodriguez, Richard. 1982. *Hunger of Memory: The Education of Richard Rodriguez.* New York: Bantam Books.

Rogin, Michael. 1971. "Voluntarism: The Political Functions of an Anti-Political Doctrine." Pp. 100–118 in *The American Labor Movement,* edited by D. Brody. New York: Harper & Row.

Rollins, Judith. 1986. "Part of a Whole: The Interdependence of the Civil Rights Movement and Other Social Movements." *Phylon* 47:61–70.

Romero, Adam P., Amanda K. Baumle, M. V. Lee Badgett, and Gary J. Gates. December 2007. *Census Snapshot: United States.* Los Angeles: Williams Institute.

Romero, Mary. 1992. *Maid in the USA.* London: Routledge.

Roos, Patricia A. 1985. *Gender & Work: A Comparative Analysis of Industrial Societies.* Albany: State University of New York Press.

Roos, Patricia A., and Barbara F. Reskin. 1984. "Institutional Factors Contributing to Sex Segregation in the Workplace." Pp. 235–260 in *Sex Segregation in the Workplace: Trends, Explanations, Remedies.* Washington, D.C.: National Academy Press.

Roscigno, Vincent J. (1992). "Conservative and Critical Approaches to the Power Structure Debate: An Assessment and Critique of Empirical Findings." *Journal of Political and Military Sociology* 20:63–81.

Roscigno, Vincent J., Steven H. Lopez, and Randy Hodson. 2009. "Supervisory Bullying, Status Inequalities and Organizational Context." *Social Forces* 87:1561–1589.

Rosenfeld, Dana. 2009. "Heteronormativity and Homonormativity as Practical and Moral Resources: The Case of Lesbian and Gay Elders." *Gender & Society* 23:617–638.

Rosenfeld, Jake. 2010. "Economic Determinants of Voting in an Era of Union Decline." *Social Science Quarterly* 91:379–395.

Rosenfeld, Rachel A. 1992. "Job Mobility and Career Processes." *Annual Review of Sociology* 18:39–61.

Rosenfield, Sarah. 1989. "The Effects of Women's Employment: Personal Control and Sex Differences in Mental Health." *Journal of Health and Social Behavior* 30:77–91.

Rospenda, Kathleen M., Judith A. Richman, and Stephanie J. Nawyn. 1998. "Doing Power: The Confluence of Gender, Race, and Class in Contrapower Sexual Harassment." *Gender & Society* 12:40–60.

Ross, Catherine E., and John Mirowsky. 2001. "Neighborhood Disadvantage, Disorder, and Health." *Journal of Health and Social Behavior* 42:258–276.

Ross, Catherine E., John R. Reynolds, and Karlyn J. Geis. 2000. "The Contingent Meaning of Neighborhood Stability for Residents' Psychological Well-Being." *American Sociological Review* 65:581–597.

Rossi, Peter H., and James D. Wright. 1989. "The Urban Homeless: A Portrait of Urban Dislocation." *Annals of the American Academy of Political and Social Sciences* 501:132–142.

Rostow, W. W. 1960. *The Stages of Economic Growth.* Cambridge: Cambridge University Press.

Roth, Guenther, and Claus Wittich, eds. 1968. *Max Weber: Economy and Society.* 3 vols. New York: Bedminster Press.

Roth, Louise Marie. 2004a. "Engendering Inequality: Processes of Sex-Segregation on Wall Street." *Sociological Forum* 19:203–228.

Roth, Louise Marie. 2004b. "Bringing Clients Back In: Homophily Preferences and Inequality on Wall Street," *Sociological Quarterly* 45:613–635.

Roth, Wendy. 2005. "The End of the One-Drop Rule? Labeling of Multiracial Children in Black Intermarriages." *Sociological Forum* 20:35–67.

Rothenberg, Paula S. 2008. *White Privilege*. New York: Worth.

Rothman, Barbara Katz. 1984. "Women, Health, and Medicine." Pp. 70–80 in *Women: A Feminist Perspective,* edited by J. Freeman. Palo Alto, CA: Mayfield.

Rothstein, Bo, and Eric M. Uslaner. 2005. "All for All: Equality, Corruption, and Social Trust." *World Politics* 58:41–72.

Rouse, Stella M., Betina Cutala Wilkinson, and James C. Garand. 2010. "Divided Loyalties? Understanding Variation in Latino Attitudes Toward Immigration." *Social Science Quarterly* 91:856–882.

Rubenstein, Ruth P. 2001. *Dress Codes.* Boulder, CO: Westview Press.

Rubin, Lillian Breslow. 1976. *Worlds of Pain: Life in the Working-Class Family.* New York: Basic Books.

Rubin, Marcie S., Cynthia G. Colen, and Bruce G. Link. 2010. "Examination of Inequalities in HIV/ AIDS in the United States from a Fundamental Cause Perspective." *American Journal of Public Health* 100:1053–1059.

Rudra, Nita. 2004. "Openness, Welfare Spending, and Inequality in the Developing World." *International Studies Quarterly* 48:683–709.

Rupp, Leila J. 1985. "The Women's Community in the National Women's Party, 1945 to the 1960's." *Signs: Journal of Women in Culture and Society* 10:715–740.

Ryan, William. 1981. *Equality.* New York: Random House.

Ryff, Carol D., Corey L. M. Keyes, and Diane L. Hughes. 2003. "Status Inequalities, Perceived Discrimination, and Eudaimonic Well-Being: Do the Challenges of Minority Life Hone Purpose and Growth?" *Journal of Health and Social Behavior* 44:275–291.

Rytina, Steven. 2000. "Is Occupational Mobility Declining in the U.S.?" *Social Forces* 78:1227–1276.

Saad, Lydia. May 25, 2010. "Americans Acceptance of Gay Relations Crosses 50% Threshold." *Gallup Poll Briefing,* 1.

Sabol, William J. 2007. *Prisoners in 2006.* Washington, D.C.: U.S. Department of Justice.

Sacks, Karen. 1975. "Engels Revisited: Women, the Organization of Production, and Private Property." Pp. 211–234 in *Toward an Anthropology of Women,* edited by R. R. Reiter. New York: Monthly Review Press.

Safran, Claire. 1992. "The New Faces of Poverty." *Redbook* 179:84–87.

Sahlins, Marshall D. 1968. *Tribesmen.* Englewood Cliffs, NJ: Prentice Hall.

Sakamoto, Arthur, Jeng Liu, and Jessie M. Tzeng. 1998. "The Declining Significance of Race among Chinese and Japanese American Men." *Research in Social Stratification and Mobility* 16:225–246.

Salin, Denise. 2003. "Ways of Explaining Workplace Bullying: A Review of Enabling, Motivating and Precipitating Structures and Processes in the Work Environment." *Human Relations* 56:1213–1232.

Sampson, Robert J. 1986. "Effects of Socioeconomic Context on Official Reaction to Juvenile Delinquency." *American Sociological Review* 51:876–885.

Sampson, Robert J. 2008. "Moving to Inequality: Neighborhood Effects and Experiments Meet Social Structure." *American Journal of Sociology* 114:189–231.

Sampson, Robert J., and Patrick Sharkey. 2008. "Neighborhood Selection and the Social Reproduction of Concentrated Racial Inequality." *Demography* 45:1–29.

Sampson, Robert J., and William Julius Wilson. 1995. "Toward a Theory of Race, Crime, and Urban Inequality." Pp. 37–54 in *Crime and Inequality,* edited by J. Hagan and R. D. Peterson. Stanford, CA: Stanford University Press.

Samuelson, Robert J. August 2, 2010. "The Big Hiring Freeze." *Newsweek,* p. 26.

Sanday, Peggy Reeves. 1981. *Female Power and Male Dominance: On the Origins of Sexual Inequality.* Cambridge: Cambridge University Press.

Sanderson, Stephen K. 2005. "World-Systems Analysis After Thirty Years: Should It Rest in Peace?" *International Journal of Comparative Sociology* 46:179–13.

Sandler, Bernice R. 1986. "The Campus Climate Revisited: Chilly for Women Faculty, Administrators, and Graduate Students." Washington, D.C.: Association of American Colleges.

Sassen, Saskia. 2000. "The State and the New Geography of Power." Pp. 49–65 in *The Ends of Globalization,* edited by D. Kalb, M. van der Land, R. Staring, B. van Steenbergen, and N. Wilterdink. Lanham, MD: Rowman & Littlefield.

LSave the Children. 2004. *State of the World's Mothers 2004.* Westport, CT: Save the Children.

Savin-Williams, Ritch C. 1996. "Dating and Romantic Relationships among Gay, Lesbian, and Bisexual Youths." Pp. 166–80 in *The Lives of Lesbians, Gays, and Bisexuals,* edited by R. C. Savin-Williams and K. M. Cohen. Fort Worth, TX: Harcourt Brace.

Savin-Williams, Ritch C., and Kenneth M. Cohen. 1996. "Psychosocial Outcomes of Verbal and Physical Abuse among Lesbian, Gay, and Bisexual Youths." Pp. 181–200 in *The Lives of Lesbians, Gays, and Bisexuals,* edited by R. C. Savin-Williams and K. M. Cohen. Fort Worth, TX: Harcourt Brace.

Savin-Williams, R[itch] C., and R. G. Rodriguez. 1993. "A Developmental, Clinical Perspective on Lesbian, Gay Male, and Bisexual Youths." Pp. 77–101 in *Adolescent Sexuality,* edited by T. P. Gullotta, G. R. Adams, and R. Montemayor. Newbury Park, CA: Sage.

Sawhill, Isabel V. 1988. "Poverty in the U.S.: Why Is It So Persistent?" *Journal of Economic Literature* 26:1073–1119.

Sawhill, Isabel V. May 27, 2008. "Spending America into Fiscal Collapse." *Akron Beacon Journal,* A7.

Scanlan, Stephen. 2009. "Coal Sludge, Toxics, and Trash: Facility Siting, Inequality, and Environmental Justice in Appalachia." Paper delivered at Annual Meeting of American Sociological Association, August 2008.

Schaefer, Richard T. 2006. *Racial and Ethnic Groups.* Upper Saddle River, NJ: Pearson Education.

Schafer, Chelsea E., and Greg M. Shaw. 2009. "Tolerance in the United States." *Public Opinion Quarterly* 73:404–431.

Schauer, Edward J., and Elizabeth M. Wheaton. 2006. "Sex Trafficking into the United States: A Literature Review." *Criminal Justice Review* 31:146–169.

Schein, Virginia, Ruediger Mueller, and Carolyn Jacobson. 1989. "The Relationship between Sex Role Stereotypes and Requisite Management Characteristics among College Students." *Sex Roles* 20:103–110.

Schellenberg, E. Glenn, Jessie Hirt, and Alan Sears. 1999. "Attitudes towards Homosexuals among Students at a Canadian University." *Sex Roles* 40:139–152.

Schervish, Paul G., Platon E. Coutsoukis, and Ethan Lewis. 1994. *Gospels of Wealth: How the Rich Portray Their Lives.* Westport, CT: Praeger.

Schieman, Scott, and Gabriele Plickert. 2008. "How Knowledge is Power: Education and the Sense of Control." *Social Forces* 87:153–183.

Schlegel, Alice, ed. 1977. *Sexual Stratification: A Cross-Cultural View.* New York: Columbia University Press.

Schneider, William. July 1992. "The Suburban Century Begins." *The Atlantic Monthly,* 33–44.

Schnittker, Jason. 2007. "Working More and Feeling Better: Women's Health, Employment, and Family Life, 1974–2004." *American Sociological Review* 72:221–238.

Schnittker, Jason, Jeremy Freese, and Brain Powell. 2000. "Nature, Nurture, Neither, Nor: Black-White Differences in Beliefs about the Causes and Appropriate Treatment of Mental Illness." *Social Forces* 78:1101–1130.

Schnittker, Jason, Bernice A. Pescosolido, and Thomas W. Croghan. 2005. "Are African Americans Really Less Willing to Use Health Care?" *Social Problems* 52:255–271.

Scholte, Jan Aart. 2000. *Globalization: A Critical Introduction.* New York: St. Martin's Press.

Schooler, Carmi, Mesfin Samuel Mulatu, and Gary Oates. 2004. "Occupational Self-Direction, Intellectual Functioning, and Self-Directed Orientation in Older Workers: Findings and Implications for Individuals and Societies." *American Journal of Sociology* 110:161–197.

Schram, Sanford F., and Joe Soss. 2001. "Success Stories: Welfare Reform, Policy Discourse, and the Politics of Research." *Annals of the American Academy of Political and Social Science* 577:49–65.

Schultz, T. Paul. 1998. "Inequalities in the Distribution of Personal Income in the World: How It Is Changing and Why." *Journal of Population Economics* 11:307–344.

Schwalbe, Michael. 2008. *Rigging the Game.* New York: Oxford University Press.

Schwalbe, Michael, Sandra Godwin, Daphne Holden, Douglas Schrock, Shealy Thompson, and Michele Wolkomir. 2000. "Generic Processes in the Reproduction of Inequality: An Interactionist Analysis." *Social Forces* 79:419–452.

Schwartz, Christine R. 2010. "Earnings Inequality and the Changing Association Between Spouses' Earnings." *American Journal of Sociology* 115:1524–1557.

Schwartz, John. November 9, 2010. "Gay Couples Planning Legal Attack on Federal Marriage Law." *New York Times,* A22.

Schwartz, Michael, ed. 1987. *The Structure of Power in America.* New York: Holmes & Meier.

Scott, Janny, and David Leonhardt. May 15, 2005. "Class in America: Shadowy Lines That Still Divide." *New York Times,* A1, A16.

Scott, Sarah. November 1, 2000. "The Deepest Cut of All." *Chatelaine,* 191.

Scully, Diana, and Pauline Bart. 1981. "A Funny Thing Happened on the Way to the Orifice: Women in Gynecology Textbooks." Pp. 350–355 in *The Sociology of Health and Illness: Critical Perspectives,* edited by P. Conrad and R. Kern. New York: St. Martin's Press.

Secombe, Wally. 1973. "The Housewife and Her Labour Under Capitalism." *New Left Review* 83:19.

Sedgwick, Eve Kosofsky. 1998. "What's Queer?" Pp. 183–187 in *Gender Inequality,* edited by J. Lorber. Los Angeles: Roxbury.

Segovia, Fancine, and Renatta Defever. 2010. "The Polls—Trends." *Public Opinion Quarterly* 74:375–394.

Seider, Maynard S. 1974. "American Big Business Ideology: A Content Analysis of Executive Speeches." *American Sociological Review* 39:802–815.

Seidman, Ann. 1978. *Working Women: A Study of Women in Paid Jobs.* Boulder, CO: Westview Press.

Sellers, Robert M., Cleopatra H. Caldwell, Karen H. Schmeelk-Cone, and Marc A. Zimmerman. 2003. "Racial Identity, Racial Discrimination, Perceived Stress, and Psychological Distress among African American Young Adults." *Journal of Health and Social Behavior* 43:302–317.

Sennett, Richard, and Jonathan Cobb. 1973. *The Hidden Injuries of Class.* New York: Vintage.

Sentencing Project. 2003. *Annotated Bibliography: Racial Disparities in the Criminal Justice System.* Washington, D.C.: The Sentencing Project.

Sentencing Project. 2005a. *Felony Disenfranchisement Laws in the United States.* Washington, D.C.: The Sentencing Project.

Sentencing Project. 2005b. *Racial Disparity in Sentencing: A Review of the Literature.* Washington, D.C.: The Sentencing Project.

Serbin, Lisa A., K. Daniel O'Leary, Ronald N. Kent, and Illene J. Tonick. 1973. "A Comparison of Teacher Response to the Preacademic and Problem Behaviors of Boys and Girls." *Child Development* 44: 796–804.

Seshanna, Shubhasree, and Stephane Decornez. 2003. "Income Polarization and Inequality Across Countries: An Empirical Study." *Journal of Policy Modeling* 25:335–358.

Sewell, William H., Archibald O. Haller, and George W. Ohlendorf. 1970. "The Educational and Early Occupational Status Attainment Process: Replication and Revision." *American Sociological Review* 35:1014–1027.

Sewell, William H., and Robert M. Hauser. 1976. "Recent Developments in the Wisconsin Study of Social and Psychological Factors in Socioeconomic Achievement." Center for Demography Working Paper No. 76–11. Madison: University of Wisconsin.

Sewell, William H., and Vimal Shah. 1967. "Socioeconomic Status, Intelligence, and the Attainment of Higher Education." *Sociology of Education* 40:1–23.

Shamir, Ronen. 2005. "Without Borders? Notes on Globalization as a Mobility Regime." *Sociological Theory* 23:197–217.

Shanahan, Michael J., Richard A. Miech, and Glen H. Elder, Jr. 1998. "Changing Pathways to Attainment in Men's Lives: Historical Patterns of School, Work, and Social Class." *Social Forces* 77:231–256.

Shapiro, Thomas M. 2004. *The Hidden Cost of Being African American.* New York: Oxford.

Shaw, Greg M., and Robert Y. Shapiro. 2002. "The Polls—Trends: Poverty and Public Assistance." *Public Opinion Quarterly* 66:105–128.

Shepelak, Norma J. 1987. "The Role of Self-Explanations and Self-Evaluations in Legitimating Inequality." *American Sociological Review* 52:495–503.

Shepelak, Norma J., and Duane Alwin. 1986. "Beliefs about Inequality and Perceptions of Distributive Justice." *American Sociological Review* 51:30–46.

Shifman, Pamela. 2003. "Trafficking and Women's Human Rights in a Globalized World." *Gender and Development* 11:125–132.

Shihadeh, Edward S., and Raymond E. Barranco. 2010. "Latino Employment and Black Violence: The Unintended Consequenceof U.S. Immigration Policy." *Social Forces* 88:1393–1420.

Shihadeh, Edward S., and Nicole Flynn. 1996. "Segregation and Crime: The Effect of Black Social Isolation on the Rates of Black Urban Violence." *Social Forces* 74:1325–1352.

Shils, Edward A. 1970. "Deference." Pp. 420–428 in *The Logic of Social Hierarchies,* edited by Edward O. Laumann, Paul M. Siegel, and Robert W. Hodge. Chicago: Markham.

Shirley, Carla, and Michael Wallace. 2004. "Domestic Work, Family Characteristics, and Earnings: Reexamining Gender and Class Differences." *Sociological Quarterly* 45:663–690.

Shostak, Sara, Jeremy Freese, Bruce G. Link, and Jo C. Phelan. 2009. "The Politics of the Gene: Social Status and Beliefs about Genetics for Individual Outcomes." *Social Psychology Quarterly* 72:77–93.

Simon, Angela. 1998. "The Relationship between Stereotypes of and Attitudes toward Lesbians and Gays." Pp. 62–81 in *Stigma and Sexual Orientation,* edited by G. M. Herek. Thousand Oaks, CA: Sage.

Simon, Lawrence H. 1994. *Karl Marx: Selected Writings.* Indianapolis: Hackett.

Simon, Robin W. 2002. "Revisiting the Relationships among Gender, Marital Status, and Mental Health." *American Journal of Sociology* 107:1065–1096.

Singleton, Judy. 1998. "The Impact of Family Caregiving to the Elderly on the American Workplace: Who Is Affected and What Is Being Done?" Pp. 201–214 in *Challenges for Work and Family in the Twenty-First Century,* edited by D. Vannoy and P. J. Dubeck. New York: Aldine de Gruyter.

Sitkoff, Harvard. 1981. *The Struggle for Black Equality, 1954–1980.* New York: Hill and Wang.

Sivaramayya, B. 1983. "Equality and Inequality: The Legal Framework." Pp. 28–70 in *Equality and Inequality: Theory and Practice,* edited by A. Beteille. Delhi: Oxford University Press.

Skocpol, Theda. 1988. "An 'Uppity Generation' and the Revitalization of Macroscopic Sociology."

Pp. 145–159 in *Sociological Lives,* edited by M. W. Riley. Newbury Park, CA: Sage.

Skocpol, Theda. 2007. "Government Activism and the Reorganization of American Civic Democracy." Pp. 39–67 in *The Transformation of American Politics,* edited by P. Pierson and T. Skocpol. Princeton, NJ: Princeton University Press.

Slater, Courtenay M., and Cornelia J. Strawser, eds. 1998. *Business Statistics of the United States.* Washington, D.C.: Bernan Press.

Slevin, Peter. May 10, 2009. "In Toledo, Downturn Empties Offices." *Washington Post,* p. A4.

Sloane, David Charles. 1991. *The Last Great Necessity: Cemeteries in American History.* Baltimore: Johns Hopkins University.

Smeeding, Timothy. 2009. "Differences in Higher Education: Investments, Costs, and Outcomes." *LaFollette Policy Report* 18:1–4.

Smeeding, Timothy M. 2005. "Public Policy, Economic Inequality, and Poverty: The United States in Comparative Perspective." *Social Science Quarterly* 86:955–983.

Smidt, Corwin. 1980. "Civil Religious Orientations among Elementary School Children." *Sociological Analysis* 41:24–40.

Smith, Dorothy E. 1987. *The Everyday World as Problematic: A Feminist Sociology.* Boston: Northeastern University Press.

Smith, Dorothy, E. 2009. "Categories are not Enough." *Gender & Society* 23:76–80.

Smith, James D. 1987. "Recent Trends in the Distribution of Wealth in the U.S.: Data, Research Problems, and Prospects." Pp. 72–89 in *International Comparisons of the Distribution of Household Wealth,* edited by Edward D. Wolff. Oxford: Clarendon Press.

Smith, James P., and Barry Edmonston, eds. 1997. *The New Americans: Economic, Demographic, and Fiscal Effects of Immigration.* Washington, D.C.: National Academy Press.

Smith, Kevin B., and Robert A. Bylund. 1983. "Cognitive Maps of Class, Racial, and Appalachian Inequalities among Rural Appalachians." *Rural Sociology* 48:253–270.

Smith, Sandra Susan. 2010. "Race and Trust." *Annual Review of Sociology* 36:453–475.

Smith, Sara J., Amber M. Axelton, and Donald A. Saucier. 2009. "The Effects of Contact on Sexual Prejudice: A Meta-Analysis." *Sex Roles* 61:178–191.

Smucker, Philip. February 25, 2001. "Egyptian Women Fight Circumcision: Activists Making

Gains against Ancient Rite of Mutilation." *Pittsburgh Post-Gazette,* A4.

Snipp, C. Matthew. 2003. "Racial Measurement in the American Census: Past Practices and Implications for the Future." *Annual Review of Sociology* 29:563–588.

Snyder, Eloise C., ed. 1979. *The Study of Women: Enlarging Perspectives of Social Reality.* New York: Harper & Row.

Sobolewski, Juliana M., and Paul R. Amato. 2005. "Economic Hardship in the Family of Origin and Children's Psychological Well-Being in Adulthood." *Journal of Marriage and Family* 67:141–156.

Solt, Frederick. 2008. "Economic Inequality and Democratic Political Engagement." *American Journal of Political Science* 52:48–60.

Soltow, Lee. 1975. *Men and Wealth in the United States.* New Haven, CT: Yale University Press.

Sontag, Susan. 1973. "The Third World of Women." *Partisan Review* 60:201–203.

Sorensen, Aage B. 2000. "Symposium on Class Analysis: Toward a Sounder Basis for Class Analysis." *American Journal of Sociology* 105:1523–1558.

Spaeth, Joe L. 1976. "Cognitive Complexity: A Dimension Underlying the Socioeconomic Achievement Process." In *Schooling and Achievement in American Society,* edited by W. H. Sewell, R. M. Hauser, and D. L. Featherman. New York: Academic Press.

Spain, Daphne. 1992. *Gendered Spaces.* Chapel Hill: University of North Carolina Press.

Spain, Daphne. 1993. "Built to Last: Public Housing as an Urban Gendered Space." Paper presented at the Urban Affairs Association, April 21–24, Indianapolis, IN.

Spector, Malcolm, and John I. Kitsuse. 1977. *Constructing Social Problems.* Menlo Park, CA: Cummings Publishing.

Spencer, Herbert. 1892/1946. *The Man versus the State.* Caldwell, ID: Caxton Printers.

Spencer, Herbert. 1897. *The Principles of Ethics.* Vol. II. New York: D. Appleton.

Spencer, Herbert. 1909. *The Principles of Sociology.* Vol. II. New York: D. Appleton.

Spencer, Herbert. 1961. *The Study of Sociology.* Ann Arbor: University of Michigan Press.

Spilerman, Seymour. 2000. "Wealth and Stratification Processes." *Annual Review of Sociology* 26:497–524.

Srinivasan, U. Thara, Susan P. Carey, Eric Hallstein, Paul A. T. Higgins, Amber C. Kerr, Laura E. Koteen, Adam B. Smith, Reg Watson, John Harte, and Richard B. Norgaard. 2008. "The Debt of Nations and the Distribution of Ecological Impacts from Human Activities." *Proceedings of the National Academy of Sciences of the USA.* February 5:1768–1773.

Stack, Steven, and Delores Zimmerman. 1982. "The Effect of World Economy on Income Inequality: A Reassessment." *The Sociological Quarterly* 23:345–358.

Stainback, Kevin, and Donald Tomaskovic-Devey. 2009. "Intersections of Power and Privilege: Long-Term Trend in Managerial Representation." *American Sociological Review* 74:800–820.

Stainback, Kevin, Donald Tomaskovic-Devey, and Sheryl Skaggs. 2010. "Organizational Approaches to Inequality: Inertia, Relative Power, and Environments." *Annual Review of Sociology* 36:225–247.

Staples, Brent. February 15, 2007. "How 'Black' is Barack Obama?" *Akron Beacon Journal,* A13.

Steensland, Brian. 2006. "Cultural Categories and the American Welfare State: The Case of Guaranteed Income Policy." *American Journal of Sociology* 111:1273–1326.

Steffensmeier, Darrell, and Stephen Demuth. 2000. "Ethnicity and Sentencing Outcomes in U.S. Federal Courts: Who is Punished More Harshly?" *American Sociological Review* 65:705–729.

Steffensmeier, Darrell, and Chris Hebert. 1999. "Women and Men Policymakers: Does the Judge's Gender Affect the Sentencing of Criminal Defendants?" *Social Forces* 77:1163–1196.

Steil, Janice M. 1984. "Martial Relationships and Mental Health: The Psychic Costs of Inequality." Pp. 113–123 in *Women: A Feminist Perspective,* edited by J. Freeman. Palo Alto, CA: Mayfield.

Stephenson, Charles, and Robert Asher, eds. 1986. *Life and Labor: Dimensions of American Working-Class History.* Albany: State University of New York Press.

Stern, Michael J. 2010. "Inequality in the Internet Age: A Twenty-First Century Dilemma." *Sociological Inquiry* 80:28–33.

Stern, Philip M. 1988. *The Best Congress Money Can Buy.* New York: Pantheon.

Stevenson, Betsey, and Justin Wolfers. August 19, 2008. "Economic Growth and Subjective Well-Being: Reassessing the Easterline Paradox." Unpublished paper.

Stolte, John F. 1983. "The Legitimation of Structural Inequality: Reformulation and Test of the Self-Evaluation Argument." *American Sociological Review* 48:331–342.

Stolte, John F. 1987. "The Formation of Justice Norms." *American Sociological Review* 52:774–784.

Stolzenberg, Ross M. 2001. "It's About Time and Gender: Spousal Employment and Health." *American Journal of Sociology* 107:61–100.

Strathern, Marilyn. 1980. "No Nature, No Culture: The Hagen Case." Pp. 174–222 in *Nature, Culture and Gender,* edited by C. MacCormack and M. Strathern. Cambridge: Cambridge University Press.

"Study Examines Rural Low-Income Families in Light of Welfare Reform." June 6, 2002. *The Wayne Journal,* 28.

Sturm, James L. 1977. *Investing in the United States, 1798–1893.* New York: Arno Press.

Substance Abuse and Mental Health Services Administration. 2010. *Results from the 2009 National Survey on Drug Use and Health; Mental Health Findings.* Rockville, MD: Office of Applied Studies.

Sue, Derald Wing. 2010. *Microaggressions and Marginality.* Hoboken, NJ: Wiley.

Suicide Prevention Resource Center. 2008. *Suicide Risk and Prevention for Lesbian, Gay, Bisexual, and Transgender Youth.* Newton, MA: Education Development Center, Inc.

Sutphin, Susanne Taylor, and Brent Simpson. 2009. "The Role of Self-Evaluations in Legitimizing Social Inequality." *Social Science Research* 38:609–621.

Swanson, Guy E. 1974. *The Birth of the Gods.* Ann Arbor: University of Michigan.

Swartz, Teresa Toguchi. 2009. "Intergenerational Family Relations in Adulthood: Patterns, Variations, and Implications in the Contemporary United States." *Annual Review of Sociology* 35:191–212.

Sweeney, Richard. 1993. *Out of Place: Homelessness in America.* New York: HarperCollins.

Swift, Adam. 2004. "Would Perfect Mobility be Perfect?" *European Sociological Review* 20:1–11.

Swim, Janet K., Robyn Mallett, and Charles Stangor. 2004. "Understanding Subtle Sexism: Detection and Use of Sexist Language." *Sex Roles* 51:117–128.

Szafran, Robert F. 1982. "What Kinds of Firms Hire and Promote Women and Blacks? A Review of the Literature." *The Sociological Quarterly* 23:171–190.

Szasz, Andrew, and Michael Meuser. 1997. "Environmental Inequalities: Literature Review and Proposals for New Directions in Research and Theory." *Current Sociology* 45:99–120.

Szymanski, Albert. 1978. *The Capitalist State and the Politics of Class.* Cambridge, MA: Winthrop.

Tabb, William K. 1970. "Black Americans: Internal Colony or Marginal Working Class." Paper presented at the Seventh World Congress of Sociology of the International Sociological Association, September 4–11, Varna, Bulgaria.

Tausig, Mark, and Rudy Fenwick. 1999. "Recession and Well-Being." *Journal of Health and Social Behavior* 40:1–16.

Taylor, Catherine J. 2010. "Occupational Sex Composition and the Gendered Availability of Workplace Support." *Gender & Society* 24:189–212.

Taylor, Paul, Cary Funk, and April Clark. 2007. *Americans and Social Trust: Who, Where and Why.* Washington, D.C.: Pew Research Center.

Taylor, Timothy. 2002. "The Truth about Globalization." *The Public Interest* 147:24–44.

Taylor, Verta. 1989a. "Social Movement Continuity: The Women's Movement in Abeyance." *American Sociological Review* 54:761–775.

Taylor, Verta. 1989b. "The Future of Feminism: A Social Movement Analysis." Pp. 473–490 in *Feminist Frontiers II: Rethinking Sex, Gender, and Society,* edited by L. Richardson and V. Taylor. New York: Random House.

Teachman, Jay, and Lucky M. Tedrow. 2004. "Wages, Earnings, and Occupational Status: Did World War II Veterans Receive a Premium?" *Social Science Research* 33:581–605.

The Gallup Report, January/February 1987. Report No. 256–57, p. 14.

Thebaud, Sarah. (2010). "Masculinity, Bargaining, and Breadwinning." *Gender & Society* 24:330–354.

Thoits, Peggy A. 1983. "Multiple Identities and Psychological Well-Being: A Reformulation and Test of the Social Isolation Hypothesis." *American Sociological Review* 48:174–187.

Thurow, Lester C. 1969. *Poverty and Discrimination.* Washington, D.C.: Brookings Institution.

Thurow, Lester C. June 1999. "Building Wealth." *Atlantic Monthly,* 57–69.

Tillman, Robert, Kitty Calavita, and Henry Pontell. 1997. "Criminalizing White-Collar Misconduct." *Crime, Law & Social Change* 26:53–76.

Tilly, Charles. 1998. *Durable Inequality.* Berkeley: University of California Press.

Tilly, Charles. 2003. "Changing Forms of Inequality." *Sociological Theory* 21:31–36.

Tittle, Charles R., Wayne J. Villemez, and Douglas A. Smith. 1978. "The Myth of Social Class and Criminality: An Empirical Assessment of the Empirical Evidence." *American Sociological Review* 43:643–656.

Tocqueville, Alexis, de. 1969. Quoted in *Democracy in America,* edited by J. P. Mayer. New York: Doubleday.

Tolbert, Charles M., II. 1982. Industrial Segmentation and Men's Career Mobility." *American Sociological Review* 47:457–477.

Tomaskovic-Devey, Donald, Catherine Zimmer, Kevin Stainback, Corre Robinson, Tiffany Taylor, and Tricia McTague. 2006. "Documenting Desegregation: Segregation in American Workplaces by Race, Ethnicity, and Sex, 1966–2003." *American Sociological Review* 71:565–588.

Tomaskovic-Devey, Donald, Dustin Avent-Holt, Catherine Zimmer, and Sandra Harding. 2009. "The Categorical Generation of Organizational Inequality: A Comparative Test of Tilly's Durable Inequality." *Research in Social Stratification & Mobility* 27:128–142.

Törnblom, Kjell Y., and Riel Vermunt. 1999. "An Integrative Perspective on Social Justice: Distributive and Procedural Fairness Evaluations of Positive and Negative Outcome Allocations." *Social Justice Research* 12:39–64.

Trei, Lisa. 2006. "'Black' Features Can Sway in Favor of Death Penalty, According to Study." *Stanford Report,* May 3. Accessed online on October 8, 2008, at http://news-service.stanford.edu.

Treiman, Donald J., Heidi I. Hartmann, and Patricia A. Roos. 1984. "Assessing Pay Discrimination Using National Data." Pp. 137–154 in *Comparable Worth and Wage Discrimination,* edited by H. Remick. Philadelphia: Temple University Press.

Tropman, John E. 1989. *American Values & Social Welfare: Cultural Contradictions in the Welfare State.* Englewood Cliffs, NJ: Prentice Hall.

Troshynski, Emily L., and Jennifer K. Blank. 2008. "Sex Trafficking: An Exploratory Study Interviewing Traffickers." *Trends in Organized Crime* 11:30–41.

Tumin, Melvin M. 1953. "Some Principles of Stratification: A Critical Analysis." *American Sociological Review* 18:387–394.

Turk, Austin T. 1969. *Criminality and Legal Order.* Chicago: Rand McNally.

Turner, Bryan S. 1986. *Equality.* New York: Methuen.

Turner, Jonathan H. 1985. *Herbert Spencer.* Beverly Hills, CA: Sage.

Turner, Jonathan H., Royce Singleton, Jr., and David Musick. 1984. *Oppression: A Socio-History of Black-White Relations in America.* Chicago: Nelson-Hall.

Turner, Margery Austin, and Felicity Skidmore. 1999. *Mortgage Lending Discrimination: A Review of Existing Evidence.* Washington, D.C.: Urban Institute.

Turner, Richard. May 17, 1999. "The $25 Million Secret." *Newsweek,* 35.

Turner, William H. 1986. "The Black Ethnographer 'At Home' in Harlem: A Commentary and Research Response to Stephenson and Greer." *Human Organization* 45:279–292.

Uggen, Christopher, and Amy Blackstone. 2004. "Sexual Harassment as a Gendered Expression of Power." *American Sociological Review* 69:64–92.

Uggen, Christopher, and Jeff Manza. 2002. "Democratic Contraction? Political Consequences of Felon Disenfranchisement in the United States." *American Sociological Review* 67:777–803.

Umberson, Debra. 1993. "Sociodemographic Position, World Views, and Psychological Distress." *Social Science Quarterly* 74:575–589.

United Church of Christ. 1987. *Toxic Wastes and Race: A National Report on the Racial and Socio-Economic Characteristics of Communities with Hazardous Waste Sites.* New York: United Church of Christ.

United Nations. 1995. *The World's Women 1995: Trends and Statistics.* New York: United Nations.

United Nations. 1998. *Human Development Report 1998.* New York: Oxford University Press.

United Nations. 2007. *Human Development Report 2007/2008.* New York: United Nations Development Programme.

United Nations. 2010. *The World's Women 2010: Trends and Statistics.* New York: United Nations.

U.S. Bureau of the Census. 1979. *The Social and Economic Status of the Black Population in the*

United States: An Historical View, 1790–1978. Current Population Reports, Series P-21, No. 80. Washington, D.C.: U.S. Government Printing Office.

U.S. Bureau of the Census. August 1987. *Male-Female Differences in Work Experience, Occupation, and Earnings: 1984.* Current Population Reports, Series P-70, No. 10. Washington, D.C.: U.S. Government Printing Office.

U.S. Bureau of Labor Statistics. January 21, 2011. *Union Members—2010.* Washington, D.C. U.S. Department of Labor.

U.S. Census Bureau. February 2002. *The American Indian and Alaska Native Population: 2000.* Census 2000 Brief, No. 01–15. Washington, D.C.: U.S. Government Printing Office.

U.S. Census Bureau. August 2004. *Income, Poverty, and Health Insurance Coverage in the United States: 2003.* Current Population Reports, Series P-60, No. 226. Washington, D.C.: U.S. Government Printing Office.

U.S. Census Bureau. 2005. *Statistical Abstract of the United States: 2004–2005.* Washington, D.C.: U.S. Government Printing Office.

U.S. Census Bureau. May 2007. *The American Community—American Indians and Alaska Natives: 2004.* Washington, D.C.: U.S. Government Printing Office.

U.S. Census Bureau. August 2008. *Income, Poverty, and Health Insurance Coverage in the United States: 2007.* Current Populaiton Reports, Series P-60, No. 235. Washington, D.C.: U.S. Government Printing Office.

U.S. Census Bureau. 2009. *Statistical Abstract of the United States: 2010.* Washington, D.C.: U.S. Government Printing Office.

U.S. Census Bureau. 2010. "Data on American Factfinder." *2007 Survey of Business Owners.* Available at www.census.gov/econ/sbo/index.html.

U.S. Census Bureau. September 2010a. *Income, Poverty, and Health Insurance Coverage in the United States: 2009.* Current Population Reports, Series P60, No. 238. Washington, D.C.: U.S. Government Printing Office.

U.S. Census Bureau. September 2010b. *Poverty: 2008 and 2009.* American Community Survey Briefs. Washington, D.C.: U.S. Government Printing Office.

U.S. Census Office. 1903. *Statistical Atlas of the United States, 1900.* Washington, D.C.: U.S. Government Printing Office.

U.S. Conference of Mayors. 2010. *Hunger and Homelessness Survey.* Washington, D.C.: U.S. Conference of Mayors.

U.S. Department of Agriculture. March 2008. *Expenditures on Children by Families, 2007.* Washington, D.C.: U.S. Government Printing Office.

U.S. Department of Agriculture. October 2010a. *Characteristics of Supplemental Nutrition Assistance Program Households: Fiscal Year 2009 Summary.* Washington, D.C.: U.S. Government Printing Office.

U.S. Department of Agriculture. October 2010b. *Characteristics of Supplemental Nutrition Assistance Program Households: Fiscal Year 2009.* Washington, D.C.: U.S. Government Printing Office.

U.S. Department of Commerce and Labor, Bureau of Statistics. 1911. *Statistical Abstract of the United States, 1911.* Washington, D.C.: U.S. Government Printing Office.

U.S. Department of Health and Human Services, Administration for Children & Families. *Characteristics and Financial Circumstances of TANF Recipients: Fiscal Year 2008.* Available at www.acf.hhs.gov/programs/ofa/character/FY2008/indexfy08.htm.

U.S. Department of Housing and Urban Development. 2010. *The 2009 Annual Homeless Assessment Report.* Washington, D.C.: U.S. Department of Housing and Urban Development.

U.S. Department of Labor, Women's Bureau. 1947. *Women's Occupations through Seven Decades.* Washington, D.C.: U.S. Government Printing Office.

U.S. Department of Labor. August 2000. *A Comparison of the Characteristics and Spending Patterns of Food Stamp Recipients and Nonrecipients.* Summary 00–14. Washington, D.C.: U.S. Government Printing Office.

U.S. Department of Labor. September 2007. *Highlights of Women's Earnings in 2006.* Report 1000. Washington, D.C.: U.S. Government Printing Office.

U.S. Department of Labor. 2008. *Occupational Outlook Handbook.* 2008–09 edition. Washington, D.C.: U.S. Government Printing Office.

U.S. Department of Labor. September 2009. *Women in the Labor Force: A Databook.* Report 1018.

Washington, D.C.: U.S. Government Printing Office.

U.S. Department of Labor. January 2010. *Employment & Earnings*. Washington, D.C.: U.S. Government Printing Office.

U.S. Department of Labor. January 27, 2010. *Mass Layoffs—December 2009, Annual Totals 2009*. USDL-10-0098. Washington, D.C.: U.S. Government Printing Office.

U.S. Department of Labor. June 2010. *Highlights of Women's Earnings in 2009*. Report 1025. Washington, D.C.: U.S. Government Printing Office.

U.S. Department of Labor. March 2010. *Consumer Expenditures in 2008*. Report 1023. Washington, D.C.: U.S. Government Printing Office.

U.S. Department of Labor. January 2011. *Employment & Earnings*. Washington, D.C.: U.S. Government Printing Office.

U.S. General Accounting Office. 1983. *Siting of Hazardous Waste Landfills and Their Correlations with Racial and Economic Status of Surrounding Communities*. Washington, D.C.: U.S. Government Printing Office.

Urban Institute. 2000. *A New Look at Homelessness in America*. Washington, D.C.: Urban Institute.

Urban Institute. June 2009. *Low-Income Working Families: Updated Facts and Figures*. LIWF Fact Sheet. Washington, D.C.: Urban Institute.

Useem, Michael. 1978. "The Inner Group of the American Capitalist Class." *Social Problems* 25:225–240.

Useem, Michael. 1979. "The Social Organization of the American Business Elite and Participation of Corporation Directors in the Governance of American Institutions." *American Sociological Review* 44:553–572.

Useem, Michael. 1980. "Which Business Leaders Help Govern?" Pp. 199–225 in *Power Structure Research,* edited by G. W. Domhoff. Beverly Hills, CA: Sage.

Useem, Michael. 1984. *The Inner Circle: Large Corporations and the Rise of Business Political Activity in the U.S. and U.K.* New York: Oxford University Press.

Uslaner, Eric M., and Mitchell Brown. 2005. "Inequality, Trust, and Civic Engagement." *American Politics Research* 33:868–894.

Valdes, Francisco. 1995. "Queers, Sissies, Dykes, and Tomboys: Deconstructing the Conflation of 'Sex,' 'Gender,' and 'Sexual Orientation' in Euro-American Law and Society." *California Law Review* 83:129–204.

van den Berghe, Pierre L. 1985. "Review of J. S. Chafetz's Sex and Advantage." *American Journal of Sociology* 90:1350.

van der Toorn, Jojanneke, Mihaly Berkics, and John T. Jost. 2010. "System Justification, Satisfaction, and Perceptions of Fairness and Typicality at Work: A Cross-System Comparison Involving the U.S. and Hungary." *Social Justice Research* 23:189–210.

van Leeuwen, Marco H. D., and Ineke Maas. 2010. "Historical Studies of Social Mobility and Stratification." *Annual Review of Sociology* 36:429–451.

Vanneman, Reeve, and Fred C. Pampel. 1977. "The American Perception of Class and Status." *American Sociological Review* 42:422–437.

Vaught, Sabina E., and Angelina E. Castagno. 2008. "'I Don't Think I'm a Racist': Critical Race Theory, Teacher Attitudes, and Structural Racism." *Race Ethnicity and Education* 11:95–113.

Veblen, Thorstein. 1953. *The Theory of the Leisure Class*. New York: New American Library.

Venkatesh, Sudhir Alladi. 1994. "Getting Ahead: Social Mobility among the Urban Poor." *Sociological Perspectives* 37:157–182.

Verba, Sidney, Nancy Burns, and Kay Lehman Schlozman. 2003. "Unequal at the Starting Line: Creating Participatory Inequalities across Generations and among Groups." *The American Sociologist* Spring/Summer:45–69.

Verba, Sidney, and Norman H. Nie. 1972. *Participation in America: Political Democracy and Social Equality*. New York: Harper & Row.

Verba, Sidney, and Gary R. Orren. 1985. *Equality in America: The View from the Top*. Cambridge, MA: Harvard University Press.

Verbrugge, Lois M. 1983. "Multiple Roles and Physical Health of Women and Men." *Journal of Health and Social Behavior* 24:16–30.

Verbrugge, Lois M. 1999. "Pathways of Health and Death." Pp. 377–94 in *Health, Illness, and Healing,* edited by K. Charmaz and D. A. Paterniti. Los Angeles: Roxbury.

Veum, Jonathan R. December 1992. "Accounting for Income Mobility Changes in the United States." *Social Science Quarterly* 73:773–785.

Vincent, Wilson, John L. Peterson, and Dominic J. Parrott. 2009. "Differences in African American and White Women's Attitudes Toward Lesbians and Gay Men." *Sex Roles* 61:599–606.

Vogel, Lise. 1983. *Marxism and the Oppression of Women.* New Brunswick, NJ: Rutgers University Press.

Volgy, Thomas J., John E. Schwarz, and Lawrence E. Imwalle. 1996. "In Search of Economic Well-Being: Worker Power and the Effects of Productivity, Inflation, Unemployment and Global Trade on Wages in Ten Wealthy Countries." *American Journal of Political Science* 40:1233–1252.

Von Braun, Joachim. December 2007. *The World Food Situation.* Washington, D.C.: International Food Policy Research Institute.

Wacquant, Lois J. D., and William Julius Wilson. 1989. "The Cost of Racial and Class Exclusion in the Inner City." *Annals of the American Academy of Political and Social Science* 501:8–25.

Waddoups, Jeffrey, and Djeto Assane. 1993. "Mobility and Gender in a Segmented Labor Market: A Closer Look." *American Journal of Economics and Sociology* 52:399–411.

Wade, Robert Hunter. 2004. "Is Globalization Reducing Poverty and Inequality?" *World Development* 32:567–589.

Wadsworth, Tim, and Charis E. Kubrin. 2004. "Structural Factors and Black Interracial Homicide: A New Examination of the Causal Process." *Criminology* 42:647–672.

Wagmiller, Jr., Robert, Li Kuang, Lawrence J. Aber, Mary Clare Lennon, and Philip M. Alberti. 2006. "The Dynamics of Economic Disadvantage and Children's Life Chances." *American Sociological Review* 71:847–866.

Wakefield, Sara, and Christopher Uggen. 2010. "Incarceration and Stratification." *Annual Review of Sociology* 36:387–406.

Waldman, Amy. April 29, 2005. "Mystery of India's Poverty: Can the State Break its Grip?" *New York Times,* A4.

Waldner, Lisa K., and Jillian Berg. 2008. "Explaining Antigay Violence Using Target Congruence: An Application of Revised Routine Activities Theory." *Violence and Victims* 23:267–287.

Wallace, Geoffrey L. 2009. "The Effects of Family Caps on the Subsequent Fertility Decisions of Never-Married Mothers." *Journal of Population Research* 26:73–101.

Wallace, Michael. 1997. "Revisiting Broom and Cushing's 'Modest Test of an Immodest Theory.'" *Research in Social Stratification & Mobility* 15:239–253.

Wallerstein, I. 1974. *The Modern World-System.* New York: Academic.

Wallerstein, I. 1979. *The Capitalist World-Economy.* Cambridge: Cambridge University Press.

Walsh, Mary Williams. April 25, 2003. "I.R.S. Tightening Rules for Low-Income Tax Credit." *New York Times,* A1, C4.

Wang, Qingfang. 2008. "Race/Ethnicity, Gender and Job Earnings Across Metropolitan Areas in the United States: A Multilevel Analysis." *Urban Studies* 45:825–843.

Ward, Kathryn B. 1993. "Reconceptualizing World System Theory to Include Women." Pp. 43–68 in *Theory on Gender/Feminism on Theory,* edited by P. England. New York: Aldine de Gruyter.

Warner, David F., and Mark D. Hayward. 2006. "Early-Life Origins of the Race Gap in Men's Mortality." *Journal of Health and Social Behavior* 47:209–226.

Warren, John Robert. 2009. "Socioeconomic Status and Health Across the Life Course: A Test of the Social Causation and Health Selection Hypotheses." *Social Forces* 87:2125–2154.

Watkins, Nicole L., Theressa L. Labarrie, and Lauren M. Appio. 2010. "Black Undergraduates' Experiences With Perceived Racial Microaggressions in Predominately White Colleges and Universities." Pp. 25–57 in *Microaggressions and Marginality,* edited by D. W. Sue. Hoboken, NJ: Wiley.

Weaver, Jay. 2010. "Medicare Fraud: Defying Justice." *AARP Bulletin* 51:12–14.

Weber, Max. 1964. *The Theory of Social and Economic Organization,* edited by Talcott Parsons. New York: The Free Press.

Webster, Murray, Jr., and James E. Driskell, Jr. 1983. "Beauty as Status." *American Journal of Sociology* 89:140–165.

Weede, Erich. 2008. "Globalization and Inequality." *Comparative Sociology* 7:415–433.

Weeden, Jason, Michael J. Abrams, Melanie C. Green, and John Sabini. 2006. "Do High-Status People Really Have Fewer Children?" *Human Nature* 17:377–392.

Weeden, Kim A. 2002. "Why Do Some Occupations Pay More Than Others? Social Closure and Earnings Inequality in the United States." *American Journal of Sociology* 108:55–101.

Weinreb, Linda, Richard Scott, and Craig Gundersen. 2002. "Hunger: Its Impact on Children's Health and Mental Health." *Pediatrics* 110:e41.

Weiss, Michael J. 1988. *The Clustering of America.* New York: Harper & Row.

Weitzer, Ronald. 2000. "Racialized Policing: Residents' Perceptions in Three Neighborhoods." *Law & Society Review* 34:129–153.

Weitzer, Ronald, and Steven A. Tuch. 2004. "Race and Perceptions of Police Misconduct." *Social Problems* 51:305–325.

Weitzer, Ronald, and Steven A. Tuch. 2005. "Racially Biased Policing: Determinants of Citizen Perceptions." *Social Forces* 83:1009–1030.

Welch, Kelly, and Allison Ann Payne. 2010. "Racial Threat and Punitive School Discipline." *Social Problems* 57:25–48.

"The Well-Heeled: Pricey Sneakers in Inner City Help Set Nation's Fashion Trend." December 1, 1988. *Wall Street Journal,* A1, A6.

Werner, Paul D., and Georgina Williams LaRussa. 1985. "Persistence and Change in Sex-Role Stereotypes." *Sex Roles* 12:1089–1100.

Wertz, Richard W., and Dorothy C. Wertz. 1981. "Notes on the Decline of Midwives and the Rise of Medical Obstetricians." Pp. 165–183 in *The Sociology of Health and Illness: Critical Perspectives,* edited by P. Conrad and R. Kern. New York: St. Martin's Press.

Wessel, David. May 13, 2005. "As Rich-Poor Gap Widens in the U.S., Class Mobility Stalls." *Wall Street Journal,* A1, A7.

West, Candace, and Don Zimmerman. 1987. "Doing Gender." *Gender & Society* 1:125–151.

West, Cornel. 1993. *Race Matters.* Boston: Beacon.

Western, Bruce. 1993. "Postwar Unionization in Eighteen Advanced Capitalist Countries." *American Sociological Review* 58:266–282.

Western, Bruce, and Christopher Wildeman. 2009. "The Black Family and Mass Incarceration." *Annals of the American Academy of Political and Social Science* 621:221–242.

Western, Mark, and Erik Olin Wright. 1994. "The Permeability of Class Boundaries to Intergenerational Mobility among Men in the United States, Canada, Norway and Sweden." *American Sociological Review* 59:606–629.

Weston, William. 2010. "The Power Elite and the Philadelphia Gentlemen." *Society* 47:138–146.

Wheaton, B. 1980. "The Sociogenesis of Psychological Disorder: An Attributional Theory." *Journal of Health and Social Behavior* 21:100–124.

Wheeler, Stanton, David Weisburd, and Nancy Bode. 1982. "Sentencing the White-Collar Offender: Rhetoric and Reality." *American Sociological Review* 47:641–659.

White, Jack E. 1997. "I'm Just Who I Am." *Time,* May 5:34.

Wildeman, Christopher, and Bruce Western. 2010. "Incarceration in Fragile Families." *The Future of Children* 20-157–177.

Wiley, Mary Glenn, and Arlene Eskilson. 1983. "Scaling the Corporate Ladder: Sex Differences in Expectations for Performance, Power and Mobility." *Social Psychology Quarterly* 46:351–359.

Wilkinson, Richard G., and Kate Pickett. 2009. "Income Inequality and Social Dysfunction." *Annual Review of Sociology* 35:493–511.

Williams, Kirk R. 1984. "Economic Sources of Homicide: Reestimating the Effects of Poverty and Inequality." *American Sociological Review* 49:283–289.

Williams, Kirk R., and Robert L. Flewelling. 1988. "The Social Production of Criminal Homicide: A Comparative Study of Disaggregated Rates in American Cities." *American Sociological Review* 53:421–431.

Williams, Roberton. 2010. "Why Nearly Half of Americans Pay No Federal Income Tax." *Tax Notes.* Washington, D.C.: Tax Policy Center.

Williams, Robin M., Jr. 1970. *American Society: A Sociological Interpretation.* New York: Knopf.

Willie, Charles Vert. 1979. *The Caste and Class Controversy.* Bayside, NY: General Hall.

Willson, Andrea E. 2003. "Race and Women's Income Trajectories: Employment, Marriage, and Income Security over the Life Course." *Social Problems* 50:87–110.

Wilson, George, and Vincent J. Roscigno. 2010. "Race and Downward Mobility from Privileged Occupations: African American/White Dynamics Across the Early Work-Career." *Social Science Research* 39:67–77.

Wilson, Rick K., and Catherine C. Eckel. 2006. "Judging a Book by its Cover: Beauty and Expectations in the Trust Game." *Political Research Quarterly* 59:189–202.

Wilson, William J. 1970. "Race Relations Models and Explanations of Ghetto Behavior." Paper presented at the Seventh World Congress of Sociology of the International Sociological Association, September 14–19, Varna, Bulgaria.

Wilson, William Julius. 1982. "The Declining Significance of Race-Revisited But Not Revised." Pp. 399–405 in *Majority & Minority: The Dynamics of Race and Ethnicity in American Life,* edited by N. R. Yetman and C. H. Steele. Boston: Allyn & Bacon.

Wilson, William Julius. 1987. *The Truly Disadvantaged: The Inner City, the Underclass, and Public Policy.* Chicago: University of Chicago Press.

Wingfield, Adia Harvey. 2009. "Racializing the Glass Escalator." *Gender & Society* 23:5–26.

Wolf, Naomi. 1991. *The Beauty Myth: How Images of Beauty Are Used against Women.* New York: Morrow.

Wolfe, Barbara, Jessica Jakubowski, Robert Haveman, and Marissa Courey. 2010. "The Income and Health Effects of Tribal Casino Gaming on American Indians." *La Follette Policy Report,* Spring: 11–14.

Wolff, Edward N. May 1992. "Changing Inequality of Wealth." *American Economics Review* 82:552–558.

Wolff, Edward N. 1998. "Recent Trends in the Size Distribution of Household Wealth." *Journal of Economic Perspectives* 12:131–150.

Wolff, Edward N. April 2000. *Recent Trends in Wealth Ownership, 1983–1998.* Working Paper No. 300.

Wolff, Edward N. May 2002. "Recent Trends in Living Standards in the United States." New York: New York University and the Jerome Levy Economics Institute.

Wolff, Edward N. 2007. *Recent Trends in Household Wealth in the United States: Rising Debt and the Middle-Class Squeeze.* Working Paper No. 502. The Levy Economics Institute of Bard College.

Wolff, Edward. 2010. "Recent Trends in Household Wealth in the United States: Rising Debt and the Middle-Class Squeeze—an Update to 2007." Working Paper No. 589. Levy Economic Institute.

Wolniak, Gregory C., Tricia A. Seifert, Eric J. Reed, and Ernest T. Pascarella. 2008. "College Majors and Social Mobility." *Research in Social Stratification and Mobility* 26:123–139.

"Women of Islam, The." December 3, 2001. *Time,* 50.

Wong, Raymond Sin-Kwok. 1994. "Postwar Mobility Trends in Advanced Industrial Societies." *Research in Social Stratification and Mobility* 11:121–144.

World Health Organization. June 2002. *Gender and Mental Health.* Geneva: World Health Organization.

World Health Organization. 2005. *Mental Health Atlas 2005.* Geneva: World Health Organization.

World Health Organization. 2008. *World Health Statistics 2008.* Geneva: World Health Organization.

World Hunger Education Service. 2008. World Hunger Facts 2008. Accessed online on October 1, 2008, at www.worldhunger.org/articles/Learn/worldhungerfacts2002.htm.

Worts, Diana, Amanda Sacker, and Peggy McDonough. 2010. "Falling Short of the Promise: Poverty Vulnerability in the United States and Britain, 1993–2003." *American Journal of Sociology* 116:232–271.

Wright, Erik Olin. 1997. *Class Counts.* New York: Cambridge University Press.

Wright, Erik Olin. 2006. "Two Redistributive Proposals—Universal Basic Income and Stakeholder Grants." *Focus* 24:5–7.

Wright, Erik Olin, Janeen Baxter, and Gunn Elisabeth Birkelund. 1995. "The Gender Gap in Workplace Authority in Seven Nations." *American Sociological Review* 60:407–435.

Wright, Erik Olin, and Donmoon Cho. 1992. "The Relative Permeability of Class Boundaries to Cross-Class Friendships: A Comparative Study of the United States, Canada, Sweden, and Norway." *American Sociological Review* 57:85–102.

Wright, Erik Olin, and Rachel E. Dwyer. 2003. "The Patterns of Job Expansions in the USA: A Comparison of the 1960s and 1990s." *Socio-Economic Review* 1:289–325.

Wright, Erik Olin, and Bill Martin. 1987. "The Transformation of the American Class Structure 1960–1980." *American Journal of Sociology* 93:1–29.

Wright, Erik Olin, and Luca Perrone. 1977. "Marxist Class Categories and Income Inequality." *American Sociological Review* 42:32–55.

Wright, James D., and Julie A. Lam. 1987. "Homeless and the Low-Income Housing Supply." *Social Policy* 17:48–53.

Wrong, Dennis H. 1959. "The Functional Theory of Stratification: Some Neglected Considerations." *American Sociological Review* 24:722–782.

Wrye, Harriet Kimble. 2009. "The Fourth Wave of Feminism: Psychoanalytic Perspectives Introductory Remarks." *Studies in Gender and Sexuality* 10:185–189.

Yamaguchi, Kazuo. 2009. "Black-White Differences in Social Mobility in the Pat 30 Years: A Latent-Class Regression Analysis." *Research in Social Stratification & Mobility* 27:65–78.

Yamaguchi, Kazuo, and Yantao Wang. 2002. "Class Identification of Married Employed Women and Men in America." *American Journal of Sociology* 108:440–475.

Yanagisako, Sylvia Junko, and Jane Fishburne Collier. 1987. "Toward a Unified Analysis of Gender and Kinship." Pp. 14–50 in *Gender and Kinship: Essays toward a Unified Analysis,* edited by J. F. Collier and S. J. Yanagisako. Stanford, CA: Stanford University Press.

Yang, Alan S. 1997. "Attitudes toward Homosexuality." *Public Opinion Quarterly* 61:477–507.

Yang, Yang, and Linda C. Lee. 2009. "Sex and Race Disparities in Health: Cohort Variations in Life Course Patterns." *Social Forces* 87:2093–2124.

Yen, Iris. 2008. "Of Vice and Men: A New Approach to Eradicating Sex Trafficking by Reducing Male Demand Through Educational Programs and Abolitionist Legislation." *The Journal of Criminal Law & Criminology* 98:653–686.

Yoo, Grace J. 2008. "Immigrants and Welfare: Policy Constructions of Deservingness." *Journal of Immigrant & Refugee Studies* 6:490–507.

Young, Leslie. 2009. "The Global Trade in Electronic Waste: Interactive Map." Available at www.pbs.org/frontlineworld/stories/ghana804.

Zakaria, Fareed. 2005. "Does the Future Belong to China?" *Newsweek,* May 9, 28–40.

Zandvakili, Sourushe, and Jeffrey A. Mills. 2001. "The Distributional Implications of Tax and Transfer Programs in the U.S." *Quarterly Review of Economics and Finance* 41:167–181.

Zastrow, Charles. 1982. *Introduction to Social Welfare Institutions: Social Problems, Services and Current Issues.* Homewood, IL: Dorsey.

Zavodny, Madeline, and Marianne P. Bitler. 2010. "The Effect of Medicaid Eligibility Expansions on Fertility." *Social Science & Medicine* 71:918–924.

Zeitlin, Irving. 1968. *Ideology and the Development of Sociological Theory.* Englewood Cliffs, NJ: Prentice Hall.

Zieger, Robert H. 1986. *American Workers, American Unions. 1920–1985.* Baltimore: Johns Hopkins University Press.

Zigler, Edward, and Susan Muenchow. 1983. "Infant Day Care and Infant-Care Leaves." *American Psychologist* 38:91–94.

Zillien, Nicole, and Eszter Hargittai. 2009. "Digital Distinction: Status-Specific Types of Internet Usage." *Social Science Quarterly* 90:274–290.

Zimmer, Michael J., Charles A. Sullivan, Richard F. Richards, and Deborah A. Calloway. 2000. *Cases and Materials on Employment Discrimination.* New York: Aspen Law & Business.

Zimmerman, Don H., and Candace West. 1975. "Sex Roles, Interruptions and Silences in Conversation." Pp. 105–129 in *Language and Sex: Difference and Dominance,* edited by B. Thorne and N. Henley. Rowley, MA: Newbury House.

Zipp John F. 1994. "Government Employment and Black-White Earnings Inequality, 1980–1990." *Social Problems* 41:363–382.

Zmerli, Sonja, and Ken Newton. 2008. "Social Trust and Attitudes Toward Democracy." *Public Opinion Quarterly* 72:706-724.

Zuckerman, Mortimer B. 2006. "Playing Fair on Taxes." *U.S. News & World Report,* May 1, 64.

INDEX